FOR CIVIL SERVICES EXAMINATION

3e

WORLD HISTORY

A Comprehensive Study of the Modern World

Krishna Reddy
*Former Director of Hyderabad Study Circle,
Hyderabad.*

Ajay Kumar C.M.
*Faculty of History of prominent
IAS academies across India.*

Mc Graw Hill

McGraw Hill Education (India) Private Limited

Published by McGraw Hill Education (India) Private Limited
Registered Office: Anjana Complex No: 5/90 A, Butt Road, St. Thomas Mount, Chennai 600 016

World History: A Comprehensive Study of the Modern World, 3e

Print Edition:
ISBN-13: 978-93-5532-526-6
ISBN-10: 93-5532-526-6

E-Book Edition:
ISBN-13: 978-93-5532-527-3
ISBN-10: 93-5532-527-4

1 2 3 4 5 6 7 8 9 7101558 27 26 25 24 23

Printed and bound in India.

Typeset at Transcend Content Solution, 163F Jaigirghat Road, Panchanantala, Kolkata – 700 063 and printed at Magic International Pvt. Ltd., Plot No. 26E, Sector-31, (Industrial), Site-IV, Greater Noida 201306

Cover Designer: Anita Kanojia
Cover Image Source: Shutterstock
Visit us at: www.mheducation.co.in
Write to us at: support.india@mheducation.com
CIN: U80302TN2010PTC111532
Toll Free Number: 1800 103 5875

COUNTER THE COUNTERFEIT & BUILD A STRONG FOUNDATION FOR SUCCESS

Books are our best friends, is the adage we have grown up with. However, the pirates of piracy are continuously forging 'our best friends'. Our books and their supplementary online resources are copyrighted, and we don't lend any right-to-copy. Piracy is synonymous to stealing books.

Knowledge comes real, let's not encourage its counterfeit. Therefore, we appeal all our readers to discourage pirated books and **choose authentic ones**.

HOW TO IDENTIFY THE PIRATED BOOKS?

1 Cover and Spine

- Look and feel (new or used book)
- Blurred images on the cover
- Hologram pasted on front
- Defective spine (wrinkles) or air pocket at its bottom
- Unclear ISBN/bar codes
- Missing/non-operational Unique Coupon Code for exclusive access to McGraw Hill Edge

2 Text/Printing/Binding

- Uneven inking of pages
- Poor quality or blurred photographs/images/charts
- Substandard paper quality and opacity
- Misaligned pages
- Missing pages
- Inferior binding quality

You can further watch this video on How to identify a pirated book

For more information about identifying piracy, visit **https://www.mheducation.co.in/piracy**

To report a pirated book, send 'Hi' on WhatsApp code given on the back cover or write to us at **support.india@mheducation.com**.

Reported pirated books are examined to combat their piracy.

Let's fight the Pirates of Piracy and resolve to go for original!

About the Authors

Krishna Reddy graduated in History from Loyola College, Chennai, and obtained his postgraduate degree in the same subject from Jawaharlal Lal Nehru University (JNU), New Delhi, in 1982. He was the Founder Director of KRISP (Krishna Reddy's IAS Study Point). He was also the former Director at Hyderabad Study Circle (HSC), Hyderabad. He had authored several books on History in English, Hindi, and Telugu. Late Dr. K Krishna Reddy taught the subject to aspirants of Civil Services Examination at various institutions across the country.

Ajay Kumar C.M is a Post Graduate in History and has been mentoring aspirants of Civil Services Examination for the last 17 years in prominent institutes across the country.

Dedicated to
Late Professor Rizwan Qaiser,
Department of History,
Jamia Milia Islamia,
A Liberal, A Nationalist, A friend.
Krishna Reddy

Dedicated to My Parents
Ajay Kumar C.M.

Preface to the Third Edition

This book is written for a specific audience – the candidates of the Civil Services Examination. Hence, it is a tailor-made product to meet the needs of three segments of this examination. First, it provides a simple yet clear-cut view of Modern World History to meet the requirement of the General Studies Paper I of the Main examination. Second, with its extensive analytical coverage, this book will be an asset for students with History as their optional in the Main examination. Third, this book is also a foundational material to the aspirants in their current affairs preparation. An in-depth analysis of the contemporary history, that is history from the 20th century – such as the World Wars, the Cold War, Decolonisation, disintegration of the Soviet Union, the Israel–Palestine conflict, Communist Revolution in China, European Union, etc. – will enable the aspirants to construct a historical perspective on current developments worldwide.

It is with immense satisfaction the third edition of 'World History – A Comprehensive Study of the Modern World' is being brought out. This new edition has been revised to incorporate the changing requirements of the Civil Service Examination and to ease further the effort of the students. A comprehensive timeline at the beginning of the book, summary at the end of each chapter and inclusion of the latest UPSC questions are some notable additions in this edition. The feedback and reviews from the students and the teachers alike show that the book has been immensely of help as a single-point source material on a vast subject like the world history in a demanding examination as that of the UPSC.

In writing this book I have been immensely benefited from the valuable lessons learned during my teaching career in various IAS institutes across the country. I am indebted to all those great minds – students, teachers and colleagues of these institutes – who in one way or the other contributed to the conceptualisation and fulfilment of this project. I also express my deep gratitude to the 'Team McGraw Hill' especially to Mr. Tanweer Ahmad, Mr. Nikhil Wadhera, Ms. Anwesha Roy, Ms. Sarita Yadav and Mr. Raman Vashisth who extended their constant support and expertise in making this project a reality.

Ajay Kumar C. M.

Preface to the First Edition

This book is intended for Civil Services aspirants for whom not only knowledge, but also a well-planned strategy is important to conquer the examination. When they have a well-defined goal like cracking the Civil Services Examination, they require a focused and systematic acquisition of knowledge and channelling it into goal-oriented objectives. The strategy they should adopt, should ideally consist of two steps: extensive preparation followed by internalisation of concepts. The former enables candidates to acquire all the necessary information, while the latter is meant to give a proper understanding of the subject. This book not only helps candidates to acquire knowledge systematically, but also acts as a tool for understanding of concepts deeply.

Methodology

The strategy for the Main Examination necessarily involves developing a proper perspective and thorough understanding of the subject. In other words, attention should be paid to honing the analytical capability rather than mere collection of information. To enable readers to acquire a thorough understanding of *Modern World History*, in this book the following pertinent questions have been posed and duly answered on each and every theme/topic of the subject. In carrying out the above task, some standard textbooks have been consulted.

Questions	Answers
1. What is it? (or) What happened?	Meaning / features / nature
2. Why was it done? (or) Why did it happen?	Causes / factors / origin
3. How was it done? (or) How did it happen?	Course / manner
4. What was the outcome / impact?	Results / significance

In every topic/theme, there is a "General Survey" that gives a panoramic view of the topic, followed by "Detailed Analysis" which covers the topic from all possible angles in an analytical manner. I have adopted this "Self-assessment" method to make history more interesting and absorbing for both teachers and students. Besides, practice questions on almost all the topics have been provided at the end of each chapter.

Question-analysis

The other part, in fact a more crucial one, for the preparation for the Main Examination pertains to the question-analysis. In the past, several types of questions have appeared in the examinations. Based on the terms and words attached to them, the questions can be classified into the following categories/types:

Of the above five categories of questions, the analytical types are most frequently asked, accounting for almost 50 per cent and potentially high-scoring.

The other four categories together make up the rest and are average in scoring.

Typology	Terminology	Requirement
I. Analytical	Discuss / comment / analyse / assess / appraise /evaluate / estimate / judge / critically examine	Merits and demerits/advantages and disadvantages/failures achievements/for and against
II. Descriptive	Describe / elaborate / narrate / give an account of / enumerate / list out	Going into the details or elaboration
III. Explanatory	Elucidate / illustrate / explain	Explaining with the help of relevant examples
IV. Causal	Account for	Giving reasons or causes
V. Chronological	Trace out	Dealing in a chronological order

Answer-writing

In writing answers to all types of questions, three factors are important. Every answer is evaluated for its relevance, clarity and precision.

Relevance shows subject command; clarity of thought gets expressed in lucidity of presentation; and precision demonstrates not only comprehending skills but also articulation. So, after acquiring a thorough understanding of the subject, a candidate should concentrate on the ways and means of applying it to the examination in the most effective fashion. Writing answers to as many previous and potential questions as possible and getting them evaluated is indispensable and highly rewarding in this examination.

In the end, I would like to express my gratitude to all my well-wishers and readers, whose unstinted support and encouragement has kept me going as a teacher and author of history for the past three decades. Finally, I would like to thank McGraw Publications in general, and Tanmoy Roychowdhury and Shukti Mukherjee in particular, for their constant support and encouragement in bringing out this book in record time.

Krishna Reddy
Former Director
Hyderabad Study Circle

Contents

Timeline of Modern World History

1448

Johann Gutenberg invented movable-type metal causing an information revolution and unprecedented mass-spread of literature. It directly impacted the development of the Renaissance and Reformation as it 'meant more access to information, more dissent, more informed discussion and more widespread criticism of authorities'.

1488

Bartolomeu Dias reached the tip of Africa and effectively discovered the sea route between Europe and Asia.

1492

Christopher Columbus explored the Caribbean Island of Espanola on his first voyage inaugurating a period of exploration, conquest and colonisation that lasted for centuries which also brought the Americas into the European sphere of influence.

1498

Vasco da Gama reached Calicut, in south-western coast of India sailing around the Cape of Good Hope in Africa.

1513

The Prince written by **Machiavelli.**

1517

The ninety-five theses of **Martin Luther** and the beginning of the Reformation.

1543

Copernicus publishes his work **'On the Revolutions of the Heavenly Spheres'**. This work marked the beginning of modern astronomy.

1687

Isaac Newton published his work 'Principia Mathematica'

1767

Invention of **Spinning Jenny** by James Hargreaves. It was monumental in initiating the factory system in cotton manufacturing and in the subsequent Industrial Revolution.

1776

The **Declaration of Independence** by which the 13 American Colonies declared their independence from Britain.

1789

Beginning of the **French Revolution**

1804

Napoleon crowned himself as the Emperor of the French.

1815

Napoleon defeated at **Waterloo** and was exiled to St. Helena

1829

Greece became independent from Turkey

1830

Construction of the first railway line in England. Railways enabled Britain to become the 'Workshop of the World' by reducing transport costs of raw materials and of finished goods. It also contributed to the transformation of Britain from a rural to a predominantly urban society.

1832

The Reform Bill expanded voting rights in Britain.

1839

Beginning of the **Opium War.** The war resulted in the defeat of the Chinese and opening of China to Western trade.

1848

The Year of Revolutions. Publication of **'The Communist Manifesto'** by German philosophers Karl Marx and Friedrich Engels

1853

The **expedition of Commodore Perry** of the United States to Japan forcing Japan to open its territories for foreigners and led directly to the establishment of diplomatic relations between Japan and the western Great Powers.

1862

Bismarck as Chancellor of Prussia

1867

Second Reform Bill doubled the electorate in England

1869

The **Suez Canal** was opened offering ships a direct route between the North Atlantic and the Indian Ocean via the Mediterranean Sea and the Red Sea, reducing the journey distance from the Arabian Sea to London by more than 9000 kilometers

Timeline of Modern World History

1882 — Formation of the **Triple Alliance** between Germany, Austria-Hungary and Italy.

1884 — The **Berlin Conference** on Africa.

1904–1905 — Japan defeated Russia in the **Russo-Japanese War**

1914 — Archduke Ferdinand of Austria was assassinated in Sarajevo which provided the spark for the **outbreak of the First World War**.

1918 — Russia signed the **Treaty of Brest-Litovsk** and withdrew from the World War I (March). Austria-Hungary and Germany signed armistice with the Allies and the World War I came to an end (November)

1919 — **Paris Peace Conference** (January). Germany signed the Treaty of Versailles (June)

1929 — **Great Depression**

1939 — **Invasion of Poland** by Germany and declaration of war by Britain and France against Germany and the World War II began

1940 — **France surrendered** (June) before the officials of Nazi Germany and Germany established a German occupation zone in Northern and Western France that encompassed about three fifths of France.

1941 — **Japan attacked Pearl Harbor** in Hawaii in December, leading to the entry of the United States in the World War II

1942 — Three **great battles of the World War II**-Midway, Stalingrad and El Alamein turned the tide in favor of the Allied Powers.

1945 — **Establishment of the United Nations** (April). Germany surrendered unconditionally (May). Japan surrendered (August) after the U.S. dropped atomic bombs in Hiroshima and Nagasaki.

1947 — **Truman Doctrine**, which became the foundation of American foreign policy and often described as the start of the Cold War.

1948 — Establishment of the **State of Israel** and the beginning of a series of wars between the new state and its neighbouring Arab states resulting in destruction, disputes over territory and exodus of refugees.

1950 — The **Korean War** began.

1961 — **Berlin Wall** built dividing the city of Berlin

1962 — The **Cuban Missile Crisis** which is often considered the closest the Cold War came to escalating into a full-scale nuclear war.

1968 — The **Prague Spring** in Czechoslovakia with its slogan "Socialism with a human face".

1969 — **Détente in the Cold War** and relaxation in tension in East-West relations

1979 — **Invasion of Afghanistan** by the Soviet Union

1985 — **Mikhail Gorbachev** as the leader of the Soviet Union. His reforms, in little more than six tumultuous years lifted the Iron Curtain and decisively altered the political climate of the world.

1991 — **Disintegration of the USSR.**

1992 — The **Maastricht Treaty** and formation of the European Union. The Treaty came into effect in 1993.

2001 — Al-Qaeda terrorists hijacked four planes, crashing two into the twin towers of the World Trade Centre in New York City, the third plane into the Pentagon in Washington, DC, and the fourth plane is downed on the outskirts of Pennsylvania. In this terror attack, also known as the **September 11 attack**, 2,996 people, including 2,977 victims and 19 hijackers, died. Invasion of Afghanistan by the United States to depose the Taliban, who had harboured al-Qaeda terrorists marked the beginning of the American-led "Global War on Terror".

Timeline of Modern World History

2002 — Circulation of physical Euro coins and banknotes (1 January). The **African Union** was launched (9 July) replacing the Organization of African Unity.

2008 — **Barack Obama** is elected to become the first black President of the United States (November). The Mumbai terror attack which lasted for four days (November), by Lashkar-e-Taiba killing more than 150 people.

2009 — **Sri Lankan Civil War** ended

2010 — Beginning of the **Arab Spring**

2011 — **Osama bin Laden** killed by the United States Navy SEALs in Pakistan (May)

2016 — Barak Obama visited Cuba and became the first U.S president to visit Cuba since Calvin Coolidge in 1928 (March). The **United States withdrew its troops from Afghanistan** after 15 years (December).

2018 — China's National People's Congress voted to abolish presidential term limits, enabling **Xi Jinping** to rule for life. He is also the General Secretary of the Chinese Communist Party, the highest position without term limits.

2019 — **COVID 19** (coronavirus disease 2019) caused by severe acute respiratory syndrome coronavirus 2 (SARS-CoV-2). The virus was first identified in an outbreak in the Chinese city of Wuhan (December).

2020 — **Britain formally withdrew from the European Union.** The COVID-19 pandemic spread from China to the rest of the world infecting millions of people and also triggered the COVID-19 Recession, the worst economic crisis since the Great Depression.

2022 — Russian **invasion on Ukraine** (February). **Protests in Sri Lanka** (March) against the economic mismanagement by the government, shortages of fuel and essential items, power cuts, high inflation, the rapid rise in the cost of living and against authoritarianism, corruption and nepotism of the Rajapaksa family.

2023 — Croatia adopted the euro and become the 20th member state of the Eurozone. **Political crisis in Brazil** as supporters of former president Jair Bolsonaro storm the Brazilian National Congress, the Supreme Federal Court and the Presidential Palace of Planalto in the capital, Brasília a week after the inauguration of his leftist rival, President Luiz Inácio Lula da Silva (January).

CHAPTER 1

Emergence of the Modern World

In this Chapter

A. The Renaissance
1. Introduction
2. What was the Renaissance?
3. Medieval Period
4. Background to the Renaissance
5. Why in Italy
   i. Historical Past
   ii. Political Conditions
   iii. Social Conditions
   iv. Economic Factors
   v. Geographical Factors
6. Renaissance Features
   i. Humanism
   ii. Secular Outlook
   iii. Individualism
7. Renaissance in Various Fields
   i. Art
   ii. Literature
   iii. Science
   iv. Religion
8. The Spread of the Renaissance
   i. The Legacy of the Renaissance

B. Reformation
1. Introduction
2. Background to the Reformation
3. Causes of the Reformation
   i. Religious
   ii. Intellectual
   iii. Political
   iv. Economic
   v. Socio-Cultural
4. Reformers Before the Reformation
5. Martin Luther
6. Beginning of the Reformation
7. Response from the Papacy
8. Stages in the Reformation
   i. Urban Reformation
   ii. Peasants War
   iii. Princes Reformation
9. The Counter Reformation
10. Spread of the Reformation
11. Role of Women in Reformation
12. End of the Reformation
13. Impact of the Reformation
14. Renaissance and Reformation in Comparison

C. The Age of Discovery
1. Introduction
2. Causes of the Explorations
   i. Legacy of the Renaissance
   ii. Fall of Constantinople
   iii. Commercial Considerations
   iv. Technological Advances
   v. Increased Geographical Knowledge
   vi. Religious Factor
   vii. Political Motives
3. Major Discoveries
4. Impact of the Discoveries
5. Reasons for the European Success

A. The Renaissance

1. Introduction

The Renaissance denotes a great wave of cultural and intellectual pursuits that swept through the Italian peninsula from the 14th century. This historical phenomenon was characterised by efforts to rediscover and apply the learning of classical antiquity and to move away from the artistic conventions, religious superstitions and narrow world view of the Middle Ages. It marked the transition between the medieval and the modern Europe.

'Renaissance' is a French word meaning '**rebirth**', its Italian equivalent is ***Rinascimento***, and refers to a revival of art and learning. It originated in **Tuscany**, centring in the city of Florence in Italy. In the 15th century, the Renaissance spread rapidly from its birthplace in Florence to the rest of Italy and soon to the rest of Europe where it evolved and existed up to 17th century. The invention of the printing press (around 1440) by a German printer **Johannes Gutenberg** accentuated the rapid transmission of the Renaissance ideas. As it spread, its ideas diversified and changed, being adapted to the local culture.

It was only in the 19th century, after the publication of the book, *The Civilization of the Renaissance in Italy*, the French word Renaissance began to gain wide acceptability to describe the **self-conscious cultural movement** originated in Italy. In the 20th century, scholars began to break the Renaissance into regional and national movements to describe periods of cultural rebirth as 'renaissances' such as the Bengal Renaissance in the case of India.

> ***The Civilization of the Renaissance in Italy*** is a work by **Jacob Burckhardt**, a Swiss historian and scholar of art and culture. Published in 1860, the work initiated the term 'the Renaissance' and discussions on it. The book contained a synthesis of opinions about the Renaissance.

The Renaissance was both a cultural movement and a period in history. As a movement it originated in the city-states of Italy and spread to the rest of Europe influencing literature, philosophy, art, music, politics, science, religion and other aspects of intellectual enquiry. It involved a revival of interest in Latin and vernaculars, application of linear perspective and other techniques in painting to impart more realism in the depiction of the natural world, increased reliance on observation and inductive reasoning in science and education.

As a period it ran from 1300 to 1600. During this period the European Civilisation experienced a fundamental transformation with the disintegration of outlook and institutions of the Middle Ages and creation of distinctly modern features in which individuals were more concerned about the worldly life and were consciously aspiring to shape their destinies. As this process of transformation was ignited by the Renaissance, the Renaissance is considered as the **'point of departure for the modern world'**.

At the same time there are scholars who consider the Italian Renaissance not as the punctuated end of the Middle Ages and the beginning of the modern world. They argue that the Renaissance was an extension of the Middle Ages that the revival of classical learning had already been visible in the High Middle Ages and that the scholastic and legal studies in the Italian universities of Padua and Bologna had contributed much to the emergence of the Renaissance. As per these scholars, rather than a period with definitive beginning and end and consistent contents in between, the Renaissance was a movement of practices and ideas in different times and places. In their view the Renaissance was a network of diverse, sometimes converging, sometimes conflicting cultures, and not a single time-bound culture. Likewise, the Marxist interpretations of the Renaissance differ from the general perception. The Marxists historians view the Renaissance developments in material terms and hold that the changes in art, literature and philosophy were part of general economic transition from feudalism towards capitalism during which the bourgeoisie class with leisure time and wealth became patrons of arts and culture.

2. What was the Renaissance?

The Renaissance, in essence, was an attempt by artists and scholars to recover and apply the learning and standards of ancient Greece and Rome. Thus, it marked a **cultural rebirth** of the classical age at the close of the Middle Ages and the rise of the Modern World.

The Renaissance scholars sought out historical and literary texts of antiquity in the monastic libraries of Europe. The **Fall of Constantinople** in 1453 accentuated the interest in ancient manuscripts as the fleeing wave of Greek scholars had brought with them precious manuscripts of classical era. These developments paved way for the innovative flowering of Latin and vernacular literature and increased focus on translating and studying the Classical works from Latin and Greek. Many writers imitated the methods and styles of ancient Greek and Roman scholars such as Homer, Plato and Cicero. This **revived interest in the Classics** led to the first archaeological study of Roman remains by the architect Brunelleschi and the **rediscovery of the Classics** lost to the Europeans for centuries inspired revival of classical precedents in architecture, painting and sculpture.

The Renaissance also represented a **break from the Middle Ages**, rejection of certain elements of the medieval outlook and also formulation of a **modern understanding of humanity** and its place in the world. The Medieval Period is generally depicted as a 'time of ignorance and superstition' that placed 'the word of religious authorities over personal experience and rational activity'. In contrast, the Renaissance thinkers and artists were people with fascination for the cultural forms and the secular spirit of Greece and Rome. They stood for full development of human talent and exploration of possibilities of life in this world. The Renaissance activities were this worldly and human centred, instead of religious and dogmatic approach of the preceding period. In short, the Renaissance could be viewed as an attempt by intellectuals to study and improve the secular and worldly, both through the revival of ideas from antiquity and through novel approaches to thought.

The Renaissance was also a period of emergence of distinctly **modern attitudes**. It found expressed in Humanism and secular treatment in art and literature, assertion of reason over revelation and theology and scholasticism loosening its ground to rationalism and science. This was a new vision, about man, as a creative individual who could shape his own destiny without depending on god and about the world as a worthy place to live-in with all the attractions of earthly life. It is because of this importance given to worldly attributes and human potentials that the Renaissance is termed as the **'rediscovery of the world and of man'**.

For the Renaissance scholars the Middle Ages was a period of decline from the high culture and civilisation of the Classical world and they believed that they were experiencing a revival of cultural greatness. Renaissance artists and writers themselves were well aware of the transformations that were taking place and had a feeling of **'self-congratulation on living in a golden age'**.

3. Medieval Period

In the history of Europe the period from the 5th to the 15th century is considered as the Medieval Period. This period coincides with the fall of the Western Roman Empire and merges into the Renaissance.

The Middle Ages in Europe was characterised by distinctive view of the world and the individual. This outlook was totally different from both the ancient Greco-Roman and the modern scientific-secular views. In the Middle Ages a perfect life meant not of this world but that of the higher world after the union with the God. This age also emphasised the point that reason that was not supported by revelation was either wrong or inadequate.

Further, the medieval view of the universe was based on the **geocentric theory** that postulated the earth as the centre of the universe. Under this theory the universe was sharply differentiated between a higher world of perfection, realm of grace, and a lower world of imperfection, the earthly realm. This earth-centred conception of the universe was in conformity with the Christian idea that the God created the universe for man and woman and attainment of salvation as the essential aim of life.

The medieval **conception of individual** was one that of wretched and sinful creature. The dominant view was that human beings were weak and sinful and they could remove their sinful nature and could attain salvation with the God's love and grace alone. This approach that the God as the central aspect in the existence of the world was known as **theocentricism**, which was the hallmark of medieval philosophy.

Another characteristic feature of the Medieval Period was **scholasticism**. Scholasticism refers to the method of critical thinking in the medieval Europe. It gave emphasis in applying reason to revelation and to prove through reason, what they already held to be true through faith. In other words, the proponents of Scholasticism used reason not to challenge faith but to buttress and clarify the faith. To the medieval thinkers, reason had no independent existence but had to be intertwined with the ecclesiastical and scriptural knowledge. Similarly the literature of the Medieval Period written in both Latin and vernaculars consisted of religious hymns and dramas depicting the life of Christ and saints. Best example of this genre 'The Song of Roland' that depicted Christian's devotion to his faith and the vassal's loyalty to his lord. All these were expressions of an age which emphasised the geocentric nature of universe, salvation-oriented existence of human beings and church-ordained principle of morality and values. Many scholars consider these as features of 'Dark Age' and the Medieval Period as an 'Age of Darkness'. It was in this socio-cultural milieu of the Medieval Age that the Renaissance took birth highlighting new approaches and values and transforming the European civilisation to the Modern Age.

4. Background to the Renaissance

As an intellectual and cultural movement the Renaissance originated in the background of a matrix of factors which were taking shape in the late Middle Age itself. Important of these were the **Crusades**, which brought the Europeans in to contact with the highly developed culture of the Orient, the **Fall of Constantinople**, the capital of the Eastern Roman Empire to the Turks in 1453 during which large number of scholars fled to Europe in order to escape the intolerable treatment of the Turks, **geographical explorations** which created a spirit of adventure and broadened the mental horizons of the Europeans, rise in **global trade** leading to the emergence of urban centres, **decline of feudalism** as a socio-economic-political system based on inherited social ranks and inherent socio and economic privileges and obligations, **spread of education** through the medium of universities like **Bologna, Padua, Pisa, Oxford and Paris** which created atmosphere of curiosity and thinking, contributions of thinkers like **Peter Abelard** (the French philosopher of 12th century) who championed the use of reason in matters of faith, **Roger Bacon** (the English philosopher of 13th century) who, inspired by Aristotle, advocated scientific method to the study of nature, writings of **Boccaccio, Chaucer and Dante** (literary figures of the Late Medieval Period) that paved the way for innovativeness in intellectual life and finally, the invention of **printing press** in 15th century by Johannes Gutenberg facilitating dissemination of ideas and democratisation of learning.

High Renaissance: Refers to a period of about three decades in the Renaissance from the 1490s. During this period the Renaissance activities revolved around three towering figures, Leonardo da Vinci, Michelangelo and Raphael, and visual arts of the Renaissance reached its apogee. The artistic creations of the High Renaissance were marked by great emphasis on classical tradition, gradual attenuation of figural forms leading to the development of a style called Mannerism-stylised and exaggerated approach in painting and sculptor and an expansion of networks of patronage.

5. Why in Italy

The Renaissance originated in northern Italy. Combinations of factors are attributed for the rise of the Renaissance in Italy starting with the city-state of Florence.

i. Historical Past

Italy was historically connected to its Roman past and its grandeur. Reminders of ancient Rome's greatness were visible all over Italy. Many of its cities stood among the ruins of ancient Roman monuments. Many artefacts, manuscripts of antiquity and other Roman cultural symbols were still in existence in Italian peninsula. These historical pieces, monuments and the Roman roads connected the 14th Century Italians with their Great Roman past and intensified their yearning for its revival. Hence, in all probability it seems likely that the classical nature of the Renaissance was linked to its origin in the Roman Empire's heartland, that is Italy.

ii. Political Conditions

Italy did not exist as a single political entity in the early modern period, instead was divided into smaller city-states. Political structure of many of these city-states was **republican** or **oligarchic** in nature. These city-states had developed a fairly uniform republican self-government around the office of a chief magistrate. Growth in private wealth as a result of expanding commerce and participation in the administration of these city-states had instilled the spirit of individual self-consciousness among the citizen of these city-states. These republics held both the monarchs and the church at bay and were devoted to the notion of liberty, which was a sine qua non for a cultural movement like the Renaissance to take its birth. Even though it has to be admitted that these republics bore little resemblance to a modern democracy, the relative political freedom they afforded was conducive to academic and artistic nourishment.

iii. Social Conditions

Compared to other parts of Europe, the city-states of Italy especially those of Northern Italy were prosperous urban centres whose unusual social climate allowed the emergence of a rare cultural efflorescence. Cities often being centres, where people exchange ideas, emerged an ideal breeding ground for an intellectual revolution.

Certain essential features of the urban life in Italian city-states facilitated the emergence of the Renaissance. Business class played a leading role in the political and cultural life of the cities. People of these urban centres had wealth, inclination to cultivate the arts and willingness to enjoy the fruits of worldly life. These rich sections proved to be the patrons and promoters of the Renaissance in Italy. For the urban class, art served as a focus of civic pride and patriotism and the rich families competed with each other in patronising artists and scholars. A fine example in this regard is the role of **Medici family** in Florence that commissioned many painters and scholars that gave fillip to the Renaissance. Cosimo de'Medici, one of the prominent members of this family, set new standard for the patronage of the arts.

Predominance of urban life in Italian city-states also meant **less importance to feudalism** than they did in other parts of Europe. By the 14th century Italy appeared to have exited from feudalism and thereby reduced the feudal values of birth, status on the basis of military powers and the lord-vassal hierarchical social structure. The loosening of feudal values was replaced with values of individual talents, individual assertion and individual achievement which all acquired dominance in the urban civic life.

Urban life in Italian city-states was also marked by the **emerging secular outlook**. For the urban population, especially the richer sections of them, the medieval preoccupation with salvation became a secondary factor, while the material world and worldly pleasures they could enjoy with their money became prime motive.

The change of outlook was also reflected in the treatment of artists and thinkers. In the Middle Ages the artists were seen as craftsmen who performed lowly labour. With the decline of feudal outlook in Italian cities, this conception about artists changed and artists began to be held in high esteem. This resulted in the emergence of large number of patrons of arts. In order to be memorialised, the rich sections and even the church authorities like Pope commissioned artists to have their portraits or sculpture to be produced. **Emergence of 'portraiture'** as a distinct genre in painting during this time is a testimony to this. Popes and the patricians alike thus became generous patrons of the Renaissance, as the works of Michelangelo and Raphael testify.

It is to be noted that the urban dwellers were not people of anti-religion or atheists but were people who were intrigued and excited by the challenges and opportunities of living a life of fullness in this world than a promised heaven.

Urban life also promoted **individualism**. Here, people were freed of feudalistic and religious constraints and were looking for expressing their talents to win fame and glory. This individualistic outlook pervasive in Italian city-states, especially in Florence, is of utmost importance in the context of Renaissance, as it was a movement that gave importance to what was distinctive and superior in an individual, not what was common to all. People of talents in the cities tried to place themselves apart, by being unique and dignified human beings. This idea of 'individuality' that a person could separate from the crowd by his creative genius was the hallmark of the period which was abundantly nurtured by the urban environment of the Italian city-states.

It is also pertinent to note that Italy especially Florence was blessed with the **presence of 'Great Men'**. Leading figures of the movement Leonardo da Vinci, Botticelli and Michelangelo were all born here.

iv. Economic Factors

In the emergence of the Renaissance in Italy, **economic prosperity** and flourishing commercial centres played significant role. Fifteenth-century Italy was one of the most urbanised areas in Europe. Accumulation of wealth in Italy, as a result of expansion of trade since the 14th century had facilitated emergence of urban centres with its unique urban culture and rich families. Flow of luxury goods from the Eastern World during the Crusades had facilitated the prosperity of towns like Florence, Genoa and Venice. Establishment of the Medici Bank which was the largest bank in Europe in the 15th century brought unprecedented wealth in the city of Florence. As already seen above, this urban culture was in tune with the notions of individualism, humanism and enjoyment of the worldly pleasures. Moreover, during the Renaissance, money and art went hand in hand. Artists depended on their patrons (many times rich merchants and banking families), while patrons required artists in order to be memorised and to be glorified.

v. Geographical Factors

The location of Italy at the cross roads of two great civilisations – the Eastern and the Western – was another factor in the emergence of Renaissance in Italy. The Crusades had reopened the Mediterranean to commerce and travel, facilitating exchange of ideas, not just of goods. The main trade routes from the east passed through the Italian cities of **Genoa, Pisa** and **Venice**. Luxury goods imported from the east could then be resold throughout Europe making the Italian cities richest urban centres. The trade routes that converged in Italy also emerged as conduits of culture and knowledge.

After the **fall of Constantinople** in 1453 a wave of migration of scholars, grammarians, musicians, poets and so forth, to Europe took place in which Italy acted as a bridge. These émigrés brought the far greater preserved and accumulated knowledge of the Greek civilisation. These scholars searched monastic libraries for ancient manuscripts and also ignited the Renaissance interest in linguistic studies through the newly opened academies in the Italian cities.

6. Renaissance Features

i. Humanism

The most important intellectual characteristic of the Renaissance was humanism. It was based on the classical Greco-Roman concept of ***Humanitas*** which mean the qualities that make men and women human with its maxim **'Man is the measure of all things'.**

It meant development of human virtues like benevolence, prudence, judgement, eloquence and rhetoric. The purpose of humanism was to create a universal man, a combination of intellectual and physical excellence, who was capable of functioning honourably virtually in any situation. Humanists aimed at transfiguration of 'Dark Age' into a new order that would reflect and encourage full development of the human potentials.

> Humanism was an intellectual movement that focussed on human potentials and achievements. Followers of this tradition were known as the humanists and they popularised the study of subjects such as history, literature and philosophy – common to classical education and these subjects are known as humanities or ***studia humanitatis*** (humanistic studies).

Humanism in Italian Renaissance found expressed in many ways. In practical terms, it was an educational and cultural program to recover, interpret and assimilate the language, literature, learning and values of ancient Greece and Rome. As such the Humanists gave emphasis on the study of ancient literature and history under the belief that the classics provided moral instruction and an intensive understanding of human behaviour. Renaissance humanists valued the classics for its own value and studied them as a guide to the good life in this world. This outlook was in contrast to that of the medieval scholars who had subordinated the classics to the requirements of the Christian doctrines. Interest cultivated by the humanists in classical learning was aimed at nourishing their attitude to worldly life, to write well, to speak well, to achieve self-cultivation and above all to live well.

Humanism was also an ethical stance which gave emphasis to human beings – individually and collectively. It emphasised critical thinking (rationalism) and evidence (empiricism) over superstition and dogma. Humanism was thus characterised by the idea of human freedom and human's ability to progress and asserted 'the genius of man . . . the unique and extraordinary ability of the human mind'. To the humanists, human life was an opportunity of achieving excellence through individual striving and it was their duty to pursue it as the end of life. This was in contrast to the medieval view that humans were incapable of attaining excellence without divine will which became one of the most characteristic doctrines of the Renaissance.

> Scholars of the Renaissance introduced the concept of the ideal individual, a **'universal man'**, a person who excelled in almost every area of study and later called as the **'Renaissance Man'**. ***The Courtier,*** a work by Baldassare Castiglione published in 1528, prescribed qualities of such a person. He should be well educated in the classics, excel in music, dance and singing and also should be a skilled rider and wrestler. The Courtier also conceptualised the **'Renaissance Woman'** as the one who was to be charming and well versed in the classics.

Humanistic expressions were visible in art pieces of the time too. For example, Michelangelo's 'God Giving Life to Adam' or his painting in Sistine Chapel, 'the Last Judgment', were religious works which celebrated humanity.

Influence of humanism and humanists were found in the prevailing view of history also. The scholastic view that history as an unfolding of God's will was challenged by the humanists who emphasised that the human will and human authors are determinant factors in the unfolding of history. The humanists viewed the period preceding their own as period of decline from classical heights and their own period as a period of rebirth of classical wisdom and ideals. The periodisation of history in to ancient, medieval and modern is attributed to the Renaissance scholars. This periodisation of history could be possible as the Renaissance humanists straddled two worlds – the classical and their own modern age. Contrasting the features of the Middle Ages to that of classical antiquity and of their own, they labelled the Middle Ages as a period of darkness.

To spread these ideals the humanists used literature, art and drama. They also founded their own schools to impart the new curriculum and were also involved in teaching in numerous grammar schools and universities.

Petrarch (1304–74) is considered as the Father of Humanism, for his devotion to the study of Greek and Roman works. Petrarch and his followers conducted systematic efforts to discover the classics. His rediscovery of Cicero's (the ancient Roman orator) letters is often credited with initiating the Renaissance. Like Cicero, Petrarch exhorted that education must consist not only learning but also learning how to communicate one's knowledge and to use it for public good. He encouraged his students to master the Greek language and setup schools to promote Ciceronian ideal. The comment that 'the Renaissance was above all things, a revival of Cicero, and only after him and through him of the rest of classical antiquity' points to the role played by Petrarch in the Italian Renaissance by reviving the Ciceronian ideals. Petrarch is also known for being the first to develop the concept of 'Dark Ages' referring to the Middle Ages. Petrarch is best known for his Italian poetry notably the 'Songbook' and the 'Triumphs'. He also wrote large number of introspective essays, letters and other scholarly works in Latin language.

Giovanni Pico della Mirandola's (the 15th century Italian Renaissance philosopher) ***Oration on the Dignity of Man*** (1486) is considered as the **'Manifesto of the Renaissance'**. In this book Pico attempted to remap the human landscape to centre all attention on human capacity and human perspective. In this, Pico depicted man as a unique creation in the 'chain of being'. God created man without any slot in the chain; instead they were made capable of learning from and imitating any existing creature. When man makes use of his talents he ascends the chain of being and attain final communion with God and when he fails to use his talents he vegetates. It was argued by Pico that with free will, human beings had the capability to change themselves, while all the other changes in nature were the result of some outside force acting on whatever it is that undergoes change. This idea of human ascend by the exercise of their intellectual powers was a profound endorsement of the dignity of human existence and one of the greatest contributions by the Renaissance humanists.

ii. Secular Outlook

Another characteristic of the Renaissance was its secular approach. Renaissance scholars moved away from the religious orientation of the Middle Ages and treated human conditions in secular terms. Hence, it is said that the Renaissance represented celebration of secular over piety. The Middle Age was characterised as a period of feudalism and an oppressive church, wedged between the golden ages of the Roman Empire and the Renaissance. In contrast, the Renaissance approach was secular and this-worldly. This secular orientation of the intellectual life of the Renaissance was a reflection of the contemporary society itself whose urban upper class considered the challenges and pleasures of this world more exciting than waiting for a promised heaven.

> It is important to note that the Renaissance secularism was not irreligious per se. While opposing the conventional authority including the scholastic theologians they did not challenge the Christian faith itself. They were practical moralists who presented a moral code for the newly emerging urban population.

This secular approach to life could be seen in the writings of scholars like **Poggio** (1380–1459) who defended acquisition of wealth and justified usury both of which had been condemned by the orthodox as un-Christian. Similarly **Lorenzo Valla** (1406–57), in his work ***On Pleasure***, condemned Christian injunction against pleasure. This emphasis on secular morality and glorification of human nature went into creating an idea not just of individualism but also an ideal of public man.

Another example of this secular approach to life is seen in **Niccolo Machiavelli** (1469–1527), observer and writer of the Italian Renaissance. As a known observer of the contemporary Italian politics, Machiavelli informs us that the Italian princes made no efforts to justify their policies on religious grounds. In his book ***The Prince*** (1513) he expounded a new political theory based on cold light of reason, free of religious and moral illusions and portrayed the emerging modern secular state. Machiavelli looked at this world as a natural entity and rejected divine origin nature of the state, hence he rejected the medieval view that the rulers are bound by the moral precepts originating in a higher world or the values prescribed in religious scriptures. Machiavelli in his book expounded a new political theory, which was secular in its approach, in order to guide the rulers how to prepare and expand the state's power. Machiavelli argued that than being morally right, a ruler should look for what was politically effective. This approach to statecraft indifferent to moral and religious considerations initiated a trend of thought that now we recognise as modern. For this reason, Machiavelli is seen as the prototype of a modern empirical scientist. He emancipated politics from theology and moral philosophy and he undertook to describe what rulers actually did and thus anticipated what was later called the scientific spirit in which the observer attempts to discover only what really happens instead of treating them as good or bad.

Machiavelli

iii. Individualism

An associated feature of Humanism was individualism – the assertion of the individual which became the hallmark of the Renaissance society. Urban life and wealth had released people from the old constraints and values of the feudal manor and Christian religion. Hence, people sought to assert their own personalities, express their emotions and demonstrate their unique talents. This faith in uniqueness of individuals and their potential is also found expressed in pursuits of praise and reputation. Humanists stood for fame and glory that came with their meritorious deeds. In other words, they emphasised on human creative power to attain excellence in every sphere and attainment of fame and glory in the material world became an end in itself to the humanists. In the writings of Dante and in the doctrines of Petrarch and Machiavelli and also in the essays of Montaigne the virtues of intellectual freedom and individual expression emerged as the most persuasive and eloquent statement of human life. Since then individualism is a deeply embedded aspect of the Western values and social life.

7. Renaissance in Various Fields

i. Art

Renaissance essentially found expressed in different art forms – painting, sculpture, and architecture. Main characteristics that differentiated the Renaissance art were its stress on humanism, a heroic vision of human beings, depiction of the ideal of beauty of nude, return to classical models in architecture and the importance given to proportion, balance and harmony in conceptualising space and spatial relations. It is pertinent to note that though the Renaissance art took as its foundation the art of classical antiquity, it transformed that tradition by absorbing contemporary development in art and scientific knowledge.

The medieval art was inspired by spirituality and had given importance to the eternal world. Renaissance art though did not stop expressing spirituality; its settings were totally different. It was set in this world where people live, aspire, act and worship. By giving importance to this world as the stage in which the humans find their spiritual destiny as they fulfil their human one and by reducing the importance of the 'perfect world' the Renaissance art marked a conscious revolt against the art of the Middle Ages.

Similarly, Renaissance artists tried to revive the classical antiquity in art and architecture. The architect **Filippo Brunelleschi** (1377–1446) and sculptor **Donatello** conducted the first archaeological study of the Roman remains. Brunelleschi designed the Dome of the Cathedral of Florence on the classical model. He also developed the rules of linear perspective in art and architecture and in doing so placed emphasis on **symmetry, proportion, geometry** and the **regularity of parts** as they were demonstrated in the architecture of Greco-Roman classical antiquity. Thus, by giving emphasis to visual space and the relationship between the object and the observer and also by defining it in mathematical terms the Renaissance art paved way for the development of the modern scientific approach.

The Renaissance art while stressing on humanistic value of the world gave importance to the ancient ideal of beauty as the beautiful nude. Excellent examples were the **'Vitruvian Man'** of Leonardo da Vinci and **'David'** by Michelangelo. In taking inspiration from the ancient art the Renaissance artists studied anatomy to represent things as they are or at least as they are seen to be.

Giotto 1270–1337: The first major contributor to Renaissance painting was Giotto, belonged to Florence. Giotto drew all his figures and their postures according to nature, hence they appear remarkably alive. Giotto's best works were frescos, and the masterpiece is the decoration of the Scrovegni Chapel in Padua depicting the 'Life of the Virgin' and the 'Life of Christ'.

Leonardo da Vinci (1452–1519), Michelangelo Buonarroti (1475–1564) and Raphel (1483–1520) were three other prominent Florentine figures of Renaissance art.

Leonardo da Vinci: He was a polymath having interests in wide subjects like painting, architecture, science, music, engineering, astronomy, history and so forth that enabled him to be called as the '**Universal Genius**' or '**Renaissance Man**'. Considered as one of the most diversely talented individuals ever to have lived, he was an individual of 'unquenchable curiosity'. His ability of close observation and his psychological insights enabled him to create works, which were nothing but of an unsurpassed genius. Among the most important paintings of Leonardo are **'The Last Supper'** and **'La Gioconda'** (the Mona Lisa). The Last Supper represents the scene of the last supper of Jesus with his apostles and is one of the most recognisable paintings in the world. In this painting Leonardo depicted the consternation that occurred among the Twelve Disciples when Jesus announced that one of them would betray him. The painting is also brilliant as it shows the personalities of Jesus' disciples through facial expressions. Mona Lisa is a half-length portrait painting which is described as the best known, the most visited, the most written about, the most produced work of art in the world. The painting technique invented by Leonardo in Mona Lisa is *sfumato*, blending of colours without the use of lines or borders, in the manner of smoke to produce a soft transition between colours and tones. Apart from the technique of painting, the subject's expression which is enigmatic also makes the painting a unique piece in the world art.

Leonardo da Vinci

Michelangelo: Apart from being a painter, architect and poet, Michelangelo was also a sculptor of par excellence. Well known for the portrayal of human body in painting and sculpture, Michelangelo created figures that were forceful and of heroic grandeur. His idea of sculpting was to release the form from the marble than imposing form on marble. Michelangelo's greatest sculptures are 'David', 'Moses', 'Pieta' and the 'Dying Slave'. David a marble statue of the Biblical hero David came to symbolise the defence of civil liberates embodied in the Republic of Florence. Pieta another sculpture in marble depicts the body of Jesus on the lap of Mother Mary after the crucifixation. Michelangelo's two great paintings are in the form of frescos in the Sistine Chapel in Rome. On the ceiling of the chapel, nine scenes from *The Book of Genesis* have been painted of which **'The Creation of Adam'** is the most famous. On the altar wall of the Chapel, Michelangelo painted **'The Last Judgment'** depicting the second coming of Christ and the final judgement by God. As an architect Michelangelo designed the dome of the new St. Peter's Basilica in Rome.

Michelangelo

Raphael: He was the last of the three giants of the Florentine Renaissance. His best known work is 'The School of Athens', a fresco depicting philosophy and is considered as the perfect embodiment of the classical spirit of the Renaissance. Raphael depicted famous Renaissance figures, such as Michelangelo, Leonardo and himself, as classical philosophers and their students. Raphael is well known for his paintings on Madonna (Madonna and the Child, Madonna of the Pinks and so forth).

> Though the Renaissance society had restricted women's roles, there were some women painters and writers such as Anguissola, Gentileschi and Vittoria Colonna. Anguissola painted portraits of her sisters and of prominent people such as King Philip II of Spain and became the first woman artist to attain international reputation.

ii. Literature

Literature of the Renaissance either reflected the time or was a self-expression of the writer or was a portrayal of the individuality of their subjects, thus imitating trends that modern writers still follow. Writers of the time wrote in Latin, in Italian and also in vernaculars. **Petrarch** and **Boccaccio** were two prominent Renaissance writers. While the former was famous for his sonnets – 14 line poems – the latter is best known for the ***The Decameron***, a series of realistic stories depicting both tragic and comic views of life.

iii. Science

The spirit of Renaissance was not confined to art alone. It found expressed in scientific studies and experiments. Great advances occurred in fields like geography, physics, astronomy, anatomy and engineering. Even though, during the initial years, the humanists had favoured the study of humanities over natural science and applied mathematics, scientific outlook was discernible even at this stage. In 1450, **Nicholas Cusanas** (German) anticipated the heliocentric world view of Copernicus. In 1492, discovery of the Americas by Christopher Columbus challenged the classical world view. Gradually a suitable environment developed to question previously held truths and the search for new answers.

Leonardo da Vinci made observational drawings of anatomy and nature and conducted controlled experiments in medical dissection, water flow and aerodynamics. In 1543, Nicolaus Copernicus published his book *On the Revolutions of the Heavenly Spheres* which offered an alternative model – **'heliocentric theory'** – of the universe as against Ptolemy's 'geocentric theory'. Scientific studies by Galileo Galilei (Italy), Johannes Kepler (German) and Tycho Brahe (Denmark) significantly advanced the Renaissance understanding of the universe. Andreas Vesalius the 16th century anatomist and physician considered as the founder of modern human anatomy published his *On the Fabric of the Human Body*, describing anatomy of brain and other organs. The English physician William Harvey further contributed to the studies in anatomy and physiology and provided the first systemic description of the circulatory system. Such significant developments in the 15th and the 16th centuries are described as the **Scientific Renaissance** which facilitated the Scientific Revolution of the 17th century during which the scientists shifted their focus from recovery to innovation.

iv. Religion

In the field of religion too the Renaissance had profound impact, especially in the way how people perceived the relation between man and God. Giovanni Pico has God saying to man 'We have made you a creature as the free and proud shaper of your own being'. The Renaissance scholars attacked scholasticism for its preoccupation with trivial questions, and instead stressed on purer form of Christianity based on the direct study of the Bible. They undermined the traditional loyalties and temporal authority of the pope through critical enquiry. In this context the essay ***On the Donation of Constantine*** by Lorenzo Valla in 1440 was seminal. In this work he proved that the donation of Emperor Constantine I, the whole of the Western Roman Empire to the Roman Catholic Church in the fourth century, as gratitude for curing of leprosy was based on a forged document of eighth century. Many of the theologians like Erasmus, Thomas More, Martin Luther and John Calvin were followers of humanism. Erasmus called as 'Prince of the Humanists', through his work ***In Praise of Folly***, made a satirical attack on superstitions and traditions of the European society. This work was to inspire the Protestant Reformation in later course of history.

8. The Spread of the Renaissance

From its birthplace in Italy, the Renaissance spread to other parts of Europe in late 15th and 16th centuries. This spread of the Renaissance north of the Alps is known as the **Northern Renaissance**. The velocity of transmission of the Renaissance ideas throughout Europe was factored by the invention of the printing press which facilitated availability of books including the Bible in vernaculars. In its migration to other parts of Europe, the Renaissance adapted itself to the conditions of the time and space.

In many cases the spread of the Renaissance to other parts of Europe was through the agency of Italian scholars. For example, the French king Francis I imported Italian art and commissioned Venetian artists including Leonardo da Vinci. The trade and commerce between Italy and other countries too facilitated the spread of the new ideas as was in case of the Low Countries (Belgium and Netherlands). Moreover many Northern European artists who studied in Italy carried the Renaissance ideas back to their homelands.

In Europe, the leading protagonists of the humanism were theologians and other members of the clerical order, which was in contrast to Italy where professionals had played a dominant role giving it a secular character. Another feature of the Northern Renaissance was that it took place under increasing centralisation of political power, whereas in Italy it was dominated by independent city-states. Also, the Northern Renaissance was closely linked to the Protestant Reformation which further accentuated changes in social, cultural, religious and political life of Europe.

> The Elizabethan Age or the period of Queen Elizabeth (1558–1603) was the period of spread of Renaissance in England. Queen was well educated and was a linguist, who knew French, Italian, Greek and Latin. She supported art and literature. Greatest playwright of all time, William Shakespeare was the most important literary figure of Elizabethan Age, his works such as Julius Caesar and King Lear depict Renaissance values – heroism, honour and constant fight against fate and fortune in ample measure.

The Northern Renaissance used the cultural tools of humanism to attack dogma, ritual or clerical power, not to undermine the faith but to restore it to its purity. They were less concerned about the revival of classical values. The Northern Humanists used the Renaissance ideas to examine the traditional teachings of the Church, were critical of it for its failure to inspire the followers to live a true Christian life and had a more focus on reform of society. This group called as the **Christian Humanists** gave emphasis on the discovery of accurate Biblical texts in order to initiate a great religious awakening, hence an effort to construct **Scriptural**

Christianity in place of Scholastic Christianity. It can be said that by reassessing the Christian theology, the Christian Humanists set the stage for the Reformation. Two important Christian Humanists were **Desiderius Erasmus** of Holland and **Thomas More** of England. In his book, *The Praise of Folly* also known as ***In Praise of Folly*** (1509), Erasmus criticised greedy merchants, quarrelsome scholars and pompous priests and argued for Christianity of heart and not of ceremonies. Thomas More in his book ***Utopia*** depicted an imaginary land devoid of greed and war.

i. The Legacy of the Renaissance

Since its origin in the Italian city-states, the Renaissance ideas transformed the socio-cultural and political landscape of Europe. The Renaissance emphasis on dignity of individual facilitated gradual rise of democratic ideas.

In art, the Renaissance painters and sculptures revived the techniques and styles of the classical Greece and Rome making their creations more realistic and lifelike. These scholars and artists created brilliant works containing both secular and religious themes. Vernacular languages gained popularity as the scholars used these languages as the medium of their expression.

In social field, emphasis on individualism and belief in human ability to achieve wisdom and glory prompted an increased desire for learning and consequent rise in literacy throughout Europe. The books of the Renaissance scholars, the published accounts of new discoveries and the new technology of printing which made information inexpensive facilitated further discoveries in different fields. General increase in awareness about the man and the world enabled the people to question political structures and religious practices and also set the tone of modern age.

SUMMARY

The Renaissance – means 'rebirth' and it marked cultural rebirth of ancient Greece and Rome, as the artists and scholars in Italy attempted to recover and apply the learning and standards of these civilisations of antiquity.

Background to the Renaissance – Matrix of factors such as the Crusades by facilitating Europeans' interaction with the Orient, the Fall of Constantinople which forced large number of scholars from Eastern Roman Empire to flee to Europe, geographical explorations by broadening the mental horizons, emergence of urban centres by giving emphasis on individualism and worldly pleasures, decline of feudalism which shattered inherited social ranks and privileges, spread of education by creating an atmosphere of curiosity and thinking and the invention of printing press by disseminating ideas and by democratising learning created an atmosphere congenial to the birth of the Renaissance.

Why it originated in Italy – Historical past, political structure and the city-states, social climate in urban centres, economic prosperity of Italian cities and geographical factors such as location of Italy at the crossroads of the East and the West.

Features of the Renaissance – Humanism, secular outlook and individualism.

Renaissance in various fields – In art emphasis was given on humanism, ideal of beauty of nude, return to classical models, importance to the worldly life and also on incorporation of developments in mathematics and scientific field to project balance, proportion and harmony in conceptualising space and spatial relations in their work. Some of the prominent personalities associated with these developments were:

In art – Filippo Brunelleschi, Donatello, Giotto, Leonardo da Vinci, Michelangelo and Raphael.

In literature – Petrarch and Boccaccio.

In science – Nicholas Cusanas, Leonardo da Vinci, Nicholas Copernicus, Galileo Galilei, Kepler and Tycho Brahe.

In religion – Renaissance transformed peoples' perception of the relation between man and God. Renaissance Humanism also influenced theologians such as Erasmus, Thomas More, Martin Luther and John Calvin.

Spread of the Renaissance – From the late 15th century the Renaissance spread to other parts of Europe. The Northern Renaissance and the Christian Humanists were the two major currents of it. The Elizabethan Age was the period of the spread of the Renaissance in England.

Legacy of the Renaissance – It caused transformation of socio-cultural–political landscape of Europe. It upheld dignity of individual, revived classical styles and techniques in art, popularised vernacular languages, increased the desire for learning and expanded awareness about the man and the world.

Questions of Previous Years Civil Services Examination

1. Give reasons for the origin of the Renaissance in Italy. (2007)
2. 'The Renaissance scholars laid the eggs which Luther, the Father of the Reformation, later on hatched'. Discuss (2006)
3. The Renaissance was the discovery of the world and of man. (1990)
4. 'The Renaissance was not a political or religious movement. It was a state of mind'. (1994)
5. What is meant by the 'rediscovery of ancient civilisation'? Show how the 'New Learning' was a major element in the beginning of Modern Europe. (1986)

B. Reformation

1. Introduction

Reformation, also known as the Protestant Reformation refers to the reform efforts in Christianity initiated by **Martin Luther**, a German monk and professor of theology in the 16th century. The Lutheran rebellion against the authority of the Church shattered irrevocably the religious unity in Christianity and marked the beginning of a new religious outlook. To the Protestants it was a reformation of their religion, to the Catholics–a schism and to the historians–a revolt with larger implications in history.

The Reformation started with the publication of the ***Ninety-Five Theses*** by Luther in 1517 and dominated the European history throughout the 16th century. In response to the Protestant Reformation the Catholic Church initiated a Counter Reformation leading to a sharp schism in Christendom. As a result of the Reformation, the Northern Europe came under the influence of Protestantism and the Southern Europe remained Catholic, while the Central Europe underwent a period of fierce conflict culminating in the **Thirty Years War** (1618–48).

2. | Background to the Reformation

Though the core reason behind the Reformation had been theological, other factors such as the rise of nationalism and nation-states, erosion of loyalty to the Catholic Church due to the Western Schism in 14th and 15th centuries and the impact of humanism and the 'New Learning' of the Renaissance had also been factors that contributed to its origin and development.

The church had been absolutely central to the medieval society. The Roman Catholic Church centred in Rome was central to the European life in the Medieval Period and had transcended geographic, ethnic, linguistic boundaries in its power and influence. Though a religious institution, the Catholic Church had many features that could not avoid having implications on social, cultural, economic and political life of Europe. Hence, what Luther did by initiating the reform was to challenge an institution that exercised ideological control on behalf of the whole feudal order. The Reformation in this sense acquired a dual nature one that of **moral** and the other that of **political**. In moral sense the Reformation aimed at purging the Christianity of its later innovations and in its political sense depriving the papacy of its political power.

3. | Causes of the Reformation

i. Religious

The Roman Catholic Church's commitment to holiness in this world and salvation in the next had been waning in its preoccupation with power and wealth. The clergy from the pope to down had been the centre of criticism for their preoccupation with the material world and corrupt practices. For example, the **Pope Leo X** (1513–21) is alleged to have said 'since the God has given us the papacy, let us enjoy it'.

Similarly, Christianity itself had undergone many changes by this time and many customs and rituals which were alien to its original character had crept into it distorting and corrupting the original teachings of Jesus and the Apostles as expounded in the Bible. Some of these features were indulgences (the documents that absolved people from their sins), intermediation of priests between believers and God, the holding of many bishoprics, sexual indulgences of the clergy (as in the case of Pope Alexander VI, who admitted that he had fathered several children) and worship of Catholic saints through statues and shrines.

ii. Intellectual

The Renaissance had created a background of spirit of enquiry and quest for reform of the static and decaying society. An environment of openness in which questions could be asked and truth could be sought had been one of the impacts of the Renaissance. Though there had been opposition to the corrupt practices of the Roman Catholic Church and attempts to reform, even before, such as those of **Peter Waldo** (12th century 'Waldensians'), **Jan Hus** (14th century 'Hussitism') and **John Wycliffe** (14th century 'Lollards'), they had not been successful in tearing apart the church and the society in an era of blind faith and superstitions. Now the conditions were changing gradually but definitely. Humanists like Erasmus had denounced worldliness and vulgarity of the clergymen in his book ***In Praise of Folly***. Considering these aspects, it can be said that the Reformation was one of the by-products of the Renaissance.

iii. Political

It was also a period of increase in the power of the kings in Europe. The existence of the Holy Roman Empire, as a Christian commonwealth led by the papacy, since the Medieval Period, as a confederation of multi-ethnic states in Central Europe, was against the ambitions of the rulers of the emerging nation-states. The Holy Roman Emperor held sovereignty over these states over which pope enjoyed spiritual control. The interests of the emerging nation-states were also in opposition to that of the papacy, as the kings considered the papal interference as a menace to their authority. This could be better understood from the fact that wherever the reformers enjoyed princely patronage, the Reformation efforts were more successful.

iv. Economic

This conflict of interests was further aggravated by the issue of taxing the church property. The Church was immensely rich with acres of landed property on which the papacy claimed exemption. Further, the papal authority had been collecting huge wealth from these territories and taking it to the papal treasury in Rome depriving the kings of huge wealth. Hence, as huge monetary losses were involved, the rulers of the nation-states were eager supporters of the Reformation in most of the cases.

The **Holy Roman Empire**: It was a multi-ethnic and fragmented collection of practically independent states in central Europe. Its titular rulers were known as the Holy Roman Emperors and from the 14th century the House of Hapsburg held this title. This empire that existed from the Middle Ages ended in 1806 when it was dissolved by the French Emperor Napoleon.

v. Socio-Cultural

In an environment of social transformation, resentment of the ordinary clergy against the centralising authority of the pope grew and the right of the pope to discipline the priesthood came under challenge. The middle class which grew larger and larger in the emerging urban centres with their sophistication and the new worldview began to question the authority of the international church, its clergy and the superstitions. Technological changes as that of the printing press ensured reproduction of these ideas faster and wider. Circulation of printed books had also enabled many Europeans to read religious books and form their own opinion about the church.

4. Reformers Before the Reformation

Even before Luther, there was a long tradition of criticism against the Roman Catholic Church on issues like corruption, nepotism and other evils within it. Theologians like **Peter Waldo** (France), **John Wycliffe** (England) and **John Huss** also known as Jan Hus (Bohemia) had attacked the church's authority and its ability to control an individual's destiny. Many of these people had to work underground or to face punishment for heresy. John Wycliffe had attacked the privileged status of the clergy, the luxury and pomp of the local parishes and had advocated translation of the Bible to the vernaculars so that ordinary people could read and understand directly from it. Wycliffe's followers known as the Lollards are considered as the precursors to the Protestant Reformation and John Wycliffe is considered as the **'evening star of scholasticism'** and the **'morning star of the Reformation'**. Similarly, many of the Northern Humanists, such as **Erasmus and Thomas More**, had added their voices of the growing criticism of Church.

5. Martin Luther

Martin Luther was born in 1483 in Saxony, in the Holy Roman Empire. He was a dropped out law student at the University of Erfurt. He was attracted towards theology and philosophy and entered the St. Augustinian Monastery in Erfurt in 1505 in search of spiritual emancipation. After being awarded his Doctor of Theology in 1512 he was appointed into the senate of the theological faculty of the University of Wittenberg in the German state of Saxony the same year.

Martin Luther

As a monk Luther sought union with God. He participated in the sacraments of the church rigorously, believing in the Church's teaching that salvation depended on faith, actions (charity and fasting) and grace. But these methods did not satisfy Luther. In search of salvation he increasingly turned to reading the Bible. Luther found hope for his own salvation in certain passages in the Bible. These passages revealed to Luther that faith, freely given by God through Christ, enables the recipient to receive salvation. This **doctrine of justification by faith** (*Sola fide* in Latin) rather than by works was a crucial factor that instilled a reform outlook in Luther.

6. Beginning of the Reformation

The Reformation started in 1517 with Luther's attack on the Church's practice of selling indulgences. In Roman Catholic Church **indulgences** were a grant, by the pope, of remission, of the temporal punishment in purgatory (a place or state of suffering inhabited by the souls of sinners who were expiating their sins before going to heaven). The Catholic Church taught that the sinners will go to heaven only after spending time in purgatory. Indulgences were meant to remit portions of that time and were granted to individuals by the church in return for their prayers, attendance at Mass and acts of charity which included monetary offerings to the church.

In 1516, the Roman Catholic Church sent Johann Tetzel as papal commissioner for indulgences to Germany to sell indulgences to raise money to rebuild St. Peter's Basilica in Rome. On 31 October 1517, Luther launched an attack on the sale of indulgences by writing a protest letter to his bishop and by posting on the door of the Wittenberg castle church the '**Disputation of Martin Luther on the Power and Efficacy of Indulgences**' which came to be known as the ***Ninety-Five Theses***. In the theses Luther questioned many of the practices existed in the Roman Catholic Church. For example, in Theses 86 he asked 'Why does the pope, whose wealth today is greater than the wealth of the richest Crassus, build the basilica of St. Peter with the money of the poor believers rather than with his own money?' Luther argued that, since God alone could grant forgiveness, those who claimed that indulgences absolved buyers from all punishments and granted them salvation were in error. Luther insisted that selling indulgences was not only morally corrupt but also theologically unsound. Basic to Luther's argument was the **doctrine of justification** – God's act of declaring a sinner righteous – by faith alone (***sola fide***) through God's grace alone (***sola gratia***). Luther declared that 'this one and firm rock, which we call the doctrine of justification is the chief article of the whole Christian doctrine, which comprehends the understanding of all godliness'. Luther also challenged the authority and the office of the Pope by his argument that the Bible as the only source of divinely revealed knowledge from God (***sola scriptura***).

In his propositions Luther differed from the views of the Catholic Church on many aspects. Firstly, Luther believed that an individual achieves salvation through inner religious feeling and by trusting God's mercy. In contrast, the church held that both faith and good works were required for salvation. Further, Luther insisted that every individual was capable of discovering the meaning of the Bible unaided by the clergy. On the other, the church believed that only the clergy could read and interpret the Bible. Moreover, Luther found no difference between the clergy and the laity, but for the church the clergy were intermediaries between the God and the laity. In short, Luther questioned the church's claim that it alone provided the way to eternal salvation and argued that clergy and church rituals do not hold the keys to salvation.

Luther's teachings

1. **Salvation** is only possible by faith in God's gift of forgiveness
2. **Bible** as the sole basis for all teachings of the Church
3. **All people** – clergy and layman – are equal and therefore priests need not interpret Bible for people.

The Latin Theses were translated into German by the friends of Luther and was circulated widely. Students thronged to Wittenberg to hear Luther speak. By 1520, Luther published his three more works – *To the Christian Nobility of the German Nation*, *On the Babylonian Captivity of the Church* and *On the Freedom of a Christian*. Lutheran action initiated the Reformation, leading to the founding of Christian churches that discarded the authority of pope.

7. Response from the Papacy

Luther's confrontation with papal power turned him as an enemy of the pope. Luther had proclaimed the pope as Antichrist and the 'church as the most lawless den of robbers'. A case of heresy was drafted against Luther and a Cardinal was sent as papal legate to examine Luther. In June 1520, the pope issued a papal bull against Martin Luther warning him excommunication unless he recanted his attack against the Church including the Ninety-Five Theses. But Luther publicly set fire to the bull at Wittenberg on 10 December 1520. Luther was excommunicated by Pope Leo X on 3 January 1521.

The Diet of Worms, a general assembly of the estates of the Holy Roman Empire, was convened in 1521, at Worms (a city on the Rhine in Germany) under Charles V, the Holy Roman Emperor, to decide the fate of Martin Luther. Here, Luther was to answer to the charge of heresy and was asked to recant. Luther refused to recant and replied 'Unless I am convinced of error by the testimony of the Scriptures or by clear reason .... I cannot and will not recant anything since it is neither safe nor right to go against conscience'. In order to protect the authority of the Church and the Pope the ecclesiastical officials convinced Charles V that Luther was a threat and demanded his condemnation by the Holy Roman Empire. Consequently, the Diet of Worms issued the **Edict of Worms** (a decree) on 25 May 1521 declaring Luther an outlaw, made it a crime for anyone in Germany to give food or shelter to Luther, permitted anyone to kill Luther without legal consequences and banned his literature. Luther went in to hiding with the help of Frederick III, a prince and the elector of Saxony, who sheltered Luther in one of his castles. During that one-year period of his hiding at Wartburg, Luther translated the New Testament to German.

Luther's Bible with notes and prefaces by Luther played a major role in the spread of Luther's doctrine throughout Germany and also contributed to the evolution of the German language and literature. On account of rising public support for Luther among the German people and due to the protection offered to Luther by many German princes, the Edicts of Worms was never enforced and Luther eventually emerged from the Wartburg castle.

Luther returned to Wittenberg in 1522 and instead of continuing to seek reforms in the Catholic Church formed a separate group – **the Lutherans**.

In 1529, at the **'Diet of Speyer'** six princes and representatives of many imperial free cities of the Holy Roman Empire protested against an imperial ban against Martin Luther and proscription of his works and teachings. These states came to be known as the Protestants and in course of time this term came to be applied on those who opposed the Roman Catholic Church.

> Since the Reformation, Protestantism is a branch of Christianity. Three prominent and distinct branches of Protestantism emerged soon. These were Lutheranism in Germany, Calvinism in Switzerland and Anglicanism in England. In course of time further differences in beliefs and practices gave birth to new denominations in the Protestantism such as Methodist and Pentecostal in Anglicanism.

8. Stages in the Reformation

Scholars of the Reformation distinguish **three different stages** in the German Reformation – an Urban Reformation, a Peasant Reformation and a Princes Reformation.

i. Urban Reformation

The urban phase of the Reformation was centred in cities of Germany once Luther became famous after he defied the emperor at the Diet of Worms in 1521. These cities were run by oligarchies and had their own grievances against the church such as tax exemption claimed by the clergy which meant more burden of tax on others. Apart from rich merchants and aristocrats, the cities had a social layer of a mass of students, craftsmen and smaller traders who were sick of paying to clergy and hence they forced the towns' ruling bodies to carry through religious changes. It is estimated that the two-thirds of the imperial cities of Germany adopted the new religion and Luther ascribed the success of his doctrine to divine will.

ii. Peasants War

The second stage known as the **German Peasant War** or the revolution of the common man took place from 1524 to 1525. The war which was both religious and social began with separate insurrections in south-western part of Germany. The war was led by the German peasantry, who were under heavy tax burden, placed at the lowest stratum of the society and were put under generations of servitude. Now they were inspired by Luther's successful confrontation with the authorities. Impromptu armies comprising thousands sacked monasteries, assaulted castles and tried to win over countryside. The rebels drew up lists of grievances comprising religious demands like the right of local communities to appoint their own pastors and utilisation of tithes and also their livelihood demands such as abolition of serfdom and end to encroachment on common land. The Revolt spread over one-third of Germany and more than three lakh people took up arms against their masters.

But the lordly class was unwilling to make concessions that would undermine its own class position. By mobilising mercenary armies they suppressed the revolt. Martin Luther was horrified by the rebellion, was not ready to take the risk of alienating the nobility who supported him and urged the lords to take extreme forms of vengeance-'knock down, stab and strangle' the rebels. Luther even wrote a pamphlet *Against the Murderous, Thieving Hordes of Peasants.* Luther in this instance proved to be a political conservative who hesitated to challenge secular authority. The peasants' movement which did not have a command structure, artillery or cavalry was put down by the sword by 1525. Though failed, the revolt 'was the most important mass uprising in pre-modern Europe' and also the largest and most widespread popular uprising in Europe, prior to the French Revolution.

iii. Princes Reformation

One of the most significant implications of crushing the peasants' revolt was the strengthening of the position of the territorial princes. During the peasant revolt the knights, the urban oligarchies and the urban middle class had supported the princes. The urban middle class though embraced the new religious ideology of Protestantism were not ready to make an assault on the old order and they supported the princes. Similarly Lutheranism had strengthened the position of the princes who sought to use it as a double-edged weapon against the Catholic Holy Roman emperor Charles V, who sought to encroach on their power and on the other against the masses to keep an ideological hold on them. Although some princes were genuine believers in Luther's ideas, some others saw it as a good opportunity to seize the Church property. As a result, the Reformation of the princes began from 1525 onwards. The first state to formally adopt the Protestant faith was the Duchy of Prussia (1525) which was followed by large number of Princes in the Holy Roman Empire. The Holy Roman Emperor, Charles V, fought wars against these Protestant princes. The conflict ended only in 1555 by the **Peace of Augsburg** by which the princes were given right to determine religion of their subjects.

9. | The Counter Reformation

The Counter Reformation or Catholic Reformation was a response by the Catholic Church to the Protestant Reformation. It started with the Council of Trent convened by Paul III (pope from 1534 to 1549), in 1545, and aimed at presenting a theological and material challenge to the Reformation. The Counter Reformation had been characterised by features like defence of Catholic sacraments, ecclesiastical reconfiguration, establishments of religious orders, new emphasis on spiritual movements and also political initiatives.

> The Council of Trent was a commission of cardinals formed by Pope Paul III with an aim of reforming the Church and defending it from Protestantism. It existed from 1545 to 1563. It defended the basic structure, sacraments and doctrine of the Catholic Church and condemned actions of the Protestants as heresies and issued a decree that the church shall be the final arbiter of the Bible. It also ruled that indulgences as valid, but prohibited false selling of them.

Starting with the **Council of Trent** the Counter Reformation defended the sacramental practices in the church. It reaffirmed the basic tenets of the Roman Catholic Church and upheld 'salvation by grace through faith and works of that faith' claiming that 'faith without works is dead'. By upholding practices like pilgrimages, veneration of saints and relics, the use of venerable images as spiritually commendable practices (all these were the ire of the Protestant reformers), the Counter Reformers also rejected any compromise with Protestantism. Reforms also included proper training of priests, prescriptions given on pastoral care and on the administration of the sacraments.

Education was given prime importance in the Counter Reformation, as capable priests were required for educating the faithful. Hence, large numbers of seminaries were established to prepare the clergy for a more austere life in the service of the church. Measures were also taken against luxury of clergy, appointment of relatives to church office and the absence of bishops from their dioceses. Establishment of new religious orders was also fundamental part of the reforms. These orders focussed on aspects like regeneration of clergy, devotion to the traditional works of mercy, checking the spread of heresy, care for the poor and the sick and set examples of Catholic renewal. Orders like **Capuchins, Discalced Carmelites** and **Jesuits** were some prominent of these orders.

Further, emphasis was also given on mysticism focussing on interior conversion (a life of intimate and friendly relation with and in the presence of God) to

Christ, deepening of prayer and commitment to God's will. **Ignatius of Loyola, Teresa of Avila** and **John of the Cross** became major figures of this spiritual revival of the Counter Reformation.

Ignatius of Loyola, a nobleman from Loyola, Spain, founded the Society of Jesus in 1534. Its members were called as Jesuits, which became the backbone of the Catholic Reformation. They mainly focussed on three activities – founding superb schools to impart quality education for the common good, conversion to Christianity and to stop the spread of Protestantism.

A system of tribunals known as the Roman Inquisition was created by the Roman Catholic Church for prosecuting individuals accused of religious crimes (heresy). Methods of persecution and censorship were also resorted to and an 'Index of Forbidden Books' was created in 1559 to combat anti-Catholic books. Another major emphasis was on missionary endeavours in newly colonised parts of the world like Asia and the New World. Attempts were also made to reconvert areas such as Sweden and England that were at one time Catholic.

10. Spread of the Reformation

From Germany the Reformation soon spread to other parts of Europe, the printing press acting as the agent for rapid dissemination of religious material in vernaculars. Depending on the country the Reformation had varying causes and background, but in general it could be said that it was an urban phenomenon and prospered where the local rulers supported it and where the distance from Rome was greatest. It was strong in northern Europe–northern Germany, Scandinavia, Switzerland, Hungary, the Netherlands and England and Scotland.

Calvinism was an important Protestant group. John Calvin, a French scholar and theologian in the 16th century, founded this group. Calvinism emphasised **predestination** (some are destined for salvation others for damnation) and the absolute sovereignty of God in salvation of the human soul. Calvin exhorted people to rigorously obey God's law, to pursue social and moral righteousness earnestly and to control human emotions strictly. This stern theology of the Calvinists produced men and women who assumed that unfailing dedication to God's law alone as sign of salvation.

Calvin's ***Institutes of the Christian Religion***, published in 1536, contained the summary of his views on the Christian theology. Calvin wrote that men and women are sinful by nature and that God chooses a very few people to save. In Geneva, a prosperous Swiss city near the French border, Calvin established a Protestant church closely regulating his followers' personal and social lives. In the 1540s, under him, Geneva became a theocratic city and the centre of international Protestantism from where the Protestant reformers of many countries carried back these ideas to their homelands.

The Calvinists were the first to publish cogent arguments opposing monarchy in modern times. Calvin believed that the ideal government was theocracy. Calvin also taught that if rulers rise up against God, they lose their divine right and must be deposed. For the Calvinists, work was a means to express their gratitude to God and economic success was a visible sign of God's grace. Calvinists in France began to be known as **'Huguenots'**, in England as **'Puritans'**, in Scotland as **'Presbyterians'** and in America as 'Methodists'.

The Reformation was initiated in the Swiss Federation by **Huldrych Zwingli**. A reformed understanding of the Bible and rationalist, humanist education were the basis of Zwinglian reforms, which was also influenced by the writings of Erasmus. He was killed in a battle between the Swiss Protestants and Catholics in 1531. He is often considered as the 'Third Man of the Reformation' after Martin Luther and John Calvin.

Protestantism was illegal in France after 1534 but a well-organised underground movement of the Huguenots under the protection of powerful nobles fought against the Catholics. The **French Wars of Religion** from 1562 to 1598 between Catholics and Protestants were the most brutal religious wars in Europe. By the Edict of Nantes in 1598, Henry IV, the French king permitted substantial religious and political freedom to the Huguenots. But under Louis XIV and Louis XV persecution of the Protestants was revived with new vigour leading to huge emigration of the Protestants to the neighbouring countries. In 1789, the 'Declaration of the Rights of Man and of the Citizen' declared the Protestants as equal citizens.

In England, the Protestantism was the result more of political and personal issues than of religious. Here, Henry VIII (1509–47) the king himself initiated the Reformation. It largely resulted from the changes in government policy which was accepted by the public gradually.

Though the English Reformation was a political act by a self-confident king, there was a long tradition of heresy and anticlericalism in England since the medieval times as in the actions of **Wycliffe**, a 14th century theologian. But in the 16th century, circumstances were different. The Tudor king **Henry VIII** wanted a divorce from his wife, the Spanish princess **Catherine of Aragon**, and to marry **Anne Boleyn**, a lady at his court in his desire to have a male heir to secure the Tudor dynasty. He and his wife Catherine of Aragon had one living child, Mary, but no woman had succeeded to the English throne till then.

The **Pope Clement** VII refused to grant him an annulment of his marriage, as the pope did not want to offend Catherine's nephew, the Holy Roman Emperor Charles V. In 1529, Henry called the English parliament into session (known as the **Reformation Parliament**) which passed a set of laws by which the papal power was removed from the English Church. The Parliament passed a series of Acts including the **Act of Appeals** (1532) forbidding all appeals to the Pope in Rome on religious or other matters and making the King the final authority in England and the **Act of Supremacy** in 1534 which made the king supreme head of the Church of England. In 1536, Henry dissolved the monasteries in England and confiscated their property. These properties were distributed or sold to nobles, thus creating vested interest which acted as a powerful force in support of the reforms. By involving the Parliament and the gentry in his rebellion against the papacy, Henry turned the Reformation into a national movement. Meanwhile, Henry married Anne Boleyn in 1533.

> Henry's desire for a son did not materialise even after he married Anne Boleyn. As Anne Boleyn gave birth to a daughter, Elizabeth, Henry imprisoned her on charges of treason and she was executed in 1536. In 1537, Henry married another woman, Jane Seymour, who gave birth to a son, Edward.

Henry VIII was succeeded by his son **Edward VI** in 1547 under whom the Reformation advanced further. He abolished clerical celibacy and the Mass and imposed compulsory services in English. Edward VI introduced the Book of Common Prayer containing complete forms of service for daily and Sunday worship in English.

But under his sister **Mary I**, (Henry VIII's daughter by Catherine of Aragon) who succeeded Edward in 1553, aggressive attempts were made to reverse the Reformation. She was the first woman to successfully claim the throne of England. Her five year tenure (1553–58) was marked by her pursuits to restore the Roman Catholicism in England and severe persecutions of the Protestants hence she is called as the 'Bloody Mary'.

In 1558, **Elizabeth I**, Henry VIII's second daughter (by Anne Boleyn), became the queen and the last ruler of the Tudor dynasty. As a moderate Protestant she was opposed to Catholicism but not to Catholics. She went for a 'via media', a middle way between the Catholic and the Protestant traditions in religious issues which was characterised by a belief in reason, esteem for continuity over the Reformation divide and hospitality towards sacramental modes of thought. Known as the **Elizabethan Religious Settlement**, it contained two enactments of the Parliament – the **Act of Supremacy** of 1559 re-established independence of the English Church from Rome (Queen Mary had repealed the earlier Act of Supremacy in 1555) and the **Act of Uniformity** of 1559 provided the form and method for the English Church. The priests in the Anglican Church could marry and could deliver sermons in English; and to please the Catholics some of the rituals of the Catholic service such as rich robes were continued. In the end the Anglican Church differed to only a limited degree in its customs and ceremonies from the Roman Catholicism it replaced.

11. | Role of Women in Reformation

Though there had been instances of women contributing to the Reformation, they were mostly in supporting roles. Katharina von Bora, wife of Martin Luther, had actively supported Luther in his reform measures. Certain princesses and noblewomen had provided shelters to the reformers during the early years. Once the Protestant branches became formal, the male leaders narrowed down women's roles. Even Luther had commented 'God's highest gift on earth is a pious, cheerful and God-fearing and home-keeping wife'. Looking from this angle, it was no wonder that no woman leader emerged in the whole period of the Reformation.

12. | End of the Reformation

The Reformation is considered to have ended with the **Peace of Westphalia in 1648**. In that year a series of treaties were signed in the city of Westphalia in north-western Germany officially ending the European Wars of Religion. Three treaties were signed in Westphalia, ending one of the most tumultuous periods in the European history and on the other inaugurating the modern international system based on the concept of the sovereign states.

By the Peace, the **Thirty Years' War** (1618–48) fought in the Holy Roman Empire between the Hapsburgs and their Catholic allies on one side and the Protestant powers (Sweden and Denmark) and France (Catholic but anti-Hapsburg) on the other came to an end. The treaties also ended the **Eighty Years'** War (1568–1648) between Spain and the Dutch Republic by which Spain recognised the independence of the Dutch Republic. The signatories were to recognise the **Peace of Augsburg** signed in 1555 which had provided for the right of each prince to determine the religion of his own state (in Latin it was termed as ***cuius regio, eius religio*** means 'whose realm their religion'). Apart from that, the treaties also recognised the Catholics and the Protestants as equal before the law and provided legal recognition to Calvinism. The treaty also provided for increased autonomy for the states in the Holy German Empire.

The Thirty Years War was a series of wars fought from 1618 to 1648. These were fought initially by the Catholic and Protestant states in the Holy Roman Empire but later on were joined by other European powers. The Reformation had caused a division of the Holy Roman Empire, which was a loose federation of largely independent states, into Catholic and Protestant. Now, the Holy Roman Emperor tried to restore Catholicism as the only religion in the Empire igniting the War. France, though was Catholic, joined the War as it was concerned about its encirclement by its powerful neighbours – Spain and the Holy Roman Empire. The War was one of the most violent and bloodiest episodes in history in which more than 10 million are believed to have perished of which more than half in combat. Because of the involvement of many parties, state and non-state actors, regular and irregular armies and for its enormous destruction and also for its lasting impact the Thirty Years War is considered by many as an example of total war and the Peace of Westphalia as the Peace of Exhaustion.

In two other aspects too, the Peace of Westphalia was significant in world history. The treaties inaugurated a new international system based on the **concept of sovereign** states and established the precedent of making peace by **diplomatic congress**. The signatories, by recognising the exclusive sovereignty of each party over its territories and people and by prohibiting interference in another state's internal affairs, inaugurated the concept of co-existing sovereign states. The treaty also effectively ended the papacy's pan-European power. The treaty also initiated the first step in making peace by delegates representing various interest groups and states assembled in a congress. As these concepts were formed at a time when the European influence was spreading across the globe, they had ramifications not just in Europe but in international order and in international law in course of time.

The Peace of Westphalia and the nation-states: The Peace of Westphalia is considered as instrumental in giving birth to the concept of modern nation-state. This is mainly for two reasons. Firstly, it demarcated fixed boundaries for the participating countries and recognised the full territorial sovereignty of the member states. Secondly, it decreed that residents of a state as subjects to the laws of that state alone and not to any authority whether secular or religious.

13. Impact of the Reformation

The Reformation had both positive and negative and also direct and indirect consequences. It contributed substantially to the shaping of the modern world by freeing the people from blind religious faith and from the injustice and tyranny of the clergy. It was also significant in its contributions in politics, economy and in individualistic ethics which all became characteristic of the modern world.

In religious terms the Reformation **weakened the church** and reduced its moral and political power considerably as a principal institution of the Middle Ages. With establishment of national churches the power and influence of Rome was considerably reduced. On the other hand, it **revitalised Christianity** through the Counter-Reformation by which evils were sought to be purged to make it more attractive to the people. At the same time the Reformation **divided the Christendom** into hostile camps leading to violence, persecutions and wars that destroyed peace and social harmony and the Christian unity of Europe.

Political consequences of the Reformation were also significant. It was one of the key factors in the emergence of the modern nation-states which were both free and secular. Protestant rulers repudiated the pope's claim to temporal power and increased their wealth and power by severing connection with Rome. Though Protestantism did not create the modern secular state, it augmented its emergence by freeing the state from subordination to religious authority. It was also seminal in the **development of nationalism** which was strengthened by the establishment of national churches. Political liberty was another indirect impact of the Reformation. The Reformation provided a basis for challenging monarchical authority and also religious justification for rebelling against tyrannical authority. The English Revolution of the 17th century and the American Revolution of the 18th century were instances in this regard. It can also be said that the Protestant view which held all as masters of their own destiny was also in conformity with the emerging constitutional government.

Protestantism encouraged entrepreneurship and facilitated the growth of **capitalism**. Though capitalism was in existence in Europe even before, the Reformation gave a new dynamism to it. German sociologist Max Weber was to define the spirit of capitalism as ideas and 'esprit' that favour the **rational pursuit of economic gain**. Belief of The Protestant businessmen that they had a religious obligation to make money and to progress coupled with the Calvinist belief that hard work, diligence, efficiency, frugality and a disdain for hedonism as signs that God was working through them encouraged money making and business a way of life. Thus, the Reformation profoundly affected the view of work, dignifying even the most mundane professions as adding to the common good and thus blessed by God.

The Reformation also contributed to the emergence of **individualistic ethic** – a characteristic feature of the modern life. The Protestant belief in 'double predestination' in which God chooses some people for salvation and others for damnation drove them to believe that God had chosen them to be saved which in turn resulted in inner confidence and assertiveness. The belief that success in this world and salvation in the next is possible through inner faith and self-discipline unaided by the church promoted individualistic ethic or **'religious individualism'** which emerged as a counterpart of the **'intellectual individualism'** of the Renaissance. It is also important to note that as both Catholics and Protestants gave emphasis to education in promoting their beliefs, large number of schools, colleges and universities sprang up in Europe. Last but not the least, the tradition of questioning of authority and of the established beliefs continued by these reformers strengthened the groundwork for the Enlightenment.

14. Renaissance and Reformation in Comparison

- Renaissance revitalised intellectual life, while reformation marked a new outlook in the religious life.
- The Renaissance aimed at reinvigorating the wisdom of ancient times, while the Reformation wanted to restore the spirit of early Christianity.
- The Renaissance was not started by any single person, but the Reformation was initiated by a monk – Martin Luther.
- Renaissance had an elite circle of scholars as its proponents, while the Reformation had ordinary people of religion as its followers.

- Renaissance had its origin in the 15th century in Italy, while the Reformation started in the 16th century in Germany.
- The Renaissance did not lead to division of Europe and the society, but the Reformation led to schism in the Christianity, division of Europe on Protestant and Catholic lines and wars of religion.
- Both had Humanism as a value. Renaissance had facilitated the way for Reformation. It also had evoked a spirit of enquiry which initiated attack on questionable practices including that of religion.

European wars of religion were a series of wars waged in Europe in 16th and 17th centuries in the wake of the Protestant Reformation which was intensified with the Counter Reformation initiated by the Catholic Church. Though the root cause of the wars had been religious, other factors like revolts and territorial ambitions of rulers too were factors. The wars caused devastation of the continent and death of more than 10 million people and culminated in the Thirty Years War (1618–48). The Treaty of Westphalia finally ended the conflicts and Catholicism, Lutheranism and Calvinism were recognised as three separate Christian traditions in the Holy Roman Empire.

SUMMARY

The Reformation – It refers to the efforts to reform Christianity initiated by a German monk, Martin Luther in the 16th century.

Causes of the Reformation – Religious-corrupt practices and preoccupation with the material world by the Catholic clergy; intellectual-spirit of enquiry and quest for reform initiated by the Renaissance scholars; political-interests of the rulers of the emerging nation states; economic and socio-cultural factors-such as tax exemption to the church property, resentment of the ordinary clergy against the centralising tendency of the Pope, emergence of middle class with a new world view and spread of education and circulation of printed books which enabled people to form their own opinion about their religion and about the church were significant.

Stages in Reformation – Urban Reformation, Peasants War and The Princes' Reformation.

Counter Reformation – It was the response from the Catholic Church to the Protestant Reformation. It started with the Council of Trent. It aimed at defending Catholic sacramental practices and to present a challenge to the Reformation. Education was given importance. Tribunals known as the Roman Inquisition punished people accused of heresy.

Spread of Reformation – Calvinism based in Geneva, Huguenots in France, Puritans in England, Presbyterians in Scotland, Methodists in America and Huldrych Zwingli in the Swiss Federation were different expressions in different countries.

Impact of the Reformation – It weakened the church which was an important moral and political structure since the Middle Ages, revitalised Christianity, accentuated the emergence of the modern nation-states, facilitated emergence of the concept of nationalism and the rise of national churches, instilled dynamism in capitalist system. It also laid the groundwork for the Enlightenment.

Questions of Previous Years Civil Services Examination

1. 'The Renaissance and the Reformation are the two springs of modern history, rival sources of the intellectual and moral freshening of modern life' (1995)
2. 'Of all forms assumed by the Protestant Reformation, Calvinism has been the most far-reaching in its scope and the most profound in its influence' (2000)
3. 'The Peace of Westphalia ended the reign of theology over the European mind and left the road obstructed but possible? For the tentative of reason' (1997)
4. 'Protestantism contributed substantially to the rise of capitalism' (1994)
5. 'His (Martin Luther's) rebellion was essentially popular and national' (1991)

C. The Age of Discovery

1. Introduction

'To serve God and His Majesty, to give light to those who were in darkness and to grow rich as all men desire to do'. These were the words of Bartolomeu Dias, one of the early Portuguese explorers while explaining his motives for voyages. It synthesises the spirit of the Age of Discovery–attainment of God's grace by propagating religion, add to the glory of the nation by establishing colonies and accumulate wealth for oneself.

The period from 1450 to 1750 was a period of overseas explorations by the Europeans. This period is known as the **Age of Discovery** or the **Age of Exploration.** It marked the beginning of globalisation and also adoption of **colonialism** and **mercantilism** as national policies by the European states. Its implications, **political**-conquest and colonialism of Asia, Africa and the New World; **economic**-emergence of a world economy based on Eastern spices, African slaves and American silver; **social**-end of an era of secluded manors and walled towns and the emergence of a capitalist society in its place; and **cultural**-exchange of new ideas and products worldwide, all were crucial in directing the flow of the history of the world since then. **Portugal** and **Spain** were the pioneers in geographical explorations followed by other European powers – Britain, France and others.

2. Causes of the Explorations

i. Legacy of the Renaissance

The Renaissance had liberated men's mind from medieval ideas and outlook. A **Spirit of enquiry** was one of the legacies of the Renaissance. Under this spirit, the young men undertook voyages in unchartered seas to discover unknown lands. This spirit of enquiry now turned into **spirit of adventure** and the European adventurers wanted to test the limits of human ability by exploring the unknown regions. The Spaniards and the Portuguese possessed an adventure craving mind for unchartered distances and everything unknown and dangerous. This desire to surpass the mundane preoccupations of ordinary life and pleasantries was expressed through exploratory missions.

Further, assertion of the clergy that the earth was flat was disputed by the thinkers of the time and they wanted to test whether the earth was round or flat kindling their desire for explorations.

ii. Fall of Constantinople

The Europeans had been introduced to spices and other luxury goods from Asia since very early times. **Constantinople**, the capital of the **Eastern Roman Empire**, was the conduit of trade between Europe and the East till 1453. In that year Constantinople fell into the hands of the Ottoman Turks and resultant disruption of trade compelled the Europeans to look for alternative trade routes to the Eastern world. Will Durant's comment that the 'failure of the Crusades compelled the discovery of the Americas' makes this point clear.

iii. Commercial Considerations

Another significant force behind geographical explorations had been commercial interest and profit from the Eastern trade. Since time immemorial, trade between Europe, Africa and Asia had been taking place but was through intermediaries (Arabs and the Venetians) which affected profits on the Europeans end. Now the Western Europeans sought to break the monopolies and intermediaries by going directly to the source – to **West Africa for gold and slaves** and to **India for spices and silks**. Moreover, by 15th century there was an ever increasing and insatiable demand for Eastern luxuries like spices, silk, precious stones, sandal wood and perfumes that form the affluent sections of the European society. Naturally the European merchants desired for direct sea routes to procure these items and to make enormous profit.

iv. Technological Advances

It was not just desire to explore new regions but technology needed for such exploration too was in favour of the Europeans. Introduction of the **Caravel** (a small ship able to sail windward), in the 1400s, advanced the navigation capability by which ships could sail safely on the open seas. The Europeans possessed armed sailing vessels (ships fitted with guns) which were also more manoeuvrable and faster compared to those possessed by the Chinese or the Arabs. The gunned ship gave the Europeans naval superiority against the opposition as demonstrated by the Portuguese victory in the **Battle of Diu** in 1509 in which a joint fleet of the Sultan of Gujarat, Sultan of Egypt and the Zamorin of Calicut were defeated by the Portuguese. Ships were also made with improved hull design which could ride out ocean storms. The voyages were also facilitated by the invention of the **Mariner Compass** and improvement in map making. Though used in China much early, the Europeans began to use the magnetic compass by 13th century only. Development of better navigational instruments like **astrolabe**, which could tell north and south of the equator by the position of the stars, expedited the explorations.

v. Increased Geographical Knowledge

Increased knowledge about geography also gave impetus to the discoveries. In the 12th century, **Muhammad al-Idrisi**, an Arab geographer, created a world map for the King of Sicily. This work, known as the ***Tabula Rogeriana***, inspired a number of adventurers to undertake explorations. As a result, from the late 13th century many travellers explored Eurasia and beyond mainly using the pre-existing trade routes by land leading to increased knowledge of the world. Further, several books based on travel accounts were also published kindling more interest in explorations. Books like ***A Merchant's Handbook*** (14th century), the Latin translation of ***Ptolemy's Geography*** (15th century), were important in this context.

vi. Religious Factor

Desire to spread Christianity to other parts of the world was another factor behind the sea voyages. In most of the cases, the flag of Christianity followed the flag of explorers in the newly discovered lands with an aim to replace the 'pagan' rituals of these lands with Christianity. For example, the early systematic evangelisation in Mexico was known as the **'Spiritual Conquest of Mexico'**.

The missionary zeal was in many instances supported and strengthened by rulers and merchants who had found a common cause in explorations. For example, Prince Henry the Navigator expected that the Portuguese expansion into Africa would lead to the discovery of gold and the spread of Christianity at the expense of Islam. Thus, explorations to various 'savage' lands in order to 'save' the natives became an obsession of the missionaries.

Further, persecutions during the Reformation, the Counter-Reformation and the European Wars of Religion too compelled many Christian sects to look for safe havens in different corners of the globe.

vii. Political Motives

The 'Age of Discoveries' coincides with the emergence of powerful centralised monarchs in Europe and was an important factor in explorations. Apart from the wealth, gold, silver and profit from trade, these rulers looked for extending their control overseas. Excellent examples were **Ferdinand and Isabella** of Spain (who funded the voyages of Christopher Columbus) and **Prince Henry**

the Navigator of Portugal (son of Portuguese king John I and sponsor of Portuguese voyages).

There was also competition between various evolving empires of Europe in terms of economy, religion and power (Gold, God and Glory) and this competition accelerated the exploratory missions.

3. | Major Discoveries

During the 15th and 16th centuries Portuguese and Spain pioneered the geographic explorations.

At the beginning of the 15th century, it was Prince Henry the Navigator (1394–1460) who initiated voyages of explorations. In 1419, Henry started a navigation school on the southwestern coast of Portugal to train navigators in perfecting their skills. Initially Portuguese expanded into islands of the Atlantic Ocean like Madeira (1419) and the Azores (1427) in search of farmlands and slaves.

For centuries slave and gold trade routes linking West Africa with the Mediterranean had passed through the Western Sahara Desert, controlled by the Moors of North Africa. Now the Portuguese under this young prince wished to trade directly with West Africa by sea and also to probe whether it was possible to reach the Indies, the source of the lucrative spice trade, by sea.

In the middle decades of the 15th century, they discovered **Cape Verde** and other remaining islands in the Atlantic and moved down to the west African coast to the mouth of the Congo river and beyond. In 1488, **Bartolomeu Dias** travelled around the southern tip of Africa, which he named the **Cape of Storms** and proved that the Indian Ocean was accessible from the Atlantic. The king John II of Portugal renamed the cape as the '**Cape of Good Hope**' as the discovery offered possibility of a sea route to India. A decade later, **Vasco da Gama** sailed around the Cape of Good Hope and across the Indian Ocean to India and landed at **Calicut** (1498). By discovering an all sea route to the East, the Portuguese broke the commercial monopoly enjoyed by Genoa and Venice on Eastern goods. In 1510, the Portuguese captured **Goa** on India's western coast. In 1511, **Alfonso de Albuquerque** reached **Malacca** (the Spice Islands), then the centre of Asian trade. In May 1513, **Jorge Alvares** reached **China.** To enforce their monopoly on eastern trade the Portuguese conquered **Muscat** (1507) and **Hormuz** (1515) in the Persian Gulf, as they connected the Persian Gulf with the Arabian Sea. In 1543, the Portuguese became the first westerners to reach and trade with **Japan.**

Spain was another European country to engage in elaborate geographical explorations. **Christopher Columbus**, an Italian explorer, expected to reach India by sailing west across the Atlantic and enlisted support of Isabella, the queen of Spain for the mission. Instead of reaching Asia, he landed on a Caribbean island (in 1492) which he named **Espanola** (Little Spain) and called the inhabitants, 'los indios' or Indians. In 1493, Columbus set out for his second journey not as an explorer but as an empire builder. His aim was to convert the Caribbean islands into colonies.

Vasco da Gama

In 1500, **Pedro Alvares Cabral**, a Portuguese explorer, landed in Brazilian coast and claimed the land for his country. Next year, **Amerigo Vespucci** an Italian explorer under the service of Spain (and later under Portugal) conducted voyages to the east coast of South America demonstrating that Columbus had not reached Asia but had found a 'new' continent. In 1507, this continent was named as the 'Americas' by a German mapmaker probably after Amerigo Vespucci.

In 1519, **Hernando Cortes**, a Spaniard, defeated the Aztecs, the native rulers of Mexico, and a decade later **Francisco Pizarro** captured the mountain kingdom of the Incas in Peru for the Spanish crown. The Spanish became the first European settlers in the Americas. These **conquistadors** added glory to the Spanish Empire by capturing the gold hoards accumulated over the centuries by the rulers of these regions. The Spaniards also discovered silver at Potosi in Upper Peru and Mexico, and the annual treasure fleets sailing to Spain became the financial bedrock of the Spanish Empire.

During 1519–22 an expedition under **Ferdinand Magellan** (a Portuguese explorer) was undertaken by the Spaniards for **circumnavigation of the globe**. This expedition travelled west, made an arduous trip through a 600-km strait (now known as the Strait of Magellan), crossed the Pacific and reached the **Spice Islands**. Though Magellan was killed in a local war in the Philippines in 1521, the fleet returned to Spain in 1522 under **Juan Sebastian Elcano.** This round-the-world voyage produced valuable knowledge of the globe and its oceans which facilitated further explorations and settlements.

The **Treaty of Tordesillas** was signed in 1494 between Portugal and Spain to avoid conflict in explorations. The treaty divided the new world between these two powers: Portuguese receiving areas east of a line, known as **the Line of Demarcation**, an imaginary line that ran near the Cape Verde islands in the Atlantic Ocean, and Spain receiving areas west of that line.

By 17th century other European nations the **English, French and the Dutch** (the Netherland) entered in the race and eroded Portuguese control of the Asian region. The British established their first trading post at Surat in 1607, focussed on trading in Indian cloth and at the same time fought with the French for supremacy in India. Britain went on to build the biggest overseas empire, on which, as they claimed 'the sun never set'.

French acquired some settlements in India such as Chandernagar, Yanam, Karaikal, Mahe and Pondicherry.

In 1619, the Dutch captured Batavia in Java and soon captured the port of Malacca and the Spice Islands from Portugal. By 1700, the Dutch controlled much of Indonesia and the Cape of Good Hope in Africa.

French, England and the Netherlands also claimed territories in **North America**. St. Lawrence, Montreal and Quebec (France); Jamestown, Plymouth, and Massachusetts Bay (England); and Hudson Bay, Hudson Strait and Manhattan (Dutch) were initial settlements of these European powers in America. In the **Caribbean** the French seized Haiti, Guadeloupe and Martinique and the British took over Barbados and Jamaica. In 1634, the Dutch captured Antilles and Aruba. On these islands the European colonisers built huge sugar and cotton plantations with the help of enslaved Africans.

The New World and the Old World

The New World refers to the Americas (including nearby islands like Caribbean and Bermuda) and Australia (Oceania). The term originated in 16th century after the Europeans discovered new parts of the world as a result of global explorations. The Old World refers to Africa, Asia and Europe also known as Afro-Eurasia. These regions had contact and cultural exchanges with each other since ancient times.

Overseas Explorations

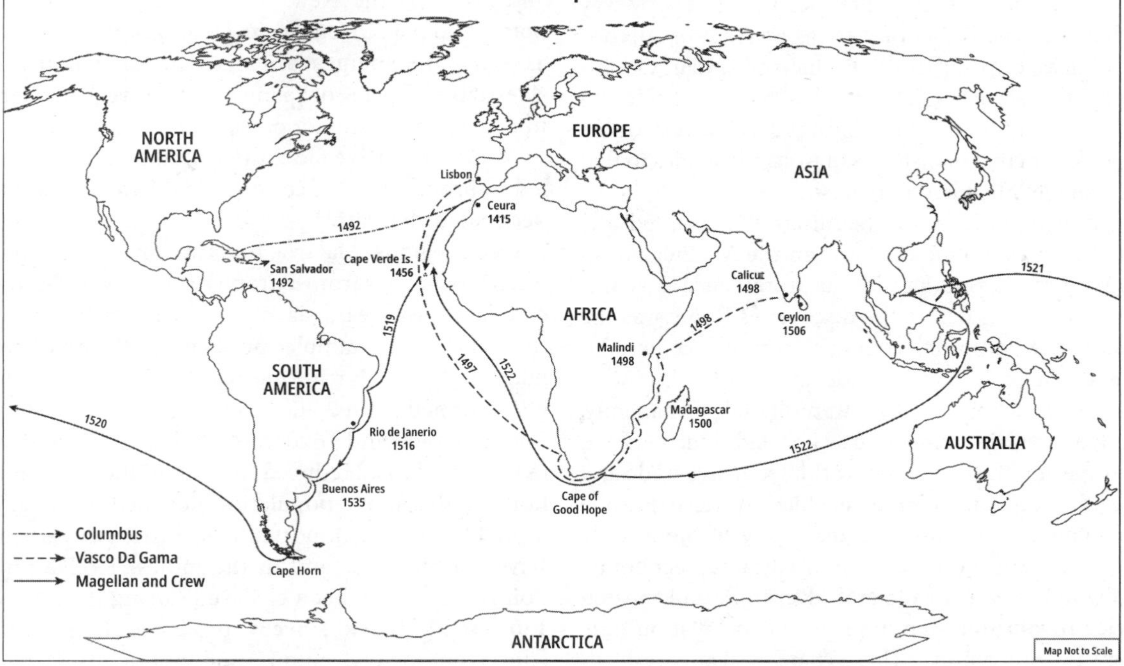

4. Impact of the Discoveries

The geographical discoveries had profound impact in the history of the world. It altered the political balance of the world, led to the foundation of colonies by the European powers, widened the mental horizons of the people, increased the wealth of nations and diminished the power of the nobles accentuating the decline of feudalism.

The geographical discoveries of the 15th and 16th centuries gave birth to the emergence of **European hegemony** in world politics. The new trans-oceanic links and their domination by the Europeans enabled them to control most of the planet. Soon the Western Europe emerged the lord of the sea lanes and master of the land masses throughout the globe. Overseas explorations essentially led to the founding of the **European colonial empires.** Starting with Portugal and Spain the European states initiated the process of colonisation of the newly discovered territories. It also inaugurated period of **Mercantilism and globalisation** and also caused mutual rivalry between the European powers over colonies leading to innumerable wars.

The discovery of both America and direct sea route to India widened the European's view of the world, stimulated further explorations and satisfied European hunger for land by facilitating emigration.

The achievements of European explorers by way of circumnavigation of Africa, exploration of two Americas, crossing of the Pacific and Indian Oceans and establishment of a network of bases and colonies throughout the world transformed the history of the world from that of histories of isolated peoples to that of a single integrated human society.

In **economic field** the discoveries shifted the European economic centre from the Mediterranean to Western Europe. Italy lost its prominence as a commercial power. Before the discoveries Rome was the hub of the European economic activities, Venice and Genoa emporium of its trade and Florence home of its arts and letters. All these were altered permanently.

Explorations tremendously boosted trade between Europe and the rest of the world. Extensive trade and wealth from the colonies enabled Western Europe to come out of subsistence economy of the Middle Ages and enter on a course of sustained economic growth. Increase in gold and silver in Europe created **price revolution** – an unprecedented inflation during the 16th century. These changes also gave birth to a new economic system – **mercantile capitalism** – which ultimately paved the way for the Industrial Revolution in the 18th century.

> **Price Revolution:** Europe experienced an unprecedented level of inflation especially in foodstuffs during the 16th century. Population growth which almost doubled during this period meant more number of mouths to feed than what agriculture sector could produce. Huge influx of silver into Europe from the New World was another factor for the Price Revolution, as it meant too many people with too much money chasing too few goods.

In the field of **geography**, the discoveries brought about changes that revolutionised the understanding of the world, shape and size of the earth and about the dimensions of the continents and the countries. The developments facilitated global mapping resulting into a new world view.

In **cultural sense** the geographical discoveries were one of the most significant global events. The geographical discoveries facilitated contact between the Old and New Worlds resulting in the **Columbian Exchange** in which goods, plants and animals unique to one hemisphere were transferred to another. For example, the Europeans while bringing cattle, horses and sheep to the New World took back tobacco, potato and maize from there. **Demographic changes** as seen in the emergence of mixed population such as **'Mestizo'** (offspring of Spanish and Native American) in America was another outcome.

On the **negative side**, the Columbian Exchange led to propagation of **communicable diseases** that decimated the native population of the newly discovered regions. Malaria, hookworm and smallpox were introduced from Europe to the newly discovered lands, where the natives had little or no natural resistance. For example, population of one of the native tribes in North America, the **Massachusetts**, had dropped from 24,000 to less than 700 by 1631. Between 1500 and 1600, the number of the natives in the New World reduced from 20 million to 2 million. As the native population declined, more and more blacks were imported from Africa to work as slaves in the fields and in the mines. Twelve million Africans had been enslaved during the period 1500–1860. **Black slavery** produced large scale effects on society, culture and politics that exist to the present day. The discoveries also led to the spread of the European culture – music, art and architecture – throughout the world.

Lastly, as observed by a historian 'Christendom is also the proper perspective from which to view the religious drive behind the justification for empire'. From the very beginning of the colonisation, the Catholic priests had accompanied the explorers in search of converts. Missionary activities expanded the reach of Christianity throughout the world and Christianity emerged as the world's largest religion.

Atlantic Slave Trade

Transportation of African people as slaves to Americas during 16th–19th centuries was known as the Atlantic Slave Trade. The Portuguese were the first to start the Atlantic slave trade in 16th century and followed by other European countries. These slaves were treated as commodities to be sold in Americas to work in plantations, mines, rice fields, construction sector and so on. By mid-17th century, slavery hardened with offspring of slaves being treated as slaves and as the property of their owners. Between 1500 and 1600, more than three lakh Africans had been taken to the Americas and by the time the Atlantic Slave Trade ended, almost 12 million African slaves had been transported to the Americas. By the end of 18th century, opposition against the slave trade grew and many states ended the slave trade. Denmark became the first country to ban slave trade through legislation in 1792 followed by Britain in 1807, the United States too abolished import of slaves in the same year but its internal slave trade continued up to the 1860s. By the time it ended, the slave trade had devastated African families, cultures and societies while contributing to the economic and cultural development of the Americas.

5. Reasons for the European Success

One of the principal factors in the success of European expansion had been their **supremacy over the oceans**, especially in long-range transport. Advances the Europeans made in naval technology, naval artillery and in scientific knowledge facilitated their dominance in the Atlantic, Pacific and Indian oceans.

Another factor was the European superiority in warfare and methodology in organised violence. Between 1500 and 1750, a Military Revolution took place in Europe. Emergence of the **Siege Warfare** (fortress built on scientific basis) and **Siege Artillery** along with a **Revolution in Field Warfare** (infantry equipped with armour penetrating firearms) facilitated this Revolution and placed the Europeans much ahead of their enemies. They used gunpowder, steel helmets and fire arms. The Western forces were also trained in tactical discipline which facilitated much cohesion and control in the battlefield than their adversaries.

The modern state structures in the forms of centralised monarchy, professional bureaucracy, standing army and emerging socio-economic institutions such as international finance and erosion of feudal elements too were significant positive factors on the European side.

In contrast to the technological superiority of the Europeans, the native populations of the conquered territories were followers of lower level technology and believers in religious and magical elements for success in war. For example, the Aztecs of Mexico used arrows and wooden clubs, while the Incas of Peru fought unsuccessfully against the Europeans with clubs and by throwing stones from slings. Import of horse from Europe gave mobility to the Europeans while creating psychological shock to the Native Americans who had never seen horse before. In the culture of warfare too there were differences. While the Europeans aimed at killing the enemy and destruction of their settlements, the natives aimed at capturing the enemy.

Another disadvantage to the natives was that they had no immunity against the diseases introduced by the Europeans. For example, the aborigines of Australia died in large numbers infected by smallpox, measles, influenza and tuberculosis. Similarly, the Europeans brought with them measles, mumps and smallpox to the Americas which had devastating effect on the native population such as the Aztecs. On political side it could be said that, as the non-European polities were fragile entities they could be broken easily by using one against the other by the Europeans.

Thus, the extension of European hegemony over much of the world – between 1500 and 1800 they had acquired more than 35% of the global land – was caused by a combination of technological, socio-cultural and strategic factors as it was also with political.

Colonialism and Imperialism: Both were forms of conquest and domination aimed at economic and political control. Colonialism is the practice of establishing a colony. The term Colony derives from the Latin word *colonus* which means 'farmer' thus implying domination over the native inhabitants by the settlers (physical control). The term imperialism derives from the Latin word *imperium* which means 'to command'. In imperialism one country maintains a command over another either directly or indirectly. Important examples of colonies were that of European settlements in North America, Australia and New Zealand with large number of permanent European residents. Examples of imperialism were territories acquired by the European nations in Africa in the second-half of the 19th century and the American control over Philippines and Puerto Rico in which foreign governments controlled these territories without significant settlements.

SUMMARY

Geographical Discoveries – The period from 1450 to 1750 was a period of overseas explorations by the Europeans and hence known as the Age of Discovery.

Causes of the Explorations – The Renaissance legacy of the spirit of enquiry, the Fall of Constantinople, commercial requirements, advances in technology, increased knowledge about geography, religious factors and political intentions.

Major Discoveries – Achievements of Prince Henry the Navigator, exploration of the southern tip of Africa in 1488 by Bartolomeu Dias, discovery of a direct sea route to India from Europe in 1498 by Vasco da Gama, discovery of the route to the Spice Islands in 1511 by Alfonso de Albuquerque and explorations and discoveries by Christopher Columbus, Pedro Alvarez Cabral, Amerigo Vespucci, Hernando Cortes, Ferdinand Magellan were significant.

Impact of the Discoveries – Boosted trade and commerce of Europe with the rest of the world, shifted the economic balance in favour of Western Europe, caused the Price Revolution, facilitated the emergence of mercantile capitalism, expanded our knowledge about the world, promoted cultural interaction, facilitated the spread of Christianity and to the Columbian Exchange. On the negative side it caused propagation of communicable diseases, decline in the number of native population and strengthening of the Black Slavery.

QUESTIONS OF PREVIOUS YEARS CIVIL SERVICES EXAMINATION

1. 'The era of discovery and exploration was but another aspect of the Renaissance interest in the world and man' (1996)
2. One great effect of the geographical discoveries of the 15th century was 'the growing belief that America, Asia and Africa were to be used extensively for the benefit of the Europeans' (1998)
3. 'The sponsors of the overseas exploration of Europe were national monarchies' (1992)
4. Portugal and Spain, the pioneers in world exploration, were also first in the race to conquer overseas countries. (1999)

CHAPTER 2

Transition to Modernity – Role of Ideas

In this Chapter

1. Introduction

Human beings are problem-solving animals and have the habit of developing ideas and institutions. They are the tools which enable us to move beyond our inheritance and shape our destiny. Thinkers and scholars gave birth to these ideas and people acting in the name of these ideas and arguments were instrumental in shaping the modern world. Many of these ideas continue to have great influence on groups, institutions and nations even today. In this chapter, we will discuss some of these important ideas that in one way or the other shaped events and institutions in the modern period.

2. The Scientific Revolution

The Scientific Revolution was a new approach of looking at the world by careful observation and experimentation. It involved two significant aspects – the **scientific outlook** and the **scientific method**. These in turn led to the development of scientific theories and new discoveries.

The scientific outlook envisaged a mechanical conception of the world. Scholars of the time tried to explain the nature in mathematical terms, which in their view was composed solely of matter, and its motion occurring in space and measurable in time was determined by the laws of force. Advances in mathematics such as algebra, trigonometry and geometry enabled the scientists to prove earlier abstract theories with logical evidence. This scientific view of nature as mechanical, analytical, mathematical and something that could be mastered gave birth to two major developments that became characteristic of the modern era. Applied to commercial practices it gave birth to **Industrial Revolution** and at intellectual level inaugurated the **Age of Enlightenment**.

These approaches to comprehend the world in scientific manner gave birth to the scientific method – a systematic procedure for collecting and analysing evidence. This logical procedure of testing ideas through observation, formation of a hypotheses and experimentation leading to formulation of general laws began to be known as the scientific method. Two scholars who contributed to the development of the scientific method were **Francis Bacon** and **Rene Descartes**. The English thinker Francis Bacon exhorted the scientists to conduct experiments and to draw conclusions instead of depending on ancient knowledge. He emphasised on inductive reasoning, that is, proceeding from the particular to the general. The French thinker Rene Descartes emphasised on reasoning to find truth. He exhorted people to doubt everything until proved by reason, as is evident from his maxim, 'I think, therefore I am'.

A. Factors that Caused the Scientific Revolution

The Renaissance which had ignited a spirit of enquiry, along with the Reformation with its questioning of accepted ways of thinking created an environment of inquisitiveness in Europe. The geographical explorations which had brought to light new lands and people unknown to the Europeans till then opened the European mind to the possibility of more truths in existence and a desire for their discovery. Moreover, the geographical explorations had fuelled research and developments in navigation, astronomy and mathematics. Resultantly, these new discoveries and developments of instruments arouse curiosity to develop more. The advent of printing press helped circulation of these new ideas far and wide in Europe spreading the spirit of inquisitiveness.

First of the important developments in the Scientific Revolution was the formulation of a **Heliocentric Theory** or the sun-centred theory of the universe by **Copernicus**, a Polish astronomer. In his book published in 1543 ***On the Revolutions of the Heavenly Bodies***, he reasoned that stars and planets revolved around the sun.

> Geocentric Theory – Earth-centred view of the universe was the basis of the understanding of the natural world till the modern era. According to this belief, the earth being the heaviest object lay stationary at the centre of the universe and the sun, the moon and the planets all moved in circular paths around the earth. This theory came from **Aristotle**, the Greek philosopher of the fourth century B.C., and was further expanded by the Greek astronomer **Ptolemy** in the second century A.D.

In the 17th century, **Johannes Kepler**, a German mathematician, demonstrated mathematically that the planets revolve around the sun in elliptical orbit. In the same century, an Italian scientist, **Galileo Galilei** built his own telescope and made many astronomical observations, which supported the theories of Copernicus. Galileo's discoveries appeared in his book ***The Starry Messenger***, published in 1610.

The scientific spirit was further advanced by the findings of **Isaac Newton,** a student of Cambridge University. In 1687, in his book ***The Mathematical Principles of Natural Philosophy*** also known as the *Principia*, Newton propounded the **law of universal gravitation** as per which all objects in the universe attract each other. This Newtonian discovery of universal gravitation was the culmination of the Scientific Revolution, as the universe could be described as matter in motion and the forces behind it could be expressed mathematically.

Isaac Newton

The scientific approach to life also led to developments in new discoveries. Some important developments and instruments that caused spectacular advances in the spread of Scientific Revolution include the invention of the first **microscope** in 1590 by Zacharias Janssen, a Dutch maker of eyeglasses, development of **mercury barometer** by Evangelista Torricelli in 1643, developments of **mercury thermometer** by the German physicist Gabriel Fahrenheit in 1714 and a Swedish man, Anders Celsius (Celsius scale) in 1742, development of a **vaccine against smallpox** by British physician Edward Jenner, formulation of the **Boyle's Law** by Robert Boyle in 1661, where he explained how the volume, temperature and pressure of gas affect each other, and the demonstration by William Harvey (1628) that blood circulates in the human body because of the pumping by the heart muscles.

It was this outlook, one based on reason when applied to human conditions and social practices ushered in a movement called the Enlightenment.

3. The Enlightenment

The Enlightenment was an intellectual movement that attempted a rational analysis of society, its beliefs, practices and institutions. The Enlightenment scholars sought to bring change by changing ideas and outlooks. It was the culmination of a new outlook initiated by the Renaissance humanists, who had given emphasis to potentials of individual and to the worldly life. In continuation to it, the Enlightenment attacked the medieval scholastic learning and initiated modern liberal thought and helped to shape modern outlook. At the same time it is important to note that the Enlightenment thinkers were not revolutionaries but proponents of reform who resorted to waging a battle of ideas. Nevertheless, these ideas became backbone of many of the revolutions including that of the American and the French.

The Enlightenment was both a **'set of ideas'** of progress and of reason, and a '**movement**' to bring into a moral and intellectual revolution. The movement reached apex in the mid-18th century, hence, this century is known as the **Age of Enlightenment, the Century of Lights, the Century of Philosophy** or the **Age of Reason.** Immanuel Kant, a German philosopher of the 18th century, was to describe the Enlightenment as 'man's release from his self-incurred tutelage' and 'mankind's final coming of age, the emancipation of the human consciousness from an immature state of ignorance'. And immaturity to Kant was 'the inability to use one's own understanding without the guidance of another'.

In giving birth to Enlightenment, ideas of Thomas Hobbes and John Locke, the English political thinkers of the 17th century, were significant. Other important figures associated with the Enlightenment were Jeremy Bentham (England), Adam Smith (Scotland), Montesquieu, Voltaire Rousseau, Diderot and Condorcet (France), Beccaria (Italy), Immanuel Kant (Germany) and Thomas Paine and Thomas Jefferson (America).

> Hobbes in his ***Leviathan*** (1651) depicted humans as naturally selfish and wicked, and human lives in the state of nature as brutish and short. He argued that to create order in society humans entered into an agreement – social contract – by which they handed over their rights to a strong ruler who in return promised to safeguard their lives. He supported absolute monarchy as it alone could impose order and demand obedience.

> The English philosopher John Locke conceptualised **'tabula rasa'** or **'clean slate'** and argued that every person is born with a blank mind and they are moulded by environment and experiences. If environments were changed, people could be changed to create a better society. Locke argued that human nature is essentially good and thus differed from the view of Hobbes. He too talked about social contract but was differed from Hobbes' in his idea of the state of nature. In his state of nature there are three natural rights – life, liberty and property – with which people are born and government's duty is to protect them. If government fails in this, Locke said, people have the right to overthrow it. This concept, that the government derives its power from the governed, became the corner stone of modern democracy and inspired struggles for liberty and democracy in Europe and in the Americas.

These scholars tried to promote a **'republic of letters'** fostering communication between intellectuals stretched across the national boundaries while respecting differences in language and cultures. The intellectuals of the Enlightenment expressed deep confidence in science and reason, believed in humanitarianism and stood for religious liberty and freedom of thought and person. They combined these values with a secular orientation and a belief in human progress. The thinkers of the Enlightenment could be seen in all major European cities, but Paris was their major centre of concentration.

A. Features of the Enlightenment

a. Faith in Scientific Methods of Investigation

The methods of natural science – observation, experimentation and critical enquiry – had strong influence on Enlightenment. The Enlightenment scholars resorted to these methods of enquiry in order to study society, to test traditions and practices and to question blind obedience to authority – of both religious and secular. They resorted to **critical scrutiny** of all received forms of knowledge. They also conducted observation and critical enquiry to **systematically explain** the natural world and their society. For example, Montesquieu attempted to link political system of a country with its physical features such as its climate and demography. In his conviction, the world was like a machine that function on certain general laws, as observed by Montesquieu 'everything which exists has its laws', the Enlightenment scholars believed that by imitating the methods of natural science they could discover laws that govern society and human nature. They wanted experimental method to be applied in the study of society in order to develop laws of human nature and of social development.

b. The Idea of Progress and Happiness for All

Two significant ideas of the Enlightenment were progress and happiness. The Enlightenment scholars believed that their period was better and more advanced compared to the past. They formed this belief from the changes that were taking place in the socio-economic life of the time. Scientists such as Copernicus, Kepler, Newton and Galileo had inaugurated a series of **scientific discoveries** which had made a better understanding of this universe and better control of natural forces possible. **Technological advancement** had resulted in better production and also had improved infrastructural facilities such as roads, canals, trade and communications. All these convinced them that they were at the threshold of a new era that would ensure all inhabitants of this planet a happy existence which would be 'the best of all possible worlds'. Moreover, they also believed that technological innovations of the time had released men from the bondage of labour and the commercial revolution had facilitated diffusion of wealth, which in turn resulted into a more equal diffusion of happiness and freedom. David Hume, one of the proponents of the Enlightenment, said 'happiness was the end to which all human life was directed'.

By promulgating the idea of progress and happiness in this world and urging people to seek happiness in this world, these scholars rejected the medieval notion of seeking happiness in next world.

c. A Social Order Based on the Principles of Reason and Liberty

For the Enlightenment theorists, reason was a tool to interrogate all received forms of knowledge, and also a non-authoritarian source of knowledge which would help liberate men from the oppressiveness of religion and state. They argued that any knowledge should be subjected to the probing of unfettered mind. Effective application of reason also enables better control of physical and social environment leading to improvement in human conditions of life.

The Enlightenment scholars cherished liberty and hence stood for ending slavery, social inequality and for a more democratic form of government. Emphasis placed by the Enlightenment scholars on freedom was found reflected in economic realm too. Freedom of individual when transformed into freedom of enterprise promotes the interest of society as a whole. For example, Adam Smith argued that the activities of human beings in pursuit of self-interest would create opportunities and benefits to others too.

d. Opposition to Religion and Absolute Monarchs

Enlightenment scholars believed religion as one of the hurdles to progress as it gave a fixed view of the world and as detrimental to reason. They viewed religion as a source of oppression and promoter of hatred among men throughout history. They attacked intolerant institutions of religion, questioned blind faith in dogmas and also its emphasis on the other world.

At the same time they were not irreligious or atheists and many of them had accepted the role of a Supreme Creator for this world and had the belief that all creatures in this world were His creations. Many scholars such as Voltaire believed that without belief in God, who punishes evil, the moral fabric of the society would be undermined.

They presented an alternative to the existing religions in the form of **Deism** – a natural religion of humanity – based on the principles of tolerance and equality of all persons and devoid of rituals and supernatural elements. Deists viewed the universe as a giant clock and God is its creator, the clockmaker, who allowed it to run on its natural laws. At the same time, the Deists, while retaining a belief in the Creator, rejected clerical authority, revelation and miracles. These scholars conducted a systematic assault against the dogmas in Christianity that defied logic and also against fanaticism and intolerance. For instance, Thomas Jefferson in his book ***The Life and Morals of Jesus of Nazareth*** or the ***Jefferson Bible*** (1820) excluded all miracles by Jesus and tried to extract the practical Christian moral code of the New Testament.

These scholars also made efforts to separate Church from the state. This idea was propounded by John Locke in his social contract principle that the liberty of conscience was a natural right and government does not have any authority in the realm of individual conscience. These ideas were to influence the makers of the American constitution who called for a 'wall of separation between the church and the state'.

As the enlightened minds cherished liberty, they were critical of despots. In their view, 'consent of the people' had to be the sole basis of power. Liberty at the same time was not a licence for unchecked pursuit of one's own interest and whims which would lead to anarchy. Hence they advocated importance of law for protecting liberty by putting restraint upon passions of individuals to violate the natural order.

e. *Spirit of Optimism*

The enlightened mind believed that reason and science had liberated people from 'the empire of fate' and had emancipated them to a world where men could shape their future. By reposing confidence in **rationalist will and humanist pride** in overcoming all hurdles, they concluded that there is no limit on what humans could achieve. Enlightenment theorists articulated a new conception of man, history and nature. For them history was marching from the dark ages to the civilised or enlightened existence of the present – an advancement from the 'barbarous rusticity to the politeness of our age'.

High Enlightenment: The Enlightenment was a dominant feature in France in the 18th century. Here, these scholars were known as the 'Philosophes'. The period between the 1750s and the 1780s during which the *Encyclopedia* was published and Paris emerged as the capital of Enlightenment is known as the High Enlightenment.

Though the Enlightenment was a Europe-wide intellectual trend, its prominent leaders were French scholars referred to as the 'Philosophes' of which Voltaire, Montesquieu and Rousseau were the most notable ones. Montesquieu published ***Spirit of the Laws*** (1748) and argued for separation of governmental powers into legislative, executive and judicial functions. Voltaire in his ***Letters Concerning the English Nation*** (1733) supported reform-minded kings – the enlightened despots and praised constitutional monarchy and religious toleration existed in England. Rousseau authored ***The Social Contract*** (1762) containing his political philosophy. He stated that 'man is born free, but everywhere he is in chains'. He believed in the goodness of nature and argued that civilisation corrupts men and distorts his natural freedom and equality. Like Hobbes, Rousseau too talked about social contract by which people surrender individual freedom and create government by the 'general will' and such a government, he argued, would restore the balance through civil liberty and equality. But Rousseau's social contract was different as it was an agreement among free individuals to form a government, while Hobbes' social contract was an agreement between a society and government.

Encyclopedia a collection of knowledge on various topics, edited by **Diderot** and **Jean d'Alembert** and published between 1751 and 1765 in multiple volumes, was the main medium of dissemination of the Enlightenment ideas in France initially and then in Europe.

f. *Spread and Impact of the Enlightenment*

The Enlightenment spread beyond Europe to America and to other European colonies such as India and Latin America. Ideas of Enlightenment especially its emphasis on individual conscience, religious tolerance and the concept of social contract were influential in American colonies. These ideas inspired the American Revolution, the Declaration of Independence and the US Constitution of 1787. In turn, the American Revolution influenced the French Revolution.

In political sphere, many European monarchs modelled their administration on these ideas. Catherine of Russia, Frederick the Great in Prussia and Joseph II in Austria (all of them in the 18th century) were some of the monarchs who tried to push through some reforms on enlightenment thought and came to be known as **'enlightened despots'**. The Enlightenment scholars had argued that all people have natural rights such as equality before the law, freedom of speech, freedom of religion, freedom of the press and freedom to pursue happiness. Enlightened rulers were monarchs that promoted these rights while retaining their royal powers intact.

It heralded a new era of political rights such as popular sovereignty, respect for law and human rights. The Enlightenment also inspired emergence of a broad **spectrum of ideologies** ranging from liberalism to socialism and communism.

The Enlightenment initiated socio-cultural changes in Europe. One of the primary effects of the Enlightenment in society was the emergence of the **public sphere**, a realm of communication in the form of debates and discussions in cafes and salons. The public sphere discussed the domain of common concern, was founded on reason and opened everything to criticism. The expansion of public domain also facilitated cultivation of arts. Increasing number of artists and musicians including women availed public concerts to express their talents and to gain fame and income. It also gave rise to individualism – the importance of individual in society and their ability to solve human problems.

> Salons were elegant drawing rooms in the mansions of the aristocrats of Paris. These were centres of social gatherings hoisted by wealthy women in Paris. In the 1700s, Paris was the cultural and intellectual capital of Europe, talented youngsters from around Europe and Americas gathered here to discuss and share ideas. In the cultural and intellectual circles of Paris germinated new ideas which soon spread throughout Europe.

The Enlightenment also affected the **domain of value** in European society. A strong belief in humanitarianism and opposition to slavery were two important outcomes to note. Thinkers like Montesquieu condemned torture as inhuman and irrational method to determine guilt or innocence. They also severely criticised slave trade thriving on both sides of the Atlantic at that time and Rousseau condemned slavery as a violation of the natural rights of man.

The Enlightenment also inspired the formulation of economic theories of which the most important was the **'laissez-faire'**. It was conceived as a way to unleash human potential through the restoration of the natural system, a system unhindered by governmental restrictions. It was an extension of the idea of liberty expounded by the Enlightenment intellectuals into the field of economics. Adam Smith applied the Enlightenment ideas to economy. These ideas shattered economic doctrines of protectionism and mercantilism and paved way for the emergence of capitalism.

Though these were noble ideals, the Enlightenment intellectuals had to face obstacles and even imprisonment. Voltaire and Diderot had been imprisoned, as powerful interests of the time viewed any questioning as deeply subversive. Rousseau had to flee from France. Many of their books had been banned in several countries as they posed threat to the established socio-political setup. Immanuel Kant observed in 1784, though 'he was living in the Age of Enlightenment; the age itself was not enlightened'. In spite of many such hurdles, the Enlightenment scholars by aspiring for a society based on rational principles, for a government that exits to enhance human happiness and with their strong belief in the infinite possibility of human progress heralded a new epoch in history.

4. | Mercantilism

Mercantilism refers to a state-controlled economic policy of regulation of trade and commerce of the nation to ensure prosperity and political power of that nation. The term 'Mercantilism' was coined by **Adam Smith.** Maximising the trade of a nation and accumulation of gold and silver were two important elements of the policy. Rulers believed that a country's power depended on its wealth, to be precise, the amount of gold and silver in its treasury. Hence, they aimed at maximising wealth through a **favourable balance of trade** by encouraging exports and restricting imports and also by **establishing and exploiting colonies**. As colonies played a vital role in the accumulation of wealth, mercantilism went hand in hand with **colonialism**. It was followed by many of the European nations during the 16th–18th centuries.

Under this policy, state intervened in economic activities through measures such as high tariffs, subsidies to new industries, by chartering new companies with freedom in overseas trade and by building up of fleets, all of which in turn accentuated the emergence of **Mercantile Capitalism** or **Commercial Capitalism.** Other components of Mercantilism were bullionism (acquirement of precious metals), paternalism (interference and control with an attitude of superiority) and economic nationalism (set of practices aimed at protecting national economy in world market).

Mercantilism was a significant factor in the formation of monopolistic trading companies such as the East India Company, behind commercial and military rivalries and wars such as the Anglo-Dutch

Wars (17th–18th centuries), high prices of finished goods and consequent smuggling of those goods and one of the causes of the American Revolution.

5. | Laissez-Faire

Laissez-faire means 'leave alone' or 'let do' and stands for minimum state interference in the economic life of individual and society. The Laissez-fairists believed that a nation's wealth is measured by its annual output of goods and services. Hence, government should allow business to operate freely. They stood for free market unregulated by government. The theorists argued that state should restrict itself to maintenance of order (police function) and ensuring of security (military function) apart from enforcing contracts and providing civil necessities.

Laissez-faire stemmed from the Enlightenment and the term is usually associated with the French economists known as the '**Physiocrats**'. This policy received strongest support from the classical economists. In 1776, **Adam Smith** published his book ***The Wealth of Nations*** and argued that freedom in economic activities leads to economic progress. Smith propounded **three natural laws** of economics.

1. The **Law of Self-interest:** Human beings are self-interested and work for their own benefit.
2. The **Law of Competition:** Competition in economic activities results in better product.
3. The **Law of Supply and Demand:** A free market produce goods at the lowest possible price to meet the demand.

The ideas of Adam Smith were further elaborated by British economists **Thomas Malthus** and **David Ricardo**. These thinkers opposed government initiatives such as fixing of minimum wage or better working conditions as they would upset the free market system and check the production of wealth in society.

Critics argue that laissez-faire would lead to inequality of wealth and income and instead of creating a level playing field for all, would lead to the emergence of vested interests and monopolies.

6. | Capitalism

Capitalism is an economic system in which the factors of production are in private hands and is carried through the process of competition aimed at profit. The term derives its origin from the word **'capital'** which means an asset which can generate income for the owner. The term capital is derived from the Latin word **'caput'** and denotes stocks of merchandise, money or money carrying interest and the term **'capitalist'** refers to those who own capital.

The dominant features of capitalism are-

1. the **private ownership** and control of the means of production,
2. the inputs and outputs of production are **determined by markets**,
3. the central reason for production is **profit motive**,
4. the division of society into **two classes** – capitalists and workers.

Capitalism emerged gradually over centuries. Different stages in its evolution are provided below.

Merchant or Commercial Capitalism: This is the early stage in the evolution of the capitalism, in which capitalism was dominated by commercial activity. It emerged out of commercial surplus invested in various economic activities. At this stage, merchants themselves became entrepreneurs to cater to market demands. As per the Marxist historians the roots of Commercial Capitalism can be traced back to the accumulation of wealth out of the profits through trade, from the late Medieval Period. It gained momentum from the 16th century onwards with extension of trade on a world scale supported by geographic explorations and lightning expansion of Europe to far and wide.

Two important results of Commercial Capitalism were the evolution of **Industrial Capitalism** and emergence of **Scientific Revolution**. Commercial Capitalism with its increased demand for goods – both consumer and capital goods – facilitated emergence of markets and towns and prepared ground for the emergence of Industrial Capitalism. Side-by-side, the expanding commerce put high demands on ship building and navigation technology, spurring inventions in compass and other instruments leading to Scientific Revolution.

Agrarian Capitalism: It developed out of agricultural surplus and existed side-by-side with the Commercial Capitalism. Interconnection of Agrarian Capitalism with Commercial and Industrial Capitalisms was too great that in some cases agricultural surplus was channelised to promote commercial activities and in other cases it was invested for industrial development.

Industrial Capitalism: This is the classical stage of capitalism during which capitalism coincided with industrialisation in its full-fledged form.

State Capitalism: It is a system of production in which the state-owned industries play a significant role within the market economy in the interest of the state. Though private firms have a key role in economy, they are subject to economic planning and interventionism by the state. In other words, it is an economic system combining capitalism with ownership or control by the state, for example, China.

Supporters of the Capitalist system argue that it promotes efficiency, innovation and economic growth apart from transforming individual self-interest into collective good. The socialists criticise capitalism alleging that it facilitates exploitation, domination, alienation, inefficiency and inequality. The capitalist economies are also characterised by boom and bust cycles, in which economy undergoes tremendous growth followed by a period of economic contraction and recession.

7. | Utilitarianism

It was the English philosopher **Jeremy Bentham** who propounded a new philosophy called Utilitarianism. His work *An Introduction to the Principles of Morals and Legislation* was published in 1789. The basic postulate of the theory was that, any action not only of private individual but of every measure of government is right, if it **maximises happiness** to everyone affected by it, and wrong if it produces the reverse of happiness, that is, pain. In other words, the morally right action is the action that produces the most good. It also argued for judging a particular idea, institution or action on the basis of their utility. For example, if any law does not do any good, it should be scrapped. By utility, it is meant general well-being or happiness which is a consequence of a good action. It called for government actions to promote greatest good for the greatest number of people. In other words, people should be left free to pursue their goals and the government should interfere only if such interference promotes greater good to the public.

Utilitarianism as a doctrine could be interpreted in both ways. The industrial class argued that industrialisation promoted greatest happiness for the majority of the people and any governmental intervention would hamper the proliferation of greater happiness. The early Utilitarians had opposed government interference in trade and industry on the assumption that, if left alone, economy would produce greatest welfare to greatest number.

The later Utilitarians modified their stance and argued for governmental action to correct the evils of private enterprise and became basis for interventionist reforms aimed at expanding education and to increase wages. **John Stuart Mill**, the English philosopher of the 19th century, questioned unregulated capitalism and argued for policies to ensure a more equal division of profits and reforms in legal and educational systems such as woman suffrage, free speech and education for all under the initiative of the state. In his work *Utilitarianism* (1861), John Stuart Mill presented Utilitarianism as an ethical doctrine not only for individual behaviour but also for state actions. As the Utilitarians gave emphasis on everyone's happiness it could be considered as an egalitarian doctrine. The question the Utilitarians ask, **'What use is it'** emerged as completely secular approach and cornerstone of policy formulation since then.

8. | Socialism

It is an economic system in which the factors of production are owned by the public and operated for the benefit of all. It thus stands for social ownership of means production and distribution. Socialists were a new group that emerged in industrialised European society. It emerged as a challenge to capitalism and as a proposal for replacing it. They espoused distribution of resources for the general good of society and argued for government interference in economic activities.

A. Rise of Socialist Ideas

Early socialist thinkers stood for social reorganisation on utopian schemes to overcome the evils of capitalism. They visualised a society that is both industrial and at the same time humane. Some of the early Utopian socialists were:

Saint-Simon (1760–1825): Simon, a French aristocrat argued for public ownership of productive property. Simon also called for harnessing of technology for the betterment of society. He argued that scientific knowledge would bind the modern society into a technocratic society, just as Christianity had unified the society in the Middle Ages.

Robert Owen (1771–1858): As a mill owner from Scotland, Owen improved working conditions and living conditions of his labourers and argued for replacement of competition by harmonious group living in which members will be rewarded solely on the basis of their actual labour. To implement this idea, he founded a cooperative community called **New Harmony**, in Indiana in the United States in 1825.

Charles Fourier (1772–1837): He was a French reformer who argued for abolition of wage system and complete equality between the genders. **Phalansteries** were the communities of few hundred people envisaged by Fourier, where men and women could engage in tasks of their interest and enjoy life. In the 1840s, many phalansteries were established in the United States based on Fourier's ideas.

Louis Blanc (1811–82): A French politician, Blanc was another thinker who opposed exploitation of workers of the industrial society. He argued for universal male suffrage as a solution by which he expected workers could gain control of the state. He also visualised a system in which an association of workers, called as 'Association of Production', would control the factories leading to withering away of both private enterprises and the state.

Pierre Proudhon (1809–68): Another Frenchman who advocated setting up of institutions to produce goods whose price shall be determined solely on the basis of amount of labour devoted to produce it and also for regulatory role of the state in the form of taxes.

But all these socialist community ideas and efforts were opposed and rejected by Karl Marx and Friedrich Engels as 'utopian', on the argument that path to socialism cannot be paved through establishment of model communities but through class struggle alone.

9. | Marxism

Marxism is radical type of socialism as expounded by Karl Marx. Its major difference with socialism is its adherence to revolutionary zeal to attain socialism. Friedrich Engels called Marxism as 'scientific socialism' and differentiated it from 'utopian' strains of socialism.

Basic elements of Marx's theory were derived from German philosophy of G.W.F. Hegel, French socialism and British economics. The communist ideology had reflections of certain developments in Europe. It subscribed to the Enlightenment belief in science and progress; the French Revolution, with its red flag and the slogan 'liberty, equality and fraternity' and the Industrial Revolution which created contradiction of poverty amidst wealth.

Marxism and Communism: Marxism is Karl Marx's theories about communism and methods to achieve it. It is a socio-political-economic theory, while Communism is the practical expression of Marxism in the form of a political system. In other words, Marxism is a theoretical model to construct a political system and a classless society. Marx defined communism as a form of complete socialism in which means of production would be owned by the community and all goods and services would be distributed equally. As per Marx, communism is the **final phase of social evolution** in which production and distribution of goods would be based on 'from each according to his ability, to each according to his needs'.

Socialism and Communism: There is no crystallised definition to both. Both talk about ideals that are assumed to be the best way to organise society, both oppose capitalism and advocate a post-capitalist order. While socialism is a general philosophy that advocates social ownership of means of production rather than by a small class of owners, Communism can be seen as an offshoot of Socialism, whose roots can be traced to 'The Communist Manifesto' which visualises establishment of a classless and stateless society after the inevitable proletarian revolution. In other words, socialism is the first phase of the communist society and communism proper is its final stage.

Karl Marx

Karl Marx (1818–83): Marx was born of German-Jewish parents in Prussia (Germany). Marx received his doctoral degree in philosophy at Jena in 1841 and became the editor of a newspaper. In 1843, Marx shifted to Paris where he met Engels, another critic of capitalism initiating a lifelong collaboration of two ardent critics of capitalism. As he was forced to leave France for his radical views, Marx lived in London from 1849 till his death in 1883. Marx viewed capitalism both as a progressive stage in history and as an exploitative system. It is progressive in the sense that, it unleashed productive power and transformed the world. It is exploitative as the capital class reaped the profits of the toils of the working class.

Friedrich Engels

Friedrich Engels (1820–95): Engels was a German businessman. Though himself a capitalist and owner of a factory in Manchester, England, Engels had been appalled by the poverty and injustice done to the workers and had portrayed it in his work, ***The Condition of the English Working Class*** (1844). Engels edited the second and third volumes of Karl Marx's Das Kapital after Marx's death. Engels' other works include 'Socialism: Utopian and Scientific' (1880) and 'The Origin of the Family, Private Property and the State' (1884).

In 1848, Marx and Engels published ***The Communist Manifesto***, a 23-page pamphlet intended as a program of action and organisational principles of a radical group known as the **Communist League**. The opening lines of the manifesto laid the basis of Marxism '*The history of all hitherto existing society is the history of class struggle*'. It called for the overthrow of the capitalist system and its replacement by a society in which all property would be publicly owned. To inspire the working class in attaining this objective, 'The Communist Manifesto' proclaimed, '*the proletarians have nothing to lose but their chains. They have a world to win*' and it also exhorted '*working men of all countries, unite*'.

The Communist Manifesto reflected converging of ideas of Engels and Marx and formed the basis for the communist movement. The authors by arguing that a series of class struggles would destroy capitalism, and will be replaced by socialism, followed by communism predicted an eventual communist triumph. The ideas contained in the Manifesto reverberated with increasing force around the world in the subsequent years and by 1950, nearly half the world's population lived under Marxist governments.

Marx further developed his critique of the capitalist system in ***Das Kapital*** or ***Capital*** (1867) and argued, '*philosophers have only interpreted the world in different ways; the point is to change it*'. In 1864, Marx was involved in organising the **International Workingmen's Association** also known as the **First International**. It was aimed at forging an alliance of international working class to overthrow capitalism. It was during the existence of the International, **Paris Commune** took place in 1871 in which the citizens of Paris rose in rebellion against the government. Marx considered the development as the first battle in the class war he had predicted.

Paris Commune was a radical government that ruled Paris from March to May 1871 after the defeat of France in the Franco-German War.

A. Main Elements of Marxism

Historical materialism: Marx rejected all religious and metaphysical interpretations regarding the world and treated it in strict materialist terms. He argued that it is possible to understand the world rationally and to change it. Marx also argued that economic and technological factors as moving forces in history what he called as **economic determinism.** Marx held that historical developments could be understood in materialist terms by recognising **the means of production**, that is, means of material production in that society. 'Before men can do anything else, they must first produce the means of their subsistence'. Thus, for Marx, material production was the nectar of life and of human actions.

In means of production there are two essentials. These are **'the forces of production'**, this includes the raw materials and tools and **'relations of production'**, this includes the division of labour.

Marx designated history into four stages of development on the basis of social relations of production.

1. **Primitive communism** of classless tribal societies
2. **Slave society** of ancient times in which aristocracy was born
3. **Feudalism** of medieval times and the lords were the ruling class
4. **Capitalism** of modern times and the capitalists are the ruling class

In Marx's view, capitalism was inevitable stage in the development of human society, made possible by remarkable scientific and technological changes. The problem with the capitalist system is its unfair distribution of wealth as the capitalists siphon off the surplus value, that is, profit.

As per Marx, capitalism creates-

1. inequality,
2. poverty,
3. false consciousness. This happens because the ideas of the ruling classes are projected as common sense and natural. Due to 'false consciousness' the exploited class may fail to understand their true interests and exploitation continues to remain hidden and
4. alienation of worker in the workplace, from his product and from their humanity.

Though capitalism produces material abundance, they are inequitably distributed. While the workers receive only a fraction of the value of goods they produce as wage, the **surplus value**, that is, profit is accumulated by the capitalists. Appropriation of the surplus value by the capitalists, as per Marx, represented the measure of capitalist exploitation. Moreover, the capitalist's desire for more profit will lead to over production and consequent fall in profit for the capitalists, which in turn would create economic crisis and unemployment. Such 'contradictions' of the capitalist system would instil class consciousness in the proletariat and their opposition to the exploiting class.

Class conflict: Marx observed that 'The history of all hitherto existing human society is the history of class struggle'. For Marx, history was successive stages of conflict between classes. This conflict between those who controlled the means of production (**the haves**) and those whose labour was exploited (**the have-nots**) had been a dominant force in history. In ancient time the struggle was between the master and slave, in medieval period between the lord and serf and in modern period between the capitalists **(bourgeoisie)** and working class (**proletariat**). In each stage a dominant class controls the means of production. But the inherent internal contradictions lead to the overthrow of the ruling class and its replacement by another.

For Marx, mode of production meant organisation of economic production in a given society and capitalism is a mode of production based on private ownership of means of production. Marx also postulated that the **mode of material production** determines the general character of the social, political and intellectual processes of life. Historically, it was the class with economic power that held the state power which also controlled the **'mental production'**. In this context he observed that 'the ruling ideas of every epoch are the ideas of the ruling class'. In modern period control over wealth enables the bourgeoisie to control government.

Dialectical view of social transformation: Marx drew from the dialectical view of human consciousness of German philosopher Hegel to construct his historical materialism. Hegel had argued that human thought has evolved from simple to higher forms of thought. Contradictions of an age give birth to a new age by smoothing over of these contradictions.

Hegel and Marx: In developing his theory of history, Marx owed much to the German philosopher **Hegel** and his idea of 'dialectic'. Dialectic is a method of reconciling ostensible paradoxes to reach at absolute truth. Hegel had outlined history as development of socio-political institutions as a result of dialectic, that is, 'thesis' (a clearly delineated proposition) and 'antithesis' (contradictory proposition) producing 'synthesis' (higher level of truth). But the major difference between them was that Hegel's dialectic was of ideas, that is, history can be understood in terms of ideas that is characteristic of each historical stage, whereas Marx's dialectic was of economic forces, that is, history as a succession of economic systems or modes of production.

Proletarian revolution: Capitalism being a volatile economic system undergoes series of recessions and depressions and would lead to unemployment and misery to proletariat. The crisis would instil a class consciousness in the proletariat and would convince them that their interests are opposed to that of bourgeoisie. This class consciousness and realisation would intensify their hatred of capitalism and eventually lead to a revolution and the proletariat will seize means of production and institutions of state power. To pre-empt a counter revolution by the displaced bourgeoisie, initially rule by the proletariat will be established. This transitional stage from capitalism to communism would be that of the **'Dictatorship of the Proletariat'**. This is a **stage of cooperative living** and payment would be in accordance with the work performed. But once the threat of counter revolution disappears, the state also would wither away resulting in the emergence of **classless communist society**, the final goal of historical evolution. In Communist system, wages would be abolished and everyone would be expected to work and receive a proportion of the wealth produced. 'From each according to his ability, to each according to his need' would create a condition of production – consumption equilibrium. With the withering away of the state, national boundaries too will disappear leading to the emergence of a global community based on workers solidarity.

Marxism thus offered a new perspective in the study of human society which had tremendous influence in disciplines such as sociology, political science and economics. Marxism also strengthened the idea of socialism and the socialist parties, beginning with Europe and then in other parts of the world. Marxism was instrumental in bringing out the Russian Revolution and was the basis of the Soviet Union. Marxism also provided a ray of hope to the downtrodden all over the world by investing them with a sense of worth as human beings and by instilling confidence of their role in the historical process. The workers in turn held the Marxian theory as rational explanation for the reasons of their plight and solution it offered as an assurance that capitalism was bound to fade away.

After the death of Marx in 1883, Engels became the chief votary of Marxism. Marx was the brilliant theoretician of the two, but it was Engels, as the apt promoter of Marxism directed attention of the intellectual world to Das Kapital through his reviews of the book, and implanted the thought that it was their "Bible." Engels also made extensive correspondence with German social democrats, perpetuating the image of Marx and fostering a degree of conformity among followers of Marxist philosophy. Engels also contributed to promote Marxism by demolishing the influence of Karl Eugen Duhring, a Berlin professor who threatened to supplant Marx's position among German social democrats by writing a book 'Herr Eugen Duhring's Revolution in Science', also known as 'Anti-Duhring' in 1878. As an encompassing presentation of Marx's thought the book probably did most to promote Marxian thought. Engels also made efforts to fill gaps in Marx's system and extended it to other fields. In particular, Engels stressed historical materialism, assigning it a character of scientific discovery. After the death of Engels in 1895, Marxists split into **revisionists**, who favoured a gradual and evolutionary transition to socialism and **'purists'** who stood for revolution.

One of the prominent revisionist leaders was the German Social Democrat leader **Eduard Bernstein** (1850–1932). In his book ***Evolutionary Socialism***, Bernstein pointed out that the standard of living of the European workers had improved since 1850 and that franchise to workers had offered opportunity of reform of the existing system by the ballot. Similarly, the **Fabian Socialists** in England too believed in 'the inevitability of gradualism' in achieving socialism. **Vladimir Lenin** of Russia was the most prominent of the purists.

B. Criticism of Marxism

1. Marx viewed history on materialistic terms and claimed economic forces influenced the flow of history. But reducing all historical developments into economic framework is wrong as factors such as nationalism, religion, ethnic loyalties had also decided the flow of history.
2. The gap between the rich and poor has not widened as predicted by Marx and Engels, consequent to reforms of governments and efforts of labour unions. For example, the English Reform Bill 1867 enfranchised the urban male workingmen.
3. Moreover, as demonstrated in history the struggles that characterised the 20th century had not been between classes but between nations.

4. Emergence of strong middleclass consisting of professionals, civil servants and others also negates Marx's theory of polarisation of society into two opposing classes – the capitalists and the workers.
5. Marx's prediction that communist revolution would happen first in industrialised countries such as the United Kingdom or the United States also proved wrong as it was the underdeveloped or feudal Russia and China that saw communist revolutions.
6. Last but not least, in countries where communist captured power the state has not withered away, as predicted by Marx. On the contrary, the state became more centralised and authoritarian.

10. | Romanticism

Romanticism was a cultural movement that emerged in the last decades of the 18th century, was in many aspects negation of Enlightenment and became influential in European cultural life in the 19th century.

In contrast to rationalistic approach to life by the Enlightenment scholars, the Romantics stood for exaltation of imagination and human feelings. One of them, **John Keats**, emphasised this point when he exclaimed, '*O for a life of sensations rather than of thoughts*'. Romantics while challenging the Enlightenment rationalism pleaded for the liberation of **human emotions** and for free expression of personality. They gave importance to the emotional side of human nature, which had been overlooked by the Enlightenment philosophers. The Romantics criticised the Enlightenment rationalism for turning the human beings into soulless thinking machines. In other words, the Romantics stood for 'natural' man against the mechanistic world view and the scientific rationality. For example, Keats argued that reducing rainbow to prismatic colours deprive it of its poetic and aesthetic values. Thus, Romanticism was a move away from the Enlightenment's rational to emotion and intellectualism to imagination.

Similarly, the Romantics gave importance to **individuality, uniqueness** and also to **diversity in humanity**. For the Romantics, individuality and uniqueness meant departure from social norms and conventions. This was in opposition to the Enlightenment view of generalisation of human beings and emphasis on elements shared by all people in general.

The Enlightenment had articulated a clear, critical and controlled mind and had set the standards of aesthetics considered to be universal. In contrast, the Romantics believed that writing poetry or painting a picture is not learned by textbooks or by set rules but by following one's own imagination and instincts. The Romantics tried to recapture the pristine freedom and creativity in the human soul by demolishing the standards erected by the civilisation. Similarly, for the Enlightened the world could be understood fully by human mind and man was in control of his destiny but for the Romanticists the world was full of turbulence and its uncertainties beyond human comprehension.

They believed that the inner mind or the unconscious state as the wellspring of creativity and more powerful than reason. Sense perceptions were, as per the Enlightened, basis of knowledge, while the Romantics believed that not just sense perceptions but the **innate sensibility** of an individual that constituted knowledge. In other words, it was the product of both innate feelings and external perceptions. Men and women were expected to interpret nature in terms of their own individual perception of it. '*By looking within ourselves, into our inner consciousness we come to understand and know the truth*', they claimed.

In matters of religion, though many of the Enlightenment scholars had not denied God but had reduced Him to the position of a watchmaker – a detached observer of a mechanical universe. But, for the Romantics God was an inspiring spiritual force and religion was an expression of human nature and feelings.

In their views on history too, the Romantics differed from the Enlightenment. While the Enlightenment regarded the Middle Ages as an era of darkness and the medieval institutions and practices as barriers to progress, the Romanticists valued the Middle Ages for its heroic deeds and celebrated the past.

For the Romantics, the universe is a mélange of times, tones, moods and places. In their search for universal principles and standardisation of culture, Enlightenment had neglected myths and folk traditions. But, for the Romantics, these were rich sources of cultural vitality, creativity and identity. This factor, that is, recognition of distinctiveness in peoples and cultures by the Romanticists, became instrumental in shaping modern nationalism.

At the same time, the Romantics attack on reason and their glorification of non-rational aspects of cultural life and native soil paved the way for ultra-nationalism.

Some prominent figures in European Romantic Movement in different fields were Shelly, Wordsworth, Keats and Byron in England, Victor Hugo in France, and Schiller and Beethoven in Germany.

11. Conservatism

Conservatism was a counterweight ideology to the Enlightenment. It was championed by the traditional ruling class and orthodox segments of the European society in the post French Revolutionary period. The British philosopher Edmund Burke's ***Reflection on the French Revolution*** (1790) is considered as the beginning point of Conservatism.

The core concept behind Conservatism was **veneration of tradition** and **rejection of revolution**. The Conservatives believed in the limitations of reason in solving human issues and argued that wickedness is inherent in human nature which could be controlled by traditional institutions such as religion, values and beliefs.

In similar vein, the Conservatives rejected the Enlightenment articulation of 'individualism' and argued that such a conception would lead to fragmentation of social fabric and consequent emergence of self-seeking isolated individuals.

Conservatives also opposed equality and held that the universe is naturally hierarchical as people are different by virtue of birth, intelligence, talents and so on and hence they supported a social hierarchy of inherited aristocracy.

In short, the Conservatives were defenders of the status quo who championed tradition over reason, hierarchy over equality and the community over the individual. They viewed the French Revolution as an event that opened the door to anarchy and terror and the *philosophes* as people who deprived the French society of its old habits and moral leadership.

12. Liberalism

Liberalism and nationalism were two important ideological forces of the 19th century. Both had their origin in the Enlightenment and the French evolution. They also represented gathering of forces against conservatism that had engulfed Europe after the defeat of Napoleon.

Liberalism was a political movement aimed at protecting individual rights against oppression of governments. It was the expression of political philosophy of the bourgeoisie. Liberals stood for **liberty and equality** as proclaimed in the French Revolution.

Two related currents in Liberalism were **political liberalism** and **economic liberalism**. The most important proponent of the 19th century liberalism was the English thinker **John Stuart Mill**. He argued for unfettered individual freedom and that freedom shall be curtailed only to prevent harm to others. **Adam Smith**'s *The Wealth of Nations*, **Thomas Malthus's** *Essay on the Principles of Population* (1798) and **David Ricardo's** *Principles of Political Economy* and his idea of 'Iron Law of Wages' were theoretical bases of economic liberalism.

Major characteristics of Liberalism were-

1. government by consent, that is, constitutional monarchy or democracy,
2. policies that promote peace and free trade,
3. individual liberty,
4. rejection of classification of people as commoners and aristocrat on the basis of birth,
5. the importance of reason in creating free institutions and responsible citizens,
6. liberals stood for written constitution as a protection against absolutism of kings and also as a guarantor of individual freedom, freedoms of expression, religion and property,
7. liberals stood for freely elected parliament and distribution of power between various organs of government and
8. in economic sphere the Liberals stood for free economy and competition, dismantling of mercantilism and supported the laissez-faire theory of Adam Smith and held that the 'best government is one that governs least'.

13. Radicalism

Radicalism is a philosophy that stands for complete change. The term is derived from the Latin word 'radix' which means 'root', hence, imply **'root and branch'** changes instead of gradualism. Both Liberalism and Radicalism traces their origin to the Enlightenment and were aimed at liberating humanity from the

Conservatives, but they differed in approach. While the Liberals stood for protection of individual rights, the Radicals argued for socio-economic and institutional restructuring. In the 19th century, the Radicals demanded for republican government and universal male suffrage. Though generally the term is associated with left-wing political groups, radicalism is also used to describe extreme right-wing groups such as the Fascists and the German Nazis.

14. Realism

Realism was a new current in art and literature that emerged at the mid-19th century. The Realists were obsessed with the **empirical world** who wanted to analyse and depict the familiar details of everyday life – how people looked, worked and behaved. In doing so the Realists revolted against the Romanticists' exaltation of inner life, emotions and intuitions. In painting, the movement was also known as '**living art**' as it depicted commonplace scenes and people without attempting any glorification. In literature, the Realists portrayed social abuses and inequalities. For example, **Ivan Turgenev,** a prominent Realist, in his ***Sketches*** (1852) depicted rural conditions in Russia and brutalities of serf's life.

15. Darwinism

This is a theory propounded by Charles Darwin (1809–82), an English naturalist, as a scientific 'theory of evolution by natural selection'. By this, Darwin constructed a universal theory about the origin and development of living species.

Charles Darwin

Charles Darwin developed his theory based on his observation, experiences and extensive evidences collected during his circumnavigation survey mission in a ship named **HMS *Beagle*,** between 1831 and 1836. It was the British biologist **Thomas Henry Huxley** who coined the term 'Darwinism' in 1860 to describe the discoveries of Darwin.

Darwin published his ideas in two books. In 1859, he published ***Origin of Species by Means of Natural Selection*** and in 1871 another book ***The Descent of Man***. The first book dealt with general theory of evolution of animals and plants and not particularly of humans, while the second discussed the human evolution in its physical and psychological aspects.

Basic postulates of the theory were-

1. All species mutate and change over time. Human beings too are products of evolution from lower, nonhuman forms of life.
2. Changes in organisms are the result of natural selection, in which each slight 'variation', if useful, is preserved increasing an organism's chances of survival. In other words, no two offspring of an organism are exactly alike. Slight variations are crucial in securing food and fighting enemies and organism favoured by nature is more likely to survive. Such favourable characteristics get transmitted to the descendants and become more pronounced over many generations and results in the evolution of species.
3. There is a competition for survival within each species and that the individuals with favourable features for that environment survive and less adaptable eliminated.
4. Reproductive isolation will lead to origin of new species.

Darwinism revolutionised the science as was the case with early contributions to science by Galileo, Copernicus and Newton. The theory offered a new understanding of ourselves as humans, our origin and development as a species apart from defining the place of humans in the universe. The theory also facilitated emergence of social sciences such as psychology, economics and sociology as scientific methods now increasingly came to be applied to the study of human society. Another effect of Darwinian Theory was separation of science from religion and secularisation of life and thought. With the 'evolutionary theory' human origin now had a scientific explanation as the one evolved from lower nonhuman forms of life, which was contradictory to 'creationism' – the explanation found in the religious scriptures.

16. Social Darwinism

This theory emerged as a result of application of Darwinian principles to society. If nature was a matter of competition, so was society and nations. The Social Darwinists postulated that nations and races are engaged in a struggle for survival and that only fittest of them alone would survive. They also emphasised on anti-philanthropic social and economic life.

By distorting Darwin's theory the Social Darwinists claimed that not only the fittest had survived but that only the fittest had the **'right to survive'**. The most articulate advocate of Social Darwinism was **Herbert Spencer** (1820–1903), the English philosopher, who opposed any support especially by government to the poor or weak as it is against the evolutionary process and the struggle for survival. Herbert Spencer also coined the phrase '**survival of the fittest**'.

Supporters of Social Darwinism claimed superiority of their races such as Anglo-Saxon (British and American) and Teutonic (German) and their right to **expansion and domination** of other lands and its peoples – Africans, Asians, American Indians and the Poles whom they considered as inferiors.

The theory influenced many of the 19th and 20th century developments such as militarism, imperialism, ultra-nationalism, racism and the Holocaust, all of which produced catastrophic results in the annals of history. Social Darwinism also accorded 'scientific' justification for **genocide** by the Nazis. In times these theorists believed that through '**civilising missions**' the inferiors could be brought at par with the European civilised life, hence a justification for imperialism, while at other times they resorted to '**cleansing**' of inferior groups as '**final solution**' in the '**struggle for existence**'.

17. Nationalism

Nationalism is a consciousness of belonging or a feeling of strong attachment by a group of people who share a common culture and history. It provides people a sense of identity and a cause worthy of self-sacrifice.

The **French Revolution** with its principle that sovereignty derives from its people as citizens of a nation inaugurated the concept of nationalism. **Romanticism** by awakening the pride of people in their shared language, literature and folk traditions further strengthened it in the form of cultural nationalism. This was particularly true of the German thinker Johann Herder (1744–1803) who stimulated national consciousness among the German people. Herder maintained that 'there is only one class in the state, the Volk (the people) and the king belongs to this class as well as the peasant'. Similarly, **Liberalism** by its emphasis on the right to self-rule as an extension of the rights of the individual further strengthened nationalism. They held that states formed of popular sovereignty would end domination by foreign groups and tyrant princes and such a state would protect the rights of the individuals.

> **Nation and State:** A nation is an ethnic or cultural community, whereas a state is a political entity having sovereignty. While many states are nations in themselves, many nations are not sovereign states. For example, ethnic minorities living in a state, as in the case of Native American Iroquois though constitute a nation, does not form a state.

Translation of nationalism as a sentiment into political power can be called as nation building. The concept of nationalism manifested politically in the 19th century, in the form of demands for autonomous political communities based on the nation. This in turn threatened the existence of multinational and autocratic states such as Austria, Russia and Ottoman Turkey.

Nationalism gave birth to **nation-states** which was the product of the amalgamation of the nation (a community of citizens) and the state (the political entity) into autonomous political communities. A nation-state is a state with majority of its people sharing the same culture and that its cultural boundaries are in congruence with its political boundaries. The nation-state entails two principles – the **state sovereignty** and the **national sovereignty**. The state sovereignty is the right to govern its territories without external interference and the national sovereignty means the right of its people to govern themselves. Hence, the nation-states are 'states of and for particular nations'.

SUMMARY

The Scientific Revolution – The Scientific Revolution refers to a new approach of looking at the world by careful observation and experimentation. The **scientific outlook** and the **scientific method** were two basic features of it which in turn led to the development of scientific theories and new discoveries.

The Enlightenment – It was an intellectual movement of the 18th century Europe that gave emphasis on a rational analysis of society, its practices, beliefs and institutions. Faith in scientific methods of enquiry, belief in the idea of progress and happiness for all, effort to construct a social order based on the principle of reason and liberty, opposition to blind faith in religion and to absolute monarchs and a spirit of optimism that articulated a new conception of man, history and nature were its main features.

Mercantilism – It refers to a policy of regulation of trade and commerce of the nation, to ensure prosperity and political power of that nation. Proponents of it stood for maximising nation's wealth by maintaining a favourable balance of trade and by establishing and exploiting colonies.

Laissez Faire – It means 'let do' and stand for minimum state interference in the economy and for a free market unregulated by government.

Capitalism – It is an economic system where production is carried through the process of competition and for profit by the private hands who own the factors of production.

Utilitarianism – It is a philosophy which argues that any action of private individual or of government should be aimed at maximum happiness to maximum people.

Socialism – It is a philosophy and an economic model in which factors of production are owned by the public and is operated for the benefit of all. It emerged as a response to the evils of Industrial Revolution and as an alternative to capitalism.

Marxism – It is a radical type of socialism as expounded by Karl Marx. Historical materialism, class conflict, dialectical view of social transformation, proletarian revolution which leads to establishment of a classless communist society are the major aspects of Marxist thought.

Conservatism – It was an ideology that emerged as a counterweight to the Enlightenment and stood for veneration of tradition and rejection of revolution.

Liberalism – It was a political movement aimed at protection of individual rights against oppression of governments and stood for liberty and equality.

Romanticism – It was a cultural movement emerged in Europe in the late 18th century in opposition to the ideas of the Enlightenment and stood for exaltation of imagination and human feelings.

Radicalism – It is a philosophy that stand for complete change and for socio-economic and institutional restructuring and in opposition to gradualism.

Realism – It was a cultural movement that stood for depiction of familiar details of everyday life.

Darwinism – It refers to the 'theory of evolution by natural selection' developed by the English naturalist Charles Darwin.

Social Darwinism – This was a theory that emerged by applying Darwinian principles to society. This theory argued that only the fittest have the right to survive and was also influential in the rise of militarism, imperialism, ultra-nationalism, racism and the Holocaust.

Nationalism – It is a feeling of belonging to a nation by a group of people who share a common culture and history. The French Revolution, Romanticism and Liberalism have contributed in the growth of nationalism since the 18th century.

Questions of Previous Years Civil Services Examination

1. Marxian socialism claims itself to be a scientific socialist theory capable of explaining the history of humankind. Discuss. (2023)
2. Enlightenment was not confined to scientific revolution alone, but humanism and ideas of progress too were its inseparable constituents. Examine. (2023)
3. The impact of industrial revolution on the middle-class world view is reflected in the views of Adam Smith, Thomas Malthus and Jeremy Bentham. Comment. (2023)
4. 'Rousseau kindled a hope which became the spirit of the Enlightenment'. Critically examine. (2022)
5. Engels did much more than Marx himself to popularise the ideas of Marxism. Critically examine. (2022)
6. What was 'enlightened' about the Age of Enlightenment? (2021)
7. 'The principles of Enlightenment were in some ways a continuation of the discoveries and theories of the Scientific Revolution'. Critically examine. (2020)
8. How would you explain the nature of Pre-Marxian Socialism? Critically examine. (2019)
9. 'The arguments of the free traders were a curious mixture of economic hard-headedness, social benevolence, cosmopolitan idealism and class prejudice'. Critically examine. (2019)
10. Explain the major ideas of Enlightenment. Discuss the contribution of Rousseau in Enlightenment. (2018)
11. 'With the writings of Karl Marx, Socialism assumed the form of Scientific Socialism'. (2018)
12. 'Karl Marx applied his critical intelligence to Wealth of Nations. Where Smith had seen only the sunlight, Marx saw only the shadows thrown upon the human scene by the unimpeded exercise of individual liberty…' Elucidate. (2016)
13. 'France was even more fertile than Britain in producing new socialist theories and movements, though bore less concrete results in France than Britain'. (2015)
14. 'Rousseau strove to reconcile the liberty of the individual and the institution of government through a new vision of the Contract Theory of Government'. (2014)
15. 'Enlightened despots (Europe) were not necessarily politically liberal'. (2014)
16. 'For Kant, Enlightenment is mankind's final coming of age, the emancipation of the human consciousness from an immature state of ignorance and error'. (2013)
17. 'The despotic rulers of Europe were influenced by philosophy of enlightenment and began to follow a benevolent policy towards their subjects'. (2012)
18. 'The promptings of the heart are more to be trusted than the logic of the mind'. Rousseau (2011)
19. 'He (Voltaire) was living in the Age of Enlightenment….The age itself was not enlightened'. E. Kant. (2010)
20. 'Rousseau's political philosophy contains the seeds of Socialism, Absolutism and Democracy'. (2004)

CHAPTER 3

The Industrial Revolution

In this Chapter

1. Introduction

Industrial Revolution refers to the revolutionary changes that took place in the field of industrial production from the latter-half of the 18th century. Though the technological advances were the most apparent feature, the Industrial Revolution was the result of a **complex interplay of changes** in technology, economy, society and culture.

The Revolution unfolded in the forms of invention of machine tools, replacement of hand craft by power-driven production, use of steam power and the rise of factory system. It marked a revolutionary transition from the previously known home-based production (also known as the **putting out system** involving physical labour and skill to produce pieces of goods) to bulk production of goods in factories that housed huge machinery run on water or steam power.

The remarkable changes were inaugurated in cotton and iron industries and spread to coal mining and then to the building of roads, canals and railways accelerating economic growth in an unprecedented manner. These changes in the method and scope of industrial production tremendously influenced the course of world history, and transformed every aspect of human life – economic, socio-cultural and political in every part of the globe sooner or later.

> **Putting-out system** was a form of production of proto-industrialisation period in which production was subcontracted to workmen who worked in their homes or in workshops. Money and raw materials were provided by the merchant, who in turn received the finished product. This was also known as the **workshop system** or the **domestic system**. Under this system workers could work in their own speed while at home and supplement their income by continuing cultivation in their small plots or farms and also could engage in household tasks.

In the global context, the Industrial Revolution caused a shift in the balance of power in Europeans' favour. It also increased the global inequality by widening the gap between the nations – the industrialised and the non-industrialised. Moreover, it also encouraged competition between the industrialised nations and paved way for imperialism, which was born out of the cycle of industrialisation, the need for raw materials and development of new markets. The Industrial Revolution was, thus, a development that transformed not just a country but the whole world itself.

> The term ***revolution industrielle*** or the Industrial Revolution was first used by the French scholars in the 1820s. It acquired general acceptability only after the publication of the book ***Lectures on the Industrial Revolution in England*** by **Arnold Toynbee** in 1884. He commented that 'the Wealth of Nations and the steam engine…destroyed the old world and built a new one'.

Industrial Revolution by facilitating bulk production of goods with the help of machines solved the question of production, while at the same time inaugurating large number of issues for the human community to cope with. The factory system with no concern for the safety and well-being of labourers created new issues in urban life, concentration of the wealth in few hands gave birth to grave economic disparities in society, while pollution caused both by factories and slum dwellings of the industrial labourers caused grave health issues and concerns.

All these issues sparked off protests, forcing the governments to initiate legislative and administrative steps to ameliorate the conditions of the masses of urban poor. The Industrial Revolution thus caused a complex set of economic, technological and social changes that developed over a substantial period of time and with its both positive and negative impacts marked a major turning point in history.

2. Roots of the Industrial Revolution

By the 18th century the Western Europe was wealthier than much of the world. The **Commercial Revolution** of the 16th and 17th centuries had led to the **accumulation of capital** in Europeans' hands. It was through this thriving commercial class, who had emerged as the world's prominent manufacturers and traders, who in the process had also enlisted the support of their rulers, that the Industrial Revolution was unfolded. Another factor that led to the European leadership in the Industrial Revolution was the **military and commercial rivalries** between different European states. As a result, industrial production and trade in goods such as weapons, uniforms and ships increased. Moreover, since the beginning of the 16th century, **overseas explorations** had opened up new lands for European penetration and economic exploitation. Availability of the resources – both human and material – in the New World, Africa and Asia, fuelled the fire of the Industrial Revolution in Europe. Overseas expansion also meant availability of markets.

Moreover, **developments in agricultural sector** contributed greatly to the emergence of industrial age in Europe. In Western Europe agriculture had become a capitalist enterprise, **agrarian capitalism**, paving way for increased efficiency in agriculture production. By the 18th century, traditional agricultural practices and patterns were witnessing a restructuring in Western Europe and agriculture was emerging as a capitalist enterprise catering to the requirements of the market rather than for the family or for the village.

In the 18th century, there was an enormous growth in the **population** of European states, which ensured both consumer and labour. More efficient agricultural production meant more births, better health and fewer deaths. Population also increased due to decline in the number of deaths from war, famine and diseases. Decline of serfdom and manorial obligations and efficient practices in agriculture had freed many people for new forms of labour required in the emerging factories.

In the realm of **ideology** too Europe had certain advantages. European cultural traditions – the '**spirit of individualism**' and the '**idea of reason**' – provided much needed push in the emergence of Industrial Revolution. The spirit of individualism with its emphasis on the right of the individual to freedom and self-realisation produced hard driving merchants, bankers and entrepreneurs who acted as the driving force of the Industrial Revolution. An emphasis on rational understanding of the nature gave the Europeans confidence about this world as something that is stable and predictable and a mastery over this material world leading to invention and adoption of new technologies. Thus having the advantages of individualistic ideology and a rational approach to the worldly life, the Europeans, 'broke down the resistance of inherited ways and made change a positive good'.

3. Industrial Revolution in England

Industrial Revolution originated in Britain in the mid-1700s and developed and spread to other parts of the globe in the next hundred years. England during this period was '**swept by a wave of gadgets**'. Of the European nations, Britain was placed at the most suitable position to witness the origin of Industrial Revolution. These factors can be classified into the following.

A. Geographical

One of the important factors for the origin of the Industrial Revolution in England was its **geographical location** and availability of **natural resources.** Britain had the advantage of being an island and was separated from the wars and turmoil that ravaged the European mainland.

Britain was blessed with extensive coast lines and navigable rivers and canals. In an age of water transport as the easiest mode of transportation, this factor facilitated Commercial Revolution at first and Industrial Revolution later.

Moreover, advantages enjoyed by Great Britain in matters of natural resources had placed it in the lead in the Industrial Revolution. Britain had the advantage of having highest quality coal in Europe and a long tradition of metallurgy and mining. Britain was also blessed with excellent coking coal and high-grade iron ore in the same basins or in some cases in the same seams. The close proximity of many of these coalfields with ports facilitated delivery of goods almost straight into ships. Local supplies of iron, lead, copper, tin, lime stone and water power provided excellent conditions for the emergence and expansion of industries in Britain. Historians also attribute damp, mild weather conditions of the north west of England as the ideal condition for cotton spinning which provided a natural starting point of the revolution in textile industry.

Human resources too played significant role in Industrial Revolution in Britain. It had a dense population for its small geographical size which provided ready supply of labour for industries and ready market for its products. British population grew upto 280% during 1550–1820, while the rest of the Western Europe grew 50–80% during the same period.

B. Economic

By the 18th century, there was a general economic prosperity discernible in England. By this time Britain had sufficient capital available for investment in the new industrial ventures. The **Commercial Revolution** and the **Atlantic Slave Trade** had created a class of rich merchants and the **Enclosure Movement** and the **Agricultural Revolution** had created wealthy land owners who were ready to invest in technological innovations and industrial enterprises. In other words, it was the existence of commercial capitalism and agrarian capitalism that metamorphosed into industrial capitalism under favourable circumstances in England.

Agricultural Revolution

From the mid-17th century, Britain experienced an unprecedented increase in agricultural production which is called as the British Agricultural Revolution. This revolution was the result mainly of two factors – **enclosure** and the development of **scientific agriculture**. The Agricultural Revolution preceded the Industrial Revolution and was partly responsible for its origin.

Enclosure refers to consolidation of small landholdings into larger farms and fencing off the land of the community for private use. Enclosed lands were under the control of the landlords who were free to adopt better farming practices in large fenced estates (enclosed). More secure nature of the land and its ownership enabled the owners to make innovations that improved their yields and increased labour productivity. Further, by cycled use of land in the form of grain production to soil restoring crops of legumes and to pasturage, the land began to be utilised all the time rather than leaving some fallow, as had been the past practice. It also facilitated transformation of feudalism into capitalism under which the subsistence agriculture was transformed into profit-oriented production for commodity markets and the transformation of small peasant proprietors and serfs into agricultural wage labourers. In 1801, the British

Parliament passed the **Enclosure (Consolidation) Act** to provide legislative support to the Enclosure movement.

Indirectly, it also accentuated the origin of Industrial Revolution. The more productivity in the enclosed estates meant requirement of fewer farmers in an estate. These villagers without land or grazing rights or job opportunity in the villages were pushed to the cities in search of work in the emerging factories. Another result of the Enclosure was the expansion in population. Greater availability of food and improved living conditions could support a growing population. An increasing population in turn boosted demand for goods such as cloth. The increased efficiency in agricultural production also meant creation of surplus for the market.

Development of **scientific agricultural practices** too contributed to agricultural revolution. In this context, invention of **seed drill** in 1701 by **Jethro Tull**, an English agricultural scientist, was significant. It replaced much less efficient method of scattering seed by hand. With the seed drill now farmers could sow seeds in well-spaced rows boosting crop yields. Similarly introduction of **crop rotation** as a practice of cultivating different crops in the same area in sequential seasons had many benefits. For example, by the mid-18th century, the farmers in England started cultivating turnips which not only enriched soil but also provided food for livestock. The practice was intended to restore the plant nutrients and reduce the pathogens and pests that occur when the same plant is cultivated continuously. It also facilitated the use of labour at the optimum level. In Britain a four-course rotation of crops greatly increased crop and livestock yields by improving soil fertility and maximisation of land in use.

Moreover, introduction of **scientific breeding** of cattle and sheep further accentuated revolutionary changes in agriculture. For example, in the 1700s, **Robert Bakewell** increased his sheep meat output by allowing only his best sheep to breed. Soon other farmers followed the method, yielding rich dividends. Along with these, selective breeding of livestock to obtain animals with desirable characteristics dramatically increased size and quality of farm animals.

Other Factors: Agricultural Revolution in Britain had also been facilitated by certain practices such as **conversion of pasture land** into arable land, for example in 1531, the King Henry VIII dissolved the monasteries after declaring himself as the Supreme Head of the Church of England. Monasteries were the principal landowners in Britain and about 2,000,000 acres of land taken from the monasteries were sold out to aristocracy and landed gentry leading to the maximum exploitation of the land. From 16th century onwards Britain began to witness expansion of roads and inland waterways. One estimate shows that road transport capacity in Britain during the period 1500–1700 A.D. grew by four times. The expansion of transportation facilities facilitated emergence of a **national market** in England. As a result vast majority of agricultural goods were produced for market rather than for the consumption of the farmers. Further measures such as use of iron-tipped Chinese plough pulled with fewer oxen, soil restoration, canal building and land reclamation measures too were instrumental in heralding this Revolution.

British labourers had enjoyed a higher standard of living than their continental counterparts providing them with more purchasing power. England's general prosperity, growing overseas trade and a climate of progress in the 18th century ensured an expanding market for goods produced by the industrial units.

In contrast to the Continental Europe, England did not have a system of internal tolls and tariffs which meant goods could be transported freely to fetch the best price. Increased agricultural output on account of enclosure of fields, pasture and waste lands into large fenced tracts of land under the capitalist landlords ensured food supply to feed an ever-increasing urban population. Britain's expanding middle class provided a home market for emerging industries, as was the case with overseas colonies that acted as markets and sources of raw materials, particularly of cotton.

Financial and fiscal features such as a single currency, lower interest rates on loan, turnpike constructions and existence of joint stock companies all boosted the process of industrialisation. The financial requirements to establish the new industrial enterprises were met by elaborate banking system that emerged in England by this time. This financial support was provided by the **Bank of England** which was established in 1694 and hundreds of provincial banks whose number grew more than 600 by 1820. By the end of the 17th century, money had been in wide circulation in England and salaries, and wages were being paid in cash rather than in goods leading to the expansion of the market for the sale of goods.

Commercial Revolution

Rapid growth in trade and commerce during the 16th and 17th centuries is known as the Commercial Revolution. Since the 14th century Europe had witnessed a growth in trade and commerce, during which there were discernible increase in general commerce and financial services such as banking, insurance and investment. The **Crusades** had created a desire in European mind for eastern goods like spices and silk which were rare in Europe, leading to expansion of trade to procure these goods. Moreover, the newly emerging European states discovered **new trade routes** in the 15th and the 16th centuries leading to the build up of vast international trade networks. The inspiration for trade expansion was also provided by ideologies of **mercantilism and colonialism** by which the European states tried to acquire new sources of wealth and prestige. At the same time the **rivalry between the European states** gave rise to intense competition for the creation of colonial empires and accelerated the desire to sail out of Europe.

The population of Europe almost doubled between 1460 and 1620 and **population growth** exceeding the capacity of local food production stimulated trade in food items. Consequently income of landlords, merchants and peasants also rose leading to a raise in the standard of living and subsequent demand for more consumer goods. Simultaneously, growth of the European states and strengthening of monarchies having huge tax revenue created demand for weapons, uniforms and ships spurring further commercial activities.

As a result of these developments markets began to expand from **local** to **regional** then to **national** and finally to **international**. Growth in volume of trade gave rise to **merchant-capitalists** whose trade operations spread across national boundaries. During this period international trade in the form of **Triangular Trade** developed between Africa, America and Europe in which African slaves were taken to the Americas to work in plantations, in gold and silver mines and also as domestic servants, raw materials such as cotton, sugar and tobacco from Americas then taken to Europe where these were turned into finished goods, and these goods were sold back to Africa.

The governments of European countries actively promoted the commercial revolution. **Public policies** were framed to support the interests of the business community. For example, in England after the transfer of power from king to Parliament economic policies were enacted which reflected the interests of the business community who had dominance in Parliament. Governments subsidised new industries, removed internal tariffs and guild regulations and companies were chartered to explore international markets.

Commercial Revolution paved way for Western Europe's hegemony as the lord of the sea lanes, master of lands in every part of the globe and the banker and profit earner in an emerging world economy. The Commercial Revolution also laid the foundation of wealth of which the **mercantile capitalism** was an expression which later paved the way for the **Industrial Revolution** and provided the economic thrust for **European hegemony** in world affairs since then.

C. Political

In a period of disturbances and wars, Great Britain was relatively at peace. Since the Glorious Revolution of 1688, Britain had enjoyed a period of political stability. Though Britain had fought many wars during the 1700s none of them had been on British soil. Britain was the only European nation that was not ravaged by the political upheaval of the French Revolution and the Napoleonic wars. It also possessed largest navy of the times which ensured protection of its colonial, trade and industrial interests intact. Other factors such as unification of England and Scotland (in 1707), absence of trade barriers between England and Scotland, existence of common laws and existence of the rule of law providing for the sanctity of contracts had created political and legal environment in England for the industries to emerge and grow. Moreover, the British parliament members – many of whom were businessmen themselves – eagerly supported governmental measures that would directly or indirectly encourage commerce and industry.

Glorious Revolution: It took place in England in 1688 with the overthrow of King James II by the English Parliament. The two major factors for the Revolution were the political battle between

Catholicism and Protestantism and the concept of divine right of kings and the political rights of the English Parliament. The Revolution ended any prospect of Catholicism re-established in England. The Revolution also marked the beginning of the English parliamentary democracy and the passage of the **Bill of Rights** in 1689. The Glorious Revolution is also known as the **Bloodless Revolution** as it involved less bloodshed compared to many other revolutions of the period.

D. Socio-Cultural

Industrial Revolution was not just a matter of political stability or of material prosperity. It required outlook and habits that would encourage inventions, investment and risking in ventures of enormous potential for gain. The English as a nation respected the sensible, the practical and the financially successful people and pursuit of wealth was perceived by Englishmen as a goal to be cherished for in this life. Consequently, England turned out to be an example for how individuals' desire to acquire worldly success through innovations and investments worked to produce prosperity for the country as a whole. In other words, the values of **self-interest, self-realisation and entrepreneurship** were found in huge measures in Englishmen of the 18th century. Existence of this entrepreneurial class is often related with Protestantism. The Protestants re-conceptualised worldly work as a duty, which benefits both the individuals and society as a whole, and this attitude went into channelising other resources, to produce more and more for individual and common good.

The German sociologist **Max Weber** described the habits of hard work, discipline, frugality as 'Protestant Work Ethic', in his work ***The Protestant Ethic and the Spirit of Capitalism*** (1904). **Max Weber** described the psychological make-up of the Puritans as **'rational restlessness'** which was the outlook required in a capitalist entrepreneur. The Puritans believed, argued Weber, that the best way to fulfil their moral obligation to God is to help others in this world for which accumulation of wealth is religiously sanctioned.

E. Ideological

The **colonial ideology** of Great Britain was another factor for the emergence of the Industrial Revolution in England. Throughout the 18th century, England's foreign policy was directed to uphold its commercial interests. In each of the wars that England fought during this period, it wrested overseas territories (except in North America where it lost its colonies). This colonialist ideology of the British augmented its worldwide markets, widened international trade and strengthened free trade. These factors along with **capitalist ideology** created conducive atmosphere for the origin of the Industrial Revolution in England.

Encouragement to capitalist spirit had also been provided by **Adam Smith** and the **Enlightenment** philosophy. Smith in his book published in 1776, ***An Inquiry into the Nature and Causes of the Wealth of Nations*** popularly known as ***The Wealth of Nations*** had argued for division of labour and had expounded upon how rational self-interest and competition could lead to economic prosperity which was similar to the ideas about the natural state of things of the Enlightenment. Smith put forward the concepts of natural laws of production and exchange, and also of demand and supply. He argued that left to their own devices these laws will regulate economy in the best possible way and thus laid the foundations of free market economic theory. Government, in his view, should not regulate economic activities other than providing a stable environment for the economy and enforcing of the laws. In similar sense, he argued that each individual should be left free to follow his own economic self-interest, 'by pursuing his own interest he frequently promotes that of the society more effectually than when he really intends to promote it'. Adam Smith used the term **'invisible hand'** to describe the unintended social benefits that results from an individual's self-interested actions and argued **'private vice yields public virtue'**. Under the influence of the arguments of Adam Smith and other economists Britain moved away from mercantilism

Adam Smith

and embraced laissez-faire economics and free trade which was perfectly in tune with the interests of new entrepreneurs of the Industrial era.

F. Technological

It was in England most of the inventions and innovations which gave birth to Industrial Revolution took place as the English entrepreneurs and technicians were ready to take advantages enjoyed by England and to respond to the compulsions of the time. Hence, these discoveries and inventions were to prove crucial in heralding a revolution in industrial production.

In inaugurating these inventions **Newtonian science** and the **Scientific Revolution** too were significant. Newton's explanations on motions in universe and motions on earth had promoted a notion of a mechanical universe which in turn had boosted a drive to mechanise human activities and a desire for the development of new machinery. It was this application of mechanical science to production by a class of industrial entrepreneurs that made Industrial Revolution possible.

a. Textile

In textile industry, a series of inventions took place, inaugurating revolutionary changes in industrial field. Earlier, Britain had produced mainly linen and wool and depended on cotton textiles imported from India. In 1707, the British Parliament imposed 50% tariffs on Indian goods and by the **Calico Act 1721** prohibited import of cotton textile from India in order to protect its domestic industry. At the same time cotton textiles were gaining more acceptability among the public, as cotton clothing was less expensive and easier to clean than wool or linen. These factors served to spur the demand of domestic cotton goods and inventors and entrepreneurs responded readily, living up to the dictum '**necessity is the mother of inventions**'.

The first important discovery was John Kay's **flying shuttle** in 1733 which enabled weavers to double their output. The flying shuttle made it possible to weave broader fabrics in less time and greatly speeded up the process of weaving than the spinners could spin. At the same time it created imbalance between spinning and weaving.

In 1767, James Hargreaves invented **spinning jenny**, a compound spinning wheel on which a single person could spin several threads of yarn simultaneously to produce as much as 16 threads at a time and resolved this imbalance.

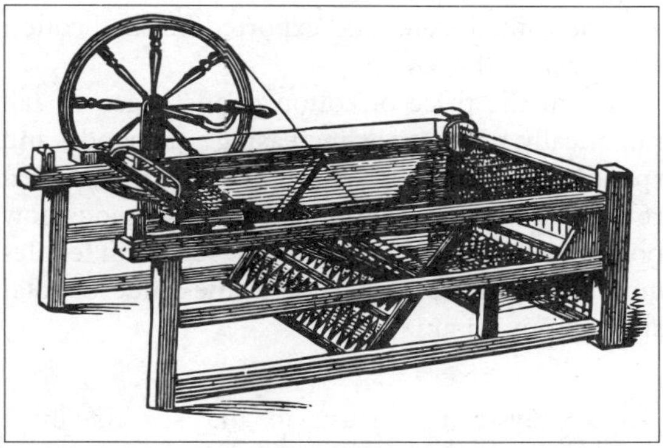

Spinning Jenny

Richard Arkwright's **water frame** spinning machine (in 1769) could produce stronger thread than before and also to weave pure cotton fabrics rather than linen and cotton mixed fabrics.

Samuel Crompton's **spinning mule** (in 1779) facilitated spinning of strong and fine yarn thus increasing cotton productivity. These developments increased the rate of cotton spinning by two to three hundred times.

In 1787, Edmund Cartwright developed **power loom** which was easy to work and could weave any kind of material.

> In 1793, Eli Whitney, an American, invented cotton gin which separated seeds from cotton fibre mechanically. This invention kept American slave plantations profitable as there was increasing demand from English entrepreneurs for raw cotton which in turn increased the demand for slave labour in America.

All these inventions resulted in increase in cotton production by ten times between 1760 and 1785 and another 10-fold between 1785 and 1825. As cotton production exceeded the domestic demand, the British began to explore markets in the New World.

The growth of slavery in the United States had been generating huge demand for cheap cotton textiles in the United States in order to clothe the slaves, while the raw cotton from America became less expensive after Eli Whitney's invention of the cotton gin in 1793. As a result, the British cotton trade became a two-way enterprise in which the British manufacturers imported most of their raw cotton from the United States and exported finished cotton goods back to that country.

Though the price of cotton goods began to fall dramatically, the ever-increasing demand and expanding market for cotton textiles meant that profits continued to grow. English cotton goods now flooded the world market and by 1815 cotton textiles amounted to more than 40% of the value of total exports from Britain.

Factory System: Increase in the size of the machines, use of water to power the machines, low cost of operating a large plant, efficiency improvement by bringing workers under one roof were initial factors that led to the emergence of factories replacing cottages and smaller workshops. In this context, Richard Arkwright's water frame could be considered as the crucial development as it could bring many workers together to work under one roof. The factory system concentrated labourers and their families near the factories and towns grew up centring around these factories. **Manchester**, a textile production centre in England, became the first modern industrial city of the world.

Developments in textile sector spurred other industrial improvements. James Watt, a maker of scientific instruments at the University of Glasgow invented the **steam engine** in the 1760s, which was perfected by 1778.

The development of steam engine was an important step in the Industrial Revolution. Before the steam engine, the mills had run with water power but steam engines allowed flexibility in locating mills anywhere and not just close to water as it ran on coal or wood. Moreover, water availability was variable and was not always available in a year. The introduction of steam engines also improved productivity and technology and facilitated creation of smaller and better engines in a wide variety of industrial fields from mines to mills and at a later stage in boats, railways and in road vehicles.

Steam engines also changed the pattern of work because less skilled or younger or weaker workers could be engaged to perform simple tasks required to run the machine, thereby encouraging employment of larger number of women and children in factories.

In 1807, **Robert Fulton**, an American inventor, built the first steamboat called the **Clermont** and ferried passengers in New York's **Hudson River**. Clermont was fitted with a steam engine made by **James Watt.**

b. *Coal and Iron*

For centuries, charcoal was used for smelting iron from iron ore. But the charcoal-based smelting had many limitations. As charcoal had impurities, the iron obtained was of poor quality and also charcoal could not generate high temperatures. Also, charcoal was short in supply and could not meet the growing demand. In this background, by a series of inventions a family of iron masters called **The Darbys** revolutionised the metallurgical industry. Grandfather, father and son of this family all called **Abraham Darby** of Shropshire invented, modified and applied their skills in this field. In 1709, the first Abraham Darby developed **blast furnace** which used coke (which was derived from coal) rather than charcoal. Darby's blast furnace could generate high temperature and melted iron from these furnaces was of higher quality. In 1756, Abraham Darby II developed **wrought-iron** (an iron alloy with low carbon content which was also tough, corrosion resistant and easily welded) from pig-iron. In 1779, the third Darby built the world's **first iron bridge** in Coalbrookdale, England.

Henry Cort, another iron master, developed two significant iron manufacturing processes: rolling in 1783 and puddling in 1784. His **puddling furnace** and the **rolling mill** used steam power to roll purified iron into bars. In the 1780s, production of wrought iron was perfected, which solved demand of a stronger metal in steam power-based units and became the most widely used metal until the emergence of steel in the 1850s.

c. *Transportation*

Industrial Revolution introduced tremendous changes in the transportation sector also. The combined forces of steam engine, iron and later on steel inaugurated a new era in transport. Britain's transport infrastructure with canal and waterway network, turnpike road network and the railways accentuated the revolution in the industries not only by facilitating transportation of bulk goods over long distances but also by fuelling demand for coal, iron and steel and steam engines.

Turnpike Roads: These were roads constructed by Turnpike Trusts who had the right to collect road tolls, hence, also known as **toll ways**. During the 18th and 19th centuries turnpike was the major mode of road construction in England which was also adopted in different colonies of Britain and in the United States. The coming of the railways led to the decline of the turnpike roads.

Water transport: Canals and waterways allowed transportation of bulk material over long distances economically. The first canal in United Kingdom known as the **Bridgewater Canal** was built in North West England in 1761 to carry coal from the coal deposits at Worsley to Manchester. Within a year the price of coal in Manchester fell by half and the success of the new waterway inspired a period of intense canal building known as **Canal Mania.** During the last decades of the 18th century and early decades of the 19th century, more than 4000 miles of canals were built in England. Britain's canal network together with its surviving buildings is one of the remnants of the early Industrial Revolution in England.

Road transport: Large numbers of roads were also constructed in England during this period. Majority of these road networks were under turnpike mode. New engineering methods were initiated in road construction by **John Metcalf, Thomas Telford** and **John McAdam**. Of these John McAdam pioneered a new way of constructing enduring roads. This 'macadamised' road construction involved placing single sized small angular crushed stones in shallow lifts and covering with a binder to keep dust and stones together. The first macadamised road was constructed in Bristol in 1816.

Railways: The invention of railways took the industrialisation process to the second stage. Introduction of inexpensive **puddled iron** by 1800, the **rolling mill** for making rails and the development of **high pressure steam engine** were instrumental in making railways a reality. Development of railways had two incentives. Quicker and cheaper transportation of heavy goods across long distances and as a new avenue for capitalists to invest their surplus profit they accumulated from other ventures.

In September 1825, **George Stephenson**, renowned now as the 'Father of Railways', and his son **Robert Stephenson** built the '**Locomotion No.1**', the first steam locomotive to carry passengers on a public rail line, the **Stockton-Darlington Railway.** On 15 September 1830, the **Liverpool-Manchester Railway**, the first **intercity railway** in the world to run exclusively on steam power, was opened, which is considered as 'opening the epoch of railways which has revolutionised the social and commercial intercourse of the civilised world'.

Success of this railway ignited the so-called '**railway mania**' between 1830 and 1850 during which more than 6,000 miles of railway was opened in Britain. The railway boom gave further fillip to Industrial Revolution as they required vast amounts of coal and iron and manufactured goods such as carriages and switches, provided employment to large number of people and boosted activity in the construction and related industries apart from opening up world market for wider penetration of industrialisation.

d. Other Sectors

Other sectors too underwent profound changes mostly in response to the developments in the textile and metallurgical sectors. In the field of industrial chemistry, new methods of dyeing and bleaching were developed. Production of chemicals to meet the industrial requirements was another development during the Industrial Revolution. Production of **sulphuric acid** by the lead chamber process by Englishman **John Roebuck** in 1746 was the first important step in this regard. The development of **bleaching powder** by Scottish chemist **Charles Tennant** in 1800 dramatically reduced the time required for bleaching, thus revolutionising the textile industry further. In 1824, **Joseph Aspdin** patented a chemical process for making **Portland cement** and in 1816 **safety lamp** for coal miners was invented by **Sir Humphry Davy**.

4. Nature of the Industrial Revolution

The Industrial Revolution in England was in the nature of long evolutionary process involving two or three generations with varying paces in different sectors. For example, cotton industry growing at a rapid rate was the leading sector in the first phase of the Industrial Revolution. With the introduction of railways in England and its expansion in the British colonies iron and steel sector expanded rapidly.

Further, the new industries did not easily displace traditional industries and the old tools and methods were not immediately replaced by new ones. Moreover, the pace of change in the traditional industries like pottery, food processing, tanning, and so forth was not induced by steam engines or developments in metallurgy but by seemingly ordinary and small innovations.

It is also of interest to note that the technological changes did not have immediate acceptability or dramatic spread across the industrial landscape as the new technology was expensive, not as effective as their inventors claimed, repair was costly and also because the industrialists were cautious in their approach in adopting them. For example, steam engine patented by James Watt in 1781 had no buyers for many years, which shows that even a very significant technology that enhanced productivity manifold was slow to be accepted.

Finally, the revolution was made possible from a very limited knowledge base. Education in basic sciences like physics or chemistry was extremely limited in England of the time and except in chemical industry progress was not related to scientific research. The inventions were by and large the results of practical men searching for ways to improve efficiency and profit. Their determination, interest, curiosity and many times even luck were decisive in the inventions. In many cases, these innovators and inventors had to overcome disabilities while pursuing their mission. The road builder John Metcalf who planned and surveyed for roads was blind and the canal builder James Brindley was illiterate. George Stephenson, 'Father of Railways', could not even read until he was 17.

5. Consequences of the Industrial Revolution

Industrial Revolution was a mixed blessing as it had **both positives and negatives** and also **short- and long-term** impacts. Rapid industrialisation brought plentiful of goods and jobs but caused unhealthy working conditions, air and water pollution apart from igniting class tensions. In the long term, it offered a better quality of life to most of the world population.

A. Factory System

Industrial Revolution transformed rural handicraft economy to the one dominated by machine-driven manufacturing. In place of cottage industry, the Industrial Revolution inaugurated factory system, in which production was carried out by group of workers, organised on the basis of division of labour and with the help of machines, originally powered by water or steam and later by electricity.

The main features of the factory system were-

a. **Use of machinery:** Inventions of number of machines led to the replacement of hand production to machine production.
b. **Centralisation of production:** The factory system gave birth to concentration of production in large buildings employing large number of employees.
c. **Division of labour:** Division of labour provided for specialisation of tasks, and was unlike the previous mode of production in which the whole good was produced by a single person. Division of labour facilitated employment of unskilled people in production by training them to perform a part in the production chain.
d. **Capitalist production:** As factory system required huge investments in land, building, machinery and in raw material, a new class, the capitalists with financial power and ability to invest emerged.
e. **Economy of scale:** Reduction in the average cost of a product when a factory increases its output, as a result of low input cost is known as economy of scale. Factory mode of production enabled production in large quantities with less manpower per unit of production thus reducing the product cost.
f. **Standardisation and uniformity:** Machines facilitated precision and standardisation of component parts of a product, leading to uniformity in the final goods.

B. Labour Conditions

The Industrial Revolution caused concentration of labour into factories, mills and mines. At these places life was not easy for those whose labour contributed to the production revolution. Labour was plenty as peasants and vagrants tramped to cities in large numbers in search of a living. As the labour was plenty wages were low. In many industries, labour demand was seasonal. Another depressing feature of the working class life was its unstable nature as economic depressions were regular occurrences and workers could be laid off, without any compensation to sustain them.

A labourer had to work for long hours, sometimes 14 hours per day in miserable conditions. The factories **lacked basic amenities** and were dirty, hot and unventilated. Dangerous conditions were in existence in factories where safety measures like fencing of dangerous machines were not the norm. For example, in mines, explosions, cave-ins and deadly gas fumes persisted as a threat to the life and safety of the labour. The use of poisonous lead in glazed pottery factories was a grave hazard to workers. A boiler explosion or injury to arm by the drive belt were all common hazards.

Moreover, under division of labour, job of a worker was monotonous and dull. Workers could be fired at the will of the employer or foreman and could be fined for mistakes and even for accidents. In simple terms workers did not enjoy work safety or job security.

Equally upsetting as the physical conditions of work was the **psychological readjustment** demanded of a factory worker. The socialisation avenues were absent in the factory system as they were fined for talking to each other, for lateness and were under the watchful eyes of foremen who always pushed the workers to work hard and efficiently to match with the machines. Similarly, they had no organisation or sense of comradeship and in many instances were competitors to each other in order to keep their jobs. Under such deplorable conditions, life span of workers happened to be very short and was lower than that of any other people in cities.

C. Urbanisation

Urbanisation is the process of city building and movement of people to cities. As factories were established in clusters near to the source of energy such as coal and water, industrial cities emerged, grew in number, size and population.

The factory system initiated **migration of millions** of people from rural parts of the country to towns and cities, leading to urbanisation in the industrial countries. In England, the number of cities with a population of over 50,000 were just 2 in 1750 which rose to 29 in 1850. Similarly, population of cities too grew rapidly. It is best illustrated in the case of **Manchester** in England nick named **'Cottonopolis'** and the world's first industrial city. Manchester witnessed a six times increase in its population between 1771 and 1831. Cities grew in size and number between 1800 and 1850 in other European countries also once the steam engine made it possible to bring people in large numbers to work in the factories.

This pace of growth of urban centres was not matched with provisions for basic amenities like clean water or adequate housing. Most of the new factory towns expanded rapidly, without planning or regulation and had no municipal government. Obvious results of **sudden growth** in number and size of the cities **without planning or control** were little sanitation, no lighting, wretched housing and little security. An expanding population had to be accommodated in buildings of several stories located as near the factories as possible. Many a times the whole family lived in one room or had to share a room with another family.

Public Health Act 1848

It was the first law dealing with the public health to be passed in England. The act was passed in the context of growing concerns of urban life in industrialised England. It established a Central Board of Health responsible for improving sanitation and living standards in urban and populous areas in England. The Act is also seen as a move away from the laissez-faire (no intervention in economic affairs) and an emphasis on state's duty to ensure public health and social security.

Smoke from factories, railway and domestic chimneys, innumerable slums, garbage and filth left on the surface to ferment and rot were sufficient enough to turn urban life miserable and unhealthy. Overcrowded and unhygienic urban environment was a fertile ground for diseases such as cholera, typhus and tuberculosis.

Governments of European countries encouraged emigration especially to the Americas as a way to ease the overcrowding. Legislative measures were also initiated in latter-half of the 19th century to rid cities of their worst slums and to improve their sanitary conditions.

D. Social Impact

In social context, the Industrial Revolution transformed class structure, family, daily life and social values.

One significant social impact of the Industrial Revolution was the permanent destruction of the old division of society into clergy, nobility and commoners. Correspondingly, the Industrial Revolution created two new classes in society – **bourgeoisie** and the **proletariat**. These two classes were fully conscious of their class status had their own interests and had a belief that the interests of men and women in other classes were contradictory to that of their own. One particular lesson that industrialisation and urbanisation taught was this class consciousness.

The **bourgeoisie** middle class comprised of people engaged in trade and capitalist ventures, bankers, factory and mine owners. It also included shopkeepers, managers, professionals like lawyers and doctors and bureaucrats. The middle class carried the virtues of work, thrift, ambition and caution. Movement within the ranks of bourgeoisie was possible, as this class believed that it was possible to get ahead by means of intelligence and serious devotion to work. Once the importance of industrial wealth grew, this class became influential in socio-economic and political fields of the European life.

Residential areas of middle class were often located beyond the areas of unpleasant sights and smells of industrialisation. They lived in multi-storey town houses or large apartments or in free standing villas. Their houses, furnishings and lifestyles reflected the material security they attained. This bourgeoisie class celebrated the city as their own creation and source of their profit.

Like the middle class, the **proletariat** was also a heterogeneous class comprised of different segments of economic life such as the industrial workers, miners and rural labourers. The industrial workers included both skilled workers in crafts and workers in the new industrial units. It also included lakhs of unskilled workers such as coal potters and cleaning women. Their living conditions and dwelling places were miserable as we have seen already.

Women were employed in large number in factories, who also offered their service as domestic servants. These were two most visible evidences of redefining of gender roles by the industrialisation. Women were preferred labour force wherever possible as they could be paid less and were easier to manage. They would be less agitated about their poor working conditions and low wages.

Children were employed in large numbers in textile factories for the fact that their small body allowed them to move between machines and in coal mines to reach deep coal faces where the approach path was too narrow for adults. Moreover, from the viewpoint of children there were very limited opportunity for education, and hence they were expected to work. Children employed in mines and hazardous industrial units developed lung diseases, eye infections and lived in constant danger of explosions of gas, chemicals and machinery, threatening their limbs and lives.

Charles Dickens

Charles Dickens (1812–70) in his novels such as *Oliver Twist* and *Hard Times* immortalised the life of industrial workers of the 19th-century England. Dickens himself had been forced to leave school to work in a factory at the age of 12. His works challenged middle-class polemics about criminals and highlighted the life of forgotten poor and disadvantaged within society. Karl Marx was to comment that Dickens's works contained 'more political and social truths than have been uttered by all the professional politicians, publicists and moralists put together'.

Urban life also caused transition to nuclear family and romantic marriages emerged as the new norm. Urban environment with its anonymity, loneliness and economic compulsions encouraged prostitution and also fostered crime.

Alteration of social values was another significant social impact. New social realities destroyed aristocratic power structure, values and privileges and created the new ones. Recognition of individual talents and opportunity for social advancement on merit became new norms. It also boosted secularisation of urban life, as world was being reshaped by technology belief in religious mysteries and salvation in other world became matters of distant concerns to the urbanites. Industrialisation also accentuated democratisation, as the urban middle class and the workers gained right to vote and opportunity of political participation, though gradually.

E. Standard of Living

The standard of living of people of the Industrial Revolution has been a matter of dispute. Some scholars argue that the real impact of the Industrial Revolution was that for the first time in history the living standards of masses of people began to undergo sustained growth. The Industrial Revolution, they argue, was the first period in history that witnessed simultaneous increase in both population and per capita income. But, large number of scholars counter this view by stating that during the Industrial Revolution the bulk of the population who were at the bottom of the social ladder suffered severe reductions in their living standards.

It is pointed out that in some cases workers' life standards in the city compared to their lives in the countryside would have improved, particularly if the whole members of the family who migrated from the village could find work. But this was not a norm.

Further, in industrial cities the **working conditions and living conditions** were terrible. In villages from where they migrated they were socially connected to family, relatives, church and to local celebrations. But such socialisation avenues were absent in industrial towns. Thus, it was a historical paradox – of poverty amidst progress – while machines churned out so many products and created huge wealth poor people continued to remain numerous and their conditions so terrible.

F. Impact on Environment

The Industrial Revolution inaugurated an era of water and air pollution. Emergence of factory system and immense growth in coal consumption resulted in unprecedented level of air pollution. The discharge of factory effluents to atmosphere, open fields and water bodies were the first environmental calamity caused by the Industrial Revolution. The environmental degradation was doubled when untreated human waste too found its way to water bodies.

As a response to degradation of environment, movements for preventing degradation too found their emergence. Responding to the threat caused by uninhibited growth of factory system and uncontrolled anti-environmental practices by the factory owners, the governments initiated legislative measures. The first important law to protect environment from degradation by the factories was the **Alkali Act 1863** in Britain, aimed at controlling air pollution. Since then large number of legislative measures such as the **Public Health Act 1875** were initiated to meet the threat to environment and public life from industrial activities. The tremendous power acquired by the humans with the help of technology for exploiting nature and destructive consumption of the natural resources also generated counter currents which call for **sustainable development** and **responsible stewardship of nature.**

G. Positive Impacts of Industrial Revolution

As seen above, the Industrial Revolution was a **mixed blessing**. On positive side, it revolutionised production of goods, raised the standards of living, created new opportunities for social advancement and also offered a hope for improvement in people's lives.

Industrial Revolution fostered invention of new gadgets, expedited technological progress and facilitated the transition to modern way of life. Abundance of **consumer goods** which would have been considered as luxuries previously, healthier diets, better housing, speedy and cheaper transport all these emerged as proof of the blessings of industrialisation.

Industrial Revolution also generated a huge job market not just for workers but also for others such as engineers, clerks and professionals. It also **revolutionised educational sector** not only by the expansion of education but also by introducing new fields such as **scientific and technical education**. Industrial Revolution contributed to the **wealth of nations**. Tax revenues greatly strengthened the hands of rulers and now governments could invest these revenues to improve the standard of living of the general population. And on the side of the working class, it could be mentioned that, in the long run they began to enjoy higher wages, shorter hours and better living conditions.

6. | Responses to Industrialisation

Luddites: The English working class' discontent with the Industrial Revolution found expression in Luddites in the 19th century. This movement was started by the charismatic leader Ned Ludd.

Luddites were group of English textile workers and weavers who resorted to destruction of weaving machinery as a form of protest. The Luddite movement took birth in the harsh economic climate of the Napoleonic Wars and a response to the difficult working conditions in the new textile factories. They demanded minimum wage, right to form trade unions and work for those who lost their job because of the coming of machinery. Luddites resorted to burning of mills and machinery. The British government sought to suppress the Luddite movement with mass trials in 1813 and with legislative measures like **Frame Breaking Act** of 1812.

Trade Unionism: Trade union or labour union was another response to the miseries of industrialisation. Starting with England from the mid-1820s, artisans and skilled workers formed **Friendly Societies** as co-operative groups as forum for collective bargaining. The National Association for the Protection of Labour (1830) and the Grand National Consolidated Trades Union (1834) were initial steps in constructing labour unions. Government measures such as transportation of the organisers of the Grand National and requirement of signing of pledge by the workers not to join a union were hurdles before the trade unionism. Finally, the **Trade Union Act of 1871** legalised trade unions and their funds were protected in England.

Chartism: Chartism was a working class movement in England during 1838–48. The movement emerged in 1838–39 in the background of economic depression, unemployment and the Poor Law Amendment Act.

Even in the late 1830s, only 18% adult male population in Britain had votes. The working-class people realised that without a voice in parliament they could not change their situation. Foundation of **London Working Men's Association** in 1836 by William Lovett and Henry Hetherington provided the platform for the movement. They sought to secure '**equal political and social rights by every legal means**' by campaigning for six key changes. This document known as the '**People's Charter**' contained the following demands-

1. Universal manhood suffrage
2. Vote by secret ballot
3. Annual parliamentary elections
4. Payment of salary to members of the House of Commons
5. Equal electoral districts
6. Abolition of property qualification for membership in parliament

These demands were signed by millions, presented to the parliament and was accompanied by mass meetings. The first petition was presented in 1839 which was rejected by the parliament. Petitions were presented in 1842 and 1848 too. Faced with the spectre of open class conflict, the government suppressed the movement.

The ruling class and almost all those who had the vote ridiculed the Chartists and portrayed them as a source of danger. Lack of unity and disagreement over tactics, as some of them wanted peaceful '**moral force**' while others wanted to resort to '**physical force**' to achieve the points in the Charter, poor management and increased prosperity of the skilled workers after the mid-century were factors that caused decline of the movement.

Though the Chartists failed in getting their demands implemented in immediate terms, they generated the notion that reforms were inevitable. The Reforms Act of 1867 enfranchised the urban workingmen, secret voting was introduced in 1872 and the MPs were paid since 1911 and by 1918 except annual parliamentary elections all other Chartists' demands were fulfilled.

7. Spread of Industrialisation

Following England, the European continent began to undergo industrialisation in the 19th century. The process was bit delayed due to many factors but gained momentum after 1815. Reasons for this delay were:

Political: Europe, especially Central Europe, had been fragmented into tiny principalities. German states were a good example. Large number of local tolls and tariffs in these states hindered free movement of goods which erected hurdles in the emergence of industrialisation.

Geographical: From the viewpoint of raw materials, the European continent was not as blessed as of England. Coal, which was the fuel of the time was not abundant in the continent. Timber continued as the main fuel because of its huge availability hence no intensive exploration of coal was undertaken. Similarly, compared to England's transportation system that of the continent was not well developed and navigable rivers were less.

Socio-cultural: Social environment of the continent was not conducive enough to incite risk taking and entrepreneurship. The socio-economic distinctions on the continent were greater and stronger than in England. Aristocrats in the continent believed that investment in industrial enterprises was against tradition and would damage their social status. As against Britain, money was not a social solvent in France and Germany, as it was also the case with entrepreneurial spirit which was again low in these countries.

Historical: Large number of wars, the French Revolution and many battles that followed had ravaged Europe, destroyed production units and disrupted efforts towards industrialisation. Fearful of disruptions and uncertainty of future that each war brought in its train, the Continental businessmen were more cautious in risk taking. Though the wars increased demand for weapons, the manufacturing techniques remained the old. The Continental System of Napoleon and the destruction of the French merchant shipping by the British navy also caused heavy damages to the European commerce delaying further the emergence of industrialisation.

By 1815, atmosphere conducive to industrialisation was developing in European continent. In the first-half of the 19th century, European population almost doubled ensuring not only labour force but also consumers. The Napoleonic wars had improved transportation in the continent in the forms of new roads and canals. After 1840, the introduction of railways expanded the markets for the Western European producers, giving fillip to industrialisation.

The influences of **Napoleonic reforms** were also discernible in the emergence of industrialisation in the Continent. Napoleon had initiated rationalisation of the French institutions and state intervention in economic sector. The **Napoleonic Code** had guaranteed freedom of contract leading to the establishment of the joint-stock companies. This model of state intervention acted as a model for other rulers to play a more direct role in economic life in their countries and to state's active support and intervention in industrialisation. For example, in almost all Continental countries railway transportation was built with financial assistance of the state.

Similarly, the Continental states reoriented their educational system to produce well-trained people who could expedite the development of industrial technology. This last point is important when we consider the fact that the British were reluctant in sharing their technology with other countries. The British artisans were under prohibition from emigrating to other countries until 1825 and also until 1842 innovative machineries could not be exported from Britain. Hence, it is observed that the European continent had to proceed with a design and strategy to industrialise, what Britain had achieved almost by chance. Nevertheless, by the mid-19th century, Europe emerged as the most industrialised portion of the world – a world which had been by this time divided into two producers of the industrial goods, that is Europe itself and suppliers of the raw materials, the rest of the globe.

A. Belgium

It was Belgium that became the second country in the world, after England, to undergo Industrial Revolution and the first in the Continent. The process was started in the late 1820s and gained momentum after Belgium became an independent nation in 1830. In the Continent, industrialisation was often modelled after England. Technology developed in Britain and British engineers and entrepreneurs were roped in wherever possible to pave the way for industrialisation. This point is best exemplified by the case of the Englishman **William Cockerill** who illegally made his way to Belgium in 1799, carrying secret plans for making spinning machinery. His son, **John Cockerill**, started integrated steel factories in Belgium, using blast furnaces and coke instead of traditional charcoal. Soon, **Wallonia** in southern Belgium emerged as the second industrial hub in the world capitalising on its extensive deposits of coal and iron as well as fine waterways for transportation, after England.

B. Germany

Political disunity, pervasive conservatism, economic isolation, scattered resources and lack of technological base delayed German industrialisation. The beginning of the Industrial Revolution in Germany happened in textile industry which had been facilitated by **Zollverein,** which eliminated tariff barriers in 1834. Aspiring to catch up with Britain, Germany imported British equipment and engineers apart from sending meritorious children to England to learn industrial management. The 1840s witnessed **introduction of railroads** revolutionising the economic life of Germany, stimulating investments in coal and iron, increasing demand for engineers, managers and skilled mechanics and also opening new markets for local products. The **German unification** in 1870 caused rapid growth of industries in which the state also played a supporting role in the form of nationalisation of the companies. Another distinctive feature of German industrialisation was existence of **cartels** by which groups of firm controlled prices and markets and also accentuated the rate of capital formation. As a result of all these, by the 1880s, the newly unified Germany became both an industrial and military giant.

> Zollverein was German Customs Union formed by a coalition of German states in 1834 as per the Zollverein treaties of 1833. It was intended to manage tariffs and economic policies of the member states.

C. France

Compared to Belgium or Germany the pace of industrialisation was far low in France, as it had a dominance of agrarian economy. **Traditionalism and paternalism** were two important characteristics of French business practices under family firms, which stood against adopting modern practices at the early decades of the 19th century. Historians also attribute the persecution of the Protestant Huguenots in the 17th century that caused large-scale flight of entrepreneurial and mechanical talents from France as one of the reasons for its slow pace in industrial march. Moreover, the prestige associated with the production of luxury goods since the time of Louis XIV had encouraged entrepreneurs to invest in luxury craftsmanship than producing for mass markets, hence in the neglect of large factories and giant corporations. As a result, the French industrialisation was characterised by comparatively small industrial units and relatively slow expansion of capital intensive large-scale production even in the mid-19th century.

D. Sweden

Sweden was another country in Europe that underwent industrialisation, from the first-half of the 19th century. A specific feature of Swedish industrialisation was the regional specialisation in production of goods, for example mining in **Bergslagen** and forestry in **Norrland.** Mandatory and **free public schooling** introduced in 1842 (thus Sweden became the first country in the world to do so) created base for technical and scientific knowledge. Certain **institutional reforms**, such as abolition of national monopoly on trade in handicrafts in 1846 and abolition of most tariffs and other barriers to trade, too facilitated the industrial process of Sweden.

E. The United States

While the Industrial Revolution was taking shape in England, the United States remained agrarian. The industrial units that were in existence in the United States during this time were mainly resource processing semi-industrial units.

In the industrial sector America had many advantages. During 1800–1900 both the **population and area** of the United States had expanded immensely transforming it from a nation of few states on the Atlantic coast to a nation of continental dimension stretching all the way to the Pacific Ocean. It had vast land and literate labour, diversity of climate, **abundance of natural resources**, navigable rivers and coastal waterways (for example, the eastern coast of the United States, with a great number of rivers and streams along the Atlantic seaboard, provided many sites for construction of textile mills necessary for early industrialisation), absence of landed aristocracy and the social acceptance of entrepreneurship and free market. A well-established **legal system** also facilitated business operations and guaranteed contracts.

An early landmark moment in the Industrial Revolution in America came in 1789, when **Samuel Slater**, an English man illegally migrating to the United States built a spinning machine from memory and partial design. Slater founded the first United States cotton mill in Beverly, Massachusetts and for his contributions he is known as '**Father of the American Industrial Revolution**'. Slater's mill started in 1793 like many of the mills and factories that sprang up in the next few decades, was powered by water, which confined industrial development to the northeast at first. The concentration of industry in this region led to the development of transportation systems such as railroads and canals, which encouraged commerce and trade.

The real impetus for America's Industrial Revolution was provided by the **Embargo Act of 1807** and the war with Britain in 1812. The Embargo Act 1807 was imposed by the United States against Britain and France during the Napoleonic Wars in response to the violations of the United States' neutrality. It prohibited any trade relation with these countries. The embargo created scarcity of European goods which in turn stimulated American industry. Eventually, America went to **war with Great Britain** in 1812. Developments during the war made it apparent that America needed a better transportation system and more economic independence, resulting in expansion of manufacturing.

Growth of the transportation infrastructure and a confluence of technological innovations before the American Civil War facilitated an expansion in organisation, coordination and scale of industrial production.

Some crucial inventions in the industrial sector took place in America accelerating its industrial production. First of this long line of innovations was the **cotton gin** by Eli Whitney in 1793. This machine separated cotton fibres from their seeds thereby making cotton available at a lower price. Eli Whitney also developed **interchangeable parts** in 1801 for the firearms of the United States military. The development of interchangeable components which are identical and could fit into any assembly of the same type facilitated easy repair of existing devices. Oliver Evans invented **automated flour mill** in the 1780s using control mechanism and conveyors doing away the need for labour. These developments were crucial in the origin of assembly line in the next stage of industrial development.

Industrialisation efforts were supported by the US government, which adopted policies that supported industrial development by providing land for construction of railroads and maintaining high tariffs to protect American industry from foreign competition. And, by around the beginning of the 20th century, American industry had superseded its European counterparts.

F. Japan

The industrialisation of Japan started with the **Meiji Restoration** in 1868. Apart from economic imperatives, an important factor that prompted the Meiji leadership to initiate industrialisation was its concern that Japan might become a colony of Western powers. Rapid modernisation to boost its economic strength and to reinforce its military was seen as essential step to protect it from Western domination.

With the Meiji, the central government initiated an ambitious program to industrialise the country on modern lines and introduced modern forms of enterprise aimed at fostering capitalism in Japan. It financed sectors such as textiles, shipping and operated many factories. The Bank of Japan founded in 1882 utilised taxes to fund **model factories.** The government also inaugurated land reforms, improved roads and built railroads.

The Meiji regime encouraged private companies to invest in industries and accorded special privileges to them. One such company was **Mitsubishi,** founded in 1870, which ensured that Japanese shipping could compete with Western companies.

Education was expanded, a **Western-based education system** was introduced and Japanese students were sent to study in the West were important steps aimed to catch up with the industrialised nations of the West. Moreover, **compulsory primary schooling** for the masses and university education for deepening engineering and scientific knowledge ensured ready supply of learned labour force. In 1871, the **Iwakura Mission,** consisting of politicians and scholars, undertook a journey of observation and learning to the Europe and the United States. On their return to Japan this mission guided the modernisation efforts of Japan. Japan also hired hundreds of Western technicians and teachers to teach science and technology and western languages in Japan. The government also conducted Domestic **Industrial Expositions**, starting from 1877 aimed at promoting modern industry and trade.

In 1869, the first telegraph line connected Tokyo with Yokohama, in 1871, a modern postal service was established and, in 1877, Japan joined the International Postal Union, linking its postal service to the world. In 1872, rail service was started between Tokyo and Yokohama and by the end of the century it had spread the whole of Japan.

All these steps ensured Japan undergoing an Industrial Revolution in light industry by the end of the 19th century and also that within 30 years after the Meiji Restoration emerging as a capitalist economy.

G. Soviet Russia

Industrialisation in the Soviet Russia is known as the **Socialist Industrialisation** as economic principles and policies sought to be employed were aimed at establishing a socialist state. Fundamental restrictions on private property, state's role in regulation of production, finance and trade and establishment of a Planned Economy in which economy was regularly mapped to indicate priority sectors were salient features of the socialist industrialisation. More about the Soviet industrialisation is given in the chapter on Russian Revolution and the history of the USSR.

8. The Second Industrial Revolution

The accelerated pace of industrialisation in the latter-half of the 19th century is known as the Second Industrial Revolution. It followed on from the First Industrial Revolution. This stage in industrialisation was characterised by further **technological advances**, changes in **scope and scale** of production and **reorganisation of the capitalist system.**

Large-scale iron and steel production (as a result of inventions of **Bessemer and Siemens-Martin** processes), construction of elaborate railroads, greatly increased use of steam power, use of petroleum and the beginning of electrification (invention of the electromagnetic generator in 1866 expedited the process) were notable technological developments at this phase. Intensification of industrial production by the application of scientific knowledge in chemical industries and perfecting of **combustion engine technology** by **Daimler and Carl Benz** were other two technological advances in this stage. This phase also witnessed introduction of **assembly-line technique** which ushered in mass production of automobiles and the birth of '**automobile age**'. Advent of telegraph, telephone and radio revolutionised communication and became major landmarks in this phase of industrialisation.

The nature and scope of **industrial operations** also underwent a change during the Second Industrial Revolution. By this time, the standard of living of the general population in Europe had increased. As there was greater demand for consumer goods, there was enormous increase in the volume of their production. Greater the scale of operation, greater was the demand for more efficiency. Consequently organisational methods emerged. The '**scientific management**' of labour theory by Frederick Winslow Taylor was foremost of these.

Emergence of giant **industrial corporations** with global interests was another development. These firms run by board of directors who were called as the 'captains of industry' not only commanded economic power but also influenced political decisions. Compared to the First Industrial Revolution, the ownership of means of production during the Second became wider through the purchase of stocks of **Joint-Stock Corporations** by individuals and institutions. The stage also witnessed emergence of **finance capital** in the form of specialised banks and financiers. Further, in contrast to the laissez-faire approach in the First Industrial Revolution, the governments generally moved into socio-economic intervention policies in the Second.

In the Second Industrial Revolution Britain lost its position as the leading industrialised nation and the United States and Germany became the frontrunners in the race. The Second Industrial Revolution is also characterised as **the Gilded Age**, a period of great extremes – great expansion and deep depression and great wealth and widespread poverty.

SUMMARY

The Industrial Revolution – It refers to the revolutionary changes that took place in the field of industrial production from the latter half of the 18th century. It began in England and then spread to other parts of the globe in the next hundred years.

British origin of the Industrial Revolution – Geographical, economic, political, socio-cultural, ideological and technological factors were favourable to the British.

Consequences of the Industrial Revolution – Factory system-in which production was carried out in factories. Major characteristics of factory system were centralisation of production, use of machinery, standardisation and uniformity in production, division of labour, capitalist mode of production and economy of scale. Explicit positive gains of the Industrial Revolution included factors such as invention of new gadgets, production of consumer goods in abundance, promotion of education and technical education and contribution to the wealth of nations.

Conditions of labour class – Factories lacked basic amenities; as labour was plenty, wages were low; job was unstable in nature as depressions and lay off were common, under the division of labour job of a worker was monotonous and socialisation avenues were less and industrial worker had to make lot of psychological readjustments.

Urbanisation – Industrial Revolution accentuated Urbanisation or city building caused by migration of huge mass of people from rural areas to industrial centres. Urban centres lacked basic amenities as most of the cities grew up without any planning or control. Overcrowding, slums, garbage and filth, lack of sanitation and security were other features of early industrial cities.

Social impact – Emergence of two new classes called bourgeoisie and proletariat, enrolment of women in workforce as both as factory workers and domestic servants, changes in standard of living, transition to nuclear family and changes in social values were significant changes in society.

Responses to Industrialisation – The Luddites, the Chartists and trade unionism.

Spread of Industrialisation – In the 19th century industrialisation spread to the European continent starting with Belgium and followed by other countries such as Germany, France and Sweden. It also caused transformations in the United States, Japan and the USSR. These countries, unlike Britain had to proceed with a design and strategy to industrialise what Britain had achieved almost by chance.

The Second Industrial Revolution – It took place from the latter half of the 19th century and was characterised by further technological advances, changes in scope and scale of industrial operations and in the reorganisation of the capitalist system.

Questions of Previous Years Civil Services Examination

1. "The Chartist Movement not only fulfilled some of the demands of the middle class, but its ramifications were felt among the working class and the colonies as well". Critically examine. (2023)
2. Do you agree that the economic effects of the Industrial Revolution were to add enormously to wealth and capital on the one hand and to degrade the masses to permanent poverty as the other? Elucidate. (2022)
3. There were many reasons why the Industrial Revolution first happened in England. Critically examine. (2021)
4. The Chartist Movement failed to achieve its stated objectives, but succeeded in seeding the idea that a representative democracy should include all citizens. Critically examine. (2021)
5. 'Industrial Revolution had far-reaching social and political consequences with the advent of assembly line factories, urbanisation and rise

of the urban working class'. Critically examine. (2020)

6. How did the policies of governments facilitate the process of industrialisation in Europe? (2019)
7. Discuss how Japan industrialised after the Meiji Restoration. What were the consequences for its neighbours? (2018)
8. 'The Industrial Revolution put mobility in place of stability'. Explain. (2018)
9. Explain why England became the harbinger of Industrial Revolution. Also throw light on its social consequences. (2017)
10. 'The roots of the Chartist Movement in the Great Britain were partly political and partly economic'. Explain. (2017)
11. 'The oppressive exploitation of the working class in the wake of Industrial Revolution had jolted the social conscience of England'. Elucidate. (2015)
12. Why did the industrial revolution first occur in England? Discuss the quality of life of the people there during the industrialisation. How does it compare with that in India at present? (2015)
13. '"Latecomer" Industrial Revolution in Japan involved certain factors that were markedly different from what West had experienced'. Analyze. (2013)
14. 'The process of industrialisation in some other countries of Europe was different from that in England'. Explain. (2012)
15. 'Whoever says Industrial Revolution, says cotton'. Comment. (2011)
16. Review the background of the Chartist Movement. Despite its failure how had their demands been met in the succeeding years? (2004)
17. The Industrial Revolution brought about great changes in the social and economic life of Europe. Explain. (1998)
18. The Industrial Revolution 'changed England in character and culture'. Explain. (1996)
19. Trace the growth of capitalism in Britain in the 17th and 18th centuries. Why was France, as compared to Britain, late in developing the capitalist spirit and the institutional framework of capitalism? (1985)
20. Give an account of the revolutionary developments in agriculture in Western Europe between the 16th and 18th centuries. How far is it correct to say that it paved the way for the Industrial Revolution? (1980)
21. The period 1500 and 1700 in Europe has been called 'the heyday of the Commercial Revolution'. Explain the causes that led to this Revolution and examine of its impact on society. (1979)

CHAPTER 4

The American Revolution and the Constitution

In this Chapter

1. Introduction
2. Britain and Its North American Colonies
3. Causes of the American Revolution
   A. Idea of liberty
   B. Political
   C. Ideological
   D. Religious
   E. Economic Factors and Taxation Policies
4. British Legislations on the Colonies
   A. The Navigation Acts
   B. The Sugar Act of 1764
   C. The Currency Act 1764
   D. The Stamp Act 1765
   E. The Townshend Acts of 1767
   F. The Tea Act of 1773
   G. The Intolerable Acts of 1774
5. The First Continental Congress 1774
6. Beginning of the War
7. The Second Continental Congress
8. The Declaration of Independence
9. The Revolution as Civil War
10. End of the Conflict
11. Factors for American Success
12. Results of the American Revolution
13. American Constitution
14. Major features of the US Constitution
   A. Federal Republic
   B. Written Constitution
   C. Elected President
   D. Separation of Powers and Checks and Balances
   E. Dual Citizenship
   F. Rigid Constitution
15. The Enlightenment and the US Constitution

1. Introduction

The **American Revolution** or the **American War of Independence** or the **Revolutionary War** 1775–83 was an insurrection by 13 British colonies in North America. It was a long and hard fought struggle between a well-trained professional army of the most powerful nation of the world and its colonial subjects aspiring for liberty, property and sovereignty. The fight extended for eight years and by the time it ended in 1783, more than 27,000 colonists and 10,000 Britishers had lost their life.

At the end of the war, the colonies became independent and emerged as a new nation – the **United States of America.** It was for the first time a nation was formed on two moral principles: that all men are created equal and that all the powers of the government are derived from the consent of the governed.

2. Britain and Its North American Colonies

In the 17th and 18th centuries, the eastern coasts of North America had become English settlements. These settlements were established by the Great Britain to harvest raw materials such as lumber, fur and fish. These settlements emerged as 13 colonies with enlargement of population (from 2,50,000 in 1700 to 21,50,000 in 1770) and prosperity mainly on its trade with European nations. Though the colonists were British subjects, they enjoyed great amount of freedom and each of the 13 colony had its own government. The British government did not have official policies in place vis-a-vis with American colonies and the colonies for long governed themselves with very little supervision from Britain.

In 1651, Britain passed the Navigation Act, providing that all goods shipped to and from the colonies had to be carried on English ships alone. More Navigation Acts were passed subsequently enlarging scope of trade restrictions which included the provision that ships heading to the American colonies should visit ports in England for inspection and to pay extra duties. Even then the British did not enforce these laws rigidly and followed a policy of **Salutary Neglect**. It meant an intentional laxity in enforcing trade laws in the colonies. This policy was based on the assumption that if the colonies were left alone, they would flourish which in turn can be beneficial for Britain in the forms of increased trade, tax and profits.

In **immediate terms** it was the French and Indian War that ignited the conflict. Now, Britain wanted to replace Salutary Neglect with **Parliamentary Sovereignty** causing conflict of interests between the colonists and the mother country. The struggle was between the colonial capitalism and the British mercantilism. Conflicts of interests led to skirmishes such as the Boston Massacre, Boston Tea Party and finally in violent eruptions at Lexington and Concord which became the 'first shots heard' in the Revolutionary War.

The 13 Colonies were founded in the 17th and 18th centuries along the Atlantic coast by emigrants, especially those escaping from religious persecution in Europe. Many were also sent to America against their will – people such as political prisoners, convicts and also slaves from Africa. As the seaboard, navigable rivers and the northern lakes were crucial for travel and trade most of the colonists lived in ports such as Boston, New York and Philadelphia. These 13 colonies were Massachusetts, New York, Connecticut, New Hampshire, Rhode Island, Pennsylvania, Delaware, Maryland, New Jersey, Virginia, North Carolina, South Carolina and Georgia.

3. Causes of the American Revolution

Causes of the American Revolution can be grouped into **long-term causes** and **immediate cause**. The long-term causes were:

A. Idea of liberty

Britain had allowed colonies to develop without much interference. Now, they were aiming to tighten control over the colonies. By subduing nature the colonists had acquired self-reliance, and by time they also had lost feudal inheritance of Western Europe and had developed individualistic outlook. As the colonists believed that their economic prosperity and liberty were under threat, they opposed the new regulations of the British.

B. Political

The American colonies were administered by governors, captains and colonels who were appointed by the British crown. Though the colonies had their own elected assemblies, the governors were not responsible to them. This caused conflict between the executive and the legislative branches and was resented by the colonists.

At the same time, years of Salutary Neglect had promoted sense of independence and self-sufficiency among the colonists who had also become accustomed to governing themselves. Now, the colonists had their own ideas about the nature of government, sovereignty and constitution which was different from that of British.

Further, the colonists' tradition of self-governance had given shape to a sense of separate identity from Britain and many colonists saw themselves as Pennsylvanians or Virginians not as British.

By latter-half of the 18th century, barriers between colonies had been greatly reduced by roads, increased coastal shipping, trade and circulation of newspapers all of which promoted a feeling of togetherness among the colonists.

C. Ideological

The **English Revolution** (the Glorious Revolution of 1688) and the **Enlightenment** were two influencers on the colonists. The English Revolution by creating a constitutional monarchy in England had set a precedent of rebellion against the monarchy. Many of the revolutionary leaders were admirers of Enlightenment ideas such as the social contract, limited government, the separation of powers and the consent of the governed. Under the influence of the Enlightenment, the colonists demanded for the same rights as the people in England had been enjoying. But the British crown refused any concessions and imposed more restrictions on the colonies. The colonists now realised it is

The Thirteen British Colonies in North America

their right to rebel against an unjust ruler who broke the social contract. As commented by John Adams, 'The revolution was affected before the war commenced. The Revolution was in the minds and in the hearts of the people'.

D. Religious

Puritan religious tradition of dissent and resistance was another factor. As was in England, Puritans in America believed in infallibility of Bible and it as their right to oppose any authority – political or religious – which in their view was unjust.

E. Economic Factors and Taxation Policies

To the English, the colonies were there for the service of the mother country. The Navigation Acts of 1651, 1660 and 1680, for example, gave monopoly to the English ships to carry goods to and from the colonies. Moreover, the colonies were not permitted to produce certain items such as paper, steel and woollen goods so that they might not compete with the British in these goods. Further, the colonies could import woollen and hardware goods only from England and had to export items like cotton, coffee, sugar, tobacco, etc., to England alone. Although these mercantilist measures were harmful to the industrial and commercial development of the colonies, the colonists did not oppose these as long as they were not strictly enforced. However, King George III who ascended the throne in 1760 wanted strict implementation of these Acts.

It was in this background that the French and Indian War or Seven Years War (1756–63) took place. The War had been an expensive conflict for Britain and to pay off the debts, British tried to raise revenue by measures such as the Stamp Act of 1765, the Townshend Acts of 1767 and the Tea Act of 1773 to which the colonists were opposed. Thus, it is said that the road to American Revolution was paved with taxes.

French and Indian War (1754–63): This was conflict between Britain and France for domination in North America. Expression of this conflict in Europe from 1756 is known as **The Seven Years War**. In 1761, Spain entered the war on the side of France and in retaliation Britain captured Spain's colonies of Cuba and the Philippines. Britain defeated France and seized almost all French possessions in North America and except for some islands the French influence in North America was eliminated. By surrendering Florida to Britain, Spain secured back Cuba and the Philippines.

4. British Legislations on the Colonies

A. The Navigation Acts

As already seen, in 1660s, Britain had passed Navigation Acts to prevent exploitation of colonial trade by foreign countries. These acts which made it illegal for the colonists to trade with foreigners were an expression of the British mercantilism. Even then, in the century before the Revolution, Britain had followed a policy of laxity in enforcing trade regulations and imperial supervision in internal affairs of the American colonies. This policy, known as **Salutary Neglect**, unintentionally promoted autonomous outlook in the colonies.

But after the **Seven Years War**, Britain reversed this policy in order to recoup the cost of the war. In the same year (1763), the new Prime Minister George Grenville came into office and mandated that the Britain should shift some of the cost of the War to the American colonies. In line with this policy, the British parliament passed a series of acts – the **Sugar Act of 1764, the Currency Act of 1764 and the Stamp Act of 1765** together known as the **Grenville Acts.**

B. The Sugar Act of 1764

This Act imposed duties on sugar and molasses imported into the colonies. The British also stringently enforced the law by stopping and searching colonial ships for trafficked goods. Despite protests by the colonists, the Sugar Act remained in force.

C. The Currency Act 1764

It aimed at regulating paper money by forbidding the colonies from issuing paper currency. This was seen by the colonists as an effort by the British government to gain control of the monetary policies of the colonies.

D. The Stamp Act 1765

As per this act, the colonists had to pay a tax to Britain to obtain official stamp on posters, wills, deeds and other contracts. The colonists opposed the Stamp Act on two grounds. First, the colonists had not paid any tax directly to British government. This was the first effort by the British Parliament to impose direct taxation. Second, it violated the natural rights of the colonists as they did not have their representatives in British Parliament. The colonists argued that only their own assemblies and not the British parliament had the right of taxation over colonies. Hence, they raised the slogan '**no taxation without representation**'. The representatives from nine colonies convened the **Stamp Act Congress** and petitioned the British King George III to repeal the Stamp Act. This also became the first act against which the colonists took to the streets for public protest.

Many colonists felt that instead of thanking the colonists for their support and participation in the French-Indian War, the enactment of new laws and imposition of new taxes more like a punishment. Further, the American colonists had fought side by side with the British soldiers in the French-Indian War. But by the **Royal Proclamation of 1763**, Britain prohibited the colonists from expanding beyond the Appalachians. Though this measure was to prevent any conflict between the colonist and the Native Americans, the colonists detested the policy as they believed that vast territories acquired during the war was being denied to the colonists.

Treaty of Paris (1763) was signed between Britain on one side and France and Spain on other, and with it ended the Seven Years War. By this, French renounced to Britain all French territories in North America (excluding New Orleans), the West Indian Islands of Saint Vincent, Grenada, and Dominica and Tobago and all French conquests in India and East Indies since 1749. Spain ceded East and West Florida to the British. France in return received back West Indian islands including Guadeloupe and Martinique and Spain received Havana and Manila.

E. The Townshend Acts of 1767

Violent outbursts and strong opposition forced Britain to withdraw the Stamp Act in 1766. But **Charles Townshend**, the new Chancellor of Exchequer, in order to assert Britain's right to impose tax on the colonies, introduced import duty by the Townshend Act in 1767 on certain goods such as tea, paper, paints and glass imported into the colonies. The Acts also allowed the officials to enter any place in search of evidence for smuggling and to seize property without following due process. Protests and tension mounted in colonies and culminated in **Boston Massacre** (March 1770), when British soldiers fired at and killed five protesting colonists. Once again strong opposition forced Britain to repeal the duties in April 1770, except the one on tea, retained as symbolic of Britain's right to impose tax on the colonists.

How the French-Indian War caused the American War of Independence?

- It removed threat from France against the colonies. Montcalm, the French general who lost Quebec to the English, had predicted 'England will soon repent of having removed the only check (by conquering Canada from the French) that could keep her colonies in awe'.
- The American soldiers and leaders gained military experience during the war, e.g. George Washington.
- Defeat of France by Britain caused France's desire to revenge and their decision to support the colonists in the War of Independence.

F. The Tea Act of 1773

The British parliament next passed the Tea Act in 1773 by which no new tax on tea was imposed but the English East India Company was granted monopoly on import and sale of tea in American colonies. This step was taken under the initiative of the new British Prime Minister **Lord North** to help the almost bankrupt East India Company. The measure was opposed by the colonists on the ground not only that they did not want British telling them where to buy tea but also they wanted to be able to trade with any country they wanted. The colonists also feared that the Tea Act would set a precedent to keep the colonial merchants out of their business. As protest mounted, in December 1773, a riotous group known as **'Sons of Liberty'** dumped large number of tea chests into the sea from a ship anchored at Boston harbour. The incident known as **the Boston Tea Party** provoked the British to close the Boston port to all commerce and to station troops there.

Sam Adams was one of the passionate defenders of colonial rights. Graduated from Harvard College, he was the main organiser of the Sons of Liberty in Boston. Later on, his cousin John Adams became America's second President.

Daughters of Liberty was the women counter part of the Sons of Liberty. Members of this group stopped drinking British tea, spun their own cloth and propagated that wearing homespun as a sign of patriotism.

G. The Intolerable Acts of 1774

Also known as Coercive Acts, these acts were a series of four acts passed by the British Parliament and became the immediate cause of the revolution. These were-

1. **The Boston Port Act** – provided for the closure of the Boston Port until the payment for damages from the Boston Tea Party.
2. **Massachusetts Government Act** – Governor's Council was made an appointed body replacing the elected council and the city was put under military rule.
3. **Administration of Justice Act** – British official were made immune to criminal prosecution in Massachusetts.
4. **The Quartering Act** – by which the colonists were required to quarter British soldiers in unoccupied buildings.

These acts were in response to the Boston Tea Party and were intended to punish Massachusetts and to end colonial challenge to the British. The British also stationed 2000 troops in the region to enforce the acts. By these measures, the British aimed to isolate the Bostonians from the rest of the colonies. Instead of abandoning the Bostonians, the other colonists rallied behind the Bostonians and assembled at Philadelphia for a united resistance against the British.

5. The First Continental Congress 1774

55 Colonial delegates from every colony (except Georgia) such as George Washington of Virginia, John and Samuel Adams of Massachusetts and John Jay of New York assembled in Philadelphia in September 1774. The Congress issued the **Declaration of Rights and Grievances** which declared their loyalty to the king but condemned the Coercive Acts. They protested against the Boston incident, denounced taxation efforts of the British and the maintenance of British army in the colonies. The Declaration marked the most revolutionary expression of American rights yet articulated and the first colonial document to articulate the right to 'life, liberty and property'. The Congress also decided to boycott British goods, formed a **Continental Association** to enforce boycott of British goods and decided to convene another Continental Congress in 1775.

6. Beginning of the War

The War started on 19 April 1775 with **the Battles of Lexington and Concord**, in Massachusetts, when the British troops sent to confiscate military stores of the colonists clashed with the local militia. This incident marked 'the shot heard round the world'. The first shots were fired in Lexington near Boston by the British and the first fighting took place at Concord.

7. The Second Continental Congress

It was convened in May 1775 and was in response to the outbreak of hostilities in Massachusetts. The Congress sent a petition known as the **Olive Branch Petition** (July 1775) to the British King declaring their loyalty to the king and requested the repeal of the unjust laws and taxes and called for the end of hostilities. The petition was a last ditch effort to prevent the conflict from escalating into a full-blown war. But the king refused any compromise and the Continental Congress now started acting as an independent government. The Congress also organised the **Continental Army** out of the local militias and George Washington was appointed as its commander. It also established a postal system, formed a Continental Navy and negotiated with the native people for their support. What began as a fight against British economic policies now evolved into a fight for political independence.

George Washington

In response, the British King issued the **Proclamation of Rebellion** in August 1775 stating that the colonists were in an 'open and avowed rebellion' and 'levying war against us'. The **Prohibitory Act** was passed in December 1775 designed to strike at the economic viability of the colonies by imposing a naval blockade against the colonies and shutting down trade with them. It also provided for seizure of all American ships and cargoes as if they belonged to an enemy power.

It is pertinent to note that even in 1776, when open war had erupted, many Colonists did not want independence. But bungling British policies such as burning of towns by the British army, blockade of colonial ports, recruitment of native Indians, slaves and foreign mercenaries to fight against the colonists, promise of freedom to the slaves if they support the British, rejection of all efforts at conciliations and finally the publication of Thomas Paine's pamphlet **'Common Sense'** in 1776 tilted the public opinion in favour of independence. Paine questioned the logic of a tiny country such as Britain controlling a huge continent of North America and declared that America had a sacred mission to the world. He accused George III as tyrant and argued that all the monarchies were formed by seizing power from the people. Arguments of Thomas Paine convinced the Congress the necessity of independence for the colonies.

8. The Declaration of Independence

The colonial governments now instructed their congressional delegates to vote for independence. A five-member committee of the Congress headed by Thomas Jefferson drafted the **Declaration of Independence** which was adopted on 4 July 1776. It declared the colonies as the United States of America, contained a Preamble which emphasised the natural rights, equality and social contract principles, enumerated 27 grievances of the colonists and finally declared their independence from the mother country.

> The Indian state of Mysore ruled by Haider Ali too had declared support to the American colonists in the War of independence. It was the cause of the Second Anglo-Mysore War 1780–84.

This document was based on the ideas of John Locke and the Enlightenment and expression of natural rights. It declared '*that all men are created equal, that they are endowed by their Creator with certain unalienable rights that among these are life, liberty, and the pursuit of happiness*'. The Declaration also proclaimed as they '*are absolved from all allegiance to the British crown*'. The declaration became the rallying point for the colonists, which also changed the whole character of the war as the colonists had now a cause to fight for.

The Declaration of Independence also allowed the colonies to seek alliances with foreign nations – with France in 1778 and with Spain in 1779. France entered the War to avenge their defeat in the Seven Years War and Spain entered the War to regain their territories of Florida, Gibraltar and Minorca from the British. In 1782, the Dutch Republic too joined the war as an ally of the colonists. Entry of France and Spain turned the struggle a global conflict as now Britain had to deploy its soldiers and resources around the globe. Now the Colonial Revolution became secondary for Britain as they had to fight war across the globe in India, West Indies and Europe.

> The Declaration of Independence along with the American Constitution and the Bill of Rights are three founding political pillars of America. It also inspired many political movements including the French Revolution. The Declaration of Independence which was titled as 'The unanimous Declaration of the thirteen United States of America' had four parts.
>
> 1. Preamble – Explains the reasons that impelled them to separation.
> 2. Declaration of Natural Rights – Declared that all men are created equal and that they are endowed by their Creator with certain unalienable rights such as Life, Liberty and the pursuit of Happiness and the governments derive their just powers from the consent of the governed. John Locke's ideas were hugely influential in the declaration of natural Rights as he had held in 1690 that people had the right to rebel against the government that did not protect their life, liberty and property. What Locke had prescribed for individual, the colonists proclaimed as a body politic.
> 3. List of Grievances – Accused George III as tyrant and listed usurpations on colonial rights by the British.
> 4. Resolution of Independence by the United States – Declared these 'United Colonies' as the 'United States of America' as 'Free and Independent States' and as absolved from all allegiance to the British Crown.

9. The Revolution as Civil War

The American Revolution was not just a fight between the colonists and the British. The War of Independence caused division of the colonial population into three categories – Tories, Patriots and those remained neutral. **Tories or Loyalists, Royalists or King's Men** were loyal to the British King and wanted the colonies to remain under Britain. They consisted King's officers or beneficiaries and were older generation with education and wealth but with conservative outlook. In many times the loyalists opposed the patriots and supported the British through propaganda, military service and insurrectionary measures. The **Patriots or Whigs** were people who were opposed to the British rule and consisted of lawyers, merchants, urban workers, farmers and artisans. The Patriots met the Loyalist threat by arresting them and confiscating their property. Thus, the American Revolution was not just a war between the British and their colonists but was also a civil war between Patriots and Loyalists. But majority of Americans remained **neutral** and were ready to support whoever won the struggle. At the end of the war, the Loyalists went into exile especially to Canada and to other parts of the British Empire.

10. End of the Conflict

Of the many battles fought between the colonial and British forces, the **Battle of Saratoga** fought in October 1777 was the most important in which the British army commander Burgoyne surrendered. In the Battle of Yorktown (1781) Lord Cornwallis surrendered before Washington. The peace negotiations started in April 1782 and concluded with the **Treaty of Paris** in September 1783 by which Britain recognised independence and sovereignty of American colonies as the United States. The treaty also demarcated boundaries between the British Empire in North America and the United States of America. Separate peace treaties were also signed between Britain and the nations that supported the colonies – France, Spain and the Dutch Republic and was collectively known as the Peace of Paris. Last of the British uniformed troops left the east coast cities in November 1783 marking the end of British occupation of the American colonies.

11. Factors for American Success

1. The colonies were defending their homeland and were more motivated.
2. Americans were supported by countries such as France and Spain. French fleet proved invaluable to the colonies by which the colonists could inflict disaster on the British such as at Yorktown.
3. Britain had to transport war material and supplies across 3,000 miles of ocean. Moreover, while the colonists were well acquainted with the terrain, the British soldiers found their task difficult in a forest-clad and vast country. For the British, fighting an overseas war too was highly expensive, this prompted tax-weary British citizens to put pressure on their government to end the war.
4. Military mistakes committed by the British generals too were important. For example, General Howe, who had some initial success did not follow up the initial advantages he gained. Moreover, the British administrators had overrated their own ability and resources while underestimating those of the colonists.
5. Leadership of the colonists provided by persons such as George Washington and Thomas Jefferson too was significant in colonial success.

12. Results of the American Revolution

- New Political Ideas: It inaugurated an era of new ideas such as popular sovereignty, civil liberty and religious freedom.
- New State Constitutions: The declaration of independence caused constitution making and state building. The 13 states drafted their own written constitutions, provided for regular elections and each state experimented with new ways to realise the goals of the Revolution.
- Expansion of Voting Rights: Independence offered opportunities for political participation for more number of people as they gained right to vote. The American society also became more egalitarian and meritocratic.
- Freedom of Religion: Legal institutionalisation of religious freedom became another highlight of the American independence.
- American Society: At the same time the principles of life, liberty and pursuit of happiness were not immediately extended to all people in

America – rights of women remained unaffected, slaves continued as slaves and the white men without property continued to remain poor and disenfranchised.

Slaves had been enlisted by both the British army and the Continental army during the Revolution and more than 1,00,000 slaves had deserted their masters, attaining their freedom during the Revolution without formal emancipation. After the war, the British military commanders evacuated Loyalist former slaves to Canada, the Caribbean and to England.

The Revolution did not end slavery but caused the dawn of an organised abolitionist movement. The revolutionary rhetoric of 'equality' gave birth to a 'revolutionary generation' of slaves and free-blacks that demanded abolition of slavery leading to Civil War in the next century. As far as the Native American tribes such as Cherokee, Iroquois and Shawnee were concerned, the American independence meant the end of their own independence as the land hungry colonists resorted to brutal expansion into western territories leading to displacement and disappearance of native tribes.

- It ended the mercantilist economy and opened up the economy for new opportunities and free trade. Expansion of territory to westward offered new sources of raw materials and domestic market which were significant in the emergence of the United States as an industrial giant.
- Emergence of American Culture – Creation of a new nation adhering to the principles of civil liberty and religious freedom resulted in the emergence of one of the most diverse countries in the world. Apart from the Native Americans, who were the original inhabitants and the English who colonised the land, this 'melting pot' of cultures had been shaped by huge immigration of Europeans, Latin Americans, Africans and Asians since then.

American Revolution inspired colonial peoples in other parts of the world. In 1804, the enslaved Africans in the French held Caribbean island of Saint Domingue – the present day Haiti – rose in rebellion and became independent. Haiti thus became the second nation in the American continent to attain independence from colonial rule.

13. American Constitution

In November 1777, the Continental Congress had adopted the **Articles of Confederation**, the first constitution of the United States establishing the United States as a collection of 13 sovereign states having an equal voice in Congress. The Articles were ratified and put into effect in 1781. The **Congress of the Confederation** was the government established by the Articles of Confederation. Under this system the power of the central government was extremely limited as there was no executive branch to enforce any acts passed by the Congress, did not have power to regulate foreign and inter-state commerce and had no provision of national court system. It had to depend on the states for the money necessary to operate as it could not raise any funds itself and in the Congress any decision of consequence required unanimous vote. The situation demanded formulation of a new constitution for which delegates from 12 states (Rhode Island did not send representative) met in a **Constitutional Convention** in May 1787 in Philadelphia and drafted a new constitution. On 17 September 1787, 39 of the 55 delegates or 'the Framers' signed the Constitution and these 39 signatories are known as 'the Signers'.

Founding Fathers: These were a group of American leaders who made significant intellectual contributions to the development of independence and nationhood of American colonies and to the drafting of the US Constitution. Some of them were members of the Constitutional Convention as George Washington, the president of the Convention, and James Madison who drafted the Constitution and the Bill of Rights. Others though not members of the Convention, such as Thomas Jefferson, who wrote the Declaration of Independence, and Thomas Paine whose pamphlet 'Common Sense' had immeasurably influenced the philosophy reflected in the Declaration of Independence, are also included in the group.

The new constitution required the approval of at least 9 of the 13 states. While many states supported the new constitution as it provided a balance between the state powers and national interests, some states and leaders argued that the powers were tilted towards the central government and demanded protection of the rights of individual citizens from encroachment of government. Most of the state constitutions had included an explicit protection of individual rights safeguarded from intrusion by government and they wanted such a mechanism to be incorporated in the Constitution. The supporters of the Constitution were known as the **Federalists** and the opposing group – the **Anti-federalists**. Finally, a compromise was reached – the **Massachusetts Compromise** – in which Massachusetts agreed to ratify the Constitution but stood for certain amendments. This cleared the deadlock as four more states – Massachusetts, Maryland, South Carolina and New Hampshire – ratified the Constitution and with the five already ratified states (Delaware, Pennsylvania, New Jersey, Georgia and Connecticut) met the minimum requirement of 9 states and became effective from 4 March 1789. George Washington was sworn in as the first President of the United States on 30 April 1789.

The First Congress in September 1789 passed 10 amendments introduced by **James Madison** which are now known as the Bill of Rights. They guarantee certain basic individual rights such as freedom of speech, assembly and religion and right to bear arms and also impose limitations on the government. These rights which are fundamental to America were based on the rights defined in the Magna Carta, the English Bill of Rights and the ideals of the Enlightenment.

14. | Major features of the US Constitution

A. Federal Republic

The United States is a federation of states which means that powers are divided between the centre and the states. The 13 colonies that originally constituted grew into 45 states by 1900 and five more – Oklahoma (1907), Arizona and New Mexico (1912) and Alaska and Hawaii (1959) joined the federation making the total number 50. All these states have their own state capital and government while they also share power with the Federal government located at Washington.

B. Written Constitution

Framers created a written constitution (framed in 1787 and enforced in 1789) moving away from the British model of unwritten constitution and became the first written constitution in the world.

C. Elected President

In giving shape to a new nation the colonists rejected both monarchy and hereditary aristocracy as the head of the nation and constructed a republic reposing their faith in an elected president.

D. Separation of Powers and Checks and Balances

Three equal and coordinate pillars of the government are the legislature, executive and judiciary – the Congress, the President and the Supreme Court, respectively. They work separately from each other and are based on the principle of separation of powers and are harmoniously balanced with each branch being checked by others – the system of checks and balances. For example, the President and his cabinet members are not members of the Congress, while the President has to submit the most important of his appointments and all his treaties to the Senate for ratification. The Congressional enactments are not to become law until approved by the President. Further, though the President can veto laws, Congress can overrule it by two-thirds majority in both the houses. The President could be removed by Congress by impeachment but the President cannot dissolve Congress. Similarly while the Supreme Court has the power to decide all cases arising under federal laws and has the power to declare a law unconstitutional, the judges are appointed by the President which requires confirmation by the Senate and the judges could be impeached by the Congress.

E. Dual Citizenship

A citizen of the United States is also a citizen of the state where they are domiciled.

F. Rigid Constitution

US Constitution is one of the most rigid constitutions in the world as it provides for a special and difficult procedure involving both the Congress and the states and requires super-majorities at both the proposal and ratification stages for its amendment.

The Congress is the federal parliament of the United States and is entrusted primarily with the task of legislation. It has two chambers – the House of Representatives and the Senate. Members of both are elected by universal suffrage. 'The House' has 435 members elected for two years from electoral districts of roughly equal population, while the Senate has 100 members two each elected from the 50 states and elected for six years with one-third retiring every two years. All legislative proposals require a simple majority in both the houses and a joint conference can be held in case of disagreement between the two houses. Further any treaty with a foreign country requires ratification by the Senate by two-thirds votes. It is located on Capitol Hill in Washington D.C

The President heads the executive branch of the United States. He is the head of state and Commander-in-Chief of the armed forces. The President controls the civil services, conducts foreign affairs, signs treaties with foreign countries and appoints his own cabinet members, ambassadors and judges. President is elected every four years through an electoral college consisting of 538 electors. The President and the First Family live and work in the White House located in Washington D.C. George Washington was the first President of the United States. Franklin D. Roosevelt was elected President four times and is the only President ever to have served more than two terms

The Supreme Court is the highest court in the United States, the only judicial body specifically required by the constitution and is the final judicial arbiter on matters of federal law. All justices are nominated by the President, confirmed by the Senate and hold office for life, i.e. remain in office until they resign, pass away or impeached by Congress. The total number of Supreme Court justices are not stipulated by the Constitution but is decided by the Congress. Since 1869, there are nine justices including one Chief Justice. The Supreme Court building, also referred to as 'the Marble Palace', is located at One First Street, Washington D.C, and is the official residence and workplace of the Chief Justice and other justices of the Supreme Court.

15. The Enlightenment and the US Constitution

Many of the American leaders such as Thomas Jefferson were adherents of the Enlightenment. Under its influence they believed it as their right to rebel against a tyrant authority. The Declaration of Independence issued by the Second Continental Congress in 1776 was another example of eloquent expression of the Enlightenment especially that of Locke. The Declaration proclaimed 'that all men are created equal' and stood for unalienable natural rights 'life, liberty and the pursuit of happiness'.

The Enlightenment had huge influence in the drafting of the US Constitution too. **John Locke** had argued that government derives its power from the consent of the governed. This concept is found in the Preamble of the US constitution in the words 'We the people of the United States', in provisions to limit governmental powers and in the creation of representative government. **Montesquieu**'s vision of separation of powers found expressed in division of powers between the three branches of government, formation of a federal system and in checks and balances. Direct democracy preached by **Rousseau** found expressed in the direct election of the President and elections to the Congress. Another Enlightenment figure **Voltaire** had argued for freedom of speech and religious freedom. These rights were enshrined in the Bill of Rights.

Legacy of the American independence

1. Inaugurated a precedent of overthrowing monarchy and colonial governments by the colonists.
2. Framed the first written constitution in the world.
3. Established a new state with its number of civil liberties.
4. Inspired large number of revolutions such as the French Haitian and Latin American revolutions.

Washington, D.C. is a city and the capital of the United States. The city, located on the River Potomac, is coextensive with the District of Columbia and was established in 1790 as the permanent seat of the federal government. The city was designed by Pierre Charles L'Enfant, a French army engineer who fought in the American War of Independence.

SUMMARY

Britain and its North American Colonies – Since the 17th century the eastern coast of North America had been settled by the British and by the 18th century there were 13 colonies of England. These were Massachusetts, New York, Connecticut, New Hampshire, Rhode Island, Pennsylvania, Delaware, Maryland, New Jersey, Virginia, North Carolina, South Carolina and Georgia.

Causes of the American Revolution – Long-term causes include the idea of liberty, political, ideological, religious and economic causes. Immediate cause was the French and Indian War and the new taxation policy initiated by the new Prime Minister of England George Grenville. The Sugar Act of 1764, The Currency Act of 1764, The Stamp Act of 1765, The Townshend Act of 1767, The Tea Act of 1773 and The Intolerable Acts of 1774 were the most important steps initiated by Britain to tax the colonists but was opposed by the colonists.

The Declaration of Independence – This was drafted by a committee of the Continental Congress and was adopted on 4 July 1776. It declared the colonies as United States of America and declared independence from Britain.

Salient features of the American Constitution – Federal Republic, written constitution, elected President, separation of powers, checks and balances, dual citizenship and rigid constitution.

Questions of Previous Years Civil Services Examination

1. "The American War of Independence finally ended in 1783 when Britain acknowledged the independence of the United States of America". Critically examine. (2023)
2. Do you understand that the lack of statesmanship in London during the 1760s and the 1770s was, an important contributory factor in precipitating the American Revolution? Analyse. (2022)
3. The American War of Independence transformed Europe as well as America'. Explain. (2018)
4. Explain the main features of the US Federal Constitution. (2016)
5. American Revolution seems to have come with remarkable suddenness. A roster of talented leaders emerged during 1763 to 1775 to make it happen'. Elucidate. (2014)
6. 'American Revolution was an economic revolt against mercantilism'. Substantiate. (2013)
7. The American Revolution was essentially an economic conflict between American capitalism and British mercantilism'. Explain. (2012)
8. No taxation without representation'. Explain. (2006)
9. The American War of Independence 'deprived Great Britain of one empire; but it strengthened the foundations of another'. Explain. (1998)
10. The American Revolution 'was a natural and even expected event in the history of a colonial people who had come of age'. Explain. (1995)

CHAPTER 5

The French Revolution

In this Chapter

1. Introduction

The year 1789 marked a seminal event in the history of the world and it was the French Revolution. Occurred as a result of cumulative factors, the revolution overthrew the monarchy and established a republic and transformed France from a 'kingdom of subjects' into a 'nation of citizens'. Eventually it culminated in the dictatorship under Napoleon, who tried to conquer and disseminate the ideals of the Revolution to the rest of Europe.

The French Revolution destroyed the Old Regime and initiated a new era that promised the fulfilment of the ideals of the Enlightenment. It tried to refashion institutions in accordance with reason and justice and upheld the ideas of equality, liberty and fraternity. It unleashed forces of nationalism and set out to create symbols of it. With all these ingredients the Revolutionary France emerged as a laboratory of social and political theories and became a source of inspiration for many of the subsequent movements worldwide.

The Revolution became the beginning point of all modern political ideologies like liberalism, nationalism, secularism and radicalism. As the Revolution unleashed forces that were bound to influence the course of human history, William Wordsworth, the English Romantic poet, while walking through the Revolutionary France expressed his emotions and hopes in glowing language:

Bliss was it those days to be alive
To be young was very heaven

2. Background of the French Revolution

In the 18th century, France was the most populous country in the Continental Europe, the leading centre of arts and literature and also the focal point of the intellectual current known as the **Enlightenment**. But, the rulers of France were despots who glorified kingship and emphasised '**divine right**' of kings – that the kings were selected by the God to rule. They sidelined the nobility, reduced the significance of the **Estates General** – the representative assembly of clergy, nobility and the common people and also eliminated interference by the Church in state affairs. And by a policy known as '**raison d'état**', which meant 'reason of state', the Bourbon kings of France suppressed all anti-monarchical elements.

Louis XIV (1643–1715): In the age of absolutism Louis XIV's France was a leader in centralisation and he boasted '***I am the state***'. He was called as the Grand Monarch of Europe and also as the '**Sun King**'. The royal palace of Louis XIV at Versailles with splendour and grandeur was built to create awe in his subjects and to convey the 'divine right' status of the king.

Bourbon Dynasty: A royal family that traced its origin to 1268. The French Revolution broke out during the period of Bourbon king Louis XVI who was later executed by the revolutionaries. After the defeat of Napoleon in 1814 the Bourbon dynasty was restored to the kingdom of France with Louis XVIII, brother of Louis XVI appointed as the new king.

Louis XV: Louis XIV was succeeded by his great grandson **Louis XV** (1715–74). Given to vice and wine and controlled by a succession of female favourites and mistresses, Louis XV's rule was characterised by disorder and confusion. Under him the state affairs were neglected, policies were inconsistent and administration was inefficient. France was also defeated in the **Seven Years War** (1756–63) by Britain. This failure shattered the prestige of France in Europe, ended French dream of colonial empire in India and America and undermined the loyalty of the people to the absolute monarchy. As criticism began to mount against his rule, Louis had the intuition of the coming storm and reported to have commented '***after me deluge***'.

Louis XVI (1774–93) succeeded his grandfather in 1774, and it was under him, the long accumulated evils and anomalies of absolutism rose to an exploding point. His decision to support the American colonies against the British pushed France to near bankruptcy and drastic reforms were necessary to prevent it. To tide over the financial crisis the king attempted rationalisation of tax system and its extension to the huge land holdings of the nobility and the church. The outraged aristocracy demanded the summoning of the Estates General, which alone was, in their view, competent enough to impose tax.

In 1789, king agreed to the reactionary demand of the aristocracy and this concession to the aristocracy forced the other classes to organise themselves. The aristocracy, who considered themselves as the natural leaders of the French society, was under the illusion that they could bend the government to their will with the popular support. But the representatives of the Third Estate – dominated by the bourgeoisie such as lawyers, bankers, businessmen – were in no mood of surrender and were in a state of self-assertion. The aristocrats looked back to the past to defend their privileges against all changes and the other group looked forward towards a society built on equality and liberty. These conflicting attitudes came out open, once the Estates General was convened and gave birth to Revolution.

3. Causes of the French Revolution

The French Revolution was the outcome of interaction of various forces. Broadly these can be classified into the following heads.

A. Political

The political system that existed in France before the Revolution had been called as the **'Old Regime'**. The political structure in the 18th-century France was **monarchical absolutism** with no check on the absolute authority of the kings. The state was personal and hereditary domain of the dynasty. People did not have any voice in the governance of the country. Though France had some representative institutions in the past, by the 18th century they had been either dysfunctional or been under the king's control. The Estates General was one such institution that had not met since 1614.

Old Regime: Also called as the Ancient Regime. It was a political and social system that existed in France from the middle ages to the Revolution. The term also used to refer similar feudal systems existed in other parts of Europe. Some of its characteristics were absolute monarchy, feudal privileges and dominance of religion in the lives of the people.

Efficiency of governance in a highly centralised monarchical system depended on the exceptional ability of the ruler. Louis XIV was able and decisive. But his successor Louis XV was weak and frivolous, under whom the state power was held by a horde of courtiers. Corruption and bad governance coupled with military failure of Louis XV had shaken the loyalty of the subjects to the cause of the royalty. With strong leadership, France would have been able to sail through the crisis.

The next ruler, Louis XVI though honest and well-intentioned, was weak and indecisive and was under the undue influence of his wife Marie Antoinette, who often interfered in the government. About Louis XVI it was commented that 'his reign was a succession of feeble attempts at doing good, shows of weakness and clear evidence of his inadequacy as a leader'.

Under the weak king evils of despotism began to surface eroding people's faith in despotic rule.

This **authoritarian, autocratic and inefficient** political system was now in conflict with the aspirations of the people who were under the influence of the Enlightenment ideas.

B. Administrative

The administrative system in the 18th century France was complex, confusing and ineffective. The practice of selling the state offices by the king had given rise to incompetency in administration. The lack of uniformity in administration and in taxation was hampering trade and commerce. Overlapping and conflicting law systems had made administration of justice unjust and arbitrary.

The monarchical absolutism was also reflected in the form of severe oppression of the general population. By issuing warrants called '**Lettres de cachet**' king could imprison any person suspected of creating discontent among the people.

C. Social

The division of French society into inequal and antagonistic groups was another crucial factor for the Revolution. The French society was graded into three orders from the top to bottom and was characterised by glaring inequality and wide variations in rights between them. These orders known as **the Estates** were the Clergy, the First Estate, the Nobility, the Second Estate, and all others that constituted about 96% of the population the Third Estate.

The first two Estates were the **privileged classes** that enjoyed total or partial exemption from taxation and had monopoly over positions and honours under the state.

The third Estate was a **heterogeneous group of unprivileged people** consisted of wide sections of the population – the bourgeoisie or the middle class, urban labourers, artisans and peasants. While the Third Estate was kept away from positions and honours of the state, the whole tax burden was thrust upon them.

The privileged classes had rights but no obligation and the unprivileged classes had all obligations but no rights. This semi-feudal social structure caused tensions in society and was a major factor in precipitating the Revolution.

The **Clergy** – men of religion under the Roman Catholic Church – constituted the First Estate. Although the church possessed huge wealth (church owned 10% of the land in France) and its land brought immense revenue, it paid no taxes to the state but made a 'free gift' to the king which was an amount determined by the church itself.

The Clergy themselves had been divided into upper clergy and lower clergy. The **upper clergy** were recruited from the nobility. This group had monopoly over lucrative church offices. But they were the men of the world and hence were indifferent to their spiritual duties. The **lower clergy** were commoner by birth, which did the real work of spiritual consolation and religious instruction and had moderate means of living, but were devoid of any avenues for promotion. This gross inequality within the First Estate was one reason that prompted many priests to sympathise with the Revolution, once it broke out.

The **Nobility** was the second privileged Estate. They accounted just 2% of the population but owned about 30% of the land. They had monopoly over highest positions in government, army and in the church. Even though they possessed one-third of the total land and exercised feudal privileges of hunting and forestry, they were exempted from most taxes. From the peasants they could also collect manorial dues and exact 'corvee' (forced labour).

Within the nobility too there existed gradations. The highest of the nobles were '**nobles of the race**' – noble families that traced their aristocratic status back to immemorial times. The other group '**nobles of the robe**' were the group newly created by the monarchy by selling the titles of nobility to the wealthy families. In the 18th century, the nobility sought to regain their aristocratic privileges lost under Louis XIV. Further, when the cost of maintaining a luxurious life rose, the nobility set out to enforce the feudal rights more vigorously by taking over parts of the common property of peasant villages and resisted any measure by the state to bring them under taxation. It was this **'feudal reaction'** that triggered the Revolution.

In feudal times, the nobility had enjoyed privileges and were exempted from taxation in return for the services they rendered to the state. With the centralisation of monarchy, the nobles had been deprived of their local powers, but continued to enjoy privileges of feudal era which was anomalous. It is this anachronism of feudal rituals that gave rise to the comment that the Revolution was not against the feudal system as such but against the 'effete survival of parts of it'.

The Third Estate comprised of **bourgeoisie, peasants and urban labourers.** The bourgeoisie consisted of lawyers, doctors, bankers, merchants and manufacturers and government officials of lower ranks. These were the '**men on the make**' – people prepared to grab any opportunity to get ahead. Although they had piled up wealth, they did not enjoy social prestige and political privileges. They had no influence at the court or could not hold any high political office. They wanted all positions under the state and the church to be opened to men of merit, a parliament to debate the issues of the nation, a constitution to limit the powers of the king, freedom of thought and expression and non-interference with business. This discontent class with worldly aspirations and imbued with the ideals of the Enlightenment was to provide leadership in the Revolution.

Peasants in France were better off compared to their counterparts in other European countries, where serfdom still existed. In France, serfdom had almost disappeared, but the lords continued to demand obligations from the peasants including '**Corvee**' and also payment of part of his produce to the lord. Lord also exercised hunting rights on peasant lands which meant trampling of crops by the hunting party. Ultimately, the peasant who had to pay **feudal dues** to his lord, '**tithes**' to the church and **taxes** to the state was left with bare minimum and many times starvation starred him at the face. Their misery doubled, in times of inflation or in times of crop failure.

Urban labourers of pre-industrial France were the poorest group within the Third Estate and consisted of craftsmen, day labourers, and artisans whose life as that of the peasants had worsened in the second-half of the 18th century. Paid low wages and frequently out of work, they often faced starvation. Between 1787 and 1789 urban unemployment in France was as high as 50 percent. During the decade before the revolution the cost of living had increased by 62%, while wages rose only by 22%. In the times of food shortages and rising prices particularly that of their staple food – bread – the urban labourers were driven to desperation and acts of violence. This desperate section was to influence the course of the Revolution decisively once it broke out.

D. Economic

In the background of absolute despotism and semi-feudal social order it was economic factor that precipitated the crisis and gave birth to the Revolution.

By the 1780s, France's once prosperous economy was in decline. Economic crisis gripped France, as was evident from the sharp rise in **cost of living**, heavy **burden of taxes** and **huge debt**. The privileged sections were more or less exempted from taxation, while the commoners were overburdened with taxation. The heavy burden of taxes made it almost impossible to do business and was a great concern to the segments of the Third Estate such as merchants. Moreover, widespread crop failure in 1870s caused **severe shortage of food grains** resulting in starvation.

In the second-half of the 18th century, France was also on the brink of bankruptcy on account of-

1. The wars of Louis XIV. Even by 1787 the enormous debt incurred during the wars of Louis XIV had not been paid off.
2. Favouritism and nepotism of Louis XV by way of granting pensions, gifts and favours to his favourites.
3. Extravagant spending of Louis XVI and his queen Marie Antoinette.
4. Debt burden on account of the French participation in the American War of Independence (1775–83) and aid provided to the colonists in the American Revolution. France's support to the American colonies was intended to avenge the loss of French colonies in America and India during the Seven Years War and to weaken its chief rival England.
5. Inefficient and unjust taxation with considerable sums being siphoned off by the 'tax farmers' – private individuals who purchased the right to collect tax.
6. Obstinate resistance of the aristocracy against any tax reform that would have affected their privileges.

In the decade before the Revolution, the cost of servicing the national debt had amounted to 50 per cent of the nation's budget. The **impending bankruptcy** and **adamancy of the aristocracy** left the king with no option, but to summon the Estates General. This provided the much needed spark to the accumulated grievances of the population to explode. Hence, it is observed that the 'fiscal causes lay at the root of the French Revolution' and that 'the train which had been laid by philosophy was fired by finance'.

E. Ferment of Ideas

By giving shape and substance to the existing discontent the philosophers of the Enlightenment played significant role in the outbreak of the French Revolution. The Enlightenment thinkers had exhorted people to discard blind obedience to authority, whether that of the ruler or religion, as for them nothing was sacred and beyond critical scrutiny. They also exposed the fallacies of the divine right theory, intolerance of the church and inequalities and anomalies of the Old Regime. By doing so, the **Philosophes** (as the scholars were known in France) prepared the mind of the people for a revolutionary change. Arguing for legal equality, representative institutions and for cultural and religious freedom they pressed for change and progress. These thinkers Montesquieu, Voltaire, Rousseau and others circulated humanistic and rationalistic ideas to a wide spectrum of the French population, especially to the literate middle class. The French Revolution thus can be seen, as an inevitable result of the radical opposition created between the Old Regime and the men of letters of the Enlightenment. Their 'literary politics' promoted a discourse of equality which was in fundamental opposition to the monarchical regime.

Montesquieu (1689–1755), in his work **'The Spirit of the Laws'**, had subjected royal absolutism to severe criticism. This book published in 1748 argued, inter alia, for constitutional monarchy, separation of powers, humane laws, rule of law, freedom of thought and religious toleration. Though neither a proponent of revolution nor an advocate of democracy, Montesquieu, by exposing the absolutism of its evils and by projecting an alternative of **limited monarchy** to the French people, paved seeds of discontent in their minds. The ideas of Montesquieu had already inspired the American freedom fighters in overthrowing the colonial yoke and in drafting a constitution containing noble ideals like liberty, toleration and separation of powers.

Montesquieu

Voltaire (1694–1778), a **rationalist** to the core, denounced the irrational institutions of France with his satirical style of writing. His appeal for **humanity** as the touch stone of civilisational life created irresistible impression on French population and heightened their desire for change. His criticisms undermined the respect for authority and freed the minds of the people from the hold of the church and the state. Victor Hugo's comment *'to name Voltaire is to characterize the entire 18th century'* is not an exaggeration for his ideas had moved like a flame over the continent and had stirred millions of people. This is also attested by Will Durant, when he commented that *'Italy had a Renaissance, and Germany had a Reformation but France had Voltaire, he was for his country both Renaissance and Reformation and half the Revolution'.*

Voltaire

Jean Jacques Rousseau (1712–88) in his work **'The Social Contract'** published in 1762 declared that **'man is born free and yet everywhere he is in chains'**. As a champion of **democracy** and supporter of **liberty** he argued that the state owes its origin to the contract of the people and that the governments should be an expression of the popular will. Rousseau taught that men would be free, wise and good in the **'state of nature'** and that instinct and emotion when not distorted by the unnatural limitations of civilisation are nature's

Rousseau

voices and instructions to good life. In his hypothetical 'state of nature' men were good and free. For him, renouncing liberty was to renounce being a man, to surrender the rights of humanity and even its duties. He exhorted people not to entrust law making to a single person or to a small group but to the general will of the population. Of all the thinkers of the time, ideas of Rousseau were the most dangerous to the Old Regime as they were a direct challenge to royal absolutism, church and the privileged. And, it is no wonder that the revolutionaries in France in its second stage, especially the Jacobins, invoked his name to justify their actions as steps to implement that 'general will' and as celebration of 'liberty'.

Inspiration for a better future also came from beyond the French boundaries. The **English Revolution** of 1688 and the limited monarchy and parliamentary government that resulted from it had been an inspiration to many of the intellectuals in France. The **American Revolution** (1783) and the **Declaration of Independence** by the American colonies had been widely admired in France. Many French men, like **Marquis de Lafayette**, had participated in the American Revolution on the side of the colonists and returned to France with dreams of establishing a state based on liberty and democracy in their own country. England and America thus provided alternative models to the Frenchmen against the tyrannical and semi-feudalistic state of affairs existed in their own country.

A group of economic theoreticians known as the **'Physiocrats'** too gave voice to the emerging middle class in France, by arguing for freedom in economic activities. They popularised the phrase 'laissez-faire' which meant 'let them do' to convey the message of free trade. They argued that transactions between private parties should be free from government interventions such as privileges, tariffs and regulations. The Laissez-Faire idea had a fertile ground among the bourgeoisie segment in France.

In the 18th century, rapid expansion in publication of books and periodicals allowed fast and wide circulation of these ideas to large number of people. Moreover, the emergence of the **'public sphere'** in France in the form of Masonic lodges, coffee houses and reading clubs, where the people discussed and debated issues, acted as the channels of dissemination of the ideas. Though initially confined to cultural questions, the 'public sphere' inevitably created a belief that the public opinion had the right to decide political questions of the country as well.

Why did the revolution happen in France and not in any other European state?

1. Feudalism with its class privileges had been prevalent in Europe but in France they had become anomalous.
2. France was the centre of the Enlightenment.
3. France had a large enlightened middle class.

4. Origin and Development

Trajectory of the French Revolution can be divided into **four stages.**

- The first from 1789 to 1792 – **The Moderate Stage**
- The second from 1792 to 1795 – **The Radical Stage**
- The third stage from 1795 to 1799 – **The Period of the Directory**
- The fourth stage from 1799 to 1804 – **The Period of the Consulate**

A graphical presentation of important developments during these stages is given on the next page.

A. The Moderate Stage (1789–92)

As seen above, France was on the verge of bankruptcy. Radical reforms of the fiscal system alone would have saved France. The king's ministers proposed fiscal reforms that included a proposal to the nobility and church to surrender some of their tax exemptions. As the privileged classes resisted these proposals, the King ordered the summoning of the Estates General.

Timeline of the French Revolution

1789

May: Summoning of the Estates General
June 17: Declaration of the National Assembly by the Third Estate
June 20: Oath of the Tennis Court
July 14: Storming of the Bastille
July: The Great Fear
August 4: Surrender of their privileges by the nobles
August 27: Declaration of the Rights of Man and Citizen

October: March on Versailles by Parisian women
November: Confiscation of Church lands by the National Assembly
1790
July: Civil Constitution of the Clergy
1791
June 20: Arrest of Louis XVI while fleeing France
September 3: Adoption of its first written constitution by France. It provided for a constitutional monarchy
1792
September: Abolition of monarchy, declaration of French Republic and the September Massacres
1793
January 21: Louis XVI guillotined
February: Declaration of war by France against Britain, Holland and Spain
April: the Committee of Public Safety
1794
The Reign of Terror
July: Execution of Robespierre
1795–99
The Directory
1799:
November: coup d'état by Napoleon and the establishment of the Consulate leading to the fall of the Directory and the end of the Revolution

The **Estates General** met at **Versailles** on 5 May 1789 and the Third Estate demanded that the three orders to meet as single body representing the whole nation. They also demanded decisions of the Estates General to be taken on individual vote. The Third Estate had an equivalent number of delegates the nobility and the clergy put together, as such it was expected that it would dominate the proceedings of the Estate General, hence was stubbornly resisted by the clergy and the nobility which formed the other two Estates.

On June 17 as the stalemate continued, the Third Estate declared itself as the **National Assembly** – an assembly not of the Estates but of 'the people' and invited other orders to join them. On June 20th, the Third Estate took an oath in a nearby tennis court (as the customary meeting hall had been locked out for them) known as the **Tennis Court Oath**. They took the oath '**Wherever we meet, there is the nation**' and the vow not to disband until a constitution was drafted. Soon, reform minded members of the clergy and the nobility joined the Assembly. In response to these developments the King Louis XVI stationed his mercenary army around Versailles.

There was a perceived threat of suppression of the National Assembly by the King. There was also public restlessness on account of soaring prices of the essential commodities. Moreover, calling of the Estates General had aroused expectations of the people intensifying their hopes of reform. In this background, on July 14, the Parisians in search of weapons and gunpowder stormed and captured the Bastille, a state prison and symbol of despotism. **Storming of Bastille** signalled the overthrow of despotism and triumph of liberty, as the Bastille was one of the dominant symbols of the Old Regime. This act created panic among the court nobles hostile to the Revolution who fled the country. This **revolutionary act of Parisian crowd** saved the National Assembly from annihilation by the king as the king now ordered the withdrawal of the royal troops reigning Paris.

French Revolution Main Events

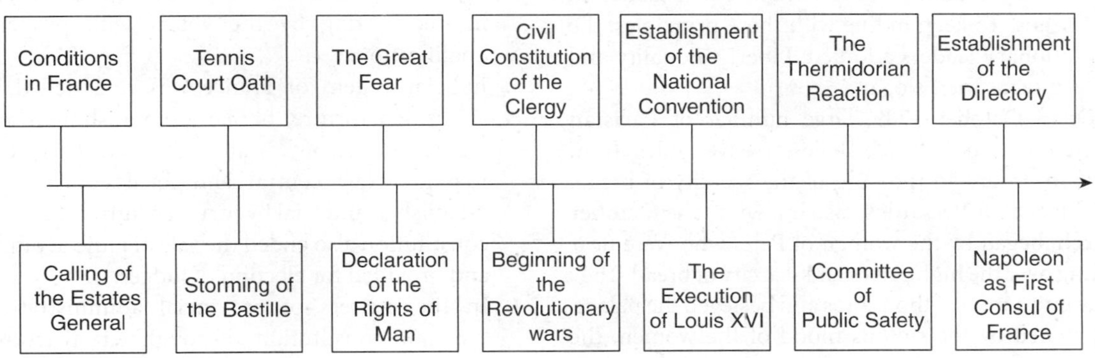

Fall of Bastille 1789 is considered as the first great turning point in the French Revolution. On 14 July 1789, crowds from the lower sections of the city of Paris attacked this symbol of absolution. Since then the Bastille Day, July 14, is a French national holiday celebrated with parades and fireworks and is remembered as the Republic Day.

The Parisian mob now created a new municipal government in Paris and a militia called the **'National Guard'** to maintain order in the city. Other cities followed the example of Paris and setup municipal governments. Soon revolution spread to provinces. Emboldened by these developments and fuelled by wild rumours that the nobles were hiring criminals to terrorise the commoners, the peasants in the provinces formed militias and attacked the chateaux (the manor house) of the nobles and set fire the records. The **violent uprising by the peasants** created consternation among the aristocracy and on 4 August 1789 the aristocrats, surrendered their feudal rights. Consequently, the National Assembly abolished feudalism and privileges, tax exemption, hunting rights, monopoly of highest offices, 'corvee' and manorial courts by issuing decrees known as the **August Decrees**, making commoners equal to the clergy and the nobles.

As the next step in ending the Old Regime and founding of a new era, the National Assembly adopted the **'Declaration of the Rights of Man and of the Citizen'** on 26 August 1789 as a statement of principles of the revolutionaries. It held that sovereignty rested with the people. It declared that ***'Men are born and remain free and equal in rights'*** and these rights included ***'liberty, property, security and resistance to oppression'***. It also guaranteed freedom of speech, freedom of religion and equal justice to all citizens. To keep in line with these principles, the revolutionary leaders adopted 'Liberty, Equality and Fraternity', as their slogan.

On 5 October 1789, large number of **Parisian women** marched to Versailles, twelve miles from Paris to protest to the king of the scarcity of bread. The **March on Versailles**, also known as the **October March**, began by the women of Paris who were near rioting over the high prices and scarcity of bread. They grew into a mob of thousands and besieged the palace. Frightened by the riotous mood of the women, the king approved 'the Declaration of the Rights of Man and the Citizen'. The next day, the crowd compelled the king and his family to return with them to Paris.

These events ended the king's independence and signified the change of power. The attack by common people removed forever the aura of invincibility that once cloaked the monarchy. The event was 'one of those defeats of royalty from which it never recovered' and the March on Versailles proved to be a defining moment of the French Revolution similar in significance as that of the fall of the Bastille. These developments were also clear signs that the Revolution was not merely a middle class affair but of concern to **urban workers, peasants and women.**

In July 1790, the Assembly passed the **Civil Constitution of the Clergy** by which far-reaching reorganisation of the church was introduced. Bishops and priests were to be elected by popular vote. Thus, clergy was transformed into government officials and to be paid by the state. The clergy had to take an oath of loyalty to the nation. The constitution abolished 'tithes' and nationalised all church property. By these measures the Catholic Church in France lost both its lands and independence. The proceeds from the sale of the Church properties were used to pay off nation's huge debt.

The National Assembly, now known as Constituent Assembly, drafted a **constitution** and presented to the public in June 1791. This constitution was the first written constitution of France and had the following features:

1. It provided for an administrative structure with the king as the head of the executive and a parliament to be known as Legislative Assembly, thereby providing for separation of legislature from the executive. King had only suspensive veto power.
2. Legislative Assembly was to be elected through indirect voting by the voters with property qualification.
3. Judicial system of France was remodelled by abolishing torture, barbarous punishment and 'Lettres de cachet' – all remnants of the Old Regime. New central and local courts were established and trial by jury was introduced. The constitution also ended the sale of judicial offices and provided for election of judges.
4. In the matters of provincial administration, the new constitution thoroughly restructured

France. The country was divided into 83 Departments of uniform size. The Departments were further divided into Districts, Cantos and Communes. Elected councils administered the Departments and other local units. Thus, the constitution restructured a highly centralised government into uniform sized local units with fair amount of local self-governance.

5. In Financial sector all tolls and duties on transportation of goods within the country were abolished. Uniform system of weights and measures were introduced and the labourers were prohibited from forming unions.

The Constitution and other measures of the Constituent Assembly were a reflection of **Enlightenment liberalism** and **middle-class interests**. Property qualification to vote, enclosure of common lands for capitalist agriculture, abolition of guilds and trade unions for unfettered economic exploitation, and restructuring of local governments and provision of election of local officials as a measure to prevent aristocratic domination were some clear examples that show, that it was the middle class that emerged winners in the first phase of the revolution.

Dismayed by these developments, **Louis XVI tried to escape** from the country along with his family. He was discovered near the border at Varennes and was brought back to Paris. The king was made to accept the constitution and to swear an oath to the constitution. After completing its duty of framing the constitution, the Constituent Assembly dissolved itself to make way for working of the new constitution. In accordance with the provisions of the constitution, the **Legislative Assembly** was created in October 1791. Members of the Legislative Assembly were divided into too many groups of which the most important were the **Girondins** or the moderate republicans and the **Jacobins** or the radical republicans.

> Classification of political groups as the Left, the Right and the Centre emerged during this period. People who stood for radical changes were called the Left, those who wanted few or no changes were the Right and people with moderate views were the Centrists. These terms derived as they sat in the left, the right and the centre sides of the Legislative Assembly hall.

Meanwhile, a **counter revolution** emerged in France. There were many sections such as royalists, aristocrats and clergy who still opposed the Revolution and wanted to destroy it. The nobles and the clergy who could not reconcile with the revolutionary developments now joined hands with the strongly catholic peasants in the countryside, who were opposed to the drastic changes embodied in the Civil Constitution of the Clergy, in a conspiracy against the Revolution. Many of them fled France, (the **émigrés)** seeking support of the neighbouring countries and started conspiring against the Revolution in organising a counter revolutionary army.

On their part, the monarchs in many European countries were watching the developments in France with alarm. The French Revolution with ideas of democracy, liberty and radicalism was a threat to the other countries of Europe. This threat, that similar revolts might breakout in their own countries, was perceived as potent and real, created panic in the courts of the despotic European kings, and they started supporting the **'emigres'** in organising a counter revolution.

The Prussian king in alliance with Austria (Marie Antoinette, the French Queen was the sister of Leopold II of Austria) issued the **Declaration of Pillnitz,** in August 1791, expressing solidarity with the French king and calling for an armed intervention to save the French monarchy. The commander of the Austro-Prussian army the Duke of Brunswick crossed into France with a huge army and issued a manifesto known as the **Brunswick Manifesto** in July 1792 that if the royal family were harmed, he would wreak terrible vengeance on the Parisians.

This threat of counter revolution backfired. There was a general feeling among the people that the foreign invasion threatened everything they gained in the previous three years. Driven by panic, led by patriotism and moved by the suspicion that the royal family was in conspiracy with the invading foreign powers, thousands of people including the **sansculottes** (urban labourers and artisans) with the support of the **Paris Commune** (local government in Paris city started after the fall of the Bastille) marched to the **Tuileries Palace** in August 1792 where the king lived and imprisoned Louis XVI, Marie Antoinette and their children. The Legislative Assembly suspended the king and called for a National Convention to frame a new constitution.

The **National Convention** was elected by universal suffrage on the 20 September 1792 to draft a new constitution, which also became the de facto new government in France.

B. The Radical Stage (1792–95)

The Revolution which had remained a moderate affair till 1792 now took a radical turn. Apart from the counter revolution, suspicion that the king was in collusion with foreign rulers and threat of foreign invasion, the most important factor that tilted the revolution towards radicalism was the discontent of the **'sans-culottes'**. They had played significant part in the revolution so far, but had gained little. They looked at the bourgeoisie as a group that cornered the benefits of the Revolution. They believed that the **privilege of wealth** was taking the place of the **privilege of birth**. While in 1789 the bourgeoisie had been demanding equality with the aristocrats, in 1792 the sans-culottes had been demanding equality with the bourgeoisie. They demanded economic reforms such as wage increase, price control, end of food shortage, political reform that would give the lower section a voice in the government and social reform ensuring dignified existence. 'The Revolution prepared by the savants was to be carried out by the men of the slump.' The Jacobins supported the cause of these common people and the Revolution moved from its moderate stage to a radical one, which is also known as the **Second French Revolution.**

Meanwhile the foreign army had advanced deep into France. The revolutionaries decided to meet the threat on two fronts by sending a large army of revolutionary volunteers, to check the advancing enemy at the front and to stop further coups by royalists and aristocrats at the rear.

In order to terrorise the supporters of the royal cause and those who were suspected of conspiring with the advancing foreign army, the Commune of Paris carried out a series of massacres. These massacres were known as the **September Massacres** as they took place in September 1792 during which hundreds of royalists, Catholic priests and other 'enemies' of the Revolution were killed. The Paris Commune then sent circular to other cities asking them to follow the example.

The National Convention now **abolished monarchy** and declared **France a republic** (21 September 1792). In December 1792, Louis XVI was placed on trial, conducted by the National Convention itself, and was declared guilty of treason. He was executed on 21 January 1793 by the guillotine.

The revolutionaries gained success on both the fronts. They got rid of the traitors within the country through the massacres known as the **September Massacres** (1792) and the revolutionary army defeated the Prussian army in **the Battle of Valmy** in September 1792 and turned the tide in favour of the Revolution.

Girondins: They were moderate republicans in France during the Revolution. During 1791 to 1792 they were prominent in the Legislative Assembly and in the National Convention where they came in conflict with the Jacobins. The Girondins were executed during the Reign of Terror. Both the Girondins and the Jacobins came from bourgeoisie class. Girondins were staunch defenders of 'liberty', while Jacobins were proponents of 'equality'.

Jacobins: The Jacobins were members of a political organisation known as the Jacobin Club, with radical republican ideology. Prominent leaders of the Jacobins were **Jean-Paul Marat**, who edited a radical newspaper 'Friend of the People', **Georges Danton**, a lawyer known for his devotion to the rights of the downtrodden of Paris and **Maximilien Robespierre.** They were responsible for the September Massacres, execution of Louis XVI and the Reign of Terror. They were also known as **the Mountains** as they sat at higher plane in the Convention Hall. In 1794, Thermidorians ousted Jacobins from power and the Jacobin Club was also closed.

The National Convention under the dominance of the Jacobins initiated a period of terror – the **'Reign of Terror'** (June 1793–July 1794). The period of Terror was a period of ruthless dictatorship and was aimed at protecting the Republic both from foreign invasion and domestic anarchy. During this period harsh measures were taken against those who were considered as enemies of the Revolution. Overall, more than 40,000 people were executed during the Terror. It was the darkest and terrible period of the Revolution. It was unearthed under their most important leader Maximilien Robespierre.

The Jacobins aimed at establishing a **'republic of virtue'** by wiping out every trace of France's past. They confiscated property of enemies of the revolution and distributed among the lower classes and introduced a new calendar dividing the year into 12 months of 30 days each and renamed each month. They decreed the **Law of Maximum**, to fix prices of essential goods. They formed a twelve member **'Committee of the Public Safety'** with Robespierre as its leader and invested it, with unlimited executive power.

The **Committee** took vigorous steps to save France and the Revolution from the internal and external threats.

1. It formulated the **'Law of Suspects'** by which any pro-monarchist or anti-republican could be imprisoned.
2. It set up **'Revolutionary Tribunal'** to expedite the trial proceedings of any enemy of the Republic.
3. It carried out executions by **Guillotine** of the enemies of the Republic. The victims included Marie Antoinette – the queen of Louis XVI – and eminent leaders of the Girondins.

By these measures the Jacobins could suppress the **federalists** who opposed a strong central government, **Girondins** who challenged the Jacobin policies, the **reactionary nobles and priests** who were trying to subvert the Republic and the leaders of sans-culottes known as **'enrages'** who pushed for more social reforms threatening an insurrection against the Jacobin rule.

4. To meet the foreign threat, the Jacobins raised an army introducing **'Levée en masse'** (conscription) – recruiting men of 18–40 age and with this army of more than 8 lakh men routed the allied forces and destroyed the coalition of European kings.
5. It introduced the concept of **'La patrie'**, i.e. love for the fatherland. The French people were reminded of their duty to the nation in the schools, at rallies and through newspapers and art forms which conveyed the notion that the 'citizen is born, lives and dies for the father land' and heralded the era of nationalism.

The Republic of Virtue: It was a republican society envisaged by Robespierre to be founded on reason, patriotism and good citizenship. Such a society would have no kings or nobles and would substitute 'all the virtues and all the miracles of the Republic for all the vices and all the absurdities of the monarchy'. He believed that fundamental virtue of the Republican France would be the virtue 'which is nothing more than the love of the fatherland and of its laws'.

Within a year the revolutionary force attained success against its enemies. But the Jacobins were divided on the issue of excesses and brutalities of that period. Many of the Jacobins opposed continuation of the Terror. But Robespierre, who governed France virtually as dictator, considered his fellow leaders as less radicals than himself and looked at them as the 'enemies of the Revolution'. He guillotined large number of them including Georges Danton.

At last, the opponents of Robespierre, in the Convention, known as the Thermidorians, ordered the arrest and execution of Robespierre and his adherents. They were guillotined on 27 July 1794. This incident is known as the **Thermidorian Reaction**, as it took place on 9 Thermidor (27 July 1794) of the French Republican Calendar and was a reaction against the Reign of Terror. The Reign of Terror – the most radical phase of the Revolution too came to an end with the end of Robespierre.

Now, the Thermidorians became supreme in the Convention and they did away with the vestiges of the Reign of Terror. The Commune of Paris was dissolved, the Revolutionary Tribunal was suspended, Committee of Public Safety was deprived of its powers and the Jacobin Club was closed. Thermidorians were property owning bourgeoisie and their reaction was a counter revolution. True to their bourgeoisie interests they re-established property qualification for voting, abolished the law of maximum prices and the law against the 'suspects'.

The violence of the Reign of Terror was also replaced by a counterterror – **the White Terror.** Following the Thermidorian Reaction violent attacks took place across France, against the followers of Robespierre or against those who had associated with the Reign of Terror. The perpetrators of the White Terror were those whose relatives or friends had been victims of the Great Terror, supporters of the Girondins, monarchists, those who opposed the Civil Constitution of the Clergy or those who were otherwise hostile to the political agenda of the Jacobins. The White Terror was essentially a series of un-coordinated attack by local people against their common enemy.

C. The Directory (1795–99)

The people of France had grown weary of terror, were tired of skyrocketing prices and were looking for peace, order and stability. In this background, the National Convention drafted a new constitution in 1795. The new constitution created a bicameral legislature and a five-member executive – the Directory. Members of the Directory were moderates, not revolutionary idealists.

The new government had to face internal unrest of a population maddened by hunger and burdened by wars. It also had to face opposition from the Jacobins on the left and royalists from the right. Finances of the nation were in total disarray. A sagging economy and the threat from foreign countries, which had formed the Second Coalition, were other challenges before the Directory.

The Directory succeeded in suppressing the riots and counter revolutionary activities with the help of the army. But the army in turn gained prominence under one of its generals Napoleon Bonaparte. **Abbe Sieyes** – one of the Directors – joined hands with **Napoleon** and organised a coup dětat and overthrew the Directory in November 1799. They replaced the Directory with a three-member Consulate consisting of Napoleon, Abbe Sieyes and Roger Ducos as members.

> The **Estates General**: It was the general assembly of the three Estates before the Revolution.
>
> The **National Assembly**: It was composed of representatives of the Third Estate. Declaration of this assembly initiated the Revolution.
>
> The **Legislative Assembly** (1791–92): It was a unicameral house composed of all the three estates. It established a constitutional monarchy.
>
> The **National Convention** (1792–95): It succeeded the Legislative Assembly and its members were elected by universal male suffrage. It abolished monarchy and declared France a republic.
>
> The **Directory** (1795–99): It was the successor to the National Convention and consisted of five 'Executives'.
>
> The **Consulate** (1799–1804): It was the last phase in the republican experiment in Revolutionary France. The Consulate drafted a new constitution for France.

D. The Consulate (1799–1804)

The Consular constitution had the following features–

1. Executive power was in the hands of a three-member Consulate.
2. One of the Consuls was to be designated as the 'First consul' and had power to appoint all civilian and military officers and ministers and to make war and peace. Other two Consuls were to have merely consultative roles.

In 1799, Napoleon was chosen as the First Consul and Napoleon took measures to establish himself as the head of a more authoritarian and centralised government in France. As commented by a historian, '*In 1789, the French had created a Republic, under the name of a monarchy. Ten years later, they created a monarchy under the name of a Republic*'.

5. Napoleonic Era

Napoleonic Era refers to the period from the capture of power by Napoleon after a **coup** on 9 November 1799 till 28 June 1815, when he was finally defeated at the **Battle of Waterloo.** Napoleonic Era is considered as the last phase of the French Revolution during which he enforced political stability in France, implemented wide ranging reforms and sought to extent his authority and the ideals of the Revolution throughout Europe.

Napoleon

Napoleon Bonaparte was born on 15 August 1769 on the island of Corsica, as the son of a noble. He was an artillery officer when the French Revolution broke out. Making use of the opportunities presented by the Revolution, he rose through the ranks of the army and became a general at the age of 24. In 1796, he was given the command of the French army in Italy against the Austrians. Napoleon demonstrated a dazzling talent in military planning and leadership and conquered the Italian peninsula within a year. In 1798, he was appointed as the head of a military expedition to Egypt, to disrupt British trade with India. Stagnation of Egyptian campaign and development of political instability back home prompted Napoleon to return to France and make a bid for power.

He orchestrated a coup in November 1799, by surrounding the national legislature with his troops and forcing out most of its members. The remaining members voted to dissolve the Directory and to establish a Consulate in its place. The Consulate had three members and Napoleon became the **First Consul of the Republic.** As the First Consul, Napoleon monopolised power in his hands and in 1802 he was elected **the First Consul for Life.** During this period, Napoleon faced many assassination attempts led by the royalists and the Jacobins. Napoleon used these assassination attempts to justify creation of an imperial system and got himself declared **Napoleon I, Emperor of the French** on 2 December 1804 in a magnificent ceremony at the Cathedral of Notre Dame in Paris, which was given a colour of popular approval through a referendum. It is commented that Napoleon established **dictatorship by plebiscites** as he resorted to regular electoral consultations by conducting plebiscite among the French people on his way to the French throne.

It was a historical paradox that the French people who had led a bloody revolution against despotism of the Bourbon kings readily surrendered before another dictator. In reality, the French people had been worn out by the turmoil of the Revolution and political experiments that had followed and were looking for an able ruler. People believed quite sincerely that Bonaparte whether as Consul or Emperor would exert his authority and save them from the perils of anarchy, hence did not worry much about the loss of liberty. The astounding victories of Napoleon too had been testaments of his abilities which enabled him to win the support of the French people.

It is also worthy to note that the socio-economic injustices were the main causes behind the revolution than the political grievances and people were satiated when socio-economic ideals of the Revolution were preserved by Napoleon. Though not a revolutionary himself, Napoleon preserved many ideals of the Revolution and supported most of the ideas of the Enlightenment. He pursued a middle path by avoiding a return either to the days of Louis XVI or to radicalism, while at the same time preserving major achievements of the Revolution thus reconciling the French people to his rule. Hence, it is commented that, Napoleon was '*at once the heir of the Revolution and the product of the reaction against it*'.

A. Reforms of Napoleon

Napoleon's efforts were aimed at reconstruction and pacification of France, ravaged by the Revolution and wars. He could be considered as a ruler belonging to the 18th century enlightened despots for he believed in **centralisation, efficiency and uniformity** in administration. A strong **centralised government** was the tool Napoleon instituted for ensuring efficiency, political stability and strengthening of the state. A centralised administrative system in which officials reaching up to village linked the entire nation with the central government and enabled Napoleon to concentrate powers into his hands. By appointing Prefects, Sub-Prefects and Mayors at Departments and other local administrative units, Napoleon perfected centralisation and autocracy and restored efficiency and order. Napoleon opened up careers to talent, implemented equality under the law and established a state with secular outlook.

At the same time he rejected representative institutions and the idea of political liberty. He censored the press in order to prevent hostile criticism to his rule and to promote support for his policies. Further, Napoleon used **instruments of police state** – secret agents, arbitrary arrests and summary trials against his opponents. All such measures were to be adopted by the 20th century dictators much more ruthlessly, hence Napoleon was also a precursor to them.

The Code of Napoleon: Napoleonic Code was a civil code established by Napoleon in 1804. By this, Napoleon aimed at establishing a comprehensive system of laws by eliminating many of injustices of the time and to institutionalise many of the gains of the Revolution.

It consisted of clearly **written and accessible laws** which gave France a common system of law in place of numerous and conflicting laws existed in pre-revolutionary France. The Code consisted of over 2,000 articles. Napoleon incorporated many **ideals of the Revolution** such as equality before law, religious toleration, protection of property rights, abolition of serfdom, provisions for coherent family life in this Code and emerged himself as the real inheritor of the Revolution.

Certain general **principles of the Rule of Law** had been incorporated in the Napoleonic Code. It provided that laws could be in force only if, duly promulgated and officially published, thus doing away with chances of arbitrary and secret laws in force. It prohibited 'ex post facto' laws being implemented and provided for interpretation of laws by the judges. The Code required division of the inheritances among all sons and daughters as against assigning all property to the eldest son which was the practice in feudal era.

At the same time, the Code reflected patriarchal view as it assigned a legally subordinate and dependent position to women and children on their husbands or fathers. Certain other provisions of the Code such as inferior position of wives in matters of property, divorce and adultery, unequal role envisaged for workers in their dealings with their employers also show that Napoleon was not free from the pulls, pressures and prejudices of the period. Similarly, the freedom of speech and of the press, established during the Revolution, were limited under this Code as it gave importance to order and authority over individual rights. Its provisions for drafting of contracts and forming stock companies and prohibitions on trade unions were supportive to business class.

Greatness of this Code can be understood from the fact that it had been adopted by much of the European countries and still form the basis of the legal system in many countries world over. Napoleon himself had commented that 'My true glory is not to have won forty battles…but what will live forever, is my Civil Code'.

Educational Reforms: Napoleon restructured the education sector in France. His educational reforms were a synthesis of the best elements of the Enlightenment and the Revolution. Napoleon was pioneer in establishing a system of **secular and public education** that featured scholarships and strict discipline and thus laid the foundation of a modern system of education in France which was later adopted by a wider world.

1. Napoleon made education secular and a state responsibility. Education was placed under the state control unlike in the past when education was provided by religious orders.
2. Introduced standardised curriculum.
3. Founded University of France and French was made the only official language.
4. Special attention was given to centres of advanced studies such as 'Ecole Polytechnique' which provided both military expertise and research in science.
5. All students were taught the sciences along with classical and modern languages. For Napoleon, education was not just a method of transmission of knowledge to new generations but also a way for indoctrination of obedience and loyalty to the state.

Economic Reforms: Economic reforms of Napoleon were aimed at two objectives, the first to strengthen the finances of the country and the other to retain the support of the bourgeoisie, the group that supported his capture of power.

1. Napoleon initiated efficient system of tax collection and established a national banking system including the founding of the **Bank of France.**
2. He dismissed corrupt officials. Graduates were appointed to public offices on the basis of merit and established government public schools known as 'Lycees' to ensure supply of trained graduates to the government.
3. For the promotion of industry and commerce he instituted loans, constructed roads and bridges and implemented favourable tariff measures.
4. Abolished the guilds of merchants and craftsmen to facilitate entrepreneurship.
5. To prevent further revolution due to scarcity of bread, food items were provided at low prices.

In addition, measures were taken to stimulate employment, and peasants were permitted to keep the lands they obtained during the Revolution. All these measures ensured him the support of large section of his subjects.

Religious Reforms: In religious sphere Napoleon disregarded the changes introduced by the Revolution and tried to fill the gap between the state and the Catholic Church that existed since the Revolution. Both the lay followers and the clergy had resented the changes introduced by the Revolution vis-à-vis with the Church in France.

Hence, in 1801, Napoleon negotiated an agreement with Pope Pius VII which is known as the **Concordat of 1801** by which Catholicism was declared as the religion of the great majority of France (not as the official religion of the state). The Pope in return concurred with the confiscation of the church property by the state during the Revolution. Bishops were to be nominated by the state and had to take an oath of fidelity to the government but were to be invested by the Pope. Catholic clergy returned from exile. Further, it provided for complete religious freedom to all sects.

Thus, the Concordat of 1801 recognised the influence of the Church, but rejected Church control in state's affairs. It secured Napoleon the support of the mass of France who were devoted to their Catholic Church and of people who were owners of the former church lands and also of the religious minorities. Even after the Concordat the balance of the Church–State relations had tilted in favour of Napoleon who opined that 'skillful conquerors have not got entangled with priests, they can both contain them and use them'. This way Napoleon made a political use of religion.

Social Reforms: Napoleon's reconciliatory approach was also well evident in repealing of the decrees against the 'emigres' and against the non-jurying clergy who were admitted back to the country. Moreover, by destroying all aristocratic privileges based on birth, by creating an aristocracy of merit in the form of **'Legion of Honour'** (a title to be conferred by the state) and throwing open careers to talent Napoleon inaugurated mobility in French society.

At the same time Napoleon was opposed to the idea of liberty under the guise of which France had been pushed to chaos. He also discarded with another principle of the revolution – the principle of popular election and the idea of self-government and replaced it with selection of officials. Napoleon thus consolidated the Revolution of its more valid fruits and removed frictional contours of it and emerged at once as heir to the Revolution and at the same time a product of the reaction against it. All these measurers attested Napoleon's statesmanship and administrative acumen.

Pro-Revolutionary measures of Napoleon: He emphasised equality in social and fiscal matters (as evident in the Code of Napoleon and in the modernisation of tax system which prohibited tax exemptions to clergy and nobility), weakened clerical power, secularised education, granted religious freedom, threw careers open to talent thus erasing aristocratic privileges.

Anti-Revolutionary measures of Napoleon: He opposed political liberty, curtailed freedom of speech and press, deprived local bodies of self-governing powers and opposed nationalism while dealing with foreign states.

Reconciliatory measures of Napoleon: He sympathetically treated the émigrés and the non-jurying clergy, signed the Concordat to heal the wounds of the Catholics while at the same time showing toleration to all religious sects.

B. Expansion of the Napoleonic Empire in Europe

In a series of wars collectively known as the **Napoleonic Wars**, Napoleon extended French power and influence in Europe. By 1810, his domination over the Continent was complete except for the Balkans. This Grand Empire which is also referred to as **the First French Empire** consisted of annexed territories, vassal states and cowed allies and it 'stretched without interruption across the continent and from sea to sea'.

The **annexed territories** included Belgium, the left bank of the Rhine, Rome, Geneva, coastal areas of Germany, Dalmatian Coast and large areas of Italy. The **vassal states** of the Grand Empire were the kingdom of Holland ruled by Napoleon's brother Louis Bonaparte, the kingdom of Naples by another brother Joseph and the kingdom of Westphalia ruled by his yet another brother Jerome and the kingdoms of Spain and Italy. It also included the 16 German states formed into the Confederation of Rhine (1806), by bringing German princes together, who were part of the Holy German Empire and the Grand Duchy of Warsaw (1807) formed by adding Polish lands to territory taken out of Prussia. By creating vassal states Napoleon encircled France with a protective ring of states that were subordinate and supportive to him.

The Grand Empire of Napoleon also consisted of defeated and **cowed allies** – Austria, Prussia and Russia, Sweden and Denmark.

The Grand Empire enabled Napoleon to emerge as the master of Europe and to make Paris the political capital of Europe. Now, the continent of Europe was subjected to the will of a single man. Peoples of different ethnicity, language, religion and culture lived under the same laws and marched in the same armies. Thus, the ideal of a universal empire though desired by many had been almost attained by Napoleon even though for a short period of time.

C. Influence of Napoleon in the European Context

Napoleon extended the ideas of the Revolution beyond the borders of France. He conquered extensive territories in Europe with the help of huge conscripted armies, infusing them with the ideas of the Revolution – 'liberty, equality and nationalism' and a commitment to fight for the glory of France. The Grand Empire of Napoleon was the Revolution in its European context as it destroyed anomalies of the 'Old Regime' and paved way for transplanting ideas and institutions from France to other parts of Europe.

In the areas where Napoleon's rule extended feudalism and serfdom were abolished, Code of Napoleon was introduced, careers were opened to talent, effective civil service was organised and above all equality of all before the law was implemented.

Other measures of Napoleon included abolition of guilds and internal tolls, introduction of uniform weights and measures and construction of roads and bridges all of which gave fillip to trade and commerce.

Promotion of secular education and improvement of public health were prioritised. Manorial courts and Church courts were abolished. All of these fostered the modernisation of the 19th century Europe. Thus, the fundamental ideas of modern state – such as equality before the law, meritocracy, religious toleration, secular education, sound finance, and codification of laws and so on – had been championed, consolidated and geographically extended by Napoleon. In that sense though the political existence of the Napoleonic Empire was short lived, its impact was monumental and everlasting. For these reasons, many sections of Europeans, especially the aspiring bourgeoisie and progressive youngsters, welcomed Napoleon as a liberator and it is aptly said that the Napoleonic Empire was not an interruption but an extension of the Revolution and was the last part of it.

In other ways too Napoleonic rule influenced the course of European history tremendously. By introducing administrative centralisation in Italy, the Napoleonic rule gave **fillip to the unification of Italy** in the 19th century. Similarly, Napoleon in many ways could be considered as **one of the founders of modern Germany.** Firstly, Napoleon dissolved the Holy German Empire and reduced the number of German states from 300 to 38. Secondly, as a by-product of the French occupation strong currents of German nationalism began to take shape in Germany. Moreover, in Germany the provisions of the Napoleonic Code liberated people from the shackles of feudalism and ensured human conditions and social freedom, which in turn paved way for the resurgence of Germany as a unified country in latter-half of the 19th century.

D. Europe against Napoleon

The revolutionary ideals and expansionist plans of France were a threat to the Old Regime in Europe. Hence, European powers under Austria, Prussia, Russia and Britain formed coalitions aimed at containing expansion of the French Republic and restoration of monarchy in France.

Following were some important developments in this regard. Napoleon defeated Austria in the Battle of Marengo (June 1800) and signed the **Treaty of Luneville** (February 1801) by which Austria recognised the France's right to natural frontiers and confirmed Napoleon's conquests. He signed the **Treaty of Amiens** (1802) with Great Britain ending the hostilities between the two. By the treaty Britain agreed to withdraw troops from the recently conquered overseas French colonies and promised non-intervention in continental affairs and the French assured stoppage of its expansionist policies.

Between 1805 and 1807, Napoleon won decisive battles against Austria, Prussia and Russia. Napoleon inflicted a shattering defeat on the combined armies of Austria and Russia at **Austerlitz** (December 1805). Napoleon signed the **Treaty of Pressburg** (26 December 1805) with Austria by which Austrian influence in Italy and Germany were sharply reduced.

In Germany, Napoleon reduced influence of two great states – Austria and Prussia. He created the **Confederation of the Rhine** (1806) composed of Bavaria, Württemberg, Baden and 13 minor states of southern Germany. This Confederation put an end to the Holy Roman Empire and also acted as the buffer between France on the one hand and Austria and Prussia on the other.

Next, Napoleon defeated Prussia in two battles at Jena and Auerstedt (October 1806) and Russia at the Battle of Friedland (June 1807) and signed the **Treaties of Tilsit** (July 1807) with them. By this treaty Prussia had to cede its territory on the west and east, out of which Napoleon created the Kingdom of Westphalia and the Grand Duchy of Warsaw, respectively. By the Treaty, Russia became an ally of France and agreed to join the Continental System.

E. The Fall of Napoleon

Treaty of Tilsit was the peak of Napoleon's life. From this short-lived peak Napoleon slid downhill from defeat to dethronement and finally to deportation. Following are the series of developments that led to the final defeat of Napoleon.

The English factor and the Continental System: Napoleon's most resolute opponent was Britain, whom he failed to subdue. Britain was also the central force in encouraging and financing the coalitions against France. The Treaty of Amiens had been a failure in establishing a lasting peace. In spite of this treaty, hostilities were revived between France and Britain, as the steps taken by Napoleon such as imposition of high protective tariffs to eliminate the British competition, revival of colonial policy by sending military expeditions to San Domingo (Haiti), Louisiana, India and to Egypt, were greatly alarming for the English.

Establishment of a European hegemony by France was against the interest of Britain. On the other hand, Napoleon was not ready to settle with anything less than a French leadership in the European continent.

> The **San-Domingo** was a French colony on the Caribbean island of Hispaniola. During the French Revolutionary Wars the colony managed to acquire political autonomy under a de facto dictator Toussaint L'Ouverture. To recover the colony, Napoleon sent an expedition but it ended in failure. In 1803, all the French troops left the island and the people, majority of whom were slaves, declared an independent republic called **Haiti** in 1804. A related incident to the Haitian Revolution was the **sale of Louisiana,** a large land mass under the French control in North America, to the United States. Napoleon had acquired this territory from Spain in 1800. France's inability to put down the rebellion in San-Domingo prompted Napoleon to sell Louisiana to the United States for a price of $15 million in 1803. By this sale Napoleon aimed twofold objectives – to fund his military operations in Europe and to punish Britain, the enemy of France. Napoleon predicted, 'The sale assures forever the power of the United States, and I have given England a rival who, sooner or later, will humble her pride'. As a result of the purchase of Louisiana, the size of the United States was doubled.

The English navy being the '**mistress on the seas**', it was impossible for Napoleon to defeat Britain in a naval war. The French defeat at the hands of the British Admiral Nelson in the Battle of Trafalgar in 1805 had amply demonstrated this point. France lacked sufficient naval strength to invade Britain. On the other, the British government had declared a naval blockade of the French and French coasts in May 1806. In this background Napoleon planned to destroy Britain, by a **trade embargo** which he called the Continental System.

The Continental System was intended to prevent all trade and communication between Continental Europe and Britain. It aimed to bring Britain, which was in Napoleon's opinion a **'nation of shopkeepers'** into submission by indirect means than fighting a war. As a result of the Industrial Revolution, Britain had emerged as the manufacturing and business hub of Europe. His strategy was to prohibit all countries under the French control from buying British goods.

To implement the plan, Napoleon issued the **Berlin Decree in 1806** declaring blockade of Britain and prohibiting imports of British goods at the ports of France and that of the countries under her control. In 1807, he issued the **Milan Decree** by which any ship was to be seized if it touched any British port. These two decrees formed the basis of the Continental System. The Continental System was one of the greatest blunders of Napoleon and it marked the beginning of his downfall.

The Continental System proved to be failure as–

1. First and foremost, the system **could not subdue Britain.** Though initially there were some damages to the British trade, the British traders overcame the embargo by engaging in smuggling goods in to the continental Europe and by developing replacement trade with Americas.

2. Second, in France itself **the System backfired.** Ship building and other industries that relied on overseas markets declined and many industries had to close down.
3. The system punished European lands dependent on British goods as **prices of the essential items** shot up creating discontent among the masses.
4. France or any other country in the continent did not have a naval strength to implement the system or to **prevent smuggling** and also to take up the challenge of the mighty navy of Britain.
5. Loss of Britain as a trading partner **hit the economies of the allies of France** and the governments in these countries moved away from the System thus weakening of Napoleon's coalition. For example, Russia reopened trade with Britain in 1810 and withdrew from the System.
6. **Bourgeoisie** who were generally supportive of Napoleonic rule now became anti-Napoleon as the system caused economic distress and was against their financial interests.
7. In order to enforce this system, Napoleon **had to fight successive wars** which exhausted his resources both in men and material. The occupation of Spain and the invasion of Russia were two instances in this context.
8. **Occupation of Rome** and imprisonment of the Pope by Napoleon for his refusal to accept the System turned the Catholics against Napoleon.
9. Portugal refused to join the System leading to the occupation of Portugal by Napoleon in 1807. The people of Portugal rose in rebellion against the French occupation adding trouble to Napoleon which gave birth to the **Peninsular War** leading to the failure of not only of the Continental System but also of Napoleon himself.

The Peninsular War 1807–14: In this background Napoleon's directive to implement the Continental System and to close her ports to British trade was not met by Portugal, an old ally of England. In retaliation, Napoleon in conjunction with Spanish troops occupied Portugal in November 1807. In response to an appeal by Portugal, English army under Lieutenant General Sir Arthur Wellesley landed in Portugal in 1808 and Portugal became a British base. The conflict now became a major war involving the armies of Napoleon, United Kingdom and Portugal for the control of the Iberian Peninsula, hence is known as the Peninsular War. To make matters worse for Napoleon, the people of Spain rose in rebellion against the occupation of their country by France. Thus, the Peninsular War overlaps with the Spanish War of Independence.

The Spanish Ulcer: Spain had been an ally of France in its fight against Britain. But fissures appeared in the alliance after the defeat of the combined French and Spanish fleets by the British at the **Battle of Trafalgar** in 1805. Spain resented both the loss of its fleet at the Trafalgar and the Continental System which was forced upon it by Napoleon. Now, under the pretext of Portugal conquest, Napoleon poured French troops in Spain. The Spanish people protested this action. Taking advantage of a succession dispute between the Spanish king Charles IV and his son Ferdinand VII, Napoleon captured power in Spain in 1808 and appointed his brother Joseph Bonaparte on the Spanish throne.

By this blatant violation of justice and deceitful capture of the Spanish throne, Napoleon awakened the spirit of the Spanish nation – 'a nation in arms'. Scared of French liberalism, emotionally attached to the Spanish monarchy and faithful to the Church the clergy, nobles and the overwhelmingly peasant population rose in rebellion against the invaders. This popular revolt against Joseph Bonaparte is known as the Spanish War of Independence.

Finally, after many military setbacks Joseph Bonaparte abdicated in 1813 and fled to France. Ferdinand VII was restored on the Spanish throne. In this war Napoleon lost more than 3,00,000 men. The years of fighting in Spain against resistance, guerrilla raids and ambushes caused heavy drain on French resources which led Napoleon to characterise the episode as 'Spanish Ulcer'.

Reasons for the French Failure

1. First and foremost, the Spanish struggle was a war of the people ready to sacrifice their life than to suffer loss of their freedom. A 'nation in arms' fighting as a single body was much formidable than an army of professional soldiers. Spain amply proved the dictum that 'a whole people is more powerful than disciplined troops'.
2. Mountainous, poor and rugged terrain of Spain made sustained war by a large army difficult as

transportation and procurement of provisions were extremely difficult.

3. Adoption of guerrilla warfare by the Spaniards multiplied the hardships of Napoleon's army.
4. The support provided by the British army and endurance, generalship and tact of Duke of Wellington too were factors which enhanced the spirit of resistance of the Spaniards against the French forces.
5. Napoleon could not personally control all the manoeuvres of his forces in Spain and the task was mostly handled by his generals who were mutually jealous.

The 'Spanish Ulcer' proved to be a heavy blow to the Napoleonic Empire and Spain became the graveyard of Napoleonic dreams. It caused harm to the Napoleonic Empire more ways than one.

1. The long war against Spain drained Napoleon's treasury.
2. Spanish insurrection compelled Napoleon to set aside a huge army in Spain leading to the dispersal of his forces and attention leading to his failure in other areas.
3. By providing an opportunity and a foothold to Britain to interfere in the continental affairs, it reversed the advantages gained by Napoleon against the British in early part of his career. The base in Spain enabled Britain to launch attack on southern France.
4. By initiating a domino effect the Spanish struggle inspired subjugated people of other countries to resist French occupation.

Russian Campaign: Russia had been an ally of Napoleon since the Peace of Tilsit (1807). But the relation between Napoleon and Czar Alexander deteriorated on account of:

1. Napoleon's creation of the Grand Duchy of Warsaw was against the interest of Czar. The Russian ruler feared that the revival of Polish power may lead to Polish nationalism and French influence in Russia's western border as threats to Russia's interests.
2. The matrimonial alliance between Napoleon and the Austrian Emperor's daughter Marie Louise strained the relation between Napoleon and Czar further.
3. Russia's illicit trade with Britain in violation of the Continental System aggravated the crisis.
4. Rupture was complete in 1810, with Czar issuing an edict modifying his adhesion to the Continental System.
5. Napoleon's insatiable hunger for territory and power too was a factor.

In June 1812, Napoleon invaded Russia with a Grand Army of more than 6,00,000 soldiers, the largest army he had ever commanded and expected a smashing victory. The Russians instead of fighting retreated and lured the enemy farther and farther into Russia far from their line of supply and resorted to a **scorched earth** – devastating an area while withdrawing policy. The Russians offered battle outside Moscow on 7 September 1812. This battle, the **Battle of Borodino**, is considered as the bloodiest day in the battle history until then. Even though the French won the battle, it was at a high cost and proved indecisive which made Napoleon to comment that 'the French showed themselves to be worthy of victory, but the Russian showed themselves worthy of being invincible'.

After seven days, the Grand Army of Napoleon, whose number had been greatly reduced by disease, exhaustion, desertion and intermittent fights, entered Moscow which had been set on fire by the withdrawing Russian army. Napoleon expected the Czar to surrender. But the Tsar remained intransigent and Napoleon decided to retreat before the onset of harsh winter. The Grand Army of Napoleon which had entered into an unfamiliar terrain and exposed to harsh winter was put to unbearable hard ships of hunger and exhaustion and to the harassing attacks of the Cossack guerrillas. Hotly pursued by the Russians, the remnants of the Grand Army reached back in France in December 1812. The ill-fated Russian expedition was a severe blow to the military might of Napoleon.

The German War: The German War took place close on the heels of Napoleon's disastrous Russian campaign and was also inspired from it. Subjugation of the German states by Napoleon had created hatred of the French rule and arousal of national feeling among the German people. The **Treaty of Tilsit** had completely humiliated Prussia. Reforms such as abolition of serfdom, national conscription, opening of positions in army on merit instead of birth, popular education, establishment of local self-government, abolition of cruel punishment in army, etc., had awakened the patriotic spirit and a determination to liberate Prussia from the yoke of Napoleon. Soon insurrections took place and cities like Berlin and Dresden were recovered from the French.

A new coalition was formed by Austria, Prussia, Russia, Spain, Portugal, Sweden, the United Kingdom and a number of German states in order to fight **the War of Liberation** against Napoleon. Napoleon mustered a new army by recruiting over-aged veterans and college boys as he had lost his experienced soldiers in the Russian debacle. In 1813 October, the allied forces defeated Napoleon at **Leipzig** after a three-day battle known as the '**Battle of the Nations**'. The **Battle of Nations** was the largest battle in European history before the First World War. Napoleon was offered peace on the basis of natural boundaries of France – the Rhine, the Alps and the Pyrenees, which he refused. Thereafter, allied forces attacked Paris and in April 1814 Napoleon was forced to abdicate. As per the **Treaty of Fontainebleau,** Napoleon agreed to retire to the **Island of Elba** – a tiny island off the coast of Italy. In France, Louis XVIII of the Bourbon dynasty and brother of Louis XVI was placed on the throne and a Congress to settle the affairs of Europe was convened at Vienna.

While the allies were discussing the future course of Europe and the French people were growing with discontent against the reactionary policies of Louis XVIII, Napoleon descended in France to test his luck once again, or rather to put his never-say-die attitude into practice. Napoleon did not believe that it as his destiny to die at Elba. Landing on the French coast near Cannes on 1 March 1815, he entered Paris to a hero's welcome and his old soldiers joined him. Louis XVIII fled to Belgium and Napoleon was again Emperor of France. The allied forces led by the Duke of Wellington of Britain and Field Marshal Blucher of Prussia organised a strong army and Napoleon was defeated at **Waterloo, in Belgium**, on 18 June 1815. This period from Napoleon's restoration to his final deportation is known as **the Hundred Days.** Napoleon was taken prisoner and was exiled to **St. Helena**, a lonely island in the South Atlantic, off the coast of Southern Africa. Here living a lonely exiled life, he wrote his memoirs and died in 1821.

F. Causes of Napoleon's Defeat

Insatiable Ambition: One of the important causes of the downfall of Napoleon was his insatiable ambition which almost blinded him from realising what is possible and what is not. This led him from one war to another and from conquering one country after another and thus extending his empire far and wide which multiplied his challenges and problems.

Nature of the Empire: Force was the sole binding factor that kept Napoleon's empire together. It failed in enlisting loyalty of his subjects. The despotic nature of his rule created reactions from the subjects over whom he ruled and the rulers whom he had subjugated. Once these forces stood in unity, the downfall of Napoleon was just a matter of time.

Continental System: The Continental System initiated with a grandiose purpose of making himself the master of the continent became a significant factor in Napoleon's downfall. The System caused hardships to people in the form of scarcity of goods, price rise and dislocation of trade which made him unpopular. To enforce the System he had to attack Portugal, had to conquer Spain, had to fight against Russia and also had to quarrel with the Pope. As these episodes started unfolding one by one, Napoleon had great difficulty in meeting the requirements of men and material in spite of his indomitable optimism.

Russian Debacle: The failed Russian campaign destroyed not only the army of Napoleon but also his reputation as an invincible military genius. Napoleon's debacle in Russia triggered a major shift in European situation and emboldened his enemies to join their hands once again to fight Napoleon. The Russian campaign caused additional drain of his resources as the conflict in Spain had not been abated and with the Russian campaign Napoleon committed the blunder of making war on two fronts, that too far apart.

Maltreatment of Pope: In 1809, Pope Pius VII was placed under house arrest for his refusal to close the Papal ports to the British ships. The humiliating treatment to the Pope created a shock wave throughout the Catholic world and undermined the moral foundations of the Napoleonic rule.

Hostility of England: Another factor was persistent hostility of England towards Napoleon. England, with her supremacy on the seas, encouraged the enemies of Napoleon and engaged in fighting against Napoleon till his final defeat. It was this enmity towards Britain that propelled Napoleon to launch his ill-conceived Continental System and attack on Portugal. It is also worth mentioning that it was the British commander the Duke of Wellington that played leading role in the defeat of Napoleon in the Waterloo.

Nationalism: It was the concept of Nationalism that made France invincible in Europe during the revolutionary period. But later on, France itself was beaten with the same weapon by the other nationalities. Directly or indirectly the French Revolution had caused dissemination of the concept of nationalism in other parts of Europe. This national spirit and the national pride provoked anti-Napoleonic wave in subjugated nations like Spain, Germany and Russia and proved to be one of the most potent causes of Napoleon's downfall.

6. Legacy of the French Revolution

1. The French Revolution left ever-lasting legacy in the history of the world. It transformed the dynastic ancient regime in France into a modern state which was liberal, rational and secular. It destroyed the old political, socio-economic and cultural structures and replaced them with new ideas, ideals and institutions. Monarchical absolutism, aristocratic privileges, feudalistic practices were destroyed and a modern state based on national, liberal, rational and secular ideals was inaugurated first in France and then followed in by other countries.
2. The central elements of the Revolution were **'Liberty, Equality and Fraternity'** and **'The Declaration of the Rights of Man and the Citizen'.**

   Liberty – both personal and political since then became a universal creed and found recognised and expressed in abolition of serfdom, enfranchisement of the commoners, freedom of speech, abolition of divine right to rule, etc. Equality – in both legal and social terms as set by the French Revolution through examples were emulated by nations all over the world as marks of advanced human civilisation. Fraternity emphasised harmony and community bonding of the people and put forward the argument that any man may aspire to liberty and equality, but he cannot achieve it without the assistance of other men. This concept of fraternity was to influence political organisations and ideologies especially those with socialist leanings since then the world over.
3. It destroyed aristocratic privileges based on birth which was now replaced by privileges of property and wealth.
4. Individuals, who were subjects of the king till then, now were made citizen of the nation with specific rights and duties. The **idea of nationalism** was the backbone of the French unity during the Revolution. The revolutionaries viewed nation as an association of free citizens living under a common law and as the sole source of sovereignty.

   On the other, it was the same nationalism that released a wave of resistance by the European states against France. National patriotism became the leading spirit behind the unification efforts of Italy and Germany in the 19th century and freedom movements in many countries like India. It may also be stated that nationalism when developed in the militant form was to unleash forces of destruction as witnessed in the World Wars.
5. The use of plebiscite, as a device to claim legitimacy to disputed issues, traces its origin to this period. A number of plebiscites were conducted both during the Revolution and under Napoleon to give legal sanction to arbitrary measures. For example, in 1802, Napoleon became Consulate for life and claimed legitimacy to his action by a plebiscite in which an unusually large majority voted for him.
6. The revolutionary France also witnessed the origin of the modern **totalitarian** states with the establishment of the Jacobin Republic in 1793. The Jacobin Republic with a powerful executive used terror as an instrument of state policy and justified their actions in the name of the state which were common with the totalitarian regimes of the 20th century.
7. Finally, it can be said that the most important legacy of the French Revolution was the Revolution itself as it marked establishment of free and egalitarian society and became inspiration for further revolutions as that of 1830, 1848 and even in the reconstruction of the post-colonial world after the Second World War. 'The French Revolution differed from other revolutions in being not merely national, for it aimed at benefitting all humanity'.

SUMMARY

Causes – Political – monarchical absolutism with characteristics such as authoritarianism, autocracy and inefficiency; Administrative – incompetent, ineffective and complex; Social – division of society into unequal and antagonistic groups or Estates; Economic – heavy burden of taxes, huge public debt, sharp rise in cost of living and shortage of food grains and other essentials; Role of ideas – thinkers and scholars gave shape and substance to the existing discontent. Three prominent personalities in this context were Montesquieu, Voltaire and Rousseau.

Origin and development of the French Revolution – Summoning of the Estates General on 5 May 1789, declaration by the Third Estate as the National Assembly on 17 June and the Tennis Court Oath on 20 June were the three developments with which the French Revolution began. The French Revolution developed in different stages – the Moderate Stage 1789–1792, the Radical Stage 1792–1795, the period of the Directory 1795–1799 and finally the period of the Consulate 1799–1804.

Napoleonic Era – It was the period from 1799, the year Napoleon captured power in a coup and up to 1815 when he was finally defeated at Waterloo. During this period, he built up a huge empire known as the Napoleonic Empire in series of wars known as the Napoleonic Wars. In his empire Napoleon implemented reforms such as centralisation and measures for efficiency and uniformity in administration. He also introduced the Code of Napoleon and implemented educational, economic, religious and social reforms.

Fall of Napoleon – The English factor and the Continental System, the Peninsular War, the Spanish Ulcer, Russian Campaign and the German War were the series of developments that caused the fall of Napoleon.

QUESTIONS OF PREVIOUS YEARS CIVIL SERVICES EXAMINATION

1. The philosophers and thinkers may have laid the foundation of the French Revolution, but it was precipitated by social and economic reasons. Explain. (2023)
2. 'The codification of French Law was perhaps the most enduring of Napoleon's achievements'. Critically examine. (2022)
3. Napoleon's continental system may be reckoned as the greatest blunder and may be described as a 'monument of misdirected energy'. Critically examine. (2021)
4. 'The causes of the French Revolution of 1789 included both long-term and structural factors, as well as more immediate events'. Critically examine. (2020)
5. 'Napoleon was not a revolutionary but he solidified many of the revolutionary changes of 1789–1791 and he himself supported most of the ideas and proposals of Enlightenment philosophers'. Substantiate. (2020)
6. Explain how the foundations of the modern world were laid by the American and French Revolutions. (2019)
7. How far did the Napoleonic preferential stance to help out the French economy result in embroiling France in continental conflicts? (2019)

8. 'The spirit behind the great reforms of Napoleon's Consulate at home was the transference of the methods of Bonaparte the general to the task of Bonaparte the statesman.' (2017)
9. Critically examine the statement that the French Revolution was not caused by the French philosophers but by the conditions of national life and by the mistakes of the government. (2016)
10. 'The multiple contradictions that quickly undermined the new edifice had been expressed even before the meeting of the Estates General in France. The internal conflict among Estates had manifested itself.' (2015)
11. 'The Continental blockade was a misconceived idea of economically defeating Great Britain.' (2015)
12. The connection between the philosophers' ideas and the outbreak of the French Revolution (1789) is somewhat remote and indirect. (2012)
13. How did Napoleon fuse the France of the ancient regime with the France of the post-revolutionary era? (2012)
14. To what extent did Napoleon's economic war with England become his undoing? (2010)
15. No event as encompassing as the French Revolution occurs in an intellectual vacuum. (2007)
16. The writings of the philosophers had a tremendous influence on the minds of people and created a revolutionary awakening in their minds and formed the intellectual creed of the French Revolution. (2005)
17. The French Revolution attacked privileges and not property. (2003)
18. If monarchical misrule ignited the French Revolution, lofty ideas both inspired and sustained it. (2002)
19. The Napoleonic Empire was doomed because of its inherent and self-defeating contradictions. Elucidate (2001)
20. How did Napoleon Bonaparte heal the wounds of France inflicted by the Revolution and correct the errors perpetrated by its leaders. (2000)
21. To some extent the American War of Independence inspired the French Revolution. (1999)
22. The French Revolution sought to remove both "the religious and secular props of the existing social order". Elucidate (1996)
23. Napoleon was the child of the Revolution but in many ways he reversed the aims and principles of the movement from which he sprang. (1992)

CHAPTER 6

The 19th-Century World

In this Chapter

1. Introduction

In Europe, the initial years subsequent to the dethronement of Napoleon had been that of conservatism and of efforts to restore the Old Regime. In the United States, the 19th century was a period of territorial expansion, consolidation and reconstruction after the tumultuous years of the Civil War. In the second-half of the century, the Western powers began a new stage in imperial activities inaugurating the era of New Imperialism. All these developments make the 19th century one of the important periods of the modern world.

2. Europe After Napoleon

A. The Congress of Vienna

After defeating Napoleon, European rulers looked for peace and stability and aimed at establishing a new European order based on collective security. For the purpose, series of conferences known as the Congress of Vienna were held in Vienna during the winter of 1814–15. Though most of the European states participated (more than 200 states and principalities), the four 'Great Powers', **Prussia, Russia, England and Austria**, the states that took the lead in defeating napoleon, decided the outcome of the Congress.

The Congress represented the Old Regime. Opposition to revolutionary ideals of liberty, equality and fraternity and fear of the new spirit of nationalism and democracy was the basic nature of the Congress. Territorial resettlement and suppression of liberal ideas had been its main objectives. With the **Treaty of Vienna** (June 1815) and the **Treaty of Paris** (November 1815) territorial settlements were signed.

The Chief Minister of Austria, Prince Klemens von **Metternich**, was the most influential in the conference. He had set three objectives for the Congress – containment of France, creation of balance of power and restoration of legitimate royal families on the thrones in Europe.

The **Age of Metternich** (1815–48): During this period, European politics had been dominated by Metternich, the Chief Minister of Austria. His period was characterised by-

1. Maintenance of status quo
2. Opposition to liberalism, democracy and nationalism
3. Intervention in internal affairs of countries to enforce the above aims

Metternich's measures were aimed at protecting the interests of Austria, an empire with a curious mix of many states and nationalities. Emergence

of liberal and national feelings would threaten its existence, hence Metternich followed a reactionary policy. To insulate Austria he instituted elaborate espionage, strict censorship of the press and rigid supervision of education.

a. Containment of France

This was to be achieved by surrounding France with strong countries. For this purpose, the Congress took the following decisions.

1. A **German Confederation** of 39 German states under the presidency of Austria was created.
2. The **Kingdom of Netherlands** was created by uniting the Austrian Netherlands (Belgium) and the Dutch Republic to check France in the north.
3. **Switzerland** was enlarged and its neutrality was established as an independent nation.
4. **Prussia** was strengthened as a check to France in the east by granting the Rhineland to it.
5. In Italy, the **Kingdom of Piedmont-Sardinia** was strengthened by the addition of Genoa to act as a barrier against France in the southeast.
6. The Congress also pushed back the **boundaries of France** to that of 1789, that is, as existed at the time of the Revolution and also imposed a huge indemnity on her.

b. Balance of Power

At the same time, the Congress neither humiliated France nor left it powerless. A humiliated France would opt for revenge and a powerless France would encourage some other country to emerge strong. Hence, the system devised at the Congress was to diminish the power of France, at the same time not to permit any other country to emerge sufficiently strong to overpower another. For example, to prevent Russia emerging stronger than others, Poland was divided up between Austria, Prussia and Russia.

c. Legitimacy

The principle of legitimacy meant that the legitimate sovereignty belonged to the old ruling families whom Napoleon had overthrown, hence their restoration. Consequently, ruling families of France, Spain and Portugal and of the states in Central Europe and Italy were restored to power. The Pope was also restored to his territorial possessions in Italy.

At the same time, the Congress neglected the legitimacy principle in the case of smaller states such as Venice and the German states as they were placed either under Prussia or Austria. In their desire to secure balance of power and dynastic interests, the Congress disregarded the new forces of liberalism and nationalism and neglected the interests of people. To prevent nationalism, Germany was divided into large number of states. Italian peninsula was reduced to a mere 'geographical expression' as it was divided into seven parts – Lombardy-Venetia, Naples-Sicily, Modena, Parma, Piedmont-Sardinia, Tuscany and the Papal States placed under different powers. The Austrian Empire was a polyglot mixture of German, Hungarian and Slavic populations and Russia consisted of multi-nationalities such as Finns, Poles, Ukrainians and hundreds of other minor groups.

The 'Big Four' also secured for themselves the best fruits of the settlement. For example, in order to make **Austria** strong in Central Europe, she was given Venetia and Lombardy – two richest provinces in Italy. Also, by restoring members of Austrian royal family to the Italian states of Parma, Modena and Tuscany, Austria was made a powerful force in Italy. The Federal Diet of the German Confederation was also placed under the presidency of Austria. **Prussia** acquired some Polish territory, Pomerania and territories on the Rhine. **Russia** retained Finland, Lithuania and eastern Poland. **England** gained Helgoland in the North Sea, Malta and Ionian Islands in the Mediterranean and Cape Colony in Africa and Ceylon in Asia from the Dutch. With all these measures, the Congress proved to be a 'meeting of the victors to divide the spoils of the conquered'.

d. Evaluation of the Congress of Vienna

The final outcome of the Congress of Vienna was **destruction of ideals of liberalism and nationalism** and **restoration of conservatism and monarchy** in European life. All major European states were now under monarchs, ranging from constitutional monarchy of England to despotic autocracy of Russia.

These powers also created alliances – **Quadruple Alliance** and **Holy Alliance** to preserve the ideals of the Old Regime. The **Quadruple Alliance** was formed in November 1816 by Britain, Prussia, Austria and Russia to act as the basis of **the Concert of Europe**. It was intended to coordinate the conservative efforts to eliminate any trace of Bonapartism or revolution in the continent and to maintain the Vienna settlements by the use of force. In 1818, France was admitted making it **Quintuple Alliance**.

The Alliance provided for periodical meetings of the diplomats of these countries thus initiating a system of '**diplomacy by conference**'. This period is also known as the '**Age of Congresses**' as many periodical meetings such as Aix-la-Chapelle (1818), Troppau (1820) and Verona (1822) were held to deliberate on European developments.

In the years following the Vienna settlements, the Concert of Europe became the collective mechanism of Europe – a 'league to bind Europe in chains' – for preventing revolutionary eruptions. For example, in Spain, a revolution took place in 1820 for democratic change which soon spread to Naples and Piedmont and the existing governments were overthrown. The European Concert met at Troppau in 1820 and issued a statement known as the **Troppau Protocol** by which they reaffirmed their commitment to suppress revolution in any European state. Subsequently, Austria suppressed the revolutions in Naples and Piedmont and restored monarchy and in Spain the French army did the same.

The Congress of Vienna apart from restoring conservatism in European politics '*marked not only the close of an old epoch but the beginning of a new*'. The Congress unconsciously let open the forces of unity in Italy and Germany. In Italy by acquiring Genoa the status of Sardinia had been strengthened making it the leader of Italian unity. Similarly in Germany, Prussia acquired the Rhine regions inhabited by Germans and emerged champion of the Germans replacing Austria. Moreover, the settlements of Vienna had the effect of restoring balance of power which secured peace for Europe for the next many decades. Not until the German unification in 1871, this balance was affected and not until the World War I in 1914, the peace of Europe was greatly disrupted.

The other alliance, the **Holy Alliance** was a moral compact between Christian rulers under the initiative of Tsar Alexander of Russia. It was an attempt to spiritualise politics and was aimed at preserving Christian charity and peace in Europe. But it proved nothing as the rulers except the Czar took it seriously and it ended with Czar's death in 1825. Metternich described it as '**loud sounding nothing**'.

B. Revolutions of the 19th Century

Though the reactionary forces tried their best to suppress liberal and nationalistic aspirations in the post-Napoleonic period, it was not successful in fully extinguishing the revolutionary spirit of the French Revolution. It found re-emergence in revolutions in 1820s, 1830 and in 1848.

a. Revolutions of 1820s

In the 1820s, revolutions against reactionary forces erupted in **Naples, Spain and in Greece**. Though those of Naples and Spain were suppressed by the Concert of Europe, as seen above, that of Greece became successful with the Greeks winning their independence from the Ottomans in 1829. Revolution also erupted in **Russia** in 1825 under the Russian officers who were exposed to the French liberal ideas during the Napoleonic Wars. But that too was suppressed by Tsar Nicholas I, the Russian ruler.

b. Revolutions of 1830

In France, Louis XVI's (who was beheaded by the revolutionaries in 1793) brother **Louis XVIII** (1814–24) was enthroned as the new monarch after the defeat of Napoleon. He was a sensible ruler who pursued a middle course trying to 'nationalize the Crown and to royalise the French people'. By a new constitution – **the Charter of 1814** – which he issued, Louis XVIII granted the French citizens certain fundamental rights such as freedom of religion and thought, and equality before the law apart from establishing a parliament.

But Louis XVIII's brother, who succeeded him as **Charles X** in 1824, was a diehard representative and a protagonist of the Old Regime. Being a supporter of monarchy and an opponent of liberalism, it was said that, he 'had learnt nothing and forgotten nothing' from the revolutionary times. By a series of ordinances, known as the **July Ordinances** (1930), he tried to suppress freedom of the people and wished to return to royal absolutism.

The Parisians, under the bourgeois, along with workers, intellectuals and students opposed these measures. They rose in revolt in July, hence known as the **July Revolution**, and forced Charles to resign. The crown was now offered to the Duke of Orleans, **Louis Philippe**. Louis Philippe was called as the 'Citizen King' because he owed his throne to the people and as the "bourgeoisie monarch" as his main supporters were the wealthy bourgeoisie. Though France continued to be a monarchy, known as the **July Monarchy**, it was a constitutional monarchy.

True to the comment of Metternich, 'When France sneezes, Europe catches cold', the revolutionary fervour soon spread to **Belgium, Poland and Italy**. Belgium had been added to Holland by the Congress of Vienna. But the union was unworkable as Belgium was Catholic and Holland was Protestant. Inspired by the developments in Paris, the Belgians declared independence from Holland and emerged as a separate nation with a liberal government in 1831. In Poland, revolutionaries rose up against Russian control. The Russian Czar brutally suppressed the revolt and merged Poland into his empire. In Italy though the Carbonari revolutionaries rose up in the Papal States, Prince Metternich sent Austrian troops there and restored order.

c. *The Year of Revolutions (1848)*

The year 1848 is called the 'Year of Revolutions', as the whole of Europe witnessed popular revolutions and the development was known as the '**Peoples' Spring**'.

Factors behind these revolutions were desire for political liberty and nationhood, antagonism against oppressive regimes and widespread economic distress.

- The **Enlightenment emphasis** on individual rights and popular sovereignty along with the **emphasis by the Romantics** on individualism and heroic struggle had strengthened the idea of political and individual liberty.
- Spread of Industrial Revolution meant growth in the number of **middle and working classes**, both of which were assertive of their rights. While the workers wanted an end to the miseries of the Industrial Revolution, the Middle-class liberals wanted greater role in political power.
- **Nationalists** of all regions wanted to throw off foreign control.
- Compounding all these factors, **economic distress** accentuated the outbreak of the revolutions. During 1846–47, there were economic recession and food shortages resulting from the **Great Potato Famine** of 1845.

As in 1830, it was Paris that ignited the revolutionary fervour. Louis Philippe and the ruling elite that comprised of rich bourgeoisie detested any move towards democracy or enlarging the voting rights (only 3 per cent adult males had the right to vote). At the same time, the Parisians workers, petty bourgeoisie and students stood for further reforms and took to the streets in February 1848. They demanded abolition of monarchy and universal male suffrage. This uprising is known as the **February Revolution**. The rage of people forced Louis Philippe to resign and a Provisional Republican Government was established. Though the new administration extended franchise to all adult males, removed censorship and legalised labour unions, these measures did not alleviate the economic crisis and poverty of the urban poor. At this time, the government also abolished the 'national workshops' (established to provide guaranteed work for the unemployed), terming them as breeding places of socialism and troubles. The working class was looking for **socio-economic reforms**, while the middle class were content with **political reforms** already implemented. This differing outlook of radical socialists and middle-class republicans took France to further turmoil. In June 1848, the working class of Paris once again revolted for radical social reforms. A class war between the workers of Paris and the French army supported by other sections of French society ensued and thousands were killed. The development is known as the **Bloody June Days**. Finally, army suppressed the **June Revolution**.

Immediate consequence of the street battles and bloodbaths was an aversion of French people to radicalism. Consequently, a moderate, republican constitution was drawn up in December that year and **Louis Napoleon or Napoleon III**, nephew of Napoleon Bonaparte, was elected as the president of this republic which began to be known as the **Second French Republic**. Louis Napoleon lived up to their expectation to a great extent. He implemented infrastructural projects, built railroads, encouraged industrialisation, reduced unemployment and followed an aggressive foreign policy.

French Republics

Since the French Revolution, France witnessed rise and fall of many republics. The **First French Republic** was formed in 1792 which lasted till 1804, the year in which Napoleon put an end to the Republic and established the First French Empire.

The **Second French Republic** was established in 1848 and lasted till 1852. In 1852, Napoleon III ended it and established the Second French Empire which lasted till 1870, the year in which France was defeated by Prussia and Napoleon III was deposed. Fall of this Second French Empire was followed by the formation of the **Third French Republic** in the same year which lasted until July 1940 when Nazi Germany defeated it during the World War II. After the World War II two more republics were established. The **Fourth French Republic** (existed 1946–58) and the **Fifth French Republic** established in 1958 and continues till today.

In 1848 too, it was not just France that came under Revolution. It spread to the German states, Austria and Italy. Though **Germany** had been divided into 39 states by the Congress of Vienna, the spirit of German unity and liberalism had been kept alive by the intellectuals, students and the like. The successful revolt in France in 1848 aroused the German liberals for action and uprisings erupted in the capitals of German states. The revolutionary agitation compelled princes of the German states to introduce reforms – ease censorship, remove reactionary ministers and form parliaments. Encouraged by these developments, the liberals convened a national assembly at Frankfurt. The **Frankfurt Assembly** having representatives from all German states approved creation of a German federation with the Prussian king as its head. But the Prussian king, Frederick William, refused to accept the crown, commenting that he was not ready to 'pick up a crown from the gutter' as it was offered to him by a revolutionary assembly. Making use of this state of confusion, armies of the German princes suppressed the revolutionaries.

The Austrian Empire under the Hapsburg dynasty had three major geographical divisions – Austria, Hungary and Bohemia – and was a curious ethnic mix of Germans, Magyars, Rumanians, Italians and Slavs (Czechs, Slovaks, Slovenes, Poles, Serbs, Croats and Ruthenians). Inspired by the abdication of Louis Philippe the Liberals revolted in Vienna, the Austrian capital, which soon spread to Bohemia, Hungary and Austrian part of Italy (northern Italy). Though the revolutionaries became successful in forcing Metternich to resign, who fled to England, the revolution itself was suppressed by the Austrian troops. The Russian Czar supplied a huge army to Austria to suppress the revolt in Hungary.

In Italy too, revolutions broke out forcing the rulers of Naples, Tuscany, Sardinia-Piedmont and Pope Pius IX to introduce reforms. Pope Pius IX fled from Rome in November 1848, while the revolutionaries declared Rome as a republic. Venetian people declared their independence from Austria and King Charles Albert of Piedmont-Sardinia declared war on Austria. But, the Austrians defeated Sardinia, and recaptured Venice. The French ruler Louis Napoleon destroyed the Roman Republic and reinstalled Pope on his possessions.

In spite of the pan-continental nature of the unrest, all of them were suppressed within a year and by 1850 an era of liberal revolution that had its origin in 1789 had come to an end.

d. Causes for Failure of the Revolutions

1. Even in the mid-19th century the reactionary forces were strong in Europe.
2. Existence of class divisions within the revolutionaries and differences on methods and objectives of the revolution were two other factors. While the bourgeois liberals stood for political reforms alone, the urban workers desired for social reforms too.
3. Another factor was nationalism. Equal to their hatred to absolutism was their hatred towards other nationalities. For example, while the Hungarians demanded independence on the national lines, they opposed nationalist demands by the minorities, such as the South Slavs and Rumanians living in Hungary. Similarly, the Frankfurt Assembly was opposed to the inclusion of Austria in the proposed German federation as it had many non-Germans. In other words, nationalism and liberalism were not compatible in many cases and the nationalists were indifferent to the aspirations and liberal demands of other nationalities and were ready to crush liberty of any people not belonging to their race or group.

C. British Democratic Politics 1815–50

While the Continent was enmeshed in revolutions for reforms and restructuring, England initiated a period of reform through its parliament. Realising the need for reforms to keep in tune with the times, the British political leadership embarked on a period of reform from the second decade of the 19th century and England became a modern democracy through a process of incremental reforms.

> **Rotten and Pocket Boroughs:** Boroughs were electoral constituencies in England. Rotten boroughs were depopulated election districts too small to justify their separate representation in parliament. Pocket boroughs were constituencies under the control of rich families, hence was considered as boroughs in the pocket of their patrons.

One of the keenly felt reforms was the **reform of the British Parliament**. Since its origin, the British parliament was dominated by the landed class and two-thirds of the House of Commons members were their supporters as they were elected from 'rotten' or 'pocket' boroughs of the landed gentry. With the emergence of **industrial cities and new classes** – the middle class and the working class – the demand for their representation in Parliament grew and acquired intensity in 1830s. The July Revolution in 1830 in France had convinced many leaders of eruption of violent revolution in England too, if reforms were not introduced. As a result, the **Reform Bill of 1832** was passed which was also known as the Representation of the Peoples Act 1832 or the Great Reform Act. It was the first of a series of electoral reforms and symbolised an evolving constitution that was changing from parliamentary into popular sovereignty and also the one which "opened a door on a new political world".

- It broadened property qualification to include all those who owned or rented property with an annual value of ten pounds thus including small landowners and shopkeepers and other members of the middle class as voters. But the Act still kept the working class and large sections of lower middle class out of voting right.
- Further, the Bill reallocated 143 parliamentary seats from the rural south to the industrial north providing representation to cities such as Manchester and Leeds.
- On its negative side, the Act explicitly barred women from voting by defining a voter as a male person.

During this period reforms in other areas too were initiated in England. The Parliament joined hands with the campaigners outside in pressing for reform. These measures gave birth to the principle of government's involvement in welfare position to improve the lives of the poor. By the **Cotton Mills Act of 1819** no child under the age of 9 was to be employed in cotton industries and for all those under 16 a maximum day of 12 hours was prescribed. By enacting a series of **Factory Acts** between 1833 and 1847, the British parliament prohibited employment in textile mills (the 1819 Act was only for cotton mills) of children under nine and limited the hours of older children and of women to 10 hours a day. All dangerous machinery was to be securely fenced off. In 1842, the **Mines and Collieries Act** was passed prohibiting all underground work for girls, women and for boys under 10.

The Parliament also **abolished slavery in British colonies in 1833**. The **Poor Law Amendment Act** was passed in 1834 to overhaul the old Poor Law and introduced role of the Central government in the care of the poor. In 1846, the **Corn Laws** (that imposed tariff on grain imported) long opposed by liberals and object of major reform movement, were repealed, reducing the price of bread.

D. Nationalism and Nation-Building

Though the State as a centralised, power wielding agency was in existence much early in human history, the nation and nationalism are modern concepts. Nationalism 'is a political principle that holds that national and political units should be congruent'. In this context, the term **national unit means nation** and **political unit means state**. This congruence of nation and state gave birth to **modern nation-states**. The nation-states replaced empires, kingdoms and city-states and marked transition from sovereign territorial states of early modern Europe to states based on the concept of nation. These nation-states were based on a sense of common identity and shared history or descent, among the majority of its citizens.

The American and French Revolutions in the 18th century gave birth to the concept of the modern nation-state, that is, state as an independent entity consisting of equal citizens and a written constitution. During the French Revolution, a sense of pride had been instilled in the French people who fought not as subjects of a king but as citizens of a nation. Subsequently, people in the lands conquered by the French armies discovered a sense of national identity while resisting the French over lordship.

Factors that contributed to the idea of nationalism included cultural affinity such as common language, race or religion and a shared past. Cultural expressions – art, poetry, music and stories – too promoted nationalism. For example, the Romantic poets tried to instil a sense of shared collective heritage what they considered as the basis of nation. Geographical contiguity of a group of people was another factor as people equated geography with national identity. Moreover, as a result of industrialisation, dominance of the landed aristocracy had ended and new social groups made up of industrialists, working class and professionals had emerged. The idea of national unity was espoused by these new social groups.

In the 19th century, nationalism emerged as a powerful ideology and it was this spirit of nationalism that fuelled efforts to build nation-states. In spite of the efforts by the Congress of Vienna to suppress nationalism, it grew in Europe as a force capable of breaking up of empires or of bringing together people sharing a common language, culture or religion into a nation. In that sense nationalism was a force both of division and unity.

1. Many nationalists in the **Ottoman Empire** such as the Bulgarians, Serbians, Montenegrins, Croats, Romanians and Greeks aspired to form their own nations.
2. Nationalities in **Austro-Hungarian Empire** wanted to form their own nations. It was a huge empire with large number of ethnic groups – Germans, Hungarians, Slovenes, Poles, Czechs, Slovaks, Croats, Serbs and Italians. In the 19th century with the strengthening of nationalism, the Empire faced an imminent breakup. After Austria's defeat by Prussia in 1866, Hungarians demanded independence. The Austrian emperor Francis Joseph divided Austria into two independent states – Austria and Hungary – with himself as the ruler of both.
3. **Belgium** emerged independent from Holland in 1831.
4. People of **Italy and Germany** too wanted to form a unified nation and in latter-half of the century emerged as unified nations.
5. The **Latin American** people emerged independent from their European masters.
6. The **Russian Empire** had large number of ethnic groups – Russians, Ukrainians, Poles, Finns, Romanians, Lithuanians, Estonians and Latvians – within it. During this period the Poles, Ukrainians and Finns intensified their ethnic nationalism.

Positive effects of nationalism

- National consciousness brought the people of a nation together to forget their other differences and work for common good of the people.
- Facilitated the end of colonialism
- Facilitated the emergence of democracies

Negative effects of nationalism

- Domination of majority culture over the minorities
- Emergence of extreme nationalism
- Nationalism aligned with imperialism led to wars including the World Wars.

E. Balkan Question or the Eastern Question

What should happen to the Balkans if the Ottoman Empire disappears? This question of immense importance in the 19th-century international relations was known as the Balkan Question or the Eastern Question. It was the product of complex mix of '**conflicting interests, rival peoples and antagonistic faiths**'.

In strategic point of view, the lands that rimmed the Mediterranean – as it controlled access to the Mediterranean and the Atlantic – had been important for the Europeans. With the **Ottoman Empire undergoing a steady decline** in the 19th century, European powers competed with each other for domination of the eastern Mediterranean and strategically important Dardanelles strait. It was also the time of the **spread of nationalist feelings** among the diverse subjects of the Ottoman Empire. Thus, it emerged out of both internal conflicts within the Ottomans and of aggressive designs by foreign powers. It found expressed in developments such as the **Greek Revolution** in 1820s, the **Crimean War** (1853–56) and the **Balkan Crisis** (1875–78). By infusing volatility in the emerging Balkan nations, the Eastern Question also proved to be one of the causes of the World War I.

At the root of the issue was the conflicting interests of two European powers – Britain and Russia over the region. As it was strategically located, Russia desired to take advantage of the crumbling Turkish Empire – the **Sick Man of Europe**. Russia wanted a breakthrough to the Mediterranean by controlling the Black Sea, the Bosporus and the Dardanelles strait and from there to the open oceans. Russia was also connected to the Balkan people by the ties of race (Slavs) and religion (Eastern Orthodox Church). The Russian design in the region was a threat to the British maritime route to India, Britain's most valued colony hence Britain followed a policy of preserving the integrity of the Ottoman.

> The Sick Man of Europe was a derisive term to describe the Ottoman Empire from the 19th century for its dwindling territory, declining economy and its dependence on the rest of Europe.

Other European powers too were apprehensive of Russia upsetting the balance of power by expanding into the decaying Ottomans. These powers such as Austria, Germany and France had their interests in the Ottomans. Austria being a landlocked country wanted to protect her trade interest by securing the Danube Valley from falling in the hands of the Russians. She was also apprehensive of the emerging **pan-Slavic movement** in the Balkans which had the support of Russia and the potential to erode the loyalty of the Slavs in the Austrian Empire. France, which had special trading rights in the Ottoman Empire wanted to protect her commercial interests. In the last-quarter of the 19th century, newly unified Germany too became a contender in the issue. After defeating Austria in 1866, Germany wanted to befriend Austria and make her the cornerstone of German alliance system. To secure Austria's friendship Germany opposed Russian designs in the region and intended to build a rail line connecting Berlin with Baghdad. The **Berlin-Baghdad Railway** was expected to extend Germany's economic influence into north Persia where Russia had a huge influence. Italy considered the Western Balkans, as a natural zone of her influence and wanted to annex the whole Dalmatian coast to Italy arguing that an Italian minority lived in the region. Italian interest in this region clashed with that of Austria, Serbia, Montenegro and Greece.

Ultimately, though Britain became successful in checking the Russian designs in the Balkans, she failed in preserving the integrity of the Ottoman Empire. The Empire declined in the 19th century and was dismembered after the First World War.

a. *Reasons for Ottoman's Decline*

The Ottoman Turkey, a mighty empire extended in three continents and strategically important, was on decline by the 19th century on account of-

1. Administrative inefficiency and corruption by the provincial governors and the state's agents.
2. Weakness of the Ottomans, which encouraged the powerful vassals to bid for independence.
3. Emergence of nationalism among the subject peoples.
4. The Empire was characterised by its tremendous diversity in terms of ethnicity, language, economy and geography. Failure of the Ottomans to assimilate its diverse subjects into the body politic.
5. Exploitative nature of the rule.
6. Desire of Russia for southward expansion and interference in Ottoman affairs.

b. *Break-Up of the Ottoman Empire*

1. **Serbia.** Among the subjects of the Ottomans the first to revolt for national freedom were the **Serbs.** From 1804, they revolted, and in 1817, Ottomans granted autonomy to Serbia.

2. **Greece.** Greece was a part of the Ottoman Empire. In **Greece**, the Turkish rule was seen as alien and oppressive. By the beginning of the 19th century, the Greeks, proud of their ancient kingdom and Hellenistic culture, came under national consciousness and aspired for an independent nation. In 1821, revolt started in Moldova which soon spread all over Greece. The Turkish ruler sent Ibrahim, the son of his Egyptian Pasha (Governor) Mehmet Ali, to suppress the uprising in Greece. Ibrahim's ruthless attitude towards Greece caused alarm of extinction of Greek race and the European powers – **England, France and Russia** – signed an assistance pact and intervened in the issue. Educated class in Europe and America who had studied and admired the ancient Greek culture too were in support of Greek struggle. There was also religious angle in the Greek episode. The European nations viewed the rule by Ottoman over Greek as rule by Muslims over Orthodox Christians.

In 1827, an Anglo-French-Russian naval force defeated Turkish Sultan's forces in the Battle of

Navarino. In 1829, with the **Treaty of Adrianople** the Ottomans recognised Greece as an autonomous but tributary state. By The **Treaty of Constantinople** in 1832 Greece was recognised as an independent nation.

In 1833, Russia signed the **Treaty of Unkiar Skelessi**, a defensive alliance with Turkey with which Russia guaranteed the existence of Turkey and in return secured the right of free passage to Russian warships while prohibiting other countries' warships in the Dardanelles. This development was of great concern to other European powers especially to Britain. Britain now reaffirmed their commitment to the policy that 'the Ottoman Empire was to be preserved, supported, reformed and strengthened'. British efforts led to the signing of the **Convention of the Straits** in 1841 with which the Turkish Sultan agreed to close the Turkish Straits (the Bosporus and the Dardanelles) to foreign ships-of-war in time of peace. Though Russia had been one of the signatories of the Convention, it had robbed Russia of its predominance in Turkish affairs. This Russian discontent led to the next conflict, the Crimean War.

c. **The Crimean War (1853–56):** The war was fought in the Crimean peninsula of Russia. The Russian ruler Czar Nicholas II occupied Wallachia and Moldavia, the two Danubian principalities (modern Romania) of the Ottomans in July 1853, leading to the Crimean War. On Russian refusal to withdraw from the conquered territories Turkey declared war on Russia. Britain and France entered into an alliance with Turkey and declared war against Russia in 1854. Italian kingdom Sardinia too joined the Allies. The combined forces of these powers defeated Russia in 1856.

With the Peace of Paris (1856), the Crimean war ended, which led to–

1. Neutralisation of the Black Sea, that is, it was opened up for international trade and commerce. It was closed to all warships and fortifications on its shores were prohibited.
2. Danube was opened for navigation of all countries
3. Guaranteed the integrity of the Ottoman Empire by the European powers
4. Recognition of Serbia and Romania as self-governing principalities

The War checked Russian designs on Turkey. Her dominance in Danube valley and in the Black Sea was also diminished. The demilitarisation of the Black Sea was a great blow to Russia as its southern coastal frontier was now vulnerable to attack from any enemy, especially British attack. The image many Russians had of their country – the biggest, richest and the most powerful in the world – had been shattered as it also had exposed drawbacks of almost every institution in Russia.

> Florence Nightingale was a member of a British voluntary nursing group in the Crimean War. She gained reputation as 'The Lady with the Lamp' making rounds of wounded soldiers at night. Nightingale's contribution paved the way for later developments in battlefield medicine. She is considered as the 'Founder of Modern Nursing' and her birthday is observed as the annual 'International Nurses Day'.

d. **The Balkan Crisis (1875–78):** Balkan discontent reemerged with uprisings in Bosnia and Herzegovina in 1875 and in Bulgaria in 1876 leading to meddling of international powers in the **Eastern Crisis**. The conflict led to Russo-Turkish War (1877–78) as Russia could not be indifferent to the hardships of her co-religionists and fellow Slavs. The Russian led Eastern Orthodox coalition defeated the Ottomans and with the Treaty of Berlin in 1878 the crisis ended. Success in the war enabled Russia to wipe out humiliation of the Crimean War.

The Treaty of Berlin (1878) was a great blow for the Ottomans. Three Ottoman principalities of Romania, Serbia and Montenegro now became independent. It also made Bulgaria autonomous. The Ottoman territories in Europe were reduced to Macedonia, Albania and Thrace. The Ottomans were also forced to accept new financial controls by the Europeans. With all these provisions the Treaty of Berlin decreed the dissolution of the Ottoman Empire.

3. The United States in the 19th Century

A. Expansion and Consolidation

In 1776, the United States was consisted of just 13 colonies on the eastern seaboard of North America. In the 19th century, the United States expanded its territory with great speed by methods of negotiation, purchase and war.

1. In 1783, by the Treaty of Paris, Britain handed over the **North West Territory** to the US.
2. In 1803, the US purchased the colony of Louisiana (the **Louisiana Purchase**), from France for a sum of 15 million dollar. By the Louisiana Purchase the size of the United States was more than doubled.
3. Florida was a Spanish settlement since 1565. In 1819, Spain handed over **Florida to the United States** by the Florida Purchase Treaty.
4. In 1845, **Texas** was added to the United States as the 28th state, bringing another 7,00,000 square miles to the United States. Texas was a part of Mexico but had succeeded in breaking with Mexico and emerge as the Republic of Texas in the Texas Revolution.
5. In 1846, by the **Oregon Treaty** with Britain the United States settled its Pacific Northwest border with Britain and established the 49th parallel as the border between the two. By this, the present states of Washington, Oregon and Idaho were acquired by the United States.
6. The annexation of Texas by the United States led to **Mexican-American War**. In 1848, the war ended with the Treaty of Guadalupe-Hidalgo and the United States acquired 1.3 million square km territory from Mexico which included the present day states of California, Nevada and Utah and portions of Arizona, Colorado and New Mexico. Though Mexico received 15 million dollar in the deal, its territory had been reduced by half.
7. In 1867, Russian Czar Alexander II sold **Alaska** adding 1.7 million more square km to the United States.

With all these acquisitions the United States **increased its size** by more than sixfold. During the same period, **population** of the United States more than trebled as these lands attracted European settlers. In 1850s alone, 2 million people migrated to the United States from Europe. It was also the time of great prosperity in the United States and by 1850 its **national wealth** had increased by 12 times. The Westward expansion of the United States, many Americans believed it as Manifest Destiny, was one of the defining themes in the American history but it also 'very nearly destroyed the republic' in the form of Civil War.

> Manifest Destiny was the belief among the Americans that expansion of the United States across the North American continent was preordained by the will of the Providence for the development of liberty and self-government.

B. The Civil War

The Civil War was fought between the Northern and Southern states of the United States, after decades of simmering tensions. In spite of emerging as a nation, there were many points of tension and differences between different regions of the United States. Differences over the extent of state rights and federal rights, differences in industrialisation between North and South, cultural differences and attitude towards slavery were some of these. Finally, it was the westward expansion and the thorny issue of slavery that led to Civil War. The southern states wanted to secede, while the northerners wanted to remain as one country. The North consisted of 25 states (20 Free states and 5 Border States that were slave states but did not secede) and the South was made up of 11 states. The Civil War between the **United States of America** and 11 Southern states that formed the **Confederate States of America** extended from 1861 to 1865 and more than 6,00,000 died in the war.

The US constitution had allowed slavery but by 1820s the Northern states had abolished slavery while it continued in the South, where more than one-third of its population were slaves. The Northern states were known as **Free states** and the South as **Slave states**. While the Southerners justified slavery on economic, political and moral grounds, more and more Northerners opposed to it and came to be known as **abolitionists**.

Rapid developments in infrastructure and industries had ensured a higher standard of living in the North, while the sub-tropical South remained largely agrarian. The agrarian economy of the South was heavily depended on the slaves for harvesting their major products-cotton, tobacco and rice. Apart from the above differences, cultural differences too existed between the regions. While the North had a more mobile society that valued wealth, business skills, liberty and free labour the social values of the South were based on honour and chivalry. The differences in economy reflected not only socio-cultural levels but also in economic policies of the two. The North wanted tariffs to protect its industries from competition, while the South wanted free trade to fetch best prices for its agrarian products.

Slavery was in existence in British colonies in America for more than 200 years. These slaves were transported from Africa. Slavery was legal in the original 13 colonies but by 1800 six states abolished it and by 1820 all Northern states had banned it. By 1860, of the more than 4.4 million black people in the United States, 3.9 million were slaves. All slaves were black but not all black were slaves and not all slave owners were white as free blacks could buy and own slaves themselves.

Uncle Tom's Cabin was a novel by Harriet Beecher Stowe published in 1852. It exposed cruel realities of slavery and intensified the abolitionist cause. Harriet Beecher herself was an abolitionist and her book became the most successful novel of the 19th century.

In 1860, **Abraham Lincoln**, a member of Republican Party, was elected on an anti-slavery platform as the President of the United States. To which the southern states of the Deep South whose economy was based on cotton cultivated by slave labour reacted by seceding from the federation. **South Carolina** took the lead in December 1860 by severing its connection with all other states in the United States and six other states - **Mississippi, Florida, Georgia, Louisiana, Alabama and Texas** followed. Later on **Arkansas, Tennessee, North Carolina and Virginia** seceded.

Abraham Lincoln

Abraham Lincoln was the 16th president of the United States (1861–65). He led the United States through the Civil War, succeeded in preserving the Union and abolishing slavery. Though reelected to the Presidency in 1864, he was assassinated at the end of the Civil War on 14 April 1865 by a well-known actor John Wilkes Booth while attending a play at Ford's Theatre in Washington D.C. By killing Lincoln, Booth intended to revive the Confederate cause. Lincoln was the first American President to be assassinated. Fondly remembered as a martyr for the cause of freedom and as the liberator of the slaves, Lincoln is ranked as one of the top three greatest presidents of the United States.

a. *Causes of the Civil War*

1. **Slavery:** Growing anti-slavery campaigns of the Abolitionists after 1830s had been a great concern among the wealthy landowners of the South who feared end of their economic well-being.
2. **State Rights:** The Southern states were apprehensive of the Federal government's encroachment into states' powers and rights. They argued that federal government had no power to end slavery, impose certain taxes or to force infrastructure developments. They held the view that just as each state had decided to join the Union, they had the right to secede too.
3. **Westward Expansion of the United States:** This had worried the southern states of loss of their powers. They also were apprehensive that anti-slavery laws would be extended to the whole United States. The Mexican-American War in 1848 had brought 1.3 million square km territory to the United States and the Southerners feared that limiting the expansion of slavery would put an end to the practice. During the next decade, while the two sides became increasingly polarised, the politicians failed to reach a compromise.
4. **Economy:** There existed a conflict between industry and agriculture in the 19th century United States. The economies of northern states had transformed from agrarian to industrial and large cities like New York, Boston and Philadelphia had emerged. The southern economy was largely depended on agriculture-based slave labour. The North no longer needed slaves, while for the South slavery was essential.
5. **Election of Abraham Lincoln:** He was elected in November 1860 without even being on the ballot in 10 of the southern states. He supported a strong federal government, was opposed to slavery and wanted the country to remain united.

Outbreak of the Civil War

6. **Secession:** When the southern states starting with South Carolina seceded and formed a new country, the Confederate States of America, Lincoln sent troops to force these states back to the Union and the Civil War started. Lincoln was determined to preserve the United States of America. He declared a naval blockade of the Confederate States describing them as 'states in rebellion'.

In February 1861, delegates of these rebel Southern states met in Montgomery and formed a new union, the **Confederate States of America**, drafted a constitution and adopted their own flag. The War started on 12 April 1861 at **Fort Sumter in South Carolina**. Though the North had enormous advantages of population, resources and infrastructure like railway and manufacturing including arms production, the South had a strong military tradition and commanders, and some of the best ports in North America including New Orleans, Norfolk and Wilmington. They also hoped to receive foreign aid and intervention. The war was fought mostly in the South for four years and became the deadliest military conflict in American history in which more than 6,00,000 men were killed. The Civil War was also one of the earliest industrial wars as railways, steamships, telegraph and mass-produced weapons came to be used extensively.

It ended on 9 April 1865 with the surrender of the Confederate forces under Robert E. Lee before **Ulysses S. Grant**, General of the Union forces. On 20 August 1866 President **Andrew Johnson** issued a Presidential Proclamation officially ending the Civil War.

b. *Results of the Civil War*

1. The Confederate states were dissolved and were readmitted to the United States.
2. Territorial integrity of the United States could be preserved. Supremacy of the Federal government over the states was unequivocally established.
3. Slavery was abolished nationwide and around four million enslaved blacks were freed.
4. It caused the passage of three Reconstruction Amendments guaranteeing freedom of former slaves and certain civil rights to all citizens.
5. Inaugurated the Reconstruction Era for healing the wounds of the war.

c. Reconstruction

The measures to rebuild the South after the Civil War is known as the Reconstruction and lasted from 1865 to 1877. The Civil War had caused extensive damages to the farms and properties in the South. End of the War had also posed a serious question of how the South would be rejoined with the Union. President Lincoln wanted a lenient treatment to the South, but he was assassinated at the end of the Civil War. The new President Andrew Johnson, who was from the South, too wanted a lenient stand towards the South. A significant step in the Reconstruction was three amendments made to the US Constitution. These were–

1. 13th Amendment (1865) – Abolished slavery.
2. 14th Amendment (1868) – Declared black people as the citizens of the United States and offered equal protection of the laws for all persons.
3. 15th Amendment (1870) – Granted voting right to all male citizens regardless of race.

Each rebel state had to be readmitted, on them repudiating secession and ratifying these new amendments to the Constitution. Federal troops had been positioned in the South during the Reconstruction to oversee reconstruction and to prevent another uprising. Federal government too was involved in the Reconstruction by building roads, schools for black children. In 1877, the Reconstruction officially ended and the Federal troops were withdrawn.

Emancipation Proclamation: It was an executive order of the American President Abraham Lincoln issued on 1 January 1863. It declared freedom of all those persons held as slaves in the rebellious states. It laid the groundwork for the eventual freedom of slaves all over the United States. The Proclamation also allowed the Union forces to recruit Black soldiers during the Civil War.

4. | Imperialism

Imperialism is the process by which a country seeks to extend its authority over other countries either by conquest or by establishing economic and political dominance. In this process weaker countries come under the political, economic and social dominance of the stronger countries. Imperialism is found expressed in one of the four forms – **colony, protectorate, sphere of influence** and **economic imperialism**.

Colony: A territory under the control of another country.
Protectorate: A territory with its own government but under the control of another country.
Sphere of Influence: A territory over which another country holds exclusive investment or trading rights.
Economic Imperialism: An independent territory whose policies are regulated by multinational corporates and to a lesser extent by foreign governments.

A. Stages of Imperialism

a. Mercantilism and Trading Empires

This was the first of the stages in the evolution of Imperialism. It extended from the end of the 15th century to the middle of the 18th century. For almost a century thereafter, a relative calm existed in imperial activities.

The **Age of Sail** with its discovery of so far unknown lands had promoted trade in leaps and bounds. Spectacular growth in trans-Atlantic trade which increased eighth fold between 1500 and 1550 was one such instance. Geographical discoveries and trade were followed by conquest of territories in America, Asia and Africa.

During the early stages, **Portugal** and **Spain** established settlements in different parts of the world. Spain established huge empire in the Americas especially in South America. The Portuguese explored and established settlements on the west coast of Africa. Soon the **Dutch, French** and **English** entered in the fray. Dutch colonised lands in the Pacific and Indian Ocean such as Indonesia. The French exploration of North America led to establishment of French colonies there. Establishment of colonies met the European hunger for land, stimulated trade, facilitated emigration; and bullion from the Americas increased money supply in Europe.

By the second half of the 18th century, Portugal and Spain lost their colonies. Dutch monopoly on shipping ended with the emergence of Britain as a strong contender for naval supremacy. Britain and France fought against each other for colonial supremacy which ended in British success as by 1789 all French colonial possessions in India and America had been captured by Britain. At the end, the British could claim, as their empire stretched across the globe, that 'the sun never set on the British Empire'.

b. Industrial Capitalism and Imperialism of Free Trade

In the second-half of the 19th century, with the spread of Industrial Revolution new powers emerged seeking a place in the colonial sun, accelerating the race for colonies. During this stage **Italy, Germany**, the **United States**, **Russia** and **Japan** emerged as new-comers among the imperialistic states. The spread of industrial capitalism meant need for more colonies as markets, as suppliers of raw materials and also as fields of investment and these powers competed each other to claim as much territory as possible for themselves. A natural corollary of this imperialistic rivalry was the division of Europe into two armed blocs leading to World War I.

Though, after the First World War, the League of Nations and its Mandate System put a respite on imperialist ambitions Japan renewed it by its invasion on Manchuria in 1931. In the 1930s and 1940s, the totalitarian regimes – Italy, Germany and the Soviet Union – gave a new vigour to imperialism by their policy of territorial aggrandisements.

c. Imperialism Under Finance Capitalism

During this stage, the industrial capitalism was not replaced by financial capitalism but was superimposed on it. Accumulation of capital as a result of developments in trade and industry gave birth to trusts and cartels. Indirect control, especially, financial control was the hallmark of imperialism at this phase.

d. Neo-Colonialism

This stage emerged after the World War II, with the emergence of **international donor agencies** and with the rise of **multinational companies**. This stage in imperialism is characterised by the control of less-developed countries by the developed countries through indirect means, such as economic, financial and trade policies of donor agencies, multilateral institutions and transnational corporations and the perpetuation of colonial forms of exploitation. The US policy known as the **Truman Doctrine** was one such instrument with which the United States tried to extend its sphere of influence in the world. Another feature of Neo-colonialism is the exploitation of the subject nations, not only by the developed nations but even by the transnational corporations through the operations of international capitalism.

B. The Age of New Imperialism

The last-quarter of the 19th century was known as the Age of Imperialism, as during this period the Western powers were engaged in a struggle to extend their hegemony around the world. Protection of domestic markets and hunt for more profitable investments, markets and sources of raw materials were characteristics of the period. Economic competition gave birth to economic rivalry and finally to the First World War.

This phase of imperialism is called as the **New Imperialism** to differentiate it from colonialism or **Imperialism** of the 15th–18th centuries. The New Imperialism began in the last-quarter of the 19th century and lasted to the 20th century.

The Early Imperialism, as seen above, was characterised by trading empires such as that of Portugal and Spain, and was connected with **merchant capitalism**, while the New Imperialism was associated with **industrial capitalism**. Hence, the New Imperialism coincided with the Second Industrial Revolution and, in turn, was one of the factors that drove Europeans to add lands to their control. Moreover, in New Imperialism the Europeans exerted substantial influence on the socio, economic and political life of the colonial people. It was also more intensive and expensive as it entailed substantial capital investment in mines, plantations, banks and in infrastructures in colonies. During the New Imperialism, the Europeans added one-fifth of the total land area of the globe to their overseas colonial possessions.

C. Causes of New Imperialism

a. National Pride

The 19th century was the age of nationalism and the European nations valued colonies as a measure of national greatness. The newly unified Italy and Germany too entered in the colonial race to win glory for their nations by acquiring '**places in the sun**' and to enter in the '**imperial club**'. Newly acquired national unity had instilled a patriotic pride in the people of these two countries who wanted to upgrade their status as world powers. It was as if patriotism now acquired a new definition 'from love of country into love of more countries'! For the French politicians, imperialism was a means to restore their lost prestige after the humiliation of defeat in the Franco-Prussian War of 1870–71. To the British, accelerated pace of industrialisation and search for colonies by Germany and France appeared as a threat to its leadership in world markets. Moreover by 1871, the boundaries of the European nations had been set and any expansion within Europe meant war with others. Hence, overseas expansion was the only way out for these countries to increase wealth, power and influence.

b. *Economic Factors*

Major economic incentives of imperialism were markets, raw materials, cheap labour and avenues for investment. High rate of industrial production necessitated new and **wider markets**, but erection of high protective tariff walls (taxes on imports) by the leading industrialised European nations except Great Britain, compelled other nations to search vigorously for colonies as 'sheltered markets', as safe and best kind of markets. Colonies were also seen as the best **field for investment of surplus capital**. Deep **economic depression** in Europe that began in 1873 too was a factor in intensifying the competition for colonies as overseas markets.

Further, many colonies were rich in minerals and metals. For example, Africa was rich in **mineral resources**. The Belgian Congo had huge deposit of copper and tin, while South Africa was rich in gold and diamonds. In later stages, the Europeans also developed **new business models** in the colonies by introducing cash-crop plantations such as palm oil, cotton and rubber at the cost of food crops required to feed the indigenous population.

This economic motive behind imperialism in which a small section of extremely rich and influential capitalist class in Europe were beneficiaries has forced some scholars to term imperialism as 'a depraved choice of national life'.

c. *Strategic Competition*

Side-by-side of nation-building, the European powers also were keen on preserving a balance of power in Europe. Britain and France had been long-time rivals in Europe and with the entry of united Italy and Germany into the struggle for power and influence, it became essential for these two countries to protect and enlarge their **strategic possessions**. Imperial powers were also keen to obtain bases, buffer states, natural frontiers and communication lines to ensure protection of their countries' interests. Establishment of a **protectorate over Afghanistan** in the 1880s against Russian expansion into India and another **protectorate over Egypt** to protect the control of the Suez Canal were two examples of the steps taken by Britain with strategic aims.

d. *Belief in European Superiority*

Imperialist drive was also fuelled by Europeans' belief in their racial supremacy. For many Europeans, imperialism was an expression of the basic nature of human beings and a part of natural struggle for survival. They argued that it is natural for people endowed with superior qualities to rule inferiors. Under this notion, which was a reflection of **Social Darwinism**, many Europeans believed that it was their duty and right to extend their culture and achievements to other parts of the world.

Cecil Rhodes (1853–1902), responsible for acquiring large territory for Britain in Africa, for example, declared that 'The British are the finest race in the world and the more of the world we inhabit the better it is for the human race'. The English missionary **David Livingstone** who believed that European colonisation would put an end to African slave trade and the English poet **Rudyard Kipling** who believed in Europeans' mission to civilise the 'barbaric' Afro-Asians provided legitimacy to imperialism. In this context, imperialism could also be seen as something more than political aim or official policy.

Cecil Rhodes

Cecil Rhodes was an Englishman settled in South Africa. He had made a fortune in diamond and gold mining in Africa and became one of the richest men on earth. He was responsible for founding Rhodesia, a vast territory in Africa for Britain, a factor behind the Boer war and Prime Minister of Cape Colony during 1890–96. Rhodes almost single-handedly acquired for Britain some 4,50,000 miles territory in Africa. He also established Rhodes scholarship to enable students primarily from the former British colonies to study at Oxford University.

e. ***Missionary Spirit***

Spread of Christianity was also one of the objectives that drove the Europe's desire for colonies. The Christian missionaries wanted to '**Civilise**' the non-Europeans by which they hoped to '**Westernise**' them. Westernisation, they believed, would end many of the evils and superstitions such as child marriage and cannibalism among them. This 'mission of civilising the natives', they also argued, would liberate people from tyrannical rule and would provide them with a superior way of life. Many also genuinely believed that imperialism would combat famine, filth, slave trade and illiteracy in the colonies.

D. The Scramble for Africa

Africa was the last continent to be carved up by the European powers. Though the Europeans had established contact with Africa as early as the 15th century, they had not been able to penetrate into Africa for long. Powerful African armies, wild diseases such as malaria and rivers that were difficult to navigate were some of the hurdles before the European expansion in Africa. Even as late as 1880 the Europeans could control only 10% of the African lands, mainly on the coast. Africa was the '**Dark Continent**', a terra incognita to the Europeans even at that point of time.

Africa was the Dark Continent to the Europeans not because of the skin colour of its inhabitants but as a land of mystery and for its inhospitable terrain. It was also considered as the 'White man's grave' for a variety of diseases such as malaria prevalent there.

At the middle of the 19th century, some European explorers had exposed to the world the beauty, resources and potentials of Africa. Henceforth, a vast continent rich in resources and inhabited by hundreds of mutually fighting primitive tribal groups whose archaic weapons were no match to that of the Europeans appeared to be the most attractive space for imperial expansion. **Discoveries of diamonds and gold** in South Africa in 1860s and 1880s strengthened European interest in Africa. European interest in Africa was further intensified after the construction of the **Suez Canal** in 1869. By the end of the century the whole continent had been parcelled out by the Europeans. This **rapid colonisation of Africa** within a short period of the last twenty years of the 19th century is known as the 'Scramble for Africa'.

First of the European explorers of Africa was a Scottish missionary **David Livingstone**, who ventured deep in to Africa. Next, **Henry Stanley**, a British-American journalist who had been commissioned by the **Belgian king Leopold II**, traced the course of the River Congo. Between 1879 and 1882, Stanley signed treaties with some five hundred chieftains of the Congo basin, giving Leopold the control of these lands. This colony began to be known as **Belgian Congo** and was 80 times larger than Belgium.

Acquisition of a huge African territory by a European rival alarmed other countries of Europe. The French responded to Leopold's action by establishing a protectorate on the north bank of the Congo. Now, no European power wanted to be left out of the race and the struggle for Africa became intense. To prevent a conflict between themselves, the European powers convened a conference in 1884–85, to lay down rules for partition of Africa. This conference, known as the **Berlin Conference** or the **West African Conference**, was held in Berlin. Attended by most European nations and the United States, the Conference laid down rules for division of Africa. The conference established the rule that, if any European country had to claim a territory, it first had to establish **'effective control'** over that area and had to notify other nations of its claims. It also provided for free passage to all ships on the Niger and Congo rivers. The Conference also recognized the establishment of the Congo Free State under Leopold II.

The conference set off a mad scramble for territory in Africa and in the rush, the Europeans ignored both natural and cultural boundaries while claiming territories. In the process, the Europeans rooted out native customs, suppressed rebellions and confiscated tribal lands. By 1914, the whole of Africa except **Liberia and Ethiopia** had been parcelled out by the European powers. Liberia founded in 1822, of freed slaves from the United States was a small territory on the western coast and was under the special protection of the United States and Ethiopia (Abyssinia) held off Italian invaders in 1896.

In the 'Scramble for Africa', Britain gained the most. Opening of the **Suez Canal** in 1869, which cut shipping time to India drastically, had aroused the British interest in Egypt, as ships could travel from the Mediterranean to the Red Sea and to the Indian Ocean. By making use of bankruptcy of Egyptian ruler and rebellion as excuses the British purchased controlling shares in the canal and established a **protectorate over Egypt** in 1882. From Egypt, the British expanded south into **Sudan**, supposedly to suppress a holy war against the British, by the Sudanese under Mahdi Mohammed Ahmed, leader of a sect of dervishes. British also acquired **British East Africa** (Kenya and Uganda) which extended her territory from the Mediterranean to the Indian Ocean. Other British colonies included Gambia, Sierra Leone, Nigeria, the Gold Coast, Malawi, Botswana and Somaliland. Thus, Britain took possession of most of Africa containing more than 30 per cent of African population.

A key British prize in Africa was South Africa. Here, the original settlers were the Dutch and their descendants known as the **Boers** – farmers and cattlemen (also known as Afrikaners). From their settlement at Cape Town, at the southern tip of Africa, the British expanded and forced the Boers to the north, in a migration called the **Great Trek** (1835–37). Here the Boers established independent republics – the Transvaal and the Orange Free State. The discovery of gold and diamonds in the Boer lands in the 1860s brought many British prospectors to the region which increased the conflict between the two. A full-scale war, known as the **Anglo-Boer War**, broke out in 1899 and ended in 1902 with the defeat of the Boers. The brutalities resorted to by the British during the war such as the scorched earth policy of burning crops and assets and establishment of concentration camps for imprisoning wives and children of Boer fighters turned the British public opinion against imperialism and diminished the British stature internationally. The British leaders, in order to secure the white solidarity and to restore peace in Africa, formed the **British Union of South Africa** in 1910 by joining the Boer republics with the British territories. The government had representation of both the Boers and the British but to the natives, a policy of racial separation and inequality was initiated.

Other important European colonies in Africa were as follows. **Portuguese** – Angola and Mozambique, **French** – Algeria, Tunis, Morocco, Senegal, French Guinea, the French Congo and the island of Madagascar. **Italy** began its imperial designs in Africa by seizing Eritrea on the Red Sea in 1883. Next it conquered Somaliland and to link these two possessions attacked Abyssinia, but met with defeat at Adowa in 1896. She also conquered Libya. **Germany** was the last entrant in the African Scramble but within six years (1884–90) established colonies in German East Africa (Rwanda, Burundi and Tanzania), Togoland, Cameroon and German South West Africa (Namibia).

a. Favourable Factors to the Europeans

The achievements of Europeans, in the field of science and technology, were one of the significant factors that facilitated European imperialism in Africa. In this context, developments in military technology were crucial. Shift from muzzle-loading rifles to **breechloaders** and the invention of the world's first machine gun in 1884 were notable. This gun known as the **Maxim gun** could fire eleven bullets a second and placed the Europeans much ahead of the Africans who had to depend on primitive weapons. Metal-hulled **steamships** allowed faster and cheaper transportation of bulk cargos such as crops and heavy ores. **Steamboats** enabled Europeans to navigate African rivers for deep penetration, while **railroads and cables** speeded up transport and communication within the colony and also between the colony and the empire. Laying of **submarine cables** had brought Europe and Africa closer and by 1885 London and South Africa had been linked. Developments in medicine, such as invention of '**quinine**', an effective prophylactic against malaria provided protection to the Europeans from dreaded diseases prevalent in the colonies.

On the other end, Africa had been a divided continent with various groups fighting each other. This factor enabled Europeans to play-off various ethno-linguistic and religious groups against one another. It was also important to note that state organisation was virtually non-existent in most parts of Africa. Natural disasters too were significant factor in European success in colonisation of Africa. For example, a serious drought hit large parts of Africa in 1895 resulting in the death of huge number of people and animals. During such crises the indigenous people were unable to fight while it was easy for the Europeans to conquer. In spite of such drawbacks, the Europeans' attempt to colonise their land had been tightly contested by the Africans. Herero Wars and Dervish resistance were some examples in this context. But being a fight between un-equals the Africans were bound to fail, and even in failures they wrote glorious chapters of resistance.

b. *Consequences of Imperialism in Africa*

The European control over Africa had altered the African lives – negatively or positively – forever. There is no dispute that the primary motive behind colonialism was promotion of imperial interests, which were in contrast to the interests of the colonies, while the positive effects, if any, were by-products and accidental.

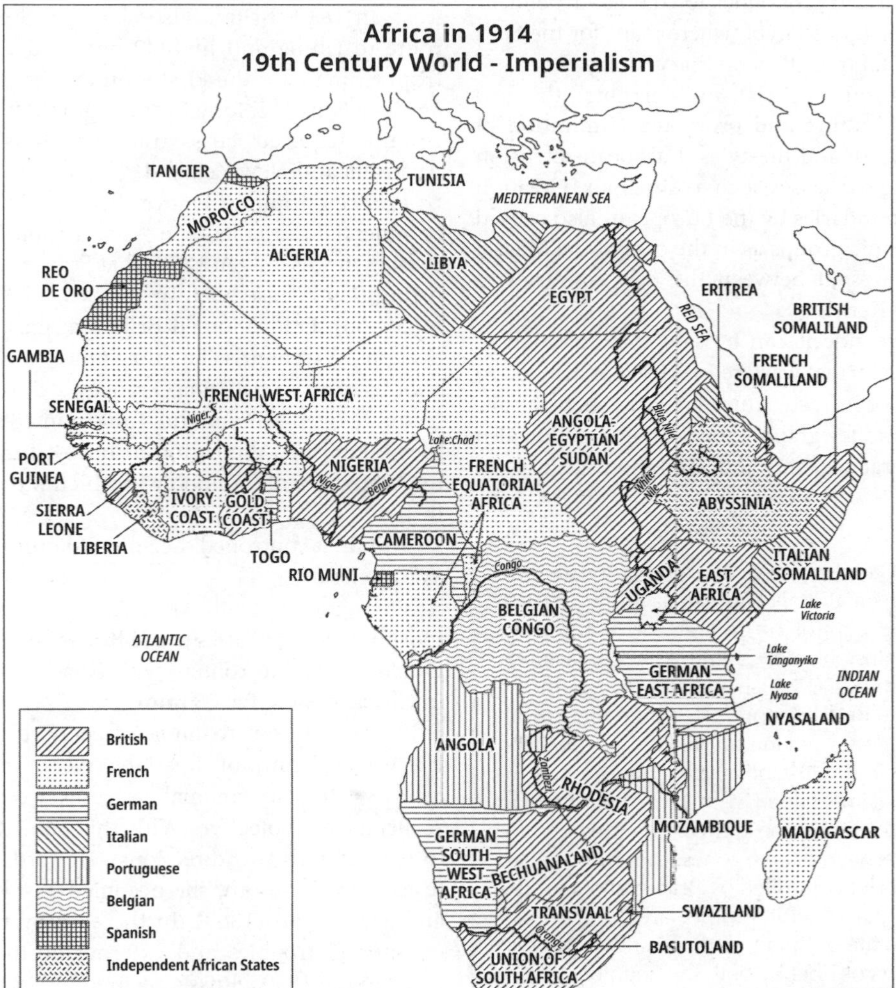

Africa in 1914

Political: Colonisation essentially meant loss of independence of the indigenous people. It also caused division of the African continent on lines of artificial boundaries and unnatural groups. The unification of rival chiefdoms was a notable example. Many ethnic conflicts that exist even today are legacy of colonial superimposition of territorial boundaries on an essential tribal society.

Colonial economy: One immediate impact of colonialism in Africa was the destruction, transformation and subordination of self-sufficient African economies. Raw materials were exploited for European industrial expansion and not for developing the industries of African nations. Further, penetration of financial capital reduced African economies to colonial dependencies. An example was Egypt, where loans for the Suez Canal had a debt trap effect on that country.

Socio-cultural: Imperialism interrupted the flow of traditional culture and promoted admiration of European culture and lifestyles. European intrusion also caused new diseases such as smallpox. Creation of artificial boundaries by the Europeans also caused division of ethnic groups as in the case of the Maasai who were now split between the new countries of Tanzania and Kenya.

On positive side it can be said that colonialism greatly reduced tribal warfare in Africa. It also led to development of infrastructure facilities such as railroads, dams and telegraph. European interaction also improved literacy, health and sanitation facilities in Africa.

The Great Game in Asia. It refers to the intense rivalry between Britain and Russia from 1830 to 1907 for the control of Central and South Asia. Russia's expansion into Central Asia was a threat to the British-India, which was the 'jewel in the crown' of the British Empire. To secure this 'jewel' Britain invaded Afghanistan twice in the 19th century, aiming to establish a friendly regime in Kabul. The Game ended with the **Anglo-Russian Convention** of 1907. The Convention provided for division of Persia into three zones – north controlled by Russia, south controlled by Britain and an independent central zone. It also declared Afghanistan as a protectorate of Britain and non-interference in internal affairs of Tibet by both the countries.

E. Imperialism in Asia

The European countries colonised most of Asia except Japan and Thailand. China escaped being colonised but had been forced to grant ports and trading rights to European powers, Japan and to the United States.

Britain: The British had started their conquest of India in 1757 with the **Battle of Plassey**. They also pre-empted efforts by the French to dominate India in a series of wars known as the **Carnatic Wars**. Securing this priced possession from other imperial powers had been of concern to Britain. To this end Britain secured India's frontiers by acquiring **Burma** in the east and **Baluchistan** in the west. In 1819, Britain also acquired **Singapore** en route to China and in 1842 obtained **Hong Kong** from China after the First Opium War. Malaya was another British colony in the region. In the Pacific, Britain acquired large tract of lands including Australia and New Zealand.

France: Though France had established their commercial settlements in Asian region by the 17th century, it was only in 1850s that France started colonizing South-East Asia. In the Second Opium War (1856–60), France joined Britain against China and occupied **Vietnam** as an entry point to China. After another war with China, France established a protectorate over **Annam and Tonkin** in 1885. In 1887, they established the **Union of Indo-China** comprising Vietnam and Cambodia to which was added Laos in 1899.

Dutch: It controlled the **Spice Islands** now known as Indonesia.

Portuguese: By the 19th century, Portugal lost most of their territories to the British, French and the Dutch and had to content with **Goa** in India, **Macau** in China and the **East Timor**.

Russia: Access to an ice-free port was a long cherished dream of Russian rulers. In the 19th century, Russian colonial ventures were aimed at securing this objective. With this aim, Russia tried to expand into two directions – towards south and to east. In the south, she occupied Tashkent (1864) and Samarkand (1868). In the east, by making use of internal troubles and external hostilities China faced in the 1850s, Russia secured territory in China up to the Amur River (1858). She also acquired territory further east along the Pacific coast up to the Korean boundary. Here Russia built a port – **Vladivostok** (meaning 'Dominator of the East') – and aimed at penetrating further into Manchuria which aim clashed with that of Japan's colonial designs and led to the Russo-Japanese War.

F. New Imperialism in Latin America

With the emergence of the United States as an industrial nation, it was imperative for the American businessmen to look for sources of raw materials and new markets. Many Americans also believed in the racial and cultural superiority of the Anglo-Saxon, and it as their duty to spread the light of civilisation to the 'backward' peoples of the world. The United States entered in the imperial race in the latter-half of the 19th century by abandoning its century long commitment to isolationism. Initially the American focus was in Latin America and the islands in the Pacific.

In 1823, the US President James Monroe had issued a doctrine, the **Monroe Doctrine**, stating that any effort by European nations to take control of any independent state in North or South America would be viewed as 'the manifestation of an unfriendly disposition towards the US'. It also declared that the United States would recognise and not interfere with existing European colonies nor meddle in the internal concerns of European countries. The objective of the Monroe Doctrine was to free the newly independent colonies of Latin America from European intervention and avoid situations which could make the **'New World'** a battleground for the **'Old World'** powers. In the 1880s, the US Secretary of state James G. Blaine formulated the '**Big Brother**' policy which was an extension of the Monroe Doctrine. The Big Brother policy aimed at rallying Latin American nations behind the US leadership and to open their markets to US business

Cuba in the Caribbean was a colony of Spain. By making use of Cubans' rebellion against Spain – the **Cuban War of Independence** – the United States declared war against Spain in 1898 apparently to protect the Americans living in Cuba. Spain was defeated and by the Treaty of Paris (1898) Spain handed over the control over **Cuba** and ownership of Spanish colonies of **Puerto Rico**, **Guam** and the **Philippine islands** to the United States. Though American forces withdrew from Cuba in 1902, the Cuban government had to agree to incorporate eight conditions as laid out in the Platt Amendment in the Cuban Constitution.

Platt Amendment: These were conditions passed by the US Senate in 1901, for withdrawal of American troops from Cuba and to regulate its relations with Cuba. It permitted the United States to oversee Cuba's international relations, economy and internal affairs apart from granting the United States the right to establish a naval base at Guantanamo Bay on Cuba's southeastern coast. Cuba incorporated the Platt Amendments in its 1901 constitution and the United States withdrew from Cuba in 1902 leading to the establishment of the Republic of Cuba. In 1934, American President F.D. Roosevelt as part of his 'Good Neighbour Policy' abrogated these provisions except that of the naval base.

In 1893, the American settlers who controlled the **Hawaii's** sugar-based economy overthrew the Hawaiian queen and established the Republic of Hawaii. In 1898, Hawaii was annexed as a territory of the United States. It was granted statehood as the 50th state of the United States in 1959.

Another expression of American imperialism in Latin America was the construction of the **Panama Canal**. The war with Spain had demonstrated the need to move the naval forces quickly between the east and west coasts. As there was no air power at that time, supremacy in the world meant ability to control oceans and constructing this canal was a geopolitical strategy to make the United States a dominant power in the world. A passage from the Atlantic to the Pacific, doing away the need to travel around the South America, was also good for trade. Panama region was part of Columbia but Columbia was unwilling to yield to the US demand. Now the Americans instigated the Panamanians to rebel against Columbia leading to the creation of the Republic of Panama in 1903. With the new government the United States signed a treaty to construct the canal which was completed in 1914.

Panama Canal: It is an 82-km artificial lock-type waterway connecting the Atlantic and the Pacific Oceans through the Isthmus of Panama. The United States started its construction in 1904 after signing an agreement in this regard with the newly declared Republic of Panama and completed it in 1914. The canal symbolised technological prowess and economic might of the United States and is considered as 'one of the seven wonders of the modern world'. Though under the control of the United States till 1999, the canal is now administered by the Panama Canal Authority, under the government of Panama.

Effects of Imperialism

1. In political sense, it caused emergence of European dominance in the world.
2. Economically, it fostered an interdependent world economy.
3. In socio-cultural terms, imperialism caused dislocation of thousands of indigenous societies, uprooting of tribal cultures and imposition of western culture.

SUMMARY

The Congress of Vienna – It refers to a series of conferences convened in Vienna by the European rulers during 1814–1815. It had three main objectives – containment of France, maintenance of balance of power and restoration of legitimate royal families on the thrones of European states.

Revolutions of the 19th Century – The 19th century was a century of revolutions as revolutionary spirit found its re-emergence in 1820s, 1830 and in 1848. But the revolutionaries could not achieve much as the reactionary forces were strong enough to suppress them.

British democratic politics 1815–1850 – During this period Britain witnessed reforms and restructuring of its political system. The Reform Bill of 1832 which broadened the voting rights and reallocated the parliamentary seats was the most significant. Other measures such as the Cotton Mills Act of 1819, series of Factories Acts and abolition of slavery in 1833 in British colonies too were adopted by the British statesmen of the time and these incremental reforms transformed Britain into a modern democratic state.

Nationalism and Nation-building – The 19th century witnessed the concept of nationalism emerging powerful and fuelling the efforts to build nation-states. Aspirations of different nationalities of the three dominant empires of the time – the Ottoman Empire, the Austro-Hungarian Empire and the Russian Empire were expression of the same.

Balkan Question or the Eastern Question – It refers to a serious debate in the 19th century international relations on 'what should happen to the Balkans and who would dominate the Balkans if the Ottoman Empire collapse'? The Greek Revolution in 1820s and its independence from the Ottoman Empire in 1829, the Crimean War (1853–1856), the Balkan Crisis (1875–1878) were different expression of the Eastern Question which also became a catalyst for the outbreak of the World War I.

Imperialism – The 19th century was also a period of imperialism as the Western powers were engaged in a mad race to extend their hegemony by establishing colonies around the world. National pride of the Western powers, economic incentives such as new markets, sources of raw materials and cheap labour and avenues for investment, competition for possession of strategic locations, missionary spirit and the belief in European superiority were the major factors that boosted the Western nations' drive for colonies.

Questions of Previous Years Civil Services Examination

1. "The Revolutions of 1848 were shaped by the ideas of democracy and nationalism". Critically examine. (2023)
2. "The British Imperialism in South Africa from 1867 to 1902 was influenced to a large extent by the capitalist mining of diamonds". Critically examine. (2023)
3. 'The first Reformation Act (1832) occupies a significant place in the constitutional development of Britain'. Critically examine. (2022)
4. What were the causes and consequences of the revolutionary upsurge of the 1840s in Europe? (2021)
5. In the American Civil War, the victory of the North had many consequences. Some of them were direct and obvious. However, its indirect effects on American development were perhaps even more important. Comment. (2021)
6. 'Lincoln's main thesis was that the Slavery issue had to be decided one way or the other and could no longer be evaded by compromise'. Comment in the light of his role in the American Civil War. (2020)
7. 'The 1848 revolutions frightened the crowned heads of Europe and caused several to abdicate. Those who remained were cognizant of the threats posed by liberalism, nationalism and socialism'. Comment. (2020)
8. Discuss how agrarian crisis accompanied by severe industrial depression triggered the Revolution of 1848. (2017)
9. What is Metternich System? Assess its impact on Europe. (2016)
10. 'A house divided against itself cannot stand. I believe this government cannot endure permanently, half slave and half free'. Explain Abraham Lincoln's perspective. (2016)
11. 'The Berlin Congress (1878) failed to unlock the Eastern Question though there was no major war in Europe for nearly three decades after the treaty it contained the seeds of many future wars'. Critically evaluate. (2015)
12. 'The whole episode, that is, known as the July Revolution (1830) was fought and won not for the establishment of an extreme democracy but to get rid of the aristocratic and clerical attitude of the restored Bourbons'. Discuss. (2015)
13. 'The language of narrow nationalism held at Frankfurt destroyed the German Revolution; as the fatal idea of aggrandizement of the House of Savoy destroyed the Italian Revolution'. Discuss. (2014)
14. 'The passing of the "Reform Act" marked the real beginning of modern party organization in England ... in a real sense, the present political system of England dates from 1832'. Discuss. (2014)
15. To what extent did the expansion of European Powers in the late 19th century help in the modernization of Africa? (2014)
16. Discuss the nature of American overseas expansion in Asia and explain the consequences. (2014)
17. 'New Imperialism was a nationalistic, not an economic phenomena'. Critically examine. (2013)
18. 'Africa was chopped into states artificially created by accidents of European competition'. Analyze. (2013)
19. What do you understand by Imperialism? State briefly its unique features in case of Africa. (2010)
20. 'The Eastern Question has always been an international question'. Elucidate. (2010)
21. 'In all the long annals of Imperialism the partition of Africa is a remarkable freak'. Discuss. (2009)
22. Discuss the emergence of neo-imperialism in the late nineteenth century. (2009)
23. Trace the various stages of European imperialism in Africa in the 19th century. (2001)
24. 'The simultaneous expansion of European power overseas during the last quarter of the 19th century brought them into frequent collisions at remote points all over Africa and Asia'. Discuss. (2000)
25. 'For a tired and timid generation Metternich was the necessary man'. Elucidate. (1993)
26. Examine the issues involved in the American Civil War. Was it a contest between two separate nations? (1991)

CHAPTER 7

Unification of Italy and Germany

In this Chapter

A. Unification of Italy

1. Introduction

For centuries, Italy was a fragmented country, divided into a number of petty states dominated by foreign powers and the battleground of intriguing dynasties. In the 19th century, it was a conglomeration of about a dozen large states and a number of smaller states. In the northwest the kingdom of **Sardinia** (also known as Piedmont) was the only native dynasty in the whole Italy. In the northeast **Lombardy and Venetia** were under the Austrian Empire. Austria also controlled smaller states of **Tuscany, Parma and Modena**. In central Italy a cluster of small states were under the control of the pope and these were known as the **Papal States**. The southern part of the peninsula known as Naples along with the island of Sicily constituted the **Kingdom of the Two Sicilies** and was under the rule of a branch of the Bourbon dynasty of France.

Another feature of the 19th century Italy was the lack of homogeneity across the peninsula. As there were huge differences between the north and south regions of Italy in terms of economy, physical conditions and social structure, there was very little cultural and emotional connection between the people of these regions. In spite of such hindrances, liberal and nationalistic ideas took roots in the minds of many Italians. They aspired to unify Italy and transform it into a modern state.

Italian unification took place in different stages starting from 1848 and was completed in 1871 with Rome being declared as the capital of the Kingdom of Italy. In this long process, three personalities contributed significantly – these were **Giuseppe Mazzini, Giuseppe Garibaldi** and **Count Cavour**. Mazzini was the prophet, Garibaldi, the sword and Cavour the brain of the Italian unification. It was patriotism infused by Mazzini, the wars of Garibaldi and diplomacy of Cavour that proved crucial in the Italian unification.

The Risorgimento

The movement for the unification and consolidation of fragmented states of the Italian peninsula was known as the 'Risorgimento' or the **Resurgence**. It was both an ideological and literary movement aimed at arousing the national consciousness of the Italians. 'Risorgimento' was also the name of a newspaper edited by Count Cavour.

2. Italy and Napoleonic Influence

The ideas of French Revolution had significant impact in Italy. They aroused feelings both against foreign rule and despotism that existed in Italy. Newspapers and pamphlets, in spite of vigilant censorship by the Italian authorities, propagated the developments of the French Revolution as a **struggle between monarchy and revolutionaries** and instilled hope of revolutionary change in their own land too.

During the Napoleonic Era, all of northern and central Italy had been conquered by Napoleon. Under Napoleon the Italian peninsula came to be divided into three parts. The northern parts – Piedmont, Parma, Tuscany, Liguria and Piacenza – were annexed to France. The central parts – Lombardy, Venice, Modena, Romagna, Reggio and the Marshes – were consolidated in 1805 as the **Kingdom of Italy** with Napoleon himself as the king. In southern part, the Kingdom of Naples was placed under his brother Joseph Bonaparte. In 1809, he also annexed Rome and the Papal States and abolished temporal power of the pope.

Napoleon's rule was a novel experience to the Italians, for whom their country was a battle ground of contending nations and mutual jealousies of petty states. Napoleon's occupation resulted in overthrow of the old ruling orders and destruction of last vestiges of feudalism. It also introduced the ideals of freedom and equality. Under **Napoleon's centralised system**, the Italians for the first time experienced a **sense of national unity**. The Napoleonic rule provided to the Italians benefits such as excellent codes of law, a fair system of taxation, better economic conditions, religious and intellectual toleration. Though the Italians had to pay higher taxes, they gained, in return, a network of new roads and improved services which hastened socio-economic transformation and cohesion. The old physical, economic and intellectual barriers were now removed and the Italians began to be aware of a common nationality.

In other words,

1. French Republic had spread republican ideas, institutions and citizenship in Italy.
2. Napoleonic campaigns in Italy had destroyed old structures of feudalism.
3. At the same time, there was reaction against Napoleon's choice of outside rulers to rule Italy which in turn strengthened nationalistic sentiments in the Italians.

3. Italy and the Congress of Vienna

The Congress of Vienna restored the pre-Napoleonic patchwork of independent states in Italy, either directly ruled or influenced by other European powers – especially by Austria. Italy was divided with Austria securing Lombardy and Venice – two richest provinces in Italy. The House of Hapsburgs also controlled smaller states like Tuscany, Modena, Parma and Luca. The Bourbon dynasty was restored in Naples. In the new system, Italy was reduced to merely a '**geographical expression**' – a collection of petty states over whom Austria had dominance.

In short, the Congress of Vienna–

1. created large number of petty states in Italy presided over by the old social orders.
2. placed despotic rulers in these states, many of whom were of foreign dynasties.
3. erected a watchful eye of Austria over the Italian states.
4. suppressed Liberalism and constitutionalism in Italian states.

The restored conservative order enforced strict censorship and practiced severe suppression of liberal and nationalistic thoughts. As a result many intellectuals and liberals fled from the country and some others formed underground societies espousing the cause of Italian unity. The **Carbonari** was one of such secret political groups that originated this time. It had large number of middle-class youngsters, businessmen and intellectuals as members.

In 1820, the Carbonari incited a revolt against despotism in Naples but was suppressed. Similar efforts were also made in Piedmont and in the Papal States but that too were suppressed under the initiative of Austria.

In the **1830s, the European revolutionary fervour** found its resurgence in Italy too in the form of series of insurrections. These took place in Modena, Parma, and in the Papal States like Bologna and Ferrara. The revolutionaries planned to create a United Italian Provinces. But at the request of Pope Gregory XVI, the ruler of the Papal States, the Austrian army marched across the Italian peninsula and crushed the insurrections.

4. The Revolutions of 1848 and the First Italian War of Independence

In 1846, the new pope, Pius IX, enacted numerous reforms in the Papal States. He granted amnesty for political prisoners, relaxed restrictions on the press and modified ecclesiastical nature of his state. These reforms aroused enthusiasm among the people of other Italian states for such reforms. As seen in the previous chapter, it was also the period of revolutionary waves throughout Europe.

All Italy rose up against Austrian domination and for liberal principles. **Charles Albert**, the king of Piedmont-Sardinia, assumed leadership of the national movement and joined Venice and Lombardy in driving the Austrians out of Italy. But Austria defeated Charles Albert and crushed the national insurrection of the Italians at Custoza in July 1848. A humiliated Charles Albert abdicated in favour of his son **Victor Emmanuel II**.

> The kingdom of Piedmont-Sardinia was the largest and most powerful state in Italy. It adopted a liberal constitution in 1848. Apart from being the only constitutional ruler in Italy, the Piedmont king was the only native ruler in whole Italy.

Soon Italian national struggle assumed the form of republican character. '*The war of the princes was finished, that of the people was begun*' as Mazzini organised people on a national level. In Rome the revolutionaries set up a republic under the leadership of Mazzini. Pope Pius IX, who had introduced some reforms, withdrew from the Italian national struggle as he was opposed to a war of liberation against the Catholic Austria and fled from Rome. The flight of the Pope from Rome stirred the Roman Catholic world. In an effort to gain popularity among the powerful Catholic group, Louis Napoleon, the newly elected ruler of the French Republic, sent an army against the Roman Republic. After a two-month defence under Garibaldi, Rome capitulated in June 1849 and the Pope was restored. Garibaldi and Mazzini were forced to flee the country.

Though the movement of 1848 had ended in failure, it had advanced Italian nationalist cause in many ways. The cumulative result of the insurrections of 1848 had been that it provided to the Italian national cause a '*dynasty to represent it and a people to defend it*'.

1. It brought to the forefront, the leadership of the king of Piedmont belonging to an Italian dynasty Charles Albert at first and his son Victor Emmanuel II later. Significant role played by Charles Albert in the national struggle in 1848 had convinced the people that the unification had to be based on a strong monarchy and their choice was Piedmont.
2. It brought all Italians together as people belonging to a single nation devoid of narrow provincialism.
3. Anti-Austrian or for that matter anti-foreign feelings were further strengthened in Italy during this period.
4. Patriots also realised that the Pope was an enemy of Italian unity and could never be the leader of the nationalistic efforts.
5. It also taught them a lesson that Mazzini's romanticism and republicanism and his approach of an armed uprising by the masses will not be workable as they were no match for the Austrian army.
6. The Italians were also convinced of their military weakness and that fragmented small Italian states as no match to the forces of France and Austria. This realisation ignited their desire to enlist support of a powerful foreign ally and to abandon the long time motto of the Italian nationalists that *Italia fara da se* (Italy will act by herself).

5. Count Cavour and the Second Italian War of Independence

The second phase of the Italian unification took place under the leadership of **Piedmont**. In 1852, **Count Camillo di Cavour** was appointed as the

Prime Minister of Piedmont. Under him, the Italian unification efforts were taken from the realm of ideals to the planes of 'Realpolitik' – 'the politics of reality'.

As seen above, the Piedmont's defeat at the hands of Austria in the First Italian War of Independence was an eye opener. Cavour was convinced that Italian unity would come only by expelling Austria and that would only be possible with the support of a great military power of the time. To meet this objective, Cavour took steps to secure the sympathy of two Great European powers – France and Britain. In 1855, Cavour joined the **Crimean War** on the side of England and France against Russia. As a result, Piedmont could assume a place among the victors at the **Congress of Paris** 1856, convened to discuss the peace. Here, Cavour raised the plight of Italy, and declared that the only threat to peace in Italy and the basic cause of subversive plots was the Austrian over-lordship. Cavour, thus brilliantly converted Italian issue as an issue of European concern by raising the whole Italian question before the assembled diplomats and denounced Austria for occupying the Italian lands.

Secondly, Cavour was also convinced that the Italian unification shall be undertaken under the leadership of Piedmont. His comment 'Piedmont would gather to itself all the living forces of Italy and would lead our mother country to the high destinies to which she is called' illustrated this point. To claim this role, Piedmont had to be transformed both economically and politically. Steps such as encouragement to agriculture, promotion of trade and commerce, abolition of privileges and immunities of the clergy, building up of railways and steamships, reorganisation of currency system and taxation were implemented. In polity, he developed parliamentary government on English model. He also initiated ecclesiastical, army, judicial and fiscal reforms. Within a few years Piedmont became a progressive modern state and also a model state to be emulated by other Italian states, placing it at the leadership role in the Risorgimento.

i. The Compact of Plombieres

The prestige of Piedmont had been strengthened with its military's role in the Crimean War. Side by side the diplomatic manoeuvre at the Congress of Paris had won it the sympathy of Europe. Cavour now concluded a secret agreement known as the **'Compact of Plombieres'** (1858) with Napoleon III, by which Napoleon agreed to support Piedmont, if it was attacked by Austria. After the war, Piedmont was to acquire Lombardy and Venetia by expelling Austria and France was to obtain Nice and Savoy from Piedmont as reward.

Napoleon III had his own reasons to conclude the Plombieres Agreement.

1. First, Napoleon III was keen to correct the humiliation of France at the Vienna Congress of 1815.
2. Second, a war against Austria was expected to bring military glory to France and humiliation to Austria which in turn was expected to raise the status of France among the European nations.
3. Third, on an ideological level Napoleon believed that supporting Italian nationalist aspirations would earn him the status of a progressive liberalist.
4. Last, on a personal level too Napoleon III was sympathetic to the cause of Italy, as he had spent his childhood in Italy and had fought as a Carbonari in 1831.
5. An assassination attempt on Napoleon III by an Italian in Paris, Felice Orsini, in January 1859 too had profound effect on Napoleon. Cavour projected the assassination attempt as an act of desperation by the people under the oppressive acts of Austria and despotism in Italian states. Napoleon now was determined to support Piedmont against Austria in order to defuse the wider revolutionary activities in Italy.

ii. Austro-Sardinian War

Having secured the support of Napoleon III, Cavour manoeuvred Austria into declaring war, for it had to appear that Austria was the aggressor. By imposing hostile tariffs, waging press attacks and starting an extensive military buildup, Cavour provoked Austria. These steps were beyond the endurance level for Austria, which sent an ultimatum to Piedmont demanding disarmament. After this demand was rejected by Piedmont, Austria declared war. Satisfied with the turn of events as expected, Cavour exclaimed that the 'die is cast, and we have made history'.

The war broke out in 1859. Supported by the French forces and aided by Garibaldi and the nationalist volunteers from all over Italy, Piedmont defeated Austria in the **Battles of Magenta and Solferino** and conquered Lombardy. At this crucial moment without consulting his ally, Napoleon III signed armistice with Austria at **Villafranca** (1859) which ended the conflict.

iii. The Truce of Villafranca

As per this agreement, Piedmont was to acquire Lombardy and Austria was to retain Venetia. The rulers of Tuscany, Parma, Modena and Romagna (one of the Papal States) who had been expelled by the people during the war were to be restored. Napoleon was not to claim Nice and Savoy as he had not taken the war to its logical conclusion.

Historians attribute many factors that caused the volte-face of Napoleon. Napoleon III was fully awake to the emerging realities. First, the French had incurred heavy losses in the war and they were also against Piedmont gaining much power at the expense of French men. Second, there was a fear of Prussian intervention on the side of Austria, as a decisive French victory in the conflict would be against the interests of Prussia. Next, the French Catholics, who were hostile to the war, were afraid of a takeover of Papal territory by Piedmont. Above all, the defeat of the Austrians had created a wave of nationalist outburst among the people of north-central Italian duchies who now expelled their rulers and demanded union with Piedmont. This emerging tendency of Italian unity was a threat to France. To Napoleon, **Italian independence** was one thing and **Italian unity** was altogether a different thing to which he had no sympathy at all. In other words Napoleon was open to the idea of independent but divided Italy under French hegemony but not to a united Italy under Piedmont.

As the Truce of Villafranca was a total disappointment to Cavour, he urged Victor Immanuel to repudiate the treaty and to continue the war until all northern Italy was united. But, Victor Immanuel opted for caution and restraint on the ground that it was wiser to take what one could get at the moment and wait for the future to unveil.

In spite of the provision in the Truce of Villafranca, in the north-central duchies of **Parma, Modena, Tuscany** and **Romagna,** the expelled rulers could not be reinstated due to strong popular opposition. People in these states demanded their unification with Piedmont. England took a policy of non-intervention and provided diplomatic support by declaring that the Italians were free to settle their own affairs. Britain now wished for a strong Italian state as a counterweight to France. Moving quickly, Cavour reopened the offer of Nice and Savoy to Napoleon III, secured his support and incorporated these states with Sardinia–Piedmont after conducting plebiscites in these states. The northern half of Italy except Venetia was united under Piedmont and freed from foreign control.

iv. The March of 'the Thousand'

Victory of the nationalists in unifying the northern part of Italy now spurred revolutionary activity in the southern kingdom of the Two Sicilies (Naples and Sicily) and in 1860 the Sicilians rose in revolt. In May 1860, Garibaldi sailed for Sicily leading his volunteer army known as '**the Red Shirts**' in an expedition known as the '**Expedition of the Thousand**' to liberate the land from its Bourbon ruler. Within three months Garibaldi liberated the entire island of Sicily and proclaimed himself as the ruler of Sicily in the name of Victor Emmanuel II of Piedmont. Next, he crossed to the mainland of Italy and occupied Naples in September 1860, while its King Francis II fled at his approach. Garibaldi now prepared to advance to Rome.

Garibaldi's brilliant success in the south and the march to Rome was a matter of concern to Cavour and a threat to the Italian unification efforts in more ways than one. Cavour's comment that 'Italy must be saved from foreigners, evil principles and mad men' reflected this concern.

- Cavour considered Garibaldi too impulsive and rash under whom the movement would acquire a republican character. Opposed to it, Cavour wanted a **constitutional monarchy** under the leadership of Piedmont.

- Cavour also feared that a republican twist to the unification effort would lead to **civil war** leading to the destruction of the national cause.
- Cavour also had realised that an assault on Rome by Garibaldi would lead to **French intervention** as Napoleon III had pledged the protection of the Pope's lands and had stationed a French force in Rome since 1849. Moreover, an attack on Rome would have caused profound indignation among the Catholics around the world.

To foster the unification of Italy by checking Garibaldi's march to Rome and thus to save Italy from foreign intervention, influence of 'evil principle' of republicanism and impulsive actions of mad men, Cavour dispatched king Victor Emmanuel II to preempt Garibaldi. Cavour believed that Napoleon III would not interfere so long as Rome was respected and Pope was unharmed. Victor Emmanuel II defeated the Papal army and captured the Papal States of **Umbria and the Marches**. Rome and its surrounding regions continued to remain under papal rule. Victor Emmanuel continued his march towards south to meet Garibaldi and his Red Shirts. Victor Emmanuel and Garibaldi met at Teano on 26 October 1860 which is famously known as the **'Handshake of Teano'**. Garibaldi turned over his conquest to Victor Emmanuel hailing him as the King of Italy.

Meanwhile plebiscites were held in the former Papal and Bourbon provinces which resulted in overwhelming support for their union with the Kingdom of Sardinia-Piedmont. The Kingdom of Sardinia expanded into the **Kingdom of Italy**. Victor Emmanuel was officially declared the King of Italy in March 1861 by the first Italian Parliament representing all Italy except Rome and Venetia.

6. The Third Italian War of Independence

Though Cavour died in 1861, unification efforts were continued. The two states – Venetia held by Austria and Rome held by Pope and protected by the French troops – remained outside the new Italy. In 1866, the **Austro-Prussian War** broke out between Austria and Prussia for the position of leadership among the German states. Italy sided with the Prussians and attacked Austria. After being defeated by Prussia at the **Battle of Sadowa**, Austria was compelled to surrender Venetia to Italy.

7. The Franco-Prussian War and the Completion of Italian Unification

On the outbreak of the **Franco-Prussian War** in 1870, the French forces were withdrawn from Rome for their redeployment against Prussia. Victor Emmanuel II now marched in with his troops and occupied Rome in September 1870. After conducting a plebiscite, Rome was annexed to the Kingdom of Italy. The event marked the final step in the long process of Italian unification. In July 1871, the capital of Italy was shifted from **Florence to Rome**.

> After annexation of Rome to Italy, Vatican City, a part of Rome, became an independent territory governed by the Pope. 'The Roman Question', the dispute regarding the status of Pope as a temporal authority, emerged and existed till the Lateran Treaty of 1929. By this treaty pope acknowledged Italian sovereignty over the former Papal States and Italy recognised sovereignty of pope over Vatican City. Now known as the Vatican City State, it is the smallest state in the world by both area and population.

8. Aftermath of Italian Unification

'Now that we have made Italy, we must make Italians', this was the comment about the situation in Italy after its unification. The unification of Italy was more about Piedmontisation of Italy in the form of extension of Peidmontese monarchy, legal system, tax system and appointment of Piedmontese officials all over the peninsula. These measures mostly benefitted the industrial north, while exacerbating the problems of poverty and famine in south which in turn caused disunity within the country.

Many sections in Italian society such as the aristocrats were not fully impressed by the revolutionary ideals. Pope too was against the Italian state till Mussolini came to power. The socialists and liberals were at loggerheads even in matters of basic issues of legislation and administration all of

Italian Unification

which hampered Italy's emergence as a powerful nation.

Italian Irredenta was a movement in Italy even after the unification. This movement aimed at taking back those territories which the Italians considered as their own but 'lost' in some point of time. At the end of the First World War Italy annexed some more territories – Trentino, Trieste and South Tyrol as part of irredentism.

Mazzini was born in Genoa in 1805. He was a prolific writer, romantic and liberal. After graduating in law he joined the **Carbonari**, a secret revolutionary group, aimed at political regeneration of Italy. In 1831, Mazzini started a new society called **'Young Italy'** to promote Italian unity – with its aim of 'one, free, independent, republican nation'. Mazzini had been jailed many times for organising insurrections and he also had to spend many years in exile in Geneva, Paris and London. During the revolution in 1848–49, a republic was declared in Rome under Mazzini but was soon overthrown by the French forces which reinstated the pope to power. After this failure, Mazzini once again went in to exile. As a liberal he stood for republican and constitutional government in Italy. As a romantic Mazzini believed that an awakened Italy would usher in liberty, equality and regeneration of humanity. Mazzini was also a visionary who advocated a 'United States of Europe' which he visualised as a logical culmination of the Italian unification. With this aim he organised '**Young Europe**'. Mazzini's greatest contribution towards the Italian unification was of kindling enthusiasm and keeping the spirit of national unity alive in the minds of the Italians, in spite of heavy odds of the times. With his charisma and eloquence he infused spiritual intensity to the Risorgimento and prepared ground for others like Garibaldi and Cavour to take it to its logical conclusion. At the age of 67 Mazzini passed away in Pisa in 1872.

Giuseppe Garibaldi was born in Nice in the Kingdom of Sardinia in 1807. Garibaldi's meeting with Mazzini in 1833 proved to be monumental as Garibaldi became a political disciple of Mazzini. Garibaldi joined the Carbonari and after a failed rebellion in Piedmont in 1834 fled to South America. In South America he participated in revolutionary movements in Brazil and Uruguay. Amidst the revolutionary turmoil of 1848, Garibaldi returned to Italy and led his volunteer army **'the Red Shirts'** in minor campaigns. Republican forces under Garibaldi defended the Republic of Rome against the French forces in 1849. After the recapture of Rome by the French forces Garibaldi escaped to America. Garibaldi returned to Italy during the Second Italian War of Independence but was totally dissatisfied when his home city – Nice – was surrendered to France in return for crucial military assistance. In 1860, taking advantage of uprisings in the Kingdom of Two Sicilies, Garibaldi led his Redshirts – an army of red-shirted volunteers – and conquered Sicily and Naples. Garibaldi handed over all his territorial gains to the Piedmont king Victor Emmanuel II and retired to the rocky island Caprera, off the coast of Sardinia. In 1866, Garibaldi again led his volunteers during the Austro-Prussian War (the Third Italian War of Independence). Garibaldi apart from being a nationalist to the core was an expert military commander. For his military expeditions he is also known as the **'Hero of the Two Worlds'**, that is of Europe and of the Americas. Garibaldi is also considered as the global exemplar of the 19th century revolutionary nationalism. While Cavour harnessed the support of powerful groups such as Piedmontese parliament and of Napoleon III, Garibaldi gained popular support and military victories in the name of a new Italy. A true patriot and a man of action, Garibaldi died in 1882.

Count Cavour was born in Turin in 1810 as the son of a Piedmontese noble. In his early years, he edited a newspaper advocating liberal reforms in Piedmont. He started his career as a military officer but resigned because of boredom of the military life. Cavour entered politics during the political upheavals of the 1848. In 1850, he was appointed as the Minister of Agriculture and Commerce and later as the Minister of Finance. In 1852, Cavour was appointed as the Prime Minister of Piedmont in which position he advanced the unification of Italy in great measure. Cavour was neither a dreamer nor a speechmaker but a realist and tough-minded task master in politics. Cavour believed that liberation and unification of Italy shall be under the leadership of Piedmont. Cavour never planned for the unification of Italy, rather his objective was to expand Piedmont. With this aim Cavour took steps to develop Piedmont as a modern state to induce other states of Italy to accept Piedmontese leadership. Special attention was given to development of railways, building up of army and navy. As he believed economic progress have to precede political change, emphasis was given to free trade and to the development of agriculture techniques. Cavour was also convinced that mass uprisings would not succeed in Italy as it was against the interest of Austria as demonstrated during the Revolutions of 1848. Cavour was also against Mazzini's goal of a democratic republic in Italy. As a practical politician

Cavour was convinced that mere enthusiasm or unaided efforts alone would not take Italy towards her historical destiny for which she required the support of a great power of Europe. He joined England and France in the Crimean War against Russia with the object of securing the friendship of Britain and France and to improve Piedmont's image in international affairs. Cavour also used his diplomatic skills in securing the French ruler Napoleon III's support for Piedmont against Austria and manoeuvred Austria into declaring war which took Italian unification effort to its next stage. Cavour's **farsightedness and diplomatic skills** were also well evident in checking Garibaldi's march in 1860, with his Redshirts to Rome, saving Italian nationalist movement turning republican and also in preventing foreign intervention in support of Rome. It is rightly observed that, if there had been no Cavour to win the confidence, sympathy and support of Europe, the efforts of others like Mazzini and Garibaldi would have added more chapters to the history of unsuccessful patriotism. In 1861, Victor Emmanuel II declared the Kingdom of Italy and appointed Cavour as his Prime Minister but Cavour died within a few months as a victim to his restless energy.

SUMMARY

Italy – In the 19th century, Italy was divided into a number of petty states dominated by foreign powers. There were huge differences between the north and south of Italy in terms of economy, physical features and social structure. Despite such hurdles Italy emerged as a united nation in 1871.

The Revolutions of 1848 and the First Italian War of Independence – In 1848 there was a revolutionary wave that swept through the European states. Italians too came under this spirit and under the leadership of Mazzini they set up a Republic in Rome upon which the Pope Pius IX fled from Rome. Now the new ruler of France Louis Napoleon in order to please the Catholic world sent an army and suppressed the Republic and shattered their dream for unity.

Count Cavour and the Second Italian War of Independence – This was the second phase of the Italians' effort for unity. Count Cavour, the Prime Minister of Piedmont (one of the states in Italy) sided with France and Britain in the Crimean War in1855 and secured sympathy of these great powers to the Italian cause. Then Cavour enlisted the support of France by signing an agreement known as the 'Compact of Plombieres' and fought a war against Austria, defeated it and acquired Lombardy from Austria. Cavour also added the north-central states of Italy – Parma, Modena, Tuscany and Romagna – with Piedmont by enlisting diplomatic support of Britain and France and by conducting plebiscites in these states. The second phase of Italian unification effort was successful to the extent that it brought the northern half of the Italian peninsula except Venetia under the control of Piedmont. The success of the nationalists in the north stirred the people in the southern Italy and a revolutionary leader named Garibaldi organised a volunteer army 'the Red Shirts' and liberated Sicily and Naples from the Bourbon monarchs and handed over to Victor Emmanuel, the ruler of Piedmont. Consequently, Victor Emmanuel was declared the King of Italy in 1861.

The Third Italian War of Independence – In the Austro-Prussian War of 1866 Italy sided with Prussia. Austria was defeated in the war and was forced to surrender Venetia to Italy.

The Franco-Prussian War and the completion of Italian unification – This was the last step in the Italian unification and took place during the Franco-Prussian War of 1870. Making use of the withdrawal of the French forces from Rome for their redeployment against Prussia Italy sent its army and annexed Rome, the only territory that remained outside Italian control. The Italian capital was shifted to Rome in 1871.

Questions of Previous Years Civil Services Examination

1. How was Italy transformed from a 'geographical expression' to a nation-state? (2019)
2. 'They have stopped me from making Italy by diplomacy from the North; I will make it by a revolution from the South'. Discuss. (2005)
3. 'The unification of Italy completed the destruction of the European order'. Discuss. (1997)
4. What were the obstacles to Italian unification till 1852? How and with what methods was the unification of Italy achieved? (1993)

B. Unification of Germany

1. Introduction

In the beginning of the 19th century, Germany was made up of dozens upon dozens of small political units (kingdoms, duchies and so forth) engaged in wars against each other. They were bound together in the name of the Holy Roman Empire. The Kingdom of **Austria** ruled by the **Hapsburgs** and the Kingdom of **Prussia** ruled by the **Hohenzollerns** were two largest states in the Holy Roman Empire. These two states rivalled for leadership of the German states which was characterised by the term **German Dualism**.

With the emergence of the concept of nationalism in the 19th century, the people of Germany too aspired for unifying their regions into a nation. This process of unifying German territories into a nation was completed by the later part of the century. The unification process was enforced from the top-down under the leadership of Prussia and its Chancellor Otto von Bismarck. Bismarck triumphed in his mission and the unified Germany announced emergence of a powerful nation in world affairs.

2. Napoleonic Influence in Germany

As seen above, the German-speaking territories in central Europe (more than 300 political entities) were part of the **Holy Roman Empire**. During his wars of conquest, Napoleon Bonaparte defeated Francis II, the Holy Roman Emperor, and by the **Treaty of Pressburg** in 1805 had forced him to dissolve the Holy Roman Empire, which was in existence for over a thousand years. Francis II also renounced his title as the Holy Roman Emperor and became the **King of Austria** with the title Francis I.

Napoleon's policy in Germany was to reduce the two powerful states in Germany – **Austria and Prussia** – into insignificance and increase the power of the smaller states, which is poetically expressed as to *abase the mountains and to exalt the valleys.* In order to bring the German states under his subordination, Napoleon created the **Confederation of Rhine** in 1806 comprising 36 states in all but, without Austria and Prussia. This system of client states of Napoleon was meant to counterpoise the power of Prussia and Austria. Napoleon, as the Protector of the Confederation, dictated foreign policy of these states, imposed mass-conscription and demanded from these states large number of military supplies. Rulers of many of these satellite states relaxed economic barriers, removed religious restrictions and servile obligations and introduced centralised administrative structures in imitation of Napoleon – all of which transformed the old ways and projected political unity an achievable possibility.

The **Napoleonic protectorate** over the German states and influence of **French revolutionary ideas and institutions** had tremendous impact in Germany. During the French occupation, French revolutionary ideas of liberty, equality, fraternity and nationalism had infiltrated among the Germans. The regions that came under the French rule experienced equality before law, freedom of opportunity and also of the advantages of efficient centralised administration. For many Germans, the triumphs of Napoleon also became an example of the great deeds that love and devotion of fatherland could inspire.

On the other hand, the **struggles against Napoleon** went into creating a unity feeling among the German people. The very presence of foreign occupiers – arrogant and avaricious – had instilled a sense of nationalism among the Germans. People of many regions with their various dialects had found 'German' as a common definition during the struggle against the French occupation. This experience of a **German-speaking central Europe** contributed to the emergence of unity feeling among the Germans. How this shared experience and common language contributed to the shaping of German nationalism is observed by the German philosopher of the time Johann Fichte in the words – 'Those who speak the same language are joined to each other by a multitude of invisible bonds by nature itself…and are by nature one and an inseparable whole'.

Sacrifices of the Germans under the Napoleonic rule further reinforced this resentment against foreign rule. Napoleon's continental system had nearly ruined the central European economy. Further, Napoleon's Russian campaign was disastrous to the German people. In this campaign more than one lakh troops from German lands had perished accentuating the German desire for a central Europe without the hegemony of Napoleon. This **anti-Napoleon feeling** caused consolidation of unity consciousness among the Germans of all classes. Youngsters formed voluntary militias such as the Lutzow Free Corps (1813) in Prussia. Thus, the experiences of Germans during their fight against Napoleon had transformed political, social and cultural relationships within the German states.

3. The Congress of Vienna and Germany

The Congress of Vienna in 1815 established a new European system on the **principle of balance of power** by reorganising Europe into **spheres of influence**. This new political and diplomatic system created by the Congress of Vienna meant suppression of nationalistic aspirations of German people.

It organised Germany into a confederation of 39 German-speaking states, the **German Confederation**, which included both Prussia and Austria. The **'Bundestag'**, its assembly of appointed representatives, was the Federal Diet and the Hapsburg emperor of Austria was the titular head of this parliament. This was highly reactionary step by the Concert of Europe and highly disappointing to the nationalist Germans, who considered it as the **'great deception of Vienna'**. Reasons were–

1. The Confederation was a union of princes and not of people.
2. It was under the leadership of Metternich (chief minister of Austria), the most reactionary leader in Europe of the time who held conservative views in politics. He was a believer in autocratic absolutism as the best form of government and a strong opponent of liberalism and nationalism.
3. The princes were against all liberal reforms and unity of people as it would have affected their interests.
4. The princes were mutually jealous of each other, which hampered any concerted effort for the well-being and unity of the Germans.
5. Moreover, through a number of decrees known as the **Carlsbad Decrees** issued in 1819, Metternich enforced reactionary restrictions in the German Confederation, which included banning of nationalist fraternities, censorship of the press and persecution of liberals and nationalists as demagogues. The assassination of a conservative German dramatist August Von Kotzebue by a radical student seeking German unification was taken as an excuse by Metternich for enforcing these decrees.

4. Emergence of German Nationalism

In spite of the efforts by the conservatives to suppress nationalist aspirations, certain developments gave shape to emerging national consciousness in Germany. First in this direction was the establishment of **Zollverein** or **customs union** by Prussia and its neighbouring states. The members of the Zollverein removed their tariff walls, established free trade among them facilitating a common fiscal policy. The economic union improved transportation of raw materials and of the finished goods across territorial borders of German states. It also brought down the number of currencies from the previously existed more than 30 to 2 and promoted inter-dependence of member states.

The Zollverein Treaties were formalised on 1 January 1834 and by 1850 it had almost all the states in Germany except Austria. The Zollverein was the most important institutional development for Germany's economic unification which facilitated regional development and changed regional fortunes by the opening and closing of markets.

The Zollverein proved to be the precursor of political union of Germany as it–

1. Instilled a spirit of inter-dependence among the German states.
2. Placed Prussia on the leadership role in German affairs, enabling it to play a lead role in the political unification in future.
3. It kept Austria (which was the greatest hurdle in German unity) out of the customs union, thus ensuring no role for Austria in the future destiny of the Germans.

It is pertinent here to ask, why Austria was exempted from this Union.

1. Prussia wanted to play a leading role in the German affairs ever since the wars against Napoleon in which she had played an important role.
2. Austria maintained a highly protective industrial sector, which was against the concept of Zollverein.
3. Prince Von Metternich, Austria's chancellor and arch-enemy of German nationalism – was opposed to the idea.

Thus, by eliminating Austrian influence in Germany and by improving economies of German states the Zollverein marked a significant step towards German unity.

The second important factor in strengthening the national consciousness of the Germans was **infrastructural developments**. Improvements in road and railway transportation promoted unity feeling among the people of different German states. By the mid-19th century, road, water and rail transportation had improved leaps and bounds in German states. Invention of macadam, helped in the construction of hard-surfaced roads, and boats with steam engine facilitated upstream navigation. By 1852, more than 16,600 kilometres of roads had been constructed in Prussia alone. By 1860, more than 11,157 kilometres of railway lines had been constructed and a network of canals from the Danube, the Weser and the Elbe rivers had been created, all of which proved to be the **'veins and arteries of the body politic'**. The railway lines apart from encouraging economic activity by creating demand for commodities and by facilitating commerce changed how cities looked and how people travelled. As people travelled more and more, it promoted freedom, prosperity and contact with each other. Importance of the railways in German unification could be best understood from the comment that 'The German Empire was founded with the construction of the first railway' by Wilhelm Raabe, one of the contemporary novelists in Germany.

In this context it is also important to note the role of natural resources in Germany. Natural resources of coal and iron from the Saar Basin provided a strong boost to industrialisation in German states especially in Prussia. Because of this fact the British economist Keynes commented that instead of 'blood and iron' it was Prussia's **'coal and iron'** that enabled German unification.

The **European Liberalism** had its own share in the growth of nationalist feelings in the German people. Liberalism as a political philosophy is based on the principles of liberty and equality and was opposed to absolute monarchy, divine right of kings and hereditary privileges. It sought to replace them with rule of law and representative democracy. This was the intellectual basis for unification efforts in Germany and also the tool to challenge dynastic and despotic models of social and political organisation.

German national identity had also been nurtured by artists, writers and linguists. Thinkers such as **Schiller and Fichte** were engaged in arousing patriotic feelings of the Germans. By identifying and emphasising the importance of tradition, education and linguistic unity of the German people, they promoted national consciousness.

Hambach Festival was one of the cultural events aimed at promoting German identity. Held at the Hambach Castle, this festival was organised as a non-political country fair. The meeting demanded civil and political rights and popular sovereignty. It also established a flag with combination of black, red and gold as a symbol of democratic movement for a united Germany which are also the colours of German flag today.

5. Revolutions of 1830 and 1848 in Germany

The July Revolution of France in 1830 had its echo in Germany and people rose up in many places demanding liberal constitutions. But Prussia and Austria – the two dominant states under absolute monarchies – suppressed these uprisings.

In March 1848, the German liberals rose in revolt all over Germany and convened an all-**German National Parliament** at Frankfurt. It produced a constitution known as the **Frankfurt Constitution** which proclaimed a **German Federation** based on the principles of parliamentary democracy and constitutional monarchy. Leadership of this federation was offered to the Prussian King **Frederick William IV**. But the king Frederick William IV declined the offer, as he was apprehensive of a hostile reaction by Austria and was also against being crowned by a revolutionary assembly, 'pick up a crown from the gutter' as he described it. He also argued that such an offer an abridgement of the rights of the German Princes.

Why liberalism failed in Germany in 1848?

1. Strong resistance by Austria was the major cause of the failure.
2. Unwillingness of Prussian king Frederick William IV to assume the throne of the German Confederation was the second important factor.
3. Idea of the rights of the people had not been penetrated deep in German conscious.
4. Princes in German states were reluctant to any move which would have endangered their position and interest.

The failure of the revolution of 1848 had far reaching repercussions on German Liberalism and its role in German unification. The liberals who had underestimated the power of the conservative old order now became disenchanted. Many Liberals fled from the country which weakened the liberal leadership. Others replaced idealism with realism and now started thinking of German unity through Prussian arms and not through liberal ideals. They held the view that the German question was now a simple alternative between Prussia and Austria. They also believed that the German question is no more a constitutional question but a question of power and of the Prussian monarchy. Prussia was fitted for the leadership role as–

1. It was Prussia that led German resistance to Napoleon in the War of Liberation and in the Battle of Waterloo.
2. Prussia was the strongest and largest of the German states.
3. The Customs Union Zollverein had placed Prussia in the economic leadership of German states and in the establishment of strong ties between them.
4. Above all, Prussia was the only power in Germany capable of challenging Austria, which was the main hurdle in German unification.
5. The Prussian kings had fashioned a rigorously trained and disciplined army, state bureaucracy was often staffed by ex-soldiers, and the Prussian throne was supported by the Junkers, the powerful aristocrats. Hence, the state apparatus of Prussia was capable of meeting its missions and objectives

6. Prussia as the Agent of Unification

In 1861, **Frederick William I** succeeded to the throne of Prussia and the first solid step for unification of

Germany was taken unintentionally. Apart from being a believer in autocracy and upholder of the prerogatives of the crown, William I was also a Prussian to the core who believed in the mission of Prussia in the destiny of German nation.

Being a military man by training, he believed that the destiny of Prussia was bound up with her army. To modernise the army the king demanded money from **the Prussian parliament – Diet**. The Diet refused the grant under the influence of liberals who feared that such reforms would strengthen the monarchy and military's role. The king dissolved the legislature, but in the general elections the liberals swept the polls. The new legislature too rejected army reform proposals creating a deadlock between the king and the parliament.

7. Bismarck and His Reforms

William I now (in 1862) appointed Bismarck as the Minister President (Chancellor) of Prussia, and with this another significant step was taken towards the unification of Germany. The outlook and aims of both the king and the Chancellor were similar and one. Both were believers in autocracy and upholders of prerogatives of the crown. Both believed in the higher role Prussia was destined to play in Germany. Both believed in the role of military in settling the issues of the time. Thus, the era of German unification under the leadership of Prussia, with the method of military might, was initiated right away with the appointment of Bismarck as Minister President.

Bismarck

Bismarck was a Junker (landed noble) of Prussia. He subscribed to Realpolitik-politics based not on morality but on power and practicality. He was destined to play a dominant role in German and European politics for the next 30 years.

Bismarck initiated **modernisation of Prussian armed forces**. Liberals who were in majority in the Diet were outraged by the domineering and authoritarian attitude of Bismarck, hence again refused the grants. Bismarck ordered collection of taxes without parliament's approval and carried on with reforms. To counter the hostile attitude of the Parliament towards his military reforms he made a speech to the Budget Committee of the Prussian Chamber of Deputies on 30 September 1862, that 'the position of Prussia in Germany will not be determined by its liberalism but by its power … ***the great questions of the time will not be resolved by speeches and majority decisions but by blood and iron***'. This speech marked a clear shift from the liberal and democratic character to more conservative realpolitik in the German unification.

As opposition to his reforms gained momentum, Bismarck dismissed the lower chamber of the legislature, introduced strict censorship on the press, dismissed liberals from civil services and arrested and jailed outspoken liberals.

8. Bismarck and the Wars of German Unification

Bismarck accomplished his aim of German unification through a series of short but decisive wars. These were – the **Danish-Prussian War (1864)**, the **Austro-Prussian War (1866)** and the **Franco-Prussian War (1870–71)**.

i. The Danish-Prussian War

Schleswig and Holstein were two duchies (a territory or domain ruled by a duke or duchess) located in the Jutland peninsula. The king of Denmark was also the Duke of these two duchies. As the people of these territories were partly Danish and partly German, both the countries desired incorporation of these two territories with them.

In 1863, the Danish king introduced a new constitution providing for the incorporation of Schleswig with Denmark and binding Holstein to Denmark with closer ties. Protests erupted not only in the two duchies but also in Germany as it was the violation of the Treaty of London 1852 which had guaranteed indissolubility of the two duchies.

To Bismarck, the Schleswig-Holstein offered a golden opportunity to carry forward his realpolitik aimed at German unification. Bismarck intended to–

1. Incorporate the duchies with Prussia as a part of his larger design of unifying Germany.
2. Silence the opponents of his 'blood and iron' policy by the aggrandisement of Prussia.

3. Use the issue to turn the tables on Austria and to expel Austria from the German affairs. Bismarck believed that 'Germany was too narrow for both Austria and Prussia'. Bismarck wanted Prussianisation of Germany for which the greatest hurdle was Austria.

As the first step of the plan, Bismarck formed an alliance with Austria to settle the Schleswig-Holstein issue and issued an ultimatum to Denmark demanding repeal of the new constitution. Austria joined hands with Prussia with an ulterior motive of preventing Prussia from annexing the territories to herself. As the ultimatum to Denmark was not complied, Austro-Prussian army invaded and defeated Denmark in 1864. The **Treaty of Vienna** (October 1864) ended the war and the Danish king ceded Duchies of Schleswig and Holstein to Austria and Prussia jointly.

Austria and Prussia, the victors of the war, could not agree as to the final disposition of the duchies. Hence, an agreement was signed between the two known as the **Convention of Gastein** (signed in Bad Gastein in Austria in 1865) which provided for–

1. Occupation of Holstein by Austria and Schleswig by Prussia.
2. Any future dispute over the duchies was not to be brought before the German Diet.

As far as Bismarck was concerned, the Convention of Gastein was a mechanism to buy time, till the emergence of a suitable moment to goad Austria into war and to expel her from the German affairs. For him, the Convention 'merely papered over the cracks'. Anticipating a show down with Austria, Bismarck made certain diplomatic moves to safeguard Prussia and to isolate Austria in the fight for supremacy in German affairs.

1. Bismarck had already secured the goodwill of the Czar of Russia by supporting Czar in the Polish insurrection in 1863.
2. In 1865, Bismarck secured French neutrality by paying a visit to Napoleon III, and by playing upon Napoleon's sympathy to nationalism.
3. Bismarck also secured the support of Italy with the promise of Venetia as reward.

Austria had no intention of keeping Holstein which was encircled by Prussian territory, hence announced her decision to refer the question of the Duchies to the Federal German Diet. Arguing that the action of Austria amounted violation of the Convention of Gastein, the Prussian troops invaded Holstein and expelled the Austrians.

ii. The Austro-Prussian War

The war between Austria and Prussia was of brief duration and is called as the 'Seven Weeks War'. Intervention of Italian forces in support of Prussia forced Austria to divide their forces. With amazing swiftness, the Prussian forces overran Austrian territory and decisively defeated Austria at the **Battle of Sadowa** or Koniggratz (July 1866). Austria signed the Treaty of Prague (1866) by which she agreed to dismantle the German Confederation and consented to the reconstruction of Germany under the Prussian leadership and also for the exclusion of Austria herself from the new Germany. Austria also agreed to handover her rights in Schleswig-Holstein to Prussia and to cede Venetia to Italy.

Bismarck now reorganised the German states. All states north of the River Main were organised into the **Confederation of North German States** under the presidency of the Prussian King. A federal council known as '**Bundesrat**', consisting representatives of the states and **'Reichstag'** a popular assembly directly elected on the basis of universal male suffrage were created.

The Austro-Prussian war advanced the unification of Germany in great measure. Apart from the annexation of **Schleswig-Holstein**, other hostile states in northern Germany like **Hanover, Nassau, Hesse-Kassel and Frankfurt** were brought under Prussian supremacy and were organised into **North German Confederation.**

It increased the prestige of Prussia among the European nations. The expulsion of Austria from German affairs settled the long standing conflict and rivalry for supremacy in central Europe between Austria and Prussia. Prussia, now with an expanded territory, with her immense military power and with her astounding victory in the war against Austria emerged as a new balance of power in Europe.

The Prussian victory had profound impact on political life within Prussia too. The tussle between the Prussian liberals and the authoritarian Bismarck ended. The Prussian success ended the chapter of constitutional struggle over army reforms in Prussia and also demonstrated **triumph for conservatism and nationalism and defeat for liberalism**. The German liberals exchanged political freedom for Prussian military glory and began to display a diminishing commitment to parliamentary principles henceforth. Before 1866, the German liberals were struggling to secure unity and freedom but after that year, they became contended with what Bismarck – a believer in **Machiavellian Principles** – gave them unity and authoritarianism.

At individual level too Prussia's success was significant. Bismarck now emerged as the man of the hour, a great hero of the German people. By appropriating the German nationalist cause from the liberals and promoting it in his own ways of authoritarianism and militarism, Bismarck emerged as the champion of German nationalism and captured adoration of all German nationalists.

Beyond the German boundaries too, the result of the Austro-Prussian war found its expression. By acquiring Venetia from Austria, Italy moved one more stage towards complete unification. The Austro-Prussian war also convinced the Austrian Emperor Francis Joseph, the need for reform of his own state. He now realised that the forces of nationalism were too strong to ignore. Austria was divided into two halves Austria and Hungary, independent of each other but with a common ruler. This reform known as **Ausgleich or Compromise** was a step to satisfy the aspirations of two dominant races of the Austrian Empire – the Germans and the Magyars.

iii. The Franco-Prussian War

After consolidating the north German states into a confederation, the task left before Bismarck was the integration of southern part of Germany with the Northern Confederation. The biggest obstacle before it was France, which considered a united Germany under the Prussian leadership a serious challenge to its interests.

The lightning success of Prussia in the war against Austria had shocked France, which was looking for an opportunity of intervention and to extract some territorial gains from it. For long, France was following a policy intended to keep Germany fragmented and weak, but the Battle of Sadowa suddenly changed those equations. The unification of north German states, formation of a new German Confederation, militarisation of Prussia, adoration of the authoritarianism of Bismarck by German people and sinking into insignificance of German liberalism - all were causes of concern to France. Moreover, for the French people it was France and not Austria that was beaten at Sadowa, as the outcome of the war had upset the balance of power and loss of pre-eminence of France in Europe. Napoleon III, the ruler of France, now began to look for some face saving measures and to re-assert the position of France in the European order. This anti-German attitude of Napoleon and the French people was resented by Bismarck and the Prussians, hence Bismarck commented that 'a Franco-Prussian War must take place before a united Germany was formed'.

Moreover, Bismarck also held the view that a war with France was necessary to arouse nationalism in southern German states and for their integration with the Northern German Confederation. Thus, both sides wanted a war – for France to restore her prestige and for Prussia to complete the German unification.

Bismarck turned to diplomacy to isolate France as a pre-condition for the Prussian success. He had ensured **Russia's friendship** by supporting Russia during the Polish disturbances and in the Russian designs against Turkey. Bismarck also bought the **friendship of Italy** with the promise of Rome to Italy which was being defended by the French army. Moreover, Bismarck had taken extra care not to humiliate **Austria** after the Battle of Sadowa. By these measures Bismarck fortified Prussia with friendliness of the neighbouring countries for an inevitable clash with France.

A cause for war arose over the **succession to the Spanish throne,** which was offered to Prince Leopold, a relative of the Prussian king. Being concerned of encirclement by an alliance between Prussia and Spain, Napoleon III, the ruler of France, objected the move. Though Prince Leopold withdrew his acceptance of the crown, the issue was put to good use by Bismarck to create indignation of the French people against Germany and to create national feeling among the Germans. The Prussian king William had met the French ambassador at the resort of Ems in Prussia to discuss the Spanish succession and had sent a telegram, the **'Ems telegram',** informing Bismarck of what had ensued. By editing and publishing it, Bismarck created the impression that the Prussian king insulted the French ambassador. The aim was to inflame French feelings against Prussia. As commented by Bismarck, the Ems Telegram produced the effect of a 'Red Flag on the Gallic Bull' and heightened fury of the French people to fever heat. What Bismarck desired was delivered by France, it declared war against Prussia. With skilful manipulation of the developments, Bismarck created a situation in which France was seen as aggressor and Prussia as the protector of German interests

The **Franco-Prussian War** began in July 1870. The Prussian army quickly and decisively routed the French army in the battlefields of Worth, Alsace, Metz and Sedan. After the defeat of the French army at Sedan, on 1 September 1870, Napoleon III surrendered to Prussia.

> Even though the French Emperor surrendered, the war was continued by rebellious republicans under their leader Leon Gambetta, who set up a Government of National Defense and proclaimed France a republic – the Third French Republic – on 4 September 1870.

The victorious Prussian troops besieged Paris. After a valiant resistance for five months, Paris capitulated and surrendered in January 1871. The victory jointly won by the German states brought them together and on 18 January 1871, in the Hall of Mirrors at Versailles in France the German princes conferred the title of **German Kaiser** (Emperor) to **William I of Prussia.**

> **The Paris Commune:** In France, hardships of the time created revolutionary conditions, leading to the formation of Paris Commune, a radical socialist revolutionary movement of workers and also of immigrants from parts of France occupied by the Germans. The Paris Commune refused to accept the authority of the French government and controlled Paris from March to May 1871. The third republican government suppressed the movement and sailed through the post-war crisis successfully. The supporters of the Commune were known as the Communards of which about 20,000 were killed during the suppression. The socialists and communists considered the Paris Commune as a model of liberated society. Karl Marx in his essay *The Civil War in France* (published in 1871) described the Paris Commune as the prototype of a revolutionary government for the emancipation of the proletariat. Future leaders of the Communist movement like Lenin and Mao were to draw theoretical lessons from the short-lived experience of the Paris Commune and perceived it as an example of 'withering away of the state'.

With the **Treaty of Frankfurt** (May 1871), the war came to an end. As per the treaty, France recognised the German Empire and William I of Prussia as the Emperor of Germany. France handed over Alsace-Lorraine region to Germany and agreed for a war indemnity of five billion Francs to be paid in five years. It also set a framework for the withdrawal of German troops from France. The treaty provisions were reflections of national security and economic requirements of the newly formed German Empire. From strategic point of view, control of Alsace region was most important, if there was a future war with France. Germany also acquired 20 per cent of mining and steel potential from the territories ceded by France.

> The Treaty of Frankfurt was deeply resented by the Frenchmen though they could not do anything against it at that time. This resentment reflected in **'Revanchist'** movement in France. A deep desire to reverse the territorial losses-Alsace-Lorraine – the 'lost provinces' – became an obsession with French leaders. This was one of the factors that propelled France to sign the Franco-Russian alliance in 1894, in the emergence of the Triple Entente in 1907 and one of the most powerful motives in France's involvement in the First World War. The French 'Revanchism' influenced the provisions of the Treaty of Versailles of 1919, by which France not only got back Alsace-Lorraine but the treaty had to be signed by the German government in the same room **'the Hall of Mirrors'** at the Versailles, where in 1871 the German Empire had been proclaimed.

a. Reasons for the French Failure and the Prussian Victory

First, in 1870, France was **militarily not prepared for a war**. Even though army reforms had been initiated, it could not be completed before the war. The French army in comparison to the Prussian army was inferior in number and in modernisation. The French army did not have previously arranged plan of campaign to meet the Prussian threat. The campaign plans prepared between 1866 and 1870 were defensive in nature.

Next, in 1870, France was **diplomatically isolated** and was without an ally. Napoleon III had expected that Austria would join in a war of revenge against Prussia, but was disappointed on this front. Napoleon also expected joining of hands by the Southern German states of Baden, Wurttemberg and Bavaria against Prussian domination of Germany. Against Napoleon's expectation, these states now under the nationalistic feeling joined with Prussia in the war. Diplomatic measures of Bismarck to isolate France from Russia and Italy too had the desired results. Thus, it was an isolated France that was goaded into the war.

On the other hand, **Prussia was fully prepared for the war** with France. As Bismarck believed that a war with France lay in the logic of history, he was amply prepared for it. The provision for conscription of every Prussian of military age had created a large population which was battle ready. The reformed and modernised Prussian army under **Albrecht von Roon**, the War Minister of Prussia had an advantage over the French army. The German forces were superior in numbers, had better training and leadership and made more effective use of modern technology of railroad, telegraph and artillery. The Prussian tactics under Field Marshal **Helmuth von Moltke** emphasised on swiftness and in battles of encirclement which produced the desired results.

Moreover, Prussia with **diplomatic manoeuvres** had insulated itself from interference of Russia and Austria and had enlisted the support of Italy. Bismarck goaded France to attack Prussia, so as to show that France as the aggressor and Prussia a victim and thus gained support of the southern German kingdoms. Thus the tactics of Bismarck, with the conviction that Europe in general believed in the dictum *'France the victor would be danger to everybody and Prussia to nobody'* ensured friendly neighbours to Prussia and also fruitful results in the war.

b. Impact of the Franco-Prussian War

The most important result of the war was the completion of the unification of Germany and the emergence of **the German Empire**. It transformed Germany from a loose confederation into a federal nation-state. The constitution of the North German Confederation was extended to all German states including of southern Germany. Berlin became the capital of the new German empire. Germany was organised into a federal empire with Bundesrat (Upper House of the delegates of the states) and Reichstag (Lower House of representatives of the people) as the legislature. The executive power was vested in the emperor. The Emperor appointed the Chancellor, the head of government.

The end of Franco-Prussian war and the creation of the German Empire **unsettled the Balance of Power** of Europe that existed since the Congress of Vienna (1815). It gave birth to a powerful nation – its people educated and industrious, its industries and commerce in mode of rapid expansion, its army modern and battle Ready. By 1900, Germany emerged the largest economy in Europe overtaking Britain and was at second position in the world only after the United States. In terms of military, it marched ahead of Britain and France based on armament production, conscription and an effective plan for the use of railway for military purposes. Intensely nationalistic, the new German Empire was eager to play a greater role in the international affairs. The new German Empire also tried Germanisation for which it started 'Kulturekampf' (cultural campaign). One expression of this policy was discrimination against the Poles.

It was a historical coincidence that, while the Franco-Prussian war completed the unification process of Germany, it also culminated in the Italian unification. During the war the French army, which had been defending Rome, was withdrawn. Rome was quickly occupied by Victor Immanuel. With the addition of Rome the Italian unification met a fruitful conclusion, and Rome was made the capital of Italy.

9. Comparison of Italian and German Unifications

- Unifications of Italy and Germany were two landmark developments in world history both of which occurred in the 19th century.

- Both the territories were divided into small states till mid-19th century and were under different dynasties.
- Before the unifications both were merely geographical expressions.
- Both experienced Napoleonic rule and imbibed ideals of liberty, liberalism and national feeling through that interaction.
- Both the countries were the victims of 'legitimacy doctrine' of the Congress of Vienna, both were dismembered into large number of states under absolutist principles.
- Both Italy and Germany had to contend with Austrian supremacy and reactionary outlook of its Chancellor Metternich.
- Both the countries witnessed efforts to set up liberal states in 1848 and in both the cases these efforts ended in failure.
- Further, in both the states national movements were under the leadership of dominant states – Piedmont in Italy and Prussia in Germany.
- It was also important that in both the countries two ministers with exceptional ability piloted the unification efforts – Cavour in Italy and Bismarck in the case of Germany.
- During the unification process, both Italy and Germany had to overcome Austrian resistance to pave the way for unification.
- Finally both completed their unification after the Franco-Prussian war 1870.

Even though similarities existed between Italy and Germany, the unification process was also characterised by contrasting differences. The principles and methods followed by the two had been different.

- While Italian unification was carried out with liberal ideals, parliamentary support and plebiscites, in the case of Germany it was authoritarianism called 'blood and iron'.
- Italy had to overcome the influence of Pope in carrying out the unification but Germany had no such hindrances.
- Compared to Italy, German unification had to be carried out by overcoming stronger local forces, for example resistance and apprehensions of southern German states, while in Italy local forces were receptive to the idea of unity.
- Finally, Bismarck did not enjoy the whole-hearted support of his king William I, while Cavour enjoyed full confidence and support of his master Victor Emmanuel II.

10. Comparison of Cavour and Bismarck

Both Cavour and Bismarck were statesmen of exceptional ability, who employed tools of diplomacy and war in augmenting their political objectives. Both occupy prominent position as the nation builders of the 19th-century Europe.

- Both of them were nationalists who placed national interests above all other interests.
- Both the leaders aimed not just the unification of their respective countries but strengthening and placing them in the forefront of European powers.

At the same time in their principles and methods both Cavour and Bismarck were figures in contrast.

- Cavour believed in liberalism and parliamentary form of government. Bismarck repudiated both.
- Moreover, Cavour flavoured the unification process of Italy by plebiscites to ensure popular support for his measures. Bismarck had no such pretensions and followed the policy of 'Blood and Iron'.
- Similarly, Cavour believed that Piedmont's liberalism and enlightenment ideals would bring other Italian states towards it. Bismarck held the view that it was the Prussian power alone that would bind other German states with Prussia. It was in this context Bismarck remarked that 'Germany is looking not to Prussia's liberalism but to her power'. As a result, the unification of Germany took place under the Prussian authoritarianism.
- Finally, Cavour was first and foremost an Italian and then a Sardinian, but Bismarck was just the opposite. He was a Prussian first and then a German, ready to assert the Prussian predominance in German nationalism.

SUMMARY

Emergence of German Nationalism – At the beginning of the 19th century Germany comprised of large number of small political units of which Austria and Prussia were the largest. Though the Congress of Vienna (1815) had organised a German Confederation consisting of 39 German-speaking states, it was a union of the princes and not of the people. The first significant step in creation of united Germany was the establishment of Zollverein (customs union) by Prussia and its neighbouring states in 1834. Infrastructural developments by the mid-19th century also promoted the unity feeling among the people of the German states. Spread of Liberalism provided an intellectual basis; and the national identity promoted by German scholars and writers such as Schiller and Fichte gave fillip for unification.

Prussia, the Agent of Unification – In the German unification it was Prussia that acted as the agent of unification. In this context succession of Frederick William to the throne of Prussia in 1861 was significant. He understood the Prussian role in Germans' destiny and initiated its modernisation especially of its army.

Bismarck and his reforms – As the Prussian Parliament – Diet opposed Frederick William's army modernisation programme, the king appointed Bismarck as the Chancellor. To carry out army modernisation, Bismarck collected taxes without parliament's approval and declared that his policy would be that of blood and iron. Bismarck then fought three wars to attain German unification. These were Danish-Prussian War (1864), Austro-Prussian War (1866) and Franco-Prussian War (1870–1871). In 1871, the Treaty of Frankfurt was signed by which France recognised the German Empire and William I of Prussia as the Emperor of Germany.

Questions of Previous Years Civil Services Examination

1. Discuss the different stages of the unification of Italy from 1848 to the occupation of Rome in 1870. (2023)
2. 'From Bismarck's "Blood and Iron" speech and his forceful actions to achieve German unification, Bismarck came to be known as the Iron Chancellor'. Critically examine. (2020)
3. At the end of the Battle of Sedan (1870), 'Europe lost a mistress and gained a master'. Discuss. (2018)
4. Was German unification achieved more by 'coal and iron' than by 'blood and iron'? (2012)
5. Examine the role of Bismarck in state building in Germany. (2018)
6. What determinant factors, along with diplomatic, shaped the process of German unification? (2017)
7. Bismarck united Germany not by majority of votes and speeches but by a policy of 'blood and iron'. In the light of this statement assess the contribution of Bismarck to the unification of Germany. (2003)
8. The political unification of Germany was accomplished solely by Bismarck. Discuss. (1999)
9. Isolation of France constituted the keystone of Bismarck's foreign policy. Elucidate. (1997)
10. The unification of Italy and that of Germany constituted a contrast in respect of the ways they were affected and the impact they left on later international politics. Elucidate. (1995)
11. 'It is one of the ironies of history that Napoleon was the creator on modern Germany'. Explain. (1984)

CHAPTER 8

The First World War

In this Chapter

1. Introduction

The First World War, also known as the Great War, 'the war to end all wars', was an international conflict of unprecedented magnitude that took place from July 1914 to November 1918. It was World War as it connected the whole world in its violence and suffering. Though the war was fought between the European powers (except Spain, the Netherlands, Switzerland and the three Scandinavian countries) along with the United States, the resources and troops from their colonies had been mobilised for the purpose.

It was '**people's war**' to which civilians along with soldiers were directly and totally committed and marked a transition from wars between kings to wars between peoples. It marked the emergence of the era of '**total war**' which encompassed the entire nation, demanding total commitment from their citizens and mobilisation of entire resources aimed at total victory. It was a man-made catastrophe that left lasting scars on the 20th century which also dismantled quite a few of the existing political, socio-economic and cultural structures of the world.

The War was fought between the **Central Powers** – Germany, Austria-Hungary, Turkey (from November 1914), and Bulgaria (from October 1915) and the **Allied Powers** – Great Britain, France, Russia (withdrew in December 1917), Italy (from May 1915), Serbia, Belgium, Romania (from August 1916), Japan and the United States (from 1917). It ended with the defeat of the Central Powers.

The First World War was also the war of many firsts. It was for the first time many of the war weapons like chemical weapons, gas masks, battle tanks, steel helmets, submarines, aeroplanes and aircraft carriers were used. It also witnessed the use of wireless communication and aerial warfare. Apart from all these, women were also enlisted in the war for the first time as nurses in the battle zones and on jobs of wartime production.

The First World War in its impact was a watershed in the history of the world in more ways than one. Most significant was the destruction it brought in. Nearly 10 million people were killed in the war or due to hardships of the war, another 20 million were wounded and much more became refugees. Politically, it caused the fall of four imperial dynasties – Russia, Germany, Austria-Hungary and Turkey. Many new nations took birth out of these fallen dynasties. It paved the way for the Russian Revolution. Further, it shook and destabilised the European society. The horrors of the War paved way for the foundation of the League of Nations. And finally, it laid the groundwork for another world war.

2. Causes of the First World War

A. Nationalism

Nationalism at this stage in history emerged as a double-edged weapon. While it served as a unifying force within a country, it also caused intense rivalry and competition among the European nations. The **unification of Italy and Germany** had given vitality to nationalism making it a potent force in politics. This trend was supported by nationalist thinkers by propagating pseudoscientific racial theories and by emphasising **Social Darwinist** doctrines, both of which glorified conflicts and justified subjugation of other peoples.

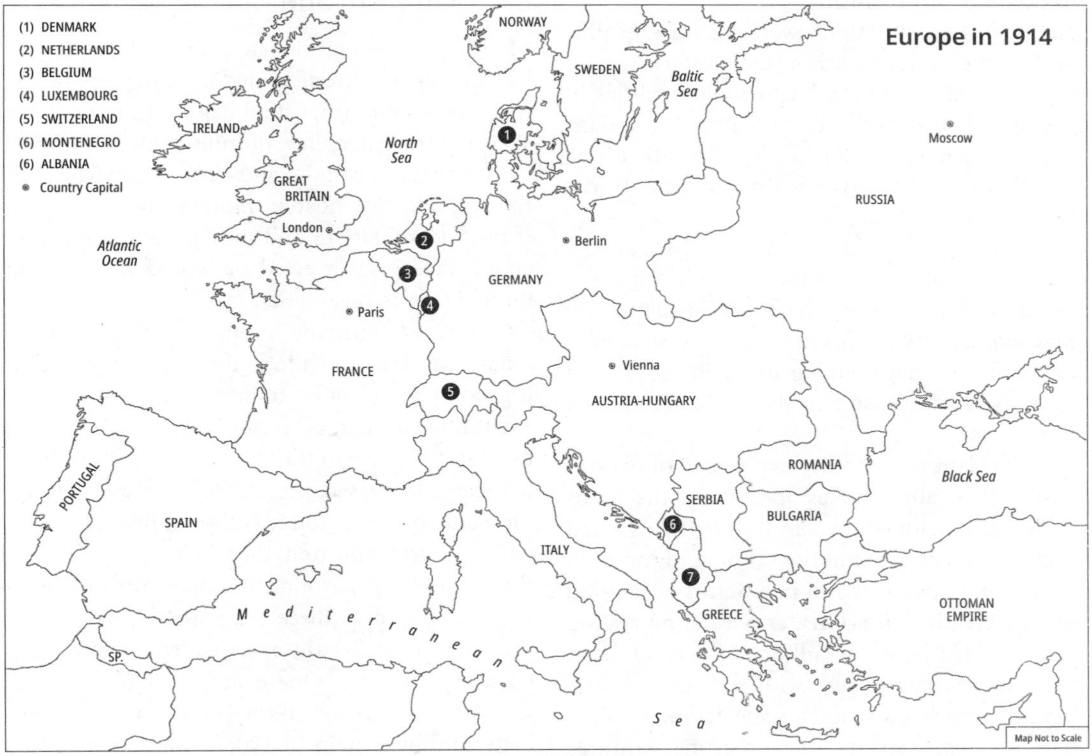

Europe in 1914

By the late 19th century, nationalism was also linked with extending areas of control by a nation in order to claim its 'rightful place under the sun'. By the end of this century, major powers of Europe – Britain, France, Germany, Austria-Hungary, Italy and Russia – had been competing for territory, materials and markets. This excess dose of nationalism had wide ramifications in the world politics and some of these were as follows–

1. It accentuated competition between different European powers in acquiring and protecting their **imperial interests** in Asia, Africa and in the Balkan part of Europe.

2. Nationalism was a dominant fuelling force behind the naval and **military competition** between the states like Great Britain and Germany.
3. Nationalism, rather the **'wounded nationalism'** of the French people after their defeat in the Franco-Prussian war (1870–71) and at the loss of Alsace-Lorraine to Germany, had turned France a bitter enemy of Germany, which also kept alive the spirit of revenge in the French people against the Germans.
4. The **Italian Ireedenta** (unredeemed Italy) and the efforts to construct a Greater Italy by acquiring the Italian-speaking territories of Trieste and the Trentino from Austria was another example of explosive nationalism.
5. Nationalistic aspirations were also discernible among the nationalities on the western fringes of the Russian Empire. Various nationalities in the region such as the Poles, Finns, Ukrainians and Lithuanians resented the **'Russification'**, and this resentment was a threat to the Tsarist Empire.
6. Most importantly, ethnic nationalism or the unmet national aspirations of the peoples in the Balkan region, such as Bosnians and Macedonians was an expression of explosive nationalism. Developments in the Balkan region were to prove decisive in the outbreak of First World War.
7. **Pan-Serbism** was another expression of nationalism. The nationalist aspirations of the Serbs under the leaderships of Serbia (which had become independent of the Ottoman Empire in 1878) found expressed in pan-Serbism. It stood for the creation of a Greater Serbia, by adding their racial kin – seven million South Slavs – that lived in Austria-Hungary with Serbia.
8. On the other end of the spectrum, opposition to nationalism was a strong **counter current**. Growth of militant nationalism compelled Austria-Hungary to oppose nationalist aspirations of its subjects, as it would have meant total destruction of the Hapsburg Empire. The **supranational Austro-Hungarian Empire** (under which there were Germans, Hungarians, Magyars, Czechs, Slovaks, Serbs and Croats and so forth) was obsolete and an anachronism in a world of states based on the principle of nationality. The anxiety among the Austrian leaders to maintain the Hapsburg Empire intact and the fear that national aspiration among its several subject nationalities would tear apart the Empire compelled Austria to pursue a forceful policy against nationalism. In the age of a heightened national feeling, tensions arising out of the multinational character of the Austro-Hungarian Empire set off the explosion in June 1914, when heir to the throne of Austria-Hungary, Archduke Francis Ferdinand, was assassinated by a member of a Serbian nationalist group called the 'Black Hand'.

B. Militarism and Military Alliances

Militarism refers glorification of military power and building up of a strong armed force in preparation for war. The second important cause of the First World War was the emergence of militarism in nations like Germany and Britain and subsequent division of Europe into two hostile military alliances by 1914. If not for militarism and military alliances, the war could have been averted or would have remained limited to Austria and Serbia.

A unified Germany represented the fulfilment of a national dream, while at the same time, the starting point for a more ambitious goal – the goal of extending German power in Europe and also to gain its 'rightful' place in the world affairs. With this aim, it greatly increased the size of her standing army. The same path was followed by countries like France which, apart from strengthening its army lengthened the term of conscription (compulsory military service) from two to three years, Russia by expanding its army, Great Britain by considerably enlarging its naval expenditure. One example of this militarism was the introduction of the powerful 'Dreadnought' battleship by Britain in 1906, which made all other battleships obsolete. This induced Germany to build its own **'Dreadnoughts'**. Such competitive arms race produced fear, suspicion and hostility among the nations of Europe.

This hostile situation was further made complicated by formation of military alliances. Though originally intended as a mechanism to keep peace in Europe, the military alliance system pushed Europe into war, instead. The origin of this alliance system could be traced to Bismarck and the Franco-Prussian War (1871). Realising that France would not forget and forgive the humiliation of the loss of Alsace Lorraine, Bismarck initiated a system of military alliances in order to keep France isolated and friendless. Bismarck believed that **'as long as it is without allies, France poses no danger to us'**. Bismarck also hoped to prevent a war between Russia and Austria, as it would have meant the breakup of the Austria-Hungary and to the Russian expansion in Eastern Europe. Aimed at these objectives Bismarck forged complex alliances, this in turn provoked counter alliances leading to division of Europe into two hostile armed camps. In international affairs the two decades before 1914 is thus considered as one of armed peace.

Following were the steps taken by Bismarck to isolate France so that she might not wage a war of vengeance against Germany, to secure the borders of Germany and to maintain the status quo in Europe–

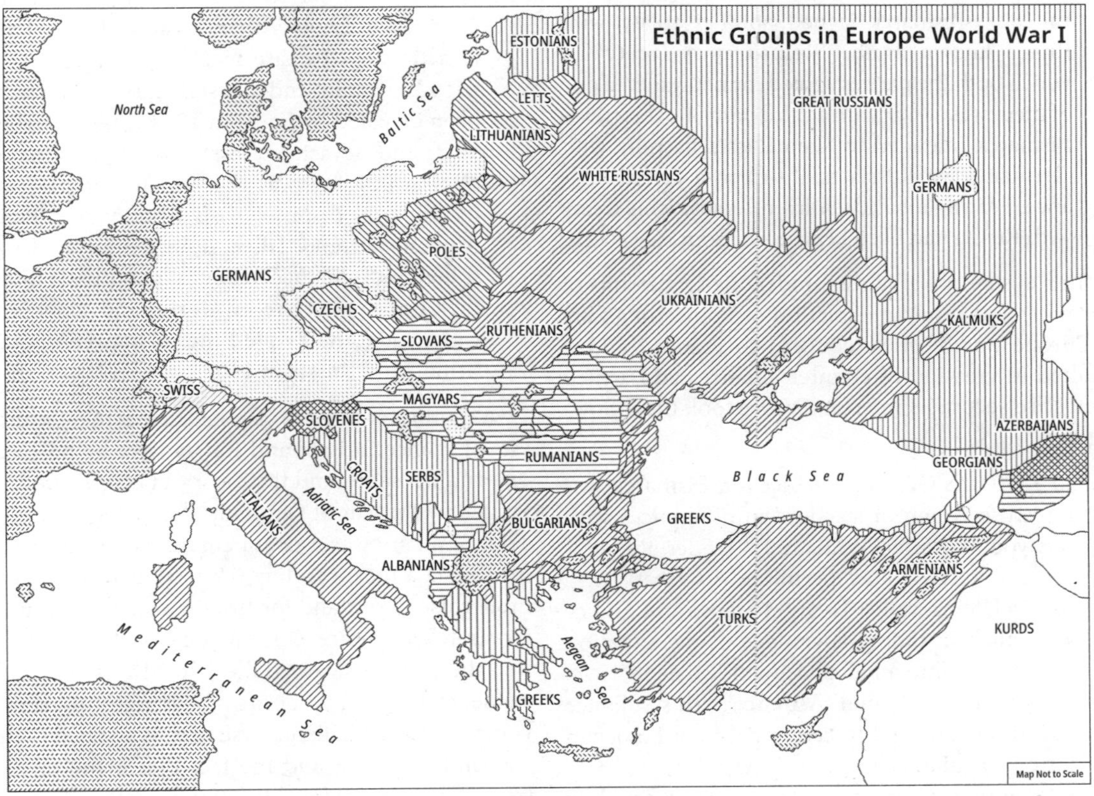

Ethnic groups in Europe

1. In 1872, the ***Dreikaiserbund*** or the **'Three Emperors' League'** was formed by Germany, Russia and Austria-Hungary. This alliance aimed at maintaining status quo in Europe, strengthen monarchy and find a solution to the Eastern Question and also to resist socialism. In immediate terms it aimed at neutralising the rivalry between Germany's these two neighbours by an agreement over their respective spheres of influence in the Balkans – Austria in western and Russia in eastern areas of the Balkans. By this friendship Bismarck could also isolate Germany's enemy – France.
2. In 1878, the *Dreikaiserbund* had collapsed after the Russian Czar withdrew from it, protesting against Germany's support to Austria on the Eastern Question. But Bismarck made use of this situation, to cement its relation with Austria by entering

into a mutual military assistance treaty, the **Dual Alliance** in 1879. Consequently, Bismarck created the famous **'Triple Alliance'** in 1882 between Germany, Austria-Hungary and Italy. To facilitate this Alliance, Bismarck made use of the wounded sentiments of Italy, when in 1881 France had seized Tunis in North Africa, which had been aspired by Italy too. By fomenting Franco-Italian rivalry Bismarck drew Italy close to Germany and strengthened the military alliance against France.

3. In 1887, Bismarck signed another treaty with Russia known as the **'Reinsurance Treaty'** by which both the parties agreed for neutrality, if one of them was at war with a third party. By this treaty Bismarck intended to keep Russia friendly with Germany, lest Russia might form a French alliance. Fearing a backlash from Austria, this treaty with Russia had been kept secret from Austria.

This system of alliances under the leadership of Germany and resultant isolation of France in affairs of Europe was of grave concern to France, and it resulted in creation of counter alliances and armed camps. To secure its interest, France took the following steps–

1. In 1890, the German Chancellor, Bismarck was forced to resign on account of differences with the young Kaiser William II. Under the new leadership, Germany permitted its treaty with Russia (Reinsurance Treaty) to lapse and France was quick in taking advantage of the situation by entering into an alliance with Russia in 1894, known as **'the Dual Alliance'**. This alliance ended the long and forced isolation of France in European affairs.
2. Like France, Great Britain was also alarmed by Germany's growing military might, its buildup of a great navy, its spectacular industrial growth, expansion of trade and military alliances. Germany's increased efforts to become a great colonial power too was a cause of concern to Britain. In this background France took superb diplomatic initiatives to bring Britain to its side and signed an agreement or entente – the **Entente Cordiale** in 1904. This treaty ended the self-imposed 'splendid isolation' (the policy followed by Britain since the Crimean War of keeping away from European entanglements) of England in European affairs. To reach this agreement both the countries sorted out their colonial differences over Egypt and Morocco. France recognised the British position in Egypt and England supported the special position of France in Morocco apart from defining the frontier of Nigeria in France's favour and demarcating the French and British zones of influence in Siam (Thailand).
3. France, in order to fortify its alliance against Germany's Triple Alliance, now initiated diplomatic steps to ease tensions between its new friends Britain and Russia. Russia, which had been defeated by Japan in 1904 (Russo-Japanese War) and devastated after a working-class revolution in 1905, was more than ready to settle its imperial disputes with Britain over Persia, Afghanistan and Tibet. Both demarcated their spheres of influence in Persia, and Russia undertook not to interfere in Afghan and Tibet. Thus was created the **Triple Entente** between France, Britain and Russia in 1907.

A significant point to be noted here is that the interests of France, Britain and Russia were by no means one and the same, and their spirit of cooperation was ignited by the fear of Germany alone. For France, the Triple Entente was a continental security apparatus, for Russia a means to buy time to catch up with the modernised West and for Britain a step to defend its far-stretched empire which it alone could not defend. But, the Germans viewed the Triple Entente as encirclement, designed to destroy their rightful claim to world power. The alliance system thus aroused mutual fear and suspicion and the fact that many of these treaties were secret heightened the tensions.

Germany now came to conclude Austria-Hungary as its only reliable ally, and if Austria falls from the ranks of Great Powers, Germany would have to fight a lonely battle against its enemies and hence resolved to protect it at any cost. But the German conclusions were fraught with grave miscalculations. First, the Triple Entente was not for waging a war against Germany, but to protect their interests against burgeoning economic, military and diplomatic power of Germany. Second, by linking the German security concern with Austria, Germany rather precipitated the war than preventing it. The Hapsburg Empire of

Austria-Hungary, which contained several nationalities often with conflicting aspirations, might well choose war as the only option to prevent its disintegration. Assured of German support, Austria was more likely to do so and fearful of Austrian destruction Germany was sure to support Austria.

By 1907, Europe was divided into two hostile armed camps, the Triple Alliance – Germany, Austria-Hungary and Italy – and the Triple Entente – Great Britain, France and Russia. Each group looking for outplaying the other accelerated the outbreak of First World War. It also meant that a dispute between any of the nations of the two groups could draw all the European nations into war.

C. Economic Causes

Germany, after its unification by the policy of 'Blood and Iron', was an industrial power house and a military giant. Now, many industrialists in Germany, it is argued, looked for a war with Britain, which owned half of the world's tonnage of merchant ship, which they believed was necessary for German economic mastery of the world. On the other, a resurgent Germany now emerged as a competitor in the international trade and commerce, which was of great concern to Great Britain. This **'Made in Germany complex'** among the British created a feeling of animosity towards Germany and any German action on economic, colonial or military spheres created alarm in Great Britain.

D. Imperialism

Imperialism means the practice of building up of an empire by a nation by seizing overseas territories. The last decades of the 19th century witnessed great burst of imperialistic expansion by the European nations. For example, in 1876 just 10% of Africa was under European control but by 1900 more than 90% had been colonised. The aim was not merely to get new markets or sources of raw materials. At a time when the greatness of a nation in Europe was decided on the basis of the value and extent of its overseas possessions, colonies became the barometers of a nation's status. By this time Britain, France and Russia had built up huge colonial empires and had practically parcelled out the non-European world among themselves and any increase in one's area of control could be possible by 'reordering' the world at the expense of another.

The unification of Germany in 1870–71 gave birth to a powerful and ambitious nation which was ready to claim its rightful **'place in the sun'**. Germany had been left out in the imperial race and hence she tried to find out outlets for expansion in every direction, and this unsatisfied imperialist ambition was the main cause of international crises in the decade before 1914.

3. Drift Towards the War

The decade preceding the outbreak of the First World War witnessed several crises which tested the competing alliances and pushed Europe closer to war. The Europe during this period was **'skating on the thinnest of ice,** and that the peace of Europe was at the mercy of a chapter of unforeseen and unforeseeable accidents'.

A. Moroccan Crisis (1905–06)

Morocco was an independent country and one of the few areas in Africa not captured by a European power. It was situated adjoining the French colony of Algeria. As per the Anglo-French Entente Cordiale (1904), Britain had recognised Morocco as a sphere of influence of France and right to economic penetration and politico-administrative interference by France in that country.

Germany protested against the French activity in Morocco and offered assistance to the Sultan of Morocco to maintain his independence. Germany also called for an international conference to discuss the matter. The International Conference of Powers met at Algeciras in Spain in 1906. Here, Britain, Russia, Italy and Spain supported the special rights of France in Morocco while affirming the policy of **'Open Door'** in which all countries were to have equal trading rights in Morocco.

The result of the development was that Germany met with a diplomatic defeat on Moroccan issue and, on the other, it strengthened the Anglo-French friendship.

> The Balkan Peninsula in the south-eastern corner of Europe is a mountainous region. It was a part of the Ottoman Empire, which was on decline by the beginning of the 20th century. The Balkans had an assortment of ethnic groups each with nationalist aspirations and a long history of clashes. Hence, the region was known as the **'powder keg of Europe'**.

B. Bosnian Crisis (1908)

This was the first crisis in the Balkans. Taking advantage of the **'Young Turk' Revolution** of July 1908, Austria annexed the Turkish provinces of Bosnia and Herzegovina. To the neighbouring state of Serbia this was a deliberate blow as the Serbs had been dreaming of a Greater Serbia by incorporating Bosnia which contained 3 million Serbs in its mixed population of Serbs, Croats and Muslims.

Russia threatened to take steps against Austrian aggression and a serious crisis erupted, which made war a near possibility. With the German declaration of military support to Austria and still suffering from the effect of defeat at the hands of Japanese (1905), Russia swallowed her wrath which led to the withering away of the crisis. The Austrian annexation of Bosnia became an accepted reality and was a triumph for the Austro-German alliance. But Serbia continually vowed to take Bosnia-Herzegovina from Austria-Hungary and in turn Austria vowed to crush any such Serbian attempt to undermine its influence in the Balkans.

> The Young Turks were modern, educated (mostly in the West) and reform-minded Turks. The Young Turk Movement stood for modernisation of Turkey, freeing it from the influence of the foreign powers and strengthening of Turkish nationalism. In 1908, through a bloodless revolution, they forced the Sultan in granting a constitution and implementing liberal reforms.

It had two unfortunate results which were to influence the outbreak of the First World War. As Serbian nationalist feeling had been wounded, they remained bitterly hostile to Austria. The Russians having learned a lesson from the crisis embarked on a massive military build up to pre-empt any further humiliation in case conflict with Austria and Germany erupt in future. The incident also brought Serbia and Russia further closer.

C. Agadir Crisis (1911)

In spite of Algeciras Settlement in 1906, crisis erupted in Morocco again in 1911, when the French troops occupied Fez, the capital of Morocco on the plea of putting down a rebellion by tribesman against the sultan. In order to pressurise the French into giving Germany some territorial compensation preferably in the French Congo and also as a warning to France, that she was not the sole arbiter of the fate of Morocco, Germany sent a gunboat **'the Panther'** to the Moroccan port of Agadir. Military preparations were hurried forward in both Germany and France and Europe was on the edge of a war. The British, who were worried about the German naval presence in Agadir, with which it could threaten Britain's trade routes and also under its commitment to support France under the Triple Entente, issued a strong warning that it would not remain as a spectator to the developments 'where her interests were vitally affected' and sent a cruiser to match the Panther. Germany not willing to push the matter to a war withdrew the gunboat and agreed to recognise the French protectorate over Morocco in return for a small territory in the French Congo.

The Agadir Crisis had serious repercussions and was a forecast of the First World War. First, it strengthened the Triple Entente. Second, it increased the French hatred and suspicions of Germans. In Germany, it enhanced the anti-British feeling, as it was the firm stand taken by the British which compelled Germany to settle for a compromise. Finally, Germany was dejected and came to conclude that their legitimate position as a world power had been compromised after the Agadir Crisis, as the French could establish their protectorate over Morocco and British could flex its naval muscle, while the German interest was sacrificed.

D. The First Balkan War (1912)

The Balkan Peninsula was a part of **Turkish (Ottoman) Empire**. This region with intermix of variety of ethnic, religious and linguistic populations emerged as a veritable powder magazine in the following ways–

1. In the background of emerging ethnic nationalism, regions in the Balkans expected to emerge as independent nations with their own identity. By the early 20th century, many regions in the Balkans such as Bulgaria, Greece, Montenegro, Romania and Serbia attained independence from the Ottoman Empire.
2. At the same time, large elements of the ethnic populations of these nations remained still under other parts of the Ottoman Empire, which they hoped to annex in order to create pan-ethnic

nations. For example, Serbia, which had a large Slavic population, hoped to absorb all the Slavs of the Balkan region.

3. Tensions were also bound to increase as these nations were intensely jealous of each other and hoped to eliminate the other.
4. Both Russia and Austria had been keeping an eye on this disintegrating region of the Ottoman Empire to expand their influence and territory.
5. The policy of **'Turkification'** – the uncontrolled domination and senseless persecution of the subject races by the Ottoman authorities – had created widespread resentment among the people of this region.

Under these circumstances, Bulgaria, Greece, Montenegro and Serbia formed the **Balkan League** in 1912 and declared war against the Ottoman Empire and defeated it. The Treaty of London (1913) ended the war and the settlement divided up the Ottoman's European territory among the Balkan states. However, Serbia was not satisfied with the settlement. Landlocked Serbia expected to annex Albania, which would give Serbia an outlet to the sea. But Albania was made an independent state, at the instance of Austria, in a calculated step to prevent Serbia becoming more powerful. For Serbia, this Austrian stand was another expression of a keen anti-Serbism, which had already been found expressed in the annexation of Bosnia in 1908. This development strengthened anti-Austrian mood in the Serbia.

E. The Second Balkan War (1913)

This war broke out as a result of dissatisfaction by Bulgaria over war spoils after the First Balkan War. Even though she hoped for Macedonia, it had been secured by Serbia. Bulgaria attacked Serbia, but was defeated and the Treaty of Bucharest (1913) formally ended the war. Bulgaria lost most of the territories it had gained after the First Balkan war.

The Second Balkan War brought the world war within a measurable distance as–

1. It strengthened Serbia and enlarged her territory. Victory in the war instilled confidence in Serbia to move forward with her designs of Greater Serbia.
2. It intensified Austro-Serbian feud. Austria had been following a policy of containment and if possible destruction of Serbia as found expressed in her support of independence of Albania after the First Balkan War. The outcome of the Second Balkan War brought Austria to the end of their patience with Serbia.
3. The incensed Serbian nationalists accelerated their pan-Serb campaign and terrorism among the Serb-Croats within Austria which was in their view the obstacle in their dream of Great Serbia. This redoubled pan-Serb agitation was of great concern to Austria, as she feared that the loyalty of millions of Serb-Croats in the Austrian Empire would be impaired by Serbia's appeal to Pan-Slavic sentiments. This Austrian attitude was shared by Germany, which saw Serbia as a satellite of Russia. Emboldened by the German support, Austria was looking for an opportunity to end the Serbian threat once and for all and this opportunity came on June 28, 1914.
4. As Russia was convinced that any further humiliation would cause irreparable damage to its prestige, vowed to back Serbia in future. The Balkan war had ended the Balkan League, which was a vital arm of Russian system of defence against Austria-Hungary. Russia, for centuries had been focussing on access to the **'warm seas' of the Mediterranean.** But the Balkan Wars ended this hope with the breakup of Balkans League and with Bulgaria moving closer to the Central powers. Russia, having lost all allies in the Balkan region, had no alternatives but to unconditionally support Serbia, its last ally in the Balkans.

Thus, while the ingredients for a war between Austria and Serbia were in the making, there were undisputable signals to show that such a war might easily draw in Russia and Germany. And as there were alliances and counter alliances, such a war would not be remaining a local war, it would be a war with the involvement of and consequences to the total world.

4. Immediate Cause of the War

In this background, **Francis Ferdinand,** nephew of the Austrian Emperor and heir to the Austrian throne, was assassinated in **Bosnian capital Sarajevo,** on 28 June 1914. The Prince and his wife were on a state visit to Sarajevo. The assassin, **Gavrilo Princip,** was a member of the **'Black Hand'** (also known as 'Union or Death'), a Serbian nationalist society. The Austrian government convinced that the Serbian government was behind the murder, issued a severe ultimatum consisting eleven demands, on 23 July to the Serbians. The Austrians, assured of German backing, were determined to use the incident as an excuse for war.

For Austria, yearning for a war with Serbia, in order to end the agitation for the union of the Serbs, this was the opportunity to strike. The Austrian people denounced the Serbians as a **'nation of assassins'**. With the Germans granting a **'blank cheque'** in the matter, Austria issued a forty eight hour ultimatum to Serbia. In spite of the fact that the terms of ultimatum were too harsh, Serbia accepted greater part of it apart from offering to refer the question to a conference of Great Powers, if so desired by Austria.

Austrian leaders, it seemed, had already decided on war and refused negotiation. Assured of German support, Austria rejected Serbia's offer and declared war on Serbia on 28 July 1914. Austria's action now set off a chain reaction within the alliance system, enlarging the conflict into a world war. The horror, destruction and trauma of a world war were soon to unfold and as prophesied by a statesman of the time **'The lamps were going out all over Europe'**.

Austria's action drew Russia, a Slav power in to the picture, as she could not remain indifferent to an Austro-German effort to liquidate Serbia – a Slav kingdom in the Balkans. Moreover, strategically too an Austro-German domination of the Balkans – a region bordering Russia – was unthinkable to Russia. Finally, Russia after repeated failures in foreign affairs was not ready to tolerate any more humiliation. On 30 July, Russia ordered mobilisation of its troops.

The action of Russia brought Germany into the scene, as she was bound to Austria by the Triple Alliance. One more reason for German mobilisation was that Russia had mobilised its forces along the German border expecting that Germany would join Austria. On 1 August 1914, Germany ordered mobilisation and declared war on Russia. Believing that France would support its Russian ally, Germany declared war also on France on 3rd August.

The German battle plan, known as the **'Schlieffen Plan'**, was based on two fronts attack against both Russia and France. The strategy aimed at rapidly concentrating bulk of its army in the West, defeat France within six weeks and shift the forces to the East, before the Russians could invade Germany. As success of this strategy depended on quick mobilisation, the Germans demanded a free passage for its forces through the Belgian territory to outflank French border defences and destroy the enemy by attacking their rear. When Belgium refused passage, the German army invaded Belgium in the night of 3–4 August 1914.

German invasion of Belgium brought England, which had remained aloof till then, into the war. Britain viewed the invasion as a violation of the **Belgian Neutrality**, as in 1839, along with the other great powers Britain had signed a treaty that guaranteed neutrality of Belgium. Moreover, for a century or more it had been one of the cardinal principles of the British foreign policy to prevent domination of the Low Countries (Holland and Belgium), lying directly across the British Channel, by any powerful continental nation, as it would be a serious menace to the safety and interests of England. Consequently, on 4 August, Great Britain declared war against Germany.

Soon other nations joined the war. The Montenegrins joined with their kinsmen, the Serbs, fighting against Austria on 7 August, Japan declared war against Germany on 23 August, because of its alliance with the Great Britain and also for capturing the German possessions in the Far East. In November 1914, the Ottoman Turkey entered the war on the side of the Central Powers. Italy though a member of the Triple Alliance remained neutral insisting that the Germans were not fighting a defensive war, but entered into the war in May 1915 on the side of the Triple Entente hoping to seize Austria's Italian-speaking provinces as well as territory along the eastern shore of the Adriatic Sea.

> Two rivals of the World War I had been the Central Powers and the Allied Powers. Germany and Austria-Hungary were the Central Powers and was known so, because of their location in central Europe. Bulgaria and Ottoman Empire later on joined the group. The Allied Powers were Great Britain, France and Russia. Japan and Italy joined the group during the course of the war.

The diplomatic manoeuvres and military calculations in the weeks just before the outbreak of the First World War have been characterised as a **'tragedy of miscalculations'**. Most of the politicians and leaders of the time failed to assess the developments in proper context. Many of the Generals believed that the war would be short and decisive. Germans believed that they could crush France within six weeks, but their plan failed and had to face full-scale war on two fronts. They also made the crucial mistake of giving a 'blank cheque' to Austria on the basis of which Austria risked a major war. Austria miscalculated that the Russians would not support Serbia. Leaders in both Russia and Germany made miscalculations by assuming that mobilisation would not necessarily mean a war.

5. | Ordeal of the Battle

A. War as Celebration

An extra-ordinary phenomenon that occurred with the outbreak of the War was the great excitement it aroused in civilians, soldiers and the intellectuals alike. To many civilians the war was an escape from the dull routine of daily life and pointlessness of society which had grown old, cold and weary. To others who were welded together by nationalism, the war was an outpouring of patriotic sentiments and a way to devote body and soul to the nation in the hour of need. Excited young men enlisted themselves for the war in huge numbers. Young soldiers bound for battle acted as if they were on a great adventure and yearned for glory by experiencing life at its most intense moments. Many of the European intellectuals were also captivated by martial mood and glorified the war as one of the divine elements of the universe and a condition for progress. They held the view that the war would unify the nation in a spirit of fraternity and self-sacrifice. Preparations for the war were also accompanied by extensive propaganda in the form of posters, newspaper articles and songs and so on.

It must be emphasised that many of these yearnings for war had sprung from the expectation that the war would be a short, decisive and gallant conflict. It also was a reflection of their failure to foresee a barbaric senseless bloodletting in the name and for the glory of fatherland that would get extended for four years. In the end, it turned out that the war was neither short nor glorious.

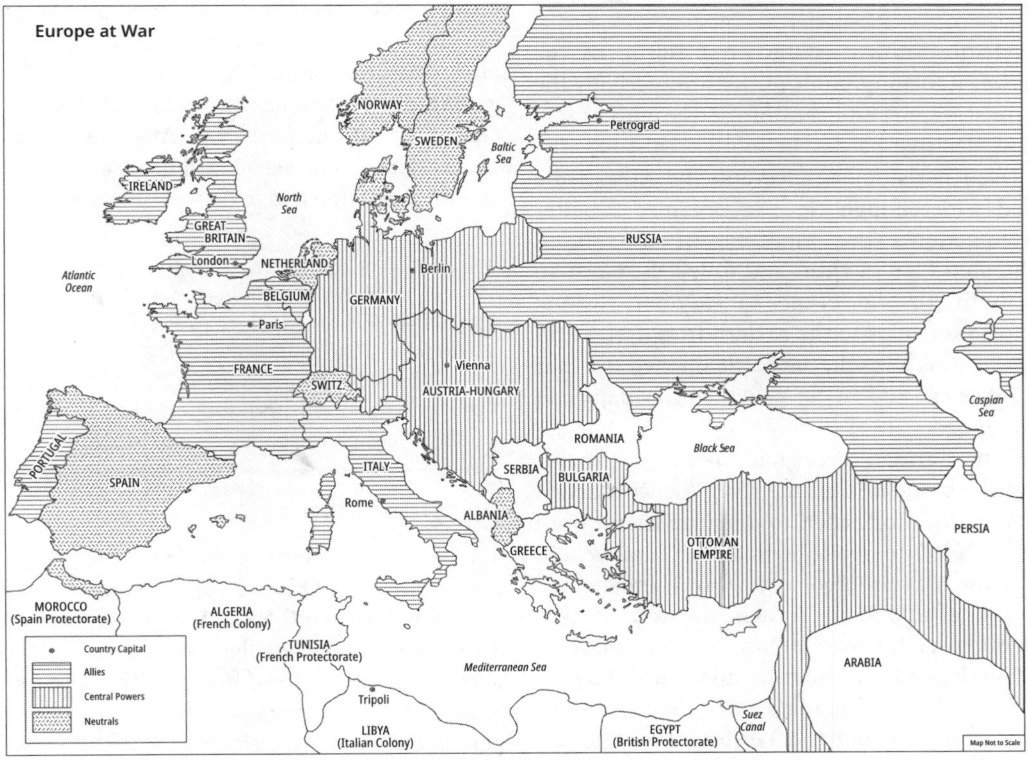

Europe at War

B. The Western Front

The battles of the First World War were fought in different parts of the world, but the battles in Europe were the most important. The war began with the **German invasion of Belgium.** In spite of gallant resistance by the Belgians, the German army swept across Belgium and entered France. By September, the German forces had reached the Marne River, forty miles from Paris aiming to knock them out of the war. With their capital at their backs, the French forces aided by the British fought with astounding courage and compelled the Germans to retreat from the Marne to the northern side of the river Aisne.

> The Schlieffen Plan had been formulated by German General Alfred von Schlieffen, much before the outbreak of the World War. It visualised German vulnerability in a two-front war, hence France had to be occupied in six to eight weeks in an overwhelming attack and then had to move the whole army to the Eastern Front to drive the Russians out.

This battle known as the **First Battle of the Marne** was a turning point in the war, perhaps the single most important event of the war and one of the most decisive battles in modern history. The battle saved Paris and France and the Allies were provided with enough time to organise a better concerted action against the Central Powers. It left the Schlieffen Plan in ruins and foiled the German plan of both crushing France quickly and rushing the victorious troops to the eastern front to take on the Russians. As a result, the battle opened two war fronts – Western and Eastern – which Germany had never intended.

Now, the German forces had to entrench themselves at the battle line on the river Aisne to defeat the attempts of the French to dislodge them. Both the sides failed to make any decisive move. As a result, the war entered a new and unexpected phase, the deadlock of **trench warfare**. Across northern France for over 400 miles from **the Alps to the North Sea** both the sides constructed a network of trenches and readied for a long stubborn trench warfare turning the Western Front into a '**terrain of death**'.

C. The Eastern Front

On the Eastern Front, Russia had mobilised more quickly than the Germans expected, but made the mistake of attacking both Germany and Austria simultaneously. The Russians were successful against Austria and could occupy the province of Galicia, but they met with terrible defeat at the hands of the Germans at Tannenberg and were drawn out of Germany. Soon the Germans beat back the Russians from Galicia, captured Warsaw and the whole of Poland and established a line from north to south inside the Russian territory.

By this time, Germany had induced Turkey to join the war against the Allies and the Ottoman Turkey entered in the World War on 29 October 1914 by launching raids on Russian ports on the Black Sea. Turkey now cut the Russian trade and main supply route through the **Dardanelles** – a narrow strait in north-western Turkey, linking Aegean Sea with the Black Sea.

In April 1915, to open this vital supply line to Russia, a combined force of British, French, Australian and New Zealand troops launched the **Gallipoli Campaign** on the European side of the Dardanelles. But the campaign was a total disaster as the Turks offered fierce resistance and prevented the Allies from getting off the beaches and taking the heights. The Gallipoli Campaign cost the Allies more than two lakh casualties and was a big blow to the Allied morale and the campaign had to be withdrawn in December.

> Serbia, whose dream of establishing a Greater Serbia which precipitated the outbreak of the World War, had gallantly resisted Austrians in the first year of the war. But in 1915, Serbia was captured by a combined Austro-German force attacking on the north and supported by a Bulgarian attack through the south.

D. Other Battles

The battles of the First World War were not confined to Europe alone. Outside Europe, battles were fought in **North Africa and West Asia.** Here, Germany and Turkey threatened the Allied possessions, while Britain and France resisted these attempts. They also fomented Anti-Turkish Arab risings in the Ottoman Empire. As part of this plan a secret agreement 'the **Sykes-Picot Agreement**' was signed between Britain and France in

May 1916 to partition 'the sick Man of Europe', that is the Ottoman Empire into their spheres of influence.

Soon the German colonies in Asia and Africa were seized by the Allied Powers. Japan acquired control over German spheres of influence in China and also captured Germany's Pacific Island colonies.

The Asian and African colonies of Britain and France emerged as the recruiting grounds of soldiers and labourers for different theatres of World War I. People from India, South Africa, Egypt, Algeria, Indochina and Senegal fought in the battlefields or kept the front lines supplied with weapons and food items.

E. The War at Sea

Soon after the outbreak of the war, Britain had initiated a **naval blockade** of Germany. Their strategy was aimed at putting the Central Powers under blockade by cutting off vital military and civilian supplies to them, keeping the British trade routes and interests safe and open and transporting troops, munitions and supplies of all sorts to the many fields of the war. This strategy was highly successful for the British as they could destroy nearly all German armed surface ships by the end of 1914. Germans retaliated with mines and submarine attacks against the British ships.

In May 1916, the **Battle of Jutland** took place, in which the main battle fleets of Britain and Germany participated and was the only first-class naval warfare during the whole First World War. The British sustained greater losses in both ships and men than the Germans, and it was the bloodiest chapter in British naval history. In spite of this fact, the battle failed to make any changes in balance of power in European waters, as the Germans failed in inflicting sufficient losses on their adversary.

The British strategy of denying German navy access to both the United Kingdom and the Atlantic turned to be successful. The German surface ships had been successfully contained by the British. On the other hand, Germany failed in reducing the Royal Navy's numerical advantage. All these resulted in food shortage in Germany, provoking Germany to embark on a new policy of **'unrestricted submarine warfare'**. By this, Germany aimed at depriving Britain of war supplies and to starve them into submission. Launched in January 1917, this was to prove fatal for Germany and was also a decisive turning point in determining the final outcome of the war.

As part of this campaign, Germany declared that the waters around Great Britain and Ireland including the English Channel and western portion of the North Sea as war zone and any vessel entering this zone was subject to destruction without even a warning. Since the Battle of Jutland, the Germans had been concentrating on the production of **U-boats (submarines)** which they now used against all enemy and neutral merchant ships in the Atlantic. At its peak, German tactics were successful as by April 1917, they could sink 430 ships and Britain was down to six weeks' corn supply. The Germans were well aware that unrestricted submarine warfare would invite hostility on the part of the neutral countries and would bring the United States into the war, but were also convinced that Britain and France could be starved in to surrender before the Americans could affect the course of the War.

The German submarine campaign prompted the United States to enter the war on 6 April 1917. The submarine campaign was now undermined with the beginning of convoy system, in which large number of merchant ships sailed together protected by escorting warships. The convoy system drastically reduced the losses for the Allies. At the same time, the advances made in anti-submarine warfare like the introduction of the depth charge, hydrophones for locating the noise of submarine's engines and the use of aeroplanes for reconnaissance increased the number of German submarine losses. All these resulted in the failure of German submarine campaign against the Allies.

The naval war of World War I, though did not witness decisive fleet actions, was nevertheless crucial part of the War. First and foremost, supremacy of the British navy ensured protection of the British shores from German raids. On the other hand, the British economic blockade of Germany could inflict great damage to the German war effort. Germany's use of submarine warfare against international commerce drew the United States into the conflict. Finally, the naval war held great ramifications in future warfare, as many of the tactics and practices were to be used in the Second World War.

F. The War of Attrition

On the Western Front, with the failure of the Schlieffen Plan the German forces had entrenched along the River Aisne. By November 1914, as armies dug themselves in long unbroken chain of opposing trenches and barbed wires, stretching 400 miles across northern France from the Alps to the North Sea, the war entered a period of a long stalemate which is known as the war of attrition. Neither side could dislodge the other for about four years. Situated between the opposing armies was **'no man's land'**, a wasteland of mud and shattered trees on which attacking troops tried to advance only to be decimated by heavy artillery and machine gun fire of the enemy.

Both sides tried to break the stalemate with the help of scientific advances. One of such developments was the use of poison gas, first used by Germany in 1915, on the Western Front with the use of **chlorine gas**. Tanks were also developed in 1916 to break the stalemate. From 1915, aeroplanes were used for reconnaissance. The new tools of war – machine guns, artillery, tanks and poison gas – did enable to kill greater number of people more effectively but failed in delivering a fast success to any side. Despite much heroism, sacrifice and death, little land changed hands and victory was nowhere in sight.

> *All Quiet on the Western Front* by **Erich Maria Remarque**, a German World War I veteran, is a novel portraying his own experiences of trench warfare. In the dedication page of the book, Remarque states that the book is 'neither an accusation nor a confession, and least of all an adventure, for death is not an adventure to those who stand face to face with it' which sets the whole tone of the book. The war of attrition and life in the trenches had destroyed all hopes of the end of the trauma for soldiers in these trenches, who called themselves as Never-endians – those who believed the war would never end. Since then the usage 'all quiet on the Western Front' is a metaphor for stagnation and lack of any visible change.

As neither side could break the deadlock of trench warfare, the Germans now modified their strategy. The strategy was to **'bleed France white'** of all able bodied-men and force them to surrender by inflicting massive casualties. In February 1916, the Germans attacked Verdun – the French city of ancient fortress and the gateway to Paris, knowing well that France would never permit a retreat from this city for reasons of national pride and strategy 'for the retention of which the French Command would be compelled to throw in every man they have'. Verdun was an important stronghold surrounded by a ring of forts, that lay near the German lines and it guarded the direct route to Paris. This battle – the **Battle of Verdun** that lasted from February to December 1916 – turned out to be one of the longest and bloodiest battles of the First World War. Though the Germans could make initial gains, once the French mounted their counter-attacks matters returned to the starting point and Verdun became a symbol of French determination and self-sacrifice.

Meanwhile in July that year, British opened a major offensive along the Somme River to relieve pressure on the French at Verdun. The **Battle of Somme** witnessed some of the fierce fighting of the First World War. The horrific bloodshed on the first day of the battle (1st July on which more than 60,000 British soldiers were either dead or wounded, 'the heaviest loss ever suffered in a single day by any army in the First World War') since then became a glaring example for futile and indiscriminate slaughter. In spite of technological advancement and heavy bloodbath, by the time the battle ended in November 1916, the Allies could make only limited advance of seven miles across the front.

But the real importance of the Battle of Somme lies in the fact that it inflicted a severe blow to the German morale as they realised that Britain was a military power to be reckoned with. By this time, condition in Germany was also worsening, as the Allied blockade had created scarcity of food and raw materials.

The Battles of Verdun and Somme had a huge toll on European lives as lakhs of people died on both the sides and military situation continued to remain essentially unchanged. Further attempts were made in the form of **Nivelle Offensive** (April-May 1917) after the failure of which there were widespread mutinies in the French army, **Battle of Passchendaele** (also known as the **Third Battle of Ypres** July–November 1917), the **Battle of Cambrai** (November–December 1917). In spite of all these, the only victor in the war was the war itself, which had by this time devoured Europe's youth at an alarming rate.

6. Russian Withdrawal from the War

Russia had entered into the war to protect the imperial interest of the royal family, but had not prepared morally or materially for a gruelling war of this nature. The Russian army – poorly trained, poorly armed, poorly supplied and poorly commanded – met with long series of defeats.

In March (February) 1917, a revolution ended the autocratic monarchy in Russia and brought to power a provisional government. The provisional government decided to continue the war under the assumption that, a victory against the Germans would enhance the new government's credibility. Russia also had obligations towards their Western Allies. However, by 1917, more than 5 million Russian soldiers had been killed, wounded or taken prisoner and

Russian losses by the Treaty of Brest-Litovsk 1918

the Russian morale was at the low ebb. As a result the war-weary Russians refused to fight. Parallel to these developments, the provisional government's authority and influence rapidly declined and anarchy spread over Russia. Many of its regions were on the course of claiming autonomy or independence from Russia either spontaneously or at the prompting of the Germans in occupation of these regions. In this background another revolution by the Bolshevik Party under Lenin took place in November (October) 1917 and the provisional government was overthrown.

The new government signed an armistice in December 1917 and concluded the **Treaty of Brest-Litovsk** in March 1918 with Germany by which Russia withdrew from the war. By the treaty Russia surrendered to Germany all her western provinces including the Baltic provinces, Poland, Finland and the Ukraine. The treaty provided many advantages to Germany. They could transfer large number of troops to the Western Front. Germany also gained 34 per cent of Russia's population, 32 per cent of its farmland, 54 per cent of its industrial power and 89 per cent of its coal mines, thus securing a huge command over material resources.

7. The American Entry

In explicit terms, the reason for the United States' entry into the First World War, in the words of its president **Woodrow Wilson,** was to **'make the world safe for democracy'**. But, the real reason for the US entry into the war on the side of the Allies was its concern to maintain international balance of power as they believed that the security of the United States depended upon a balance of forces in Europe which in turn was based on Britain's ability to prevent any nation from achieving supremacy in Europe. And the British ability was based on their naval supremacy. In the World War, German navy posed a great threat to British naval supremacy and had the potential to unsettle the balance of power. Moreover, the Americans had a special bonding with the English. They shared a common ancestry and language and were followers of similar democratic institutions and legal systems. The overthrow of the Tsar in March had removed an obstacle – the American hesitation about siding with an autocratic regime. The discovery that Germany was trying to persuade Mexico to declare war on the United States **(Zimmermann Telegram)** with the promise of support to recover the territories of Texas, New Mexico and Arizona in return too accentuated American decision to enter in to the war.

> Arthur Zimmermann was Germany's foreign secretary during the World War I. The US officials intercepted a telegram sent by Zimmermann, promising to help Mexico to 'reconquer' the lands it had lost to the United States, if Mexico ally with Germany.

The direct cause of American entry in the First World War was the **U-boat warfare** of the Germans. For the Germans, U-boat was one of their most valuable weapons which they used against the British, to blockade and starve them into submission even by torpedoing neutral vessels headed for the British ports. The ships from the United States used to supply war materials clandestinely to British, in passenger ships. In January 1917, Germany started a campaign of 'unrestricted submarine warfare' which was against the interests of the United States hence the United States declared war against Germany. 'The world must be made safe for democracy. Its peace must be planted upon the tested foundations of political liberty. We are but one of the champions of the rights of mankind'. These were the words of the US President Woodrow Wilson to the Congress, while announcing his decision to enter the War. On 2 April 1917, the United States entered in the War.

The US entry into the war was the turning point of the war, and had three important effects. It ensured **supply of war materials,** food and enormous extension of credit for the Allied Powers. Second, the supply of troops in great numbers by the United States strengthened Allied lines and uplifted their morale and prevented an immediate and decisive victory for Germany which it was desperately aiming for. Third, Germany's most effective weapon against the Allies – the submarine warfare – could be neutralised with the construction of new ships by the United States to replace the lost ones. It can also be said that the US entry into the war set an example to other states in the Western Hemisphere such as Cuba, Brazil, Peru and Uruguay to declare war against Germany.

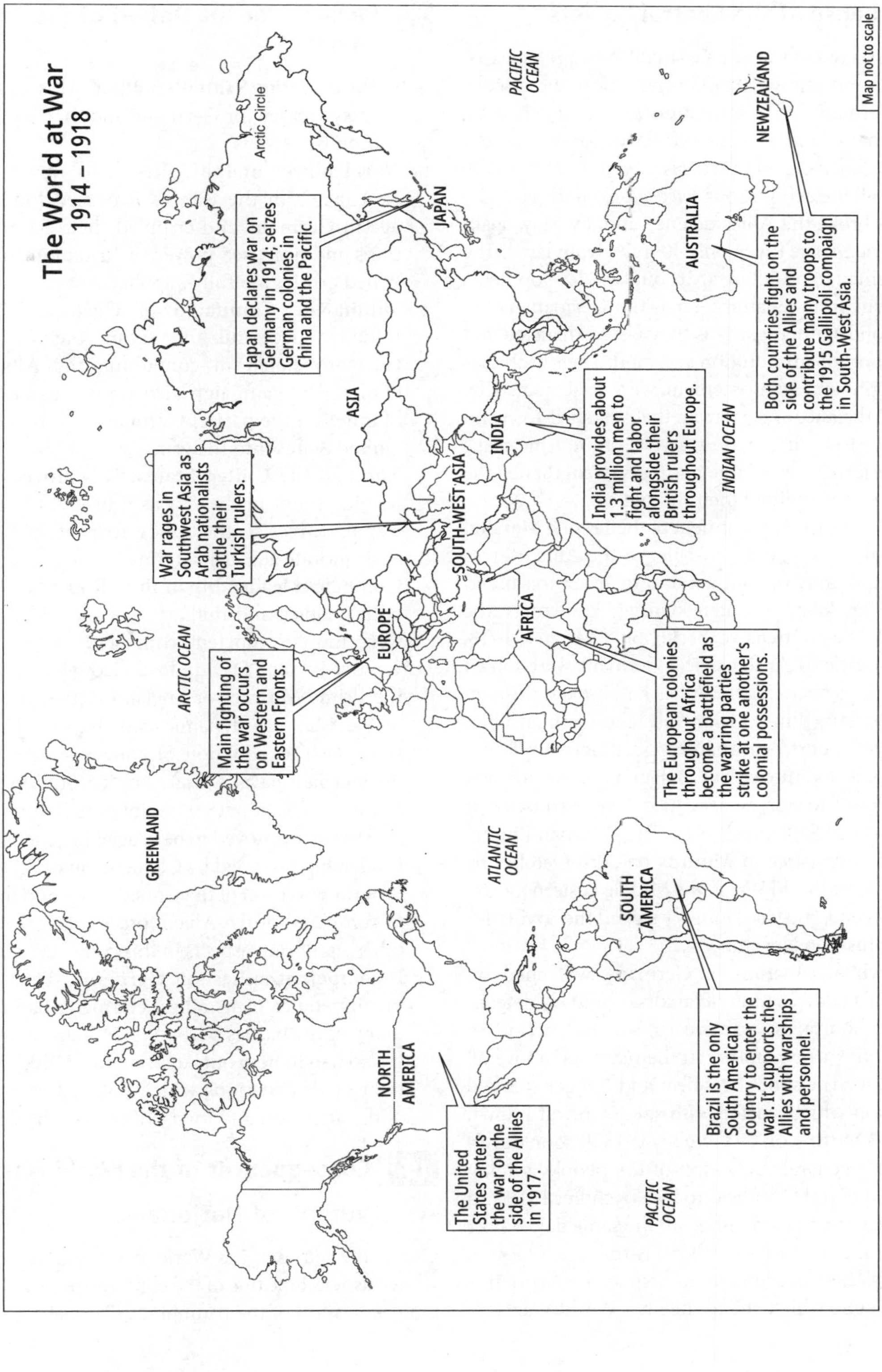

The World at War

8. Collapse of the Central Powers

With Russia out of the war, Germany now prepared for a decisive and immediate offensive before the discontent in Germany led to revolution. On 21 March 1918, the Germans launched an offensive (known as **the Spring Offensive**) aimed at decisive victory in the west. Drawing all the extra troops released from the east, the Germans broke the Allies defence and, by May, again reached the Marne River, only 40 miles from Paris. The Allies seemed to be falling apart but two developments saved them from calamity. First, the Germans could not consolidate their gains as they were exhausted and were in short of ammunition and food. Their problems of re-supply and reinforcement were exacerbated by increased distance and a terrain that was shell-torn and impassable to traffic. Second, arrival of the Americans and American arms in large numbers strengthened the Allied lines and uplifted their morale.

Meanwhile, the appointment of the **French Marshal Foch,** as the commander-in-chief of the Allied forces had brought unity of command in their approach and tactics. The Allied counter-offensive known as the **Hundred Days Offensive** began on 8 August 1918, with the **Battle of Amiens.** The Germans were forced back and by September the Allies had broken through the Hindenburg Line. Meanwhile, the German allies deprived of support form a hard-pressed Germany found it unbearable and moved out. Bulgaria became the first Central Power to sign an armistice – the **Armistice of Salonica** on 29 September 1918. The Ottoman Empire signed the **Armistice of Mudros** on 30th October by which the First World War in the Middle Eastern theatre came to an end. Austria-Hungary signed the **Armistice of Villa Giusti** on November 4.

Meanwhile, situation in Germany worsened on account of a combination of factors – military defeats, dire food shortages, war weariness, destruction of morale in the army, mutiny in the navy and above all a revolution. The shock of defeat and hunger sparked a revolution which started with sailors' revolt known as the **Kiel Mutiny** on 29 October 1918. It soon developed into a general revolution of the people, forcing Kaiser Wilhelm II to abdicate on 9 November 1918 and the proclamation of a republic on the same day. Kaiser fled to Holland. On November 11, the new German Republic signed an armistice known as **the Armistice of Compiegne** which ended the First World War.

9. Reasons for the Defeat of the Central Powers

a. **Failure of the Schlieffen Plan.** This prevented an easy victory for Germany and they had to face war on two fronts.
b. **Naval power of the Allies.** This was a significant factor in the war, as it caused food shortage in Germany and crippled their economy. At the same time, sea power of Britain ensured the Allied armies are fully supplied.
c. **Submarine Campaign of Germany.** Though initially successful the submarine warfare of Germany failed in containing the Allied war efforts. The campaign also proved to be a great blunder on the part of Germany as it brought the United States into the war.
d. **Entry of the United States.** This proved to be a turning point in the war as it brought enormous war resources to the Allies apart from boosting their morale at a crucial time.
e. **Competent leadership of the Allies.** The leaders – both political and military – of the Allied Powers were more competent compared to that of the Central Powers. David Lloyd George, who became the Prime Minister of England during the course of the war, was dynamic and decisive. His decisions such as adoption of convoy system against the German naval warfare and constitution of the Ministry of National Service for mobilisation of men into the army proved to be crucial in Allied success. Leadership provided by Clemenceau of France and Woodrow Wilson of the United States and the unity of command of the Allied forces under Foch were other significant aspects in this context.
f. **Incompetent allies of Germany.** Due to the incompetence of its allies, Germany had to fight many of the battles of the World War I by its own. It also had to help out Austrians and Bulgarians in their crisis situations which resulted in diffusion of the attention and forces of the German army.

10. Consequences of the World War I

A. Triumph of Nationalism

One of the causes of the World War I was nationalism, which also became one of the consequences of the War. One expression of the triumph of nationalism was the formation of new nations. Many new nations emerged after the War. **Estonia, Latvia, Lithuania, Finland and Czecho-Slovakia** were created from the old Russian and Austrian empires. The Enlargement of Serbia as Yugo-Slavia and restoration of Alsace-Lorraine to France were other important expressions of the triumph of nationalism. Moreover, in the context of awakened nationalism Britain was compelled to withdraw its protectorate in Turkey in 1922 and also to consent establishment of an **Irish Free State** in Ireland in 1921.

B. Fall of Empires

The end of the War also witnessed the collapse of four empires. These were Romanov of Russia, Hohenzollerns of Germany, Hapsburgs of Austria and the Ottomans of Turkey. Collapse of these absolute monarchies marked the culmination of a process that had begun in France in 1789.

C. Spread of Democracy

With the fall of autocratic regimes, a period of democracy was followed in European nations, leading to the formation of parliamentary governments throughout eastern and central Europe. These developments raised the hope that liberalism would thrive throughout Europe as the World War had put an end to the autocratic regimes.

The War also caused intensification of demand for democracy in colonies such as India, as the colonial powers had claimed that the World War had been fought for strengthening of democracies throughout the world.

D. Catalyst for the Russian Revolution

The First World War radically reshaped the political map of Europe. Apart from ending the Russian, German, Austro-Hungarian and Ottoman empires as seen above, it became a catalyst for a revolution in Russia. The Bolshevik Revolution in Russia also became an inspiration for people of many other nations such as Germany, Austria and Hungary in the 1920s, resulting into polarisation of people on the Left and Right.

E. Rise of Dictatorship

Emergence of democracies had been an immediate political outcome of the First World War, which had aroused the hope that Europe has finally come out of autocratic regimes. But the history of Europe of the 1920s and 1930s proved these expectations fragile, as in an extraordinary turn of events democracy was thrown into the death throes and authoritarian governments came to power in Italy, Germany, Spain, Portugal, Russia and in many other newly created central and eastern European states.

In many instances, the newly formed democratic governments were incapable of solving multitudes of problems of the post-war period and it was out of this despair that people began to repose their faith in dictatorship. These totalitarian regimes were known by different names – Fascism, Nazism or Bolshevism – but exhibited common traits such as authoritarianism, extreme nationalism and opposition to democracy.

F. Women Emancipation

During the war, women had played major role in war efforts, by replacing men in wartime production, in factories and in offices. Their ability to work hand-in-hand with men had earned them wider acceptance for their claim to **gender equality.** As a result, women found more opportunities and greater equality in socio-economic and political fields. One expression of political emancipation of women was the right to vote. In 1918, women over 30 years of age were granted voting right in Britain and in 1928 full suffrage was given to them. The United States enfranchised women in 1920. In other countries such as Germany, USSR, Hungary, Poland and Czechoslovakia too women won the right to vote.

G. Economic Impacts

The war dislocated the international economy which had taken decades to build up. The depth of economic destruction and dislocation caused by the war can be gauged from the economic terminologies of the post-war years. These words such as reconstruction, recovery, restoration of the gold standard and so forth had a prefix 're', which pointed to the task left before the world community in rebuilding the ravaged world economy.

The war also ended European industrial supremacy and triggered the emergence of the United States as an industrial powerhouse. By the end of the War, Europe had also become a debtor to the United States. The war time demand had also spurred the capitalists of countries such as India, Japan and the Latin America to develop industries in their own countries.

H. Social Consequences

The war triggered profound changes in social relations, in the family and in the workplace. Severe economic hardships, mass displacement, disillusionment and demoralisation were visible expressions of the impact of the War on society.

I. Formation of the League of Nations

The horrors of the War led to a rethinking on the war and the need for an international organisation in which the states of the world, both great and small, were expected to join for preserving peace and in promoting cooperation. The League covenant was incorporated with each of the five peace treaties signed after the war and the League of Nations was established as a 'league of all nations' and 'league for all nations'.

11. Total War

Total war means a war that encompass the entire nation, that devout all their resources – economic, social and technological – to the war effort. Such a war is without limits and can end only in the unconditional surrender of the enemy. The total war redefined the concept of warfare by introducing novelties in how wars are fought, to what end and how the belligerents mobilise their resources.

It is **unrestricted warfare** in terms of the weapons used, the territory involved, combatants participated or the objectives pursued. It is also characterised by the lack of distinction between fighting lawful combatants and civilians. In effect, outcome of the total war is not just decided by military strength but by the staying power of the entire nation.

Total war **aims** not just the defeat of the rival armies but total destruction of enemy's political and economic edifices. In such a war, targets are not only military personnel and installations but include infrastructural facilities, industrial centres and civilian populations for total destruction of the public morale. Thus, the total war involves civilian massacre as an instrument of military strategy that aim at extermination. Example in this context is German submarine warfare against the Allied commercial shipping during the World War I. Terms such as blitz, carpet bombing and mass population transfers are inseparable aspects of total war. The massacre of 1.5 million Armenians by the Turkish government in 1915 exemplifies the brutal nature of total war on the general population.

In terms of participation too, total war is unique and marks a sharp departure from the previous wars. It involves **mass mobilisation** of a nation's population – both male and female – for war purposes and thus is also called as 'people's war'. This is in contrast to the wars up to the end of the 19th century, which in essence were an affair between professional armies. Thousands of women replaced men in factories and shops apart from serving near the war fronts as nurses.

Apart from the total mobilisation of population, total war involves **reorganisation and mobilisation** of economy for the war effort. This reorganisation takes different forms such as printing more paper money, increased borrowing from foreign markets, high taxes, food rationing, transfer of vital machinery from less to more important industries and conversion of factories into munitions production units. All these mean that the outcome of total war is determined by the capacity of a nation's economy to mobilise, reorganise and produce in tune with the war needs. To illustrate this point Russia is an example. Russia's incapacity to produce for the war was a major factor in its rout in the First World War.

Another feature of the total war is unprecedented **mobilisation of scientific resources** and efforts aimed at constant improvements in communications, aeronautics and war weaponry. As a result tanks, fighter aircrafts and other weapons of mass destruction were developed aimed at annihilation of enemy with greater effectiveness and ruthlessness. Thus, total war was genocide of brutal nature made possible by impersonality of technological innovations.

12. Legacy of the First World War

The First World War, by ushering the notion of war on a grand and global scale, marked a significant point in the modern world. The War profoundly altered the course of human civilisation by putting a question mark on the idea of ever-expanding human progress. It also weakened human confidence in future. The **senseless slaughter and destruction,** the War brought along its course clearly indicated how fragile and perishable are all those human achievements and how barbarian the humans could become.

The most important legacy of the War was the destruction and horrors it caused both in human and material terms. The war caused the death of more than 10 million soldiers and in the wounding of another 20 million. Being the total war it also caused death of countless of civilians by way of slaughter, starvation and diseases.

Devastation of the **European economy** was another legacy of the World War I. Apart from the destruction of homes, factories, farmlands, villages and cities, it is estimated that the War cost a staggering $338 billion which drained the treasuries of the belligerents.

At social and psychological level too, the Great War left a deep legacy. A sense of **demoralisation and disillusionment** was the immediate impact on the social level. For the survivors violence, cruelty and suffering seemed to be acceptable components of human existence. And the old beliefs in the blessings of science and in the perfectibility of humanity now gave way to insecurity and despair as was reflected in the art and literature of the time. Novels such as *The Trial* (1925) and *The Castle* (1926) of the Czech-born author **Franz Kafka** depict the condition of people caught in threatening situations about which they could neither understand nor escape. In painting, a new movement known as **Dadaism** expressed this postwar mood of disorientation and despair. The Dadaism viewed life as absurd.

Franz Kafka

The emergence of **totalitarian movements** was another legacy of the World War I. The War had loosened faith in liberal-democratic values and in the parliamentary institutions in solving socio-economic problems. Many, consequently, turned to fascism as an alternative saving faith. A generation of young people who had fought in the War and had reached their maturity in combat now became ready adherents of this ideology. These youth with a fascination for violence and contempt for life yearned for excitement of the battle. It is to be of significance that both Hitler and Mussolini themselves were ex-soldiers.

The **outbreak of another world war** was another legacy of the World War I. The World War I had not only failed in diffusing either militarism or nationalism but on the other hand intensified the nationalist hatreds. Consequently Germany looked for revenge and Italy felt aggrieved. Further, the peace treaties resulted from the World War I, though aimed at security and peace, instead had prompted anger and resentment which were directly connected to the factors that led to the outbreak of the World War II.

SUMMARY

Causes of the First World War – Nationalism, militarism and military alliances, economic factors and imperialistic motives were the major causes of the World War I

Developments that led to the War – Moroccan Crisis 1905–1906, Bosnian Crisis 1908, Agadir Crisis 1911, the First Balkan War 1912, the Second Balkan War 1913 were the major developments in international relations before the World War I

Immediate cause of the War – Assassination of Francis Ferdinand, nephew of the Austrian emperor and heir to the Austrian throne in Bosnian capital Sarajevo on 28 June 1914 was the immediate cause.

Development of the War – Western Front–Eastern Front–War of Attrition–Entry of the US–Collapse of the Central Powers.

Reasons for the Defeat of the Central Powers – The first important factor was failure of the Schlieffen Plan denying Germany an easy victory that the Germans expected. Other factors such as Naval power of the Allies, Submarine campaign of Germany which brought the United States into the war on the side of the Allies, competent leaders of the Allies and incompetency of the allies of Germany proved crucial in the defeat of the Central Powers.

Consequences of the World War I – The war upheld the spirit of nationalism. It also caused the fall of Empires, spread of democracy and later on the rise of dictatorship. It also factored as a catalyst for the Russian Revolution. The destruction and magnitude of the suffering caused a rethinking on the war and led to the founding of the League of Nations. It also had economic and social consequences such as dislocation of international economy and emancipation of women apart from ending the European industrial supremacy.

Total War – World War I was a Total War. It encompassed the entire nation and mobilisation of all the resources of the participating nations. Total War also meant unrestricted warfare in terms of weapons, territory and combatants. The aim of War was not just defeat of the enemy but total destruction. It also involved mass mobilisation of the participating nations' population, reorganisation of their economy and constant improvement of scientific and technological resources for the war efforts.

Questions of Previous Years Civil Services Examination

1. Europe was at war with itself in the first half of the 20th century with a long cease-fire. (2021)
2. 'There are many ways in which the war of 1914–18 was unprecedented and in human history entirely novel'. Critically examine. (2019)
3. Why was the First World War termed as the first Total War in modern history? (2017)
4. How far is it correct to say that the First World War was fought essentially for the preservation of the balance of power? (2015)
5. 'Any single explanation for the outbreak of First World War is likely to be too simple. An amalgam of factors intellectual, social, economic as well as political and diplomatic contributed to this horrifying conflict of monumental proportion'. Explain. (2012)

CHAPTER 9

The Russian Revolution and History of the Soviet Union

In this Chapter

1. Introduction

'Europe is pregnant with revolution. The coming years in Europe, precisely because of the predatory war, will lead to popular uprisings under the leadership of the proletariat'. These were the words of the Russian revolutionary in exile, **Vladimir Lenin**, in January 1917 while addressing workers in Zurich, Switzerland. As he prophesied, revolution erupted in Russia, which turned out to be one of the seminal events of the 20th century in terms of its historical impact.

The Russian Empire spread over one-sixth of the land surface of the globe was the most conservative of the Great Powers in Europe. By the end of the 19th century, Russia was fundamentally different from the Western Europe. The great movements that reshaped Western Europe – the Renaissance, the Reformation, the Enlightenment, the Scientific Revolution and the Industrial Revolution – did not have much impact in Russia. The vast majority of its people were illiterate. Though uprisings had erupted in Russia since the 19th century over the persistent issues of **autocracy, poverty, inequality** and **inhumane working conditions**, they all had ended in failure. Finally, people's discontent exploded in 1917 in two stages in March and October. The **March Revolution** ushered in a short period of liberal government by ending the Czarist regime and the **October Revolution** overthrew the liberal government and inaugurated an era of 'dictatorship of the proletariat'.

2. History of Russia

A Russian state first emerged in the 9th century centred in Kiev as a loose federation of East Slavic and Finnic peoples in Europe. Prince Vladimir, the Great (980–1015 A.D.) introduced Christianity with his own baptism and accepted **Eastern Orthodox Christianity** from Byzantium in 988 A.D. Since then, the state and the Orthodox Church were closely entwined in Russia. The Russian rulers took the title *tsar* or *czar* (the Russian equivalent of the Latin Caesar) and became the head of both of the state and the Russian Orthodox Church. The **Romanov** was the last dynasty of the Tsars that ruled from 1613 to 1917 – the year in which the Revolution overthrew it.

3. Causes of the Russian Revolution

The Russian Revolution has been equated to a firecracker with a very long fuse. Though the explosion took place only in 1917, resentment against oppressive rule of Czars had been widespread since the 19th century.

A. Political Causes

a. Autocracy

Russia under the Tsars was autocratic and ineffective. Throughout the 19th century, waves of discontent had erupted against autocracy and for political reforms. The Russian officers, who had been exposed to the western civilised life during their fight against Napoleon, had aspired for such features in their country too and had turned revolutionaries. In December 1825, a small group of conspirators rose in rebellion demanding a constitution. But these uprisings known as the **'Decembrists Uprisings'** were suppressed and the **Tsar Nicholas** I (1825–55) followed a policy called 'official nationality' for Russification (uniform Russian culture) of his Empire.

> The 'Decembrists' were intelligent and patriotic young men of the aristocracy who aspired for constitutional and judicial reforms and abolition of serfdom in Russia. The uprising took place in December 1825 in the interregnum between the death of Tsar Alexander I and the ascension of Tsar Nicholas I. The Decembrists uprising had been described as 'an attempted revolution on the people's behalf by a section of the educated elite'.

This policy had three components – Orthodoxy, Autocracy and Nationality. The Russian people were taught to believe that the Orthodox creed of the Russian church, the autocratic rule of the Czar and Russia's Slavic nationalism and culture as superior to the West. '**For Faith, Tsar and Fatherland**' became the common public motto enforced by the emperor, and it was the Russian version of a general European ideology of restoration and reaction that followed the Napoleonic Wars. To enforce this decree, Nicholas I created secret agency of police spies and created a monolithic country centred on the monarch.

> **Russification:** Policy followed by the Tsars of Russia under which they tried to extend the language, religion and culture of Great Russia over all the subjects of the Tsars with measures such as compulsory teaching of the Russian language throughout the empire, prohibiting the use of minority languages such as Polish in schools and patronisation of Eastern Orthodox Church. Russification also meant repression which many a time turned to pogroms, that is, wholesale massacres, and was mainly aimed at the Poles, Finns and Jews as these nationalities were considered most dangerous to the state.

Nicholas' successor **Alexander II (1855–81)** too was autocratic but was in favour of initiating some reforms. He granted local self-government, introduced trial by jury, constructed rail roads, permitted import of western goods and capital. Above all he liberated the serfs by granting legal rights to more than 22 million serfs on some land and liberated them from the bondage to the nobility in 1861 for which he was known as '**Alexander the Liberator**'. Alexander II also instituted local government structures called ***mir*** or village communes and ***zemstvos*** or elected provincial councils. Though these bodies did not pass real authority into peoples' hands, nevertheless provided opportunities for debating on political issues and caused political awareness.

But apprehensive of the spread of Liberalism, Tsar Alexander II called a halt to reforms and substituted censorship and repression in its place. The *zemstvos* were forbidden from discussing political issues and censorship was extended to the press and to educational institutions. Angry over these developments, some revolutionaries assassinated Tsar Alexander II in 1881.

The rule of the next Tsar, **Alexander III (1881–94)**, was a reaction against the entire policy of reforms, and he strengthened autocracy and implemented ruthless Russification. He perfected the police state, stiffed dissent, curtailed the powers of the local assemblies and subjected villages to government by wealthy nobles who were appointed by the state. Political prisoners were sent to Siberia, a remote region of eastern Russia. All these suppression forced many intellectuals to find refuge in countries such as Switzerland.

Under **Nicholas II (1895–1917)**, the son and successor of Alexander III, despotism continued unabated in Russia. He was conservative, irresolute and weak, and was under the undue influence of his wife **Alexandria** and her spiritual mentor, the monk **Rasputin**. Rasputin's relationship with the Tsarina and his influence in administration led to disastrous ministerial appointments and corruption.

Unmindful of the potential strength of the new forces – the liberal and revolutionary ideas – that were surging around him, Nicholas II continued the traditional ways of the Russian autocracy, accentuating the revolution.

Rasputin was a self-professed 'holy man' who claimed to have magical healing powers. He was close to the Empress Alexandria and eventually became the real power behind the throne. His opposition to reform, drunkenness and numerous affairs with court ladies had caused public criticism. In 1916, some nobles killed Rasputin.

b. *Emergence of Political Parties*

In the last decades of the 19th century, Russia witnessed great progress in industrialisation. Between 1863 and 1900, the number of factories in Russia more than doubled. The industrialisation gave birth to a new wage earning class – the industrial workers – who had to toil hard in crowded towns under intolerable circumstances. They were marched to and from factories, where the average working day was up to 15 hours and conditions in factories were unsafe and unhealthy. These harsh realities of industrialised urban life instilled a deep discontent and class consciousness among the workers of Russia.

During the same period, socialism and the teachings of **Karl Marx** began to take roots among the factory workers through the writings and preaching of radicals like the novelist **Maxim Gorky**. It was also the period of emergence of political parties in Russia. The first was the **Workmen's Social Democratic Party** in 1895. The Russian peasantry organised **Social Revolutionary Party** in 1901 with the aim of confiscation of estates of the nobility and distribution of it to the peasants. In 1902, the middle-class businessmen and professionals formed **Constitutional Democratic Party** with aims like formation of elected parliament and promotion of liberalism and westernisation.

In 1903, the Social Democratic Party split into **Bolsheviks** and **Mensheviks**, on questions of party discipline and strategy. The Bolsheviks (the majority group, because they had majority on the questions that caused the split) stood for a strongly centralised party of hardened professional revolutionaries, extreme measures to bring in a revolution and for establishing the dictatorship of the proletariat. This group opposed any co-operation with middle class as they did not recognise any class other than that of the proletariat. They were under the leadership of a dedicated revolutionary Vladimir Ulyanov better known as Nikolai Lenin. The Mensheviks (the minority group) stood for a broad-based and inclusive formula and were less radical in their views and methods. They resembled European revisionist socialists and believed in slow and gradual progress towards socialism and were ready to co-operate with other classes and parties in overthrowing autocracy in Russia.

Apart from these, a growing number of people in Russia espoused the doctrines and teachings of the anarchist Mikhail Bakunin calling themselves as **Nihilists** and resorted to violence for political change. The Nihilists held the view that 'the passion for destruction is also a constructive passion' and favoured freeing individuals from all religious, political and family obligations. In actions described as **'propaganda of the deed'**, the Nihilists assassinated many government officials as part of their political strategy.

Thus, by the first decade of the 20th century, the political landscape of Russia had been planted with large number of political parties with varied aims such as establishment of representative democracy, end of autocracy and the establishment of the dictatorship of the proletariat.

B. Socio-Economic Conditions

Another important factor that created conditions for a revolution in Russia was the socio-economic conditions marked by a **wide cleavage between the rich and poor**.

The two classes that comprised the Russian society were the **nobles and serfs**. The nobility, which possessed vast tracts of land, occupied most of the offices of the state and lived a life of luxury. On the other, serfs were miserably poor and were 'hewers of wood and drawers of water' under the nobles. Even through the serfs had been liberated from bondage to the nobility in 1861, as seen above, their economic conditions had not improved much. With the best lands in the country remaining in the hands of the nobility, agrarian sector remaining technologically backward and with the taxing the peasantry even for raising the capital for industrialisation, the condition of the Russian peasantry was miserable. In 1900, almost 90 percent of the Russian population was peasants and two-thirds of the population was illiterate. This discontent class of peasantry was ready to participate in any movement that would take them out of their miseries.

The strides made by Russia in industrialisation in the last decades of the 19th century had added one more discontent class in Russia – the **industrial workers (the proletariat)**. The industrialisation had promoted mobility, literacy and exposure to the western ideals, which in turn had facilitated awareness about exploitation and in the emergence of political consciousness. This class of industrial workers were conscious of their existence as a class and were resentful of the exploitative system. The Russian industrial worker was partly a peasant who had strong roots in. the villages. As an industrial worker he had to toil under subhuman conditions while his family in the village had to bear the crushing burden of the land tax and redemption payments. Another group was the **bourgeoisie**, the emerging middle class, that is, industrial owners, professionals and businessmen who were believers in liberalism. They aspired for constitutional government on western lines.

Under such cleavages of class and wealth, **liberal, socialist and revolutionary ideas** had a fertile ground in Russia and these sections with varying aims and deep discontent of the existing system were to provide impetus to the revolution.

C. Influence of Ideas

Before the material revolution, Russia had undergone a revolution in the realm of ideas. **Liberal ideas** of democracy, elected parliament, limited monarchy and also **radical socialist ideas** like class struggle had been filtering into Russia in spite of the efforts by the Russian emperors to immunise its subjects from such influences. Writers like **Leo Tolstoy (War and Peace), Ivan Turgenev (Fathers and Sons), Fyodor Dostoyevsky (Crime and Punishment)** and others, through their works, profoundly influenced the minds of the educated class called the intelligentsia. During this period the Russians thirst for learning and education had been on the rise as they absorbed reading matter whether socio-economic theories or philosophies, as observed by a contemporary scholar 'like hot sand drinks water'.

The ferment of ideas had awakened the imagination of the Russian youth who now began to aspire for a glorious future replacing the wretched condition that was under the Tsarist autocracy.

D. Military Failures

The incompetence of the Tsar had been well demonstrated in areas other than administration too. Russia had been defeated in the **Crimean War** (1853–56) by an alliance under the leadership of the Ottoman Empire. The failure of Russia in the Crimean War had shattered the image of the Russian Empire and had shaken confidence of Russian subjects in their masters.

Russo-Japanese War (1904–05) was another military set-back for Russia that further eroded the confidence of the Russians in their ruler. For many Russians, the shock of unexpected humiliation at the hands of an Asian country was a metaphor for the shortcomings of the Romanov autocracy. Popular discontent exploded in a revolution in 1905, but the Tsar could tide over it.

The Revolution of 1905. Russian losses in its war with Japan gave b rth to a revolution in 1905. In January 1905, hundreds of people were killed when soldiers opened fire upon a crowd that assembled before Czar's Winter Palace in St. Petersburg demanding reforms. This incident known as the **'Bloody Sunday'** provoked strikes and violence throughout Russia. The strikers at St. Petersburg went to the extent of forming a Council of Workers' Deputies known as the St. Petersburg Soviet under Leon Trotsky and called on the country to stop the payment of taxes to the Tsar. Under threat of a revolution Nicholas II was forced to make concessions. He issued the **October Manifesto**, promising more freedom and creation of Duma (an elected parliament). The split in the opposition groups and the loyalty of the armed forces saved the Tsar from the crisis. Though he created the Duma, it was reduced to a mere consultative forum.

Finally, it was Tsar's inefficiency and ineffectiveness in leading Russia's campaigns in the **First World War** that gave the much needed spark to the accumulated discontent to explode. The Russo-Japanese war had shaken the foundation of the Czarist regime and the First World War by bringing to a head the gathering discontent destroyed it.

Russia had entered the War unprepared to handle its military and economic cost and the result was defeat after defeats. The defeats in turn resulted in devastating loss of morale both in Russian army and in the general population multiplying the dissatisfaction with the Romanov family. Tsarina Alexandra, who was the real power centre, was German born, causing suspicion in peoples' mind of her collusion with Germany.

Russian army proved incapable of winning the battles of the World War. Soldiers went hungry, did not have sufficient shoes, munitions and even weapons. Result was rampant discontent which lowered the morale of the soldiers which was further aggravated by a series of military defeats. A vivid sign of the disaster was the high casualty rate. For example, by the end of 1914, only five months in to the war almost 4 lakh Russians had lost their lives and 10 lakh men had been injured.

Aggravating the crisis, the railway system broke down leading to the collapse of transportation and communication and shortage of food and fuel. Situation was further inflamed by inflation, caused as a result of printing millions of rouble notes to finance the war. High prices caused riots of peasants in the country side, strikes of workers in cities and desertions of soldiers in army. As situation worsened, people of all classes were clamouring for change and an end to the war.

4. | Origin of the Revolution

The crisis erupted in the capital city of **Petrograd** (St. Petersburg had been renamed during the war as Petrograd) in March 1917 with bread riots by women. They were joined by strikers of factories. The troops sent by Tsar refused to fire at the unarmed crowd and turned on their officers and mutinied. The local protest now exploded into a revolution known as the **March Revolution**. The Tsar tried to prorogue the Duma, accusing this body of instigating the strikes. In defiance the Duma formed a Provisional Government. On 15 March 1917, Tsar Nicholas II abdicated in favour of his brother, but he refused to take up the crown and the Russian monarchy came to an end. The Romanov dynasty that ruled Russia for three hundred years (1613–1917) ended.

The Russian Revolutions of 1917 are known as the February and October Revolutions on the basis of Julian calendar of Russia or March and November Revolutions on the basis of Gregorian calendar of the West.

5. | The Provisional Government

A Provisional Government first under **Prince Georgy Lvov** and later under **Alexander Kerensky** was set-up. It was a government of liberals comprised of the bourgeoisie or the middle class. Their aim was establishment of a constitutional monarchy under the middle-class leadership. They were opposed to the social revolution that could result in the seizure of private properties and destruction of class structures.

Unfortunately, the provisional government could not cope up with the enormous crises on all fronts and misunderstood the mood of the people. The measures of the provisional government did not satisfy large sections of people, leading to a second revolution in November 1917 which brought the Bolsheviks, to power.

Reasons for the Failure of the Provisional Government

1. Being admirers of the liberal ideas of the West, the provisional government promulgated a number of **liberal reforms** like freedom of speech, association and religion; and released thousands of

prisoners but none of these did satisfy the masses. The largely illiterate masses of Russia did not have experience of a free society and understanding of liberal ideals. And lacking the support of the masses the Russian liberalism was bound to fail.

2. While the Provisional Government **promised a constituent assembly** to decide the form of permanent government, they held the view that basic economic reforms should wait the convening of the constituent assembly. But the masses were more concerned about peace, land and bread which were the issues of concerns to their very existence than the political reforms. The masses were looking for socio-economic reforms that would uplift them from their miseries, and as these were not being implemented the revolution that began as a liberal movement drifted to socialism. As dissatisfaction with the Provisional Government grew, the workers, peasants and soldiers established alternative governing bodies called the Soviets (councils) throughout the country.
3. The provisional government decided to continue the war on the side of the Allies, in spite of **heavy military losses** being suffered on the front. The Provisional Government continued the War under the premise that domestic changes must be subordinated to the war efforts, which was against the wishes of the soldiers leading to desertions of soldiers in large numbers – almost two million – and they began to fraternise with their enemy, the Germans across the trenches.
4. The liberals were supporters of **Russian nationalism** and wanted their country to remain undivided. Hence, they opposed non-Russian minorities in Russia like Finns, Georgians, Poles and others who sought self-determination. These minorities were opposed to the Provisional Government and started asserting for their freedom.
5. The **unabated conditions** of soaring prices, scarcity of essential commodities which was difficult to remedy because of the wartime conditions and the spectre of famine multiplied the hardships and anger of the masses. The peasants seized large estates, workmen resorted to strike for higher wages and fewer hours of work and soldiers refused to obey the orders and became a mutinous rabble.
6. To make things worse, the Provisional Government could not take decisive policy decisions due to **political factionalism** which left the government open to strong challenges from both the right and the left. Ineffectiveness in governance was also the result of breakdown in the state structures. The local soviets, political organisations mostly of socialists often used discretion whether or not to implement the policies and programs of the Provisional Government. Of the adversaries of the Provisional Government the Petrograd Soviet was the most important and the most powerful. The **Petrograd Soviet** and the Provisional Government competed for power.

   Proved incompetent, the Provisional Government now blamed the Bolsheviks (the only group among the socialists that had not joined the government) for the chaos and ordered arrest of its leaders.
7. The credibility of the Provisional Government was also undermined by the **Kornilov Mutiny**. In August 1917, General Kornilov, the Commander-in-Chief of the Russian army, attempted a coup to set up a military dictatorship. But it was thwarted by the workers of the Petrograd.
8. Leadership and the promises of the **Bolsheviks were attractive and realistic**. Lenin who had returned to Russia from his exile and Trotsky, who had been Menshevik but just had become a Bolshevik understood the mood of the people and channelised their energy for another revolution. Their promises such as exit from the World War and land to peasants were attractive to the general population.

6. Lenin and the Rise of Bolshevism

Lenin

Vladimir Ilyich Ulyanov Lenin was born in 1870 in a wealthy family in Russia. Early in his life Lenin embraced revolutionary socialist politics and turned a Marxist ideologist. In 1897, he was exiled to Siberia on charges of sedition. In 1900, he moved to Western Europe and was engaged in promoting Marxist aim of the overthrow of capitalism and its replacement with socialism. In 1902, Lenin published a political pamphlet ***What Is To Be Done?*** In this, Lenin argued for a political party of dedicated revolutionaries or **'vanguard'** to spread Marxism and to convert the Russian working class to Marxism.

Russian Communism and Marxism

The Russian Bolshevism was based on the Marxian teachings as interpreted by Lenin. Lenin's interpretation had certain deviation from the original teachings of Marx, which was a reflection of conditions prevailing in Russia and is known as Marxism-Leninism.

Marx had predicted the proletarian revolution to occur in a highly industrialised country with abundant wealth and a large exploited proletariat. But Russia was one of the least industrialised nations of Europe and had a weak proletarian base. Marx had also expected that capitalist stage as a necessary pre-condition that would lead to revolution because of its inner contradictions. Here too Lenin's view was different as he held that a direct transition from a feudalistic to socialistic pattern was possible. Moreover, Karl Marx had not given much emphasis on revolutionary character of socialism, while Lenin emphasised this aspect. Further, in his conception of the proletarian rule too Lenin differed from Marx. While Marx visualised the whole working-class participation and democratic practices within that class in the 'dictatorship of the proletariat', Lenin stood for the necessity of a select minority of disciplined and dedicated party elite, a 'vanguard of the proletariat' in such a dictatorship.

He had encouraged the revolutionaries during the failed Russian Revolution of 1905. With the outbreak of the First World War Lenin campaigned for a Europe-wide proletarian revolution. In April, 1917, Lenin who had been living in exile in Switzerland returned to Petrograd with the support of Germany, who recognised his potential as a revolutionary to cause problems to their Russian enemies. On his journey from Switzerland Lenin prepared his **'April Theses'** containing 10 directives to the Bolsheviks, which included denouncement of the Provisional Government, condemnation of the World War I as a 'predatory imperialist war', call for new communist policies and also gave the slogan **'All power to the Soviets'**.

Lenin rallied the Bolsheviks, promised **'peace, land and bread'** to the people and called for the capture of power by the Soviets. The Bolsheviks now took measures to garner support of the Soviets (councils) of soldiers, workers and peasants.

The Soviets were the people's parliament par excellence and the most representative body in Russia, with members elected from factories, workshops and from the military barracks. The first Soviet had been constituted during the Revolution of 1905 at St. Petersburg, which was reconstituted after the abdication of Tsar. Soon, Soviets sprang up throughout Russia, which became 'the most spectacular centre of the revolution' whose orders and instructions had universal obedience. The Petrograd Soviet of Workers' and Soldiers' Deputies played crucial role during the revolution.

7. Bolshevik Revolution

On 6 November 1917, Lenin exhorted that 'the government is tottering. It must be given a death blow at all costs'. The next day, 7 November 1917 (25 October as per the old Russian calendar), the Bolsheviks calling themselves as **Red Guards**, occupied the Winter Palace at St. Petersburg (Petrograd), disbanded the Provisional Government and seized power. Kerensky fled from the country. For their success the Bolsheviks' owed much to the leadership of Lenin. Lenin's clarity of perspective in assessing the situation, in understanding the needs of the people, in gauging the true strengths and weaknesses of various classes and also in pointing out the revolutionary potential of the peasantry were determinant factors for the success.

Lenin took series of measures to implement the slogan of the Bolsheviks 'peace, bread and land'. **Three Decrees – the Decree on Peace, the Decree on Land** and **Decree on Workers' Control** – were promulgated. It ordered distribution of land to peasants without compensation to former owners. Bolsheviks entrusted the control of factories to the workers. They also nationalised banks, confiscated private accounts and properties, labour was made compulsory for all citizens and Orthodox Church of Russia was dismantled. Women were given equal rights with men. It abolished all ranks, titles and decorations and all local government bodies were replaced by a hierarchy of Soviets. It also negotiated a treaty with the Germans and signed the **Treaty of Brest-Litovsk** in March 1918 and withdrew from the world war.

> ***Ten Days that Shook the World*** (1919) is a book written by the American journalist **John Reed**. It is a firsthand account of the October Revolution of 1917. During the rule of Stalin the book was banned in Soviet Union as it portrayed Trotsky and not Stalin as the man who co-led the Revolution with Lenin.

The Romanov family Tsar Nicholas II, his wife Tsarina Alexandra and their five children were executed in July 1918. As these actions were antagonistic to the views and interests of many sections – both the moderates and the reactionaries – Russia soon plunged into a civil war.

> **Treaty of Brest-Litovsk:** The treaty was signed at German-controlled city of Brest-Litovsk (now in Belarus) following the Bolshevik Revolution of 1917. It was signed between the Bolshevik government and the Central Powers under Germany in March 1918 ending the Russian participation in the First World War. By this treaty Russia conceded most of Germany's territorial demands. Russia lost Finland, Poland and the Baltic provinces apart from Ukraine, its chief industrial base and the breadbasket. By the treaty, Russia lost a quarter of its pre-war population and three-quarters of its iron and steel producing areas. Though the treaty was a great humiliation to Russia, Lenin believed that the losses were temporary as the Russian Revolution was only the first stage of the worldwide revolution and the signing of the Treaty was a step to 'the world revolution'.
>
> The Treaty meant not just the end of conflict between Russia and Germany but more than that it strengthened the hands of Germany by freeing up a million German soldiers for the Western Front. Germany also acquired much of Russia's food and fuel supplies, industrial base and communications which made the German domination in Eastern Europe a reality. The Allied Powers considered the Treaty as the ultimate betrayal of the Allied cause and is also considered to have sowed the seeds of the Cold War.

8. Civil War in Russia (1918–20)

Though the peace treaty with Germany ended a major problem for the new government, it was soon beset with host of new ones. Of these, the most important crisis was the attempt by the anti-Bolshevik groups to unseat the new government leading to a civil war.

The propertied class – the landlords and the capitalists – were not happy with loss of their property. Many Russians were also dissatisfied with the humiliating provisions of the Treaty of Brest-Litovsk. There was discontent among the soldiers and the workers against the Bolsheviks' high-handedness of the Soviets. Instead of permitting the Soviets to run the town's administration and the local industry, the Bolshevik government had appointed officials known as the **Commissars**, which was seen as dictatorship from the centre. Many were also enraged over the murder of the royal family.

Two combatants in the Russian Civil war were **the Reds** or the Red Army fighting for the Bolshevik and **the Whites** or the White Army – the anti-Bolsheviks consisting of army officers, Cossacks (the elite corps in the Tsars army), Mensheviks, supporters of monarchy and of the Provisional Government and all shades of political groups ranging from moderate socialists to the reactionary. The desire to defeat the Bolshevik was the sole factor that united the White Army.

The **Allied Powers** such as Great Britain, France, the United States and Japan sent troops, so that the Communist call for a world revolution could be defeated at its source of origin. Meanwhile pro-independence movements also emerged in regions that had been parts of the former Russian Empire – in the Ukraine, Finland, the Caucasus and the Baltic.

In spite of adversities, the Red Army eventually defeated most of the anti-Bolshevik forces and extended the Communist control over the remaining parts of the former Russian Empire and emerged as the USSR or the Union of the Soviet Socialist Republics in December 1922. The Bolsheviks also renamed their party as the Communist Party.

A. Factors for Bolshevik Success

1. Greater popular support, superior political skills, compulsory military service and strict discipline in the Red Army were major factors.

2. The Red Army had more troops and had a better leadership under Trotsky. Their control over industries ensured better supply of armaments.
3. Support of the peasants, who feared that a return to the old system would mean the loss of their newly acquired land, too proved crucial in the final outcome.
4. Introduction of War Communism ensured resource mobilisation and its supply to the fighting units.
5. The Whites were divided among themselves, were loosely knit and were discredited by their association with the Tsarist regime.
6. The position of the Whites had also been discredited by their foreign connections, and Lenin could project the war as a fight between the Bolshevik national government and the foreigners.
7. Moreover the Western intervention had been half-hearted and these nations soon turned war-weary and ended their efforts to overthrow the Communist regime.

B. Results of the Civil War

The results of the civil war were enormous. Apart from huge human cost – around 14 million – in the form of war casualties, the civil war also prompted emigration of around two million people known as the **White émigrés** from Russia to the Far East and to the newly independent Baltic states. The Russian economy was also devastated due to the destruction of machines, factories and the bridges. Industrial production collapsed due to lack of fuel. On account of all these, the total industrial production in 1920 was only 13% of what it had been in 1913. All these culminated in the famine of 1921–22 which took toll of millions of life. The civil war also caused for the introduction of **'War Communism'** in 1918 to deal with the plummeting economic production, inflation and hunger in the cities.

9. The War Communism

War Communism refers to a set of economic policies introduced by the Bolshevik government in 1918 with the goal of ensuring food and weapons to the Red Army and the proletariat in the cities. It ended in 1921. Under the war communism the state took over the means of production by nationalising all industries, by introducing strict centralised management, by enforcing strict discipline for workers and also by prohibiting strikes. It also meant conscription of labour and confiscation of grain from the peasants. War Communism limited the sphere of private ownership and rationed food through centralised distribution system.

For a nation devastated by war, revolution, terror and civil war, War Communism was another step of further strangulation. It devastated the economy even further, caused depopulation of many cities and alienated workers and peasants from the regime. Adding to the misery, as already seen, there was severe famine in 1921. A series of workers' strikes and peasants' uprisings took place throughout Russia. In March 1921, an uprising of sailors at Kronstadt naval base, though suppressed by the Red Army, became an expression of dissatisfaction with the state of affairs and proved to be a turning point. In that year, the Communist party replaced War Communism with NEP or the New Economic Policy.

10. The New Economic Policy and Consolidation (1921–28)

In 1921, Lenin initiated series of measures intended to revitalise the Soviet economy by allowing greater freedom in agriculture, industry and trade. Lenin characterised this system as **'state socialism'** in which government retained control of finance, industry and transportation – **'the commanding heights of economy'** – while allowing rest of the economy to return to private sector. It permitted manufacturing and trade by private entrepreneurs on small scale, reintroduced the payment of wages, ended grain requisitioning and permitted peasants to sell their surplus grain in the open market after payment of a tax for the surplus and permitting traders to buy and sell freely. The NEP in other words was a move away from full nationalisation of certain segments of economy and a reversal to a small-scale version of capitalism.

The NEP facilitated the economic recovery of Russia which had been devastated by the World War, Revolution and the Civil War. In Lenin's words NEP was **'one step backward in order to take two steps forward'**, a strategic retreat from socialism to create economic conditions necessary for socialism eventually to evolve. NEP was successful as it increased agricultural production and could surpass pre-Revolution agricultural production. It ignited economic recovery and improved electrification in industries. By 1928, Russia's farm and factories had equalled pre-World War production level. The NEP came to an end in 1928 with re-nationalisation of much of the economy and introduction of the Five Year Plan by Joseph Stalin.

11. | Establishment of the USSR

In 1924, a constitution was adopted replacing the old imperial Russia with a new name – the **Union of Soviet Socialist Republics (USSR)** or the Soviet Union to include all the self-governing Soviet republics such as Russia, Armenia, Georgia, Ukraine and Azerbaijan under one union. The constitution, in theory, provided each nationality of the constituent republics the right to promote its own language and culture and also the right to secede from the union. Though the constitution was based on socialist and democratic principles, what soon emerged in Soviet Russia was a dictatorship of the Communist Party which was the directing force behind both politics and in governance of the union and of the constituent republics.

12. | One Party Dictatorship

The political developments of the Soviet Union, since the time of the Civil War, had been that of gross violation of democratic principles and individual liberty. The Soviets, formed during the Revolutionary period, were democratic organs in which vast masses of people had opportunity in decision-making and direct political participation. As such large number of political groups like the Liberals, Mensheviks, Socialists and Revolutionaries had flourished during this period and had active participation in the Soviets. During the Civil War, while the Communists were waging a fierce struggle against the Whites, these opposition groups were eliminated from the political life of the country. Many were terrorised into submission, and many were exiled to Siberia and much more were forced to leave the country for safe havens.

The Bolshevik Party, which came to be known as the **Communist Party of the Soviet Union**, was the sole political party in the Soviet Union and its Central Committee was the directing force both in government and in politics. The party controlled all public agencies and its leaders held the chief positions in government.

Under its constitution, the Russian Communist Party was structured as a democratic body whose organisational apparatus extended to all areas of the vast country. Its members elected delegates to the periodic party congress which in turn elected the **Central Committee** – the leadership of the party. However, power soon shifted to a small and close-knit group of professional political leaders known as the **'politburo'** which assumed dictatorial role. This body led by key leaders like Lenin, Trotsky and Stalin determined policy, assigned tasks and appointed important officials.

Similarly, the Communist Party which had a democratic way of functioning that had permitted debates and discussions within the party soon came to eliminate all democratic decision processes. In 1921, Lenin banned factionalism within the party which meant that once decision was taken after discussion within the party, all sections of the party had to abide by it. Anybody who continued with a different view from the official party line were disciplined or expelled from the party and political enemies were terrorised. In 1921, one-third of the party members were expelled and many more were forced to resign for opposing the NEP.

The Communist Party also instituted tools of oppression of which the **Cheka** (secret police) was the most ruthless. The Cheka established forced labour-camps, where it indulged in extreme terror not only against enemies of the regime but even against the general population. All these features of Russian Communism were in contravention with the human values that Marx had taken from the Enlightenment in constructing his vision of a socialist society.

Further, the **trade unions were turned into the agents of the regime** and had to do what the government told them. The workers were relentlessly reminded of their main duty of increasing production, the need for 'iron discipline at work' and 'unquestioning obedience' to the single will of the Communist Party.

In their effort to transform the Soviet Union into a modern industrialised state and a role model for the world, the Communists imposed autocracy much harsher than that of the previous Tsar regime. Under the belief that the masses always needed guidance, and also to create proper 'consciousness' of socialist order, every sphere of life in the Soviet Union came under unprecedented government control. It found expressed in the fields of education, arts and literature, and in press and radio where the ideals of Communism were highlighted, contributions of the Communist regime were glorified and Marxism-Leninism as the sole source of truth was emphasised.

It abolished the power of the Orthodox Church, reduced influences of other religions and kept them under the watchful eyes of government, so that religion would not corrupt people's mind. It tried to eliminate all other creeds of politics, religion and philosophy and insulated the minds of people from all 'subversive' elements from outside, especially from the capitalist world.

13. Legacy of the Russian Revolution

The Russian Revolution was one of the most significant events of the 20th century and is considered as a continuation of the French Revolution of 1789 in its eastern advance for it smashed autocracy, gave land to the peasants, and liberated the oppressed nationalities.

It overthrew the last absolute monarchy in Europe and established a state based on the ideals of Marxian socialism. Many of the developments in the world in that century or even after had been related to this incident. The Revolution also heralded a very **radical socio-economic and political order**. Its measures such as workers' control of industrial enterprises, compulsory labour and equality of gender all were nothing but radical. Construction of a new socio-economic order based on the Marxist ideal of egalitarianism was a significant achievement in history. No unemployment, no hardcore poverty, provisions for subsidised food, housing and transport and free health care and education greatly bridged the gap between the rich and poor. Under the Communists, the Soviet Russia quickly transformed from a rural and undeveloped economy into a **major economic, military and political power** of the world as is attested by the fact that by 1932 more than 70 per cent of Russia's national product was from industry.

The event also inspired revolutionary surge throughout the Europe in 1918 and 1919 – such as in Germany, Spain and Hungary. Beyond Europe, it inspired the tobacco workers in Cuba to form 'Soviets', and students in Argentina, Mexico and China in forming revolutionary organisations. In colonial countries such as India, the Revolution provided a boost of morale in their struggle against oppressive colonial masters.

At the same time the Revolution had replaced the autocracy of the Tsar with authoritarianism of the Bolsheviks, especially under Stalin. Instead of establishing a 'dictatorship of the proletariat' as Marx had prophesied, the Revolution established the 'dictatorship of the Communist Party'. Many of the achievements of Soviet Russia had also been at substantial cost in both **human lives** and **human rights**. The Civil War, Collectivisation, forced labour camps of Siberia, the Great Purge and many famines had a heavy toll on human lives. Freedom of expression and freedom of religion too had been major casualties in Soviet Russia. Apart from all these, the Soviet subjects had to undergo unrelenting campaign of indoctrination.

It appears as one of the ironies of history that within 20 years after the Revolution, which ended the tyranny of the Tsars, a heavier and brutal version of the same was imposed on the people of Russia. Moreover, the basic spirit of the Russian Revolution, discarding of old divisions of nationality and proclaiming of internationalism, was soon replaced by **xenophobia**. As a result, an iron curtain was erected across Europe, and the Soviet secluded itself from the capitalist world causing another war, luckily not hot, but the Cold War.

14. Emergence of Stalin

Stalin

Lenin died in January 1924 at the age of 53 leaving the task of rebuilding the nation on Communist lines incomplete. His death precipitated struggle for power between two of his lieutenants – Joseph Stalin and Leon Trotsky. The developments in Soviet Union after Lenin was that of transformation from one party rule to dictatorship under Stalin.

Joseph Dzhugashvili was born in 1879 in the small town of Georgia, as the son of poor peasants. He took the name Stalin which means **'man of steel'**, for himself. At a young age Stalin joined the Russian Social Democratic Labor Party (Bolshevik) and edited its newspaper 'Pravda'. In 1922, at the 11th Party Congress, Lenin nominated Stalin as the new General Secretary of the Communist Party. In this position Stalin could control nominations to the Council of Commissars (various departmental ministers) with party members loyal to him and thus control the government. Stalin also built up a reliable party cadre known as 'apparatchiki' or apparatus men during this period and started dominating the party.

After the death of Lenin, it was expected that **Leon Trotsky**, one of the members of the **'Politburo'**, who was an inspired orator, an intellectual and the organiser of the **Red Army**, would succeed Lenin. Trotsky's contribution in the Revolution and subsequently as foreign minister and war minister of the Soviet state was considered to be second only to Lenin's. Moreover, Lenin had considered Stalin stubborn and rude and had suggested in his will that Stalin be removed from the post of the Secretary-General of the Communist Party. Despite these, Stalin emerged victorious in the struggle for succession to Lenin. Stalin took measures to reduce the importance of Trotsky in the affairs of the Soviet state and, finally, Trotsky was expelled from the Communist Party in November 1927. As a prelude, Stalin had removed Trotsky as Commissar for Military and Naval Affairs (1925), from the Politburo (1926) and from the Central Committee in October 1927. Trotsky was exiled in 1929 and in 1940 Stalin got him assassinated in Mexico where he had been living.

15. | Russia Under Stalin – Totalitarianism

As seen already, soon after the revolution, Lenin had laid the foundation for an authoritarian state in Russia by instituting attack on rival political parties and by eliminating opposing voices with censorship and secret police. But, it was Stalin who perfected it by extending control of the party and government over virtually to every aspect of the Soviet life. Stalin aimed at creating a perfect Communist state and to realise this objective, he transformed the Soviet Union into a totalitarian state.

In the '**Dictatorship of the Proletariat**', a new type of society and a higher type of civilisation was what promised by the leaders of the Revolution. Instead, the political developments in Soviet Union took the form of **dictatorship of the party** (whose membership of about only 1 million in 1930 which was a small fraction compared to the total population of 150 million) at first and then by virtue of Stalin's domination of the party, **dictatorship of an individual**.

A. The Great Purge

Stalin took measures to eliminate political opponents and critics once and for all. The first batch of the victims were members of the party, the **Old Bolsheviks** – the most independent-minded and therefore the most dangerous to Stalin. Many founders of the Communist Party were accused of conspiring with the exiled Trotsky in setting up a 'terrorist centre' to wreck the 'socialist reconstruction' and executed. In 1932, Stalin made use of **Ryutin Platform** to expel many leaders from the party and were banished from Moscow.

> Martemyan Ryutin, an Old Bolshevik expelled by Stalin in 1930 from the Communist Party, had gathered likeminded people and had called for slowing down industrialisation, end of forced collectivisation, reinstatement of expelled party members and removal of Stalin from the leadership. This platform of Stalin's critics described him as 'the gravedigger of the Revolution'. Stalin considered this group as the enemies of Communism and as traitors to the party and the working class, who were eventually exiled to the Urals. Ryutin was executed in 1937.

Assassination of Sergei Kirov, one of his supporters and a member of the Politburo, in 1934, was used as a pretext by Stalin to launch 'the purges' – repression against everyone, even on suspicion of loyalty. Though it was almost certain that Stalin got Kirov assassinated, it was blamed on Stalin's critics. Over the next four years, Stalin instituted **'the Great Purge'** (also known as the Great Terror) a campaign of political repression in which hundreds of thousands were arrested, tortured and made to confess to crimes in which they had no role. Series of **'show trials'** were conducted which invariably found these people guilty who were then sentenced to death or were sent to labour camps. The toll of the purges was in millions (some estimate put it about 8 million) and the victims included important civil and military officials, scholars, artists, engineers, scientists, kulaks (rich peasants), professionals and national minorities who were accused of being '**fifth column**' communities.

> ***Darkness at Noon*** is a work by **Arthur Koestler** (1905–83) published in 1941. It is a firsthand description of Stalinist Russia, during the author's visit to the Soviet Union in 1933. Through the leading character of the book, the imprisoned Rubashov, an Old Bolshevik, Koestler brings out the trauma and ironies of the communist totalitarianism. The Old Bolsheviks, who had served the party faithfully, are now being tortured and denounced by Stalin as enemies of the people. Though innocent, Rubashov confesses to crimes he never committed and thus sacrifices everything for the party as its loyal servant.

Though the Great Purges officially ended in 1938, practice of mass arrest and exile continued. People from all walks of life – men, women and even children – were dragged into the net of Stalin's secret police (NKVD) to frighten the common people and to eliminate dissenters until Stalin's death in 1953. The purges achieved many objectives – eliminated any possibility of rival leadership from emerging, consolidated the authority of Stalin and could terrorise the people into submission. But all these came with a great prize – it eliminated the best brains in civil and military services, industry and society in general.

B. Totalitarianism in Socio-Cultural Spheres

Stalin envisioned total reconstruction of state and society and called for '**a new man**' – motivated and disciplined citizen as the builders of this new society. All aspects of social life – educational, cultural and religious – came under the state control and supervision, so that the innermost corners of human consciousness could be shaped in line with '**socialist realism**'. And the socialist realism meant describing the world as the party saw it or the party hoped to shape it.

All forms of information and communication such as newspapers, motion pictures, radio and others were under **strict censorship**. They could publish nothing that did not conform to the views of the state and on the other hand had to glorify communism and achievements of Stalin.

Education became a tool of the revolution, and from nursery to university it was harnessed to train dutiful and loyal citizens, deification of the leader and for indoctrinating the minds. Students had to learn the virtues of the Communist Party and state sponsored youth organisations had the task of training future party members. The Russian language was made compulsory in schools and offices, against the sentiments of the ethnic minorities.

Writers, artists, musicians and actors were forced into subservience and were expected to glorify the Soviet achievement and Soviet ideology and anyone who did not conform was persecuted.

Efforts were also made to replace religious dogmas with the ideals of communism and propagation of atheism became a state-sponsored program. The Russian Orthodox Church was subordinated to the state, most churches (of these the most important was the demolition of Moscow's Cathedral of Christ the Saviour in 1931), synagogues and monasteries were closed and the clergy persecuted.

Even the introduction of a new constitution in 1936 apparently with democratic features like universal suffrage, secret ballot, freedom of speech and of religion proved to be an illusion so long as all aspects of life in the Soviet Union continued to be determined by the Communist party and its undisputable leader Stalin.

C. Reforms in Economy

To Stalin the foremost priority was not world revolution, but the fastest possible industrialisation of the Soviet Union. Why was it so? Stalin believed that rapid expansion of heavy industry as essential to deal with the sooner or later expected attack from the Western capitalist powers. Industrialisation was also expected to boost the support for the government because the industrial workers were considered as the greatest allies of the Communists. The Bolshevik pride also required strengthening of the country as much as possible, by the Russian efforts and surpass capitalism in the shortest time possible as foreigners were unwilling to invest in a communist state. At the same time it was also necessary to produce more food to meet the requirement of the expanding industrial population and for these an integrated approach to development was envisaged in the form of Five Year Plans.

a. *Five Year Plans*

In 1928, the NEP was ended and a series of Five Year Plans were initiated. The first Five Year Plan (1928–32) focussed on rapid industrialisation and collectivisation of agriculture. The emphasis was placed on heavy industry – coal, iron, steel and machinery – and construction of railroads, power plants and production of military hardware. Consequently production of consumer goods was cut down. The two later plans continued to give importance to heavy industries though some increases in consumer goods production too was discernible.

The Five Year Plans called for a **command economy** that set elaborate system of national priorities and entailed lodging of virtually all economic decision-making like pricing, wages, output of each product in centralised departments. Obviously, the plans created **elaborate state machinery** tasked with organising and supervising the plan details at all levels. Demand and supply and other market principles had no role in the Soviet economy. The small-scale private enterprises permitted during the NEP was now taken over by the state and private ownership and control over industry and trade became extinct. Elimination of private capitalism and attainment of self-sufficiency were the stated objectives of the Plans.

b. *Rapid Industrialisation*

The resources required for industrialisation were almost entirely mobilised within the Soviet Union itself under the auspices of the state and some from grain exports. Ruthless ploughing back of profits and surpluses and strict disciplinary methods on the labour force were other instruments with which the Soviet planning was implemented. Medals were given to meritorious workmen and severe punishments including spells in forced labour camps were awarded to bad workmanship. For technological support large numbers of foreign technicians were brought and efforts were made to develop indigenous technical resources by expanding education.

The results of economic planning and industrialisation were profound. Though the first Five Year Plan had to be scrapped before completion, the subsequent Plans improved quality of planning and production and the Soviet Russia did industrialise at an incredibly rapid pace. Hundreds of industrial units and industrial townships (especially to the east of the **Ural Mountains** to be safer in case of western invasion), oil refineries in the **Caucasus** and hydroelectric dams were telltale evidences of the Stalinist command economy. By 1940, the Soviet Union had overtaken Britain in iron and steel production and was competing with Germany in industrial production.

At the same time, these achievements were attained at the expense of the tremendous sacrifices of body and spirit of the toiling masses and **'thousands wills were subordinated to one will'** – the will of one party and of one leader. Moreover, a strong tilt towards heavy industries caused reduction in consumer goods production and resultant material hardships and anguish in the general population.

c. *Agricultural Collectivisation*

Collectivisation was the tool with which the peasants were integrated into the planned economy. Collectivisation meant amalgamation of individual peasant holdings, animals and equipment into larger units of several thousand acres called **collective farms** for the sake of efficiency and large-scale production with the help of machines and tractors.

The program was started in 1929, with government seizing over 25 million privately owned farms. It had to be implemented by brute force against the peasants, who resisted attachment of their own land. Resistance was especially strong from the Kulaks, the more prosperous farmers, who slaughtered cattle and burned crops rather than allow the state to confiscate them. The forced collectivisation led to another terror as Stalin declared war on the countryside. The **kulaks** were **'liquidated as a class'**, either killed outright or deported to forced labour camps and poorer peasants were herded on to collective farms at the point of a bayonet. And by 1939, more than 90 per cent of the peasants had been living on collective farms.

Collectivisation proved to be a disaster for the country. The cattle herds declined by one-half, number of horses – crucial for rural transportation – declined by one-third and total grain production did not increase at all (except in 1930). Yet government resorted to exporting grain to pay for the importation of industrial machinery. All these resulted in a deadly famine in 1932–33 during which more than seven million people died of starvation.

Collectivisation was an accomplished fact by 1939 and was primarily an instrument to achieve larger goals of Stalin.

1. If the Five Year Plans had to be successful, the government had to get planned crops of planned quality and quantity at planned times.
2. Further, it also facilitated quick industrialisation by the migration of twenty million people from the countryside to the cities.
3. It also facilitated transition from an agrarian economy to industrial power and in bridging the economic gap with the West – one of the prime concerns of Stalin.
4. Collectivisation also enabled government to export grain to pay for the import of much needed industrial machinery.
5. The kulaks, whom Stalin considered as the enemies of Communism, could be wiped out, the peasants ever rebellious since the times of the Tsars could be cowed into submission. The ascendancy of the party over the people of Russia became complete as the peasants worked on collective farms without owning any piece of land and had to follow directions issued by the party.

Women in Soviet Union

The Communist Revolution of 1917 had declared men and women equal. The Bolsheviks had envisioned that under socialism the family would 'wither away' as would the state. It was expected that public dining rooms, kitchens and kindergartens, and so forth would free the women 'from the old domestic slavery and dependence on husbands'.

Under the Five Year Plans, women had no other choice than to join the labour force and millions of women worked along with men in factories and farms. Demand for skilled workers under a planned economy also improved educational and technical skills of women. Increased educational opportunities enabled women to prepare for careers in engineering and science as is evident from the fact that by 1950 more than 75 per cent of doctors in Soviet Russia were women.

16. International Relations of the Soviet Union

A. The Communist International

Soon after the Bolshevik Revolution, the relation between Russia and the Western nations had deteriorated. The Bolsheviks' effort to spread the revolution to other parts of Europe especially in Germany, Austria and Hungary was the basic reason for this. Consequently, the western nations under Britain, France and the United States intervened in the Russian Civil War supporting the 'Whites' in an effort to destroy Communism. Russia had also been kept out of the Paris Peace Conference, 1919, convened to prepare peace.

In these circumstances, Russia decided to demarcate her own role in the international order. In March 1919, a conference of representatives of communist parties of thirty countries was held in Moscow and formed the Communist International or **Comintern**. It stood against any co-operation or collaboration with the capitalist countries and to work for their overthrow. By the 1930s, more than sixty countries had communist parties with a strong support base among the workers and the Communist International placed Soviet Russia as the communist alternative to the capitalist West.

As a political tool for world revolution, the Communist International could not achieve much and was often seen by others as an instrument of Soviet foreign policy.

B. 'Socialism in One Country'

Stalin reversed the policy of international communism and kept the interests of the Soviet Union as supreme. He advocated the concept known as 'socialism in one country' which represented a shift in the attention of the Communist International from world revolution to the defence of the Soviet state. Stalin came to believe that success of the Soviet Russia would be the best propaganda for Communism. Peace with the Western countries was also necessary for the success of the Five Year Plans.

This reorientation of the Soviet foreign policy was reflected in measures such as efforts for economic self-sufficiency, exaltation of patriotism which was in contrast to the emphasis on internationalism of the period soon after the revolution and in the building up of an army which was doubled in size and reorganised on western European model.

In the 1930s when Germany emerged as a threat to the Soviet Union, Stalin adopted a policy of cooperation with other European powers and became a member of the League of Nations (1934) and also signed a military pact with France in 1934. In 1936, Stalin extended his support to the socialist-led **Second Spanish Republic** in the Spanish Civil War, against the Nazi-supported Spanish nationalists. However, in August 1939, Stalin, who now held the view that the West wanted to encourage Nazi aggression in the East, hoping that such a war would put an end to both the Soviet Union and Nazi Germany, signed a neutrality pact with Germany. This treaty known as the **Molotov-Ribbentrop Pact** or **the Nazi-Soviet Pact** or **Hitler-Stalin Pact** provided for non-belligerence by each party towards the other and a secret protocol to demarcate the 'spheres of influence' of both the parties in the event of re-arrangement of political boundaries in Europe.

In the Second World War, the Soviet Union played a crucial role in defeating fascism which earned them great goodwill from around the world. But, with the end of the war, a tightly integrated and controlled alliance of communist states was established under the Soviet Union in Eastern Europe. These countries – East Germany, Poland, Hungary, Czechoslovakia, Bulgaria and Romania – came to be known as the Soviet satellites. The undemocratic manner of their creation and repressive way of governance in these states eroded the goodwill the Soviets had earned during the war. And her efforts in sponsoring communist parties to engineer revolution in states like Greece, in turn contributed to the Cold War.

17. Era of Nikita Khrushchev – Period of De-Stalinisation (1953–64)

Stalin died in March 1953 but had not anointed anyone to succeed him. As a result, a system of collective leadership was initiated under the Politburo, known as the Presidium. Gradually, Nikita Khrushchev as the First Secretary of the Communist Party and one of the eight members of the Presidium emerged the leader of the Soviet Union and continued till 1964, when he was voted into retirement by the Central Committee of the party.

Khrushchev initiated de-Stalinization of the Soviet Union. A series of reforms were initiated as the revision of Stalin's policies. In February 1956, Khrushchev delivered a speech at the Twentieth Party Congress of the Communist Party of the Soviet Union. This speech known as the '**Secret Speech**' as it was delivered at a closed session of the party delegates condemned Stalin for encouraging cult of his own personality and violating the party norms of collective leadership. He also revealed the details of Stalin's purges and criticised Stalin's conduct of the World War II. He also talked of **'different roads to socialism'** than those pursued by Stalin and suggestive of conceding more freedom to the satellite states.

The speech is considered as a milestone in the history of the Communist movement in two ways. First, it initiated the so-called '**Khrushchev Thaw**' – relaxation of repression and censorship, reduction in secret police activities and more freedom for ordinary people in the Soviet Union and a change in the foreign policy in the form of **'peaceful co-existence'** with the west. Second, it became the major cause for the split in international communist movement known as the **Sino-Soviet Split**. The Chinese communist leader Mao Zedong, who continued to believe in the theory of the inevitability of war with the capitalist bloc, criticised Khrushchev as a revisionist and accused the post-Stalin leadership in Soviet Russia deviating from the path of Lenin and Stalin.

The Khrushchev Thaw thus became a clear expression of de-Stalinisation initiated by Khrushchev. Internally to the Soviet Union, the Thaw initiated irreversible transformation of the Soviet society by allowing more freedom in the media, arts and culture, improvements in prison conditions, investigation into the arbitrary arrests and executions of Stalin's period, renaming of places and buildings bearing Stalin's name, for example Stalingrad into **Volgograd** (1961), purging of the State Anthem of the Soviet Union of references to Stalin and removal of Stalin's body from Lenin's Mausoleum in Red Square, Moscow.

Many foreign movies, books, art and music were permitted in the Soviet. For example, some of the internationally recognised authors like Ernest Hemingway were allowed to publish their works in the Soviet Union, and in 1962 the Russian writer Aleksandr Solzhenitsyn's ***One Day in the Life of Ivan Denisovich***, the first uncensored book about Gulag labour camps, was published.

> *The Thaw* was a novel by the Soviet writer **Ilya Ehrenburg** published in 1954 which coined this term for the comparative liberal environment under Khrushchev. It depicted life in the Soviet Union in a more realistic way than had been projected in officially approved works of the Soviet Union.

In international relations *The Thaw* found expressed in the form of relaxation of tension between the United States and the USSR. Khrushchev under his theory of **'Peaceful Co-existence'** believed that the two superpowers and their ideologies could co-exist together without war. To make his point clear Khrushchev attended international peace conferences such as the **Geneva Summit** (1955) and travelled to USA's **Camp David** in 1959 and met the US President Dwight Eisenhower.

Even though Khrushchev advocated peaceful co-existence with the capitalist bloc and talked of 'different roads to socialism', the Soviet policy *vis-à-vis* with the Eastern Europe did not undergo fundamental changes. It was well evident during the developments in Poland and Hungary.

In June 1956, the industrial workers of Poznan in Poland resorted to general strike demanding **'bread and freedom'**. Khrushchev was not impressed by the developments and Soviet tanks surrounded Warsaw, the Polish capital. In the end Khrushchev had to compromise by accepting Wladyslaw Gomulka, a popular and reformist communist as the new leader on his assurance that Poland would remain communist.

Hungary, one of the members of the Eastern Bloc, was under the authoritarian pro-Stalin leader **Matyas Rakosi** who described himself as **'Stalin's best Hungarian disciple'**. Rakosi's regime was notorious for its brutality and repression. Thousands were purged, arrested, tortured and imprisoned in concentration camps similar to that of the Gulag camps in the Soviet Union. Encouraged by the 'Secret Speech' of Khrushchev and inspired by relative success of agitations in Poland, students and workers of Hungary took to streets in October 1956 demanding more freedom and toppled a huge statue of Stalin in the centre of Budapest. Khrushchev now appointed a reformist **Imre Nagy** as the new leader of Hungary. But the protests continued, and on 1 November 1956 Nagy declared Hungarian neutrality and withdrawal from the Warsaw Pact. On 4 November the Soviet Union invaded Hungary, suppressed the rebellion killing more than 20,000 and forcing more than 2,00,000 Hungarians to flee to Austria. Nagy was executed and the hard-liner **Janos Kadar** was appointed as the new leader of Hungary.

In economic sector, the Five Year Plans were continued but for the first time emphasis was placed on production of consumer goods like radios, refrigerators and washing machines in an attempt to improve the standards of living of the population and also a vast housing program was started. Although these measures improved the living standards of the masses, the USSR continued to remain much behind the United States and the West in these parameters. In agriculture as an effort to raise food production the **'virgin lands scheme'** was introduced in 1954 under which huge tracts of land in Siberia and Kazakhstan were brought under cultivation for the first time. Khrushchev also ordered cultivation of corn (maize) in the Virgin Lands.

In October 1964, the Central Committee of the Communist Party of the Soviet Union removed Khrushchev from his position for reasons of 'advanced age and ill health' and appointed Leonid Brezhnev as the General Secretary. The real reasons for the removal had been erosion of Khrushchev's popularity due to the failure of his agricultural policy, erosion of his prestige in the **Cuban Missile Crisis** and also the widening of his differences with China.

18. Leonid Brezhnev – Period of Stagnation (1964–82)

Leonid Brezhnev became the leader of the USSR in 1964. In his position he had a long term of 18 years (1964–82) which was second only to that of Joseph Stalin.

A. Domestic Affairs

In broad sense Leonid Brezhnev's policies were similar to that of Khrushchev. His period began with economic growth and prosperity but later on political corruption and economic stagnation emerged and the period is considered as an 'Era of Stagnation'.

In economy, he introduced certain reforms. Recentralisation of the Soviet economy by establishing several central ministries, price reform and enterprise incentive system with provision for material incentives for good performance was important in this regard. More than these, Brezhnev was reluctant to take any major initiatives. The hardliners within the Party, fearing that the reforms would weaken the Party's prestige and power, halted the reforms. By this time, industry had become notorious for slowness and poor quality and cumbersome procedures of bureaucratic administration did not provide for innovativeness and flexibility required at the enterprise level which led to stagnation.

Brezhnev continued the conventional methods of organising collective farms and imposing centrally determined output quotas. He also increased the state investments in farming which was 27 per cent of all state investments. At the same time the agriculture sector was facing multitudes of problems like shortage of skilled workers, method of payment to workers in proportion to the quantity rather than quality of the work and of low agricultural output.

In the late 1970s, the Soviet economy began to lag behind the West and by the early 1980s faced economic stagnation on account of factors like too little investment on light industry and consumer goods, decline in productivity, lack of labour discipline, high spending on military and low yield in agriculture sector. A country that had the best arable land in Europe was desperately short on grain and had to depend on American grain imports.

B. Foreign Affairs

In foreign affairs, Brezhnev followed a two-pronged approach. On the one hand, he tried to **normalise relations** with West Germany and ease tensions with the United States. On the other, he resorted to a **massive buildup of the Soviet military** power with huge expansion and modernisation of its **military-industrial complexes**.

a. Détente

The foreign policy of the USSR during Brezhnev was characterised by *Détente*. Though it had similarity with the 'Khrushchev Thaw', the *Détente* was more comprehensive as it included signing of agreement on arms control, crisis prevention and promotion of East-West trade. It was also characterised by his attempt to equalise with the military strength of the United States.

- In 1970, Brezhnev made a deal with West Germany by which the West Germany recognised the boundaries imposed by the Soviet Union in Eastern Europe.
- Another expression of the *Détente* was the **Moscow Summit** of 1972 between Brezhnev and Richard Nixon (Nixon was the first US President to visit Moscow).
- In May 1972, Brezhnev and Richard Nixon signed **SALT I** (Strategic Arms Limitation Treaty I) which limited the number of missiles (ICBMs and SLBMs) on both sides and a limitation on deployment of **ABM systems**. By this, for the first time during the Cold War, the United States and the USSR reached an agreement to limit their nuclear missiles. The Summit also witnessed the signing of the **Apollo-Soyuz Test Project** – a joint US-Soviet space flight (the flight was conducted in July 1975) as a symbol of the policy of *détente*.
- As a corollary, **SALT II** Treaty was signed in Vienna in June 1979 by Brezhnev and Jimmy Carter to limit all categories of their strategic delivery vehicles to 2250, though both the countries failed to ratify it.

b. Military Buildup

Under Brezhnev, the Soviet Union carried out unprecedented military buildup – both conventional and nuclear. The Soviet army with over 5 million troops became the largest in the world. The induction of new aircrafts, missiles and ICBMs gave parity to the USSR with the United States. The Soviet navy was upgraded from a glorified coastguard to a formidable naval force with induction of large submarines, new SLBMs and aircraft carriers. This huge expansion was clearly evident from the fact that even though the Soviet economy was half the size of the United States, its expenditure in defence exceeded the American expenditure and in 1982, the year of Brezhnev's death, it was 15 per cent of the Soviet's GNP.

c. Brezhnev Doctrine

But Brezhnev had to face serious challenges in other areas of his foreign policy – in **Czechoslovakia (1968), Afghanistan (1979) and** in **Poland (1980–81)**.

C. Czechoslovakia and the Prague Spring

In Czechoslovakia, a reformist Communist Party leader named Alexander Dubcek had been speaking about creating **'socialism with a human face'** and had initiated reforms in 1968. This brief period of liberalisation (January–August 1968) known as the **'Prague Spring'** stood for liberalisation and decentralisation and freedom of the press, assembly and travel. Brezhnev viewed the development as tantamount to counter revolution and invaded Czechoslovakia in August 1968. The invasion by the Warsaw Pact members under the leadership of the Soviet Union led to the suppression and reversal of the reforms, deposition of Dubcek and appointment of a hard line Communist leader in power.

As a response to the Prague Spring, Brezhnev formed the Brezhnev Doctrine by which the Soviet Union asserted its right to intervene in any Communist country against 'counter revolutionary' elements. The Doctrine proclaimed that if socialism was in jeopardy in any communist state, it becomes a threat to all socialist states and **'it becomes not only a problem of the country concerned, but a common problem and concern of all socialist countries'**. It further argued for economic integration, political consolidation, a return to ideological orthodoxy and inter-Party cooperation of the satellite states.

The Brezhnev Doctrine severely limited reforms in the Soviet Bloc because of which the detractors of the Soviet Union called it as the **'Doctrine of Limited Sovereignty'**. On the other hand, it is undeniable that the doctrine was instrumental in preventing the deterioration of Communist Party's control over the satellites until the reforms of Mikhail Gorbachev in the 1980s.

D. The Afghan Quagmire

Brezhnev Doctrine came to be applied in Afghanistan in December 1979 as a basis for intervention in the **Afghan Civil War** (1978–92) and in the prop up of a faltering communist government there.

In April 1978, Communists under the banner of the People's Democratic Party of Afghanistan had captured power in a coup known as the **'Saur Revolution'** overthrowing a centrist government of Mohammed Daud Khan and established the **Democratic Republic of Afghanistan**. The new government under **Nur Muhammad Taraki** replaced the national flag with a red flag, advocated equality of the sexes, followed socialist policies and initiated extensive land and social reforms. The new government also established close ties with the USSR and resorted to ruthless purges of all opposition and execution of political prisoners.

The Afghan population, which was deeply immersed in tradition and in Islamic faith, resented these measures and organised resistance which soon developed into full-scale opposition that came to be called as the **Afghan Civil War**. The anti-Communist insurgents were collectively known as the **mujahideen**.

At the same time, the communist government itself was divided along factional lines which resulted in the capture of power by the Prime Minister **Hafizullah Amin**, who, in September 1979, deposed and ordered the death of the President Nur Muhammed Taraki. Consequently, Brezhnev sanctioned Soviet military intervention in Afghanistan in December 1979. The Soviet troops killed Amin and appointed **Babrak Karmal**, another communist leader as the new President.

The mujahideen now turned their ire against the Soviet forces and the Soviet intervention in Afghanistan soon turned down to a stalemate, with more than one lakh Soviet troops controlling the cities and major towns, while the mujahideen controlling the countryside and resorting to **guerrilla warfare**. The mujahideen were aided by the United States, Pakistan, Chinese and Saudi Arabian governments. They also received huge funding from private donors and religious charities throughout the Muslim world. The fighting resolve of the mujahideen had also been strengthened by the arrival of large number of Muslim volunteers (mostly Arabs), called as the '**Afghan-Arabs**' in Afghanistan in support of fellow Muslims in their fight against the anti-religious communist regime.

Neither the government of Babrak Karmal nor the forces of the Soviet Union could resolve the Afghan quagmire and the Soviet troops had to withdraw from Afghanistan in 1989, though the Soviet backed Communist government in Afghanistan continued to survive for another three years till 1992, the year in which the communist government under **Mohammed Najibullah** was overthrown by the rebels.

Causes for the Soviet Withdrawal

The Soviet army which was trained for large-scale conventional warfare had found its task in Afghanistan difficult, where the guerrilla fighters used hit-and-run tactics in the hilly and rough terrain. Other factors like insufficient intelligence gathering, inability to hold the ground after an area was captured and alienation of Afghan population from the Soviet army on account of violence and killings of the civilians, nature of the war as the war of national liberation fought by the mujahideens against the Soviet sponsored revolutionary regime and the support they received from the Muslin fraternity around the world were factors that caused the Soviet failure in Afghan and its withdrawal.

Brezhnev's decision to intervene in Afghanistan had serious military, diplomatic, economic and political implications.

- Though intended initially as a small-scale intervention, it enlarged into a decade long war which came to be referred as the **'Soviet Union's Vietnam War'**. More than 14,000 Soviet soldiers had lost their life and much more soldiers had been wounded. It also caused huge material losses in aircrafts, tanks and others.
- The Afghan stalemate devastated the morale and legitimacy of the Russian army. The Soviet army had been perceived as glue that held the diverse Soviet Republics together and the main defender of Communism. In that sense, its defeat in Afghanistan put a question mark on the survivability of the Soviet Union itself.
- Another significant military effect of the Afghan War was that it demonstrated that the Red Army was not invincible which in turn emboldened the non-Russian republics in the Soviet Union to demand independence. In other words, the Afghan War by providing a common rallying banner to the secessionist movements in non-Russian republics accentuated cleavages between the non-Russian republics and the Soviet state.
- Politically the Afghan war proved to be an eye opener to the Russian leaders of the limitations in using military to hold the empire together and in intervening in foreign countries.
- The Soviet Union came under various embargos, sanctions and warnings by the international community such as the UN on the aftermath of the Afghan invasion. The US trade embargo on grain export to USSR and the US-led boycott of the **1980 Summer Olympics** in Moscow were two significant developments in this context.
- The Afghan War became an important factor in the disintegration of the Soviet Union. The development had disrupted the domestic cohesion and had weakened conservative anti-reform forces in the Soviet Union which in turn paved the way for glasnost and perestroika.
- The growing number of the Afghan war veterans in Soviet Russia, known as the **'Afgantsy'**, had caused arousal of feeling of anti-militarism in Russian society and a desire for reorganisation of its politico-social setup. These war veterans formed non-party organisations that challenged the legitimacy of the Soviet Communist party and created a wedge between the army and the Communist party.

E. The Polish Crisis and Solidarity

Another powerful challenge to communist rule emerged in Poland in 1980 and the Soviet Union's response to the developments was yet another affirmation of the Brezhnev Doctrine.

Poland is located in Central Europe at geographical crossroads linking North Western Europe to the sea lanes of the Atlantic Ocean and the fertile plains of Eurasia. With the end of the World War II and the expulsion of the Nazi German forces from the occupied Poland, a communist-controlled Provisional Government had been formed in Warsaw in 1945. The post-war Poland renamed as the **Polish People's Republic** became a **communist satellite state** of the Soviet Union. Nearly four decades of totalitarian rule followed during which latent popular discontent continued to exist and many Poles had adopted the attitude of 'resigned cooperation' towards their government. During this period, increasing economic and political difficulties had forced people to rise in protest in many times as in 1956 (as seen early), 1968 and in 1970.

In 1980, the discontent intensified by the rise in food prices was found expressed in workers strike in the coastal city of Gdansk (also known as *Danzig*). Here, at the huge Lenin Shipyards an electrical worker named **Lech Walesa** emerged leader of the striking community. The workers presented 21 point demands including freedom to form their own workers union which they named as **'Solidarity'** (founded in September 1980), independent of the Communist Party. Nearly twelve million workers (out of sixteen million workforce) joined Solidarity which also had the moral support of **Pope John Paul II, the first Polish pope**.

There were three strands of people that formed communist opposition in Poland – one that considered the system as contrary to liberty and democracy, the second that felt that it had not lived up to its socio-economic promises and, finally, those considered it as inimical to national and Christian values. Almost universal support the Solidarity enjoyed in Poland and a series of controlled strikes it organised to advance its demand for workers' rights, for the involvement of trade unions in decision-making process and also for free elections posed a serious challenge to the authority of the Communist Party.

Under pressure from the Soviet leadership, in December 1981, the Polish government declared martial law, declared Solidarity as illegal and arrested its leaders including Lech Walesa. But there was a major difference in the Soviet attitude towards Poland. Compared to the unrest in Hungary 1956 and Czechoslovakia in 1968, the Soviet army was not directly involved in suppressing the Polish unrest for fear of a massive national resistance by the Poles.

In 1985, Mikhail Gorbachev became the Soviet leader and in a changing political climate he chartered a new course for the Soviet Union and abandoned the Brezhnev Doctrine.

19. Mikhail Gorbachev – Decline of Communism and Disintegration of the USSR (1985–91)

After the death of Leonid Brezhnev, leadership of the Soviet Union went into the hands of two elderly politicians Andropov (1982–84) and Chernenko (1984–85). In March 1985, **Chernenko** died and Gorbachev was elected by the Politburo as the General Secretary of the CPSU. That year, at the age of 54, he was by far the youngest member of the Soviet leadership since Stalin and also the first party leader born after the Russian Revolution.

Gorbachev

A. Reforms of Gorbachev

After rapid economic growth in the initial decades, the Soviet economy had been stagnating. Gorbachev recognised that the legitimacy and stability of the Communist regime depended on its economic success. He rightly understood that the Soviet system was highly centralised which left no room for individual initiative, strongly tilted towards heavy and defence industry causing shortage of consumer goods for ordinary people and was based almost completely on state ownership and control which made them inefficient. Hence, Gorbachev's primary domestic goal was to resuscitate a stagnating Soviet economy by resorting to rapid modernisation of technology, by increasing workers' productivity and by improving bureaucratic efficiency. This initial effort to reform which he called as ***Uskoreniye*** (acceleration) aimed at accelerating socio, economic and political development of the Soviet Union. But, these superficial changes failed to yield tangible results prompting for a whole series of radical reforms.

a. Perestroika

The core of this reform program was perestroika (restructuring) of the economic and political landscape of the Soviet Union. It involved initiating economic and political changes without abandoning socialism. In other words Gorbachev wanted to replace the existing system, which was still basically Stalinist with a **humane and democratic socialism**. Under this, the role of the central planning was reduced and decision-making at the factory level was permitted and small-scale private and co-operative enterprises were allowed to operate independently of government planning. The **Gosplan's** (the state planning committee of the Soviet Union) role was reduced to providing general guidelines and national investment priorities and not to provide detailed production plans.

In 1987, the **Law on State Enterprises** was passed under which the state enterprises could determine output, based on demand and were made self-financing, that is, they had to meet their expenses through revenues.

In 1988, the **Law on Cooperatives** was enacted providing for private ownership in the services, manufacturing and foreign trade. Limited role for the free market in agriculture was also permitted as part of the reforms.

In the same year, the **Soviet Joint Venture Law** allowed foreigners to invest in Soviet Union in the form of joint ventures with state ministries, state enterprises and cooperatives.

The reforms also ended monopoly of the Ministry of Foreign Trade on trade operations by permitting individual ministries and individual state enterprises to conduct foreign trade.

b. Glasnost

Glasnost was a measure for greater **openness and candour** in government affairs and for interplay of different views in political debates, in the press and in Soviet culture. It meant opening of Soviet society to a critical evaluation of its past and present problems and to seek solutions.

Glasnost relaxed censorship and as a result, topics like joblessness, crime, drug abuse and urban blight, which all were taboo till then, began to receive coverage. Several well-known dissidents were released or were permitted to return to Moscow, long-banned anti-Stalin films and novels were published and Pravda (the official newspaper of the Soviet Union) was allowed to publish an article criticising Brezhnev – all of which were unthinkable till then. It permitted criticism of government officials, allowed the Union of Writers to sack their reactionary heads and replacing them with more independent-minded leaders. There was new freedom in news reporting. For example, when the **Chernobyl nuclear reactor** in Ukraine exploded in April 1986, the disaster was reported and discussed with unprecedented frankness. Gorbachev cited the disaster as evidence for **shoddy workmanship** and **workplace inertia**. These measures aimed at, inter alia, using mass media to publicise inefficiency and corruption in the Soviet system, educate public opinion and to mobilise support for the new policies. Thus, Glasnost was also a necessary measure (the crucial, irreplaceable weapon of perestroika as Gorbachev described it) to ensure Perestroika by alerting the Soviet population to the nature and depth of the country's problems.

c. Democratisation

Associated with Perestroika and Glasnost was 'democratisation' of the political system. It was started in 1987 with internal democracy within the CPSU by which members of the local soviets were to be elected by the people, instead of being appointed by the party. In the past, voters merely had to put stamp of approval on candidates hand-picked by the Party. Further, reforms such as multi candidate (not multiparty) competition in elections, secret elections for top party positions and elections in factories to choose managers were also introduced.

Fundamental changes were introduced in the central government structures. The Supreme Soviet (the old parliament of 1,450 deputies which met for about two weeks every year) was replaced by a **Congress of People's Deputies of the Soviet Union**. Its main duty was to elect a new and smaller Supreme Soviet (450 members) to be elected from its 2,250 members. The new Supreme Soviet acted as proper working parliament, sitting for about eight months a year and its chairman was to be the head of the state. In May 1989, Gorbachev was elected Chairman of the Supreme Soviet.

In March 1990, the Congress of People's Deputies elected Gorbachev to the **newly created post of the President of the USSR**. The President had extensive executive powers and had an 18-member Presidential Council to advise and help him which de facto replaced the Politburo. At the same session, the Congress also abolished Article 6 of the Soviet constitution ending Communist Party's constitutionally guaranteed monopoly of political power in the Soviet Union. This step ended de jure one-party state and paved the way for legalisation of other political parties.

d. International Relations – 'New Thinking'

The final element of Gorbachev's reforms was 'new thinking' in foreign policy. Soon after becoming the leader of the Soviet Union, Gorbachev spoke of a '**radical restructuring**' of foreign policy. He was shocked at the prospect of nuclear war and was aware that the Soviet Union was unlikely to win the arms race and was also convinced that continued focus on high military spending was detrimental to his desire for domestic reforms. Economic factor was also an important concern. If Moscow wanted an efficient economy and robust development, it was essential to expand foreign trade, attract technology and reduce military spending and cut back aid being given to other countries, all of which required a relaxed international environment.

To these ends Gorbachev floated a number of arms-control proposals, reduced Soviet defence spending and pulled back some troops stationed in Eastern Europe. He cultivated warmer relations with the United States and in December 1987 signed the **Intermediate-range Nuclear Forces (INF) Treaty** with the US President Ronald Reagan to destroy all existing stocks of intermediate range nuclear-tipped missiles of the two countries. In 1988–89, he withdrew the Soviet forces from Afghanistan. To develop warmer relations with Western Europe he visited United Kingdom, France, West Germany apart from meeting **Ronald Reagan** in Washington (1987), Chinese leader **Deng Xiaoping** in Beijing (1989) and the **Pope John Paul II** in Italy (1989).

B. Unrest in Eastern Bloc and the Revolutions of 1989

Gorbachev expected to make the Eastern European countries more efficient and less dependent on the Soviet Union by prodding those countries to implement their own glasnost and perestroika. Gorbachev also backed away from the Brezhnev Doctrine and emphasised 'the right of every people to choose the paths and forms of its own development'. The People of this Bloc was a discontent mass because of **authoritarianism of the communist system, economic miseries** and **low standards of living**. Increased exposure to the West and their higher standards of living was an eye opener. It was in this background the revolutions known as the **'Fall of Nations'** or the **'Autumn of Nations'** erupted in 1989 during which Communist rule was overthrown in Central and Eastern Europe.

The Soviet Bloc: These were countries in Eastern Europe over which the Soviet Union had held political hegemony since the end of the Second World War. These were East Germany, Poland, Hungary, Czechoslovakia, Bulgaria and Romania. These were also known as the Soviet Satellites as all these were modelled after the Soviet Union with features such as a single party (Communist Party), central planning and state-owned economy. All these countries were also part of a military alliance known as the Warsaw Pact. Outside this bloc Yugoslavia and Albania existed as two communist states in Europe but not under the hegemony of the Soviet.

The chain of events started in Poland in 1989 and spread to Hungary, East Germany, Bulgaria, Czechoslovakia and Romania. In **Poland**, in spite of the ban, the Solidarity had continued its activities as an underground organisation. With the deterioration of economic conditions and with emergence of new wave of strikes and labour unrest across Poland in 1988, the government was forced to conduct **Round Table Discussions** with the opposition groups, restore Solidarity and to conduct free elections in June 1989.

Flag of Solidarity of Poland

In the elections, Solidarity-led coalition won an overwhelming majority of seats in Parliament. The Communist Party lost majority in parliament and a coalition government consisting of Solidarity was formed under **Tadeusz Mazowiecki** as Prime Minister. It was for the first time since 1948 a non-communist government holding power in an Eastern European state. In December 1990, **Lech Walesa** was elected president of Poland. In October 1991, the entirely free Polish parliamentary elections (elections of 1989 had certain number of seats reserved for the communists) were held and Poland's transition from

Communist Party rule to a Western-style liberal democratic political system became complete.

Developments in Poland opened floodgates of reform in the rest of the Eastern Bloc. In **Hungary**, Polish style round table negotiations between the government and the opposition took place in Budapest in 1989. They agreed on constitutional reform, multiparty system and free parliamentary elections. In October 1989, Hungarian parliament passed legislations providing for multiparty parliamentary elections and a direct presidential election and guaranteed civil and human rights. The Hungarian Communist Party was dissolved, the word 'People's' dropped transforming Hungary from a 'People's Republic' to the **'Republic of Hungary'**, opened its border with the West on the Austrian border (opening a large hole through the Iron Curtain through which thousands of Eastern Europeans travelled to the West) and the Soviet troops withdrew from Hungary during 1990–91.

In **East Germany** or GDR **(German Democratic Republic)** a hard line communist leader, **Erich Honecker**, refused to introduce Soviet-style reforms and as a desperate measure prohibited circulation of Soviet publications viewing them as dangerously subversive! But the East Germans could not be kept away from the influence of wave of revolutions that had been sweeping through the Eastern Bloc in 1989.

In May 1989, Hungary had removed their border fence with Austria as seen above, allowing East Germans to escape to the West. Soon GDR restricted its people travelling to Hungary. Against the new restrictions a wave of demonstrations erupted all over East Germany in Dresden, Leipzig and other East German cities demanding freedom, free emigration, resignation of Honecker, legalisation of political opposition and an end to communism.

In mid-October 1989, SED (as the East German communist party was officially known) replaced Honecker with Egon Krenz as the General Secretary of SED and the leader of East Germany. On 9 November 1989, government ended travel restrictions, promised free elections and **opened the Berlin Wall** prompting hundreds of thousands of people to storm the Wall, chop it with hammers and celebrate with the rejoicing West Berliners with champagne. In March 1990, elections were held – the first in that part of Germany since 1933 and SED was thoroughly defeated and CDU (Christian Democratic Union) won an overwhelming victory.

Though the government was hoping for gradual move towards reunification of the two Germanys, surging tide of refugees from East to West Germany caused speedy unification. In July 1990, a monetary union of two Germanys with West German currency as common currency was established. A unification treaty was ratified by the parliaments of both the countries ('Bundestag' and 'Peoples Chamber') which came into effect on midnight of 3 October, 1990. The **German Democratic Republic** joined the **Federal Republic of Germany** and two parts of divided Berlin became one land. In December 1990, elections for the united Germany were held and the CDU alliance won a comfortable majority, while the communists could win only a meagre of seats. **Helmut Kohl** became the Chancellor of the new Germany.

Czechoslovakia was next in line. Czechoslovakia, one of the most successful economies of Eastern Europe, had run into trouble by the 1980s. The turmoil in East Germany 1989 spilled over to its neighbouring Czechoslovakia creating undercurrents for regime change in the form of a **Velvet Revolution**.

On 17 November 1989, students took out a march in Prague to commemorate the 50th anniversary of the suppression of a student demonstration against the Nazi forces in German occupied Prague in 1939. The march was suppressed, which in turn sparked series of demonstrations all over the country for political change and out of these demonstrations was born the Velvet Revolution. **Vaclav Havel**, playwright and co-author of **Charter 77**, formed a movement known as the **Civic Forum** on 19 November 1989 to unify the dissident forces. A general strike was observed on 27 November 1989 demanding free elections and end to one-party rule.

Vaclav Havel

Charter 77 was a document prepared in 1977 demanding human and civil rights in Czechoslovakia. It was considered as anti-state and anti-socialist document by the communist government.

Writing on the wall was clear to the government which was forced to negotiate with the opposition, and on 29 December 1989 Vaclav Havel was appointed as the interim president of the country. In June 1990, first free elections since 1946 took place and Havel was elected as the President. The Soviet troops withdrew in June 1991 and Czechoslovakia's transition from communism to democracy and command economy to market economy took place. On 1 January 1993, Czechoslovakia was divided into **Czech Republic** and **Slovak Republic**. As it was with the end of communist rule in Czechoslovakia, the dissolution of the country into Czech and Slovakia too took place in a bloodless manner, hence it was known as the **Velvet Divorce!**

On similar lines, the communist regimes were overthrown in **Bulgaria**, Albania, Romania and Yugoslavia. In Bulgaria, the communist leader Todor Zhivkov in power since 1954 was ousted by Politburo under pressure for political reform. Agreement was reached on the basis of round table talks for transition to democracy and in June 1990 free elections were held in which the Bulgarian Socialist Party emerged victorious.

Albania was a communist country since 1945 but had remained the poorest and most backward country in Europe. Demand for reform started with students' demonstrations in the capital Tirana in December 1990 which soon spread to other cities. Eventually free elections were held in March 1992 and a non-communist government came to power.

But in **Romania**, revolution took a bloody path. Here the communist regime under **Nicolae Ceausescu** since 1965 was most brutal compared to any other regime. His secret police maintained rigid controls over free speech and media and any dissent was met with brutal suppression. In the 1980s, his regime resorted to export country's agricultural and industrial products to repay the large foreign debt. The resulted shortage of food, fuel, energy, medicines and other necessities drastically lowered living standards which in turn intensified unrest.

The revolution started on 16 December 1989 in Timisoara and riots and protests followed all over the country. Ceausescu regime collapsed when the army refused to fire on anti-government protestors and defected to the demonstrators. Ceausescu and his wife Elena Ceausescu who was also the Deputy Prime Minister were captured while trying to flee and were tried by a military tribunal on charges of genocide, abuse of power and other charges. Both of them were executed on 25 December 1989 and 42 years of communist rule came to an end in Romania.

Yugoslavia (Land of the South Slavs) had emerged as an independent state after the First World War. Yugoslavia was a multi-national, socialist federal state of six republics – **Serbia, Croatia, Montenegro, Slovenia, Bosnia-Herzegovina** and **Macedonia**. Two provinces – **Kosovo** and **Vojvodina** – were associated with Serbia and had autonomous status for protecting the interests of Albanians and Magyars, respectively.

During the Second World War its people had waged a heroic resistance under their leader **Josip Broz Tito** against the Nazi occupation. After the World War II, under Tito Yugoslavia became a socialist country. Though ruled by Communist Party, it was not part of the Warsaw Pact and followed its own version of communism often referred to as '**national communism**'. During the period of Tito, Yugoslavia was able to maintain political stability, could attain strong economic growth and had played significant role in international affairs as the founding member of the **Non-Aligned Movement**.

Marshall Tito

After the death of Tito (1980), crisis emerged in the form of high inflation, huge foreign debt, unemployment and low productivity. The inefficiency and unproductive projects implemented by the poorer southern and eastern regions were resented by the wealthier northern and western regions such as **Slovenia and Croatia**, as they too were required to contribute funds to federal development programs. For them, independence meant more economic opportunity and prosperity.

There was also a wide split in the Communist regime in Yugoslavia with **liberal-decentralist group** under Croatia and Slovenia arguing for a more decentralised federation, while **conservative-centralist group** led by Serbia looking for more centralisation to protect the pan-Serb interest.

Growing **ethnic conflicts** between its diverse groups such as the Serbs, Croats, Albanians, Bosniaks and Slovenes was another factor. For example, there was a demand by Albanians in Kosovo for republican state status which was strongly opposed by the Serbs in Kosovo.

Now the collapse of communism in Eastern Europe and unification of Germany in 1990 added fuel to the discontent. The imminent collapse of the Soviet Union had removed the threat from that side which in turn gave encouragement to anti-communist and nationalist forces to strengthen their demands. On the other end of the spectrum, with end of the Cold War in sight, the Western capitalist states took least interest in Yugoslavia as a strategic intermediary between the Western and Eastern Blocs.

Free elections were held in 1990 and non-communist governments came to power. Transition to non-communist rule was followed by the dissolution of the Socialist Federal Republic of Yugoslavia into constituent republics in 1992 which was yet another expression of Balkanisation. **Slovenia** was the first to declare independence in June 1991 followed by **Croatia** and **Bosnia**. The final breakup of the federation took place in April 1992 with the declaration of independence by **Macedonia** and **Bosnia and Herzegovina**. The dissolution also caused bitter inter-ethnic war known as the Yugoslav Wars.

C. Disintegration of the USSR

The USSR, a union of 15 republics each with its own parliament, was a conglomeration of different nationalities many of which were annexed to the Russian Empire before the Revolution in 1917 or into the Soviet Union afterwards. The Soviet Union had more than a hundred ethnic groups within it. Of these, the Russians were the largest group. In all other 14 Soviet republics other than Russia, non-Russians were in majority. Once the **reforms of Gorbachev** weakened the central control and with the **collapse of Communism in the Eastern Bloc** in 1989, many of the Soviet republics aspired to be independent.

By 1990, the writing on the wall was clear that the Soviet Union could not continue as a single state. In March 1990, **Lithuania** took the lead in declaring independence which was followed by other two Baltic republics of **Estonia and Latvia**. These states had been annexed to the Soviet Union in 1940. To prevent the breakup, Gorbachev negotiated a treaty with the leaders of the republics for a decentralised union with greater autonomy to the republics.

At this point hard-line members of the Communist Party launched a coup to remove Gorbachev and reverse his reforms. On 19 August 1991, Gorbachev and his family were held under house arrest and an emergency was declared. The **coup against Gorbachev in August 1991** was a natural culmination of a conflict between the old and new political, economic and social forces that had been set in motion in 1985 when Gorbachev came to power. The coup organisers expected popular support but the public opinion was mostly against the coup and even the army was opposed to it.

Boris Yeltsin

At the same time, the coup leaders had committed the fatal mistake of not arresting **Boris Yeltsin** (the President of the Russian Federation) who managed to rally opposition to the coup and face down the plotters. On August 21, the coup leaders admitted defeat and were arrested. The coup disgraced and discredited the Communist party and accelerated the process of disintegration. Gorbachev resigned as party general secretary and suspended activities of the Communist Party in the Soviet territory. A party that captured power in a coup in 1917 now collapsed because of another coup in 1991.

The final phase of the collapse of the Soviet Union began on 1 December 1991 with a popular referendum in **Ukraine** (the second largest Soviet republic after Russia) in which 90 per cent of the voters opted for independence. On 8 December, the leaders of Russia, Ukraine and Belarus negotiated for a new union of republics and signed the **Belavezha Accords** providing for the creation of the **Commonwealth of Independent States** (CIS) and for dissolving of the USSR. On 21 December, leaders of Armenia, Azerbaijan, Belarus, Kazakhstan, Kyrgyzstan, Moldova, Russia, Tajikistan, Turkmenistan, Ukraine and Uzbekistan met in Alma-Ata (Almaty) in Kazakhstan and signed **Alma-Ata Protocol**. The Protocol contained the founding declarations and principles of the CIS and the Russian Federation was allowed to assume the Soviet Union's UN membership and its permanent seat in the UN Security Council. On 25 December 1991, Gorbachev resigned as president and the Soviet Union ceased to exist and was replaced by 15 independent states – Armenia, Azerbaijan, Belarus, Estonia, Georgia, Kazakhstan, Kyrgyzstan, Latvia, Lithuania, Moldova, Tajikistan, Turkmenistan, Ukraine, Uzbekistan and Russia.

D. Why Did the Soviet Union Collapse?

Next to the World Wars, the disintegration of the Soviet Union was the most seminal development of the 20th century. The disintegration started by the end of the 1980s with the Eastern Europe moving out of the Soviet Bloc and culminated in the disintegration of the Soviet Union itself in 1991. A seminal event like the dissolution of the USSR cannot be attributed to any single factor. It was the result of a number of internal and external factors.

Political factor: Mikhail Gorbachev was well aware of failure of institutions and need for democratisation in the USSR. Gorbachev's effort to streamline the Communist system offered promise but ultimately proved uncontrollable resulting in the dissolution of the Soviet Union. Instead of infusing a new spirit in communist thought, the reforms opened floodgates to criticism of the entire Soviet apparatus. Glasnost resulted in the Communist Party losing its grip on the media and damaging credibility of the Soviet government which in turn eroded the Communist Party's social base and undermined faith of the public in the Soviet system.

In international affair, Gorbachev had repudiated the 'Brezhnev Doctrine' in favour of 'Sinatra Doctrine' – non-intervention in the internal affairs of the Warsaw Pact allies – which accentuated the fall of communist governments in the revolutions that swept through Eastern Europe in 1989. The upheaval in Eastern Europe reverberated in the Soviet Union and along with the political consequences of Glasnost within the Soviet Union, the national consciousness in the constituent republics found a re-emergence. Massive peaceful protests in regions such as the Baltic States grew in to independence movements accelerating the pace of the dissolution of the USSR.

In the emerging environment, under pressure from both the radicals and the conservatives within his own party Gorbachev had to tread a difficult path. While the radicals like Boris Yeltsin, the Moscow party leader, stood for drastic reforms, the traditional communists like Yegor Ligachev felt that the changes were too drastic, causing dangerous split in the party at a crucial period in the history of the Communist Party.

Economic factor – An economy in decline: The Soviet economic system had been dogged by certain serious problems. Command economy deprived any initiative at local level, emphasis on heavy industries led to scarcity of consumer goods and attention on space and defence research had caused backwardness in other areas of technological advancements.

By the 1980s, the Soviet economy was facing crisis and economic stagnation had been hobbling the country. The Soviet Union was one of the world's top producers of oil and natural gas and export of these commodities had played a vital role in the growth of the Soviet economy. But the **fall in oil prices in the 1980s** dried up the external capital source of the Soviet Union which precipitated the economic crisis. Further, labour unrest, shortage of consumer goods and hoarding were commonplace. Wage hikes were supported by printing money which caused inflationary spiral.

Gorbachev's reforms were not radical enough to revitalise a chronically sluggish economy of the USSR. Though the reforms made some inroads into decentralisation, the fundamental elements of the Stalinist system – price controls, government monopoly of most of means of production and so

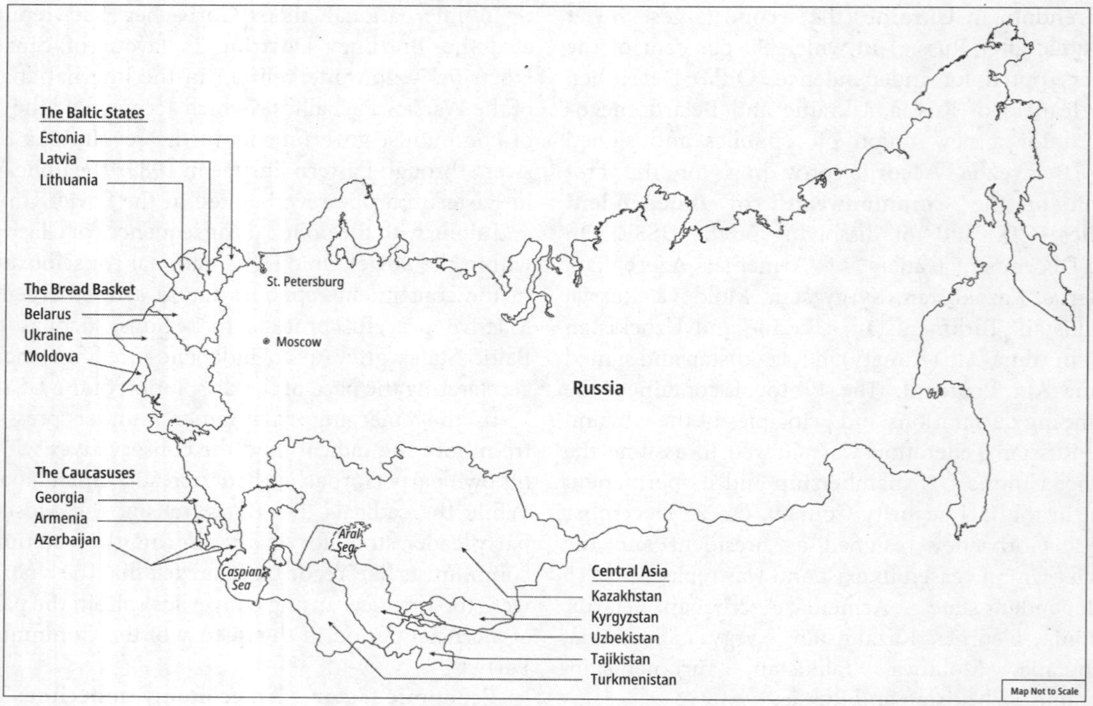

Republics of the USSR

forth – continued to exist. Continuation of consumer price subsidies and state support to unprofitable enterprises sharply increased government spending, causing further strain in economy. **The anti-alcohol campaign** reduced tax revenues and to make things worse the republics and local governments withheld tax revenues from the central government under the growing **spirit of regional autonomy**. Disillusion with the reforms grew with huge shortage of basic goods such as soap, washing powder, television and food, resulting in long queues in cities. Coal miners in Siberia resorted to strike in 1989 against scarcity and miserable economic conditions, repercussions of which soon found in other mining and industrial centres too.

Under the liberalised atmosphere of Glasnost, public dissatisfaction with economic conditions was overt and expressive. It is said that 'Gorbachev actually put the sort of final blow to the resistance of the Soviet Union by killing the fear of the people. It was still that this country was governed and kept together by the fear from Stalinist times'.

Military factor – Burden of military competition with the United States: Another factor for the crisis in Soviet Union was its high military spending. Soviet military spending was highly accelerated in response to the **Strategic Defense Initiative** of the US president Ronald Reagan. Even when the economy stagnated, the Soviet leaders ensured that military remained well funded. Though it can be said that expenditure on armaments and space research enabled the Soviets to maintain the balance of power in the Cold War era, it meant diversion of huge resources away from productive and essential sectors.

Afghan factor: By invading Afghanistan, the Soviet army had waded into a quagmire, in a region known as the **Graveyard of the Empires**. The 10-year occupation caused huge human and material cost to the Soviet, apart from causing a huge morale loss. The Afghan debacle also strengthened the divisive forces in the Soviet. Many Soviet soldiers who participated in Afghan mission from the Central Asian republics felt closer ethnic and religious ties to Afghans than with the Russians. For example, of the three major ethnic groups – the Pashtuns, Tajiks and Uzbeks in Afghanistan – the latter two were also part of the population of the Soviet Union who viewed the war as a war against their own brethrens. Similarly, to the Baltic republics the war in Afghanistan was a metaphor for the Russian occupation of their own countries which strengthened secessionist movements and declaration of independence by them in 1990.

Social factor: The Soviet public was disgusted with the widespread corruption and controls that were characteristic of the Soviet state. Once Glasnost and Perestroika ushered new ideas, concepts and opportunities, the Soviet citizens were eager to explore them which meant questioning of the drawbacks in the system and consequent erosion of popular base of Communism.

Cold War factor: The Cold War was too expensive. The cost of maintaining the Socialist Bloc by way of suppressing unrest in Eastern Europe, providing financial support to the third-world countries, and the cost of maintaining a large military force to hold the Bloc together added to the economic burden of the Soviet, precipitating its disintegration. Hence, it is said that the 'Soviet system, in harness with communism, destroyed the Soviet economy and thus hastened the disintegration of the USSR'.

Nuclear factor – Chernobyl Disaster: Chernobyl nuclear disaster occurred in April 1986, at Chernobyl Nuclear Plant in Ukraine and its fallout was 400 times more than that of atomic bomb dropped in Hiroshima. Though the Soviet authorities tried to cover-up the disaster, the extent of the catastrophe was known to the world soon. The incident exposed the real conditions in the Soviet Union, brought to light low-quality standards, destroyed the *Soviet façade* of everything great in the Soviet and put a question mark on the legitimacy of Glasnost. The Soviet Union was now a state with ruined credibility not only to the people of outside world but also to its own newly empowered citizens. This prodded Gorbachev to intensify Glasnost, and Glasnost in turn accentuated the end of the Soviet Union. Gorbachev was to ascribe later on, the disaster, than perestroika, as the real cause of the end of the Soviet Union.

Nationalist pressure: In the dissolution of the Soviet Union and in discrediting the ideal of a unified Soviet, nationalism too had been a factor. The **socialist internationalism** and the interests of the **various nationalities** were not always compatible as was evident in developments in Czechoslovakia in 1968 and Poland in 1980. Resultantly, communism collapsed in Eastern Europe which in turn enormously accelerated and radicalised nationalist feelings within the USSR. The reforms inadvertently released the long suppressed national sentiments of all peoples within the multinational Soviet state and the republics of the union started demanding greater autonomy in internal and external affairs leading to the disintegration of the USSR.

SUMMARY

Russia before the Revolution – Russia was under the autocracy of the Romanov dynasty and was the most conservative of the Great Powers in Europe. It was beset with poverty, inequality and inhumane working conditions in the industrial sector.

Causes of the Revolution – Political causes – autocracy of the Tsars on the one side and the emergence of political awareness and political parties on the other. Socio-economic conditions in Russia – wide cleavage between the rich and poor, social division of nobles and serfs and the emergence of the proletariat and the bourgeoisie as a result of industrialisation. Influence of ideas – Liberal ideas of democracy and limited monarchy along with radical ideas and socialist ideas had been penetrating in the minds of the educated class. Military failures of Russia – Russia was defeated in the Crimean War and in the Russo-Japanese War. Russia was also facing setbacks in the First World War.

Origin and development of the Revolution – Revolution erupted in March 1917 in Petrograd forcing the Tsar to resign. A Provisional Government was then established but it failed in solving enormous challenges faced by the country leading to outbreak of another revolution in November 1917. This was led by Lenin, the leader of the Bolsheviks and they succeeded in capturing power. Soon Russia underwent a period of Civil War between the Bolsheviks or the Reds and those opposed to the Bolsheviks known as the Whites. In the Civil War the Bolsheviks emerged victorious and they declared the establishment of the Union of Soviet Socialist Republics (USSR).

Russia under Stalin – Totalitarianism – Though Lenin had laid the foundation for an authoritarian state it was Stalin who perfected it. His measures such as the Great Purge, totalitarianism in socio-cultural spheres and efforts to create a 'new man', the Five-Year Plans, steps for rapid industrialisation and agricultural collectivisation were expressions of the same.

Nikita Khrushchev and de-Stalinization – He initiated a series of reforms aimed at de-Stalinization and as the revision of Stalin's policies. He held the view that there are 'different roads to socialism' and stood for peaceful coexistence with the West.

Leonid Brezhnev and period of stagnation – Though he started his regime with some reforms they were not enough to revitalise the economy. Political corruption, continuation of conventional methods such as organising collective farms and imposing centrally determined quotas; and re-centralisation of the Soviet economy all led to stagnation.

Mikhail Gorbachev and his reforms – Perestroika was an effort to restructure the economic and political edifice of the USSR; Glasnost meant more openness and candour in government affairs and opening of Soviet society to a critical evaluation, democratisation of the political system aimed at internal democracy within the CPSU (Communist Party of the Soviet Union) and new thinking in foreign relations was aimed at relaxation of international environment.

Decline of Communism and disintegration of the USSR – Gorbachev did not want to end communism, what he aimed at was replacing the existing system. But the reforms of Gorbachev weakened the central control within the USSR thus initiated a chain of events in the Eastern Bloc that started with unrest in Poland in 1989 which soon spread to other Eastern Bloc nations such as Hungary, East Germany, Bulgaria, Czechoslovakia and Romania and also in Albania and Yugoslavia. In 1990, Lithuania declared its independence from the USSR and it was followed by Estonia and Latvia. As the crisis deepened the Belovezha Accords was signed in 1991and the USSR was formally dissolved.

Questions of Previous Years Civil Services Examination

1. Discuss, how the policies adopted by Mikhail Gorbachev were responsible for the disintegration of the USSR? (2022)
2. Revolutions whether in Russia (1917) or in China (1949), are a disastrous way of transforming a country. (2021)

3. How did Stalin build on Lenin's legacy of Bolshevik Revolution and introduce new elements of totalitarianism to transform USSR as a superpower? (2020)
4. Review the policy of Glasnost adopted by Gorbachev. (2018)
5. 'By the 1980s, the communist system of the Soviet Union was incapable of maintaining the country's role as superpower'. Substantiate. (2017)
6. Examine the statement that 'the danger that of Bolshevism dominated not only the history of the years immediately following the Russian Revolution of 1917 but the entire history of the world since that date'. (2017)
7. How did Lenin achieve an abrupt transition from a Monarchical autocratic to a Socialist State? (2016)
8. In what way the political changes in Soviet Union influence the events in Eastern Europe during the closing decades of the 20th century? (2016)
9. 'The essence of perestroika is for people to feel they are country's master' – Gorbachev. Elucidate. (2010)
10. Account for the overthrow of the Tsarist regime in Russia. Examine the statement. (2009)
11. The Russian Revolution (1917) was an economic explosion hastened by the stupidity of the autocratic government. Elucidate. (2005)
12. Examine the causes of the Russian Revolution of 1917 and indicate its significance in world history. (2003)
13. Discuss the main factors leading to the collapse of the Soviet Union. (2002)
14. In Russia, Lenin was 'the father of socialism, organiser of the revolution and the founder of the new Russian society'. Examine the statement. (1998)
15. 'Stalinist Russia was a despotic regime'. Critically examine the view. (1999)
16. The Russian Revolution of 1917 was a single revolution which developed in two phases. Elucidate. (1992)

CHAPTER 10

The League of Nations

In this Chapter

1. Introduction

The League of Nations was a 'general association of nations', established on 10 January 1920. It was headquartered in Geneva, Switzerland, and was intended to be an **inter-governmental organisation for peace-keeping and international co-operation**. The League was expected to replace the old system of alliances, balance of power, secret diplomacy and war as instruments of policy in international relations. It was established by **Part I of the Treaty of Versailles** and became the first international organisation whose principal mission was to maintain world peace.

The League scored some notable successes in its first decade, but in the 1930s the authority of the League came under challenge after the Japanese invasion of Manchuria (1931) and the Italian invasion of Abyssinia (1935). After 1935, the authority and prestige of the League was further undermined as was evident in Germany's disputes with Czechoslovakia and Poland, during which the League was not even consulted.

The League ultimately proved incapable of preventing another world war which was its primary purpose and was dissolved (it had not met after December 1939) in April 1946. The League lasted for 26 years and was replaced by the United Nations, which inherited many agencies and organisations founded by the League.

The League failed to meet the expectations of its founders, nevertheless, its foundation was a significant event in the history of international relations and marked 'a forward leap of unprecedented extent and speed, accompanied by extraordinary changes in the conduct of international relations'.

2. Early Efforts Towards Global Peace

The League of Nations is often considered as the brainchild of the American President, **Woodrow Wilson**, who had included it, as the last point of his **Fourteen Points**, during the First World War. But the idea of a peaceful community of nations was in existence since the 18th century, when in 1795, **Immanuel Kant**, the German philosopher, proposed the formation of a peaceful world community in his essay titled ***Perpetual Peace: A Philosophical Sketch*** and had argued for the establishment of a 'league of peace' as the corner stone of the law of nations.

After the end of Napoleonic Wars the Congress of Vienna (1815) created the **'Concert of Europe'** to promote collective security, to maintain status quo and to prevent wars. This Quadruple Alliance (Austria, Prussia, Russia and England) inaugurated a period of collective deliberation in international affairs. At the end of the three-year long Crimean War (1853–56), the **Congress of Paris** was held in France in 1856 between the great powers of Europe at the time – France, Britain, Russia, Prussia, Austria, Sardinia and the Ottoman Empire, which resulted in a pledge by all of the powers to jointly maintain 'the integrity of the Ottoman Empire' and to preserve peace.

The 19th century also witnessed the development of international law dealing with humanitarian relief during wartime in the forms of **Geneva Convention** (1864) and governing rules of war and peaceful settlement of international disputes known as the **Hague Conventions** of 1899 and 1907.

Geneva Convention 1864 was inspired by a Swiss businessman Henry Dunant who had in 1862 proposed for the:

1. Establishment of a permanent relief agency for humanitarian aid in times of war. The proposal led to the establishment of the **International Committee of Red Cross (ICRC)** in 1863 in Geneva, Switzerland.
2. Signing of an inter-governmental treaty recognising the neutrality of the agency and allowing it to provide aid in a war zone, which led to the Geneva Convention of 1864.

> **Henry Dunant** was awarded the first **Nobel Peace Prize** in 1901 for his contribution in forming the Red Cross and in framing the Geneva Convention of 1864.

The **Geneva Conventions** are treaties and additional protocols that establish standards of international law for humanitarian treatment in war. These rules are applicable only in times of armed conflict and seek to protect people who are not or are no longer taking part in hostilities like the sick and wounded of armed forces on the field, wounded, sick and shipwrecked members of armed forces at sea, prisoners of war and civilians.

The **Hague Conventions** of 1899 and 1907 were other efforts at international level to frame statements of the laws of war and war crimes in the body of international law. These conventions were significant in the field of multilateralism as they represented the first multilateral treaties that addressed the conduct of warfare. It also set up the Permanent Court of Arbitration, for adjudication of international disputes.

The efforts of the Hague conferences to prevent war by a policy of disarmament proved to be a failure with the outbreak of the World War I, as the rules laid down at the Hague Conventions were violated in the First World War. But they gave shape to international arbitration movement to settle disputes and symbolised the civilised world's efforts for restrictions on war and the desirability of avoiding it altogether.

The next important step in the multilateralism was the IPU – the forerunner of the League of Nations. The **Inter-Parliamentary Union (IPU)** was founded in 1889 by peace activists William Randal Cremer and Frederic Passy to encourage governments to solve international disputes by peaceful means. Headquartered in Geneva, Switzerland, it was the first permanent forum for political multilateral negotiations. IPU established annual conferences to help governments refine the process of international arbitration. IPU was structured as a council headed by a President which was later reflected in the structure of the League of Nations too. The League of Nations had, thus, many precedents and models in promoting arbitration and settling international disputes. Yet, the League was a move beyond all these precedents, as it aimed at a system of collective security based on law and permanent institutions and a framework for the general co-operation of nations.

3. Origin of the League of Nations

As seen above, the League of Nations was the culmination of series of attempts initiated to avoid war and for peaceful settlement of international disputes, which gained momentum with the outbreak of the First World War.

Soon after the outbreak of the World War, schemes for an international organisation to prevent future wars had gained considerable support from **civil society**. Feminist organisations had started mobilisation against the war and had conducted protest marches in Europe and the United States. Many thinkers and groups such as the Bryce Group and the Fabian Society in England, the 'League to Enforce Peace' in the United States and the 'Women's International League for Peace and Freedom' (started in 1915 in Hague, Netherlands, and headquartered in Geneva, Switzerland) and so forth had started campaign for a neutral mediating body and for measures to avoid war.

In 1914, it was Goldsworthy Dickinson, a British political scientist and one of the founders of the **Bryce Group**, who coined the term 'League of Nations'. He also drafted a scheme for such an organisation.

Similar views were held by a number of world statesmen. **David Lloyd George**, the Prime Minister of England (1916–22) during the World War I, endorsed the desirability of such an organisation and considered it as one of the war aims of the British. The British Foreign Secretary, **Lord Arthur Balfour**, argued that 'behind international law and behind all treaty arrangements for preventing or limiting hostilities, some form of international sanction should be devised which would give pause to the hardiest aggressor'. The French statesmen like **Leon Bourgeois** advocated annual meetings of a council, to settle all disputes and formation of an 'international army' to enforce its decisions.

Lord Robert Cecil, minister in the war time coalition government in Britain, prepared and circulated a 'Memorandum on Proposals for Diminishing the Occasion of Future Wars', in the British cabinet in 1916 and urged for an alternative to war, as a means of settling international disputes and application of sanctions including blockade, to force countries to submit to peaceful procedures. **Jan Christian Smuts**, a prominent South African statesman, published *The League of Nations: A Practical Suggestion* in December, 1918, proposing the creation of a council of great powers and creation of a mandate system for territories captured during the war.

The American President, **Woodrow Wilson**, in his speech in 1918 to the US Congress on war aims and peace terms, proposed '**Fourteen Points**' to be used for peace negotiations in order to end the World War I and envisaged a world organisation that would guarantee the 'political independence and territorial integrity of great and small states alike'.

The World War I – 'the war to end all wars' – came to an end in November 1918 and putting an end to future wars became a keenly felt necessity. It resulted in the emergence of **anti-war sentiment** throughout the world and possible causes of the war were caused to be vigorously investigated so that such factors could be identified and eliminated. Arms race, militaristic nationalism, secret diplomacy, alliances and freedom of sovereign states to enter into war for their own benefit were identified as some of the major causes of the War. The creation of an international organisation with the prime aim to prevent future wars through disarmament, open diplomacy, international cooperation and restrictions on the right to wage war and penalties that made war unattractive emerged as one of the remedies that gained wide acceptability.

A. Formation of the League

At the **Paris Peace Conference in 1919**, the proposals of Woodrow Wilson, Robert Cecil and Jan Smuts were discussed. A commission under Woodrow Wilson with Robert Cecil, Jan Smuts and Leon Bourgeois among others as members was appointed to prepare a covenant. After negotiations and compromises, the final text was adopted on 28 April 1919 by the unanimous decision of the Conference and the League of Nations was established by **Part I of the Treaty of Versailles**. On 28 June 1919, 44 states signed **the Covenant** (a charter or document that lays out the granting of rights or privileges) which contained 26 articles and on 10 January 1920 the Covenant of the League of Nations came into force (the same day that the Versailles Treaty came in to existence). On 1 November, the preliminary office of the League was moved from London to Geneva, where the first General Assembly was held on 15 November 1920. The official languages of the League were English and French.

In recognition of the US President Woodrow Wilson's effort to establish and promote the League, he was awarded the Nobel Peace Prize in 1919. The first headquarters of the League of Nations in Geneva, the Palais Wilson, was named after Woodrow Wilson. It continued to be the headquarters of the League till 1936, when it was shifted to the newly constructed Palais des Nations (Palace of Nations), Geneva.

In the preface to the **Covenant of the League**, the aims of the League were stated as:

1. to **promote international cooperation**
2. to **achieve international peace and security**
   - by the acceptance of obligations not to resort to war
   - by the prescription of open, just and honourable relations between nations
   - by the firm establishment of the understandings of international law as the actual rule of conduct among governments, and
   - by the maintenance of justice and a scrupulous respect for all treaty obligations in the dealings of organised peoples with one another.

In other words, the League was to encourage international co-operation for solving economic and social problems, and to maintain world peace through collective security by restraining the aggressor either by economic sanctions or by military action.

To secure the primary objectives of the League, three articles were incorporated in the Covenant, These were Articles VIII, X and XVI.

Article VIII provided that 'the maintenance of peace requires the reduction of national armaments'. **Article X** required 'members of the League undertake to respect and preserve as against external aggression the territorial integrity and existing political independence of all members. In case of any such aggression or in cases of any threat or danger of such aggression the Council shall advice upon the means by which this obligation shall be fulfilled'. **Article XVI** stated 'should any member of the League resort to war, it shall ipso facto, be deemed to have committed an act of war against all other members of the League'. The article also provided for 'the severance of all trade or financial relations, prohibition of all intercourse between their nationals and the nationals of the Covenant breaking state' and entrusted the Council 'to recommended to the several governments concerned, what effective military, naval or air force the members of the League shall severally contribute to the armed forces to be used to protect the Covenants of the League'.

Towards the end of the Second World War, the world leaders, while considering options for a new world order, opted for a new beginning in the form of a new organisation – the United Nations, instead of revitalising the defunct League. As a result the League of Nations was dissolved on 18 April 1946 and its assets and responsibilities were transferred to **the United Nations**.

Members of the League: The League had greatest extent (membership) from 1934 to 1935 with 58 members. Membership of the League underwent much fluctuations, some recognised States completely abstained from it, while some others withdrew, making its work more complicated. Despite formulating and signing the Covenant, the United States never joined the League of Nations. The US Senate refused tc ratify the Treaty of Versailles and the US membership in the League, as there was strong opposition from isolationist members of the Congress, led by the Republican Senator Henry Cabot Lodge. The isolationists were opposed to any further United States involvement in international conflict and viewed Article X of the League Covenant as a d rect infringement on their country's sovereignty. The U.S.S.R. was the only country to be expelled by the League in 1939, following its invasion of Finland.

4. | Organisation of the League of Nations

The League of Nations was organised in the form of three main constitutional organs – the Assembly, the Council and the Permanent Secretariat, two essential wings – the Permanent Court of International Justice and the International Labour Organisation (ILO), in addition to several auxiliary agencies and commissions. Each organ's budget was allocated by the Assembly and the member states provided the financial support to the League.

A. The General Assembly

The Assembly was the plenary organ of the League. The Assembly consisted of all member states with each state allowed up to three representatives and one vote. It convened once in a year in Geneva. Its responsibilities included admission of new members, periodical election of non-permanent members to the Council, election of judges of the Permanent Court and control of the budget.

Any decision taken had to be unanimous, unless otherwise indicated. This unanimity concept was an expression of the recognition of national sovereignty and also of the fact that the League sought solution by consent and not by dictation. At the same time abstentions were not to be treated as contrary votes and that in some cases the votes of the parties in conflict did not count.

Some of the particularly relevant functions of the League Assembly as conferred upon it by the Covenant were:

a. admission of new members, to be decided by a two-thirds majority (Art. 1)
b. selection of non-permanent members of the Council and to approve any expansion of that body (Art. 4)
c. approve the appointment of the Secretary General made by the League Council (Art. 6)
d. consider 'international conditions whose continuance might endanger the peace of the world' (Art. 19)

The League Assembly inaugurated a number of practices that were to become typical of international organisations since then. Its annual sessions assured regularity and permitted development of certain routine. The practice of working in commissions, each convened every year, to deal with issues related to legal, technological and intellectual organisations, disarmament, budgetary matters, social questions and political matters including the mandates and slavery enabled the Assembly to address broad range of issues and emerge in practice as a body far more influential than initially intended.

B. The Council

The Council was the executive body, directing the Assembly's business and met more often, at least three times a year and in extraordinary sessions when required. It consisted of **permanent members and non-permanent members**. Great Britain, France, Italy and Japan were the permanent members. The non-permanent members were elected by the Assembly for a three-year term and the first non-permanent members were Belgium, Brazil, Greece and Spain.

The League Covenant provided for additional permanent and non-permanent members by the Council with the approval of the majority of the Assembly. Under which the composition of the Council was altered many times. In 1926, when Germany joined the League, it was admitted as the fifth permanent member of the council and later when Germany and Japan withdrew from the League, the Soviet Union was made a permanent member. By 1938, the League Council was composed of four permanent and eleven non-permanent members. By 1940, with the expulsion of the Soviet Union and withdrawal of Italy the only permanent members left were France and the Britain.

The number of non-permanent seats was increased to 6 (1922), then to 9 (1926) and finally to 11 (1936). The decision of the council had to be unanimous which meant each League Council members enjoyed the veto power on substantive issues.

C. The Secretariat

The Secretariat was the veritable backbone of the League, comprised of a body of experts in various spheres under a Secretary General. It was responsible for preparing the agenda for the Council and the Assembly, publishing of reports of the meetings, writing resolutions and reports for carrying out the decisions of the League. As provided in the Covenant registration and publication of international treaties was also the responsibility of the League Secretariat. It was organised into eleven sections such as Political, Financial and Economic, Mandates, Disarmament, Legal and so forth.

The Secretariat comprised of international career civil servants of high reputation and competence recruited in an equitable proportion from member states. With its permanent character the Secretariat acquired much needed expertise and experience. Being based on the principles of internationalism, independence and neutrality, the Secretariat shaped the modern understanding of the international civil service. It is also pertinent to note that the Secretariat had also established a radio station – the Radio Nations – to promote relations between the League members.

D. The Permanent Court of International Justice

It was based at **The Hague in Netherlands**. It consisted of 15 judges of different nationalities. Its judges were elected by the Council and the Assembly. The Court was to hear and decide any international dispute which the parties concerned submitted to it. It also had an advisory power on any dispute or question referred to it by the Council or the Assembly.

The Permanent Court of International Justice often called as the World Court ceased to exist since 1946 and was replaced by the International Court of Justice.

E. The International Labour Organisation (ILO)

The ILO was established in 1919 on the basis of part XIII of the Treaty of Versailles to 'secure and maintain fair and humane conditions of labour', as an affiliated agency of the League of Nations. Although subjected to the budget control of the Assembly, the ILO was an autonomous organisation with its own Governing Body and its own Secretariat.

Representation in ILO had been accorded not only to governments but also to representatives of employers and workers organisations. After the end of the League of Nations in 1946, the ILO became the first specialised agency of the UN it is headquartered at Geneva, Switzerland.

F. Other Institutions

The Covenant of the League of Nations had entrusted discretionary power to the Council and the Assembly to create auxiliary organs in the form of:

- **Technical organisation** dealing with finance and economic, transit and health
- **Advisory committees** dealing with disarmament, military questions, mandates, intellectual co-operation, traffic in women and children and so forth.

Under the above provisions the Disarmament Commission, the Health Organisation, the Mandates Commission, the International Commission on Intellectual Cooperation (precursor to UNESCO), the Commission for Refugees, and the Slavery Commission were established.

> Three of the institutions – the ILO, the Permanent Court of International Justice (renamed as the International Court of Justice) and the Health Organisation (as the World Health Organisation), were transferred to the United Nations after the Second World War.

5. Performance of the League

A. Effectiveness of the League

The League in its first decade resolved many of the political disputes referred to it. The aftermath of the First World War presented unsettled issues of national boundaries or to which country a particular region would belong. There were frequent occurrences of such crises. Some examples were:

a. Aland Islands

In the quarrel between Sweden and Finland over Aland Islands, a collection of around 6,500 islands located mid-way between Sweden and Finland in the Baltic Sea, the League was called in to interfere. In 1921, the League gave the verdict in favour of Finland. The islands were to remain a part of Finland with the guaranteed protection of the islanders including demilitarisation.

b. Upper Silesia

In 1921, the League was requested to resolve the dispute between Germany and Poland over Upper Silesia. The League recommended division of Upper Silesia between Germany and Poland in which most of the territory was given to Germany, while Poland secured majority of the regions mineral resources and industry.

c. Albanian Issue

The frontiers of Albania had not been settled till 1921, leading to clash with the troops of neighbouring countries like Greece in the south and Yugoslavia in the north. In November 1921, the League announced that the frontiers of Albania should be the same as it existed in 1913.

d. Mosul Question

Mosul was a province of the former Ottoman Empire. In 1926, dispute over Mosul emerged between the new Turkish republic who claimed the province as part of its historic heartland and Iraq which was under the British Mandate system. A League of Nations Commission of Inquiry assigned Mosul to Iraq.

e. Saar

Saar was placed under the League by the Treaty of Versailles since 1920. A plebiscite was to be held after 15 years to determine whether the province should belong to Germany or France. In 1935, referendum was held and 90.3 percent voters supported its union with Germany which was quickly implemented.

f. Columbia–Peru Dispute

There had been border conflicts between Columbia and Peru and in 1922 as per an agreement between the two governments the border town of Leticia was ceded to Columbia, giving Columbia access to the Amazon River. In 1932, an armed band of Peruvian civilians captured Leticia and forced the Columbian residents to flee. The League of Nations was asked to mediate and eventually in May 1934 a final peace agreement was signed resulting in the return of Leticia to Columbia, a formal apology from Peru for the 1932 invasion, demilitarisation of the area around Leticia, free navigation of the Amazon and Putumayo Rivers and a pledge of non-aggression by the two countries.

The Leticia incident was also significant in the sense that for the first time ever, soldiers wore the armband of an international organisation while performing peacekeeping duties. The wearing of arm bands of the League of Nations by the Columbian soldiers was a face-saving device to permit the Peruvians to leave without appearing to submit to the Columbians. This development was an antecedent of the United Nations peace keeping under its emblem decades later.

g. Greek's invasion of Bulgaria

In 1925, Greek invaded Bulgaria after a Greek army officer and a sentry were killed by Bulgarian soldiers at the border town of Petrich, southern Bulgaria. The League was swift in intervening and ordered ceasefire and withdrawal of Greek troops from Bulgaria and damages amounting £45,000 to be paid by Greece to Bulgaria.

The involvement of the League in these developments facilitated early settlement of the disputes. By the middle of the 1920s, the League emerged as the centre of international activity. France, Britain and Germany were all using the League's machinery to improve their relations and settle their differences and each of their foreign secretaries made it a point to attend the League meetings at Geneva during this period.

B. Ineffectiveness of the League

At the same time, role of the League was minimal or ineffective where the big powers were involved. Some of the developments of this nature were Corfu Incident (1923), Mukden Incident or Manchurian Incident (1931), Chaco War (1932), Abyssinia Crisis (1935), Spanish Civil War (1936–39) and the Second Sino-Japanese War (1937).

a. Corfu Incident

In 1923, the Italian forces sent by Mussolini occupied the Greek island of Corfu in violation of the League Covenant. The reason behind the occupation was killing of some Italians who were part of an international boundary commission marking out the newly decided border between Greece and Albania. At the request of Greece, the League examined the dispute but referred the matter to the Conference of Ambassadors for final decision.

Conference of Ambassadors was an inter-allied organisation of the Entente Powers which was formed in Paris, in 1920. It consisted of ambassadors of Great Britain, Italy and Japan accredited in Paris and French foreign minister. It was formed to enforce peace treaties and to mediate in territorial disputes among the European states.

Benito Mussolini defied the League of Nations during the Corfu Incident and declared that Italy would withdraw from the League, if it arbitrated in the crisis. At the insistence of Mussolini, not the League but the Conference of Ambassadors tendered an agreement favouring Italy, under which Greece had to pay fifty million Lire to Italy.

The Corfu incident thus demonstrated the League's weakness in dealing with big powers and was not a promising sign apt to a world body. The authority of the League was openly defied by Italy, a founding member of the League and a permanent member at the Council. The crisis was the first major test for the League but the League failed it.

b. Mukden Incident

Japan had spheres of interest in northern China and Manchuria since its victories in the First

Sino-Japanese War (1894–95) and the Russo-Japanese War (1904–05). The Japanese had the right over the South Manchurian Railway Zone and Japanese soldiers were stationed within the zone for security of the tracks and trains.

In 1931, the Japanese soldiers staged an explosion at the railway line owned by Japan's South Manchuria Railway near Mukden as a pretext for the Japanese invasion of north eastern China known as Manchuria. The Japanese accused Chinese soldiers sabotaging the railway and in apparent retaliation occupied all of Manchuria, renamed it as Manchukuo and set up a puppet government.

The League of Nations refused to acknowledge Manchukuo as an independent nation and rejected the Japanese claim that the Manchurian invasion and occupation was an act of self-defence. The League of Nations on the basis of its observers' report (Lytton Commission) declared Japan to be the aggressor and demanded return of Manchuria to China. In 1933, this report was passed in the League Assembly for 42-1 (only Japan voted against). In response Japan withdrew from the League (1933). Instead of obeying the League's direction and removing its troops from Manchuria, Japan continued to occupy Manchuria until 1945. Once again, the League and the idea of collective security proved to be ineffective as the League powers were unprepared, indifferent or in sympathy with the aggressor.

c. *Chaco War (1932–35)*

Latin American countries of Paraguay and Bolivia were engaged in a dispute over Gran Chaco region. The region was arid and sparsely populated but was important for both the land locked countries to have access to Atlantic Ocean through the Paraguay River. Speculation of rich deposit of petroleum in the region too intensified the claims. Though the border clashes were frequent throughout the 1920s, the League failed to prevent it developing into a war.

In 1932, war broke out when Bolivian army attacked Paraguay. In spite of appeal by Paraguay, the League did not take action, failed to impose an arms embargo, failed to arbitrate and negotiate peace between the two countries or to put a stop to the hostilities. Instead the Pan-American Conference offered to mediate in the dispute. The Pan-American Conference was an association of American states aimed at closer co-operation of the North, Central and South Americas. The war was disastrous for both the countries and a ceasefire was signed in 1935. Paraguay seized two-thirds of the disputed region but Bolivia was given a corridor to the Paraguay River and a port-Puerto Casado which was recognised by a peace treaty-Chaco Treaty signed in Buenos Aires in 1938.

d. *Abyssinia Crisis or Italo-Ethiopian War (1935–36)*

If the Chaco war demonstrated inability of the League in preventing outbreak of a war and its inaction in resolving the dispute, the Abyssinia crisis was to clearly exhibit the League's ineffectiveness in punishing an aggressor and how it could be influenced by the self-interest of its members.

Ethiopia was one of the few independent states in a European-dominated Africa, which Italy had unsuccessfully tried to conquer in 1896. This landlocked semi-feudal kingdom adjacent to Italy's existing colonies on the Horn of Africa contained fertile uplands, abundant raw material and offered path to Sudan and Suez. To Italy it also offered an opportunity of erasing the humiliation of 1986.

The border between Ethiopia (Abyssinia) and the Italian Somaliland (an Italian colony) had not been clearly demarcated. In 1930, Italy built a fort at **the Walwal Oasis** in a boundary zone between the two nations, causing skirmishes between Ethiopian and Italian forces. In the background of increasing tension and skirmishes between the Ethiopian soldiers and Italians Emperor **Haile Selassie** of Ethiopia appealed to the League of Nations for arbitration. The arbitration committee of the League absolved both parties of any culpability on the ground that each nation had believed Walwal was within its own territorial borders. Thus, the League's response was inconclusive.

In 1935, Mussolini mobilised troops in Eritrea and Italian Somaliland which were Italian colonies that bordered Ethiopia to the northeast and southeast, respectively. On 3 October 1935, Italy invaded Ethiopia, prompting Ethiopia to declare war on Italy, thus beginning the Second Italo-Abyssinian war. The modern Italian army defeated the poorly equipped Ethiopian army and captured Ethiopian capital Addis Ababa in May 1936 forcing Emperor Haile Selassie to flee. Mussolini proclaimed Victor Emmanuel III, the King of Italy as the Emperor of Ethiopia.

The League had condemned Italy's aggression and imposed economic sanctions in November 1935. The League's failure in the Abyssinian Crisis was evident in more ways than one. The sanctions imposed by the League were ineffective since they did not ban the sale of oil or block Italian access to the Suez Canal. The League could not harden its stand even after Italy resorted to the use of dumdum bullets (bullets designed to expand on impact for faster incapacitation) which had been banned by the Hague Convention, poison gas and bombardment of Red Cross units and civilian settlements which were violative of international norms.

It was also important that, in spite of lack of precedent for a head of state addressing the Assembly of the League of Nations in person, Haile Selassie addressed the League of Nations Assembly in June 1936 denouncing Italian aggression and criticising world community for standing by it, which he concluded with the words '**It is us today. It will be you tomorrow**'. His resolution to the League to deny recognition of the Italian conquest was defeated. In July 1936, the League voted to end the sanctions against Italy.

The major powers of the League too took indifferent attitude in the crisis. France appeased Italy as it could not afford to risk an alliance between Italy and Germany and the Britain followed France's lead citing its own military weakness. Thus, the Abyssinian Crisis was a clear demonstration of the failure of the League. Italy and Ethiopia were members of the League, yet the League was unable to control Italy or to protect Ethiopia when Italy violated Article X of the Covenant of the League of Nations. In the ultimate, Italy ignored the sanctions, quit the League and established control over Ethiopia by making special deals with Britain and France.

The Abyssinian Crisis had serious consequences in the international relations as it discredited the League as the small states lost all faith in it, encouraged Hitler to break the Versailles treaty and annoyed by the League sanctions, Mussolini moved closer to an alliance with Nazi Germany.

e. *The Spanish Civil War*

In July 1936, the Spanish Army, under General Francisco Franco, effected a coup d'état leading to a prolonged conflict between the **Republicans** (under the elected leftist government) and the **Nationalists** (conservatives and anti-communist rebels supported by many officers of the Spanish army) known as the Spanish Civil War. The Spanish Civil War exposed political divisions of the European continent and was also an indicator of growing instability across Europe with potentials to escalate into another world war. The right and the Catholics espoused the Nationalist cause as a way to check the expansion of Bolshevism, while the left and intellectuals supported the Republicans as a necessary battle to stop the spread of fascism. As such, the Fascists under Hitler and Mussolini provided aid to the Nationalists, the leftist under Soviet Union supported the Spanish Republic. The League of Nations response by way of forming a Non-intervention Committee and a ban on foreign volunteers in the civil war proved ineffective.

f. *Second Sino-Japanese War*

In July 1937, Japan started a full-scale attack on China. Though China appealed to the League, it could not provide any assistance. The League just referred the matter to the Nine Power Treaty Conference which was under the leadership of the United States and in which both Japan and China were members.

g. *Failure of Disarmament*

The Article VIII of the Covenant had entrusted the League of Nations, the task of reducing 'armaments to the lowest point'. Though significant efforts were made in this direction, the League failed in the task. In 1926, the League appointed a Special Commission to draw up plans for disarmament, and in 1932, the World Disarmament Conference was convened in Geneva.

The **World Disarmament Conference** was held in Geneva during 1932–34 with representatives from 60 states. Though the Disarmament Commission had obtained initial agreement from France, Britain, Italy, Spain and Japan to limit the size of their navies, no final agreement could be reached. Germany, from the outset, had demanded equality of armaments with France but the French argued that this should be postponed for at least eight years, on the ground that, German military inferiority was their only insurance from a deadly future conflict. Hitler, who by this time had become the Chancellor of Germany, used this French attitude as an excuse to withdraw Germany from the Conference and from the League itself in October 1933.

Efforts of the League towards disarmament failed as its members held different views towards the issue and on the other the fascist powers paid scant respect to the League directives. The French were reluctant to reduce their armaments in the face of Germany's attempts to overturn the Treaty of Versailles and the reconstruction of German military. As for the British and the United States they were unprepared to offer additional security commitments that France was looking for. Countries like Poland and Czechoslovakia felt vulnerable to attack from the west (that is, Germany) and thus wanted the League's guarantee against such aggression before they disarmed.

On the other hand, Germans could see no reason why their country could not enjoy the same level of armaments as others. After Hitler became the Chancellor of Germany in 1933, he intensified its armament efforts, remilitarised the Rhineland, occupied the Sudetenland and withdrew Germany from the League citing inability of the League in providing parity in arms between France and Germany.

6. Achievements of the League in Other Areas

The League accomplished much in social and humanitarian field. In this context, the works of the ILO were commendable. The **ILO**, created in 1919 on the basis of Part XIII of the Treaty of Versailles and as an agency of the League, tried to improve conditions of labour by persuading governments on issues like campaign to end child labour, adequate minimum wages, 8-hour workday and 48-hour working week, old age pension and so forth. It also collected invaluable statistics on labour.

The **Health Organisation** of the League focussed on ending leprosy, malaria and yellow fever and worked successfully with the government of the U.S.S.R to combat typhus epidemic in that country.

The **Refugee Organisation** facilitated return of former prisoners of war stranded in Russia, to their homes. It established camps in Turkey in 1922 to aid the country with an ongoing refugee crisis, helping to prevent disease and hunger. The Refugee Commission also introduced '**Nansen passport**' as a means of identification for stateless people which was an internationally recognised refugee travel document. The Commission also provided valuable help to thousands of people fleeing the Nazi persecution in Germany.

The **Slavery Commission** directed its efforts towards eradication of slavery and slave trade across the world and fought against forced prostitution. The results of efforts in this direction led to abolition of slavery by Afghanistan in 1923, Nepal in 1926, Persia in 1929 and Bahrain in 1937.

The **League of Nations Mandates** were established under Article 22 of the Covenant of the League and was based on two principles – non-annexation of territory and administration of that territory as a sacred trust of civilisation for the benefit of its native people. The **Permanent Mandates Commission** supervised League of Nations Mandates and organised plebiscites in disputed territories so that residents could decide which country they would join.

7. Reasons for Failure of the League

A. Nature of Its origin

The League of Nations was closely linked to the Treaty of Versailles and was seen by many, as an organisation especially for the benefit of the victorious powers of World War I. They viewed the League as a '**League of Victors**'.

Moreover, the League had to defend the peace settlements, which were far from perfect. The Treaty, as it resulted from conflicting needs of the time, could neither pacify nor conciliate both the victors and vanquished fully. Germany had denounced the treaty and viewed it as humiliating. Italy though was on the side of victors was disappointed of the treaty outcome. Thus, the League was entrusted with task of maintaining international co-operation and peace in an environment unsettled by the post-World War I peace treaties. The 'unmet aspirations' of countries like Italy, 'vindictive' attitude of France and 'humiliation' of Germany all were to erect insurmountable challenges before the League, which coupled with other weakness led to its failure.

B. Weakness in Its Structure and Membership

The structure of the League and its functioning, where a unanimous vote was required in the Council and the Assembly for decision to be taken, proved any effective and conclusive action difficult.

Further, though envisaged as a forum of all nations, many never joined or their membership was short and perhaps most importantly, it never enjoyed the full support of all great powers. At the beginning of the League in 1920, some countries like Germany or Soviet Russia were excluded from its membership. Germany was admitted in 1926, also as a permanent member of the Council but Adolf Hitler withdrew Germany in 1933. Japan was a permanent member of the Council but withdrew in 1933, as was the case of Italy and Spain which existed in 1937 and 1939, respectively. The Soviet Union was admitted in 1934, but was expelled in 1939. Above all, the United States whose President, Woodrow Wilson, had been a driving force behind the League's formation chose not to join, as the United States Senate rejected both the Versailles Treaty and the League, depriving the world body of a powerful member and financial support. In other words, the continued absence of the United States and expulsion or withdrawal of USSR, Italy and Japan made the League very much a French and British affair.

C. Weakness in the Covenant

a. The League had **no military force** of its own to enforce its decisions and, thus, it 'lacked teeth'. Article XVI of the Covenant required the member states to supply troops if necessary, but a decision in this regard was to be taken by individual nations. It is also important to note that, though attempts had been made to modify the Covenant and strengthen the League, these failed as it required a unanimous vote.

b. Contradictory **concepts of collective security and disarmament**. Firstly, the collective security required the member states to act in a way that might affect their national interests, sometimes even against states they considered friendly, or to support states with which they had no affinity. During the Abyssinian crisis this contradiction was exposed when Britain and France had to balance their national security interests, in which Italy's support was imperative while meeting their obligations to Abyssinia, as a member of the League. Similarly, in the face of growing German militarisation under Hitler, both Britain and France had to abandon the concept of collective security in favour of appeasement to protect their national interests. Ultimately, the League or for that matter any international organisation is only, as strong as, the determination of its leading members to stand up to aggression. But, the powers of the time were unwilling to act except where it suited their individual national interests.

In addition there was a contradiction in the League's advocacy of disarmament while at the same time advocating collective security, depriving the League itself the only forceful means by which it could uphold its authority.

Emergence of pacifism, as a strong force among both the people and governments in many nations, too acted as a barrier to decisive actions against violators of the Covenant. **'Peace at any price'** became the motto of many intellectuals and statesmen of the time, who were still tortured by the horrors of World War I.

D. The World Economic Crisis

The crisis started in 1929 found expressed in the form of unemployment, falling living standards leading to failure of democracy and facilitating the emergence of extreme right wing governments in many countries. These powers violated the Versailles Treaty provisions one after another – invasion of Manchuria, remilitarisation of Rhineland, occupation of Sudetenland and Anschluss of Austria to name a few. The League was mostly silent in the face of major events leading to the Second World War and its outbreak demonstrated failure in its primary objective, the prevention of another war.

In conclusion, it can be said that the League of Nations failed not just because the United States did not join or because of inherent weakness in its Covenant, but because the great powers were unwilling to apply sanctions – economic or military – except where it suited their national interest and also because democracy, on which the original idea of the League was based, had collapsed over half of the world within a decade of its formation.

8. | Legacy of the League of Nations

In 1943, while the Second World War was under way the Allied Powers at the **Tehran Conference** agreed to create a new body – **the United Nations** – to replace the League and intended to make it more effective. For example, the Security Council decisions are binding on all members of the UN and unanimity of decisions are not required in the conduct of the UN. The last meeting of the League took place in April 1946 in Geneva and transferred the League's assets and functions to the UN or to its specialised bodies. The **Palace of Nations**, the headquarters of the League of Nations, became the United Nations Office at Geneva.

Even though failed in its primary purpose of maintaining world peace, the League left to the posterity, a rich legacy of institutionalising international affairs as opposed to the pre-First World War methods of law and politics. Moreover, by recognising the importance of economic and social questions in international relations, the League was to influence modern forms of international co-operation tremendously. The League's contribution in areas such as in reducing international opium traffic, helping racial and political refugees in finding homes and in conducting plebiscites in disputed areas were commendable. It also strengthened the concept of collective security, paved way for new forms of statehood as the Mandate put the colonial power under supervision and above all, raised awareness regarding epidemics, slavery, child labour and refugee rights and gave voice to smaller nations of the post-World War I.

SUMMARY

The League of Nations – The League was established on 10 January 1920 as the first international organisation whose principal mission was to maintain world peace. It was established by the Part I of the Treaty of Versailles.

Early efforts towards world peace and origin of the League of Nations – League was formed as the culmination of a series of efforts for peaceful settlement of international disputes. The Concert of Europe, the Congress of Paris (1856), the Geneva Convention (1864), the Hague Conventions (1899 and 1907) and the Inter-Parliamentary Union were major early efforts to settle international disputes by peaceful means. In spite of such efforts World War broke out in 1914 and serious campaign for a neutral mediating body and measures to avoid war took place. Efforts of Goldsworthy Dickinson, David Lloyd George, Lord Arthur Balfour. Leon Bourgeois, Robert Cecil, Jan Christian Smuts and Woodrow Wilson apart from the role of civil society were the significant in this context.

Structure of the League – The General Assembly – it was the plenary body and consisted of all member states; The Council – it was the executive organ consisting both permanent and non-permanent members; The Secretariat – it provided secretarial service to the League and was comprised of international career civil servants headed by Secretary General; The Permanent Court of International Justice – it had 15 judges from different member states to settle any international dispute which the parties concerned referred to it.

Effectiveness of the League – Aland Islands, Upper Silesia, Albanian Issue, Mosul Question, Saar, Columbia-Peru Dispute, Greek invasion of Bulgaria.

Ineffectiveness of the League – Corfu Incident, Mukden Incident, Chaco War, Abyssinia Crisis, the Spanish Civil War, the Second Sino-Japanese War and Failure of Disarmament.

Achievements of the League in other areas – These were mainly in social and humanitarian field such as its efforts to promote health facilities, mitigate refugee crisis and slavery.

Reasons for the failure of the League – Nature of its origin, weakness in structure and membership, weakness in the Covenant, the World Economic Crisis.

Questions of Previous Years Civil Services Examination

1. The ineffectiveness of the League of Nations to prevent or to check Japanese aggression against China was the first serious blow to its prestige as an agency for providing security. Critically examine. (2019)
2. 'League of Nations is a League of Notions'. Comment. (2016)
3. 'The Communist International and the League of Nations both announced the end of the Balance of Power'. (1996)
4. 'The Manchurian Crisis decided the fate of the League of Nations'. Discuss. (1993)
5. 'Thus the League sought to achieve the profoundest of all psychological revolutions to transform the war mentality of man into a peace mentality'. Discuss. (1992)

CHAPTER 11

The Inter-War Years 1918–39

In this Chapter

1. Introduction

The period between the end of the First World War and the outbreak of the Second is called as the **inter-war period, inter-bellum period or between the wars period**. This period, though short, was filled with significant developments.

The period started with formulation of **peace settlements** and formation of the **League of Nations**. The First World War had destroyed economies of the nations, nevertheless situation gradually improved. Economic growth and relative peace offered confidence about the future. But, the **Wall Street Crash** of 1929 shattered the hope of an early economic recovery and of increasing material prosperity.

The 1920s and the 1930s were also the decades of disillusionment, desperation and pessimism. Literary and artistic creations of the time too reflected these moods. Oswald Spengler's ***The Decline of the West* (1926)** best illustrated this pessimism, when Spengler insisted that the Western civilisation had entered its final stage and was destined to die.

The First World War was depicted as 'the war to end all wars' and the period following it was expected to be one of peace, freedom, progress and democracy. Yet, within few years extraordinary events followed and democracy was put on its death throes. Failure of the newly created democracies in solving multitudes of crises caused their fall and in turn facilitated the emergence of dictators. In response **Appeasement** was introduced, but it failed to quench the thirst of the dictators, who took the world to another catastrophe – the Second World War.

2. The Paris Peace Conference

The First World War had come to an end, as seen already, by a series of armistices signed between the Allies and their adversaries in 1918. On 18 January 1919, the representatives of the Allied Powers assembled in the **Hall of Mirrors** at the **Palace of Versailles** in Paris, to decide the peace terms. The conference, known as the **Paris Peace Conference** or the **Versailles Peace Conference** was attended by representatives from 32 nations. Soviet Russia was not invited as it had signed a treaty with the Central Powers in 1918 and the Central Powers – Germany, Austria-Hungary, Bulgaria and the Ottoman Empire – too were not allowed in the deliberations.

The United States, Britain, France, Italy and Japan – the '**Big Five**' – dominated the Conference. But the views of the '**Big Four**' Woodrow Wilson, President of the United States, David Lloyd George, Georges Clemenceau and Vittorio Orlando, the Prime Ministers of the United Kingdom, France and Italy, respectively were decisive. Soon it reduced to the '**Council of Three**', when Orlando withdrew from the conference after Wilson refused to give Italy all it demanded.

At the conference each major power had its own agenda and their leaders had different outlooks what the peace should look like.

The United States: America's vision was set out in Woodrow Wilson's **Fourteen Points**. On 8 January 1918 Wilson, in his address to the US Congress, had laid out his ideas for a post-World War settlement. This statement of principles known as the Fourteen Points had facilitated the conditions for the armistice that brought the First World War to an end. Now they were to influence in shaping the contours of the post-war world. The Fourteen Points were–

1. **Open covenants of peace** and abolition of secret diplomacy.
2. Absolute **freedom of navigation** upon the seas.
3. Removal of all economic barriers and establishment of an **equality of trade conditions** among all the nations.
4. Reduction of **national armaments** to the lowest point, consistent with domestic safety.
5. Impartial adjustment of **colonial claims**, with equal weight to the interests of the populations and claims of the governments.
6. Evacuation of all **Russian** territory and assurance of a sincere welcome into the society of free nations.
7. Restoration of **Belgium** as a free nation.
8. Liberation of all **French** territories and restoration of Alsace-Lorraine to France.
9. Readjustment of **Italian** frontiers along the lines of nationality.
10. Self-government for the peoples of **Austria-Hungary**.
11. Restoration of Romania, Serbia and Montenegro, access to the sea by Serbia and international guarantees of the political and economic independence and territorial integrity of the **Balkan states**.
12. Assurance of sovereignty to **Turkey** but self-government for the non-Turkish peoples of the Turkish Empire and opening of the Dardanelles to the ships and commerce of all nations.
13. Establishment of an independent **Polish state** with free and secure access to the sea.
14. Formation of a **general association of nations** for the purpose of affording mutual guarantees of political independence and territorial integrity to great and small states alike.

Woodrow Wilson was an inflexible idealist and had infused his outlook into his Fourteen Points that, as seen above, trumpeted principles of democracy, liberalism and nationalism. Wilsonianism or Wilson's idealism as it began to be called was based on **liberal internationalism** hoping that the peace settlement based on liberal-democratic ideals would sweep away the foundations of future war. He interpreted the war, essentially an outcome of autocracy, imperialism and economic nationalism built on secret alliances, militarism and balance of power politics. Self-determination for all nations, democratic control of diplomacy, open negotiations, disarmament, free trade and collective security were as per Wilson, antidotes to future war.

Woodrow Wilson

Wilson also had some practical objectives in mind. Aware that any harsh treatment might prod Germany for revenge, Wilson insisted for a '**peace without victory**' – a just settlement which would encourage a defeated Germany to work with the victors, not only in building a new Europe but also in preserving peace and remake the world. Similarly, his call for **an association of nations** was aimed at establishing a permanent body for settling disputes and for preservation of justice between great and small states alike.

Wilsonianism did not have a smooth sail at the Conference. At the Conference, Wilson found 'rivalries and conflicting claims previously submerged' erecting barriers before his lofty goals.

1. Most important of these was **France's demand for security** and desire for revenge. Its Premier Clemenceau had expressed scepticism with the Fourteen Points with the comment, 'even the God Almighty has only ten'.
2. Another barrier to Wilson's mission was **intermingling of European nationalities**. As central Europe was made up of mixture of nationalities, it was well-nigh impossible to create a Europe exactly on nationalistic basis or completely free of minority issues. For example, creation of an independent Poland with secure access to sea would mean granting a strip of land to Poland but populated by Germans.
3. Also the secret treaties such as the **Sykes-Picot Agreement** (1916) drawn up by the Allies during the war too were impediments before Wilson's ideals. These secret agreements, providing for division of Ottoman, German and Austrian territories among the Allies themselves, were not in tune with the principle of self-determination envisaged in the Fourteen Points.
4. Moreover, mutual bitterness and **spirit of retribution** had continued to exist in the masses and the leaders alike even after the end of the war. In an atmosphere of desire for war spoils and punishment, spirit of compromise and moderation were hard to be fulfilled.
5. And finally, Wilson's position was undermined in his home front itself by the **victory of the Republicans** in the elections to the American Congress in November 1918. Victory by the Democrats would have signalled endorsement of Wilson's policy by the American people. Instead, the election of 25 Republicans to the Senate implied that Wilson was preaching to Europe when he could not command the support of his own people. It was also interpreted that the Republicans were not keen to involve the United States in the European affairs.

Great Britain: Britain was led by Lloyd George, a clever and witty politician who was not particularly sympathetic to European issues such as nationalism. He wished for a less severe settlement with Germany, for a united and healthy Germany would contribute to European recovery and would also balance the now ascendant power of France. But electoral compulsions, as he had just won a general election in England with slogans such as **'Hang the Kaiser'** and promise of making England 'a country fit for heroes to live in' had been pressure factors on him.

In fact, Lloyd George had an unenviable role to play as he had been accused by the Americans of conspiring with Clemenceau to promote imperialism and at the same time was accused by Clemenceau, of favouring the Germans. Lloyd George was to comment later, that he 'did not do badly, seated as I was between Jesus Christ and Napoleon Bonaparte' in reference to the idealism of Wilson and stark realism of Clemenceau at the Conference.

France: France was represented by Georges Clemenceau, leader of the Radical Party. He was cynical, suspicious of idealism and did not share Wilson's hope for a new world. Nicknamed 'the Tiger', he wanted a harsh peace to ruin Germany strategically, economically and militarily, so that it would never again threaten France.

Clemenceau, who had witnessed two German invasions on France (in 1870 and 1914), wanted to use his country's present advantage to cripple Germany and to secure safety of the French. Germany's greater population, superior industrial strength and military tradition of not resign itself to defeat all were of great concern to France. Further, certain harsh realities of the War, such as France had been summarily attacked in 1914, had suffered the most physical damages, had to sacrifice a generation of its youth and also that the entire battles on the western front had been fought in its territory – all were compelling factors for France to adopt a rigid stand.

France's rigid stand was also a reflection of threefold crises it faced in the post-war period. The threefold crisis were of **security, finance** and **industrial reconstruction**. To meet the first crisis, that is, a guarantee of its future security, Germany had to be weakened permanently. It was France's conviction that without the help of Britain and the United States, France would have been totally destroyed by Germany. Upon this realisation, France stood for an American and British guarantee of French security that wars of 1870 and 1914 would not be repeated.

France expected to tide over these crises through harsher treatment of Germany if the United States and Britain pursued their own interest at the peace conference. To tide over the second crisis, that is, shortage of financial resources for rebuilding the devastated regions, France required capital inflows by way of reparations. Third, to realise the heavy industrial expansion now made possible by the recovery of Alsace-Lorraine, France required German coal as there was a huge shortage of coal in France after the flooding of the French mines by the retreating German forces.

Italy: Italy was represented by Vittorio Orlando, whose powers of diplomacy at the conference were inhibited by his lack of English. Italy had joined the Allies in 1915 on the promise of territories by the Allies in the Treaty of London. Italy had lost more than seven lakh soldiers and had a huge budget deficit incurred from the war. Orlando and his people therefore expected full realisation of the Treaty of London and even some more favours from the conference.

3. The Paris Peace Settlements

After months of negotiations the following settlements were reached at Paris:

1. The covenant of the League of Nations (28 April 1919)
2. The Treaty of Versailles with Germany (28 June 1919)
3. The Treaty of Saint Germain with Austria (10 September 1919)
4. The Treaty of Neuilly with Bulgaria (27 November 1919)
5. The Treaty of Trianon with Hungary (4 June 1920)
6. The Treaty of Sevres with the Ottoman Empire (10 August 1920) revised by the Treaty of Lausanne (24 July 1923).

A. The Treaty of Versailles

Of the treaties, the most significant and controversial was the Treaty of Versailles, criticised even in the Allied countries for being too hard on Germans. The provisions of the treaty such as huge reparations (fixed at 6,600 million pound), disarmament and the Article 231 which imposed the guilt for the war on 'the aggression of Germany and her allies' all were not signs of dawning of a new world envisioned by Wilson. By the Treaty, Germany was punished, disarmed and humiliated. The humiliation and resentment of Germans against the treaty is considered as one of the factors responsible for Nazi electoral success and eventually for the Second World War.

The War Guilt Clause: Germany had to accept the responsibility of Germany and her allies for causing the war and all the loss and damages during the war.

Territorial Provisions:

1. The treaty stripped Germany of 25,000 square miles of territory with 7 million people. Major losses were Alsace-Lorraine to France, Upper Silesia and Polish Corridor to Poland, North Schleswig to Denmark, Memel to Lithuania and Eupen and Malmedy to Belgium.
2. As a compensation for the destruction of French coal mines, Germany was to cede the Saar Coalmines to France for 15 years. After this period, by plebiscite people of the region would decide whether to join Germany or France.
3. Estonia, Latvia and Lithuania were taken from Germany and set up as independent states. Germany had acquired these territories by the Treaty of Brest-Litovsk.
4. The Treaty explicitly prohibited the union between Austria and Germany.
5. Germany had to recognise the independence of Poland and renounce all rights and title over the territory. Germany had to cede Pomerelia to Poland to create the Polish Corridor, so that the new state of Poland could have access to sea. In effect, it cut Germany into two and left Eastern Prussia geographically isolated.
6. Germany was to cede the city of Danzig on the Baltic Sea and the delta of the River Vistula to the League of Nations to establish the Free City of Danzig.
7. Germany had to renounce its colonies and these were to be converted into Mandates under the League of Nations to be controlled by the Allied nations. Under this provision Germany lost Togoland, Cameron, Ruanda-Urundi, German South West Africa (now Namibia) and other territories in Africa and its possessions in Asia such as German Samoa.

Military Restrictions: The Treaty contained comprehensive restrictions on the German armed forces to make it incapable of a future offensive action and also aimed at promoting international disarmament.

1. The Treaty restricted the maximum strength of German army to 1,00,000 men and that of navy to 15,000. Only six battle ships were permitted. Germany was also prohibited from having an air force.
2. Further, to prevent Germany from building up a large cadre of trained men conscription was banned, the number of men allowed to retire early from army was limited, paramilitary forces were forbidden, and the police force was reduced to its pre-war size.
3. The Rhineland (its land along the French border) had to be demilitarised permanently, that is, German troops were banned from all territory west of the Rhine and within 50 kilometres east of the Rhine.
4. Germany was prohibited from manufacturing or stockpiling chemical weapon, armoured cars, tanks and military aircraft and from engaging in arms trade.

Reparations: The treaty required Germany to accept the responsibility of causing the war and to compensate the Allies for the losses and damages to the civilian population and their property. It provided for the establishment of a 'Reparation Commission' to determine the amount and form of such payment by Germany. The Commission in 1921 fixed the total German indemnity at 6,600 million pounds (33 billion US dollar).

Guarantees: In order to ensure the compliance of the provisions by Germany, occupation of the Rhineland by the Allied troops for 15 years was proposed in the treaty.

Evaluation of the Treaty

Reaction in Germany: The German President Friedrich Ebert had to sign it at the threat of resumption of war by the Allies. The National Assembly voted in favour of signing the treaty by a vote of 237 to 138.

In Germany, people of all political shades denounced the treaty and considered it as an insult to the nation's honour. It was seen as **'Carthaginian Peace'** – a peace aimed at complete subjugation of the defeated. Acceptance of the treaty was considered as surrender of German sovereignty and hence the German nationalists, conservatives and ex-military leaders could never forgive the Republic on that account.

A new theory was developed by these nationalists that the German nation had been '**stabbed in the back**' by the socialists and Jews in the government who had first agreed to the armistice and then to the treaty. It was alleged that the Jews and Communists had not supported the war and had played a role in selling out Germany to its enemies. The supporters of this theory argued that Germany had already won on the Eastern Front against Russia and had concluded a favourable treaty. In the west, Germany had seemed to have come close to winning the war with the Spring Offensive in 1918. To support this theory they pointed that while surrendered the German armies were still on the French and Belgian territories. It was the strikes and unrest in the critical military industries at the crucial moment of the war, they argued, what caused Germany's failure. Those who resorted to unrest or who opposed the German nationalism were depicted as conspirators in Germany's failure.

Treaty as violation of the Fourteen Points: First, Germany had signed the armistice in 1918, as an agreement between equals, and had expected the peace terms to be based on Wilson's vision for a new democratic and peaceful post-war world. But Germany had not been even consulted in formulating the Treaty.

Further, it violated Wilson's vision for international disarmament as Britain, France and Italy could maintain forces of their liking while Germany was to be disarmed.

The concept of national self-determination was denied to Germany, as the treaty denied Anschluss (union) with Austria. Further, many ethnic Germans now found themselves living outside the German national boundaries such as in the newly formed state of Czechoslovakia and re-formed country of Poland.

Takeover of German overseas possessions by Britain and France under the Mandate system was another violation of Wilson's plan of 'impartial adjustment of all colonial claims'.

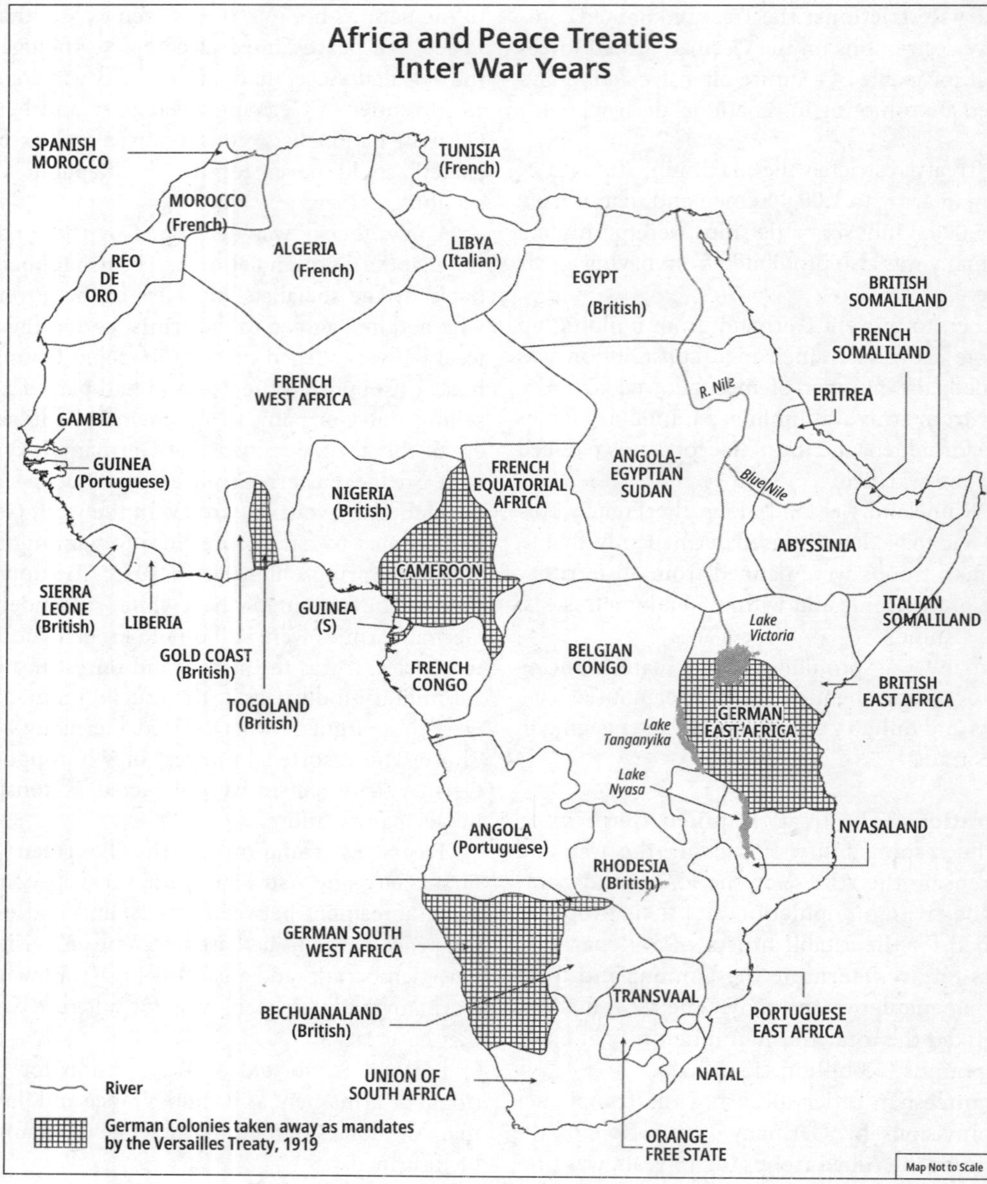

Africa and peace treaties

Treaty as a diktat: The following are illustrative of the Treaty being an imposed one:

1. Germany was not invited in the negotiations.
2. Germany's demand for the removal of certain harsh provisions like Articles 227 (constitution of a special tribunal to try the accused) and 231 (war guilt) were not only rejected but she was also threatened with resumption of war, if Germany failed to sign the treaty.
3. Germany had been issued with an ultimatum of five days' time to accept the Treaty or face an invasion if they failed to sign.
4. The treaty was presented to Germany on a 'take it or face the consequences' manner. Though

they were permitted to express their objections in-writing, these were not considered.

B. The Treaty of Saint Germain

It was signed between Austria and the Allied Powers at Saint Germain-en-Laye near Paris. The treaty officially registered dissolution of the Hapsburg Empire as the Austro-Hapsburg Empire had already crumbled at the end of the war with various nationalities in it proclaiming their independence.

With the treaty, Hungary was separated from Austria. Moreover, Austria was prohibited from union with Germany though it was inhabited by German-speaking people. Conscription was abolished and the Austrian army was limited to a force of 30,000 volunteers.

As a result of the Treaty, independent states of **Hungary, Czechoslovakia** (consisting Bohemia and Moravia), **Yugoslavia** (by incorporating Bosnia-Herzegovina with Serbia and consisting Serbs, Croats and Slovenes) and **Poland** (by acquiring Galicia) came into existence. Austria also had to surrender Trieste, Istria and southern Tirol and the Trentino to Italy. Altogether Austria lost three-fourth of its area and its people and became a small landlocked country with its population concentrated in the city of Vienna.

C. The Treaty of Neuilly

It was signed with Bulgaria at Neuilly, a suburb of Paris. By the treaty Bulgaria lost Western Thrace to Greece thus depriving her of Aegean coastline. She also lost territories on her western border to Yugoslavia. Bulgarian army was limited to 20,000 men.

D. The Treaty of Trianon

It was signed with Hungary at Trianon Palace at Versailles. The treaty was based on the idea of '**self-determination of peoples**' and attempts were made to give non-Hungarians their own national states. For the purpose, Slovakia and Ruthenia were ceded to Czechoslovakia, Transylvania to Romania and Croatia-Slovenia to Yugoslavia.

By the treaty, Hungary lost two-third of its former territory and two-thirds of its population was made a land locked state and its armed forces were restricted to 35,000 men.

E. The Treaty of Sevres

This treaty was signed with Ottoman Turkey, in Sevres, a suburb of Paris. It put an end to the Ottoman Empire and ended Turkey's rights over all non-Turkish territories.

It provided for independence of **Armenia** and autonomy for **Kurdistan**. Most of the Turkish territories in Europe such as Eastern Thrace and the Aegean islands commanding the Dardanelles and Smyrna on Turkish mainland were given to Greece. Adalia and Rhodes were given to Italy. Palestine and Mesopotamia became **British mandates**, Syria and Lebanon **French mandates** and Southern Anatolia a sphere of influence of Italy. The Straits such as the Dardanelles and the Sea of Marmara were declared open in times of peace and war alike to all vessels of commerce and war.

Mustapha Kemal

The Turkish nationalists under **Mustapha Kemal** (later called Ataturk) who had established a revolutionary government at Ankara rejected the treaty, though the sultan had signed it. They rebelled against foreign influence in Anatolia and Constantinople and chased the Greeks out of Smyrna and the Italians from Anatolia. The nationalists captured Constantinople in November 1922 and deposed the Sultan.

These developments forced the Allies to revise the settlement with Turkey. With the **Treaty of Lausanne**, signed in July 1923 in Switzerland, the borders of modern-day Turkey were redefined. Turkey regained Smyrna and Eastern Thrace, including Constantinople. With this treaty, Turkey renounced all claims on the Dodecanese Islands, Cyprus, Egypt, Sudan, Syria and Iraq. In return, the Allies dropped their demands of autonomy for Turkish Kurdistan, claims to spheres of influence in Turkey and also for controls over Turkey's finances or armed forces.

Consequently, Turkey was proclaimed a republic on 29 October 1923 with **Ataturk** as its first President and **Ankara** as the capital. The **Caliphate** was abolished in March 1924 and members of the Ottoman dynasty were expelled from Turkey.

Thus, Turkey became the first state to successfully challenge and revise the Paris Settlement, by the Treaty of Lausanne, which in course of time was to prove a durable solution to the old 'Eastern Question'.

4. Evaluation of the Paris Settlements

The Paris settlements were not conspicuous success and had the potential to generate further issues and conflict zones in world politics.

1. In immediate terms, it had the unfortunate effect of **dividing Europe** into two – those dissatisfied with the settlement hence wanted to revise it, and those who wanted to preserve it. The dissatisfied nations included not only the defeated states like Germany but also Italy, which was on the side of the Allies.
2. The manner of convening the peace conference and the signing of the final agreement was **authoritarian in nature**. In settling the peace, neither Germany nor other Central Powers had been consulted and hence was a dictated peace. After finalising the treaty, Germany was given just five days to accept it or to face invasion. Even at the signing ceremony, the German representatives were humiliated as they were 'escorted in and out of the hall in the manner of criminals' and were not even permitted to sit.
3. Even though the guiding idea behind the Fourteen Points had been 'self-determination', the Paris Peace Settlements had **violated the self-determination principles** in many respects. Some of the examples in this regard were as follows: more than three million Germans in Sudetenland had found themselves in the new state of Czechoslovakia and more than a million Germans were placed in Poland. Hitler was to use these two instances as an excuse for his territorial aggrandisement on these countries. Similarly, Transylvania had more than half Hungarian population but was incorporated with Romania. The Slovakia region had not only Slovaks but a million Magyars and half a million Ruthenians, but these territories had been detached from Hungary to create Czechoslovakia. Though these measures were, as argued by the Allies, aimed at making the newly created states economically viable, the real intention was to weaken Germany and Hungary and to strengthen the successor states. Hungary considered these as violation of its historical character which sowed seeds of resentment and ethnic conflict in the inter-war period. At the outset of the Second World War, Hungary with the support of Nazi Germany and Fascist Italy expanded its borders by dissolving Czechoslovakia and by invading Yugoslavia as part of irredentism. The **Mandate System** too violated the self-determination principle as territories of the vanquished, located outside Europe were placed under European nations and not to the people of these regions.
4. The peace settlements had resemblance more closely of a **sentence from a court** than a negotiated one. Treaty provisions such as the war guilt, huge reparations that were impossible to pay, deprivation of territory of the defeated powers in violation of the principle of self-determination all were expressions of punitive settlement.
5. The Paris settlements redrew the **geography of Europe** and its neighbourhood with huge implications in the history of the world. It broke up German, Austrian and Ottoman empires and carved new independent states – Finland, Estonia, Latvia, Lithuania, Poland, Czechoslovakia and Yugoslavia – apart from segregating Austria from Hungary. Turkey emerged as an independent republic, while Syria, Lebanon, Palestine and Iraq were placed as Mandates of Britain or France. Though theoretically these new states were based on nationality, some minorities inevitably remained in most states which became an important factor in the instability that marked Europe after the World War I, well demonstrated in the Balkans, a synonym for violent nationalist unrest.
6. **Defenders of the peace settlement** argue that, if the Germans had won the war, treaty imposed by them would have been much harsher. They point to the German war aims, which had called for German expansion not only in Europe but also in central Africa, and also to the Treaty of Brest-Litovsk that Germany signed with Russia which was very harsh. To argue their part, they also point out factors such as Germany had a population almost double that of France even after the Treaty, its territory had not been

attacked or destroyed during the war, while 10 richest provinces of France had witnessed total devastation during the War.

7. Incorporated in each of the five treaties was the **Covenant of the League of Nations** based on the principle of collective security. Woodrow Wilson had expected a functioning League, so that it could correct whatever injustices that had crept into the treaties themselves. But the League never lived up to its potential.

8. The settlements reached at Paris did not get wholehearted support from **the international community**. The United States did not ratify the settlement and Russia was not part of it. Italy felt cheated for not receiving all that had been promised to her during the war. Britain feeling guilty over the treatment of Germany had lost the will for enforcement. Eventually, responsibility for preserving the settlement rested with France alone.

Post World War I Europe

5. International Relations in the Inter-War Period

A. The French Quest for Security

During the inter-war period France, a nation of 40 million, was haunted by the memories of the brutalities of the World War I. Its economy and territory devastated and faced with an enemy of 70 million (Germany), France was in search of measures to ensure its security. Following were the steps taken by France in this direction:

- It insisted on a **harsh treatment of Germany** in the Paris Peace Settlements, to make it incapable of initiating another attack on France.
- German **reparation amount** was kept very high (6,600 million pounds to be paid in annual

instalments) to straddle her for the next 66 years. French troops also occupied the Ruhr, the German industrial region in 1923 to enforce reparation obligations.

- Though France joined the **Washington Naval Conference 1921** and agreed to limit her battleships, she refused to accept any limitations on her submarines.
- France formed military alliances known as the **'Little Entente'** with Poland (1921), Czechoslovakia (1924), Romania (1926) and with Yugoslavia (1927).
- The **Locarno Pact** was signed in 1925 between Great Britain, France, Germany, Italy and Belgium. By this France could get a guarantee from Germany that the frontiers drawn in the Versailles Settlement as permanent.
- France also took certain **conciliatory steps**. France sponsored German entry into the League of Nations (1926), granted certain concessions such as agreeing to the Young Plan (1929) which eased German reparation obligations and she also ended occupation of the German Rhineland in 1930, five years ahead of the schedule.
- France also took initiative in framing the **Briand-Kellogg Pact** in 1928. (Briand was the French foreign minister and Kellogg was American Secretary of State.) By this step 65 nations renounced war as national policy.
- In the background of increasing popularity of the Nazis in Germany, in the **World Disarmament Conference** in Geneva (1932–33), France refused to disarm as she believed that her security was based on her armaments. In response to this French stand Hitler withdrew Germany both from the Disarmament Conference and from the League of Nations.
- In the 1930s, France built **Maginot Line**, massive defence lines along its German border. It consisted of underground fortresses, blockhouses, bunkers and rail lines.
- She signed **the Franco-Soviet Pact** in 1935. This mutual assistance treaty was signed after the German declaration of rearmament in March 1935. At the same time, it is important to note that this treaty was taken as an excuse by Hitler to justify remilitarisation of the Rhineland in March 1936 and for denouncing the Locarno Pact as he was threatened by the Franco-Soviet Pact.

B. World's Search for Peace

Haunted by horrors of the World War, world community was in search of mechanisms to secure peace in the post-War period. This quest for peace was well evident in many conferences held and in treaties signed during this period.

- The **League of Nations** was formed in January 1920, with principal mission to maintain world peace.
- The **Washington Naval Treaty 1922** provided for limitation on their navies by five great naval powers – the United States, Britain, France, Italy and Japan.
- **Dawes Plan 1924:** This was a scheme devised by an international committee of financial experts headed by American banker **Charles Dawes** in August 1924, to resolve the issue of German reparations which was accepted by the Allies and Germany.

Though the Plan did not reduce total reparation obligation, it changed the rate at which Germany would pay. It provided for a series of graduated annuities beginning at 1 billion Mark in 1924–25. The German central bank was also re-organised under supervision of international financial experts.

The Dawes Plan also offered an immediate loan of £ 40 million from the United States, (total foreign loan amounted to 800 million gold mark) enabling German industry to rebuild and expand. Foreign loan enabled Germany to make its reparation payments to France and Britain, which in turn was used by these countries to service their war debts to the United States. The French troops withdrew from the Ruhr easing tensions for the Republic and once again the German industry began to undergo a period of boom.

- **Locarno Pact 1925:** Also known as the Locarno Treaties, it consisted of a series of agreements initiated in Locarno, Switzerland, whereby Germany, France, Britain, Italy, Belgium, Poland and Czechoslovakia agreed to maintain tranquillity of Europe and to extinguish hostility between Germany and France.

It provided for mutual guarantee of inviolability of Franco-German and German-Belgian borders as fixed by the Treaty of Versailles, a promise not to attack each other, to use arbitration instead as a means of resolving disputes and a guarantee by Britain and Italy to assist the attacked country, if the agreement ever broken. This eased the stressful relation between Germany and France as it met the insistent French demand for security and removed German fear of French occupation as had happened in 1923. The reconciliation between France and Germany was called as the '**Locarno Honeymoon**' which raised expectations for continued peaceful settlements and was often referred to as the '**Spirit of Locarno**'.

The Pact also contained arbitration treaties between Germany and Poland and Germany and Czechoslovakia for settling their future disputes. The success of the Locarno Agreements led to admission of Germany into the League of Nations in 1926 as a permanent member.

- The **Kellogg-Briand Pact** 1928: By this, 45 countries (later on by 65 nations), including Germany and Russia, **renounced wars as instrument of state policy** – only wars of aggression and not military acts of self-defence. It also called upon the signatories to settle their disputes by peaceful means. Frank B. Kellogg was the Secretary of State of the United States and Aristide Briand was French Foreign Minister.
- **Young Plan 1929:** The Young Plan was a revised program for settling Germany's world war reparation obligations. The Plan was prepared by a committee headed by American industrialist, **Owen Young**, in 1929.

As per the Young Plan Germany's reparation debt was reduced from 6,600 million pound to 2,000 million pound payable over 59 years. The Plan also established the **Bank for International Settlements** to handle the reparation transfer. It also provided for withdrawal of last of the occupying troops from Germany. All these developments appeared to have placed Germany on economic recovery, political stability, internal order and international support.

Nobel Peace Prize: Significance of international efforts to ease tensions during this period was also recognised by the Nobel Committee. In 1925, Charles Dawes was co-awarded the Nobel Peace Prize for his contribution to the resolution of the world crisis and in 1926 Richard Stresemann was awarded the Nobel Peace Prize for his reconciliation measures in international politics. Frank Kellogg was awarded the Nobel Peace Prize in 1929 for his role in shaping the Kellogg-Briand Pact.

- **The Lausanne Conference 1932:** At this conference, held in the background of deepening crisis of the Great Depression Britain, France and Germany reached an agreement to suspend the German war reparations. By now Germany had paid only one-eighth of the sum required by the Treaty of Versailles and the Lausanne Protocol in effect put an end to further exactions from Germany.
- **The World Disarmament Conference (1932–34).** This was convened in Geneva to discuss measures to be adopted for disarmament. But it failed in securing the objective as France refused to disarm citing threat from Nazi Germany, while Germany demanded parity in arms with France.

C. American Isolationism

Though the United States had played a crucial role in the war and in the Paris Peace Conference, the decades following these were characterised by the US isolationism in international politics. Two major reasons for this American policy were war weariness of the American people and Republican success in succession in the US Presidential elections in 1920, 1924 and 1928. The Republicans were against involving America in European affairs. Below given are some examples of this policy of isolationism:

- The United States refused to join the League of Nations.
- She also refused to write off the war debts of European nations and insisted on full repayment.
- The United States continued to maintain high tariffs making it difficult for European nations to export to the United States and to earn dollars to pay back their war debts.
- The United States refused to recognise Soviet Russia till 1933.
- In the 1930s, the United States refused to join hands with other nations to curb the acts of aggressions by Japan, Italy and Germany.
- In 1935, the US Congress passed Neutrality Acts prohibiting loans and arms to nations at war.

At the same time, the post-World War period was the period of emergence of the United States as a leading power in the world. During the war the European economy had been damaged but that of the United States had expanded. Its tremendous industrial expansion was supported by advances in science and technology. Moreover, during this period she emerged as the main creditor to the European nations.

6. Society in the Inter-War Period

A sense of disillusionment and cynicism was the pronounced factor in social life in the period. The generation that came of age during the World War I was called as **the Lost Generation**, a generation that could never fully recover from its trauma. Perturbed by the violence many turned to Pacifism and many others turned to internationalism as they were revolted at the concept of nationalism.

> ***Modern Man in Search of a Soul*** is a book by Swiss psychologist Carl Gustav Jung. Published in 1933, the book talks about 'the catastrophic results of the World War .... the shattering of our faith in ourselves and our own worth'.

The shock of the war and its brutalities had upset the European conscience and many viewed life as spiritually barren and uncertain. Art and literature too reflected this outlook. In art **abstract**, dada and surrealism acquired prominence. Abstract paintings consisted of lines, shapes and colours with no recognisable subjects. **Dadaism** as an artistic movement rejected all traditional conventions. **Surrealism** portrayed the inner workings of the mind and depicted objects in unrealistic ways. In philosophy a new movement known as **Existentialism** emphasised that there is no universal meaning to life and people by their own choices and actions make meaning to their life.

Society in the post-War period reflected new ideas and freedom. As the War had disrupted traditional social patterns, people were ready to experiment with new values. During this period there was distinct cultural shift in terms of ideas about morality and a shift in social roles. Co-educational institutions marked this transition where women in large numbers attended and more and more women entered in careers such as medicine, journalism and teaching. As careers opened up, more women worked outside their homes. Women who rejected the established moral values and enjoyed the new air of freedom were known as **Flappers**. Fuelled by the writings of the psychoanalyst Sigmund Freud which promoted an understanding that men and women have the same human impulses and sexual desires, women liberation efforts were intensified at this time. Jazz as a distinct form of music combining Western harmonies with African rhythms emerged and symbolised the new freedom.

Advances in technology had tremendous impact on society. The World War had fuelled development of new drugs and methods of treatment which were of help to millions of people now. Automobiles, air travel, radio and motion pictures transformed social life in the post-War period.

7. Economy in Inter-War Period

A. Post-World War I Economic Crisis

The World War I had been financed mainly by means of credit. The United States had provided $10.3 billion to the Allies. After the war, even though the European nations had been in a financial crisis, the United States, the prime creditor, did not wave the war debts upon which the Allies had to rely mainly on German reparations.

Another significant economic development was the emergence of a unique economic pattern. This economic pattern was based on German reparation payments, American loan and the French, British and Belgium debt. Under this pattern the Germany was to pay the reparations to France, Britain and Belgium if the Americans grant loan to Germany, which in turn was used by them to pay their war debts to the Americans. By the last years of the 1920s, the drying up of the American credit made it difficult for Germany to pay reparations and the onset of the Great Depression hammered the final blow.

At the same time, it was not just war reparations and debt that caused trouble in the post-war economy. Even though the World War had come to an end in 1918, many local conflicts and clashes such as that in Turkey and in the Balkans continued to strain the European economy.

Occupation of the German Ruhr region by the French and Belgian troops in 1923 as retaliation for default in reparations was another factor that complicated the economic crisis. Germans resorted to passive resistance upon which the French gained nothing and in Germany it caused a terrible inflation.

Further, in the aftermath of the World War, many countries had adopted welfare state measures. The onset of Great Depression and increase in unemployment put great strain on these welfare states.

Roaring Twenties: Roaring Twenties refer to the decade after the World War I. This was a period of socio-cultural and economic dynamism especially in the United States and to lesser extent in Europe. Rapid industrial growth, large-scale production of automobiles, radios, telephones and electrical appliances accelerated the consumer demand. The period ended with the Great Depression.

B. Great Depression

The United States had come out of the First World War in better financial level than before it and in the 1920s prospered further. But, underlying the prosperity, there were serious weaknesses in the US economy.

In spite of economic growth, there was **uneven distribution of wealth**, so and so that by 1929 the richest 5 per cent of the population had amassed 33% of all personal income. In other words, while the economy expanded, it left the bulk of the population impoverished creating a fundamental maldistribution of purchasing power, leaving huge sections of its population without the means to buy what was being produced.

Further, there was **overproduction** both in industry and agriculture. By 1929, America produced nearly half of the world's industrial output. Similarly, by 1929, there was an excess supply of houses that had resulted from the house construction boom of the mid-1920s. Farm machinery and scientific farming techniques had enabled American farmers to produce huge surplus while at the same time competition from Europe and Latin American farm products had caused prices and profits down. Unable to sell their products and crops many businessmen and farmers failed to pay off their loans.

It was in this background that the Federal Reserve (the central bank of the United States) increased the **interest rates** to rein in the rapid rise in stock prices. This was important because during the 1920s, large number of Americans had purchased stock on credit taking the stock prices to very high and well beyond their real worth.

Increase in interest rates in turn led to reduction in spending in housing, automobile and so forth causing a **reduction in consumption** responding to which factories reduced production and laid off workers.

Till then the American stock market had witnessed a boom in the form of soaring prices of stocks and by 1929 the stock prices had reached beyond the levels of reasonable anticipations of future earnings. In September 1929, buying of shares in the **Wall Street** slowed down supported by the spread of rumour of the end of the speculative boom. Crisis started, when some investors started selling their stocks, on the assumption that growth in share prices was far faster than the growth in physical trade. Soon people started rushing to sell their stocks before further sharp drop in their prices. This in turn resulted in lowering of share prices leading to **panic selling**. On 24 October 1924, the **'Black Thursday'** the stock market bubble burst as a result of panic selling which is known as the **Wall Street Crash** or **the Great Crash** of 1929. On October 29, Tuesday, a record 16 million stocks were sold resulting in the stock market collapse.

Another blow occurred when large number of people in financial difficulties rushed to banks to withdraw their savings resulting in what is known as the **'Banking panic'**. This hasty liquidation caused failure in the banking system and one-third of all banks vanished. Collapse of the banking system resulted in the evaporation of the life's savings of millions. Closure of thousands of banks also disrupted lending, further reducing funds available for investment and thereby strengthening a phenomenon called **money contraction**.

Cumulative impact of all these – stock market collapse, closing down of banks and business, reduction in wages and laying off – resulted in further reduction in the buying capacity of the people. In response, factories made further cuts in production resulting in more workers losing their jobs and families buying fewer goods. All these resulted in a long business slump which began to be called as the **Great Depression**. Unemployment was the main symptom of the depression and by 1933 one-fourth of the Americans were unemployed. The Great Depression became the harshest adversity faced by the United States since the Civil War (1861–65) and had devastating effects beyond the borders of America too.

How did this become a global concern?

By this time the world economy had been highly dependent on the United States because of loans, investment and trade. Now, the American bankers started demanding the repayment of their overseas loans and the American investors withdrawing their investment abroad. To tide over the crisis the US government also imposed high tariffs on import, denying American market for European goods (Tariff Act of 1930 imposed near record tax rates on imported goods). Following America, other nations too raised their tariff barriers leading to a 65% drop in the world trade. Latin America with its dependence on the United States for selling its raw materials was the first foreign region to be affected. With fall in demand, closing down of industries, drop in export, soaring unemployment, fall in government revenue and drop in international trade, the economic downturn found its reverberation all through the world. This was evident from the fact that during 1929 to 1932 the world economy had declined by 38 percent and world trade by two-thirds.

How did the world tackle this crisis?

For the world nations, the Great Depression was both a political and economic crisis. Democracies came under severe pressure, while in many countries **authoritarianism** replaced democracy as illustrated in Germany. To cope with the crisis Britain established a **National Government** consisting of major parties which adopted measures like tax increase, high tariffs and lowering of interest rates. In France too, a coalition government known as the **Popular Front** took measures to tide over the crisis but was not successful enough. The Scandinavian countries such as Norway, Sweden and Denmark strengthened cooperative bodies, increased unemployment insurance and pension for the aged apart from initiating large number of public work projects.

In the United States, the epicentre of the crisis, government initiated a multi-faceted reform program known as the New Deal. It was aimed at preserving the capitalist system. Initiated by the **Franklin D Roosevelt** administration, the **New Deal** (1933–39) involved massive socio-economic programs and projects to increase purchasing power of the masses and to combat the ravages of the Great Depression.

In 1932, Presidential elections Roosevelt as the candidate of the Democrats had promised a 'new deal' to meet the Great Depression. When implemented, these measures signalled a departure from 'laissez-faire' to government intervention in economy and caused expansion of the US federal government in its size and scope. These measures aimed at providing quick economic relief, regulation of private industry, stabilisation of economy to take America out of the crisis. These steps were in contrast to the policy of Roosevelt's Republican predecessor Herbert Hoover that government need not play an aggressive role in economic bailout.

Franklin Delano Roosevelt or **FDR** was the 32nd President of the United States. He was the cousin of the former US President Theodore Roosevelt. He was the Governor of New York for two terms before becoming the President of the United States. His promise to the people of America of 'action, and action now' and assuring words 'the only thing we have to fear is fear itself' were crucial in boosting the morale of the people in hard times. Through his radio addresses known as 'fireside chats' he communicated his ideas and programs with millions of Americans resulting in remarkable turnaround in the public confidence. Though he had been stricken with poliomyelitis at the age of 39, with indomitable confidence he won Presidential post four times – the only president elected to the office four times – from 1933 to till his death in 1945.

The New Deal can be summed up in **Three 'R's.** These were **Relief** to those affected by depression, **Recovery** of the economy through Federal spending and **Reform** of the capitalist system as a safeguard against future depressions through a series of regulatory legislations and social welfare programs.

There were two phases in the New Deal. The **First New Deal** (1933–34) started with **'The First**

Hundred Days' (March–June 1933) during which he summoned the US Congress for a nearly 100-day special session and passed series of legislations creating '**Alphabet Agencies**', called so because of their acronyms. Some of these were:

- **AAA** – Agricultural Adjustment Act (1933) was passed specifically to combat rural economic crisis. It provided subsidies to farmers to produce less and thereby to boost agricultural prices by reducing surplus.
- **CCC** – Civilian Conservation Corps (1933) provided jobs to unemployed unmarried men on federally funded conservation projects such as tree plantation and prevention of soil erosion.
- **FERA** – Federal Emergency Relief Administration (1933) provided federal grants to states to meet expenditure on direct-aid to the poor programs to alleviate household unemployment. In 1935, the Works Progress Administration and Social Security Administration replaced FERA.
- **TVA** – Tennessee Valley Authority was established in 1933 to develop the Tennessee River watershed spanning across seven states. The Authority constructed 16 dams along the Tennessee River to control floods, improve living standards of farmers and to generate electricity. Fringe benefits too were significant in the form of jobs, low-cost housing, reforestation, industrial development and recreational tourism.
- **NIRA** – National Industrial Recovery Act (1933) aimed at setting prices and wages in different industrial sectors. It recognised the right of workers to organise workers' unions. The Act also created the National Recovery Administration tasked with eliminating cut-throat competition and to promote fair codes of competition in industrial sector.
- **FDIC** – Federal Deposit Insurance Corporation (1933) was created to provide insurance coverage for bank deposits in case bank went bankrupt.
- **SEC** – Securities and Exchange Commission (1934) was established to regulate the stock market and to enforce new securities laws aimed at preventing stock manipulation.

As situation continued to be unstable, the **Second New Deal** (1935–38) was launched. During this stage, emphasis was placed on creating durable assets and financial security.

- **WPA** – Works Progress Administration (1935), was tasked with providing employment in public projects such as roads and bridges. It also ensured payment to all kinds of people including artists, actors and writers who contributed in constructing assets around the country in projects such as painting murals and preparing national park guidebooks.
- **Social Security Administration** (1935). This was aimed at combating poverty among senior citizens through a national pension fund, unemployment insurance system and by providing assistance for dependent mothers, children and the disabled.
- **Wagner Act** (1935) or **National Labor Relations Act** guaranteed right of workers to form unions, take collective actions such as strikes, and created National Labor Relations Board to supervise union elections and violations of labour law.
- **Fair Labor Standards Act** (1938) provided for hourly minimum wage, set the standard for forty hour work week and banned child labour.

> John Maynard Keynes was an English economist. In his book *The General Theory of Employment, Interest and Money*, published in 1936, he argued that depressions do not disappear of their own. He stood for aggressive action to kick start economy through 'deliberate and sustained countercyclical spending'.

The New Deal was not fully successful. It achieved some notable accomplishments but failed in ensuring full-scale economic recovery. The judiciary too put hurdles. Conservative majority in the Supreme Court invalidated many of reform efforts such as the National Industrial Recovery Administration and the Agricultural Adjustment Administration as unconstitutional as they extended the federal powers. Finally, it was quadrupling in defence production with the outbreak of the Second World War and the American entry into the World War with massive military expenditure that stimulated industrial production and took America out of the Great Depression.

What all were the gains of the new deal?
First, by putting people back to work, it restored sense of security of the American population. It also reaffirmed the Americans faith in their democratic political system. With the construction of a network of hospitals, schools, roads and others it strengthened infrastructure. By forming a framework for regulatory state, the New Deal tried to protect the interests of all Americans whether rich or poor and created an environment in which the private sector could work in a more productive way. Finally, what the New Deal did was not just adjusting interest rates, providing farm subsidies or creating short-term employment programs, it instilled a firm belief in American people that an interventionist government is good for families, economy and the nation and many of such programs such as social security and federal subsidies continue to exist in the United States.

8. | Polity in the Inter-War Period

A. End of Autocracies

As seen already, one of the direct political impacts of the First World War was the end of the absolute monarchies in Europe. These were the **Russian Empire, the German Empire, the Austro-Hungarian Empire** and the **Ottoman Empire**. The Revolution in 1917 had ended the Tsar autocracy in Russia and with the defeat of the Central Powers the German, Austro-Hungarian and Ottoman empires too collapsed.

Out of these empires emerged new states – Russia based on Communist ideology and other states based on the ideals of popular sovereignty, liberalism and nationalism. From the old Russian Empire also emerged the new states of Poland, Finland, Latvia, Lithuania and Estonia, of the old Habsburg Empire the new states of Austria, Hungary, Czechoslovakia and Yugoslavia, on the ruins of the Ottoman Empire a secular democratic republic was established in Turkey and in Germany, a democratic republic known as the Weimer Republic was established. All these countries adopted written constitutions and elected their legislatures through universal suffrage.

In Ireland, which had been fighting for freedom from Britain, an Irish Free State with Dominion status was created in 1922. For the purpose, Ireland was partitioned with Northern Ireland of six counties remaining in the United Kingdom and the southern part forming the Irish Free State. The Irish Free State later on emerged as the Republic of Ireland.

The period also witnessed the spread of democratic practices even in the established democracies with extension of voting rights to women – in Britain (1918) and in the United States (1920).

B. Decline of Democracies

But the post-World War conditions, pressures and strains were soon to result in the demise of democracy altogether in many of these countries. There were many reasons for the failure of democracies in Europe during this period.

Economic crisis was most important of these. As seen above, the world war had disoriented the economy and the newly created nations were undergoing a period of economic challenges. The misery caused by the war as a result of millions of death, injury and destruction was now multiplied by unemployment and price rise causing widespread discontent. The European nations had also been saddled with enormous national debts those owed by the Allies to each other as well as to the United States. The economic situation got further complicated by inflation and then depression. Moreover, erection of customs barriers and other protective tariff measures by the nations too were of importance.

Secondly, in spite of the efforts to create new nations on nationalistic basis, the **minority issue** had remained unresolved in these nations. Conflicts of interests of these national minorities were unlikely to create a fertile ground for democracy to take roots. Minorities, infested with nationalist sentiments, encouraged discontent in the newly established countries of Europe.

Adding to the woes of democracies was increased **class consciousness** leading to class conflicts. The common people who had contributed in great measures during the war now found their demands and interests being neglected by the governments. In most of the cases, control of the governments and formulation of the policies were still in the hands of aristocratic and industrial classes, who were not ready to surrender these to the less privileged majorities. This non-inclusive political structure, coupled with the neglect of the interests of the less privileged majorities, caused discontent among the people and opposition to the existing regimes.

Lack of democratic experiences had been another factor. The people of these new democracies, who lived under despotic monarchs for generations, did not have experience of representative government. Existence of large number of political parties, formation of unstable coalition governments and frequent changes in policies followed and proved fatal, for they failed in solving crises. Under such conditions people looked for strong and authoritarian government in place of their weak democratic systems. Further, many of these states were weak and unaccustomed to practices of tolerance, inclusiveness, compromise and incremental change which were essential for democracy to take its roots.

In the above background, it was easy for totalitarian leaders to capture the attention of the masses by preaching the destruction of the political system that failed in solving issues of economic chaos, fulfilling nationalistic aspirations and in resolving class conflicts.

C. Rise of Totalitarianism

Totalitarianism refers to a form of government in which state's power is unlimited and it imposes total control over every aspect of public and private life. Hungary under Miklos Horthy (1919) was the first post-war dictator in Europe. Poland under Josef Pilsudski (1926) was another example. In Romania, Albania, Bulgaria and Yugoslavia too authoritarian forces captured power. Russia under Stalin was another example of brutal form of totalitarianism. In Portugal, Antonio de Salazar captured power replacing a republic that had been in place since 1910. In Greece, a dictatorship was established under Ioannis Metaxas in 1936. In Spain, General Francisco Franco established his dictatorship in 1939 after a brutal civil war. The only countries that remained out of authoritarianism in Europe were Britain, France, Czechoslovakia and the Scandinavians. The destruction of democracy and the emergence of totalitarianism were best exemplified by Fascism in Italy and its German brand Nazism.

9. Origin and Features of Fascism

The term fascism is derived from the Latin word ***fasces*** denoting a bundle of rods tied around an axe which was the symbol of authority of the ancient Roman state. It symbolised **strength through unity**. The term in political context is used to denote organisations representing **radical authoritarian nationalism** and acquired prominence in the 20th century Europe. The two historical regimes that are regarded as paradigmatically fascists were Benito Mussolini's fascist Italy and Adolf Hitler's Nazi Germany. Apart from the fascist regimes, there were fascist parties too in Europe, Latin America and in the Middle East in the inter-war period.

The origin and growth of fascist movements can be viewed from different angles. One of these is to view it, as seen above, as a response to post-war conditions of **economic dislocation and political instability** prevailed in many European states. Another angle is that it was a reaction to the **failure of liberal and democratic institutions** in solving the multitudes of problems that emerged in the modern industrial society such as class exploitation, unemployment and the widening of poor–rich divide. Fascism was also a product of **anxiety and fear that the Bolshevik Revolution** would spread to other countries of Europe. Extension of Bolshevik Revolution to other European countries meant destruction of property relations and private interests. The propertied class believed the fascists as the protectors of the interests of the rich and the aristocracy, hence they welcomed the fascist groups. The fascist movements were also a clear demonstration of the fact that ideals and institutions of democracy are not easy to emulate and retain. In countries with **weak democratic traditions** people repose their faith on non-rational approaches and in charismatic leaders who promise panacea for all the ills of their country.

The fact that the fascist ideology had never been expounded by a theoretical writer as what Karl Marx did for communism makes a proper understanding of its ideological underpinnings difficult. But, there are certain features found in common in different versions of fascism.

- **Extreme Nationalism:** Fascists movements, irrespective of differences in their backgrounds, were marked by extreme nationalism. The fascists view the national identity as the foundation of individual identity. They hold nation as a **natural unifying force** of people and seeks **regeneration of nation** for solving its socio, economic and political ills. The fascists believe in the rebirth of the nation after a period of its degeneration. Hence, 'palingenesis' or regeneration of the nation, by purging of its decadence, is an idea very close to the hearts of the fascists.

- **Totalitarian State:** Fascists conceive the state as all-embracing and believe that outside of which no human or spiritual values can exist. In such a state, government attempts to arouse, mobilise and control as many aspects of people's lives as possible. A Fascist state also aims at purging of ideas that are inconsistent with their beliefs and resorts to indoctrination through education and media, glorifying the fascist policies and need for obedience to the state. For the fascists, a totalitarian state is also a strong state which guarantees totality of political unity transcending all diversity. For this reason fascists also believe that a pluralistic society as disastrous to the existence of a strong state.

Doctrine of Fascism is an essay attributed to Mussolini which was published in 1932. In the essay, Mussolini emphasised the importance of the state in the words, 'If the 19th century was the century of the individual, we are free to believe that this is the collective century and therefore the century of the state – everything in the state, nothing against the state and nothing outside the state'.

- **Opposition to Liberalism:** The fascists oppose liberalism for its emphasis on **individualism**. Liberalism denied the state in the interests of the individual, while fascism reaffirmed the state as the true reality of the individual. These contrasting conceptions regarding the individual and the state, by the liberals and the fascists was a focal point of conflict between the Liberals and the Fascists. Individualism promotes the exercise of one's goals and desires, and values independence, while opposing external interference upon one's own interests by society or by government. Individualism thus involves the **right of the individual to freedom and self-realisation** and is based on the premise that the human individual is of primary importance in the struggle for liberation.

As against this, the Fascist conception of the state is all embracing, outside of it no human or spiritual values can exist. It is a **synthesis of all values** which interprets, develops and potentiates the whole life of its people. In this sense, Fascism stood to undo the legacy of the French Revolution of 1789. Mussolini declared that 'we stand for a new principle in the world. A world which stands for the sheer, categorical, definitive antithesis to the world of democracy and liberalism, the fundamental principles laid down in 1789'.

- **Opposition to Marxism:** Fascism opposes Marxism, on the premise that **class conflicts divide a nation**. In opposition to Marxism, Fascism stood for ending class hostilities that divide and weaken a nation and thereby **integration** of the proletariat in to the nation. The fascist opposition to Marxism also sprang from the belief, that the Marxists' call for the unity of the workers of the world, as a threat to their concept of the **national community**. In other words, Marxism stood for **internationalism**, while Fascism stood for **authoritarian nationalism**.
- **Opposition to rationalism and the ideas of Enlightenment:** Fascism opposed rationality and replaced it with will, feeling and instinct. Fascists opposed rational discussion and critical analysis, as they germinate divisive tendencies in the nation, promote doubts and enfeeble the will. On the other, the Fascists stood for arousal and manipulation of brutal and primitive impulses and instinctive aggressive action.

Fascism views the rationalistic developments since the Enlightenment as a descent into depravity. It is invariably hostile to broad learning or expressing deviant or innovative points of view, since such pursuits threaten the dominance of fascist myths.

- **Exaltation of the Leader:** Fascism exalted the leader, a 'righteous' one who has total grasp of what is best for the nation. Hitler was the ***Fuhrer*** and Mussolini the ***Duce***, both words for 'leader'. The leader is the interpreter of the popular will, and his authority was often enhanced by his personal charisma. This one righteous leader's decisions in the best interests of the nation, believed the fascists, would relieve the people the trouble of participating in decision-making process. This belief in the 'righteous one' was an important component in the fascist monolithic national structure, of which one party and one national will were other elements.

- **Lower Middle Class Base:** Fascism was a mass movement with multi-class membership, but it drew its mass support from the lower middle class comprised of artisans, merchants, peasants, civil servants and white collar workers. For the lower middle class, fascism was a non-communist way of overcoming economic crises without posing any threat to their property.

At the same time the Fascists were eager to enlist the support of the elites – the landed aristocrats, industrialists and army leaders bereft of whose support, the fascists could not have captured power. This was well demonstrated in Italy and Germany where the ruling elite handed over power to the fascists.

- **Economy – the Third Position:** In economic affairs, the Fascist advocated an alternative to both international socialism and free market capitalism and put forward a third position – the **Third Alternative**, by taking elements from both.

The fascists, while rejecting **international socialism**, were receptive to the concept of **nationalist socialism**, a type of socialism that will strengthen national unity and solidarity. Class conflicts within a nation were to be resolved through the mediation of the state to secure the national interest and to strengthen national solidarity.

Similarly, the fascists, while opposing **free market capitalism**, supported **productive capitalism**. Fascism condemned only unproductive capitalism or financial capitalism. Whereas Marxism condemned capitalism as a system of exploitative property relations, the fascists criticised capitalism not for its competitive nature or for its support of private property but for its materialism and indifference to the nation. It is pertinent to note that the economic ideology of fascism does not reject the profit motive, rather it holds the view that the industries must uphold the national interest as superior to private profit. Fascists view workers and productive capitalists as part of productive segments of a nation who are in conflict with parasitic elements in society which includes corrupt financial capital, feeble people and so on.

The Fascist economics stood for a mixture of private and public ownership with **state control** and **economic planning** applicable to both the public and private sectors. The Fascist economic model also included **'corporatism'** – an economy that suppresses trade union liberty, broadens the sphere of state intervention and seeks to achieve solidarity and collaboration of the productive sectors under the control of the state or by state corporations.

By resorting to a third position, by advocating resolution of domestic class conflicts by the state and by implementing a state controlled economic model, the fascists aimed at **autarky** or economic self-sufficiency of their nations.

Similarly, the fascists criticised egalitarianism, as it preserves the weak and they were also opposed to the concept of social welfare as it encourages the degenerate and the feeble.

- **Military strength and action orientation:** Fascists promoted military values such as discipline, courage and physical strength and adopted military practices such as salutes and uniforms for their cadre. It also placed emphasis on action and legitimacy of political violence. For the fascists, political violence and war were expressions of national rejuvenation. This fascist '**Cult of Action, for Action's Sake**' dictates that action is of value in itself and should be taken without intellectual reflection. Slogans attributed to Mussolini such as 'A minute on the battlefield is worth a lifetime of peace' and 'Nothing has ever been won in history without bloodshed' are expressions of the same.

Corollary to the above, Fascism repudiates the doctrine of Pacifism and considers renunciation of the struggle as an act of cowardice. Mussolini commented that, 'war alone brings up to its highest level all human energy and puts the stamp of nobility upon the peoples who have the courage to meet it'. This fascist emphasis on violence is well evident from the fact that most fascist parties had private militias such as the **'Brownshirts'** of the German Nazis and the **'Blackshirts'** of the Italian fascists.

- **Age and gender roles:** Fascism also gave importance to youth, both in its physical and spiritual aspects. Young age was the period of energy and virility, a critical stage in the moral development and in the spiritual sense, a period of total commitment to action. In pursuance to this belief, Fascist created youth organisations to channelise the energy of the youth on fascist lines.

Regarding the gender roles, the fascists held conservative views. Women were urged to perform their traditional role as wives and mothers, as is exemplified in Mussolini's own words 'war is to man what maternity is to the woman'.

SUMMARY

The Interwar Years 1918–39 – This was the period between the two world wars and was filled with significant developments that had deep impact in shaping the modern world.

Paris Peace Conference – It was held in the Hall of Mirrors at the Palace of Versailles in Paris to decide the terms of peace. It was dominated by the Big Five – the United States, Britain, France, Italy and Japan.

The Fourteen Points – These were 14 ideas for world peace as envisaged by the American President Woodrow Wilson. These were – open covenants of peace, freedom of navigation, removal of all economic barriers, reduction of national armaments, impartial adjustment of colonial claims, evacuation of all Russian territory, restoration of Belgium as a free nation, restoration of Alsace-Lorraine to France, reallocation of Italian frontiers on national lines, self-government for Austria–Hungary, respect the territorial integrity of the Balkan states, opening of the Dardanelles to the ships of all nations, establishment of Polish state and formation of a general association of nations.

Peace settlements – Major outcome of the Paris Peace Conference was the formulation of peace settlements with the defeated powers of the World War I. These were the Treaty of Versailles with Germany, Treaty of Saint Germain with Austria, Treaty of Neuilly with Bulgaria, Treaty of Trianon with Hungary and the Treaty of Sevres with the Ottoman Empire. The Conference also formulated the Covenant of the League of Nations.

Verdict on the settlements – The settlements were authoritarian in nature as the defeated powers had not been consulted in framing them. It had the effect of dividing Europe into two groups those satisfied with it and the other non-satisfied and hence wanted to revise it. In many times the settlements violated the self-determination principle. It resembled more of a sentence from a court than a negotiated settlement by two groups. The settlements also redrew the geography of Europe. The international community did not accept the settlement wholeheartedly and one point to cite is non-ratification of the settlement by the United States.

International relation in the Interwar period – Three major features in this context were the French quest for security, the world's search for peace and American isolationism. Many steps were taken by France during this period such as insistence for a harsh treatment and huge reparation on Germany in the peace settlement, formation of a military alliance known as the 'Little Entente' with Poland, Romania, Czechoslovakia and Yugoslavia, taking initiative in framing the Briand–Kellogg Pact by which 65 nations renounced war as national policy, constructing of the Maginot Line to secure its border with Germany and signing of the Franco-Soviet Pact in 1935 were expressions of the French quest for security.

Haunted by the horrors of the World War I the world community was in search for measures to ensure peace for which steps such as formation of the League of Nations, signing of Washington Naval Treaty to limit naval strength of the five great powers, formulation of the Dawes Plan to resolve the German reparation crisis, Locarno Pact, the Kellogg–Briand Pact, the Young Plan, the Lausanne Conference and the World Disarmament Conference (1932–34) were undertaken with this aim.

Society in the Interwar period – Society reflected the post-war disillusionment and cynicism. For this generation – the Lost Generation – the war was catastrophic that had shattered their faith in themselves. This mood was reflected in arts of the time in the forms of Dadaism, Surrealism and Existentialism. At the same time the period was also of freedom and of new values about morality and of social roles. Economic dynamism and experiments in socio-cultural life is reflected in the term the 'Roaring Twenties'. Co-educational institutions and entry of more and more women in careers instilled a new spirit of freedom and empowerment among the women who began to be called as 'Flappers'. The World War induced technological advancements continued even after the war providing better avenues such as automobiles, air travel, radio and motion pictures all of which transformed social life in Europe and America.

The Great Depression – It was a period of long business slump originated in the United States with the Wall Street Crash in 1929 which had devastating global impact. In political sense, the Great Depression caused emergence of authoritarianism in many countries as the democracies failed in solving the crisis. In economic sphere, many countries initiated fiscal and monetary measures such as high tariffs, increased taxation and lowering of interest rates. In America the multi-faceted reforms known as the 'New Deal' was implemented to tide over the crisis by its President Franklin D. Roosevelt.

Rise of Totalitarianism and its features – Totalitarianism is a form of government with unlimited state power. The Interwar period witnessed emergence of authoritarian rulers such as Miklos Horthy (Hungary), Josef Pilsudski (Poland), Antonio de Salazar (Portugal), Ioannis Metaxas (Greece) and General Francisco Franco (Spain). Benito Mussolini of Italy and Adolf Hitler of Germany were two paradigmatic fascist rulers in Europe during this time. The main characteristics of fascism are – extreme nationalism, totalitarian state, opposition to liberalism, opposition to Marxism, opposition to rationalism, exaltation of the leader, dependence on military strength, lower middle-class base, conservatism in gender roles and a third position in economy.

Questions of Previous Years Civil Services Examination

1. 'Roaring Twenties' in Europe and America had many positive points. It helped women to uplift themselves in the region. Critically examine. (2022)
2. 'There arose a serious challenge to the Democratic State System between the two World Wars'. Evaluate the statement. (2021)
3. Do you agree with the view that the Treaty of Versailles was a bad compromise between a treaty based on force and a treaty based on ideas? (2016)
4. What policy instruments were deployed to contain the Great Economic Depression? (2013)

5. 'The peace of Versailles lacked moral validity from the start'. Elucidate. (2011)
6. 'The War's (First World War's) most permanent contribution to the spirit of the post-War years was disillusion'. Elucidate. (2007)
7. 'Treaty of Versailles contained the seeds of future conflict'. Elucidate. (2006)
8. 'The most important single factor…in the years following 1919 was the French demand for security'. Elucidate. (2004)
9. 'The Great Depression (1929–34) was attended by momentous consequences in the economic as well as in the political sphere'. Elucidate. (2002)
10. 'There was not only a difference of principles at Paris (Peace Conference) but a clash of personalities'. Elucidate. (2001)
11. Analyse the provisions of the Treaty of Versailles of 1919 and examine the validity of Germany's objections to the treaty. (2000)
12. Trace the rise and growth of the New European Society in the inter-war period. (1999)
13. 'President Franklin Roosevelt's New Deal had the wit to start the political economic in a fresh, more promising direction'. Do you agree? (1997)
14. 'The Treaty of Versailles was merely an armistice for twenty years'. Elucidate. (1993)
15. The treaties made at the Paris Peace Conference in 1919–20 were replete with unstable compromises, reflecting more materialism than idealism. Elucidate. (1990)
16. 'Extreme nationalism of the Fascist Variety has various faces in various countries, but it has everywhere some common characteristics'. Elucidate. (1989).

CHAPTER 12

Fascism and Nazism

In this Chapter

A. Fascism in Italy

1. Introduction

Fascism first emerged in Italy in the second decade of the 20th century. Here, *fasci* (bands or groups) had been organised as early as 1914 to mobilise people for Italy's participation in the First World War. In March 1919, Mussolini formed his **Italian Fasci of Combat** (FIC) in Milan. But in the elections of 1919, Mussolini and his party failed miserably against the socialists. Subsequently, it was renamed as the **National Fascist Party** (PNF) in November 1921, transforming it into a more coherent political group from that of a paramilitary squad.

2. Factors for the Origin of Italian Fascism

Although Italy had been on the winning side in the First World War, it faced a lot of problems in the immediate aftermath of it and appeared as a defeated nation. Such an environment provided a fertile ground for the emergence of militant and patriotic organisations, culminating in the capture of power by the fascists.

i. Disappointment with Paris Peace Settlement

As an Allied partner, Italy had contributed to the Allied war efforts. But, the treatment accorded to Italy at the Paris Peace Conference was a huge disappointment to many Italians who viewed theirs as '**mutilated victory**'. Italians believed that despite their sacrifices – close to 7,00,000 dead and one million wounded – they had been robbed of their due share of victory.

During the war, the Allies had promised territories such as the Dalmatian coast, Trentino, Adalia and some Aegean islands and protectorate over Albania to Italy. Though most of Italy's demands were eventually met, there were some exceptions such as denial of the German colonies in Africa to Italy. Similarly, Albania had also been made independent. Another cause of Italian resentment was the allocation of the Adriatic port of Fiume to Yugoslavia, which had a large Italian population. These developments inflamed Italian nationalism and left the government highly unpopular. The Italians, in general, wanted their government to follow a strong stand in foreign affairs.

ii. Economic Effects of the War

Italy was poor and its participation in the world war had made her poorer. During the war, the government had borrowed large sums, especially from the United States (the national debt had risen from 16 billion lire to 85 billion during the war) and now these debts had to be repaid. The end of the War gave birth to disorder and discontent arising from economic and financial hardships. To make things worse value of Lira too declined. Worsening economic condition was reflected in:

a. increase in the cost of living by five times
b. severe food shortage leading to discontent and violent strikes
c. massive unemployment consequent to reduction in industrial production back to pre-war level and due to closing of foreign markets
d. the spread of socialistic ideas. As a result, workers started occupying factories and peasants started squatting on the uncultivated estates or ousting the landlords after seizing their property. It was as if Italy was on the verge of a social revolution.

iii. Failure of the Governments

During such critical situation what Italy required was effective leadership and strong government. But the governments under the Liberals proved incapable of meeting the challenges. The parliamentary system threw up the shaky governments. The parliamentary system of government with votes for all men, though provided an opportunity for large number of political parties including the liberals, nationalists, communists and catholic party to send their representatives in the parliament, it resulted in an undesirable situation of **hung parliaments** and governments with shaky majorities. Within a short period (1919–22) five different cabinets came and went, under which neither consistent policy was possible nor coherent steps could be initiated. Bold leadership and visionary policies could have saved Italy from the crisis, but that did not happen. As a result contempt for parliamentary system and support for radicalism grew.

iv. Apprehensions of Revolution

Amidst multitudes of grievances, different sections in Italy were apprehensive of a revolution. The industrialists and large landowners feared that Italy was quickly moving towards a communist revolution. This fear was generated not just by the proliferation of socialist and communist parties but also by a series of strikes in 1919 and 1920. The socialist workers took over many factories to run it for the benefit of the workers. In rural areas socialist groups organised themselves into **Red Leagues** and seized property of the landlords and setup cooperatives. In the elections of 1919, the socialists captured about one-third of seats in the Chamber of Deputies. The Italian communist party was also established in 1921.

The middle class in Italy was apprehensive of government measures, while at the same time was alarmed at the surging communism in their country. The government had initiated reforms such as increased taxation to meet the crisis. But the burden fell heavily on the middle class consisting businessmen, small land owners, civil servants and professionals.

The fear of a Russian type revolution and disgust with the government for its inability in suppressing the disorder and saving the country from crisis caused resentment in the minds of industrialists, landlords and the middle class. These sections were, therefore, ready to accept totalitarianism, if it could save the country from the crisis, suppress communism and ensure continuation of the existing social order. Out of these groups of nationalist enthusiasts emerged the Fascists.

Benito Mussolini

3. Benito Mussolini

Benito Mussolini (1883–1945) was born as the son of blacksmith in Romagna. He was a socialist in early stage of his political career and had edited a socialist newspaper **'Avanti'** ('Forward'). As a socialist, Mussolini followed anti-nationalist, anti-militarist and anti-imperialist stand and opposed Italy's intervention in the First World War.

But, with the outbreak of the world war, which had resulted in a surge of Italian nationalism, Mussolini underwent a radical transformation. He now saw the war as an opportunity for himself and for Italy. Mussolini believed that the war would complete the process of **Italian *Risorgimento*** by uniting the Italians in Austria-Hungary into Italy and also by affording an opportunity to the common people to participate in the war as members of the Italian nation, hence advocated Italy's participation in the World War. Mussolini was expelled from the Italian Socialist Party for his support of Italian intervention in the war, as opposed to the Party's stand against the war. Mussolini went on to serve Italian army in the war but returned home in 1917 after being wounded.

In March 1919, he founded the Italian fascist party *Fasci Italiani di Combattimento* (FIC) or the Italian Fasci of Combat in Milan with the support of about 200 members consisting of discontented socialists, restless revolutionaries and discharged soldiers. The fascist party branches were organised as *fasci de combat* (fighting groups). A **bundle of rods with a protruding axe** became the symbol of this party. They adopted black shirt as uniform and paraded in the streets in quasi-military formats. **Blackshirt** squads raided and burned down socialists', trade union and newspaper offices. As the socialist **'Redshirts'** responded with the same kind of violence, Italy soon became a battle ground between the fascists and the socialists.

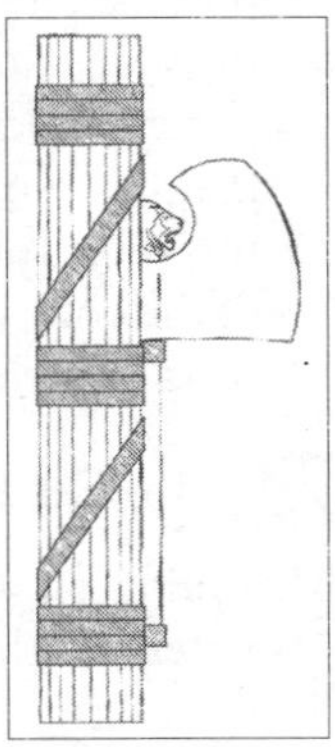

Fascist Symbol

4. Growth of Italian Fascism

Though it had very few supporters at the beginning, the fascists began to attract large number of people from the discontented, disillusioned and uprooted sections of Italian society. Fascist's ideals were attractive to many sections and the fascists exploited the situation by promising to different sections what they were looking for:

a. Fascist policies were attractive to hardened battle veterans and ardent patriots who believed that Mussolini would win for Italian nation, a rightful place of honour in international affairs.
b. The fascists also made up for their initial lack of numbers by strong determination and disciplined aggressiveness against the Socialists and others who had opposed Italy's participation in the Great War, whom they called as Italy's 'internal enemies'.
c. In Italy, 1919 and 1920 were known as the **'two red years'** during which the Socialists had made huge electoral gains, while the labour unions had unleashed a wave of strikes unprecedented in Italian history. The political culture and social order had been radically altered with the Socialists winning control of municipal governments, founding co-operatives and establishing peasant leagues which resulted in series of strikes, occupation of factories and estates. The **conservatives** denounced these as 'red terror' and as a threat of socialist revolution. These conservative elements were under the belief that the fascists would save Italy from Communism, save her from anarchy and hence started supporting the fascists.
d. The **industrialists and land owners** contributed large sums to the Fascist party. The **lower middle class**, fearful that the socialist party would destroy their property and prestige, too supported the Fascists.

e. The **university students** looking for adventure and an ideal looked at Mussolini and the fascist programmes a way to channelise their energy.
f. The **army officers**, filled with the dream of an Italian empire, considered the fascists vision for Italy in consonance with that of their own.
g. **General population** disenchanted with parliamentary democracy was reinvigorated by Mussolini's promise of stable government and by the philosophy of action. They now yearned for dictatorship as a panacea for the multitudes of ills of Italy.
h. Fascism's appeal was also based on the **personality cult** built around Mussolini and **propaganda** they unleashed. The fascists held patriotic rallies, during which Mussolini, whose style of oratory and staccato caught the imagination of the crowds.
i. Mussolini's conciliatory speeches also ironed out the differences between the Roman Catholic Church (of which Mussolini was a critic earlier) and the fascists. The Roman Catholics under **Pope Pius XI** supported Mussolini as the best bet against communism.
j. Moreover, **the king** and his supporters had also started supporting the fascists after Mussolini dropped his republican outlook and programmes by 1922.
k. The growth and consolidation of fascists in Italy were also facilitated by the fragmented and **ineffective opposition**. The anti-fascists groups like the liberals, communists and the socialists refused to co-operate with each other. For example, the socialists who had 123 seats in parliament after the 1921 elections (the fascists could win only 35 seats in this election) refused to work with the Liberal government of Giolitti (Prime Minister of Italy during 1920–21) which would have meant a stable government and a check to the fascist menace. In the summer of 1922, the socialist called for a general strike and Mussolini exhorted the fascists to suppress the strike, if the government failed to do so. The strike failed due to lack of support and strong suppression resorted to by the fascists and Mussolini was able to project himself as the saviour of the nation from communism.

Thus, **nationalism, activism, propaganda and anti-communism** of the fascists gained them gradual support from the aristocrats, capitalists, lower middle class, army officers, the church and the royalists. Realising that the wind was in his favour, Mussolini effected a **Fascist *coup d'état*** in October 1922. Mussolini declared that 'either they will give us the government or we shall take it by descending on Rome' and organised a **'March on Rome'** and convergence of fascist squads on the capital, from all over Italy. The king **Victor Emmanuel III** (1869–1947) instead of suppressing the fascists invited Mussolini to form a new government. Believing that he was rescuing the nation from terrible violence and ruinous civil war and also securing his own throne, the king accepted the revolution and appointed Mussolini as the premier on 29 October 1922, who became the **first ever fascist premier in history**.

Mussolini headed a coalition cabinet in which only 4 out of 12 ministers were fascists. In the general election in April 1924, the fascists and other right wing groups captured 404 seats in a 535 member parliament. In the previous parliament the fascists had only 35 seats.

The fascist takeover of power did not meet any strong opposition because-

a. There was a general desire for a strong and stable government in place of weak governments of the preceding years.
b. Large numbers of people were ready to forsake political liberty and were longing for the end of disorder and anarchy, which was promised by the fascists.
c. The fascists also resorted to violence and intimidation to divide and suppress the opposition.
d. The fascist takeover was also supported by a legal measure. The **Acerbo Law** passed by the parliament in November 1923, changed the rules of general elections by providing that the party or the group of parties gaining the largest share of the votes (provided they gain at least 25 percent of the votes) would automatically gain two-thirds seats in parliament.

5. | The Fascist State in Italy

Mussolini, on assuming the dual position as **Prime Minister** and the party leader, Duce, gradually established fascist dictatorship in Italy which was based on certain basic principles. These were extreme nationalism, a totalitarian government, one party state, autarchy and militarism.

The Italian Fascists believed in extreme nationalistic ideas. They believed in the rebirth of the nation and stood for building up the power and prestige of the nation. **Nationhood** was the highest form of society. The Fascists claimed theirs to be a spiritual movement aimed at the revival of the Italian soul which was in their view in existence in the grandeur of ancient Rome.

The Italian fascists also gave emphasis on a totalitarian government and tried to arouse, mobilise and control the great mass of people to promote the greatness of the state. Elected municipal bodies and other local governing councils were replaced by officials appointed by the centre. Mussolini claimed that the fascist totalitarianism was aimed at completion of the ***Risorgimento***.

The Italian fascists envisaged a single-party system and rejected democracy. In pursuance of this policy, Mussolini eliminated non-fascists from his cabinet, dissolved opposition parties and trade unions, suppressed opposition publications and newspapers and organised secret police to round up the dissidents.

The Italian fascists also stood for self-sufficiency in economic affairs (autarchy) and active intervention of the government in the economic life of the nation. Efforts were made to reduce Italy's dependence on foreign imports. Mussolini advocated agrarianism and autarchy as part of his economic battles for 'Land, Lira and Grain'. Agriculture was given vital importance by the fascists, as Italy was overwhelmingly rural and protectionist measures were initiated in this sector. Labour organisations negotiated labour relations on behalf of all its members, with the state acting as the arbitrator. In 1933, Institute for Industrial Reconstruction (IRI) was established to promote nationalisation of Italian economy. Mussolini described his economic policies as 'state capitalism' and 'state socialism' an economic system with the state directing the economic production and allocation of resources.

The Italian fascism relied on the strength of the military and sought to forge a strong Italian Empire as a '**Third Rome**' in modern period. The Fascists believed that war exalted and ennobled man, and that the nations which did not expand would eventually wither away. Hence, for the Italian fascists militarism and war were expressions of statism and nationalism.

To establish a fascist state in Italy, Mussolini took following measures.

i. Constitutional and Legal Measures

1. By passing the Acerbo Law in 1923, Mussolini ensured two-thirds seats for the fascists in parliament.
2. In 1925, the Prime Minister was made responsible only to the king and not to parliament. Mussolini also took up a new official title 'Head of Government' for himself and assumed formal powers over his ministers who became responsible to him rather than to the Chamber of Deputies.
3. In 1926, changes were made to the constitution by which power was given to the Prime Minister to rule by decree, meaning that the laws need not to be discussed in parliament. Though the Parliament was not abolished, its role was reduced to that of an advisory council.
4. The Fascist Grand Council became the decision-making body of the country and Mussolini its undisputed leader.
5. Electorate was reduced from 10 million to 3 million wealthiest of the total population.
6. Elected bodies of towns were abolished and officials were appointed in them.
7. To enforce complete state authority the National Security Militia was created in 1923 and a secret police force known as Organization for Vigilance and Repression of Anti-Fascism or OVRA was created in 1927.

ii. Censorship and Supervision

1. Mussolini introduced strict censorship of the press, radio and films.
2. Anti-fascist newspapers were banned.
3. Educational system was monitored and supervised by the state, aimed at inculcating habits of discipline, obedience and nationalistic values.
4. Text books were re-written to glorify the fascist system.
5. The press, radio and cinema were directed to project an idealised life under fascism implying that Fascism had eradicated poverty, social tensions and crimes.
6. Children and youth were compelled to join fascist organisations. Efforts were also made

to train the youngsters on the fascist motto '**Believe! Obey! Fight!**' Youth had to participate in patriotic ceremonies which were aimed at the submergence of individual identities into that of the group.

7. Teachers and university professors were compelled to swear their allegiance to the fascist ideology and government.
8. Fascist critics and 'subversive' elements (political opponents) were either imprisoned or were exiled to remote islands. Victims included Antonio Gramsci, intellectual and one of the founders of the Italian Communist Party.
9. The Fascists rightly understood the importance of influencing the minds of Italian population. To this end, propaganda measures were initiated to build up prestige and popularity of Mussolini and the fascists. In 1925, to increase acceptance of fascist rule a national recreational club known as OND (*Opera Nazionale Dopolavora*) was set up with a vast network of clubs, libraries and sports grounds to provide subsidised sports, outings and holidays. Press, posters, radio and newsreel films portrayed Mussolini as youthful, energetic leader and as an expert in wide range of pursuits.

Fascists writers, artists and scholars emphasised the point that the fascist rule as a revival and return to the greatness of ancient Rome and Mussolini as a new Caesar. This development known as the '**Romanita**' movement aimed at the 'resurrection of the empire' and creation of '**New Man**' as a modern version of the idealised **Roman centurion**.

iii. Economic Measures

1. Mussolini reorganised the economy by preaching the end of class conflict as a fascist mission, denouncing economic liberalism for promoting individual self-interest and condemning socialism for instigating conflicts between workers and capitalists.
2. Mussolini organised the **Corporate State**, under which both the labour unions and employer's associations (syndicates) were organised into corporations. The Italian economy was placed under the management of 22 Corporations, each responsible for a major industrial enterprise. They consisted of representatives from trade unions, employers and the government. These corporations determined the working conditions, wages and prices and also settled their disputes. In 1930, the **National Council of Corporations** was established with representatives from the twenty two corporations to resolve their issues on national level.

   This corporatist model was a '**third way**' between capitalism and communism and was expected to bring harmonious cooperation of workers and employers for the general good of the nation. It aimed at creating a national community, where the interests of all parts of the economy were integrated into class-transcending unity.
3. Fascists prohibited strikes and lockouts, deem these acts as prejudicial to the national interest.
4. Fascists discouraged foreign trade and supported protectionism, believing that too much dependence on international trade would make a nation vulnerable to internationalism.
5. To compensate workers, whose life had been regimented and controlled, Mussolini introduced *Dopolavoras* (after work organisations). These provided annual holidays with pay, social security schemes and other facilities like theatre and tours at cheap rates to workers.
6. To attain economic prosperity and make Italy self-sufficient (autarchy), the fascist regime imposed tariffs and other trade barriers. With the same objectives three battles – the **Battles for Land, the Lira and Grain** – were also launched.

   Under the first, Mussolini's regime launched a programme of land reclamation of marshlands and brought marginal lands under cultivation. Being labour intensive it employed large number of people. On the belief that a powerful nation could not have a weak currency, Mussolini inflated the value of the lira which made exports more expensive. Mussolini launched the Battle for Grain to make her economically strong and self-sufficient in grain and urged farmers to concentrate on wheat production. Though by 1935 wheat imports had been cut by 75 percent, it was at the expense of fruit and vegetables leading to decline in total agricultural output.

iv. Religious Measures

In 1929, **Lateran Treaty** was signed with Pope Pius XI to settle the **Roman Question** (the status of the Pope *Vis-à-vis* with Rome). Since 1870, Pope had been hostile to the Italian government for its annexation of Rome and all the territories that belonged to the Papacy (the Papal States) which had completed the unification process of Italy.

1. This treaty created the **State of Vatican City**, with pope as its head, with guaranteed full and independent sovereignty. In return the Pope recognised Kingdom of Italy with Rome as its capital.
2. Lateran Concordat (as this treaty was also known) also provided for appointment of all bishops in Italy by the Pope and the payment of salaries of the bishops and priests by the state.
3. Italy also agreed to pay a large sum of money as compensation for all his losses, repealed many of the anticlerical laws, made Catholic faith as the official state religion and also provided for compulsory religious instructions in all schools.

By the Lateran Treaty, Mussolini made a political use of religion and secured for Italy the unstinted support of the Church, a valuable aid to authority and a stabilising force against social upheavals. Throughout the 1930s – during Mussolini's invasion of Ethiopia and his intervention in Spanish Civil War – the church supported him.

It was pragmatism on the side of Pope and expediency of Mussolini that led to the Lateran Accords. The pope regarded Mussolini's regime as the best bet against communism and less hostile to church interests, while Mussolini believed that the agreement with the church would improve his image with the catholic public. The Lateran Treaty provided free hand to Italian people in matters of religion and state, as their loyalty to the state and obedience to their religion ceased to be mutually incompatible. For these reasons, many consider the settlement with the Papacy, as Mussolini's most lasting and worthwhile achievement.

v. Fascist Foreign Policy

Mussolini believed that Italy had been denied of its rightful claims as per the Treaty of London (1915), the Allies had neglected Italy in the distribution of Mandates, and victory in the First World War as far as Italy was concerned as a 'mutilated victory'. Mussolini wanted to rectify these wrongs.

Mussolini's foreign policy can be understood in the framework of two important elements in the fascist principles - its emphasis on **extreme nationalism** and **glorification of war**. As part of the first, Mussolini envisioned to forge a new Roman Empire by acquiring territories in Africa and in the Mediterranean and to secure for Italy the prestige and status of a world power. To attain the above objectives Mussolini believed in the necessity of war and glorified war as an expression of national virility and pursued an aggressive foreign policy.

As part of this policy Mussolini took some important steps:

1. In 1923, Italy invaded the Greek island of **Corfu** to avenge the murder of some Italians that were part of an international boundary delegation.
2. In 1924, Italy annexed the Free State of **Fiume** by a treaty with Yugoslavia.
3. In October 1935, Italy invaded **Ethiopia (Abyssinia)** which was the only African country to escape colonisation and proclaimed Italian King Victor Emmanuel as the Emperor of Ethiopia. Mussolini also defied the sanctions imposed by the League of Nations.
4. From 1936, Italy provided military support to the Nationalists in the **Spanish Civil War**. The Nationalists here represented the Spanish version of fascism.
5. Now, estranged from Britain and France for its invasion of Ethiopia and for its support to the Nationalists in Spain, Italy moved closer to Hitler hoping that German support would frighten Britain and France to grant more concessions to Italy and formed the **Rome-Berlin Axis** in October 1936.
6. In May 1939, this alliance was formalised by Hitler and Mussolini by signing the **Pact of Steel** in Berlin, which bound together Fascist Italy and Nazi Germany in a full military alliance.
7. Close alliance with Nazi Germany meant Italy continuing an aggressive foreign policy and becoming a junior partner of Nazi Germany. It found expressed in Italian annexation of

Albania (April 1939), and Italy's acceptance of German annexation of Austria (1938), the dismemberment of Czechoslovakia (1939), invasion of Poland (September 1939) and in its **entry into the Second World War** on Germany's side in June 1940.

6. Downfall of Italian Fascism

Though the fascists were successful in creating enthusiasm in the minds of the Italians, the average Italian had not benefitted much from the regime. In spite of censorship of the media, suppression of opposition and heavy punishment and banishment meted out to opponents, the downfall of the regime had set in long before the World War II. Italy's entry in the World War II along the side of Germany doomed its end.

Italy entered the World War II on 10 June 1940 by declaring war on Britain and France. Mussolini's immediate war aim was expansion of Italian colonies in North Africa by taking them from the British and the French.

Many Italians were opposed to the alliance of Mussolini with Hitler and for transforming Italy a German satellite. Moreover, the Italian army was comparatively depleted and weak to have played decisive role in the war. Economically too Italy was poor and incapable of waging a major war.

Once the war started the general public suffered immense hardships due to inflation, fall in wages, food rationing, increased taxation and bombardment of its cities by the Allied forces. The people expressed their resentment and opposition to the war and resorted to strikes in cities such as Milan and Turin, the first since 1922.

The Italians suffered a string of defeats in the war. Finally, the **defeat of Italian troops in North Africa** (May 1943) and the **capture of Sicily** by the Allied Forces (July 1943) compelled the King to dismiss Mussolini, who had refused to make peace, and the fascist rule came to an end.

Mussolini was imprisoned and a new government led by **General Pietro Badoglio** was formed which signed an armistice with the Allies in September 1943. Mussolini's downfall did not evoke any resistance and the people rejoiced at the news as they believed that the end of Mussolini meant the end of the war and suffering.

About two months after Benito Mussolini was stripped of power, he was rescued by the Germans in **Operation Eiche** and was shifted to northern Italy, where he setup a new fascist state – the **Italian Social Republic** (RSI). This was the second and final chapter of the Italian fascist state.

Meanwhile, the Allied armies advanced through Italy and controlled southern Italy with the help of Italian royalist forces. The Allied troops breached the Gothic Line. Imminent collapse of the Italian Social Republic in sight, Mussolini tried to flee to Switzerland, disguised as a German soldier. But he was captured and was shot dead on 28 April 1945 (two days before Adolf Hitler's suicide) by the Italian resistance force, that is, the force resisting the fascist rule. The German and RSI forces surrendered before the Allies in May 1945.

Gothic Line: It was the German defensive line of the Italian campaign during the World War II, against the Allied armies in Italy. It ran along the summits of northern part of the Apennine Mountains.

7. Verdict on Italian Fascism

It is beyond dispute that the fascist regime saved Italy from disorder and anarchy of the post-First World War years. It made governmental administration efficient and encouraged economic self-sufficiency. In the industrial sector production of iron and steel doubled by 1930, silk production increased by 10 times and hydroelectric power generation doubled. The regime implemented an impressive public work programme which included construction of roads, railways, bridges, sports stadiums and schools. Measures were also taken to increase Italy's share of world shipping and in the tourist inflow.

At the same time, there were glaring drawbacks in fascist achievements. For example, the success in the Battle of Grain meant an overall decline in the agricultural output as the farmers concentrated on the wheat production at the cost of fruit production and animal husbandry. Similarly, as a result of restriction on imports, Italians had to pay higher prices for consumer goods.

Further, whatever achievements attained by the fascist regime were secured at a heavy price, namely, political liberty and it is said that these could have been achieved just as well by a democratic government. Moreover, the Italian fascists by aligning themselves with the German Nazism dragged Italy into the Second World War and became responsible for the consequent destruction.

SUMMARY

Causes of the origin of Fascism in Italy – Disappointment with Paris Peace Settlement, economic impacts of the War, failure of the governments to meet the challenges faced by Italy, apprehension of a revolution in Italy were the major causes.

The fascist state in Italy – Mussolini established a fascist state in Italy gradually, which was aimed at Risorgimento. Major steps in Italy's transformation to a fascist state were as follows – Constitutional and legal measures such as passing of the Acerbo Law in 1923 and creation of the Fascist Grand Council; censorship and supervision; economic measures such as organisation of the Corporate State; religious measures such as signing of the Lateran Treaty with Pope Pius XI in 1929 and reorientation of the foreign policy of Italy.

Questions of Previous Years Civil Services Examination

1. Discuss, how Fascism was a response to the post-war situation arising out of political instability, thwarted nationalist hopes and fears of the spread of communism? (2022)
2. Examine the circumstances which led to the overthrow of democracy and establishment of Fascist dictatorship in Italy. (2017)
3. Discuss the main characteristics of Fascism. (2007)
4. 'The roots of the rise of Fascism lay in Peace Treaties' Elucidate. (2003)
5. 'Corporate State' was Mussolini's answer to the socio-political problems of his country. Elucidate. (1995)

B. Nazism

1. Introduction

The history of Germany up to the end of World War II can be divided into three periods-

1. German Empire (1871–1918)
2. Weimer Republic (1919–33)
3. Nazi Germany called as the Third Reich (1933–45)

The German Empire also known as Imperial Germany or the Second Reich (the Holy Roman Empire was the First Reich) had been constituted in 1871 after the unification of the German states. As Germany faced defeat in the World War I, the public opinion turned against the government. Extreme burdens of the war, strong impact of the defeat and the social tensions between the general population and the elites who led and lost the war resulted in a revolution. Known as the **German Revolution**, it erupted with sailors' mutiny in Kiel on 3 November 1918.

As the unrest soon spread to other regions and sections of Germany, the German Emperor **Kaiser William II** was forced to abdicate on 9 November 1918. It marked the end of the German Empire. Kaiser fled to Holland and a **provisional government** was set up under **Frederick Ebert**, a Social Democrat leader.

By this time communism had taken wide roots in Germany and the communists called as the '**Spartacans**' (named after the Roman Spartacus, who had led a slave revolt in 71 BC) were eager to bring out a Russian type revolution in Germany. The German Communists, under their leaders **Rosa Luxemburg and Karl Liebknecht**, launched agitations known as the **'Spartacist Rising'** (January 1919) in factories and streets as a part of their strategy to put 'pressure from the streets' to seize power.

But the socialists were opposed to a Bolshevik model revolution and were determined to suppress the 'Spartacans', who were receiving support and encouragement from Russia. With the help of army and the ***Freikorps*** or **Free Corps** (volunteer brigades of ex-soldiers and adventurers), Frederick Ebert suppressed the Spartacist Rising. Both Rosa Luxemburg and Liebknecht were murdered in January 1919, by members of the Free Corps.

Meanwhile, a National Assembly was elected by secret ballot and the Social Democrats emerged as the largest single party and its leader Friedrich Ebert assumed the first Presidency of the Republic. The new parliament met in February 1919, at Weimer, and proceeded to draw up a constitution for the new state. This constitution was signed into law on 11 August 1919 and was in existence till 1933.

2. The Weimar Republic

The new German government was known as the Weimer Republic, after the German city where the constitution was drafted as Berlin was still under unrest and political turmoil. It went through three stages during its existence.

1. The period between 1919–23 is known as the period of infancy of the Republic and struggle for survival. It had to face rebellions from both the Left and the Right wing groups.
2. The period between 1923–29 is known as the Golden Era. It was a period of recovery and hope. Under the leadership of Gustav Stresemann, the Republic achieved economic prosperity, foreign policy successes and witnessed cultural flowering.
3. The period between 1929–33 is known as the period of crisis. The onset of the Great Depression in America and its disastrous effect on Germany found expressed in unprecedented levels of unemployment and economic crisis. It was duly exploited by Hitler for his advantage resulting in the expansion of support base of the Nazis. While the Republic was struggling to overcome the crises, Adolf Hitler and his **National Socialist Party** blamed the government for all the ills of the country and promised solutions. Hitler, who was appointed by the President Hindenburg as the Chancellor in January 1933, put an end to the Weimer Republic and emerged dictator of Germany and established **the Third Reich** which lasted till 1945.

3. Features of the Weimer Constitution

Scholars consider the Weimer Constitution as the most perfect democratic constitution, at least on paper, a constitution full of ingenious and admirable devices which seemed to guarantee the working of an almost flawless democracy.

1. The constitution envisaged a **federal system** but with many centralising features.
2. It had a **preamble** which declared that the German people as the adopter and authority of the constitution.
3. The executive power was vested in the **President**, who was to be elected for a term of seven years by adult suffrage. The President could dissolve the Reichstag, submit any law passed by it to referendum and suspend civil liberties in case of emergency.
4. The President was to act on the advice of a ministry headed by **Chancellor (*Reichskanzler*)** which was responsible to Reichstag.
5. It provided for a **bicameral legislature**. The Reichstag composed of representatives elected by the people on the basis of secret ballot open to all men and women aged 20 and above. Elections were to be held on proportional representation system. The Reichstadt was the representative body of the states for national legislation and administration.

6. The Weimer constitution also laid the **basic rights** and obligations of the German people. These provisions included equality before law, gender equality, abolition of privileges based on birth or social status, right to education and so forth. An oath on the constitution was mandatory for all public servants and to members of the armed forces.
7. **Freedom of belief** and conscience were guaranteed by the constitution and was protected by the state. No state church was provided for.
8. The Weimer Constitution also guaranteed the **right to property**. It also contained that the economic life of the Reich (nation) should conform to the principles of justice, aiming a dignified life for all and securing economic freedom of the individual.
9. The constitution also had provisions of **'initiative', 'referendum' and 'recall'**.

4. | Challenges of the Weimer Republic

In the immediate aftermath of the War, Germany faced many crises. Even before its inauguration as seen above, there was the **November Revolution** (1918) that broke out with the **Kiel Mutiny** and then a **civil war** between the communists and the socialists. Moreover, various right-wing groups preferring an autocratic state opposed the Republic and to undermine its credibility, blamed the socialists and Jews for Germany's defeat in the First World War. It also had to face many coup attempts in 14 years of its existence.

i. Post War Reconstruction

The Republic had to reconstruct Germany from the devastations of the war.

The industrial sector of Germany had been destroyed during the war. Industrial production was around two-fifths of the pre-war level. It was also in the grip of crisis on account of the loss of supplies of raw material due to continental blockade, the loss of colonies and ending of the war time demand. There was severe food shortage. Grain production was less than half of the pre-war level. Around 7,50,000 had died of starvation and malnutrition during 1918–19.

Germany also witnessed outbreak of epidemic such as flu which added misery to the people and woes of the government. Moreover, Germany had a casualty of around 7 million (2 million dead and 5 million wounded) of its man power. On a psychological angle, morale of the Germans, after four years of war and struggle had been at the lowest ebb.

ii. Humiliation of the Treaty of Versailles

The Republic had begun its journey by accepting the Treaty of Versailles (signed on 28 June 1919, incidentally on the fifth anniversary of the assassination of Archduke Franz Ferdinand, which was the immediate cause of the war) which was unpopular among the Germans and humiliating to their honour. It was this resentment against the **harsh and unrealistic provisions** of the treaty that was to create fertile psychological ground for the failure of the Republic and eventual rise of the Nazi regime. Many believed that 'one thing the new Republic brought the Germans-the peace-was a form of prolonged slavery' and to the Republic it was not an encouraging start. As one historian commented, 'the fundamental significance of Versailles was emotional rather than rational'. Those who did not accept the Treaty formed patriotic associations, some of which had their own paramilitary forces and they targeted public figures with violence and intimidation.

iii. Weaknesses of the Weimer Constitution

In spite of admirable provisions contained in the Weimer Constitution, the running of the new German republic proved to be deeply problematic.

First, the structure of government was a mix of presidential and parliamentary systems and the president could assume some of the powers of monarch would have wielded. For example, by invoking the emergency decree, the president could suspend civil liberties. Later, Hitler was to use this provision for his own advantage after the Reichstag fire in 1933 to suspend civil liberties and to pursue a ruthless suppression of the Communists.

President's power to dismiss the Chancellor, even if he retained the confidence of the Reichstag, and his power to appoint a Chancellor who did not have the support of the Reichstag were again problematic. In 1933, the President appointed Hitler as Chancellor even though his party did not have majority in Reichstag.

Second, the proportional electoral system gave rise to multitude of splinter parties, making it difficult for any party to establish and maintain a parliamentary majority. The existence of multitude of parties representing the extreme ends of political spectrum contributed to frequent changes in government and associated negative fallouts. A succession of coalition governments came to power but no party could carry out its programme. Political deadlock caused Germans to lose what little confidence they had in the democratic system.

Third, the Weimer Constitution was put into implementation in an adverse socio, economic and political environment. The post-World War I realities in which the constitution was made to perform were heavily tilted towards its failure and it is said that the Weimer constitution was no worse than the constitutions of most other countries and its problematical provisions might not have mattered so much, had the circumstances been different. In other words, failure of the Republic was far more due to the course of events and to the character of social forces of the time than to constitutional defects.

iv. Lack of Democratic Tradition

The political parties in Germany did not have experience in running a democratic parliamentary government and their refusal to compromise and cooperate complicated the political climate further. '**A democracy without democrats**' was the apt description of German republic because of its limited democratic traditions.

Moreover, there was a general contemptuous attitude towards democracy from the conservatives like the industrialists, large landowners, judges, higher civil servants and army leaders. This lack of respect for democratic institutions by the traditional classes and general acceptance for the elites (army and officer class) as the rightful leaders in German society was another stumbling block to the Republic. These sections also held the view that Germany had been '**stabbed in the back**' by the democrats by signing the peace treaty. Also, the rightwing intellectuals often attacked democracy and republican government as a threat to German nationalism turning many Germans against the republic and eroding its popular support further.

v. Threat from Conspirators and Private Armies

The German Republic had to face internal threats from both the radical left and the radical right. The first of such development was the **'Spartacist Rising'** in January 1919. In this rising the communists, inspired by the success of the Russian Revolution, took to the streets of Berlin and declared the government of Ebert deposed. The government managed to tide over the threat by suppressing the Communists with the help of Free Corps. But the government's dependence on private militia was a sign of its own weakness.

In March 1920, radical right wing groups made an effort to capture power. This coup or rising known as **'Kapp Putsch'** was organised by the Free Corps, when they were ordered by the government to disband. Instead of disbanding, the Free Corps declared a new government by **Wolfgang Kapp**, as Chancellor. The republican cabinet had to flee to Dresden. The German army – the Reichswehr – many of which generals were in sympathy with the rightists, refused to suppress the putsch. Finally, a general strike called by the workers of Berlin paralysed the capital and prevented Kapp from governing and in the failure of the coup. Though Kapp was imprisoned and the Freikorps disbanded, the incident put a question mark on the loyalty of the army to the Republic and pointed to the existence of strong currents of right wing politics in the German soil.

In November 1923, another threat to government occurred in the form of **'Beer Hall Putsch'** (as it set out from a beer hall in Munich) also known as the **'Munich Putsch'** under the leadership of Adolf Hitler and a former army general Friedrich Ludendorff. They aimed at capturing power at the Bavarian state government in Munich and then overthrowing the national government in Berlin. The police suppressed the putsch and Hitler was imprisoned for 9 months.

Apart from the threats of organised groups trying to depose the government, the republic also had to face increasing lawlessness, political assassinations and expansion of private armies. All these discredited the republic in the eyes of German people, who began to long for a strong government that would establish order in society and safety of life.

vi. Economic Crisis

The Republic was constantly burdened by economic problems since its inception.

At first there was threat of bankruptcy on account of the enormous expenses of the war. To meet the deficit in the national budget, the government resorted to printing more and more money causing a drastic decline in the value of the currency, the German Mark. For example, in 1919, the Mark value was 8.9 to the dollar, while in 1923 it was 4 billion Marks to the dollar!

Economic crisis was aggravated by the issue of **war reparation**. In August 1921 after paying £50 million due, Germany requested suspension of payments until the recovery of German economy, but was bluntly refused by France. In January 1923, to recover the reparations, the French Premier Raymond Poincare ordered **occupation of the Ruhr** – the nerve centre of German coal and iron industry, by the French and Belgian troops. The Germans outraged by foreign incursion resorted to passive resistance and struck work in the Ruhr region.

The strike paralysed the economy of the Ruhr region and defeated the French aim, but caused more harm to Germany. It ruined the German industry and triggered **galloping inflation**. Workers were the badly hit as the wages failed to keep pace with huge increase in the cost of living, as was with the middle classes who lost their savings. Realising that their savings, bonds, pensions and years of toil and hard work had become worthless, people began to turn against the Republic, became more receptive to rightist ideas and intensified their search for a government that would alleviate suffering and protect their interests.

vii. Impact of the Great Depression

Gustav Stresemann as Chancellor (August–November 1923) and as Foreign Minister (1923–29) had skilfully placed the republic on the path of recovery. Stresemann's highest priority was restoration of German prestige as a leading European nation.

He stood for 'fulfilment' of its treaty obligations, called off passive resistance in the Ruhr and resumed reparation payments. He issued a new currency **'Rentenmark'** in 1924, backed by mortgage on German real estate. Inflation receded and the Republic seemed to gain stability and confidence. During 1924 to 1929 economic conditions improved drastically. High interest rates and low cost of labour attracted huge foreign investment, and iron, steel, coal and chemical production exceeded pre-war levels. Germany was also able to pay reparation instalments as provided in the Dawes plan.

But the German expectations of greater prospects were soon shattered with the emergence of the Great Depression. The crisis which began with the Wall Street Crash in the United States triggered a severe shock wave in Germany.

The revived German economy was built on foreign and short-term loans and Stresemann himself had commented that Germany was **'dancing on a volcano'**. The German recovery was much dependent on the American loans and with the Great Depression, America stopped loan and started demanding repayment of the short-term loans already granted to Germany.

The Great Depression also affected the German industry. As demand reduced, factories had to close leading to severe unemployment touching 4 million. The exports too were severely reduced. To compound all these, Gustav Stresemann, the politician best equipped to deal with the crisis died in October 1929.

The government under the Chancellor Bruning took certain measures to save the country from the crisis. The measures included reduction in salaries and pensions of government servants, high tariffs on foreign goods, buying of shares of companies affected by the slump and stopping the reparation payment. In spite of these measures situation did not improve and the government came under severe criticism as unemployment rose and peoples' life became more and more miserable.

As seen above, the Weimar Republic was fragile in all its existence and the Great Depression with its devastating impact played a major role in accentuating its downfall and its replacement by the Nazis. The Nazi promises now emerged as attractive alternative to the Germans facilitating the capture of power by the Nazis. Thus, it is said that the Great Depression was the indispensable condition for the Nazi's rise to power.

5. The Nazi Alternative

To a desperate population looking for employment, value for their money, safety of their life and honour of their country, the Nazis promised all these. It was as if the Nazi leader Hitler had grasped the inner most feelings, resentments and longings of the German population.

The Nazi alternative offered employment, prosperity, unity and honour to the Germans by ridding Germany of the root cause of the troubles – the **'November Criminals'** (leaders who agreed armistice in November 1918). The Nazis also accused Jews and the Bolsheviks as conspirators against Germany. The Nazis called for the **overthrow of the Treaty of Versailles** and for the **regeneration of Germany** as the Third Reich by uniting all Germans in Germany, Austria, Czechoslovakia and Poland.

Nazi hostility towards the communists was appealing to the industrialists and land owners as they were apprehensive of Bolshevik type revolution in Germany. Liberal funding from these groups too facilitated the growth of the Nazi party. For the youngsters, the Nazi militia known as the Storm Detachment or the Brownshirts (SA) was attractive as it offered a uniform and a small wage.

Nazi Symbol on a Flag

The SA (Sturmabteilung) founded in 1921 was the paramilitary wing of the Nazi party. They were assigned with the task of protecting Nazi leaders at rallies and to break up meetings of rival political parties such as the socialists and communists.

The Nazis correctly understood the importance of propaganda in the age of universal suffrage and a popular press, to win the support of the masses. The **Nazi propaganda** aimed at the emotions of the people. The Nazis believed that the masses were not moved by scientific ideas or by objective and abstract knowledge but by feelings and emotions. Based on this assumption, the Nazis engaged in elaborate propaganda that could attract huge support within a short period.

Hitler himself had extraordinary oratory skills and leadership qualities. His frenzied exposition/denunciations of the woes and wrongs of Germany under the Weimer Republic made the audience spell bound, while his tremendous energy and will power enabled him to pursue his aims in spite of setbacks and hurdles.

6. Adolf Hitler

Adolf Hitler (1889–1945) was an Austrian-born corporal in German army during the World War I. War time experiences had reinforced Hitler's German patriotism, apart from instilling in him qualities of discipline, leadership, struggle and ruthlessness. At the end of the war he was shocked by Germany's capitulation before the Allies, which intensified his commitment to racial nationalism. He came to believe that the German army **'undefeated in the field'** was **'stabbed in the back'** on the home front by the civilian government.

Adolf Hitler

Hitler entered into politics in 1919, by joining the **German Workers Party**. This party was renamed as the **National Socialist German Workers Party** (NSDAP) or Nazi Party in 1920. In 1921, Hitler emerged the leader of the party and set out to make it a mass movement.

As seen already, in 1923, Hitler tried to capture power in a coup – the **Beer Hall Putsch** in Munich – but failed. He was arrested and put to trial. Hitler was sentenced for five years in prison but served only nine months. In prison Hitler dictated ***Mein Kampf*** (*My Struggle*) an autobiographical work and an exposition of his ideology.

Mein Kampf: The book is a quintessence of ultra-nationalistic, Social Darwinist, anti-Semitic, anti-democratic and anti-Marxist ideas. In this book, published in 1925, Hitler highlighted race as the key to understanding world history and held that conflict between the races as the catalyst of history. Hitler's world view had two important components – racial supremacy and lebensraum – a greater German territory. Hitler believed that the world consisted of superior and inferior races pitted against each other for survival. He identified the **Aryan** as the superior race and the Jews as inferior and parasites. As descendants of the Aryans, the Germans were **'men of God'** embodied with qualities of creativity, bravery and loyalty. A greater German territory being superior were entitled to conquer and subjugate others and to establish **'Lebensraum'** or living space, a vast European empire at the expense of the Slavs and the Communist Russia. In the book, Hitler states that extermination of the weak and sick is far humane than their protection. In essence it can be stated that Hitler identified Jews and the Bolsheviks as racially and ideologically inferior and Aryans and the National Socialists as racially superior and ideologically progressive. Hitler despised parliamentary system as corrupt and its leaders as opportunists. The book is also a testimony to Hitler's opposition to individualism, liberalism, intellectualism, pacifism, internationalism and Marxism all of which he attributed to the Jews.

Political upheavals found often in history have their roots in economic crises and the Great Depression offered such an opportunity to Hitler. By making emotional appeal to an ever-increasing number of disillusioned and discontented Germans, Hitler promised them reassertion of Germany's natural greatness and an end to their economic woes. As a result, Nazi party became the second largest party with 18 percent votes (107 seats) in 1930 compared to a mere 2.6 in 1928 national elections.

Now Nazism became more than a class movement and emerged a truly national party with followers drawn from different classes and groups – unique in Germany of the time. Its promises attracted all segments – the industrialists and large land owners frightened by communism, war veterans, romantic nationalists, intellectuals, the unemployed and newly enfranchised youth yearning for a cause.

In the election in July 1932, the Nazis secured 37.3% votes and with 230 seats emerged the largest single party, but still not a majority in the Reichstag of 608. Once again political crisis emerged in Germany as no Chancellor could retain a majority in the Reichstag. Now a small clique of right-wing politicians with the support of industrialists and aristocratic land owners persuaded President Paul von Hindenburg to appoint Hitler as Chancellor. Many reasons are attributed to this momentous decision-

1. The right-wing nationalist politicians were afraid of the Nazi seizure of power by a putsch which would hamper their dream of restoration of the monarchy.
2. They also believed that Hitler could be better controlled inside the government than if he remained outside (Nazi positions would be restricted to Chancellorship and insignificant ministries).
3. It was also believed that Hitler alone could bring together a coalition that could command a majority in the Reichstag.
4. They found in Hitler a useful instrument to fight communism, to destroy labour organisations and to build up the armament industry.

7. | Hitler as the Chancellor

On 30 January 1933, Hitler was appointed as the Chancellor and he headed a coalition government of the Nazis and the Nationalist Party.

Hitler, who had no intention to rule within the constitutional framework, stood for assuming absolute power. His first opportunity came in February 1933 when the Reichstag building was set on fire by a Dutch communist. Hitler utilised this incident to stir up fear of communism and for strong measures against them. Hitler proclaimed that the arson marked the beginning of a communist uprising and persuaded Hindenburg to sign an emergency decree, suspending civil rights and freedom of the press. The **Reichstag Fire Decree of 1933** allowed Hitler to unleash violent suppression of Communists and the Social Democrats.

Next, Hitler persuaded Hindenburg to dissolve the Reichstag hoping to get overall majority for the Nazis in fresh elections. The **elections in March 1933** witnessed brutal and violent campaign and intimidation but still the Nazis could not win a majority. They could secure only 44 per cent of the votes and 288 seats, 36 short of majority in the Reichstag.

In the newly constituted Reichstag, Hitler took his next step to consolidate his power. In March 1933, Hitler bullied the Reichstag into passing the **Enabling Act**, to gain complete political power without the need of support of a majority in the Reichstag. The Act was an amendment to the Weimar Constitution and required two-thirds majority for its pass. Hitler used intimidation and the provisions of the Reichstag Fire Decree to secure the needed majority. The Communist MPs were either arrested or expelled, support of the Centre Party was obtained either by promises or intimidation and non-Nazi members were surrounded and threatened by the 'Brownshirts' in the Reichstag and the Act was passed by 441 votes to 94.

The Enabling Act permitted the Chancellor to pass laws without either parliamentary control or consent, for the next four years (unless renewed). In effect, the Act eliminated the Reichstag as an active institution of German politics which was now reduced to a mere stage for Hitler's speeches. The Act became the legal foundation of the Third Reich and formed the constitutional basis of Nazi dictatorship. In effect, these two laws – the **'Reichstag Fire Decree'** and the **'Enabling Act'** – were **Hitler's instruments of democracy** to destroy the republic and to establish his dictatorship.

In August 1934, when the President Hindenburg died, Hitler merged the office of the president and the supreme commander with that of Chancellor and assumed the titles of ***Fuhrer*** **(Leader)** and ***Reichskanzler*** **(Chancellor)** by which he became both head of state as well as head of government. He gave it a colour of popular approval by securing 88 percent of votes in plebiscite.

Thus, Hitler, within a year of his advent to power, emerged dictator of Germany which he called the **Third Reich** – the successor of the **Hohenstaufen Empire** of the Middle Ages and of the **Hohenzollern Empire** under the Kaisers.

8. | Nazi Germany or The Third Reich

Hitler followed a policy of forcible co-ordination known as *Gleichschaltung* to subjugate all political, economic and cultural aspects of the nation to the will of the party and to mould Germany into a totalitarian state. Main features of this state were as follows:

i. Leader State

Germany under Hitler was organised as a leader state in which the 'Fuehrer' became the embodiment and expression of the will of the people. Hitler called for absolute obedience of all subordinates. They were expected to 'work towards the *Fuhrer*', which meant their decisions and actions to be in line with Hitler's wishes and the goals of the Nazi party.

Another expression of this leader state was the use of extensive propaganda to develop a 'cult personality around Hitler'. Slogans such as 'the *Fuhrer* is always right' emphasised the importance of the charismatic dictator as the sole source of inspiration of the nation.

Hitler did not brook any interference in his leadership. Many leaders of his own party and of the SA (Nazi storm troopers) were eliminated in 1934 in a purge known as the **'Night of the Long Knives'** when their aspirations threatened to undermine Hitler's leadership. Thousands of persons were summarily executed in the purge which included many who had helped Hitler in his rise to power.

ii. One Party State

Nazi Germany was also a single-party state with the **National Socialists** as the sole legal party in the country. In June 1933, the Social Democratic Party was banned and other political parties were intimidated into dissolving themselves rather facing arrest and imprisonment in concentration camps.

Similarly, strikes were prohibited, trade unions were abolished, their assets seized and leaders were arrested. Their place was taken over by the **German Labour Front**, an umbrella organisation representing both the workers and the employers. This organisation was a reflection of the concept of 'national socialism' and was aimed to pre-empt a revolution against the factory owners and the National Socialist state.

iii. Police State

Nazi Germany was also a police state, which used terror as an instrument of compliance and obedience of as many aspects of life as possible. Apart from the regular police force of the state, the Nazi Germany had two paramilitary forces, the **SA** or the Brownshirts and the **SS** or the Protective Force in black uniform in pursuit of totalitarian goals. These police apparatus along with **Gestapo** (secret police) became instruments of security, surveillance and terror under the Nazis.

Members of these organisations admonished to harden their hearts to human suffering were tasked with containing 'enemies of the state'. These enemies were political opponents such as communists, socialists and Social Democrats, minority groups such as Catholic priests, Gypsies and above all the Jews. It also included homosexuals and others accused of socially deviant behaviour by the Nazis. Large number of concentration camps were opened (from 1933) where the enemies of the Reich were interned or systematically killed.

iv. Centralised State

Hitler centralised the German polity in a way that neither Bismarck nor the Weimer Republic had ventured into. In 1934, the provincial parliaments (*Lander*) were deprived of their sovereign powers and their functions were taken over by Nazi Special Commissioners appointed by the central government. These officials who had complete control over the affairs of the provinces turned them in to mere administrative districts of the Reich. Elections to local bodies were also discontinued. Similarly, in February, 1934, the Reichstadt, the upper house of the German parliament and the representative body of the states, was also abolished. The civil service was also purged of 'enemies of the state' – Jews and the Communists, claiming to re-establish a 'national' and 'professional' civil service.

v. Racism and Anti-Semitism

'Racial nationalism' was core to the Nazi ideology. And, it was based on two aspects – notion of **German racial superiority** and **hatred towards the Jews** both of which underscored the extreme fanatical nature of the Nazi totalitarian regime.

> Hitler's racial prejudice had been embedded since the time he spent his life in Vienna as a youth, where he had come into contact with Georg von Schoneres' pan German movement and had read volumes of literature that were nationalist, anti-Semitic and pan-German. Here, Hitler also acquired hatred for democracy and Marxism.

Hitler considered Aryans as superior type of humanity and the Nordic people of Germany as purest stock of Aryans. On the other hand, Hitler regarded Jews as inferior, non-Aryan sub-humans who were placed at the bottom of his concept of racial hierarchy. Hitler's hatred towards Jews also stemmed from his belief that the Jews were the source of all ills of Germany – humiliation at Versailles, the depression and communism – and claimed that there was a **'world Jewish plot'**.

The Nazi state initiated and institutionalised large number of racial measures.

Efforts were made for purification and multiplication of the **'German race'** as well as its biological separation from the 'inferiors', especially from the Jews. In 1933, the **Marriage Subsidy Law** was enacted to stimulate birth rate of Aryan race by granting loans to newly married couples to have as many children as they could. The **Sterilization Law** in 1933 provided for compulsory sterilisation of any person suffering from a hereditary disease, if medical knowledge indicated that his offspring will suffer from a hereditary disease. In 1939, the Nazi state initiated 'euthanasia' programme known as **T4 Program**, for the murder of Germans who were intellectually or physically disabled and who by their very existence violated the Nazi ideal of Aryan superiority.

But what made Nazism most unique from other forms of totalitarianism was its single-minded persecution of the Jews. In 1933 itself the Nazis had initiated boycott of Jewish business and had banned Jews from government jobs. As a result, thousands of Jewish doctors, teachers, professors, judges and lawyers had been ousted from their professions.

In 1935, the **Nuremberg Laws** deprived Jews of their German citizenship (they were designated as 'subjects of the state'). They could neither vote nor occupy public office. Marriage and sexual relations between Jews and non-Jews were forbidden. Jews were compelled to wear identifying **Yellow Star** (Star of David) while in public. All these resulted in emigration of half of Jewish population from Germany to the United States, Great Britain, Palestine and to other countries.

In November 1938, the Nazis utilised the murder of a German diplomat by a Jewish youth as a pretext, to organise an extensive pogrom, the ***kristallnacht*** or **the night of broken glass**. As part of the pogrom, Nazi troopers attacked and looted Jewish shops and synagogues, murdered hundreds of Jews and thousands more were sent to concentration camps.

The World War II was the enlarged stage for Hitler's anti-Jew hatred. In German-occupied countries such as Czechoslovakia, Poland and Russia more than 6 million Jews were put to death in gas chambers of the

Prisoners of a Nazi Concentration Camp

Nazi concentration camps such as **Auschwitz, Sobibor and Treblinka**. These genocides known as the **'Holocaust'** were the most brutal of crimes against the humanity committed by the Nazis.

> ***Survival in Auschwitz*** (originally titled as ***If This Is a Man***) is a Holocaust memoir by an Italian Jew **Primo Levi**, first published in 1947. The book is a heart shattering rendition of brutalities, human conditions and emotions in a concentration camp. The author portrays the inmates of the camp as '**hollow men**' who were deprived of everyone they love and everything they possessed and make the observation that '**he who loses all often easily loses himself**'. Still, he survived on the belief that 'there still existed a just world outside......a remote possibility of good, but for which it was worth surviving'.

vi. Religion and Culture Under the Nazis

Like other aspects of Nazi Germany, religion too was brought under the state control. In July 1933, Hitler signed Concordat with the **Pope Pius XI**. By this agreement the German Reich guaranteed noninterference with the affairs of the German Catholics in any way. In return the Pope agreed to dissolve the Catholic Centre Party and prohibited the clergy from working in and for political parties.

But promulgation of the Sterilization Law and dissolving of the Catholic Youth League by Hitler soon strained the relation between the two. When the Catholics protested, the church schools and the catholic press were closed down and large number of clergy, nuns and lay leaders were arrested and sent to concentration camps.

Similarly, Hitler targeted various Protestant groups in his effort to bring them into a **'Reich Church'** with the aim of changing traditional Christian teachings to align with the ideology of National Socialism. He believed that the Protestants were more liable to reinterpretation and receptive to his ideas. Protests from pastors against interference in their affairs and also against Hitler's treatment of the Jews strained the relation between the two. Once again Hitler resorted to persecution and many of them were sent to concentration camps.

Education in Nazi Germany was a closely monitored affair aimed at indoctrination of pupils on Nazi ideology. Textbooks were rewritten to fit with Nazi political and racial ideas and history was taught to glorify Germany. Youth organisations – **'Hitler Youth'** for boys and the **'League of German Maidens'** for girls – were compulsory and were further avenues of indoctrination.

The **Ministry of Public Enlightenment and Propaganda** under **Joseph Goebbels** exerted control over the news media, books, theatre, films, arts and information. Newspapers were censored, radio broadcasting was regulated and films that glorified war and pilloried the Jews were encouraged. In 1933, Goebbels organised first of the public book burning episodes, by burning books considered threat to Nazi regime.

On another end, **Goebbels** engaged in active propaganda – promoting the party, its programme and its leader. Propaganda, centred on the myth of the race and the infallibility of the Fuehrer – aimed to disorient the rational mind and to mould a nation to think and respond to the requirements of the leader state. Posters with Hitler's images portraying him as the saviour of Germany were circulated far and wide.

Nuremberg Rally

Annual mass rallies staged at Nuremberg and thus known as the **Nuremburg Rallies** were primarily propaganda events. Scores of thousands of true Nazi believers, the end product of Nazi indoctrination, marching to the martial music and the burning torches, symbolised the solidarity between the German people and the Nazi party and projected the regimented and disciplined Nazi movement to the rest of the world.

vii. Nazi Economy

Under Hitler, economic life of Germany was closely organised. It controlled food prices and rents, imposed compulsory membership in cartels, directed the industries what to produce depending on what the country needed and outlawed strikes and lockouts. But it did not stand for nationalisation and redistribution of wealth and hence the term 'socialism' (in National Socialist Party) was a misnomer.

Two important aims of Nazi economic policies were economic **self-sufficiency** (autarchy) and **employment generation**. It also had two supplementary features – the ideal of 'Beauty of Labor' (work as good and everyone who could work should work) and rearmament which were closely connected with and supportive to the first two.

Hitler made every effort to make Germany self-sufficient. For this, imports were discouraged, exports encouraged and raw materials were rationed. An elaborate bureaucracy was appointed to regulate imports aimed at eliminating foreign competition in German markets. Another step towards autarchy was encouragement provided to develop synthetic replacement for materials such as rubber, textiles and oil and was aimed at reducing foreign dependence. Farmers were subsidised to produce more which resulted in reduction in food imports. The Nazis held peasants in high regard as evident from the Nazi theory of **Blood and Soil**. The soil represented not only reverence for the homeland but also affection for the peasants.

For employment generation, the Nazi regime initiated large number of public works programmes such as construction of schools, superhighways known as autobahns, hospitals, the 1936 Olympic Stadium, afforestation and land improvement. The Nazis also embarked on a vast programme of military rearmament for generation of jobs. This sector grew much faster than the civilian work-creation programmes and the German military expenditure amounted to 75 per cent of national income by 1944. Jobs of the sacked Jews were given to non-Jews. All these measures transformed employment scenario from that of mass unemployment to one of labour shortage.

In industrial sector, the Nazis encouraged private ownership wherever possible. Nazi regime privatised several banks, railway lines and shipping lines. But this was permitted under increasing control of the state. Many reasons were behind Nazi support to the private sector. Of these, the most important was budget deficit of government and privatisation was one method to raise funds. Second, Hitler aspired for strong relation between government and the private sector so that economic goals of government and profit motive of the industrialists could be merged. Moreover, on an ideological level the Nazis believed that private property provided greater incentives for greater cost-consciousness and a precondition to developing creativity of the German race.

How popular were Hitler's policies?

At least in the initial years of the Third Reich, the Germans were happy with the rule. Hitler's decisive actions were in contrast to the weak and indecisive measures of the Weimer Republic. Though Hitler established totalitarianism, he had maintained legality by not repealing the constitution and abolishing the parliament. Secondly, Hitler had resolved many of Germany's economic problems and unemployment in a vigorous manner. Apart from providing employment, Hitler also took care to provide subsidised holidays and cheap entertainment facilities to the working class. To many Germans, especially to the officer class in the army, Hitler's measures for rebuilding the German army and for regaining its status in international affairs were astounding. Hence, many believed in Hitler's ability to take Germany out of defeat and depression and only a small group of people such as the Social Democrats and Communists continued opposing his regime.

Similarities and Differences between Fascism and Nazism

Both aimed at establishment of totalitarian state based on extreme nationalism, autarchy, militarism and opposition to communism. But Nazism was much deeper and stronger in the above parameters. It was also ruthless and brutal especially in its racial measures. Further, Mussolini ruled under a monarch, while in Germany Hitler was the supreme ruler. Mussolini was less successful in fashioning totalitarianism, as life in Italy was less regimented and the army and the church were not under the complete domination of the party. Individuals led their lives less fearful in Italy as evident from the fact that Pope could criticise Mussolini for his persecution of the Jews.

viii. Foreign Policy of Hitler

1. Hitler envisaged for Germany honour, power and importance in world affairs which she had enjoyed prior to the First World War.

2. His greatest ambition was reunion of the German peoples by absorbing German populated regions of Austria, Czechoslovakia and Poland in to the '**Third Reich**' or a greater German empire.
3. Closely associated with the above aim was the creation of a living space or **'Lebensraum'** for Germans by conquering and colonising Eastern Europe and its ruthless Germanisation. Hitler regarded Eastern Europe as the natural field of expansion which would provide food for the German people and an area of settlement for the excess German population. By Lebensraum Hitler also claimed the right of the 'Aryan master race' to decimate the indigenous populations such as Poles, Ukrainians, Czechs, Russians and other Slavic peoples of these regions who were, in Nazi view, 'racially inferiors'.
4. To attain these objectives destruction of the Treaty of Versailles was a prerequisite, as it had imposed huge restrictions on Germany. And, as this aggressive foreign policy of expansion and domination would lead to war, Hitler aimed at **re-armament of Germany**.
5. Hitler also used effectively, the Nazi propaganda machine as an instrument of foreign policy. To create social and political disorientation in other countries, the Nazis disseminated anti-Semitism beyond the German borders. Hitler was also portrayed as the defender of European civilisation, as champion of Europe against Bolshevism and also as a man of peace who only wanted to **remove inequalities of the Versailles Treaty**.

In order to achieve the above-mentioned objectives, Hitler initiated a series of measures which all turned out to be brilliantly successful until his fateful decision to invade Poland in 1939.

What steps were taken by Hitler to achieve his aims?

1. In 1933, Hitler withdrew Germany from the **League of Nations** and the **World Disarmament Conference**.
2. In January 1934, Germany signed a 10-year **non-aggression pact with Poland** by which both the countries pledged to refrain from aggression for a period of 10 years and to settle their issues by bilateral negotiations. The treaty normalised relations between Germany and Poland and allowed Hitler, time for re-armament. Hitler also projected this agreement as an evidence of his peaceful intentions.
3. Hitler incorporated the **Saarland** with Germany in January 1935, after a plebiscite, with over 90 per cent of voters opting for reunification with Germany. After this annexation Hitler claimed that all causes of his grievance with France had been removed.
4. In March 1935, Hitler tore up the disarmament provisions of the Treaty of Versailles by reintroducing conscription. It expanded **Wehrmacht** (German armed force) to 6,00,000 (six times more permitted by the Versailles Treaty). Side by side Hitler initiated development of an air force.
5. In June, the same year the **Anglo-German Naval Agreement** (AGNA) was signed allowing Germany to build its navy up to 35 per cent of Britain's naval strength and 45 per cent of its tonnage in submarines.
6. In March 1936, Hitler reoccupied the demilitarised **Rhineland** (on Germany's western border) which had been permanently demilitarised by the Versailles Treaty. This step was also a repudiation of the Locarno Agreements to which Germany was a signatory.
7. Hitler also launched a **Four Year Plan** (1936–40) to prepare Germany for self-sufficiency and strengthening of its military defences as prime motives.
8. During the **Spanish Civil War** (1936–39) Hitler extended his support to General Franco. The Spanish imbroglio proved to be a 'dress rehearsal for a greater drama soon to be played on an ampler stage', as it provided Germany with an opportunity to test its weapons and tactics. Moreover, it strengthened Hitler's notion that France and Britain lacked determination to fight fascism.
9. In October 1936, Hitler entered into a treaty of friendship with Mussolini which is referred as the **Rome-berlin Axis**. Ethiopian Conflict had pulled Italy away from an alignment of Britain and France, while pushing it closer to Germany. Spanish Civil war had afforded another common bond between Germany and Italy. The two countries also treated Bolshevism as abomination.

10. Hitler took an important foreign policy step in 25 November 1936, by signing **Anti-Comintern Pact** (against the Russian communism) with Japan. The treaty was facilitated by Hitler's strong anti-Bolshevik attitude and also was a reflection of his appreciation of Japan's success against China in Manchuria. To solidify his relation with Japan, Hitler recognised Japan's puppet state Manchukuo in China and renounced German claims to its former colonies in the Pacific, now held by Japan.

    Italy joined this Pact on 6 November 1937 and thus the **Rome–Berlin–Tokyo Axis** came into existence. Soon this Axis, of three seceders from the League of Nations (Japan left the League in March 1933, Germany in October 1933 and Italy in December 1937), was to emerge as the new balance of power in world politics.

11. Hitler believed that Germany's economic crisis could only be stopped by military aggression on **Austria and Czechoslovakia**. Pursuant to this belief, emboldened by lack of any resistance from the Western powers during his intervention in Spain and fortified by his new friendship with Mussolini, Hitler made two dramatic foreign policy moves in 1938. These were the **'Anschluss'** (Annexation) of Austria in March and the Munich Agreement and subsequent **annexation of the Sudetenland** region of Czechoslovakia in September.

    Austria's union with Germany had been explicitly prohibited by the Versailles Treaty. But, Hitler under the pretext of preventing violence – as there were huge demonstrations and rioting staged by the Austrian Nazis in cities like Vienna and Linz – sent German troops and annexed Austria on 13 March 1938. The annexation of Austria added about six million Germans to the Reich, whetted Hitler's territorial appetite and failure of the British and French to take action emboldened him to further acts of aggression.

    Czechoslovakia, an artificial creation of the peace treaties, had about three million ethnic-Germans in its **Sudetenland** region. Hitler declared that Sudetenland as the natural part of the Reich. Hitler also hated the Czechs for their democracy and also for the fact that it was a product of the hated Versailles Treaty. With Austria now annexed to Germany, Czechoslovakia was almost surrounded by an expansionist Germany which could now attack it from the south, west and north. Czechoslovakia rejected German demand to cede Sudetenland and a war seemed imminent.

    Britain and France anxious to avoid a military confrontation determined to negotiate. A **four-power conference** was held in **Munich** (29 September 1938) attended by Hitler, Mussolini, Chamberlain (Prime Minister of Britain) and Edouard Daladier (the French Premier). Czechoslovakia, the fate of which was to be decided, was not invited to the meeting, so was the Soviet Union which had a mutual military assistance treaty with Czechoslovakia. The four parties signed the **'Munich Agreement'** by which Germany was allowed to annex Sudetenland while at the same time guaranteeing the integrity of the rest of Czechoslovakia. Subsequently, the Sudetenland was occupied by German troops.

    Hitler now plotted to annex the rest of Czechoslovakia and encouraged the **Slovak minority** there to demand independence. In March 1939, the German troops occupied the remainder of Czechoslovakia on the pretext of protecting the Slovak people's right of self-determination and established a puppet regime in its capital Prague.

12. Emboldened by series of successes in the realm of his foreign policy, Hitler now moved to formalise the Rome–Berlin Axis of 1936, by entering into a pact – the **'Pact of Steel'** with Mussolini on 22 May 1939, obligating each other country to cooperate militarily, economically or otherwise.

13. Hitler's main foreign policy goal in 1939 was invasion of Poland. Hitler for long had resented the loss of the city of **Danzig**, which had been turned in to a 'free city' and also the creation of the **'Polish Corridor'** which separated East Prussia from the rest of Germany. Germany now demanded return of Danzig and the Corridor, which was refused by Poland upon which in April 1939, Hitler withdrew Germany from the German-Polish Non-Aggression Pact signed in 1934.

    As the British and the French had promised support to Poland 'in the event of any action which clearly threatened Polish independence' by Germany, Hitler now opted to pre-empt the possibility of Soviet opposition to his campaign against Poland, so that chances of a simultaneous fight on a second front in the east against the Soviet Union could be averted.

14. Hitler now restructured his strategy towards Moscow and signed the **Molotov-Ribbentrop Pact** on 23 August 1939. This pact, also known as **Hitler-Stalin Pact**, was a **neutrality pact** by which the two countries agreed not to attack each other and not to support an enemy of the other party. A secret protocol appended to the Pact called for the partition of Poland between Germany and the Soviet Union and division of Eastern Europe in to German and Soviet spheres of influence.

The Molotov-Ribbentrop was an extraordinary diplomatic coup by Hitler. On Hitler's part, he was fiercely anti-Soviet for its communist ideology and because of his anti-Semitism. Hitler expressed this hatred in the term 'Jewish-Bolshevism' as a movement trying to establish world domination from its place of origin. During the Spanish Civil War, the German forces had supported the Spanish Nationalists, while the Soviets had extended their support to the Spanish Republic which in turn had made the Spanish Civil War a proxy war between Germany and the Soviets. It was also in 1936, that Germany had signed the Anti-Comintern Pact directed against the Soviet Bolshevism. In spite of such conflicting interests Hitler cemented a pact with the Soviet and blocked Britain, France and the Soviet Union from reviving their First World War grand alliance against Germany.

On the Soviet side, they had failed in reaching a collective security agreement with Britain and France against the Nazi Germany because of Western distrust of the communist Soviet Union. Moreover, the appeasement measures of the Western powers and unchecked militarism of Nazi Germany had fuelled a fear in Stalin that the Western powers would strike a bargain with Hitler by diverting the Nazi expansion eastward. Stalin also held resentments towards the western powers as the Soviet Union had not been included in the negotiations of the Munich Pact. Another factor for the Soviet tilt towards the Nazi side was desire for territory. The Soviets had lost territory to Poland in 1920. Now Hitler's offer of territory in Poland and a share in the Baltic States were something irresistible to Stalin.

With the Soviets now on his side, Hitler expected that the Western powers would back down as they had done at Munich and commented that 'Our opponents are little worms. I saw them in Munich'.

15. On 1 September 1939, Germany invaded **Poland**. On 3 September, Great Britain and France responded by declaring war on Germany and the World War II began. Hitler's aggressive foreign policy, as seen above, was the primary cause of the World War II.

9. Hitler and the World War II

By employing the new military tactic of Blitzkrieg, the German army rolled into Poland from the west and by invoking the secret protocol of the Molotov Pact, Stalin invaded Poland from the east. On September 27 Poland fell and Hitler and Stalin annexed the country dividing it into western and eastern halves.

By April 1940, Hitler targeted **Norway** to secure iron mines for his war needs, which was then followed by subjugation of **Denmark, Holland, Belgium and Luxembourg** in quick succession and Hitler proclaimed the birth of the **'Greater Germanic Reich'**.

In May 1940, Germany attacked France, captured Paris on 14 June and on June 22 France signed armistice with Germany. The armistice was signed in the same railway coach in which Germany had signed its surrender in 1918 ending the World War I and Hitler gloried in his revenge. Germany occupied northern France and Atlantic coast with an eye on its naval bases.

In the summer 1940, Britain remained the only country at war with Germany which continued to reject Hitler's peace overtures. As a prelude to a full scale-invasion against Britain, Hitler launched an air campaign from August 1940, with bombing raids on British ports, airfields, defence factories and cities. This campaign known as the '**Battle of Britain**' involved hundreds of British and German planes engaging in '**dog fights**' in the sky above Britain. Faced with stiff resistance by the British air Force and suffering heavier loses, Hitler had to call off the campaign in June 1941.

In September 1940, Germany signed a **Tripartite Pact** or the **Berlin Pact** with Japan and Italy declaring their intention 'to establish and maintain a new order, calculated to promote the mutual prosperity and welfare of the people concerned'. The treaty was a **defensive military alliance** that called on the parties to assist one another with all political, economic and military means and was primarily intended to deter the United States from entering the conflict.

The next development in the World War II was directly connected to Hitler's imperial ambitions and racial prejudices. As seen already, destruction of Bolshevism and the conquest and colonisation of Soviet Russia had been a cardinal aim of Hitler's foreign policy. Hitler believed that vast resources of Russia would make Germany 'invulnerable' and guarantee access to the strategic resources needed to defeat Germany's remaining rivals. He also visualised settling of millions of people of 'pure Aryan blood' in territories west of the Urals after exterminating the Jews and enslaving the Slavs.

To secure this intended invasion on Russia, Hitler at first fortified the Balkan flank by subduing **Greece and Yugoslavia** in April 1941. Then, on 22 June 1941, in spite of the 1939 non-aggression pact (the Molotov-Ribbentrop Pact), Germany attacked the Soviet Union. The invasion named '**Operation Barbarossa**' involved a massive assault by 3 million men supported by tanks and air attack along a front that stretched more than 3,000 km. from the Baltic to the Black Sea. The Russians followed a '**scorched earth**' policy and retreated before the advancing German forces. Within few months the German troops advanced within the striking distance of **Leningrad** and **Moscow**. Hitler had hoped to defeat the Soviet before the onset of winter but heavy rains of October and severe early winter in November and December 1941 hampered German mission. Once the Soviet counter-offensive intensified in the winter of 1941 Hitler was forced to postpone the assault on the Russian capital.

Now Hitler concentrated his attack on **Stalingrad**, the prosperous industrial centre located on the Volga River. The offensive was launched in July 1942 and by November the Germans had reached in and around Stalingrad. In the **Battle of Stalingrad**, in the winter of 1942–43, the Soviet army fought doggedly and courageously for every inch of their territory and encircled the German troops. The Axis forces at Stalingrad which had been cut off from retreat, exhausted of ammunition and food, and being reduced to less than half of their original number surrendered in February 1943 under their commander Friedrich Paulus.

10. Defeat of Hitler and the End of Nazism

The success in Stalingrad boosted the Soviet morale and they followed up with more offensives forcing the Axis forces to abandon the siege of Leningrad and Moscow. Soon the Soviet army pushed the Germans out of the Soviet republics and advanced through Poland to Berlin. On 30 April 1945, while the Soviet troops were approaching the Reich Chancellery – the office of Hitler – at Berlin, **Hitler shot himself dead**. A Total War ended in Hitler's total defeat. With his death ended a period of unparalleled atrocities, human sufferings on an unprecedented scale and immeasurable destruction all of which were caused by this man who professed an ideology that was gravely immoral to the civilised world.

SUMMARY

The Weimer Republic – It was the government that came to power in Germany after the First World War. During its existence from 1919 to 1933 it went through three stages before being ended by Hitler who was appointed as the Chancellor by the German President Hindenburg.

Features of the Weimer Constitution – This constitution was drafted in the city of Weimer, Germany. Federal system, preamble, executive power vested in the President, ministry headed by Chancellor, bicameral legislature, provision for the German peoples' basic rights and obligations, religious freedom, right to property and provisions of 'initiative', 'referendum' and 'recall' were the major features of the constitution.

Challenges of the Weimer Republic – Post-war challenges of reconstruction, humiliation of signing the Treaty of Versailles, weakness of the Weimer Constitution, lack of democratic tradition in Germany, threats from conspirators and private armies, economic crisis and finally the devastating impact of the Great Depression.

Adolf Hitler and the Third Reich – Adolf Hitler (1889–1945) was a corporal in German army. The state and system of governance he constructed in Germany after his capture of power is known as the Third Reich. This was a totalitarian state and had the following main features – Leader state, one-party state, police state, centralised state, racial nationalism and anti-Semitism, state control over religious and cultural life, autarchy-oriented economic practices and an assertive foreign policy.

Hitler and the World War II – Hitler's aggressive foreign policy was the most important cause of the World War II. His measures such as withdrawal of Germany from the League of Nations, incorporation of the Saarland with Germany, re-armament and re-introduction of conscription in German army, reoccupation of the Rhineland, signing of the Anti-Comintern Pact with Japan in 1936, establishment of the Rome–Berlin–Tokyo Axis in 1937, Anschluss (annexation) of Austria and of the Sudetenland and finally his invasion of Poland in September 1939 were indirect conflict with the interests of other powers which ignited the World War II. Though Hitler employed his military tactic of Blitzkrieg and achieved commendable success in the initial stages of the war, by the year 1942 the tide of the war turned against him and he was defeated by the Allied Powers. His defeat also ended the Nazi regime in Germany.

Questions of Previous Years Civil Services Examination

1. 'Hitler did not really want a World War. His intention was only a short war with Poland'. Elucidate. (A.J.P Taylor) (2009)
2. What were the weaknesses and difficulties of the Weimer Republic? How did Hitler succeed in establishing his dictatorship? (2004)
3. 'Comparison of the Fascist regime in Italy with the National Socialist regime of Germany is almost inevitable. The similarities are obvious, but there is one point of difference which is worth mentioning'. Elucidate. (1991)
4. 'There was an element of system in Hitler's foreign policy … His outlook was continental'. Elucidate. (1995)

CHAPTER 13

The Second World War

In this Chapter

1. Introduction

The war that broke out in 1939 was another World War and in many respects was a continuation of the first, and at the same time was more destructive and transformative conflict in history. Neither the idealism of Woodrow Wilson as expressed in his **Fourteen Points** nor the **League of Nations** with its mandate to preserve peace and prevent war could save the world from drifting towards another catastrophe. In retrospect, the **Paris Peace Settlements** too proved to be no more than an armistice as prophesied by the French Marshal Ferdinand Foch in 1919, that this Treaty (of Versailles) is not peace. It is **an armistice for twenty years**.

The Second World War was a global war fought between the vast majority of the world's nations grouped into two alliances – the Allies and the Axis. At the beginning of the war the **Allied Powers** consisted of the United Kingdom, France, Poland and dependent states, such as India, and independent dominions of the British Commonwealth such as Canada, Australia, New Zealand and South Africa. The USSR joined the group in June 1941 and in the same year China officially joined the Allies. In December 1941, the United States officially joined the Allied Powers. The **Axis Powers** consisted of Italy, Germany and Japan, hence, the grouping was also known as Rome–Berlin–Tokyo Axis.

The battles of the World War II were fought across the globe – on the coasts of Western Europe, on the Plains of Russia, in the deserts of Africa, in the rugged terrains of China and in the waters of the Pacific. These battles are ever since entwined with images not only of bloodshed but also of immense suffering, sacrifice and heroism. The Second World War was also a Total War in which all the resources and activities of nations were channelised for the war purposes. Years of bloodshed, barbarity and destruction could finally be brought to an end only with the use of nuclear bombs in 1945.

2. Causes of the Second World War

A. Defects in the Paris Peace Settlements and German Desire for Revenge

One important outcome of the Paris Peace Conference had been formulation of peace settlements with the defeated nations, especially with Germany. One of the important causes of the Second World War was the defects in these settlements, which in reality created more problems than they solved. And these Settlements, instead of facilitating peace, ushered in **'twenty years of crisis'**.

The World War I had greatly weakened France, and in its weakness and fear of Germany it sought to isolate and punish Germany with the tacit approval of other victorious powers. The War being a devastating and demoralising catastrophe, the victors under the insistence of France and to avoid a repeat, had made terms of the Versailles Treaty too harsh, which left Germany destitute and its people victimised. Apart from imposing harsh terms on Germany, such as war reparations, the treaty of Versailles had saddled them with the 'war guilt' and had deprived them their rightful share in international relations.

To the Germans, for whom the War ended not in their defeat but in a stalemate, the Treaty was a humiliation and vindictive, aimed at keeping Germany economically and militarily weak, rather than working out an agreement assuring long-term peace and progress. Treaty of Versailles failed to answer the German concerns and the real danger emerged with the German unwillingness to accept its defeat as final. All these went in to exacerbating old hatreds and creating **'Revanchism'** in German population. The humiliation and resentment created by the Treaty of Versailles caused Nazi electoral successes. Adolf Hitler laid the psychological ground work in preparing Germany for another war, and his disregard for the treaty became the most important factor for the Second World War.

> The First World War had been termed as 'the war to end all wars', coined first by **H.G. Wells** in his book ***The War That will End War*** (1914). But, it turned out that neither that War nor the post-war peace treaties could prevent another war. In this context, it is pertinent to note the comment made by the British Staff Officer **Archibald Wavell**, the future Viceroy of India, on the Paris Peace Conference that 'after the war to end war, they seem to have been in Paris at making the peace to end peace'.

B. Failure of the League of Nations

The League of Nations was established after the World War I with the primary objective of preventing another world war and it marked a fundamental shift in the diplomatic scene of the preceding century. The League of Nations was a government of governments with mandate of settling disputes between nations in an open and legalist forum. The old mechanism of 'balance of power' with strong armies and secret agreements was now replaced with open covenant.

The League was supposed to prevent war through methods such as collective security, disarmament, settlement of disputes through negotiation and also through measures to improve global welfare. The League failed in many times such as during Japan's invasion of Manchuria and Italian invasion of Abyssinia in enforcing its mandate and controlling those powers that worked outside of accepted international law. The League which required unanimity in its decisions, no army of its own to enforce decisions and as a body that upheld self-interest of its leading members ultimately proved failure. And those failures were to prove fatal to the world when another world war broke out in 1939.

C. Power Politics

The First World War did not end the power politics or power struggle between nations. But on the other, power politics reappeared in international scene soon after the signing of the peace treaties.

First, the vanquished powers of the First World War considered the League of Nations itself as an alliance of the victors to promote and perpetuate their national interests. Consequently, these nations did not take the League seriously.

On the other, the victors started alliances to keep their enemies isolated and contained. France maintained the largest standing army in post-war Europe and sought to encircle Germany with a ring of military alliances. One expression of this encirclement was creation of the **'Little Entente'**, a defence alliance in 1920, consisting of France, Rumania, Yugoslavia and Czechoslovakia to keep Austria and Germany in containment. Further, as if the Versailles Treaty provisions were not enough to prevent the revival of German power, Franco-Belgian and Franco-Polish alliances were also created (1920–21). Another expression of this encirclement was the creation of a buffer zone of Baltic States, Poland and Rumania against Soviet Russia.

These alliances and measures by the victors fomented anxieties and tensions in countries such as Germany as was clear when Germany and the Soviet Russia – two 'outcast nations' among the European powers – signed the **Treaty of Rapallo** in 1922 providing for normalisation of relations between the two, trade collaborations and renouncing of all territorial and financial claims against each other, resulting from the Treaty of Brest-Litovsk. The treaty also paved way for secret military cooperation between the two. In 1926, the **Treaty of Berlin** was also signed between these two nations pledging neutrality in the event of an attack on the other by a third party.

As a result of these alliances and measures, anxiety among the European powers and mutual suspicion of each other's intensions re-emerged. At the same time neither the League nor any diplomatic measures such as the Kellogg-Briand Pact (1928) could alleviate these fears or eliminate power struggles.

D. Economic Causes

In causing the World War II economic conditions of post-World War I period too were significant. **Collapse of the German economy** and the **Great Depression** were two major economic developments in this period and were directly linked to the outbreak of the War.

By imposing huge war reparations on Germany and by occupying its industrial heartland, the Saar Basin, France, had pushed the German economy on the verge of total collapse. The economic hardships under the obligation of huge reparation, loss of industrialised territories coupled with the post-war reconstruction responsibilities had placed the Weimer Republic into an unenviable situation. The German economic recovery was retarded and inflationary pressure mounted, as Germany resorted to printing trillions of marks to meet the reparation obligations. The French occupation of the Ruhr in 1923–25, the German coal region further worsened economic condition of Germany.

Economic crisis discredited the Weimar Republic in the eyes of the majority of Germans, who were under economic hardships and national humiliation forcing them to look for a leader who could take Germany out of the chaos. Failure of the Republic facilitated capture of power by Hitler. Though Adolf Hitler had attempted *coup d'état* in 1923, it had failed. But, Hitler gained recognition as a national hero and thereby laid the foundations of Nazi party's rise to power. In 1933, he captured power with a determination to overthrow the hated Versailles settlement and to resurrect Germany not only in economic sphere but in other aspects too.

The second factor was the Great Depression, which originated in United States in 1929. It became worldwide in 1930s and in many ways contributed to the outbreak of the Second World War.

1. In Germany it halted economic recovery, caused economic downturn and widespread unemployment exposing the fragility of the Weimer Republic and facilitated the rise of the National Socialist Party of Hitler.
2. It strengthened economic nationalism. To meet the crisis of business stagnation and unemployment and to protect their economies many nations intensified economic nationalism by resorting to high tariffs so that the home market could be preserved for the home producers.
3. Nations also increased their armaments production as a means to reduce unemployment. The armaments production on a large scale to reduce unemployment and to boost business was first undertaken by Germany. As a result, Germany could reduce unemployment substantially. Other nations too followed the German armament expansion model, not simply to reduce unemployment but also to meet the perceived threat from a rearmed Germany.
4. The Depression also caused a new wave of militant expansionism. Nations now stood for expanding their territory as a means of solving their economic crisis. These expansionist steps were nothing but, as proved soon, stepping stones to the Second World War.

    a. In 1931 Japan invaded **Manchuria**, the northeast part of China, to ensure the market for its goods and adequate supply of coal, iron and other minerals. Manchuria was also seen as a base for future Japanese expansion to the rest of China.

b. In 1936, Italy under Mussolini invaded and annexed **Ethiopia** to divert the attention of the Italians from the problems of economic depression. Italy also invaded **Albania** in 1939 in similar spirit.

c. Hitler remilitarised the **Rhineland** in 1936, which had been forbidden by the Treaty of Versailles. Economic problems at home necessitated a foreign policy success to restore the Nazi regime's popularity and remilitarisation of Rhineland was the easy way out for Hitler.

d. Similarly, economic problems of Germany compelled Hitler to launch a series of wars to expand German power over Austria and Czechoslovakia and to exploit their economies to Germany's advantage. In March 1938, **Austria** was annexed and in October 1938 **Sudetenland** was incorporated into Germany. These expansionist policies partly motivated under economic conditions strengthened the hands of fascist powers and contributed directly to the outbreak of the Second World War.

E. Nationalism

Though nationalism was one of the causes of the First World War, it had failed in solving the aspirations of many nationalities. The post-World War I settlements had placed many ethnic minorities in different sovereign states. The unmet nationalistic aspirations of these groups increased the chances of another world war.

The best example in this context was Eastern Europe. In this region, ethnic minorities had been placed under different sovereign states. **Czechoslovakia**, for example (the newly created state and one of the successor states of the Austro-Hungarian Empire at the end of the First World War), had people of different ethnicities – Czechs, Slovaks, Germans, Hungarians, Poles and Ruthenians. Existence of this multi-ethnic state in the age of ethnic nationalism was bound to create fissures and instability in international relations.

F. Appeasement

Appeasement was a feeble and ineffectual response from the democratic countries against militarism and expansionism of the fascist powers. It was a policy followed by the British and later by the French in international relations by giving political or material concessions to aggressive powers of Germany, Italy and Japan in order to avoid war. It was carried through compromise and negotiations. This policy of continuous concessions was granted in the hope of reaching a point of saturation when the dictators would be willing to accede to international collaboration. But, the Appeasement was capitulation to blackmail and ultimately proved to be a failure.

This policy was based on certain assumptions on the part of western democratic nations, as given below:

1. The first was the desire to avoid outbreak of another world war. The trauma of the First World War still fresh in mind, the western democratic nations desired to avoid war by giving way to the demands of the fascist powers provided they were not too unreasonable.
2. The British leaders also believed that it could not afford a military build-up and its expenses.
3. In the post-World War I period, there existed a strong pacifist public opinion in Britain against war. For example, in 1933, the **Oxford Union** (a public forum), voted against wars and that it would not fight for 'the King and Country'.
4. The British believed that the Treaty of Versailles had been too harsh on Germany and many of its grievances were genuine. They also believed that Italy had been cheated at the Versailles. It was expected that certain concessions to these powers would remove the need for war.
5. Appeasement was also based on the conviction that economic co-operation between Britain and Germany would be beneficial for both and that the British support in economic recovery of Germany would lead to establishment of internal order in Germany and removal of feeling of humiliation of German People.
6. It was also a reflection of failure of the League of Nations and the failure of collective security it envisaged. The policy of collective security ran parallel to the international disarmament measures and economic sanctions against the aggressors. As these measures proved ineffectual, the British Prime Minister Neville Chamberlain believed that through personal contact between the leaders he could control and civilise the fascist powers.

7. The United States was more concerned about dealing with the Great Depression, hence did nothing to strengthen the resolve of Britain and France against Hitler.
8. Finally, Fascism, as believed by many people in the democratic nations, was a healthy form of anti-communism. The appeasers believed that by assisting Germany rebuild its economic, political and military power they could contain the westward advance of communism emanating from the USSR. Many Conservative leaders in Britain believed that the communist threat was greater than that of Hitler. On similar thinking, the West refused to impose sanctions against Japan, after its invasion of Manchuria as Japan too could act as a counterweight to the communist Russia.
9. Above all, the British Empire which had overextended by now was totally unprepared and unwilling to fight a full-scale war against more than one country – Japan in Asia, Italy in the Mediterranean and Germany in Europe – all at once. The United States was keeping a policy of self-imposed isolation in international affairs and France was weak. In such a circumstance, the British PM Chamberlain came to believe appeasement as the best policy, while he also speeded up the British rearmament as an effort to deter aggression from the fascist powers.

Phases in Appeasement

The appeasement emerged in the 1920s and came to an end in March 1939 with Hitler's attack on Czechoslovakia.

It developed in two phases. The first was from the mid-1920s to 1937 during which Britain, under its Prime Ministers **Ramsay McDonald** and **Stanley Baldwin** followed a policy of avoiding conflict by not taking any action against violation of the Treaty of Versailles by the fascist powers.

The second stage was from May 1937 under the new British Prime Minister, **Neville Chamberlain**, who gave a new thrust to the policy, by taking initiative to meet the fascists' demand by negotiations. The climax of appeasement reached in the Munich Conference, where Britain and France presented the Sudetenland to Hitler in a desperate move to avoid war. The appeasement as a policy to avoid war ended in 1939 when Hitler in defiance of his promises given at Munich seized Czechoslovakia compelling Chamberlain to abandon the policy of appeasement in favour of policy of resistance.

Examples of Appeasement

In its first stage appeasement found expressed in the following developments:

a. Britain tried to conciliate Germany with the **Dawes Plan** and **Young Plan** and with the **Locarno Treaties**.
b. In September 1931, Japan invaded **Manchuria** in north-east China. The League of Nations condemned the aggression and directed Japan to withdraw to facilitate a peaceful settlement. In response, Japan resigned from the League and continued its advance into China. Neither the League of Nations nor the Western democratic powers took any action and this inactivity and ineffectualness in the Far East lent every encouragement to European aggressors to pursue their similar acts of defiance.
c. Britain did not oppose the **German rearmament** in violation of the Versailles Treaty.
d. **Anglo-German Naval Agreement** – 1935. This was an ambitious attempt on the part of both London and Berlin to establish better relations by regulating the size of German navy in relation to the British Royal Navy. It fixed the total tonnage of the German Navy to 35% of the total tonnage of the British navy. By signing this agreement Germany was allowed to build a navy beyond the limits set by the Treaty of Versailles.
e. **Abyssinia Crisis** 1935–36: As part of Benito Mussolini's imperialist ambitions, Italy had acquired Eritrea and Somalia in Africa, and was looking for opportunity to conquer Abyssinia (Ethiopia).

   In October 1935, Mussolini launched an attack on Abyssinia, citing a border skirmish between Italian and Abyssinian troops near the border in Somaliland as excuse. The League of Nations declared Italy to be the aggressor and imposed sanctions. Undeterred by the sanctions, Italy captured **Addis Ababa**, the Abyssinian capital and proclaimed Victor Emmanuel III, King of Italy as the Emperor of Ethiopia (Abyssinia). During this crisis, Britain took only halfhearted efforts like sending a naval fleet in to the Mediterranean and the sanctions imposed by the League were ineffective.

f. **Remilitarisation of the Rhineland**: The Treaty of Versailles had demilitarised the Rhineland and Germany had reaffirmed this arrangement under the **Locarno Treaties of 1925**. Hitler repudiated Locarno spirit and sent German troops into the Rhineland in March 1936. France, though lodged protests with the League of Nations, did not mobilise their troops for want of backing from the British. The British Prime Minister Stanley Baldwin said Britain lacked the forces to support France. In Britain the general perception was that the Germans were merely walking into '**their own back yard**'.

g. **Spanish Civil War** 1936–39: The Spanish Civil war was a three-year long brutal fight between the **Republicans** and the **Nationalists**, ultimately the Nationalists led by **General Franco** emerged victorious.

> The Spanish Civil War has often been described as a struggle between democracy and fascism. It has also been portrayed as a struggle between leftist revolution and rightist counter-revolution that exposed political divisions in the European continent. While the right and the Catholics supported the Nationalists as a way to stop the expansion of Communism, on the left including intellectuals and labour unions considered the war a necessary battle to stop the spread of fascism.

The Spanish republic had been established in 1931. In 1936 elections, the **Popular Front**, an electoral coalition of various left wing political groups, defeated the **National Front** (a collection of right wing groups) and formed new Spanish government with **Manuel Azana**, as the president of the Spanish Republic. The new government initiated reforms such as restoration of political liberties, distribution of land to the peasants by breaking up big estates and measures to improve the conditions of industrial workers and miners.

The right wing groups and the **Falangists** (the fascist and conservative ideologists in Spain) were opposed to the reforms of the new government and planned its overthrow. In July 1936, the fascists or the Nationalists organised mutinies with the support of most of the Spanish army. The Nationalists were led by General Franco. The Nationalists received munitions and soldiers from Nazi Germany and Fascist Italy, while the Republicans received support from the Soviet Union. Finally, the war ended with the victory of the Nationalists and the establishment of a dictatorship under General Franco.

The Spanish Civil War is often portrayed as the '**Dress Rehearsal**' of the Second World War. Firstly, the civil war exposed the political division of Europe into fascist and non-fascist groups. The European fascist powers of Germany and Italy along with Portugal provided men and material to the Nationalist forces. German involvement included soldiers, powerful air and armoured units, U-boat undertakings and contribution from the German navy the Kriegsmarine. The War provided combat experience to German military in latest technology, while Spain offered a test ground for German tank tactics. Germany also made use of the Civil War to test its new weapons such as Luftwaffe Stukas and bombers proving their effectiveness. Like Hitler, Benito Mussolini too joined the war in support of Franco. The Royal Italian Navy participated in the Mediterranean blockade, in breaking the Republican Navy's blockade of the Nationalists held Spanish Morocco, apart from supplying machine guns, artillery, aircrafts and tanks.

The Soviet Union provided material assistance to the Republican forces and also sent military advisers and large number of Soviet volunteers to Spain. The Soviet Union directed communist parties around the world to organise and recruit the '**International Brigades**' in support of the Republicans. Many Europeans, often affiliated to communist and socialist entities, joined the International Brigades to assist the Second Spanish Republic during this conflict. The Latin American country of Mexico too supported the Republicans. Mexico provided diplomatic support as well as sanctuary for the Republican refugees.

In the Spanish Civil War, neither Britain nor France intervened, and they followed a policy of non-intervention in the Spanish affairs. This non-intervention was a part of the policy of appeasement aimed at preventing a proxy war in Spain from escalating into a major conflict of world powers. They tried to control materials coming into Spain, which in effect subjected the Spanish Republic to international isolation. But the efforts to stem the flow of war materials to Spain proved unsuccessful as it was mocked by Germany and Italy by providing decisive support to the rebels. Thus, the policy meant no aid to the Republicans, while the German and Italian support to the Nationalists continued unchecked. It is in this context, the comment by **George Orwell**, a famous English novelist and critic, that says 'the outcome of the Spanish Civil War was settled in London, Paris, Rome, Berlin – at any rate not in Spain' acquires significance.

In its brutalities and devastations too the Spanish Civil war was a '**Dress Rehearsal**' of the Second World War. In territories captured by Franco's forces, organised purges took place as a part of cleaning up any trace of 'leftism' in Spain. Extensive killings of non-combatants such as trade unionists, government sympathisers, Republican intellectuals and those suspected of voting for the Popular Front were carried out. The Republican militia too resorted to wanton killings of civilians, clergy, shopkeepers and industrialists, if found not sympathetic to the Republican cause. The Civil War was also infamous for its aerial bombardment of civilian areas and towns of which the most infamous was that of Guernica, a Spanish town destroyed by aerial bombing by fascist planes.

Pablo Picasso, the Spanish painter and regarded as one of the most influential artists of the 20th century and known for co-founding the **Cubist movement**, painted **Guernica** in 1937. The painting depicted the horrors of the bombing of the Guernica town and cast the Spanish Civil war into global attention.

Guernica

h. **The Anschluss** – Annexation of Austria to Nazi Germany

The post World War I treaties with Germany (Treaty of Versailles) and Austria (Treaty of Saint Germain) had prohibited the political union of these two countries. A Nazi movement had emerged in Austria, demanding their integration (Anschluss) with Germany. They conducted huge demonstrations and attempted a failed putsch in January 1938. Realising that this could be the prelude to a German invasion to his country and hence to forestall Hitler, the Austrian Chancellor Schuschnigg scheduled a plebiscite on whether or not Austria should remain independent. The plebiscite was scheduled for 13 March 1938. But before this could take place, in case the vote went against his interest, Hitler acted and annexed Austria by sending German troops on 12 March 1938.

Hitler's justification was that the German troops had been sent to Austria 'to help the brother Germans in distress'. Anschluss was Hitler's greatest success till then, which was achieved without any opposition from the western powers and exposed the weakness of Britain and France, who once again limited their response to protest. The British Prime Minister, Neville Chamberlain, held the view that the satisfaction of Germany's 'just territorial demands' would save Western Europe and maintain peace. He justified his inaction against Germany in the House of Commons with the comment that 'the hard fact is that nothing could have arrested what has actually happened, unless Britain and other countries had been prepared to use force'. Many in Britain considered the Anschluss as the natural union of one German group to another. The reaction from France and America was similar. This lack of action by the international community against the Anschluss led Hitler to conclude that he could use even more aggressive tactics for constructing the Third Reich.

The **second stage** in the appeasement unfolded under the new British Prime Minister **Neville Chamberlain**. This phase witnessed Britain negotiating with Germany to find out reasonable claims of Hitler, while at the same time speeding up the rearmament measures to deter the fascists.

i. Munich Agreement

Czechoslovakia as a sovereign state in central Europe had been established out of the old Austro – Hungarian Empire at the end of World War I. After the annexation of Austria into Germany, next in line in Hitler's aggressive design of building his Third Reich was Czechoslovakia. In security point of view, now Austria being part of Germany, Czechoslovakia was almost entirely surrounded by Germany and could be attacked from the west, north as well as from south.

Hitler's desire to destroy Czechoslovakia had many motives. First and foremost, it was a part of his dream of constructing the Third German Reich and **lebensraum** (living space) to German people. He also hated Czechoslovakia for its democracy towards which he had no sympathy. Similarly, he hated Czechoslovakia for being a product of the Versailles settlement.

As the first step to the conquest of Czechoslovakia, Hitler planned annexation of the Sudetenland, a part of Czechoslovakia with a large German population. Sudetenland was also an important industrial centre of Czechoslovakia. Hitler made himself the advocate of ethnic Germans living in Sudetenland triggering the '**Sudeten Crisis**'. Encouraged and instructed by Germany, the Sudeten Germans denounced the Czech government.

The Nazi propaganda machine had already organised the Sudeten Germans into a 'fifth column'. And as in Austria, a Nazi movement had gained momentum in Sudetenland under their leader **Konrad Henlein**. They accused the Czech government of persecuting its German minority and started agitating for autonomy and freedom to profess Nazi ideology. During the huge protest demonstrations clashes occurred between the Germans and the Czechs. Hitler accused the Czech government of discriminating against the Sudeten Germans and demanded the Czech government to cede the Sudetenland to the Reich.

Both France and Britain had their own reasons for appeasing Hitler on the Sudeten issue. In 1924, France and Czechoslovakia had entered into an agreement of mutual support in case of an attack from Germany. Logically, Czech government called on France to provide military support as promised in the treaty of 1924. But suffering under economic turmoil and internal dissension France was not in a position to fight against Germany.

On the other hand, Britain unlike France had no commitment to Czechoslovakia. Still the British could have opposed the German move, had their military preparations and policy perceptions were something different. The British forces were not battle ready as the rearmament of Britain had only just begun. The British chief of staff reported that the nation was not prepared to fight, and to buy time, sacrifice of Czechoslovakia was necessary. Many British officials believed that the Sudeten Germans are indeed a suppressed minority in Czechoslovakia, and also that the Sudetenland was not worth a war to destroy the Western Civilisation. 'How horrible it is that we should be digging trenches and trying on gas masks here, because of a quarrel in a faraway country between people of whom we know nothing?' asked Neville Chamberlain, in his radio broadcast to the English people. Many in Britain also genuinely believed that Hitler was carrying the principle of self-determination to its logical conclusion and after the integration of all Germans under the German flag Hitler would be satiated? The location of Czechoslovakia was also such that Britain and France could forcibly prevent the German occupation of the Sudetenland only by an invasion of Germany.

Faced with the prospect of war, the British Prime Minister, Neville Chamberlain, negotiated with Hitler. Hitler agreed for a four-power conference. In the meeting held in Munich, on 29 September 1938, and attended by Hitler, Mussolini, Chamberlain and Daladier (Prime Minister of France), it was decided to handover Sudetenland to Germany. At the same time the four powers guaranteed the integrity of the rest of Czechoslovakia.

The **Munich Agreement** signed by these four powers was another capitulation by Britain and France. They ignored the vital interests of a nation whose territory had been guaranteed by the Treaty of Versailles. Czechoslovakia was not even invited to the meeting and their country's representatives were left to await their fate outside the conference room in Munich. The Czechs were told that, if they refuse to the Munich decision, they would receive no help from Britain and France. For these reasons, the Munich agreement was a tragedy to the Czechs and was considered as **Munich betrayal**. Under ultimatums both from the friends and foes the Czechoslovak government had no other alternative but to accept the diktat under protest.

The Munich Agreement gave Sudetenland to Germany. Czechoslovakia now lost its defensible border with Germany and its fortifications, along with the loss of 70% of its iron and steel industry, 70% of its electrical power and more than 3 million of its population to Germany.

For Britain, it brought time to re-arm. Chamberlain returned to Britain claiming that it was '**peace for our time**' and received rapturous welcome from the public. And to Hitler, it was another development that stimulated his ferocious appetite for conquests. The Munich Agreement convinced Hitler, that the democratic nations would never put up any effective opposition to him and expressed his contempt for them in a speech to his military commanders 'our enemies are no masters, no men of action, they are little worms. I saw them in Munich'. Since then the Munich Agreement is a byword of the futility of appeasing totalitarian regimes.

Neville Chamberlain has been criticised for his surrender before Hitler in Munich. Winston Churchill called the Munich Agreement 'a total and unmitigated defeat'. Opposing Chamberlain, Winston Churchill commented, 'You were given the choice between war and dishonour. You chose dishonour and you will have war', a prophecy soon proved to be true. Critics say Chamberlain was foolish enough to believe that Hitler could be bought off by ceding Sudetenland. Contrary, Hitler considered it as sign of weakness and increased his demands. Critics also point out that, it was better to fight Hitler in 1938 than in 1939 by which time Hitler too had strengthened his military. It is also argued that, it was better to fight on the issue of Sudetenland because the Czechs had a well-trained and modern army and the Czech people were ready to fight to preserve their nation's integrity.

j. Hitler's invasion of Czechoslovakia

Next, Fuehrer planned of occupying total Czechoslovakia and encouraged the Slovak minority there to demand independence. At the same time, Hitler pressurised the Czech President Hacha to seek German help to restore peace and order. In March 1939, the German troops entered and occupied Czechoslovakia and established a puppet regime in its capital Prague.

The German action caused great anger and criticism. Hitler broke his promise given at Munich. Moreover, the invasion of Czechoslovakia was of totally different character from his previous adventures of Rhineland militarisation, the Anschluss with Austria and the annexation of Sudetenland. In all these, Hitler had a claim of self-determination of German people. But in the case of Czech, Hitler had no *locus standi* and his intention became very clear to the European statesmen that Hitler was seeking European hegemony. Chamberlain was compelled to make a radical turn in his policy of appeasement to a policy of resistance to which France too now agreed.

G. Immediate Cause of the Second World War – Invasion of Poland

Hitler next annexed the Lithuanian **Port of Memel**, which had a large German population but had been placed under Lithuania by the Treaty of Versailles. Hitler secured the Port by issuing an ultimatum to Lithuania, who considered acceptance of the ultimatum as a 'necessary evil' to preserve their independence. Next targets logically were **Danzig** and the **Polish Corridor**. The Germans had resented the loss of Danzig and the Polish Corridor, a narrow strip of land which connected Poland with the Baltic Sea. In April 1939, Hitler demanded return of Danzig and the Polish Corridor from Poland to the German Reich. Britain now promised to support Poland in the event of an attack from Germany. Britain, France and Poland entered into a formal alliance guaranteeing one another's independence and territorial integrity and with this another world war was well on the horizon.

Meanwhile, Germany and Russia signed a **Non-Aggression Pact** on 23 August 1939. The pact also known as **Nazi-Soviet Pact** or **Molotov-Ribbentrop Pact** (after the foreign ministers of the two countries who signed this pact in Moscow) delineated the spheres of interest between the two powers and a secret section of the pact provided for the partition of Poland between the two parties and the Russian control over Finland and the Baltic states of Latvia, Lithuania and Estonia. Stalin expected that the treaty with Germany would provide him time to strengthen his armed forces. Stalin was also apprehensive that the western democracies might strike a bargain with Germany by diverting Nazi expansion eastward at the expense of Russia. Apart from that Stalin was convinced from the Munich Agreement (to which Soviet Russia was not invited) that Britain and France were unreliable.

Being convinced of non-intervention by Britain and France, and Russia now being neutral, Hitler expected that Poland would quickly capitulate. Poland refused to negotiate and on **1 September 1939**, German tanks crossed the Polish border.

3. | Ignition of the War

In response to German invasion of Poland, Britain and France declared war on Germany on 3 September. Hitler employed his new military tactic – the ***Blitzkrieg*** (lightning warfare), to bring Poland in to quick submission. The *Blitzkrieg* involved the use of massive amounts of manpower, airpower and armour with speed and surprise to achieve rapid annihilation of the enemy. Hitler conquered Poland within a month and on 29 September Poland was divided up between Germany and the Soviet Union as agreed in the Nazi-Soviet Pact.

The fall of Poland was followed by a period of ***Sitzkrieg*** (sitting war) or 'Phoney War' for around six months during which there was no large-scale military action and the German force manned their defensive line, the **Siegfried Line** along the French border.

Stalin now attacked and annexed countries to the north of Poland. While **Lithuania, Latvia and Estonia** fell quickly, **Finland** put up a fierce defence against the Russian forces. But by March 1940 even Finland surrendered but only after inflicting heavy losses to the Russians.

***Blitzkrieg* and *Sitzkrieg*:** These were two tactics associated with the World War II. *Blitzkrieg* or '**lightning war**' was a military strategy of the Germans for a quick and surprise attack against their enemies with an incredible speed and coordination of air and ground attacks. *Sitzkrieg* means '**sitting war**' and also called as 'phoney war', refers to a phase in the Western Front of the same war during which France and Germany manned their respective defences – the **Maginot Line** and **Siegfried Line** – waiting for each other to attack first.

On 9 April 1940, Hitler restarted the *Blitzkrieg* and conquered **Denmark and Norway**. In May he launched another *blitzkrieg* across **Holland (Netherlands), Belgium and Luxembourg** and moving through the dense Forest of Ardennes reached on French soil. Then racing across the northern France to the sea the German forces sought to annihilate the Allied forces trapped in the French seaport of **Dunkirk** near the Belgian border.

At this point, in one of the most heroic acts of the War, some 3,38,000 British and French troops were ferried across the English Channel to safety by the British navy. The mission known as the **Dunkirk Rescue Mission**, conducted in the face of constant German Luftwaffe attack on the beaches, was a turning point in the war. By this operation more than three lakh Allied troops could be rescued to fight again instead of being annihilated by the Nazi forces. Success of the mission boosted the morale of the Allied forces and Winston Churchill used it as a propaganda tool by describing it as the '**Dunkirk Spirit**'.

The Germans now swept southwards and on 14 June 1940 captured Paris. A demoralised France whose resistance was dying out signed armistice on 22 June at **Compiegne** in the same railway coach in which Germany had signed the armistice in 1918, ending the World War I. The northern France and the coast were occupied by Germany and the French army was demobilised. In southern France a puppet government was established at Vichy under **Marshal Philippe Petain** which collaborated with the Germans.

Many factors attributed for the failure of France which include psychological, political, military and leadership failures. France as a nation had been bitterly divided between the right and the left. The right groups admired Hitler, believed the Fuhrer as a man of destiny and wanted an agreement with him. The communists too were opposed to the war in the light of the non-aggression pact in existence between Hitler and Stalin. Thus, the French were psychologically not prepared for war and their internal political disputes had destroyed the will to fight. On the military front, the French Command was content to sit behind the Maginot Line and did not move the troops to block the Germans on the River Meuse. Though France had as many planes and tanks as the Germans, they were not equal to the German Command who had mastered the psychology and technology of motorised warfare.

Charles de Gaulle (1890–1970) was a French general who escaped to London and set up a government-in-exile and organised the Free French forces that fought against the Nazis until France's liberation in 1944. He was elected as the President of France in 1958.

4. Development of the War

In the summer of 1940, with the defeat of France, Britain was the only country that remained at war with the Nazis and Hitler expected Britain to surrender. But the English under their new prime minister, Winston Churchill, proclaimed 'we shall fight on the beaches, we shall fight on the landing grounds, we shall fight in the fields and in the streets…we shall never surrender'. Churchill described the Nazis as '**a monstrous tyranny, never surpassed in the dark, lamentable catalogue of human crime**'.

Winston Churchill

Winston Churchill (1874–1965) was a Conservative politician who had served in Britain's First World War government as a Liberal. He had opposed the Appeasement and had spoken out in favour of British rearmament during the inter war years. He replaced Neville Chamberlain as the prime minister and headed a national government consisting members from the Conservative, Liberal and the Labour parties during the World War II. As a youngster, Churchill had a speech defect but emerged an exceedingly compelling orator and used the radio to communicate with his countrymen.

Now, Hitler proceeded in earnest to invade Britain. He planned landing of more than 2,50,000 soldiers on England's shores. This operation was code named as **'Operation Sea-Lion'**. The invasion of Britain to be successful, Germany required to gain control over the English Channel by neutralising the British air and naval forces. For the purpose, Hitler started an air campaign with bombing raids on British airfields, aircraft factories and naval installations. By September 1940, German air force started raiding the British cities including London to break the British morale. The British fighter pilots offered courageous resistance turning the sky above Britain with **dogfights between hundreds of aircrafts** of these two countries.

In this aerial battle known as the **Battle of Britain**, the **Royal Air Force** (RAF) inflicted huge losses on the **Luftwaffe**. Britain lost only 792 aircrafts, while Germans lost 1389. Convinced that the Luftwaffe could not destroy the British air defence, Hitler called off the invasion in May 1941 and redirected his attention to the Mediterranean and to Eastern Europe.

Among the factors that contributed to the British upper hand in the Battle of Britain were two technological devices – **radars** and a German code-making machine named **Enigma**. A network of new radar stations provided early warning of approaching German planes to the British. Enigma, a German code-making machine smuggled into Britain, enabled the British to decode German secret messages which deprived Germans the surprise factor in their operations and also allowed the RAF to launch counter attack on Germany. The limited range of the German bombers, as they could stay in the air only for about 90 minutes, and inability of Germany to make up its losses of planes too acted in favour of British side. The skill and courage of the British fighter pilots and the leadership of Churchill, whose oratory skills kept the morale of the British in high spirits, in spite of death and destruction too were undeniable factors that contributed to the British success. Churchill later on commented that '***Never in the field of human conflict was so much owed by so many, to so few***', which was a fitting tribute to the spirit of the British fighter pilots.

5. Entry of Italy

Benito Mussolini, though an ally of Hitler, had remained neutral at the beginning of the war. With Hitler's conquest of France and not wanting to be outdone by Hitler, Mussolini declared war on Britain and France. In September 1940, he sent an army from the Italian colony of Libya into British-controlled Egypt and pushed 60 miles inside Egypt. However, the British soon drove the Italians out of Egypt, pushed them back to Libya and took more than 1,30,000 Italians as prisoners. Mussolini proved to be an embarrassing ally to Hitler and Hitler had to step in to save his Axis partner. Hitler sent a crack German tank force, the **'Afrika Korps'** under **General Erwin Rommel** which drove the British out of Libya.

6. Hitler's Invasion of Russia

Unable to subdue Britain, Hitler shifted his attention, in spite of the 1939 nonaggression pact, to the Soviet Union. Though many scholars consider that invasion of Russia was Hitler's greatest mistake, Hitler had many reasons for attacking the Soviet Union.

1. Hitler 'had always wanted to establish the foundation of his thousand-year Reich by the annexation of the territory between the Vistula and the Urals'. Conquest, exploitation and colonisation of Russia by the German master race and establishment of Lebensraum had been cardinal to the Nazi ideology.

2. The extermination of the Jews and the enslavement of the Slavs were also part of Hitler's Reich.
3. He also believed that Russia's vast resources would make Germany invulnerable and would empower her to 'wage wars against whole continents'.
4. Another factor was Hitler's hatred of communism which he wanted to obliterate.
5. Hitler also feared a Russian attack on Germany, while she was still fighting the Allies in the west. In other words **'to Hitler the Russian campaign was not a luxury: it was the be-all and end-all of Nazism'**.

As a preliminary to his plan of Russian invasion, Hitler wanted to secure the **Balkan flank**. In early 1941, through the threat of force, he had brought **Bulgaria, Romania and Hungary** to the side of the Axis Powers. In April 1941, Hitler attacked and defeated **Greece** and **Yugoslavia**.

The attack on the Soviet Union, **Operation Barbarossa**, was launched on 22 June 1941. Hitler assembled more than 3 million men, 3,300 tanks and 5,000 planes along a 2000-mile front. It was another *Blitzkrieg* and the Germans drove deeply in to Russia, destroying and surrounding the disorganised and unprepared Russian forces, the **Red Army**, who were still re-equipping their army and air force after the purges of Stalin.

Though the Russians had the largest army in the world, they suffered terrible losses – on the first day itself the Luftwaffe had destroyed more than 1,200 Russian aircrafts. Within three months more than 2.5 million Russian soldiers had been killed, wounded or captured. The Germans also captured important cities such as Riga and Kiev.

But, the Russian reserve strength was far greater than what the Germans had estimated and the Russians, in spite of terrible hardships did not capitulate. The Soviet troops now resorted to a **scorched-earth policy** by burning and destroying everything in the enemy's path, as they withdrew. By the end of 1941, the Germans had conquered vast regions of the Soviet Union but failed to capture **Leningrad** and **Moscow** or to bring Stalin into submission. Hitler's plan to end the Russian war before the onset of winter thus was poised for collapse.

In September 1941, the Germans put **Leningrad** under siege and cut off it from the rest of the Soviet Union in order to starve and force them to surrender. Even though nearly one million people died in Leningrad during the winter of 1941–42, the city refused to surrender.

Failing to bring Leningrad into submission, Hitler looked to **Moscow**, the capital of the Soviet Union. By December 1941, the Nazis had reached within twenty-five miles of Moscow but the advance was stopped by the counter-attack of the Red Army. The movement of German forces was also severely hampered by heavy rains and harsh winter during which temperature fell to minus 40 degrees centigrade rendering much of the German heavy equipment useless. Far from its supply line, the German army, the Wehrmacht, was running short of fuel and food supplies and its soldiers were fighting in the bitter cold, but in summer uniforms.

7. Japan's Entry and the Pacific Theatres of World War II

Japan had initiated an expansion program in 1931, by taking over **Manchuria** in north-eastern China and had established the puppet state of **Manchukuo** in 1932. In 1937, the Japanese army swept into the heartland of China inflicting heavy casualties on the poorly organised Chinese forces and captured its cities and its principal seaports.

In September 1940, Germany, Italy and Japan signed a **Tripartite Pact** pledging to support each other in the war. It also recognised Japan's plan to create the **Greater East Asia Co-operative Sphere** by conquering territories in East Asia. In return, Japan recognised German and Italian supremacy over Europe.

Japan, now eyed European colonies in Southeast Asia-French Indochina, British Burma and Malaya and the Dutch East Indies to meet its need for oil, rubber, tin and food. The Japanese also had a belief that the European powers were in no fit state to defend their possessions in Asia, as they are engaged in a life and death struggle in Europe.

Though the United States still had not directly entered the War, the Japanese considered it necessary to secure their rear, by destroying American fleet in the Pacific as they considered it **'a dagger pointed at Japan's throat'**. Japanese aggressiveness became more apparent when **General Hideki Tojo** became its prime minister in October 1941.

On their side, the Americans were concerned about the Japanese expansion, as any such move could threaten the American-controlled Philippine and Guam. With an aim to contain the Japanese expansion, the Americans had sent aid to the Chinese who were still at war with Japan.

On 7 December 1941, the Japanese bombers attacked the US naval base at **Pearl Harbor in Hawaii**. In the attack the Americans suffered a total defeat – 188 aircraft, 8 battleships and other naval vessels were destroyed and more than 2,300 Americans were killed. Losses on Japan were minor.

Pursuant to the Pearl Harbor, the Japanese launched bombing raids on the European possessions in Asia, such as the British colony of **Hong Kong** and American controlled **Guam** and the **Wake Island**. By mid-1942, the Japanese captured vast territories such as the **Philippines, Indonesia, Burma, Malaya, Singapore and Thailand** and planned to launch a strike against India, the largest of the British colonies. The Japanese drive for a Pacific empire was at its apex.

8. | Entry of the United States

During the initial years of the World War II, the United States had been neutral. Though many Americans were sympathetic to Britain, they had opposed direct US entry into the war. At the same time, the Allies had been allowed to buy arms from the United States on cash-and-carry basis. In March 1941, the US Congress passed the **Lend-Lease Act** by which the US President could lend or lease arms to any country 'vital to the United States'. Subsequently, the US Navy also started escorting British ships carrying US arms. The US President Roosevelt and the British Prime Minister Winston Churchill also issued a joint declaration **'the Atlantic Charter'** (August 1941) as the war aim, even though the United States had not entered the war.

But, the Pearl Harbor attack by the Japanese, as seen above, brought the United States into the War. The US president Franklin Roosevelt declared it as '**a date which will live in infamy**' and declared war on Japan the next day. On December 11, Germany and Italy declared war on the United States and in turn the United States declared war on these two powers, turning the War truly a global war.

Now, immense industrial and military potential of the United States was brought to the side of the Allies. The US war machinery consisting of more than 3,00,000 aircraft and 85,000 tanks and other weapons was to prove '**the arsenal of victory**' of the Allied Powers. Industrial production in America during the World War II was a picture of one of the greatest military industrial efforts in history. It is said that "no war was more industrialized than World War II. It was a war won as much by machine shops as by machine guns". The aircraft companies increased their production from building a handful of planes at a time to building them by the thousands and aircraft manufacturing attained the first place from the 41st place among American industries in course of the war. For example, in 1939, total aircraft production for the US military was less than 3,000 planes but by the end of the war, America produced 300,000 planes. Similarly, other areas of industrial production too witnessed a huge jump in production augmenting the Allied war resources. For example, on their assembly lines the Ford Motor Company built one motor car (comprising 15,000 parts) in every 69 seconds enabling America to produce three million vehicles in 1941. With all such measures half of the world's war production came from the U.S. and the Americans could claim at the end of the war that, "We won because we smothered the enemy in an avalanche of production, the like of which he had never seen, nor dreamed possible." This fact was also attested to by Joseph Stalin who commented later on that "Without American production, the United Nations could never have won the war". By the spring of 1942, it had appeared that the Axis Powers held the upper hand, with Germany controlling Europe almost to Moscow and the Japanese conquest and establishment of a Pacific Empire in the East. But the entry of the United States, and three decisive battles – Midway, Stalingrad and El Alamein – reversed the tide of the war in favour of the Allies.

9. | The Battle of Midway

The Island of Midway, located in the Pacific, 1,100 miles northwest of Pearl Harbor, was an important **American airfield**. In June 1942, the Japanese forces made a powerful attack on the Midway with 5 aircraft carriers, 17 warships and 400 aircrafts and with an invasion force of 5,000 soldiers. On June 4, the two navies fought a **unique naval battle** entirely by carrier-based planes. Demonstrating extra ordinary courage and marked superiority over their enemies, the US pilots destroyed all aircraft carriers and 332 Japanese planes. The **Midway Debacle** seriously hampered the Japanese war initiatives as they had lost their carriers and strike planes. The Battle of Midway turned the tide in the pacific theatre of the World War II, for waging battles in the vast expanses of the Pacific, air power operating from carriers was crucial. Subsequent to the Midway success, the Americans under **General Douglas** McArthur started mission **'island-hop'** to recover the islands in the Pacific, starting with the August 1942 landings on the **Solomon Islands**. Meanwhile, the Allies had started to turn the tide in their favour both in the Mediterranean and on the Eastern Front.

10. The Battle of El Alamein

By mid-1942, the German forces had advanced to El Alamein, a village in Egypt west of Alexandria under their brilliant tank commander **General Erwin Rommel**. In October 1942, the Battle of El Alamein began with a surprise attack by the British Eighth Army commanded by **General Bernard Montgomery**. Rommel's army, though fought back fiercely, was beaten and had to retreat to west. In November 1942, a joint Anglo-American force landed in Morocco and Algeria (French colonies under the control of Vichy France allied to Germany), under the American **General Dwight D. Eisenhower**. Trapped between Montgomery's and Eisenhower's armies, Germany's **'Afrika Korps'** surrendered in May 1943. It marked the end of German and Italian presence in North Africa.

The success of this first combined Allied offensive led them to initiate steps to bring the Mediterranean under their complete control. The Allies invaded and conquered Sicily in July 1943. The conquest of Sicily toppled Mussolini from power as his fellow fascist leaders turned against him and the King Victor Emmanuel III dismissed him from prime ministership. On September 3, the Allied troops invaded southern Italy and Italy surrendered.

But the Germans seized control of northern Italy, rescued Mussolini from detention and resurrected him as the puppet ruler of a government in northern Italy under their protection. Though the Nazi forces continued to hold central and northern Italy, the **Italian resistance fighters** fought against the German occupation which continued till the fall of Germany, in May 1945.

11. The Battle of Stalingrad

After the attack on Moscow was repulsed by the Russians, Hitler in the spring of 1942, turned his attention to southern Russia – the rich agricultural and industrial region of **Ukraine** and the oilfields of the **Caucasus**. Hitler sent his Sixth Army under the command of **General Friedrich Paulus** which penetrated deep through the Crimea, but was checked at **Stalingrad** on the River Volga. With the onset of another winter, the Germans were trapped inside the city and the Soviet troops cut-off their supply lines. The **Battle of Stalingrad** fought during the winter of 1942–43 became an epic struggle in which the Russian soldiers and civilians fought for every building and every street. It lasted for five months and with his retreat cut-off, General Paulus with about 1,00,000 men surrendered in February 1943.

The Battle of Stalingrad had been described as the '***greatest single trial of strength***' of the Second World War. The battle was a catastrophe for the Germans. They lost more than 3,00,000 troops and about 1,00,000 were taken prisoner. It also shattered the myth that the Germans were invincible. The defeat also put the Germans on the defensive and they were compelled to undertake a general retreat.

12. The Second Front

Opening of a Second Front had been a consistent demand of Stalin to the Allied leaders, in order to relieve the concerted Nazi drive against the Soviet Union. Pursuant to this, the Allies built up a massive invasion force consisting thousands of planes, ships, tanks and more than three million troops. This Allied force under the command of General **Dwight D. Eisenhower** planned an attack across the English Channel on the **coast of Normandy** in German held France.

Dwight D. Eisenhower

The invasion code – named **Operation Overlord** – began on 6 June 1944 and was the largest land and sea attack in history. It involved securing the beaches and marching inland. Despite stubborn German resistance – on the first day itself about 3,000 died on the American side alone – the Allied forces consisting of British, American and Canadian troops held the beaches and landed lakhs of men, tanks and heavy vehicles. Within one month more than one million troops landed in France and marched into Paris triumphantly.

By September 1944, France, Belgium and Luxembourg were liberated, and by the spring of 1945, the Allied troops penetrated into Germany. While the Allied forces moved to Germany from the west, the Soviet forces conquered Romania, Bulgaria and Hungary, the countries allied with Germany and advanced to Germany, from the east. Warsaw, Budapest and Vienna were liberated and the Soviet forces encircled Berlin in April 1945. On 30 April 1945, Hitler committed suicide, the Soviet troops hoisted the Red Flag on the Reichstag building and the German army surrendered unconditionally. On May 9, the surrender was officially signed in Berlin and the Allied forces celebrated the **VE Day-Victory in Europe Day**.

13. End of the War

Even after the German surrender, the war continued in Asia and the Pacific. After their success at Midway in June 1942, the Allied Powers had strengthened their counter-offensive against Japan by a series of naval battles and island assaults in the region. Despite tenacious defence by the Japanese soldiers who preferred death to the disgrace of surrender, the Allied forces could capture the islands of **Iwo Jima and Okinawa** by June 1945 and were within 500 miles from the Japanese mainland.

> **The Manhattan Project**: A top-secret project by the United States to develop atomic bomb. The project was headed by **General Leslie Groves** and chief scientist **Robert Oppenheimer**. The first experimental test was conducted near Alamogordo, New Mexico, in the United States on 16 July 1945. Oppenheimer commented that, he could see 'a thousand suns' at the test.

On 26 July, Harry S Truman, then the US President, called upon Japan to surrender or to expect a ***'rain of ruin from the air'***. In the absence of any reply from Japan, the United States dropped an atomic bomb (Little Boy) on Hiroshima on August 6 and 3 days later a second bomb (Fat Man) on Nagasaki. More than 1,50,000 people were killed immediately and much more died of radiation fallout.

Harry S Truman

Truman's decision to use atom bombs was one of the most controversial actions of the entire World War II. It is argued that the Japan was close to surrender as the American naval blockade and unrelenting aerial bombardments had deprived it of essentials such as oil and rice and had caused severe devastation. But Truman argued that atomic attack was necessary as an invasion on the Japanese homeland would have cost the Allies, hundreds of thousands of lives. It was also believed that the use of atomic bomb would bring the war to the quickest possible end. Critics argue that, Truman wanted to deprive the Soviet Union of an opportunity to strengthen its influence in East Asia, for which he desired a swift end of the war.

On 2 September 1945, Japan surrendered to **General Douglas MacArthur**, aboard the US battleship Missouri in Tokyo Bay and the World War II came to an end.

14. Exploitation and Extermination – The Holocaust

The **Holocaust** was the terrible expression of the fulfilment of Nazi racial theories. It meant systematic man slaughter of Jews and other peoples judged inferior by the Nazis. The word is derived from the Greek words *holos* (whole) and *kaustos* (burned). The Nazis believed that the Germanic people as the '**master race**' and called them as Aryans. They considered most of the rest of humanity to be inferior humans deserving either extermination or enslavement. These included the Jews, Poles, Russians, homosexuals, gypsies, insane and the sick. Extermination of such races and groups became an obsession and mission with the Nazis to protect, as what they claimed, the '**racial purity**' of the Aryans.

The Nazi propaganda concentrated on the myth of race and blamed Jews for Germany's failure in the World War I, humiliation of the Treaty of Versailles and for their country's economic problems. After the Nazi capture of power, targeting of Jews became government policy and the Nuremburg and other laws denied German citizenship to them apart from imposing many restrictions on the Jews.

Discrimination and persecution forced thousands of Jews to migrate to other countries such as France, Britain and the United States. As forced emigration did not yield the desired result, Hitler herded the Jews into designated cities where the Jews had segregated areas known as the **ghettos**. With barbed wires, stone walls and sealed off from other sections, Jews lived in these ghettos under horrible conditions.

Hitler's real war of annihilation took place during the World War II in what he called as the '**Final Solution of the Jewish Problem**'. This meant nothing but genocide aimed at 'the planned biological destruction of the Jewish race in the Eastern territories'. Under **Heinrich Himmler**, a fanatic believer of Hitler's racial theories and the chief of the SS, (Hitler's elite security force) the German forces rounded up Jewish men, women and children from the Nazi occupied territories to execution grounds and killed them with machine guns.

As Nazi forces swept across Europe, Hitler tried to impose a **New Order** by exploiting men and material of these regions for the German benefit. The Nazis looted and exploited the industrial and non-industrial resources of non-German lands to the benefit of the German war economy. Further, more than seven million people from all over Europe were enslaved and taken to Germany to work in German companies such as the Krupps, Siemens and Farben.

Concentration camps, such as at **Auschwitz, Belzec, Treblinka, Buchenwald** and elsewhere, originally established for political prisoners, were turned into death camps. Jews from all over Europe were taken to these camps and upon arrival women, children, the old and the sick – those unfit for work were exterminated immediately in gas chambers. Some gas chambers as that of Auschwitz could kill 20,000 people a day. The healthy were sent to worksites where they worked till death – of starvation, disease or exhaustion. The inmates of these camps were also used for biological experiments, for testing new vaccines and for inducing new diseases.

It is estimated that more than six million Jews (two-thirds of the Jewish population), of which 1.5 million were children, had been exterminated in the Holocaust. As a result, centuries-old Jewish culture and community-life was erased from the socio-cultural landscape of many regions of Europe. The Holocaust thus inflicted a deep wound in human conscience that could never entirely heal. Apart from being a dark episode in the history of civilisation, it also was a terrible testament of human irrationality.

Nuremberg Trials: These were series of trials of Nazi war criminals held in Nuremberg, Germany, during 1945–46. The trials were conducted under an **International Military Tribunal** representing 23 nations. At the trials the term genocide was coined and came to be defined as a '**crime against humanity**'. The Nuremberg Trials also became basis for the formulation of the United Nations Genocide Convention (1948), the Universal Declaration of Human Rights (1948) and the Geneva Convention of the Laws and Customs of War (1949).

15. | Consequences

Destruction: The World War II had often been portrayed as 'the last good war' as it had a clear and noble purpose – destruction of Nazism and fascism and eradication of all the barbarities they stood for. With destruction of Nazi Germany, fascist Italy and imperial Japan and by the liberation of Western Europe from tyranny, the good triumphed over the evil. But all these implied huge cost both in men and material and was attained through horrid acts, obscene atrocities and horrifying blunders committed by both sides.

In immediate terms the end result of the World War II was the death and destruction it caused, which was more than any other conflict in history. Some of the estimates suggest the overall casualties from the war at sixty million men, women and children and about one-third of these deaths occurred in one country, the Soviet Union alone. Millions of people had also been uprooted from their homes – to work as slave labourers, interned in concentration camps or had been forced to flee from the war zones.

Material costs of the war too had been staggering. The war's direct cost in money terms was estimated at $4 trillion dollars. The ground war had destroyed much of the country side, while aerial bombardment and shelling had turned hundreds of cities to rubble. Some of these were London, Warsaw, Dresden, Berlin, Tokyo and of course Hiroshima and Nagasaki. The gigantic task of rebuilding was a major challenge faced by the nations.

The misery caused by the war continued for years after the war, as many cities had no water, electricity or sufficient food. As the fighting had ravaged the countryside agriculture had been in ruin, resulting in thousands of death by starvation and disease. The Second World War thus transformed the scope and scale of the warfare forever.

End of European domination of the world: One significant effect of the World War II was the end of European domination of the world. The western European states such as Britain, France, Italy and Germany, that played a leading role in world affairs for the last many decades were thoroughly destroyed or weakened. They with their industries in ruin, economy in shambles and in deep debts, were not longer in a position to keep their dominance.

Emergence of super powers: End of the war signalled a shift in the power balance and geopolitical structure in the world. The **United States** and the **Soviet Union** emerged as the most powerful states in the world. The United States had the largest navy and air force, had immense industrial might and had experienced great prosperity by supplying the Allies with food and war materials during the War. The Soviet Union though severely weakened after the war, retained the world's largest army and stood for protection of its interests and ideology in different parts of the world.

Political: The War caused spread of democracy throughout West Europe and spread of Communism throughout East Europe.

Division of Europe: Another feature of the post-war years had been the deepening divide between Western and Eastern Europe underpinned by different economic and social systems called capitalism and communism. The mutually conflicting interests of these powers created conditions for the Cold War – **perpetual war for perpetual peace** – leading to wastage of billions of dollars and thousands of lives and its brushes with nuclear annihilation in the decades after the war.

Decolonisation: The war caused destruction of the imperial powers of Europe which accelerated the disintegration of their overseas empires. Now, these war-ravaged countries had to concentrate on reconstruction instead of fighting new wars against Asians and Africans, who had intensified their fight for independence. Japanese occupation of European colonies in Asia had destroyed the notion of European superiority and invincibility. At moral level too, the European states who had fought against German imperialism could hardly justify colonialism any longer.

Establishment of the UN: To maintain world peace and prevent another war, the world leaders formed the United Nations in 1945. The new organisation was founded on the experiences and lessons learned from the failed League of Nations, as such it was more vivid and strong in its objectives and responsibilities.

Inauguration of the atomic age: The World War II also ushered in the atomic age. The United States was the first to possess the bomb, but soon, the Soviet Union and others acquired it. The emergence of a weapon that can destroy the entire planet became the ever present and ever terrifying legacy of the World War II.

Social changes: The War had far-reaching effects beyond the obvious negative effects. The war had socially levelling impact both in **class and gender** terms. The war though did not erode class differences weakened it, by narrowing the gap between rich and poor due to increased income tax, improved employment, increase in working-class wages and increase in state welfare measures. For women, the war was a liberating experience as it offered greater opportunities and better position in society. By serving in the armed forces (Hitler's pilot Hanna Reitsch flew plane in Berlin even when the Soviets troops were already in Berlin), in fields and factories women equalled in many fields as to men. As a result, women acquired voting rights in France and Italy in 1945 and 1946, respectively.

SUMMARY

The Second World War – It was another global war fought after a period of 20 years of peace since the end of the First World War.

Causes of the World War II – The Paris Peace Settlements and the German desire for revenge was the most significant cause. Other causes such as power struggle between nations, failure of the League of Nations, nationalism, the policy of Appeasement and economic causes such as the Great Depression too made the war inevitable.

Development of the War – The World War II was ignited with the German invasion of Poland in September 1939. In 1940 France was defeated and surrendered before the Germans. Then Hitler attempted to capture Britain by launching an operation named the 'Operation Sea Lion' but the determined resistance by the British forces defeated Hitler's objective. Japan entered the World War II by attacking the US naval base at Pearl Harbor in Hawaii in December 1941. This invasion necessitated American entry in the war and had the effect of securing for the Allied Powers the immense military and economic resources of America. In 1942, three important battles – the Battles of Midway, El Alamein and Stalingrad turned the tide of the war in favour of the Allies. In 1944, the Second Front of the World War II which was essential to relieve the Nazi drive against the Soviet Russia was opened and was named the Operation Overlord. Then the Allied powers invaded Germany both from the West and the East and being encircled by the enemy forces. Hitler committed suicide on 30 April 1945. Japan surrendered in September 1945 after it was attacked with atom bombs by the United States.

Consequences of the World War II – Death and destruction on its trail, end of the European domination of the world, emergence of superpowers, division of Europe, establishment of the UN, acceleration of the process of decolonisation, inauguration of atomic age and social changes were significant consequences of the World War II.

QUESTIONS OF PREVIOUS YEARS CIVIL SERVICES EXAMINATION

1. The Treaty of Versailles contained in itself the seeds of the Second World War. Examine. (2023)
2. Do you agree with the statement that the Second World War was history's most destructive war? Elaborate (2020)
3. Was Czechoslovakia served on a dish to Hitler at Munich? What were its implications? (2019)
4. 'Until December 1941, the battlefield of the Second World War was exclusively European and Atlantic; thereafter it became also Asiatic and Pacific'. Elucidate. (2018)
5. Show how the Spanish Civil War was a prelude to World War II. (1991)
6. To what extent can Germany be held responsible for causing the two World Wars? Discuss critically. (2015)
7. How did the policy of appeasement escalate the problem of Nazi aggrandisement? (2011)

CHAPTER 14

The United Nations Organization

In this Chapter

1. Introduction

The United Nations as an inter-governmental organisation was established on 24 October 1945 with the primary objectives of promoting international co-operation and preventing wars. And today, it has emerged as an indispensable pillar of the international system engaged in the preservation of peace, delivery of humanitarian aid, promotion of sustainable development and protection of human rights.

Emblem of United Nations

At its founding the UN had 51 members and was a replacement for the League of Nations, which had been established after the World War I with similar objectives. It is headquartered at **Manhattan**, New York in USA. Its official languages are Arabic, Chinese, English, French, Russian and Spanish. Of these, French and English are the working languages of the Secretariat and the official languages of the International Court of Justice. It now has 193 sovereign states as members, resolved to 'shape our future together'. Though the UN is headquartered in New York, it has three regional headquarters in Geneva, Vienna and Nairobi. The **United Nations Office at Geneva (UNOG)** is the second largest office outside of New York and is a centre for conference diplomacy and a forum for disarmament and human rights. The **United Nations Office at Vienna (UNOV)** looks after programmes on drugs and crimes and the peaceful uses of outer space. The **United Nations Office at Nairobi (UNON)** promotes co-operation between the UN and regional organisations apart from managing programmes on environment and the human settlements.

2. Making of the United Nations

The outbreak of the Second World War signalled the failure of the League of Nations. As such, during the Second World War itself, the great powers of the time, under the leadership of the US President **Franklin D. Roosevelt**, gave serious considerations to the idea of founding a better world-body to replace the League of Nations by eliminating some of its drawbacks and to realise the ideal of one '**world state**' so that the world nations may dwell in unity.

During the war, a number of meetings and conferences had been convened by the Allied Powers to discuss the war aims and common strategies to be pursued in the war. It was in these conferences the idea of the United Nations was conceived and consolidated, leading to its creation in 1945. These were as provided in sections below.

A. The Atlantic Conference

It was the first of a series of meetings held during the World War II. The conference was attended by the British Prime Minister **Winston Churchill** and the US President **Franklin D. Roosevelt** aboard a warship anchored at **Placentia Bay** located in Newfoundland in the **Atlantic,** where Roosevelt was holidaying. The leaders issued a joint declaration on 14 August 1941, known as the **Atlantic Charter**, defining the Allied goals for the post-war world that contained eight common principles, which are:

1. no aggrandisement, territorial or other
2. no territorial changes against the wishes of the people
3. right to self-determination
4. removal of trade barriers and access to the trade and to the raw materials for all states
5. global economic co-operation aimed at improved labour standards, economic adjustment and social security
6. establishment of a peace that will afford to all nations the means of dwelling in safety within their own boundaries and a world free of fear and want
7. freedom of the seas
8. disarmament and abandonment of the use of force by all nations of the world.

The Charter conveyed 'a message of hope to the occupied countries and held out the promise of a world organisation based on the enduring verities of international morality' and was accepted by all Allied nations and became the first step taken towards the formation of a new world body. It also became a basis and inspiration for many other international agreements in future, as the nations by accepting the Charter accepted that their internal policies were relevant to the international problems.

B. The First Washington Conference

This was the first conference after the entry of America in the World War II. It was led by Franklin D. Roosevelt and Winston Churchill, and in military parlance was known as the **Arcadia Conference.** The US President Roosevelt suggested a new name 'United Nations' to describe the Allied Powers and 26 nations described themselves as the United Nations and signed a declaration known as the '**Declaration by United Nations**' on 1 January 1942. In the Declaration, the signatory nations reaffirmed their commitment to the Atlantic Charter and resolved to:

1. employ their full resources and make every effort to defeat the common enemy.
2. cooperate with one another for the purpose, and agreed not to make separate truce or peace treaties with the enemies.

C. The Moscow Conference

Foreign ministers of Britain, America and the Soviet Union participated in this conference held in October 1943, in Moscow. The conference issued 'the **Declaration of the Four Nations on General Security**' (the fourth being Chinese Ambassador to Moscow). The declaration recognised necessity of ensuring rapid and orderly transition from war to peace and of establishing and maintaining international peace and security. They also called for the establishment of a general international organisation based on the principle of the sovereign equality of all nations and open to membership by all nations – large and small, for the maintenance of international peace and security, at the earliest practicable date. This 'Declaration on General Security' is said to mark the beginning of the Charter of the United Nations.

D. The Bretton Woods Conference

Also known as the United Nations Monetary and Financial Conference, it was held in Bretton Woods, New Hampshire in the United States in July 1944. It was attended by delegates from 44 Allied nations to discuss international financial order of the post-War world. It resulted in three agreements providing for:

1. establishment of an **International Monetary Fund** to promote stability of exchange rates and financial flows.
2. establishment of an **International Bank for Reconstruction and Development,** to speed up reconstruction and to foster economic development in the post-War world.
3. **cooperation** in other aspects of international economy.

The Bretton Woods Conference was a seminal incident in the course of emerging internationalism as by establishing two bodies, the IMF and IBRD, the conference put an end to economic nationalism and initiated encouragement to open markets.

E. The Dumbarton Oaks Conference

This was the first concrete step towards the creation of a general international organisation, as it formulated **proposals for the UN Charter**. The Conference was held in Georgetown, Washington D.C., in August 1944 and was attended by the delegates of Britain, the United States, the USSR and China to deliberate over proposals for the establishment of an organisation to maintain peace and security in the world, as had been provided in the Moscow Declarations of 1943.

The conference drafted the **Dumbarton Oaks Proposals,** also known as the '*Proposals for the Establishment of a General International Organization*' under the title 'The United Nations' and decided to meet at San Francisco in 1945 to finalise the draft of the Charter of the United Nations. The Dumbarton Oaks proposals are considered as the **blueprint** for the proposed world organisation.

F. The Yalta Conference

Held in February 1945, in **Yalta in Crimea**, in the Soviet Union, it was attended by Franklin Roosevelt, Winston Churchill and Joseph Stalin.

The Conference issued **'Declaration of Liberated Europe'** pledging to assist the countries of Europe in establishing democratic institutions (which was a reaffirmation of the Atlantic Charter promise of 'the right of all people to choose the form of government under which they live').

The Conference reaffirmed their faith in the principle of 'the Atlantic Charter', their pledge in 'the Declaration by the United Nations' and committed to create the United Nations in cooperation with other peace-loving nations dedicated to peace, security, freedom and general well-being of all mankind. The three countries also agreed to call a conference of the United Nations to draft a Charter, on the basis of the Dumbarton Oaks Proposals.

G. The San Francisco Conference

This was the last of the conferences in the making of the UN and was officially known as the **United Nations Conference on International Organization (UNCIO)**. It was held in San Francisco, California, in the USA, from 25 April 1945 to 26 June 1945 and had participation from 50 nations. The objective of the conference was to draft the Charter of the UN. At the conference delegates discussed, reviewed and amended the text agreed upon at the Dumbarton Oaks Conference.

> The US President Franklin D. Roosevelt, who had proposed the idea of United Nations, was unfortunately not a part of the San Francisco Conference as he had passed away on 12 April 1945, few days before it was convened.

On 26 June 1945, at San Francisco Opera, the delegates unanimously adopted the final text of the UN Charter by a standing ovation. The US President Truman in his closing speech to the delegates observed that 'with this Charter the world can look forward to the time when all worthy human beings may be permitted to live decently as free people'.

The United Nations officially came into being on 24 October 1945, after the Charter was ratified by the governments of the **Big Five – the United States, the United Kingdom, the USSR, France and China** – and majority of the other signatory nations. Poland which was not present at the conference signed it later and became one of the 51 original member states.

3. Charter of the United Nations

The UN Charter is an **international treaty** containing the basic tenets of international relations and also a constitutive instrument establishing its principal organs and procedures and setting out the rights and obligations of the member states.

The Charter consists of a Preamble and 111 articles grouped into 19 chapters. The Preamble starts with the words 'We the peoples of the United Nations determined' and expresses the shared ideals and common aims of all its Members.

To amend the Charter, a vote of two-thirds members of the General Assembly and ratification by two-thirds of the Members of the United Nations, including the five permanent members of the Security Council, is required.

In 1965, the Charter was amended to modify certain provisions. The Security Council membership was increased from 11 to 15 and the number of affirmative votes required for a decision was increased from 7 to 9, including the concurring vote of the five permanent members for all substantive matters. In the same year (1965), the Economic and Social Council membership was increased from 18 to 27, and in 1973 from 27 to 54 states.

4. Membership of the United Nations

Criteria for admission to the UN as set out in Chapter II of the UN Charter are:

1. All peace-loving states which accept the obligations contained in the Charter and, in the judgement of the Organisation, are able and willing to carry out these obligations.
2. Admission of any such state to the UN will be effected by a decision of the General Assembly upon the recommendation of the Security Council.

> The Charter provides for suspension or expulsion of a member for violation of the principles of the Charter, so far no such action has been taken.

5. Purposes and Principles of the United Nations

A. Purposes

1. Maintain international peace and security.
2. Develop friendly relations among nations based on respect for the principle of equal rights and self-determination of peoples.
3. Cooperate in solving international economic, social, cultural and humanitarian problems and in promoting respect for human rights and fundamental freedoms.
4. Be a centre for harmonising the actions of nations in attaining these common ends

B. Principles

1. Sovereign equality of all its members.
2. All members are to fulfil in good faith their Charter obligations.
3. Members to settle their international disputes by peaceful means and without endangering international peace and security and justice.
4. Members are to refrain from the threat or use of force against any other state.
5. Members are to give the United Nations every assistance in any action it takes in accordance with the Charter.
6. Nothing in the Charter is to authorise the United Nations to intervene in matters which are essentially within the domestic jurisdiction of any state

6. Structure of the United Nations

The United Nations Organization has six principal organs apart from the 15 specialised agencies, numerous funds and programmes as well as other entities. Those are:

1. The General Assembly - deliberative assembly of all UN member states
2. The Security Council - organ for international peace and security issues
3. The Secretariat - administrative organ of the UN
4. The International Court of Justice - universal court for international law
5. The Trusteeship Council - to administer Trust Territories

6. The Economic and Social Council - organ for global economic and social affairs

A. The General Assembly

It is the main deliberative body of the UN consisting representatives from all member nations. It is a deliberative, policy-making, supervisory and reviewing organ. It meets in regular **annual sessions** in September and in **special sessions** that may be convoked by the Secretary General at the request of the Security Council or of a majority of the Members of the United Nations or at the request of one Member, if, agreed to by a majority of the Members. **Emergency Sessions** may be convoked at the request of the Security Council, on a vote of any nine members or at the request of a majority of Members of the United Nations.

Each Member may send up to five representatives to the General Assembly but each Member has only one vote. Decisions do not require a unanimous vote, in contrast to the League of Nations Assembly. Decisions on important questions (such as those on peace and security, admission of new members and budgetary matters) require a two-thirds majority and other issues a simple majority. While the decisions of the Assembly are not a legally binding force for governments, they carry the weight of world opinion and the moral authority of the world community.

Functions and Powers of the General Assembly

a. *Maintenance of International Peace and Security*

The General Assembly may consider general principles of co-operation in the maintenance of international peace and security and **make recommendations** to the Members of the United Nations or to the Security Council or to both.

It may **discuss** any questions relating to international peace and security brought before it by any Member of the United Nations or by the Security Council or by a state which is not a Member of the United Nations but is a party to the dispute, if that state accepts the obligations of pacific settlement.

The Assembly may also **call the attention** of the Security Council to situations which are likely to endanger international peace and security.

The Secretary General also notifies the General Assembly, with the consent of the Security Council, matters related to the maintenance of international peace and security, being dealt with by the Security Council. Article 12 of the Charter provides that while the Security Council is exercising, in respect of any dispute or situation, the functions assigned to it in the Charter, the General Assembly is not to make any recommendations on it unless requested by the Council to do so. On 3 November 1950, the General Assembly adopted a resolution '**Uniting for Peace**', and decided that if the Security Council, because of lack of unanimity of the Permanent Members, fails to exercise its primary responsibility for the maintenance of international peace and security, the Assembly should consider the matter immediately and make recommendations to Members. The Assembly may meet for this purpose in emergency special session within 24 hours at the request of the Security Council by a majority or at the request of a majority of the Members of the United Nations. Transfer of an issue to the Security Council is considered as a procedural matter and is therefore not subject to veto of the P5. This resolution abandoned the sole competence of the Security Council to act within the UN system of collective security and empowered the General Assembly to intervene in circumstances that endanger international peace. So far, 10 emergency special sessions have been convened, the last being in 1997.

> This Resolution is also known as the Acheson Plan, after the US Foreign Secretary Dean Acheson who persuaded the General Assembly to claim for itself a subsidiary responsibility with regard to international peace and security.

b. *Promotion of International Political, Economic and Social Co-operation*

The General Assembly initiates, studies and makes recommendations for the purpose of progressive development of international law and its codification, realisation of human rights and fundamental freedom for all without distinction as to race, sex, language or religion and supervises the functions of another UN organ - the Economic and Social Council - in this context.

c. ***Organisational, Administrative and Budgetary Functions***

The General Assembly elects the non-permanent members of the Security Council, members of the Economic and Social Council and members of the Trusteeship Council. The Assembly and the Security Council, voting independently, elect members of the International Court of Justice. The General Assembly elects its own President and Vice-President.

It is the Assembly that appoints the Secretary-General of the United Nations on the recommendation of the Security Council. The Secretary-General appoints the staff of the Secretariat in accordance with regulations of General Assembly. Annual report on the work of the United Nations is considered by the Assembly.

The Assembly on the recommendation of the Security Council admits any state to membership in the United Nations, suspends a Member against which preventive or enforcement action has been taken by the Security Council and expels a Member which has persistently violated the Principles of the Charter.

The General Assembly considers and approves the budget of the UN and also determines the proportion of the budget to be paid by each Member. The Assembly also considers and approves financial and budgetary arrangements of the specialised agencies.

The Assembly may request the International Court of Justice to give an advisory opinion on any legal question.

The General Assembly carries out its functions in the form of Committees. The six main Committees are:

1. Committee on Disarmament and International Security
2. Economic and Financial Committee
3. Social, Humanitarian and Cultural Committee
4. Special Political and Decolonisation Committee
5. Administrative and Budgetary Committee
6. Legal Committee

B. The Security Council

The Security Council is the organ with the primary responsibility, under the Charter, for the maintenance of international peace and security. It consists of 15 members: 5 permanent (China, France, Russia, United Kingdom and the United States, also known as the P5) and 10 non-permanent members (elected by the General Assembly for a term of 2 years).

Each member has only one vote and decisions on procedural matters require an affirmative vote of at least 9 of the 15 members but on substantive matters require 9 votes and the absence of a negative vote (veto) by any of the five permanent members. If a permanent member disagreeing with a proposed resolution, but does not wish to cast veto, may abstain from voting allowing the resolution to be adopted, if it gets the required nine favourable votes.

- It is to be noted that, while other organs make recommendations to member states, only the Security Council has the power to make decisions that member states are **obligated to implement** under the Charter.
- The Security Council **function continuously** and a representative of each of its members has to be present at all times at the UN Headquarters.
- The Council on receiving a complaint concerning a threat to peace, usually recommends the parties to try to reach an agreement by **peaceful means**. When a dispute leads to hostilities, the Council's primary concern is to bring them to an end at the earliest. For this purpose, it may issue **ceasefire directives** or dispatch **military observers** or a **peacekeeping force** so that tensions can be reduced and calm can be re-established after which peaceful settlements may be sought.
- Moreover, the Council can also take **enforcement measures** such as economic sanctions, arms embargoes, financial penalties and restrictions, travel bans, severance of diplomatic relations, blockade or even collective military action.
- On **military action**, the Security Council may rely on the Military Staff Committee, a subsidiary organ established by the Charter, for advises on military requirements for the maintenance of international peace and security, employment of forces placed at its disposal, the regulation of armaments and possible disarmament.

The Security Council unanimously adopted Resolution 1373 on 28 September 2001 (following the terror attack on the United States in September 2001) and established the Counter-Terrorism Committee, as a subsidiary organ. This document is the basis of the Security Council's response to the terrorist threat since then, and the Committee is mandated to assess Member States' compliance with the resolution's provisions.

C. The Secretariat

It is the 'office-staff' of the UN, and carries out the diverse day-to-day work of the organisation. It provides secretarial services to the organs of the UN and administers the programmes and policies established by them.

The Secretariat is comprised of international civil servants recruited on a merit basis and with regard to equitable geographic distribution. They are permanent expert officials rather than political appointees of member nations. They are required to take an oath of loyalty to the UN.

The wide-ranging duties of the Secretariat includes administering of peacekeeping operations, mediating in international disputes, surveying of economic and social trends, preparing studies on human rights and sustainable developments, organising of conferences on global significance and establish clearing houses of information apart from providing facilities and information to UN bodies for their meetings.

The Secretary General of the UN: The Secretary General heads the UN and plays the roles of diplomat, advocate, civil servant and manager while providing overall guidance to the organisation. The UN Charter defines the Secretary General as the 'chief administrative officer' who acts in that capacity. The Charter empowers him to bring to the Security Council's attention, any issue that in his opinion might threaten international peace and security. The Secretary General is appointed for a five-year renewable term by the General Assembly, upon the recommendation of the Security Council where the permanent members have veto power. As the symbol of UN ideals and as a spokesperson for the interests of the world's peoples, the Secretary General must take into account the needs and concerns of the individual states and at the same time has to speak and act independently for peace.

D. The International Court of Justice

It is located at **Peace Palace,** at The **Hague**, **Holland**. Of the six principal organs of the UN, International Court of Justice is the only one not located in New York. It has 15 judges elected for 9 years terms from different countries by the General Assembly and the Security Council voting independently. It settles legal disputes between states and gives advisory opinion to the UN and its agencies. The court is not open to private persons and entities or other international organisations.

E. The Trusteeship Council

It was a replacement to the League of Nations Mandates Commission. It was created for supervision of the 11 Trust Territories and to prepare them for self-government. Its operations were suspended in 1994 as all those territories were given self-government or independence by that year.

F. The Economic and Social Council

The ECOSOC is the principal organ to coordinate the economic, social and related work of the UN and the specialised agencies and other bodies. It serves as forum for discussing international economic and social issues and for formulating policy recommendations to member states and to UN system. It is an umbrella organisation that co-ordinates the activities of large number of **specialised agencies** of the UN such as the WHO, ILO, FAO and UNESCO and the United Nations **programmes** such as UNDP, UNEP and UNICEF. It has 54 members elected by the General Assembly of which one-third retire every year. Membership is based on geographical representation - African nations get 14 seats, West European and other states 13, Asia 11, Latin America and Caribbean 10 and East Europe 6.

World Bank Group and World Bank

1. **IBRD** – International Bank for Reconstruction and Development (1944). It seeks to reduce poverty in middle-income and creditworthy poorer countries by promoting sustainable development through loans, guarantees and advisory services.
2. **IFC** – the International Finance Corporation (1956). It provides support to private sector in developing countries to mobilise capital in the international markets.
3. **IDA** – the International development Association (1960). It is the 'World Bank's

Fund for the Poorest' and provides support for health, education, agriculture, infrastructure and economic and institutional development in poorest countries.

4. **ICSID** – the International Centre for Settlement of Investment Dispute (1966). It provides forum for the resolution of disputes between governments and foreign investors.
5. **MIGA** – the Multilateral Investment Guarantee Agency (1988). It promotes FDI in developing countries by providing guarantees to investors.

While all the above five form the World Bank Group, the term World Bank refers specifically to two of the above five – IBRD and IDA.

7. How is the UN Different from the League of Nations?

The UN is a continuum and at the same time different of the League of Nations. It is a continuum in many respects as its general purpose, structure, functions and many of its agencies were inherited from the League. At the same time, it differs from the League with regard to its objective of maintaining international peace and its commitment to economic and social development.

1. The Covenant of the League was given shape by the Big Four (the United States, Britain, France and Italy) behind closed doors but the UN Charter was the product of combined effort of 50 nations, small and large alike.
2. Decision of the League required unanimous vote both in League's Assembly and in Council, but in the UN, unanimity is required only of five major powers in the Security Council.
3. League Covenant did not have any provision imposing total ban on war and the League's Council did not have sufficient powers to prevent outbreak of hostilities. The UN Charter does not recognise any circumstance under which a nation can start a war and the Security Council has power for collective measures if a 'threat to peace exists'.
4. The UN has a wider scope. The League did not have provisions for coordinated socio-economic cooperation. Compared to the League, the UN devotes larger resources and time on socio-economic issues and now more than 90 per cent of the UN expenditure is allocated for it.
5. The UN has wider membership including that of the United States.
6. It is committed to protect individual human rights, which was not a part of mandate of the League.
7. The Secretary General has more powers. As per the Charter the Secretary General is empowered to bring to the attention of the Security Council any matter that may threaten international peace and security. He also uses his good offices - including his special and personal representatives - and envoys to prevent international disputes from arising or spreading as happened in Cyprus, East Timor and Western Sahara.
8. The 'Uniting for Peace' resolution enables the UN for a more assertive role than the League had.

WHO: World Health Organization was established in 1948. It is headquartered in Geneva and is responsible for providing leadership on global health matters and on monitoring and assessing health trends.

8. Criticism of the UN

Following are some major areas and points of criticisms against the UN:

1. **Peacekeeping**: The UN was a failure in Indochina conflict during most of its existence and still could not find a permanent solution to the prolonged conflict in the Middle East. In 1995, the UN peacekeeping forces proved failure in ending the massacre of more than 8,000 of Muslims by the Bosnian Serbs.
2. **Gulf War**: The US invasion of Iraq in 2003 was without the UN Security Council authorisation.
3. **Refugee Crisis**: Though the UN had brokered the Refugee Convention in 1951 and in spite of the work of the UN High Commission for Refugees, millions of people continue to live as refugees, internally displaced or as stateless people be it in Palestine, Syria, Ukraine or in other parts of the global conflict zones. As per the 'Global Appeal 2023'-UNHCR's annual publication describing its plans and the outlook for

forcibly displaced and stateless people-there will be 117.2 million people forcibly displaced or stateless in 2023.

Refugee and Migrant: Although often used interchangeably there are distinctions between the terms "refugee" and "migrant". As per the definition of the U.N., refugees are persons who are outside their country of origin for reasons of feared persecution, conflict, generalized violence, or other circumstances that have seriously disturbed public order and, as a result, require international protection. On the other, an international migrant is "any person who is outside a State of which they are a citizen or national, or, in the case of a stateless person, their State of birth or habitual residence".

4. **Out-dated Representation**: The Security Council reflects 1945 geopolitical realities and the continued exclusion of Germany, Japan, India and Brazil is symbolic of its failure in responding to the changing world realities.
5. **Western Domination**: The UN and its agencies such as the IMF and the World Bank are dominated by Western powers which undermine their credibility and leads to the creation of rival institutions such as the Asian Infrastructure Investment Bank by non-Western nations.

FAO: Food and Agricultural Organization. This agency leads the global effort to eradicate hunger and helps developing countries in modernising and improving agriculture practices.

9. Verdict on the United Nations

The Preamble of the UN Charter describes **Peace and Security, Human Rights, Rule of Law and Development** as the four pillars of the UN. Hence, it is better to evaluate the UN mainly on these parameters.

A. Performance in Preserving Peace and Security

The former UN Secretary General Javier Perez de Cuellar defined the peacekeeping as 'the use of soldiers as a catalyst for peace rather than as the instrument of war'. In this mission, the UN principally aims for **conflict prevention, peacemaking, peacekeeping, enforcement and peace building**.

The UN has been a witness and catalyst to an extraordinary transition such as nuclear threat, the Cold War belligerence and numerous regional conflicts, since its formation. During the Cold War, the Security Council was crippled by super power tensions. Consequently, the UN was successful only when it was dealing with crises where interests of great powers were not involved as in the **West New Guinea Crisis** (1946). But in areas of super power interests, the UN has been ineffective just as the League had been. For example, during the **Hungarian Crisis** in 1956 when the USSR resorted to a brutal suppression, the UN was a total failure. The Hungarian government appealed to the UN, but the UN Security Council resolution was vetoed by the Soviet Union and the General Assembly resolution to investigate the issue was rejected by the Soviet.

Nevertheless, by sending observer missions and peacekeeping forces to the troubled spots, many a times the UN has facilitated restoration of peace and also succeeded in preventing conflict from escalating. Even in cases where it failed in preventing wars, for example the Iraq War, its role in post-war reconstruction and in ameliorating the sufferings of the people was invaluable.

In 2006, the UN created the **Peacebuilding Commission** - an inter-governmental advisory body to help countries in transition from war to lasting peace. For the same purpose a **Peacebuilding Fund** and **Peacebuilding Support Office** have also been created and all these constitute the **Peacebuilding Architecture** of the UN.

Peace and security is also sought to be promoted by measures of disarmament. The **International Atomic Energy Agency (IAEA)** works as the nuclear watch dog of the world community and ensure that nuclear material is used only for peaceful purposes. The **UNODA** (United Nations Office for Disarmament Affairs) provides support in the area of the disarmament of weapons of mass destruction (nuclear, biological and chemical weapons) and participates in the multilateral efforts to strengthen the non-proliferation of WMD.

UNESCO: United Nations Educational, Scientific and Cultural Organization. Its area of work are education, natural, social and human sciences, culture and communication and information. It also strives to create conditions for dialogue among civilisations, cultures and peoples. Apart from the above, the UNESCO has two global priorities – Africa and gender equality.

B. Performance in Other Areas

The UN is more successful in humanitarian, developmental and environmental areas. Since its origin it has served food to more than 90 million people in over 70 countries. It has also supported 30 million refugees and has promulgated more than 80 treaties and declarations aimed at protecting human rights. The role of UN in supporting children and women by providing vaccinations and maternal health practices is also commendable.

UNICEF: United Nations Children's Fund, created in 1946, is committed to protect every child's right to survival, protection and development by providing long-term humanitarian and developmental assistance to children and mothers in developing countries. It publishes 'The State of the World's Children' report every year.

a. Human Rights

The **United Nations 'Declaration on Human Rights' (UDHR)** 1948, has upheld the 'inherent dignity and of the equal and inalienable rights of all members of the human family'. Member states are expected to prepare a report on the status of human rights in their country every three years. The Declaration is the basis for more than 60 international human rights instruments that makeup a comprehensive system of legally binding treaties for protecting and promoting human rights.

The **Genocide Convention** of 1948 aimed to combat genocides (efforts to eliminate national, racial or religious groups) in war and peace time. Of recent, in the field of International criminal justice the UN has done a vital contribution by constituting the **International Tribunals for Yugoslavia and Rwanda** in 1993 and 1994, respectively, to demonstrate that grave violations of international law will not go unpunished.

In 1959, the UN Human Rights Commission formulated '**Declaration of the Rights of Child**' envisaging adequate food, free education, medical care for every child and their protection from racial, religious and other types of discrimination.

The **UN Convention on the Elimination of All Forms of Discrimination against Women, 1979** was a significant step in promoting women's rights worldwide.

The UN contribution to **end the apartheid** in South Africa by imposing measures such as arms embargo was also significant.

In 2006, the General Assembly established the **Human Rights Council,** as the main intergovernmental body for protection of human rights. The **United Nations High Commissioner for Human Rights** cooperates with governments and international, regional and non-governmental organisations in promoting and protecting civil, cultural, economic, political and social rights for all. The High Commissioner reports to the Human Rights Council and the General Assembly. The **Office of the High Commissioner for Human Rights (OHCHR)** serves as the secretariat for the Human Rights Council and other human rights organs of the UN.

The UN has **strengthened democracy** by strengthening democratic institutions and by supporting democratic elections in countries such as South Africa, Timor, Afghanistan, Congo, Iraq and Sierra Leone. By giving formal recognition to the newly independent countries, the UN accelerated the process of **decolonisation** too.

UNRWA: The **United Nations Relief and Works Agency for Palestine Refugees** was established in 1949, to mitigate the sufferings of the refugees in the Middle East. It is headquartered in Gaza and Amman in Jordan.

b. Rule of the Law

As a principle of governance, the rule of law holds that all persons, public and private institutions, including the state are accountable to laws that are consistent with international standards. The UN Charter aims to establish 'conditions under which justice and respect for the obligations arising from treaties and other sources of international law can be maintained'.

The **International Court of Justice** by its judgements and advisory opinions facilitated settlement of international disputes such as those related to territories, maritime boundaries, treatment of the aliens and prevented conflicts from escalating.

Between 1973 and 1982 the '**United Nations Convention on the Law of the Seas**' **(UNCLOS)** succeeded in framing international law of the seas and conceptualised terms and steps such as EEZ, Exclusive Economic Zones, and provisions for protecting marine resources.

> **The UN System** consists of the United Nations family of organisations – Six Principal Organs, the Funds and Programmes (these are subsidiary bodies of the General Assembly), the Specialized Agencies (are autonomous organizations coordinated by ECOSOC and are linked to the UN through individual agreements) and other Related Organizations (includes IAEA and the WTO which have their own budget and legislative bodies and address particular areas of activity).

c. Development

True to the declared aim in the Charter 'to promote social progress and better standards of life in larger freedom', roughly 70 per cent of the UN System focusses on promoting social progress and improving the well-being of people around the world. A wide variety of agencies and funds are in operation in fighting hunger, reducing poverty, ensuring health facilities and to promote development. In promoting development the UN is emphatic that development shall be sustainable. The Millennium Development Goals, Global Environment Facility and the Vienna Convention for the Protection of the Ozone Layer (1985) are some of the steps in this regard.

> The **United Nations University (UNU):** It is located in Tokyo and was established in 1975 as an international community of academics engaged in research, policy study and the dissemination of knowledge to further the UN's aims of peace and progress.

d. The Global Think Tank

By conducting research in wide areas of global issues, the UN has emerged as the leading source of information and analysis. Some of the important agencies in this regard are as follows:

The **UN Statistical Division** is engaged in compilation and dissemination of global economic, environmental, demographic, social, gender and energy statistics.

The **United Nations Development Programme** tracks human development trends and policies, prepares the Human Development Index and publishes the Human Development Report. The **UN Population Division** conducts research on global population trends and prepares demographic estimates. Other reports such as the **World Development Report** of the World Bank, the **World Economic Outlook** of the IMF, the **World Economic and Social Survey** of the United Nations Department of Economic and Social Affairs (UNDESA) also enriches our ideas and understanding of the global community.

> **UN-Women** or the **United Nations Entity for Gender Equality and the Empowerment of Women** was created by the General Assembly in 2010 to accelerate measures for empowerment of women and girls. It is based on the assumption that equality for women and girls is not only a basic human right, but a social and economic imperative. It consolidated four existing UN agencies – the UN Development Fund for Women, the Division for the Advancement of Women, the Office of the Special Adviser on Gender Issues and the UN International Research and Training Institute for the Advancement of Women. It supports intergovernmental bodies in devising policies and in implementing standards relevant to women's issues.

> **UNAOC:** The United Nations Alliance of Civilizations was established in 2005. It is a global network of partners including states, civil society and the private sector to improve cross-cultural relations between diverse nations and communities. It emerged out of the realisation that extremists were exploiting the perception of a widening gap between Islamic and Western societies. It aims to promote mutual respect for religious beliefs and traditions and overcome prejudice and polarisation, which threaten world peace.

Weaknesses of the UN

- No army of its own to enforce its decisions.
- Veto of the permanent members. Though the 'Uniting for Peace' resolution enables it to overcome the veto, much delay is caused in the process.
- Fund shortage.

10. Reforming the UN

Management reform: Improving efficiency, increasing accountability, avoidance of duplication and minimisation of waste are important in this regard.

Financial: Member nations many a times fail to meet their financial obligations to the UN either because of their financial difficulties or as a mark of disapproval of UN policies. As UN depends entirely on contributions from member states, it is imperative that member states pay their share unconditionally, in full and on time.

Security Council reform: Since 1965, when the Security Council membership was expanded from 11 to 15 it remains static, while the UN membership has expanded considerably. An expanded council which will reflect the representative nature of the UN will bring greater political authority and legitimacy in UN's actions.

Veto power reform: The privilege of any of the five permanent members to use veto, thus preventing any UN action even if other 14 members of the Council vote 'yes' and regardless of international support has harmed the UN many a times. Hence, Veto should be limited to vital national security issues or it should require support of multiple states or it should be abolished altogether. As any amendment of the UN Charter require the approval of the five permanent members any reform of Veto would be opposed by them, hence would require wide consensus.

ILO: The International Labour Organization was established in 1919 to promote social justice and labour rights. In 1946, it became the first specialised agency of the United Nations and in 1969 was awarded the Nobel Peace Prize. It is headquartered in Geneva, Switzerland.

11. India and the UN

India is one of the founding members of the UN. India supports its purposes and principles and contributes to its programmes and missions. In 1953, India's **Vijayalakshmi Pandit** became the first woman President of the UNGA. In 2007, as an expression of the UN commitment to peace and its adherence to 'non-violence', the UN declared Mahatma Gandhi's birth anniversary of October 2, as the '**International Day of Non-violence**'. In 2014, the UN also declared 21 June as the '**International Yoga Day**'.

India was the first country to raise the issues of racism and apartheid in South Africa in 1946 and the force behind the resolution against racial discrimination adopted by the General Assembly. India is one of the largest contributors of troops to the **UN Peacekeeping Missions** - to Korea, Egypt, Somalia, Congo, South Sudan, to name just a few. The UN field network consisting of its offices, programmes and funds such as FAO, WHO, UNESCO, UNAIDS, etc., has long history of activities in India and have contributed to the betterment of Indian lives. Their technical support, role in technology transfer and support in policy development were crucial in resolving many of the challenges we faced as a newly emerged nation. Some of these are attainment of food security and nutrition, preservation of historical monuments, combating AIDS, controlling diseases such as malaria and TB and eradication of diseases such as cholera.

United Nations Messengers of Peace and **Goodwill Ambassadors**. The Messengers of Peace are famous personalities from different fields such as cinema, sports, etc., who have lent their names and public recognition in support of the UN's work for a better world. Goodwill Ambassadors are those who support the ideals and objectives of the UN agencies and programmes by public appearances, contact with international media and humanitarian work. Sachin Tendulkar is a Goodwill Ambassador of the United Nations Environment Programme (UNEP), while Amitabh Bachchan, David Beckham, Lionel Messi and Jackie Chan are among the Goodwill Ambassadors of the United Nations Children's Fund (UNICEF).

The main endeavour of the permanent members of the UN had been to prevent the UNSC from taking any action against their own national interests, thus limiting the role of UN to peacekeeping and sanctions. On the belief that the UN must be an organisation for smaller powers too, to which they can look for their security and protection, India has been highlighting issues of decolonisation, nuclear disarmament, terrorism, human rights, North-South relations, South-South cooperation, equity in the international economic matters and non-alignment on the platforms of the UN.

In its desire to see the UN as a world body that responds to the emerging challenges, India had been championing its reform. In this context it is worthy to note that the '**G4 Nations**' - India, Japan, Germany and Brazil - are championing each other's bid for permanent seats in UNSC. India's claim to permanent seat is based on the size of the country, its population, economy and also its commitment and track record in the principles of the UN - peace, democracy, international cooperation, development assistance and human rights.

IPCC: The **Intergovernmental Panel on Climate Change** is the forum for clear scientific view on climate change and its potential environmental and socio-economic consequences. It put forward adaptation and mitigation options. It was jointly established by the United Nations Environment Programme and the World Meteorological Organization in 1988. This Geneva-based organisation shared the Nobel Peace Prize in 2007.

12. Role of the UN in the Emerging Global Order

The UN is the forum of world nations where irrespective of size and status, nations come together, talk and express their views. In spite of drawbacks and failures, the UN continues to be relevant as the world needs a **multilateral forum** - inclusive and effective - and a **framework of international rules** to promote peace, create order and to ensure security so that everyone live in peace, dignity and equality on a healthy planet.

Creation of lasting peace depends upon pulling together all resources to ensure economic development, social justice, respect for human rights and good governance in each country. Only the UN has the global legitimacy, multilateral experience, competence, coordinating ability and impartiality to meet the above requirements.

In emerging context of **plethora of cross border challenges and global issues** no nation can disengage itself from multilateralism. Issues such as mass migration, humanitarian crises, terrorism, climate change, natural disasters, global water and food security, pandemic like Corona and many such issues are inexorably intertwined and trans-national in nature and therefore require multilateral cooperation. It is to be noted that any nation can achieve far less in isolation than working collectively towards global welfare and the UN provides this collective forum.

The UN is only as strong as the will of its members - **the collective will** - permit. The future success of the UN will depend on how far it bridges the great gulf between what is ideal and what is politically possible in shaping that collective will.

SUMMARY

Background of the formation of the United Nations – The Atlantic Conference, the First Washington Conference, the Moscow Conference, the Bretton Woods Conference, the Dumbarton Oaks Conference, the Yalta Conference and the San Francisco Conference.

Founding of the UN – It was founded on 24 October 1945 after ratification of the Charter by the Big Five – the US, the UK, the USSR, France and China.

Structure of the UN – It consists of six principal organs (General Assembly, Security Council, Secretariat, International Court of Justice, Trusteeship Council and Economic and Social Council), fifteen specialised agencies and numerous funds and programmes.

Verdict on the UN – Despite criticism and failures in certain areas, the UN has been instrumental in shaping the contours of the contemporary world. The main criticism against the UN are outdated representation, Western domination, failure in peace keeping in the Gulf War and also its failure in resolving the refugee crisis. It was also criticised that the Cold War had a crippling impact on the Security Council and it failed to assert itself where interests of the superpowers were involved. But the UN has been doing commendable service in the field of preserving peace and ensuring security. Some of the major developments in this regard were creations of the Peacebuilding Commission, Peacebuilding Fund and Peacebuilding Support Office. The roles of International Atomic Energy Agency and United Nations Office for Disarmament have been instrumental in ensuring security and disarmament. The contribution of UN in areas such as in protecting human rights, enforcing the Rule of Law, in promoting social progress and better standards of life and by conducting research in wide areas of global issues had been remarkable and enriching of our understanding of the global community.

Questions of Previous Years Civil Services Examination

1. "UNO was the necessity of the time when the World War II ended." Critically examine its achievements and shortcomings. (2023)
2. Do you think that the United Nations Organization has played a significant role in resolving international disputes and ensuring peace in the world? (2021)
3. Discuss how far the United Nations has been successful in resolving global disputes from year 1946 to 1991. (2018)
4. The UNO was created in the light of experience of the League of Nations, but in spite of the mandate contained in the UNO constitution, its effective role in maintaining world peace has lacked cohesiveness and collective approach. Examine. (2015)
5. Examine the peacekeeping efforts of the United Nations Organization. (2009)
6. 'In spite of the careful framing of the Charter, the role of the UNO as peacekeepers and international mediator has been somewhat lacklustre and muted and that continues to be so even after the end of the Cold War'. Elucidate. (2013)
7. 'The Security Council is the heart of the United Nations'. Elucidate. (2003)

CHAPTER 15

The Cold War

In this Chapter

1. Introduction

The Cold War was a state of armed truce and geopolitical belligerence between the United States and the USSR. Originated at the end of the Second World War, it caused the division of Europe into two antagonistic spheres, **Western Europe** (under the United States) and **Eastern Europe** (under the USSR) and the spread of rivalry to the rest of the world. It lasted till the collapse of communism in Eastern Europe and disintegration of the USSR in 1991.

The Cold War originated from two opposing **ideological** underpinnings, divergent **historical** experiences, profound **economic** opportunities and incompatible **political** ambitions of the super powers in the post-World War II global order. Their belligerence was further aggravated by mutual fear, aggressive self-protectionism and collective pride. The Cold War was featured by arms race, proxy wars, ideological battles, military coalitions and economic aid to the bloc members.

The term 'Cold' is used because even though they viewed each other as mortal enemies, there was no direct fight between the two sides. Rather, they attacked each other with **propaganda, economic measures** and by supporting major regional wars known as **proxy wars**. It was **'Armed Truce'** in the sense that both the blocs were heavily armed in preparation for war and for ideological hegemony of the world.

The term Cold War was first used by the English writer **George Orwell** in his essay **'You and the Atomic Bomb'** in 1945, in which he predicted a period of 'peace that is no peace'. But it was

Bernard Baruch, an American financier, who first used the term in 1947 to describe the geopolitical confrontation between the United States and USSR.

2. Stages in the Cold War

The Cold War developed through different stages.

1. Beginning of the Cold War (1946–53): Post-Second World War realities and opportunities gave birth to Cold War.
2. The Thaw (1953–61): This period was featured by relaxation in tensions.
3. Escalation (1961–69): At this phase, confrontation rose to a terrifying climax.
4. The *Détente* (1969–79): There was visible relaxation of tension as a result of conscious efforts.
5. The Second Cold war (1979–85): Revival of Tensions
6. The End of the Cold War (1985–91): Disintegration of the USSR ended the Bi-polar world and the end of the Cold War.

3. Strategies of the Cold War

- Propaganda – Both sides used this method to extend their influence. Journals, newspapers, radio and movies came to be used extensively for the purpose. For example, Radio Free Europe broadcast its programmes into Eastern Europe.
- Foreign Aid – Financial and material aid became integral part of strategy. Marshal Plan of the United States and construction of Aswan Dam in Egypt with the Soviet aid were some examples.
- Military Alliances – NATO and Warsaw Pact were two major instances to quote.
- Espionage – Under CIA (US) and KGB (USSR) both the countries engaged in elaborate espionage, assassinations and secret operations.
- Proxy Wars – Both got themselves involved in regional conflicts by backing opposing sides.

4. Causes of the Cold War

A. Ideological Differences

Cold War was essentially an expression of the ideological differences between the communist states and the capitalist states. The **incompatibility of objectives** of these two ideologies was at the root of the Cold War.

In Russia, a communist socio-economic-political order structured upon collective ownership of the wealth, classless society, and the dictatorship of proletariat (working class) had been established after the Revolution in 1917.

On the other hand, the Western nations followed the path of capitalism emphasising private ownership of the wealth, profit-oriented production, competitive markets and preservation of the power of the private wealth (capitalist class).

The capitalist states were afraid of the spread of communism to their own countries which would lead to the end of private ownership of wealth and also the destruction of their interests and privileges. Under this apprehension, capitalist states – United States, Britain, France and Japan – had sent troops to Russia during the Russian Civil War in 1918, to assist the anti-communists. The capitalist support to the anti-revolutionary forces had made Lenin to comment that his country had been put under '*a hostile capitalist encirclement*'.

On the other, the Soviet denouncement of capitalism as a system that promoted national enmity, inequality, colonial slavery, national oppression and imperialist brutalities were of concern to the capitalist states.

Thus, the differences in ideologies and political aims led to mutual distrust, resulting in domestic and foreign policies aimed at resisting the spread of communism by the capitalists and the destruction of capitalism by the communists. After 1945, expression of this conflict in new areas with new methods and new players and above all with greater intensity is termed as the Cold War.

B. Foreign Policies of Stalin

Joseph Stalin followed a policy of expansion. In August 1939, Stalin signed the **Molotov-Ribbentrop** Pact providing for *inter alia*, the territorial rearrangement of Central and Eastern Europe between Russia and Germany. Subsequently the USSR entered the War by invading Poland and divided Polish territories between Germany and the USSR. During the war, the USSR annexed territories also of Finland and Romania apart from annexing Estonia, Latvia and Lithuania. At the end of the War, as the defeat of Germany was clearly in sight, Stalin planned of creating a **'sphere of influence'** in Eastern Europe. These measures of Stalin caused concern in the Western democratic nations. Stalin frightened the West further by his speech in February 1946 that communism and capitalism could never live peacefully together and that his aim as the ultimate victory of communism.

C. Suspicion and Hostility of the United States and Britain Towards the USSR

Since its origin the USSR had been mistrusted by the Western nations. Western countries had sent their troops, as seen previously, to Russia to destroy the communist state that had been set up after the revolution. Though this intervention ended in failure, the image of communism as a militant faith aiming for world revolution had been ingrained in the capitalist world since then. Thereafter, the Soviet Union was ostracised by most of the western nations who refused to initiate diplomatic relations with it. Though an alliance was formed between the United States, the USSR and Britain during the Second World War, it had not been free of suspicions and tensions. Though the United States had supplied all kinds of war materials to Russia under the Lend-Lease Act of 1941, the United States and Britain conducted their war operations jointly under a unified command without taking the Soviet into confidence. Out of this mistrust they also did not reveal the existence of the atomic bomb and delayed the opening of the 'Second Front' till June 1944 in order to put maximum pressure of the Nazi invasion on the Russians to bring them to the point of exhaustion.

D. Differing Goals in the Post-World War II World

The goals of the United States and the USSR were sharply in contrast in the post-War world. While the United States aimed promotion of democracy, prevention of the spread of communism, re-unification of Germany and its stabilisation for ensuring security of Europe, the Soviet Russia wanted to spread communism in other countries and to keep Germany divided so as to prevent it from waging a war again. In economic sphere, while the United States looked for sources of raw materials and new markets for its booming industries in European countries, the Soviet Russia set their eyes on Eastern Europe's resources and industrial equipment to rebuild its war ravaged economy.

5. | Run-Up to the Cold War

Certain developments during the World War II and soon after it created background for the emergence of the Cold War. These were:

A. World War II conferences
B. Emergence of the Eastern Bloc
C. Fulton Speech

A. World War II Conferences

During the War the United States, Britain and the USSR took some initiatives to reach a common action plan. These were:

a. The Yalta Conference

Also known as the Crimea Conference, as it was held in the Black Sea resort of Yalta in the Crimean region of Russia in February 1945, it was attended by Winston Churchill, Roosevelt and Stalin.

The conference aimed at shaping **post-war peace** on the principle of self-determination to the liberated peoples of post–Nazi Europe and to create a collective security order. For the purpose, the conference issued **'Declaration of Liberated Europe'** providing for 'the earliest possible establishment through free elections governments responsive to the will of the people'.

It was agreed to 'de-Nazify' and demilitarise Germany after its unconditional surrender. Further, Germany and Berlin were to be divided into four zones – under American, British, Russian and French control.

The conference also agreed to reorganise the Communist Provisional Government of the Republic of Poland that had been installed by the Soviet Union in Lublin (even through there was already a Polish government in exile in London) on Stalin's promise of free elections in Poland.

Violations of decisions reached at Yalta by Stalin were to prove crucial in causing a split in the Allied unity and the Yalta became a byword for failure and broken promises.

b. The Potsdam Conference

It was held in July–August 1945 in Potsdam, Germany, and was attended by the US President Harry S Truman, the Russian leader Joseph Stalin and the British Prime Minister Winston Churchill and later by Clement Atlee. The Conference was held to discuss the treatment of defeated Nazi Germany and the establishment of post-war order.

Since the Yalta Conference significant developments had occurred in international affairs which were decisive in determining the outcome of the Potsdam.

1. Most important development was the surrender of Germany. Serious differences emerged between the leaders over the future of Germany and the rest of Central and Eastern European states.
2. In the months following the Yalta Conference, the Soviet Union had occupied the Central and Eastern Europe and had setup pro-communist governments in countries such as Hungary, Bulgaria, Albania, Romania and Poland and also had reoccupied the Baltic states of Estonia, Latvia and Lithuania.

   Stalin claimed that Eastern Europe as a legitimate sphere of Soviet influence and establishment of puppet governments were defensive measures against possible future attack. Apart from these annexations, the Soviet had occupied regions of Germany east of Oder-Neisse Line and had expelled more than 5 million Germans living in the region.
3. Another important development was a change in the political leadership in United Kingdom. In the general elections in United Kingdom, the Labour Party emerged victorious and its leader Clement Atlee became the new prime minister.
4. Similarly there was a change in leadership in the United States. President Roosevelt had died in April 1945 and Vice President Harry Truman had assumed the Presidency of the United States. This change in leadership meant a change in attitude towards the USSR. During the war for the sake of the Allied unity, Roosevelt had expressed his confidence in Stalin and had brushed off warnings of a potential domination of Eastern Europe by Stalin. But, Truman was suspicious of the Soviet intensions and considered the developments in Eastern Europe as aggressive expansionism by Russia which was incompatible with the agreement reached at Yalta.

At Potsdam the leaders agreed upon the following- On Germany and Austria: The three heads of government agreed to divide Germany and Austria into four occupational zones (United States, Russian, British and French as agreed in principle at Yalta Conference) and also their capitals Berlin and Vienna into four zones. The leaders also issued a statement of aims of their occupation of Germany as four Ds:

a. Demilitarisation of the former Nazi forces and the German arms industry
b. De-Nazification of German society of Nazi ideals and influence
c. Democratisation through the establishment of political parties and trade unions and by the provision of freedom of speech, press and religion
d. Decentralisation aimed at the establishment of German federalism

The agreement provided for reversal of all German annexations in Europe and to redraw the eastern border of Germany to westwards to the Order-Neisse Line which meant 25 per cent reduction in the size of Germany.

It was decided to put the Nazi war criminals on trial and to impose war reparations on Germany to the benefit of the USSR towards repairing the damages they had suffered during the war. The German economy was to be decartelised (aimed at decentralisation) and to be reorganised with primary emphasis on agriculture and peaceful domestic industries.

On Poland, the leaders recognised the Provisional Government of National Unity based at Lublin, thus ending the Polish government-in-exile based at London. The western border of Poland was provisionally defined by the Oder and Neisse Rivers.

The **cooling off in relations** between the leaders of the Allied powers were clear at the Potsdam Conference that they could not even agree when or whether the four occupied zones would be allowed to form a united country again. Truman's insistence for free elections in Eastern Europe was also rejected by Stalin. Truman in turn did not inform Stalin about the exact nature of the atomic bomb though he mentioned about an unspecified '**powerful new weapon of unusual destructive force**' to Stalin. Subsequently, the United States dropped atomic bombs on Hiroshima on August 6 and Nagasaki on 9 August 1945 and ended the war quickly, suggesting that Truman did not want Stalin involve in the terms of Japan's surrender.

B. Emergence of the Eastern Bloc

The developments in Eastern Europe and the emergence of the Eastern Bloc under the USSR revived the pre-war fears of communism in Western countries. As Russia lacked natural western border, it had been invaded many times in centuries of its history. Some of these were, Poles in the 17th century, Napoleon in the 19th century and the Germans during both the World Wars. Stalin intended the Eastern Bloc governments as nothing but puppet regimes to create a buffer zone for protection against any threat to the USSR from the west. These governments reproduced command economies, denied political freedom and resorted to brutal methods of suppression against the real and potential opposition. Soviet style secret police systems were introduced in these countries which rigged elections, supervised expulsion and execution of non-communist members of the coalition governments and dissolution of other political parties. The western nations could only watch the Soviet Union tightening its grip on Eastern Europe, including over Poland, for whose freedom England had gone to war in 1939. Stalin justified his action by saying 'whoever occupies a territory also imposes on it, his own social system'.

At Yalta, Stalin had agreed to assist the liberated countries of Europe to create democratic institutions through free elections. Contrary to it, Stalin's domination of the Eastern Europe was seen as betrayal of these promises which aggravated the British and the US indignation against the USSR.

C. Fulton Speech

The Conservative Party leader and the former British Prime Minister Winston Churchill responded to the establishment of Soviet Satellites, in a speech he made at **Fulton, Missouri (USA)** in March 1946. In this speech Churchill emphasised the point that '**from Stettin in the Baltic to Trieste in the Adriatic an iron curtain has descended across the continent**' and called for an Anglo-American alliance against Soviet Russia. Stalin responded to the speech comparing Churchill to Hitler, in so far as he advocated the racial superiority of the English-speaking nations and denounced Churchill as a war monger. The Fulton Speech and Stalin's response to it widened the rift between the West and the East.

> **Cold War 'Worlds':** During the Cold War the world had been grouped into three, while the industrialised, capitalist nations constituted the First World, the Communist nations under the Soviet were the Second. The newly independent, developing nations not aligned with either of the above two were known as the Third World.

6. Beginning of the Cold War (1946–53)

A. Developments in Greece

The Cold War clouds soon emerged in Europe during the civil war in Greece. Erosion of democracy in Eastern Europe, as seen above, was of concern to the Western democracies as it was a threat to what they called the **'Free World'**. Now, the threat of Soviet penetration into the Mediterranean alarmed the United States which abandoned its traditional policy of isolationism and took up the leadership of the Free World.

During the World War II, Greece had been occupied by the fascists under Germany. While resistance against the fascists emerged in the country a Greek government-in-exile under King George II had been setup in Egypt, and was recognised by the Western Allies. After the end of the War, Greece was mired in a civil war between the royalist and the communists. The British troops which had been sent to Greece to liberate Greece from the Germans had restored the king who was brought back from exile which was opposed by the communists leading to civil war.

The Greek government army was supported by the United Kingdom, while the communists were supported by the neighbouring communist countries of Yugoslavia, Albania and Bulgaria. As Britain planned to withdraw from Greece, on account of post-war financial crisis, the United States decided to support the royalist forces in Greece. The US administration

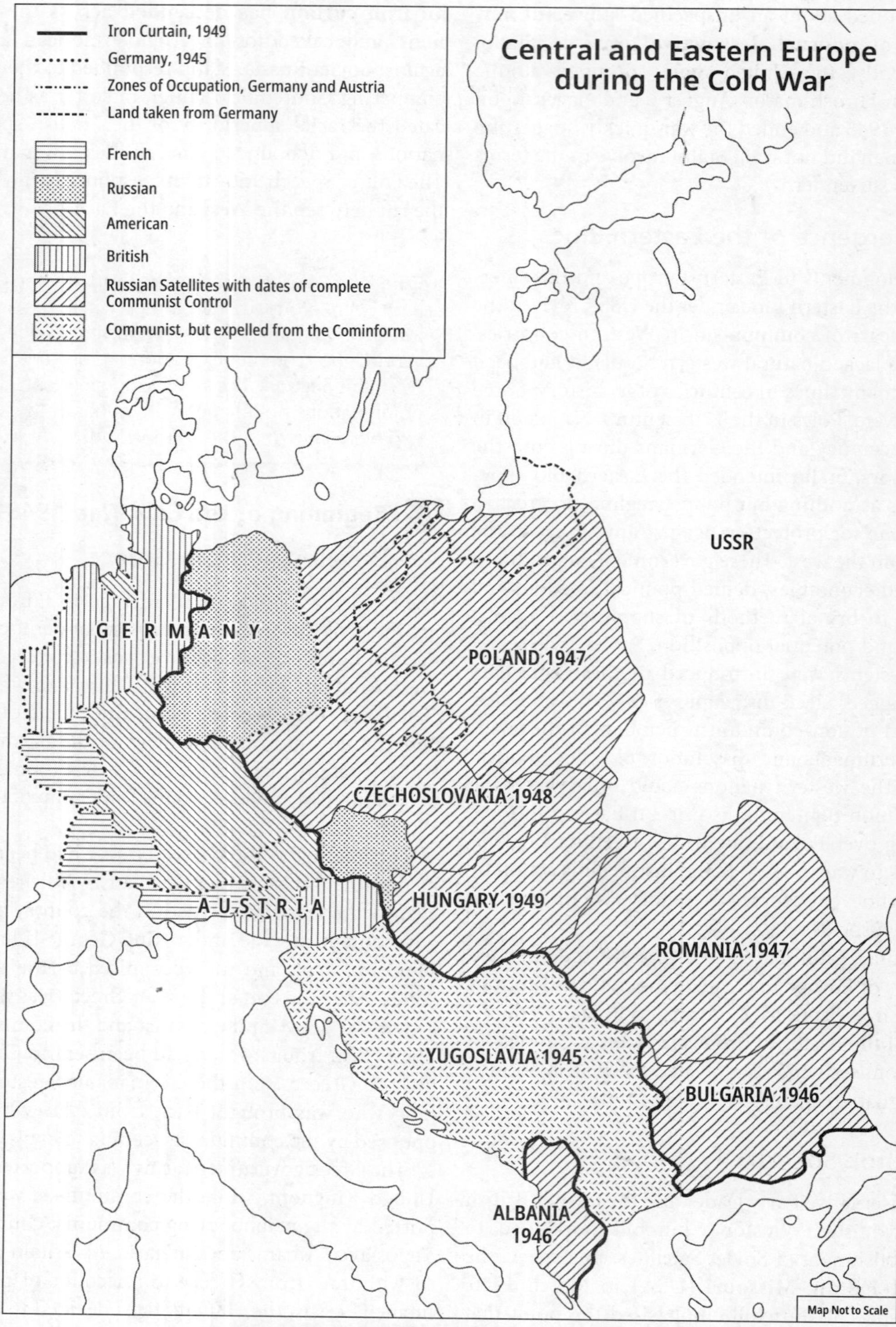

Central and Eastern Europe during the Cold War

formed the **Truman Doctrine** and Greece was supplied with massive amounts of arms and other supplies leading to the end of the civil war in 1949 and the defeat of the communists. Greek Civil War turned out to be the **first proxy war of the Cold War**.

B. Developments in Turkey

After the Second World War, Soviet Russia pressurised Turkey to open up the Straits of Constantinople, which connected the Black Sea to the Mediterranean, to the Soviet shipping and to return some border areas, it had seized from Russia soon after the Communist Revolution of 1917. In 1946, the Soviet Union also increased its naval presence in the Black Sea.

The United States decided to support Turkey as it did not want the strait to fall into the hands of the Soviet Union as it would give them a strategic gateway between the Black Sea and the Mediterranean and possibly lead to a communist Turkey. The United States believed that, if the Soviet Union succeeded in introducing its armed forces into Turkey with the ostensible purpose of enforcing the joint control of the Straits, the Soviet Union will use these forces to obtain control over Turkey.

On the appeal of Turkey, the US President Truman sent a naval force to Turkey upon which the Soviet Union pulled out most of its forces from the region by the end of 1946. Turkey abandoned its policy of neutrally and accepted $100 million in economic and defence aid from the United States, under the Truman Doctrine.

C. The Truman Doctrine

The Truman Doctrine was the foundation of American foreign policy during the Cold War. It marked a sharp departure from traditional American isolationism and is often considered as the beginning point of the Cold War. In March 1947, the US President Harry Truman went to the Congress with a request for funds '**to assist free peoples who are resisting attempted subjugation by armed minorities or by outside pressures**'. He stated that the United States 'must assist free peoples to work out their own destinies in their own way'.

The Truman's speech requesting the Congress to appropriate $400 million to 'support the free peoples' marked the adoption of '**containment**' as official US policy.

> Containment was a foreign policy initiative of the United States under Truman. It aimed at holding the Soviet power and communism within the then existing boundaries by forming alliances and helping countries to resist Soviet advances.

D. The Marshall Plan

The Marshall Plan was an economic extension of the Truman Doctrine. The plan was announced in June 1947 and was in operation for four years. The plan officially known as the **European Recovery Program** envisaged reconstruction of Europe through economic and financial help of America. It was named after the United States' Secretary of State George Marshall, who prepared the plan.

George Marshall, in his address to the students of Harvard University in June 1947, announced the Plan and explained that 'the United States should do whatever it is able to do, to **assist in the return of normal economic health to the world**'. He went on to add that 'our policy is not directed against any country, but against hunger, poverty, desperation and chaos'. He also visualised that 'the revival of a working economy in the world would permit the emergence of political and social conditions in which free institutions can exist'.

- The Second World War had devastated much of Europe. The total devastation of the European infrastructure and slow recovery of these economies especially that of the Germany convinced the United States that the economic recovery in Europe could not go forward without the reconstruction of Germany and without the European recovery and progress there cannot be lasting peace and stability.
- Another factor behind Marshall Plan was the prosperity of the United States. The only major power, whose infrastructure had not been significantly destroyed in Second World War, was the United States. Though much prosperous than before the war, its exports were a small factor in its economy. The European Recovery Program was expected to ensure markets for American exports.

- The background was also prepared by the Truman Doctrine which had argued for 'containment of communism'. It was expected that communism was less likely to get a foothold in a prosperous Europe. There was also some hope that the Eastern Bloc nations would join the Plan and thus could be pulled out of the emerging Soviet Bloc.

The **Economic Cooperation Act** was passed by the Congress to give effect to the Marshall Plan and was signed into law by President Truman in April, 1948. The 16 participating nations (Austria, Belgium, Denmark, France, West Germany, Greece, Iceland, Ireland, Italy, Luxembourg, the Netherlands, Norway, Sweden, Switzerland, Turkey, the United Kingdom) and the United States signed an agreement establishing an aid coordinating agency – the **Organisation for European Economic Co-operation (OEEC)** which later (in 1961) was to emerge as the Organisation for Economic Cooperation and Development – **OECD**. During the four years the plan was in effect, the United States donated $ 17 billion to Western European nations fostering their economies. By 1952, as the funding ended, the economy of every participant state had surpassed the pre-war levels.

Marshall Plan had important effects on the European continent and in the evolution of world history. In economic sense the Marshall Plan heralded an era of fastest growth in European history as the Western Europe embarked upon an era of unprecedented growth during which the industrial production, agricultural output and the standard of living increased dramatically. The Marshall Plan also set the stage for large amounts of private US investment in Europe, establishing the basis for modern transnational corporations.

The political effects of the Plan too had been significant. As a result of the general prosperity and with reduction of rationing and austerity measures, discontent was reduced and political stability could be established in Western Europe. True to one of its proclaimed objectives, the Plan could contain Communism to great extent, even though it could not engineer a defection in the Eastern Bloc and bring a Soviet satellite to the Capitalist Bloc.

The Marshall Plan played an important role in the European integration too. The OEEC, created in 1948 to coordinate the Marshall Plan activities, served as the testing and training ground for the structures that would later be used in the creation of the European Economic Community. The relations fostered by the Marshall Plan also facilitated the emergence of a military alliance between these nations in the form of NATO (April 1949).

Importance of the Marshal Plan in the Cold War perspective was that, it marked a clear division of the European continent into the capitalist and the communist lines. The Marshall Plan also subtly 'Americanised' the European countries by an enlarged exposure to American popular culture including the 'rock n' roll' and Hollywood.

The Soviet Union and its satellite states in Eastern Europe rejected the plan. The Soviet Union came out with an 'alternative' to the Marshall Plan known as the **'Molotov Plan'** in 1947 to provide aid to rebuild Eastern European countries. Stalin also created **'COMINFORM'** (Communist Information Bureau) in September 1947 to bind together various communist parties in Europe including that of France and Italy.

E. Developments in Czechoslovakia

By 1948, Czechoslovakia was the only Eastern European state with a democratic system. A coalition government called the **National Front** consisting of communists and non-communists had been established after free elections in 1946. But rejection of the Marshall Plan by the government and efforts by the communists to control police, civil services and the armed forces caused a split in the government. Subsequently, fresh parliamentary elections were held in May 1948, but were rigged as voters were presented with a single list of candidates – all communists. In the purged election the communists secured 89 per cent of the votes, communist leader **Klement Gottwald** became the new president and with the adoption of a new Soviet style constitution Czechoslovakia's entry into Communist Bloc became complete.

F. Developments in Germany

As seen already, Germany had been divided into four occupation zones each under the United States, USSR, United Kingdom and France and was jointly administered by an **Allied Control Commission**.

The capital city of Berlin was located deep inside the Soviet zone which was also divided into four zones.

Stalin wanted the Soviet zone with its communist, pro-USSR government as a separate entity, as a buffer between the USSR and the western powers. For Stalin, Germany was a security threat, hence wanted to make Germany weak so as to prevent it from emerging again against the Soviet Union. Stalin drained its resources away to Russia in the name of German war reparations which severely weakened the East German economy. The Soviets transported approximately 33 per cent of its industrial plant to the USSR and by the 1950s had extracted some US $ 10 billion in reparations in the form of agricultural and industrial products. Moreover, Stalin treated the Russian occupation zone as his satellite. In the Soviet zone, large landholdings were confiscated and redistributed among peasants, industries and mines were nationalised, German Communists in exile were encouraged to return, and the teaching of Marxism-Leninism and the Russian language were made compulsory in schools.

On the other hand, the United States aimed at the rebuilding of Western Germany and its integration into the world community. In the western part a capitalist economy thrived along with mushrooming of political parties and groups sharply hostile to communism and the USSR. The United States, Britain and France merged their three zones into **single economic unit**, whose prosperity was in contrast to the poverty of the Russian zone. In June 1948, the west introduced a new currency **Deutsche Mark** in their zone and in West Berlin without consulting the Russians.

The Russians, already embarrassed by the prosperity of West Berlin, amidst the poverty of surrounding areas under their own control decided to put West Berlin under a blockade in June 1948. By blocking all road, rail and canal links from Western Germany to Western Berlin, situated one hundred miles inside the Soviet Zone, the Russians aimed at forcing the West to withdraw from West Berlin by reducing it to starvation. This development is known as the **Berlin Blockade**.

In response, the Western Allies conducted massive airlift of supplies to West Berlin, known as the **Berlin Airlift**. It continued for about 11 months from June 1948 to May 1949. During the period over 2 million tons of supplies including food, fuel and machinery were airlifted to West Berlin in a colossal operation which kept the 2.5 million West Berliners life and spirit alive. In May 1949, the USSR lifted the blockade and in September 1949 the 'Berlin Airlift' officially came to an end.

Though the Blockade and airlift caused the Cold War tension to heat up, the crisis did not develop into an open war. Reasons were many. Truman's decision to airlift the supplies than sending US armoured troops into Berlin to break the blockade averted an open conflict at the initial stage itself. Technically, the Soviets could not object to the flight of cargo aircrafts as it did not pose any military threat, and the only way to enforce the blockade would have been shooting down unarmed humanitarian aircraft. Any such action from the Soviet side would have attracted retaliation from the Western powers. The Soviet, though had an advantage in conventional military, was preoccupied with rebuilding of their war-torn country and did not risk that option. The Soviet Union was also aware of the fact that the United States had stronger navy and air force and nuclear weapons, hence did not disrupt the airlift.

- As far as the USSR was concerned the 'Berlin Blockade' was a failure as it could not force the west to withdraw from West Berlin.
- For the Western powers the Berlin airlift was a great success. It provided a great psychological boost to Western powers as they could defeat the ulterior intention of the USSR which was to bring West Berlin under submission and to extend the sphere of influence of communism. It was also an expression of a successful application of the 'Containment'.
- The incident also facilitated removal of any differences between the United States, United Kingdom and the French regarding West Germany, leading to the emergence of the Federal Republic of Germany, popularly known as West Germany in 1949.
- The incident also reduced the animosities between Germany and the Western Allies as these former enemies now realised the common interests and shared values as mutually beneficial.
- The threat perceived of the Soviet Union as evident in the Berlin Blockade and the lessons learned in

coordinating the Allied military efforts during the Berlin Airlift prompted the western powers to initiate a collective defence system known as **NATO** in April 1949.

- Last but not the least, the Berlin crisis brought the relation between the West and the Soviet to the worst ever level and deepened the Cold War.

G. Formation of NATO

In March 1948, a mutual defence treaty, known as the **Brussels Defense Treaty**, had been signed by some of the Western European nations – the United Kingdom, France, Luxemburg, the Netherlands and Belgium. But the developments in 1948 – *coup d'état* in Czechoslovakia and the Berlin Blockade – strengthened the Western apprehensions regarding the intentions of the Communist Bloc and convinced the Western leaders of insufficiency of the Brussels Treaty in meeting the threat from the Communist Bloc.

NATO Emblem

In April 1949, the five Brussels Treaty members were joined by United States, Canada, Portugal, Denmark, Italy, Norway and Iceland to sign a treaty creating the NATO, providing for trans-Atlantic cooperation. Headquartered in Brussels, Belgium, NATO was envisaged as an organisation **'to keep the Russians out, the Americans in and the Germans down'**.

That is:

1. to keep the Soviet sponsored communist expansion out to Western Europe,
2. to bring in American involvement in western European affairs,
3. to keep Germany from rearming and threatening the peace again and to forbid revival of militant nationalism in Europe.

> NATO envisaged both military and non-military co-operation. Article 2 provided for non-military cooperation, while Article 5 of the Treaty provided that 'an armed attack against one or more of them shall be considered an attack against them all and that each ally would take such actions as it deems necessary, including the use of armed force'.

The formation of NATO facilitated creation of a joint NATO command to coordinate the defence of the members and also brought about standardisation in military technology, terminology and procedures of the member states. NATO signalled the abandonment of **'no entangling alliances'**, the traditional policy of the US in international affairs. In 1952, Greece and Turkey joined NATO and in 1955 the West Germany became a member.

Formation of NATO heightened the tensions of Cold War. In August 1949, the Soviet Union conducted its first successful nuclear weapon test in Kazakhstan and responded to the western challenge and also ended the US monopoly in atomic weaponry.

H. Emergence of Two Germanys

In May 1949, the three zones under the United States, United Kingdom and France were united into **German Federal Republic** known as **West Germany** with capital at Bonn. In October, the Soviet zone became the **German Democratic Republic or East Germany**.

West Germany was established as a federal parliamentary republic with market economy and re-emerged as an industrial giant with the assistance under the Marshall Plan. In 1955, West Germany was admitted into NATO and in 1957 became one of the founding members of the European Economic Community.

On the other, East Germany though democratic in name was under the political and military control of the Soviet and followed the Soviet style command economy.

I. COMECON and the Warsaw Pact

COMECON or Council for Mutual Economic Assistance was an economic forum aimed at promoting coordinating economic planning, trade and development under the leadership of the USSR. It was formed in January 1949 and was the Eastern Bloc's reply to the formation of the OEEC (Organisation for European Economic Co-operation).

The Warsaw Pact was a collective defence treaty between the USSR and seven other Soviet satellites-Albania, Bulgaria, Czechoslovakia, East Germany, Hungary, Poland and Romania. It was formed in May 1955 in Warsaw, Poland and was formally known as

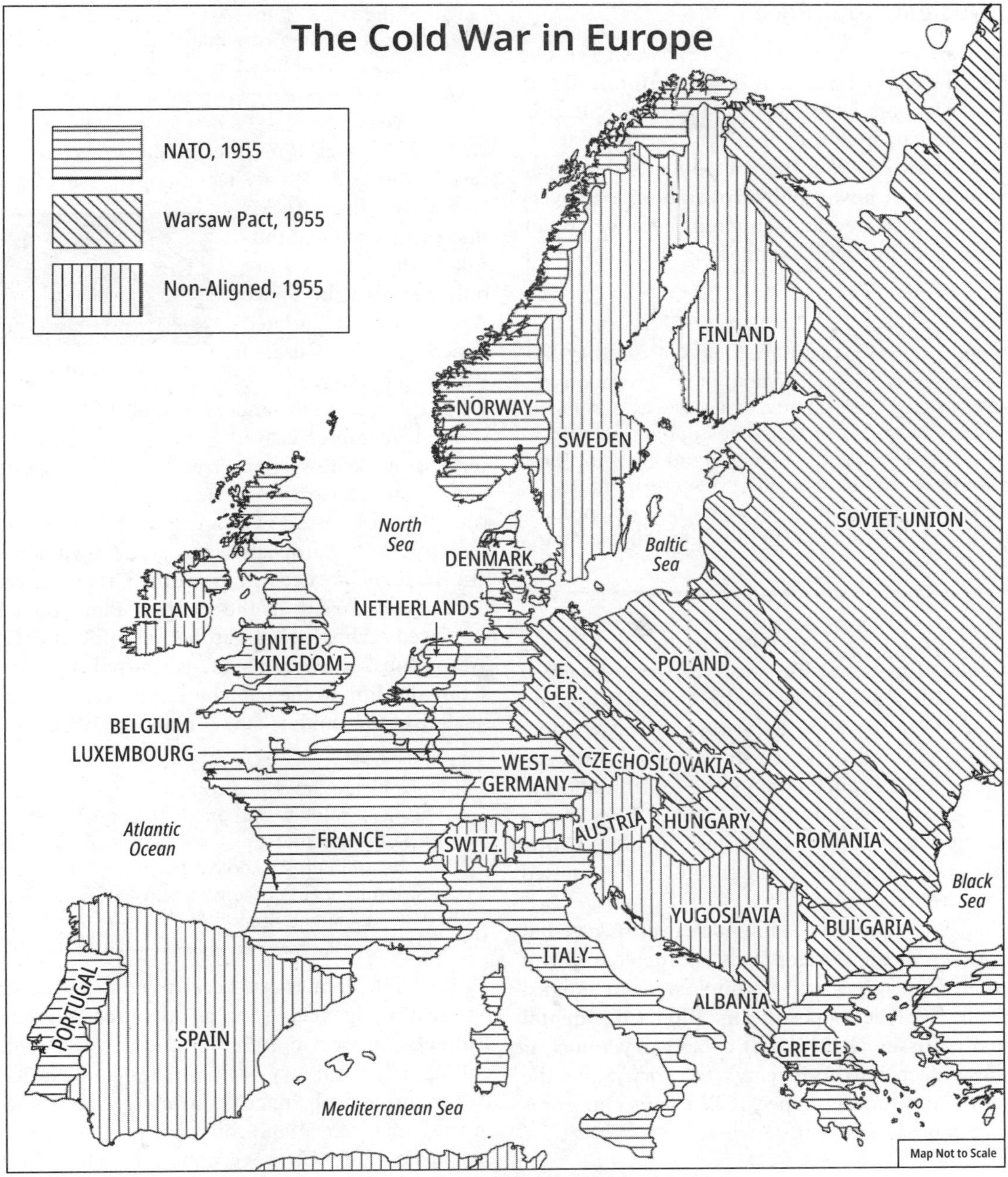

Cold War in Europe

the **Treaty of Friendship, Co-operation and Mutual Assistance**. It complemented COMECON and came to embody the Eastern Bloc. The immediate provocation for the formation of the Warsaw Pact was the inclusion of West Germany in NATO on 9 May 1955 and her remilitarisation. The Treaty provided for a unified military command and for garrisoning of the Soviet troops in member countries.

J. Nuclear Arms Race

Cold war accelerated arms race between the two blocs. The United States possessed **atomic bomb** since 1945 and in August, 1949 the USSR produced their own atomic bomb triggering a race in nuclear arms. In 1952, the United States developed the much more powerful **hydrogen bomb**. The very next year Russia developed not only hydrogen bomb but also a bomber with a range long enough to reach America.

Brinkmanship means the practice of pushing an issue or event to the threshold of confrontation in order to gain greatest advantage. It was a foreign policy tool of the United States during the presidencies of Eisenhower, Kennedy and Johnson. The concept was initiated by the US Secretary of State John Foster Dulles in 1956 when he explained it as 'The ability to get to the verge without getting into the war'.

During this period in addition to the United States and Soviet Russia, nuclear weapons were developed by their allies too. In 1952, the **United Kingdom** became the third nation to possess nuclear weapon, which it followed by successfully testing hydrogen bomb in 1957. **France** became the fourth nation to possess nuclear weapon in 1960 and in 1968 France conducted its hydrogen bomb test. In 1964, **China** became the fifth nuclear power and in 1967 tested their hydrogen bomb.

Cold War caused not only nuclear arms race but also a race in the development and deployment of associated weapons and technologies. In August 1957, the USSR developed the first **Inter-Continental Ballistic Missile** (ICBM) that could carry a nuclear warhead deep into its enemy's territory. Soon the United States too developed ICBM, larger in numbers than possessed by the Soviets.

During the Presidency of Dwight D. Eisenhower, in 1954, the US Secretary of State, John Foster Dulles, gave a new dimension to the arms race by coining the term 'massive retaliation'. The United States would massively retaliate by force disproportionate to the size of attack. It called for massive attack against the USSR, if they were to attack the Western Bloc regardless of whether it was a conventional or a nuclear attack.

Next, in October 1957, the Russians inaugurated a race in the field of space technology by successfully launching the world's first earth satellite, **Sputnik 1**. The Sputnik 1 not only heralded the **Space Age** but also inaugurated **Space Race**. The use of ICBM technology by the USSR in successfully launching Sputnik 1 into space showed unambiguously the ability of the Soviet in sending nuclear weapons from Russia to Western Europe and to North America. All of a sudden, the United States, a land with a history of geographical security from European wars, seemed vulnerable. The incident created the **Sputnik Crisis** a period of fear and anxiety in the Western Bloc about the perceived technological gap between the two Cold War groups. The Sputnik Crisis spurred America to action, leading to the launch of **Explorer 1**, the first satellite of the United States, in January 1958.

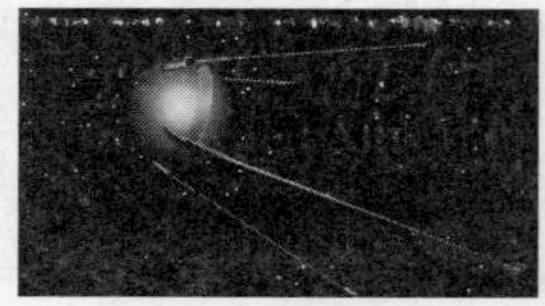

The Sputnik

Sputnik, means 'travelling companion', was world's first artificial satellite and the first manmade object to be launched into the Earth's orbit (4 October 1957). It is of interest to note that when the Russians developed their first vaccine against COVID-19 in 2020, it was named Sputnik V.

The United States also accelerated its Space Race by creating agencies such as **Advanced Research Projects Agency** in 1958, for the development of cutting edge military technologies and **National Aeronautics and Space Administration** (NASA) in the same year (1958) for space programme. The seriousness the US government attached to the Space Race was evident in the sharp increase in US government funding on scientific research and education, new emphasis on science and technology in American schools and also in the provision for low interest loans to college students majoring in mathematics and science under the **National Defense Education Act** 1958.

Subsequently both the powers developed **Submarine Launched Ballistic Missiles** (SLBMs) and by the 1960s **the triad of nuclear weapon delivery** was established with **bombers, ICBMs and SLBMs** to ensure that even if a defence was found against one method, other methods would still be available.

The Soviet Union's launching of the **first manned space flight** by Yuri Gagarin in April 1961 and the July 1969 **Apollo 11** mission by the United States for the first human landing on the moon were other important milestones in the Space Race. After landing on the moon on its south-western edge named as the **Sea of Tranquility**, Armstrong radioed his feeling to the Mission Control Centre in Texas as '**that is one small step for a man, one giant leap for mankind**'.

The super powers search for ensuring their security led to the development of **Anti-Ballistic Missiles** (ABM). These missiles are designed to intercept and destroy enemy ballistic missiles. The ABM system could allow one side to initiate a first strike and protect itself from enemy retaliation by shooting down incoming missiles. In the 1960s, both the United States and the Soviets developed their anti-ballistic missile systems **Nike Zeus** and **A-35**, respectively.

Development of ABMs undermined the MAD doctrine to some extent because a super power could resort to a first strike without fear of a retaliatory second strike by the enemy. For a second retaliatory strike to be successful the enemy needed to break the anti-ballistic missile shield. This challenge was soon overcome with the development of MIRV technology. The **Multiple Independently Targetable Reentry Vehicle** technology enabled a missile to hold many separate warheads. This meant that while an ABM relies on intercepting individual warheads, a MIRV missile can have multiple warheads (sometimes up to 12), making the interceptor – having only one warhead per missile – ineffective.

The nuclear parity attained by both the Blocs took the Cold War conflict to extreme dangerous and annihilative stage which is described by the term MAD. In 1962, Donald Brennan, an American strategist, coined the term **Mutual Assured Destruction** (MAD) to describe the nuclear weapon capabilities acquired by the super powers. The Doctrine was a key element in the US military strategy under Robert McNamara, the US Secretary of Defense during 1961–68. As per this doctrine, use of nuclear weapons by opposing sides would lead to complete annihilation of both the attacker and defender leading to apocalyptic conclusions. This doctrine further assumes that neither side will dare to launch a first strike because the other side will resort to second strike resulting in unacceptable losses to both parties. To ensure the credibility of this doctrine both the sides strengthened their arms research and development to keep nuclear parity or to retain a guaranteed second strike capability. On the positive side about the MAD, it could be said that it prevented any direct full-scale conflict between the United States and the USSR. In this aspect MAD is also referred to as **'nuclear deterrence'**.

A workable defence against MIRVs would require multiple defensive missiles for each offensive one. Further, the probability of decoy re-entry vehicles when used alongside actual warheads to reduce the chances of the real warheads being intercepted makes MIRVs more effective and render ABM systems less effective. Thus, both in military and economic sense (cost of maintaining a workable defence against MIRVs is very high) ABMs were rendered less effective.

America developed their first MIRV, **Minuteman III**, in 1970 intended to breach the Anti-Ballistic Missile system deployed around Moscow. The Soviets responded by creating their own MIRVs such as the **UR100N**, as part of their strategic missile defence program.

One of the direct results of the arms race had been the emergence of a network of **military–industrial complex** to meet the requirements of defence forces. It also caused emergence of alliance known as 'iron triangle' between bureaucrats, legislators and military–industrial firms and vested interests.

7. Cold War Conflicts in Asia

Developments such as the establishment of the **People's Republic of China** in 1949 and the **Korean War** in 1950 took the Cold War to Asia.

A. Formation of Communist China

At the end of the civil war in China between the Nationalist Kuomintang (KMT) and the Chinese Communist Party (CPP), the Communists established the **People's Republic of China** (PRC) in October 1949. The Nationalists retreated to the island of Taiwan (Formosa) establishing the **Republic of China** (ROC).

> Bamboo Curtain refers to the political demarcation between communist and non-communist states in Asia during the Cold War. To the north of this curtain communist states of China, the Soviet Union, Vietnam, Laos, Cambodia, North Korea and Mongolia and to south of it non-communist countries such as India, Pakistan, Taiwan, Japan and others situated.

Establishment of communist rule in the most populous country in the world not only aggravated the fear of communism in the Western Bloc but it also brought the Cold War tensions to the Asian continent. Since then, the US policy towards Asia was obsessed with the overthrow of the communist rule in China, restoration of Kuomintang government in mainland China and containment of the spread of communism in Asia.

The United States formed a defence pact, the **South East Asia Treaty Organization** (SEATO) in September 1954 with Britain, France, Australia, New Zealand, Pakistan, Thailand and the Philippines. In 1955, by another treaty, the **Central Treaty Organization** (CENTO), it strengthened its containment policy by bringing major Central Asian countries – Iran, Iraq, Turkey and Pakistan – to a military alliance with the United States and Britain.

The United States also kept China out of the United Nations (till 1971), refused to recognise the People's Republic of China for about three decades (till 1979) and continued its military support to Chiang Kai-Shek's Taiwan.

> The fear of Communism or the Red Scare manifested in the form of **McCarthyism** in the United States (making accusations of subversion and treason against people without proper evidence) as well as a campaign of fear of communist influence on American institutions. This anti-communist stand of the United States caused its involvement in many military conflicts in Asia (for example, in Korea and Vietnam) and to view nationalism and anti-colonial struggles in Asian countries as part of the strategy for communist expansion. The term owes its origin to the US Senator Joseph McCarthy who was responsible for stirring up anti-Communist feeling in the United States in the 1950s.

B. The Korean War (1950–53)

Korea had been under the occupation of Imperial Japan from 1910 until the end of the Second World War. With Japanese surrender, the Korean Peninsula was occupied by the USSR in north and the United States in south and the 38th parallel became the dividing line between the two zones.

Initially Korea was administered by a **US-Soviet Joint Commission** with the aim of granting independence after a five-year trusteeship. But, as in the case of Germany, Korea too was polarised along the 38th Parallel.

As the stalemate continued the United States brought the issue before the UN in September 1947. The UN passed a resolution providing for free elections in Korea, withdrawal of foreign troops from the Korean peninsula and creation of the **United Nations Temporary Commission on Korea** (UNTCOK) to oversee elections in Korea.

As the USSR did not cooperate in the elections arguing that the UN could not guarantee fair elections, the general elections were held in the South and the '**Republic of Korea**' or South Korea was setup with its capital at **Seoul** in August 1948. Next month (September 1948), Russians created the '**Democratic People's Republic of Korea**' or North Korea with a Communist system, with its capital at **Pyongyang**. Consequently, both the Soviet and the US troops withdrew from North and South Korea, respectively.

But in June 1950, clashes broke out between the two Koreas. The war started on 25 June 1950 with the Korean Peoples' Army crossing the 38th parallel. Within few days North Korean forces swept across almost the entire South Korea and captured Seoul, the capital of South Korea.

What caused the Korean War?

There is no clear evidence to show what caused the attack. Many reasons were suggested. The United States considered the attack was Stalin's doing as a part of the USSR's policy of spreading Communism. By 1950, confidence in the Communist Bloc had been boosted on account of developments such as victory of the Communists and the formation of a Communist Republic in China, withdrawal of the US forces from South Korea and the end of US monopoly in nuclear weapon after the detonation of nuclear bomb by the USSR. By this time the Soviets had also cracked the codes of communication used by Washington in their communication with their embassy in Moscow which gave the impression to Stalin that to the Americans, Korea did not warrant a nuclear confrontation. The **Sino-Soviet Treaty of Friendship, Alliance and Mutual Assistance** signed in February 1950, too had boosted Stalin's confidence. Stalin also believed that a Communist takeover of the South Korea would make up the failure of the USSR in West Berlin. Another factor behind the invasion was the support secured by **Kim Il-sung**, the ruler of North Korea, from Mao Zedong, the leader of China of his support in case of war with the South. Kim Il-sung was also under the impression that a North Korean invasion would be welcomed by the communist guerrillas and the general population in South Korea.

Truman, the US President, was convinced that Korean War was Stalin's strategy to spread communism. Truman therefore decided to stand by South Korea not just with economic help but with full military support. Truman believed if aggression went unchecked, a chain reaction would be initiated encouraging communist aggression elsewhere. Truman equated the North Korean invasion with Adolf Hitler's aggression in the 1930s and argued that 'if the communists were permitted to force their way in to the Republic of Korea without opposition from the free world, no small nation would have the courage to resist threat and aggression by stronger communist neighbors'. In August 1950, the Congress consented to appropriate $ 12 billion for military action in Korea, and Truman sent **General Douglas MacArthur** to lead the US forces in Korea and dispatched the US Seventh Fleet to Taiwan Strait to protect the **Republic of China** (Taiwan under Chiang Kai-shek).

The United Nations Security Council unanimously condemned the North Korean invasion of the Republic of Korea (in the absence of the Russian delegation). When North Korea refused to withdraw her troops, the UN asked member states to send help to South Korea.

In total 15 nations including the United States, Australia, Canada, Britain and France sent troops all of which were placed under the command of General Mac Arthur. The arrival of the UN troops led to swift collapse of the North Korean forces and the South Korea was cleared of the communist forces. The UN troops now carried the war inside North Korea by crossing the 38th Parallel as Truman wanted unification of the two Koreas and hold free elections. By the end of October the UN troops captured two-thirds of the North Korea including its capital Pyongyang and reached the Yalu River the frontier between North Korea and China.

China was seriously alarmed at this and therefore launched with the tacit support of the USSR, a massive counter-offence in October 1950 with a deployment of over 3 lakh soldiers. By mid-January 1951 the Chinese forces drove the UN troops out of North Korea, crossed the 38th parallel into South Korea and captured Seoul again.

Now, General Mac Arthur considered a nuclear attack against China. The US administration (President Truman even commented 'we are trying to prevent a world war, not start one'), in April 1951, replaced General MacArthur with General Ridgway as the Supreme Commander in Korea. General Ridgway reorganised the UN forces and in the ensuing counter attacks cleared the communists out of South Korea again and fortified the frontier at the '**Line Kansas**' just north of the 38th parallel. On 27 July 1953, the UN forces and North Korea signed cease fire and agreed for the **Korean Demilitarized Zone** (DMZ) as a buffer zone between the two Koreas which runs roughly along the 38th parallel.

Impact of the Korean War:

- Politically, the Korean War permanently sealed the division of the Korean peninsula into two countries. The existence of these two nations intensely suspicious of each other and heavily armed became a hotspot for ceasefire violations and threats of nuclear war ever since.

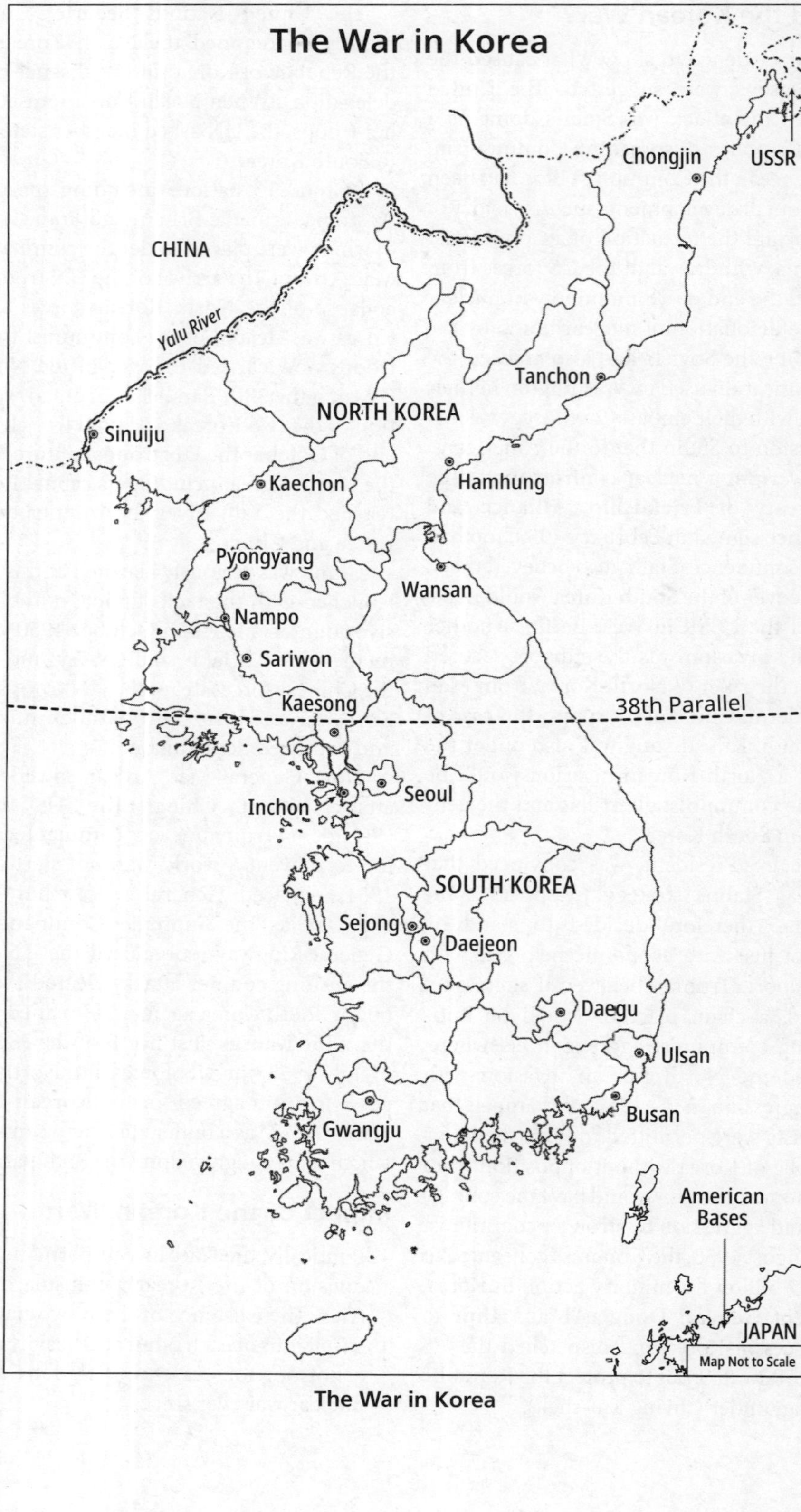

The War in Korea

- Demographically the war devastated the region. More than four million Korean soldiers and civilians had been killed during the war and five million people became homeless. During the war and in post-war period both North and South Korea had engaged in execution of their civilians in purges and as part of victimisation.
- In addition, existence of a large number of mixed race children (offspring of foreign soldiers and Korean women) became significant feature of Korean society.
- Economically, both North and South Korea suffered massive damages to their infrastructure, industries and loss of skilled workers.
- The Korean War had important implications in the international scenario. For the UN, the Korean War became the first war in which it was called upon to act. It exerted its authority, reversed an act of aggression and prevented it breaking out in to a major war.
- In the case of the United States, it could derive satisfaction for having contained communism and for deterring the Communist Bloc from pursuing military aggressions in their neighbourhood with the timely military support to South Korea. The war also initiated the practice of maintaining a heavy military presence by the United States in South Korea in the name of upholding the armistice.
- As far as China, the newly born communist nation was concerned, its impressive performance raised its status among the world nations and their leader Mao Zedong improved his own prestige in the communist international fraternity. China could prevent North Korea from falling, check the advance of the American forces across the Chinese border (Manchuria) and prevent the unification of Korea under the American influence. The Chinese military's role in engaging the strongest power in the world, forcing it to retreat, and compelling it to an armistice highlighted the abilities of the People's Liberation Army and announced the emergence of a military power. Inside China, the Korean War increased the legitimacy of the Chinese Communist Party, while weakening the anti-Communist dissent. But China failed to reunify Taiwan with the mainland China as the US President Truman had dispatched the Seventh Fleet to neutralise the Taiwan Strait and to protect the independence of Taiwan.
- To the Cold War, the Korean conflict brought new dimensions. First, it showed that the two superpowers – the United States and the USSR – could engage in a '**proxy war**' in a third country and this pattern was to repeat throughout the Cold War era in Vietnam, Afghanistan and Middle-East among others. The war strained the relations of America with China and Russia permanently. The United States started a policy of encirclement of China by establishing military bases, signing military agreements and by setting up **South East Asia Treaty Organization** (SEATO).
- On the other side, the Communist Bloc received a new member when China successfully confronted what the Communist Bloc viewed as the strongest anti-communist power in the world. China now took up the initiative in supporting the Indochinese people in their struggle for independence from France and started to offer aid to the under-developed countries of Asia, Africa and Latin America. Finally, the Korean War ingrained anti-US sentiments in the Chinese mind and fear of communism got strengthened in the Capitalist Bloc.

C. The Indochina Wars

The United States' obsession with the policy of 'containment' of communism dragged it in the Indochina Wars, a protracted conflict in South East Asia. It had **two phases**. In the first, known as the First Indochina War, the people of the region fought against their French colonial masters and became independent. The second stage is known as the Vietnam War during which civil war broke out in South Vietnam for reforms and for its unification with North Vietnam.

The Indo-China Peninsula in South East Asia consisted of **Vietnam, Laos and Cambodia** and was a French colony from the middle of the 19th century and was known as the **French Indochina**. During the World War II Japan occupied the land and destroyed the French colonial administration and declared Vietnam, Cambodia and Laos as independent states and members of Japan's **'Greater East Asia Co-prosperity Sphere'** which was a grouping of nations in Asia and Oceania conceptualised by Japan as self-sufficient bloc of Asian nations free of western powers .

During the Japanese occupation, the **Viet Minh** (the League for Vietnamese Independence), a communist-led common front of the people under the leadership of **Ho Chi Minh**, had fought against the Japanese. After the conclusion of World War II, France desired to restore its colonial rule in French Indochina leading to resistance known as the First Indochina War.

> Ho Chi Minh (means 'he who enlightens') was a communist revolutionary who had spent many years in Soviet Russia learning the means and methods of organising Communist revolution. Returning to Vietnam in 1941 Ho Chi Minh fought against the occupation forces of Japan. In 1945, he declared Vietnam's independence from France. Though lovingly called as **Uncle Ho** by the people of Vietnam, he ruled Vietnam by crushing all opposition.

a. The First Indochina War (1946–54)

With the end of the Second World War, the French reoccupied the Indochina with the support of the British. Ho Chi Minh and his Viet Minh forces organised an all-out war against the French which lasted for 8 years from 1946 to 1954. Ho Chi Minh organised guerrilla warfare and was supported by Soviet Russia. From 1949 the war turned into a conventional war with the Viet Minh forces now also supported by the newly formed Communist China.

Even though not a party at the beginning, the United States soon got involved in the conflict after the establishment of the People's Republic of China in 1949. As a communist domination over the entire region would have deep implications for American interests, the United States provided political, financial and logistic support to the French. In spite of the American support, the French were finally defeated in the **Battle of Dien Bien Phu** in May 1954. In July 1954, the **Geneva Accords** were signed by the French and Vietnamese, Laotian and Cambodian representatives providing for:

1. Ceasefire,
2. Creation of a provisional demarcation line in Vietnam along the 17th parallel and creation of a demilitarised zone on each side of the line,
3. Withdrawal of troops to its side of the line by both the groups,
4. Laos and Cambodia were to be fully independent,
5. Democratic elections for unification of North and South Vietnam, two years after ceasefire, that is, in July 1956,
6. An international commission consisting representatives of Canada, Poland and India to supervise execution of the accord.

b. The Vietnam War (1954–75)

The **Vietnam War** also known as the **Second Indochina War** was fought between the North Vietnam (capital at Hanoi) under Ho Chi Minh's Communist government and the government of South Vietnam. In the war North was supported by the USSR and China, while the South was supported by the anti-communist allies led by the United States.

The Geneva Accord was violated by both the parties within a short time. The North Vietnam violated it by refusing to withdraw all Viet Minh troops from South Vietnam. The South refused to conduct reunification elections in 1956 citing that it was impossible to hold free elections in the communist North.

The government of the South Vietnam, now known as the **Republic of Vietnam** under its leader, **Ngo Dinh Diem**, was supported by the United States. Diem ruled as a dictator, eliminated political opposition and targeted communist groups. Discrimination felt by the majority Buddhists (more than three-fourth of the population were Buddhists) under Diem, who was a Roman Catholic, was another reason for discontent. Peasants looked for land reforms as implemented in China and North Vietnam.

Discontent caused emergence of a broad-based opposition and to civil war. It started with low level insurgency which included bombings and assassinations of government officials. In December 1960, the **National Liberation Front** (NLF) popularly known as **Viet Cong** was created to bring all anti-government forces together and to demand reforms and a unified Vietnam.

Ho Chi Minh supported the Vietcong as he believed that the government of the South Vietnam was an American puppet regime and wanted its overthrow and integration of the South with the North. On the other, the US government viewed the North Vietnamese as a puppet of communist international, spread of which was to be contained, if not eliminated. The US foreign policy now directed by the currents of the **'Domino Theory'** favoured providing strong support to South Vietnam.

Domino Theory: A foreign policy outlook of the United States during its President Eisenhower (1953–61), which described the South East Asian nations like a row of dominos and if one is pushed over, it will knock over the next and so on. Similarly, if one nation falls to communism, it would lead to successive falls and expansion of Communism in South East Asia.

As the civil war intensified, America strengthened its support of South Vietnam government. Under its Presidents, Dwight Eisenhower (1953–61), John F. Kennedy (1961–63), Lyndon Johnson (1963–69) and Nixon (1969–74) the United States supplied not only arms and ammunitions but regular combat troops which climaxed to half a million by 1967. The United States also bombed North Vietnam to pressurise Ho Chi Minh to call off the campaign. To destroy the **Ho Chi Minh Trail**, the United States also bombed Laos and Cambodia enlarging the war zone. In spite of huge efforts, the United States could not subdue the Vietcong and by 1972 huge part of the country had been secured by the Vietcong.

The Ho Chi Minh Trail was a logistical supply route connecting North Vietnam with South Vietnam running through Laos and Cambodia. This was the main supply route through which the Communist North Vietnam supplied weapons, manpower and other essentials to the South Vietnam guerrillas during the Vietnam War.

Finally, ceasefire was signed in January 1973 by which the United States agreed to withdraw from Vietnam. It also provided for respecting the 17th parallel as the frontier between the two Vietnams. But the Vietcong continued the fight and devoid of American support the South Vietnam government crumbled. In April 1975, Saigon was captured which was renamed as Ho Chi Minh City and Vietnam was united with the North.

Nixon Doctrine: It was formulated by Richard Nixon administration in the background of harsh realities of the Vietnam War. The Doctrine emphasised the treaty obligations of the United States in defending its allies but entrusted basic responsibility of defence to the nations themselves, while the US support would consist of military and economic aid rather than with ground troops. As an expression of this policy Nixon initiated 'Vietnamization' – assigning larger combat role to South Vietnamese forces and steadily reducing the number of US combat forces.

The Vietnam War was one of the most brutal in terms of suffering and casualties. The total tonnage of bombs used in the war was much more than dropped on Germany, Italy and Japan in World War II. Use of defoliants such as **Agent Orange** transformed landscape, caused deaths, injuries, diseases, birth defects and poisoning of the food chain. The war had turned more than 8 million people into homeless refugees in South Vietnam alone.

Why American intervention failed? Most important factor was the widespread support of the people to the Vietcong. They supported the rebels with all kinds of provisions and hideouts. On the other hand, the South Vietnamese government the Americans defending was unpopular. Second factor was the guerrilla tactics adopted by the rebels. Support received by the rebels from the North Vietnam, China and Russia too were significant in strengthening the resolve of the rebels. Moreover, the amazing resilience showed by the rebels in the face of casualties and American brutalities convinced Americans of the hopelessness of the struggle. Finally, there was a strong anti-war campaign in the United States which compelled the government to look for a way out.

In Laos and Cambodia too communists captured power. In 1975, Laotian communists known as Pathet Lao captured power in Laos. In the same year, the Communists known as the Khmer Rouge captured power in Cambodia and renamed it as Kampuchea. Under their leader Pol Pot, the Communists established one of the most brutal communist regimes and slaughtered more than two million people in their attempt to transform it into a Communist society. Pol Pot and his Khmer Rouge zealots who were intended to create an egalitarian agrarian society liquidated their opponents, abolished private property, private households and currency, demolished temples and forced urban population to villages. The UN-sponsored peace settlement in 1991 facilitated free elections and transition to democracy in 1993.

My Lai Massacre: One of the brutal incidents during the Vietnam War in which the American soldiers rounded up, tortured and shot dead about 500 civilians of a village My Lai. The victims, whom there were women, old aged and children, were buried in mass graves.

8. Thaw in the Cold War (1953–61)

In the 1950s, there was thaw in the Cold War. Many factors contributed to the thaw.

First, after the death of Stalin in 1953, new leadership under Nikita Khrushchev wanted improved relation with the United States. Khrushchev criticised Stalin and argued for **'peaceful coexistence'** as there were only two ways, either peaceful coexistence or total destructive war and no third way ahead. He also abandoned Stalin's seclusion and travelled throughout the world which included visits to United States in 1958 and 1960 and a visit to Tito of Yugoslavia. He also began a series of summit meetings with leaders of Britain, France and the United States. Desire for reducing international tensions also grew out of the desire to prevent a perceived collapse of the Communist Bloc. Under the growing demand for easing restrictions as seen in Poland and Hungary in 1956 the Soviet leadership had to agree that there was **'more than one road to socialism'**. The thaw was also facilitated by the Sino-Soviet split which widened the ideological divergence in the Communist camp.

On his part the US President Eisenhower declared that America wanted to be friendly with the Soviets. This new attitude was partly the result of possession of hydrogen bomb by both the countries by the year 1953 and their desire to avoid nuclear catastrophe. In America, there was a revulsion against McCarthyism.

The thaw found expressed in the desire to end the Korean War in 1953, end of the Indochina war in 1954 and in other developments like dissolution of the Cominform in 1956 which meant more freedom for the Eastern Bloc nations. Most importantly, Austria was given independence by the Austrian State Treaty in 1955 and all occupying troops withdrew. Austria was prohibited from uniting with Germany and was to remain neutral in any dispute between the Blocs.

Though Khrushchev believed that ultimate triumph of communism can be attained by means other than wars, he did not reduce his guard against the Western Bloc. The Warsaw Pact was signed in 1955, the Berlin Wall was built in 1961 and missiles were installed in Cuba in 1962 leading to escalation of tension again.

Sino-Soviet Split: Emergence of China as a Communist nation was a big boost to the Communist Bloc. In 1950, Stalin and Mao signed a 30-year treaty of friendship. But differences emerged soon. China wanted to pursue its own brand of Communism. While both sought leadership of world Communist movement, they had territorial disputes between them as they shared longest land border in the world. All these led to Sino-Soviet Split.

9. Escalation of the Cold War (1961–69)

A. The Berlin Crisis of 1961

Since the division of Germany into two, there was huge exodus of people from the East to the West resulting in a massive **'brain drain'** in East Germany threatening its economic viability and political credibility as a nation. To prevent the exodus, East Germany strengthened the fortification of its boundary with the West Germany which was known as the **Inner German Border**. This border between East and West Germanys running from the Baltic Sea to Czechoslovakia over 1393 km length became one of the heavily fortified frontiers in the world, defined by a continuous line of metal fences, walls, alarm, watch towers and mine fields. The border was physical manifestation of Winston Churchill's metaphorical **'iron curtain'** that separated the Soviet and Western Bloc.

With the closing of the Inner German Border, the border between East and West in Berlin became the main route by which the East Germans left for the West. The East German government sought to stop its population leaving to the West through Berlin by erecting a wall between the East and West Berlin.

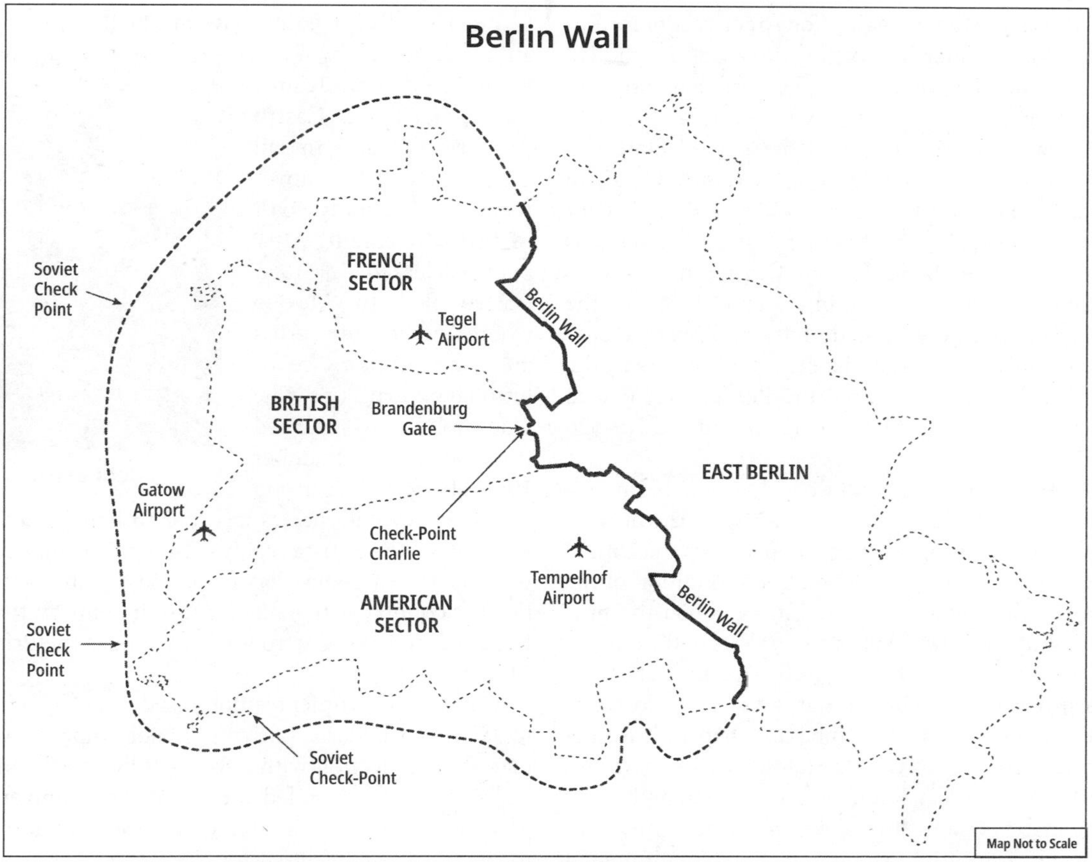

Berlin and the Wall

In August 1961, barbed wire were erected along the 156 km stretch around the three western sectors. East Germans could no longer travel or emigrate to West Germany. In 1945 Potsdam Conference, the four governing powers of Berlin had agreed that Allied personnel could move freely in any sector of Berlin. Construction of the wall restricted the movement. The East German government claimed that the wall as an 'anti-fascist protective measure' against any aggression from the West.

As tension mounted both the United States and the Soviet forces mobilised their tank units and stood facing each other at the boundary with orders to fire if fired upon. Finally, Khrushchev and Kennedy agreed to withdraw the tanks leading to relaxation in tension. Kennedy was reported to have commented that 'it was not a very nice solution, but a wall is a hell of a lot better than a war'.

Spy scare: Spy missions too were part of Cold War tactics. In May 1960, the Soviet shot down U-2 high-altitude spy plane of the Central Intelligence Agency of the United States while flying over Soviet territory.

B. Developments in Cuba

Cuba was a colony of Spain. A series of rebellions in the 19th century had failed in ending the Spanish rule. Finally, it was the Spanish-American War (1898) that resulted in the end of Spanish rule in Cuba. Americans had huge investments in Cuba and it was the major reason for America's interest in Cuba. In the latter-half of the 19th century, the US businessmen had monopolised Cuban economy and 90 per cent of Cuba's total exports and 40 per cent of Cuba's imports were with the United States. In 1898, the American battleship USS Maine, docked in Havana, exploded killing 258 which gave the spark for war with Spain. The American cry of the hour was 'Remember the Maine, To Hell with Spain'.

Spain was defeated and in December 1898 by the Treaty of Paris, the United States and Spain recognised the Cuban independence. Under this treaty the United States also acquired the Philippines, Puerto Rico and Guam from Spain for a sum of US $20 million.

After the Spanish withdrawal, Cuba became a semi-colony of the United States till 1902, the year in which it got formal independence from the United States as the Republic of Cuba. As a condition of the transfer, the Cuban constitution contained the provisions of the **Platt Amendment** (8 conditions for the withdrawal of the US troops from Cuba). By this provision the United States had right to intervene militarily in Cuba, Cuba also had to lease the Guantanamo Bay to United States.

The new Cuban Republic tried to strengthen its democratic system and develop its economy. But political radicalisation and social strife culminated in the dictatorship (1952–59) of **Fulgencio Batista**. Batista's dictatorship was a nightmare for its citizens and tragedy for the nation. Corruption of the government, brutality of the police and government's indifference to the basic needs of the people became hallmarks of Batista's Cuba. The Cuban capital Havana became 'a hedonistic playground for the world's elite' with gambling, prostitution, drug and mafia making it their haven. During this period Batista regime also executed more than 20,000 Cubans and turned democratic Cuba into a complete police state.

In the context of the Cold War the United States supported the Batista regime for his strong opposition to communism. Close relationship between the United States and the Batista regime enabled the US corporations to capture dominancy in the island's economy and by the late 1950s the US companies owned 90 per cent of mines, 80 per cent of public utilities, 50 per cent of railways, 40 per cent sugar production in Cuba.

Fidel Castro, a young law graduate, organised an armed attack by a small group of revolutionaries on 26 July 1953 against Batista but failed. Castro was arrested and in jail Castro named his movement as the '**Twenty Sixth of July Movement**'. After being released in 1955 Castro fled to Mexico where he came across an Argentinian revolutionary Ernesto 'Che Guevara'. Castro returned to Cuba in December 1956 along with a group of armed revolutionaries in order to fight guerrilla war against the Batista regime. After an all-out effort to suppress the guerrillas ended in failure Batista fled the country with a huge wealth in January 1959. In February 1959, Castro was sworn in as the Prime Minister of Cuba.

Fidel Castro

Castro's government emphasised social reforms to improve standards of living. Major emphasis was placed on education with a work-study programme, health care was expanded and nationalised, universal vaccination against childhood diseases was implemented, day care facilities for children and care centres for the disabled and elderly were started. Castro's regime was popular with workers, peasants and students who constituted majority of the Cuban population. At the same time Castro was a dictator – he executed his opponents, restricted the press and suspended elections.

By 1960, Cuba began to be embroiled in the Cold War conflicts. The increasing tilt of the Cuban government towards the Soviet Russia and the fear of spread of communism throughout the Latin America as had happened in Southeast Asia caused a change in the US attitude towards Cuba. The US administration believed that international communism was using Cuba as an 'operational base' for spreading communism in the western hemisphere. This was also seen by the United States as a direct violation of the **'Monroe Doctrine'**.

Castro agreed to provide the USSR with sugar, fruit, fibre and hides in return for crude oil, fertilisers, industrial goods and a $100 million loan. This development caused concern in the US administration. Cuban oil refineries were in the hands of the US corporations – the Shell and ESSO and they refused to process Soviet oil. Castro nationalised the refineries. In retaliation the United States cancelled import of Cuban sugar provoking Castro to nationalise most of the US-owned companies and assets including banks and sugar mills in Cuba. In January 1961, the United States terminated diplomatic relations with Cuba. The United States further tightened its opposition to Cuban government by freezing all Cuban assets on American soil and imposing an embargo on Cuba. In April 1961, a counter revolutionary (mostly Cuban exiles in America) group trained and funded by the Central Intelligence Agency (CIA) made an attack on Cuba to overthrow Fidel Castro. The invasion was launched from Guatemala and Nicaragua and the counter revolutionaries landed at **the Bay of Pigs** on southern coast of Cuba. But the invasion ended in failure. After the Bay of Pigs, Castro openly declared the revolution 'Marxist Leninist' and pursued closer relations with the USSR leading to the Cuban Missile Crisis. The US President Kennedy ordered the Pentagon to design secret operations to overthrow the Castro regime under the name **Operation Mongoose**.

C. The Cuban Missile Crisis of 1962

Fidel Castro believed that the United States would invade Cuba again, even after the failed Bay of Pigs incident and in early 1962 reached a secret agreement with Nikita Khrushchev to place strategic nuclear missiles in Cuba.

Nikita Khrushchev himself was motivated in placing nuclear missiles in Cuba on many grounds.

1. Khrushchev believed that the Americans had surrounded his country with military bases and now wanted his enemies to learn 'what it feels like to have enemy missiles pointing at you'. It was natural for the Soviet to move existing nuclear weapons to locations near to the US targets and Cuba offered a suitable option as the American territory was just about a few hundred miles away from Cuba.
2. Another reason for placing of missiles in Cuba was the belief of Khrushchev that he could muscle the west out of West Berlin, by using the missiles as bargain weapons. Nikita Khrushchev wanted also to counter the US act of installing intermediate range ballistic missiles known as Jupiter, in Turkey, which brought Moscow closer to the US nuclear strike limit.
3. On the ideological level too Khrushchev was compelled to provide protection to Cuba from any further US invasion as the loss of Cuba would do great harm to the communist movement.
4. Khrushchev was also under the impression that the US President John F. Kennedy would avoid a confrontation and accept the missiles as a fait accompli.

By mid-1962, the Soviet started construction of missile launch facilities in Cuba in a top secret mission. The US reconnaissance missions obtained photographic evidence regarding missile projects in western Cuba upon which the United States imposed a military blockade to prevent further missiles from reaching Cuba and demanded that the weapons already in Cuba be dismantled. The US President Kennedy declared in his address to the nation that 'it shall be the duty of this nation to regard any nuclear missile launched from Cuba against any nation in the Western hemisphere as an attack by the Soviet Union on the United States'.

As the world was moving towards a nuclear war, the UN Secretary General, U Thant, appealed to both the parties for restraints. After tense negotiations finally an agreement was reached between Kennedy and Khrushchev. As per this agreement the Soviet dismantled their offensive weapons in Cuba and took them back to the Soviet Union and in return the United States publicly declared not to invade Cuba again, respect inviolability of the Cuban borders and not to interfere in internal affairs of Cuba. Kennedy removed all missiles set in Turkey on the border of the Soviet Union, though this was not announced publicly. The United States announced end of the blockade on 20 November 1962.

The **Cuban Missile Crisis** also known as the **October Crisis** or the **Caribbean Crisis** of 13 days (October 16–28) is considered the peak of the Cold War confrontation which came near to escalating into a full-scale nuclear war. The crisis also had the effect of bringing both the powers to their senses leading to relaxation of tension. Leadership of both the countries realised how easily a nuclear war could have initiated and how terrible the results would have been. A **Moscow-Washington hotline** (a direct communication link between the leadership of the two countries) was created for swift and direct communication to solve such a crisis. Moreover, in July 1963 the United States and the USSR agreed and signed an agreement **Nuclear Test Ban Treaty (NTBT)** prohibiting nuclear tests except for those conducted underground. The treaty is also known as **Partial Test Ban treaty**.

10. *Détente* (1969–79)

Cold War entered a new stage known as the *détente* (means relaxation) in 1969, the year in which **Richard Nixon** assumed office as the new President of the United States. Nixon believed in 'realpolitik' and followed a practical and flexible approach in international affairs. Better communications and greater respect between the United States and the USSR took place leading to general easing of the tension between the two super powers. The *détente* ended in 1979 with the Soviet intervention in Afghanistan. The major reasons for the *détente* were:

1. Both the sides were awake to a catastrophic nuclear war in which there would be no winner if the Cold War belligerence was permitted to harden. Both sides were also aware of **economic difficulties** resulting from the diversion of resources to military research as the nuclear arms race was becoming incredibly expensive.
2. The **Vietnam debacle** was an eye opener to the Americans that there must be a better way to contain Communism than fighting hopeless proxy wars in alien parts of the world.
3. Emergence of **huge popular protests** in the United States against America's involvement in the Vietnam War was another factor. Many in the United States including some parliamentarians stood for return to the policy of 'isolationism' in the international politics.
4. The Western European nations were worried of the fact that in the event of a nuclear war between the United States and the USSR they would be at the forefront. Leaders such as the West German Chancellor **Willy Brandt** (1969–74) took steps to improve relations with the East European nations under a policy known as **'Ostpolitik'** (means eastern policy) and concluded treaties with the USSR, Poland and East Germany. The Western German government also repudiated all territorial claims east of the Oder-Neisse River which removed the fear of German revanchism against USSR and Poland.
5. On the side of the Communist bloc, it was becoming unbearable for the USSR to keep up with the United States. The Eastern Bloc nations were lagging behind in the standard of living, there were some **signals of unrest** in the Bloc as seen in Poland in the early 1970s, hence, more resources had to be allocated to bring up the living standards.
6. The **USSR and China** were not in good terms and the unity of the Communist bloc was under question.
7. The disruptions in oil supply and higher fuel prices as a result of the OPEC oil embargo and **the world oil shock of 1973** had devastated the US economy.
8. Reduction of tensions was also facilitated by the admission of West Germany and East Germany to the United Nations in September 1973.

Easing of tensions found expressed in the form of **series of summits** held between the leaders of the United States and the USSR. In May 1972, Nixon visited Moscow for a summit with Brezhnev. As a prelude and as a signal to the Soviets to be more open to the United States, Nixon visited China (he was the first US president to visit the communist China) in February 1972 and Nixon himself described the visit as **'the week that changed the world'**.

The first major breakthrough was achieved with the **Strategic Arms Limitation Treaty I** (SALT 1) signed in 1972 by Richard Nixon and Leonid Brezhnev in Moscow. It consisted of the Treaty on Anti-Ballistic Missile (ABM) Systems and an Interim Agreement and Protocol on Limitation of Strategic Offensive Weapons. The ABM Treaty limited strategic missile defences to 100 interceptors and one missile defence sites to each party and the Interim Agreement froze each side's ICBMs and SLBMs at existing levels. The effect of the SALT 1 was that it slowed down the nuclear arms race though it did not reduce the number of strategic armaments on both the sides.

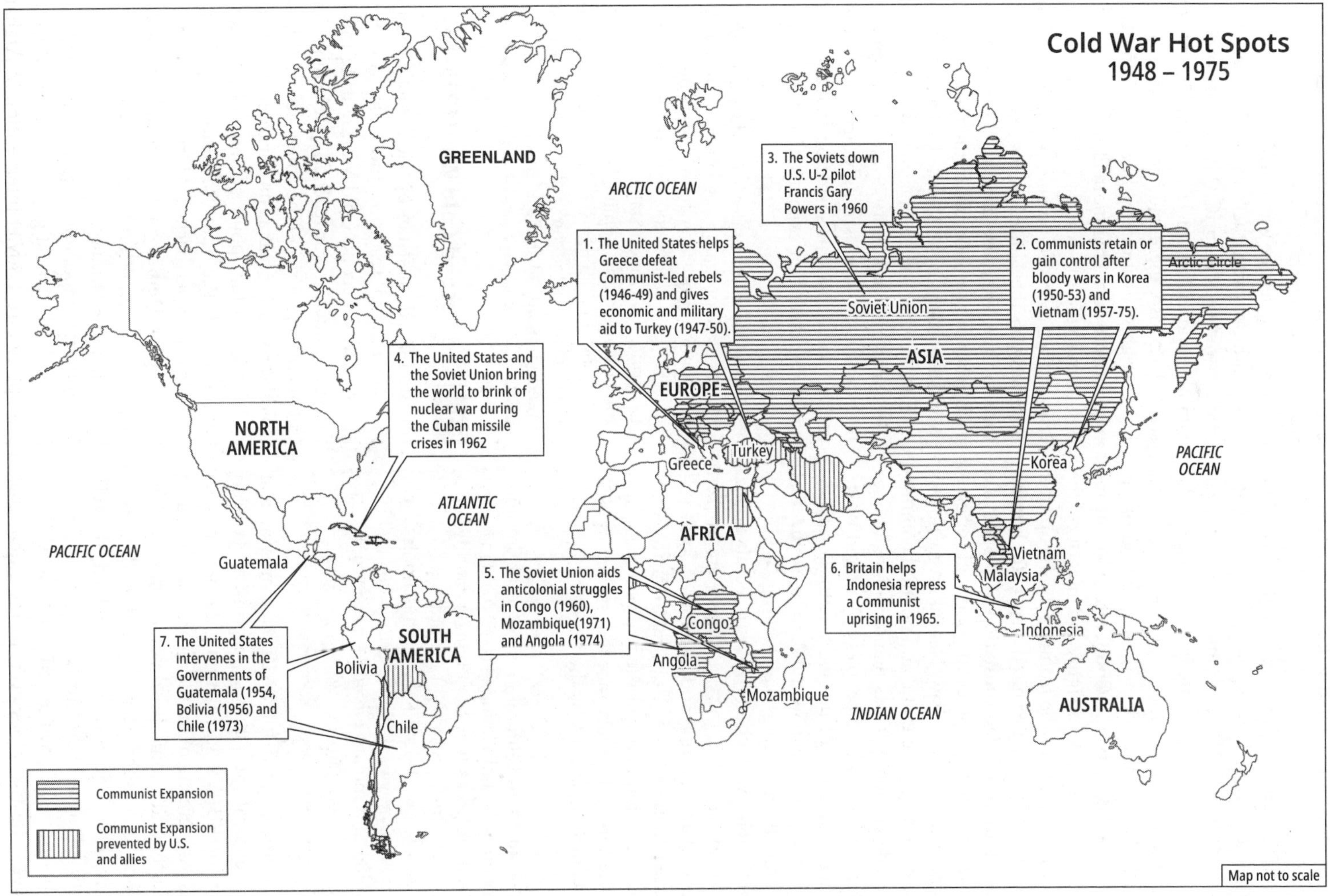

Some Developments During the Cold War

As seen above, the United States withdrew from Vietnam in 1973.

Helsinki Accords 1975 was another development. This was signed by 35 states including the United States, the USSR, Canada and all the European states except Albania in an attempt to improve relations between the Communists and the West. It was signed in Helsinki, Finland, at the conclusion of the **Conference on Security and Cooperation in Europe** (CSCE). It accepted the sovereignty and integrity of the states and inviolability of the frontiers drawn up after the Second World War. It promised **respect for human rights** and **right of self-determination** of peoples and peaceful settlement of disputes in good faith of obligations under international law. Helsinki Agreements though not binding were moral and political commitments aimed at lessening tension and opening of lines of communication between peoples of East and West.

Another expression of *détente* was the joint US-Soviet space flight known as the **Apollo-Soyuz Test Project (ASTP)** involving the docking of the US spacecraft Apollo with the Soviet spacecraft Soyuz. Conducted in July 1975, the two ships were docked in space, exchanged crew and conducted joint scientific experiments before returning to earth. Apart from easing tension between the two powers, it also marked the end of the space race that started in 1957 with the launch of Sputnik by the USSR.

Cold War in Socio-Cultural Life: The ever-present threat of nuclear annihilation was reflected in daily life of Americans as they built bunkers and bomb shelters in their backyards. Mock drills known as 'Duck and Cover' air-raid drills, in schools and public places, movies depicting arms race, nuclear devastation and mutant creatures were reminders of the ever present threat of war.

Talks were initiated for **SALT II** aimed at real reduction in strategic nuclear weapons, to contain expansion of MIRVs and banning of new missile programs. An agreement in this regard was signed by Jimmy Carter and Leonid Brezhnev, in June 1979, in Vienna. But six months after the signing, the Soviet Union invaded Afghanistan after which the US Senate refused to ratify the Treaty.

The period also witnessed **extensive trade ties** between the two blocs even to the extent that approximately 70 per cent of the Soviet Union's grain import was from the United States.

In fact, the *détente* was a shallow affair as both sides had continued with their war readiness by keeping nuclear warheads atop ICBMs, SLBMs and by maintaining hundreds of nuclear armed aircrafts on constant alert. Also, there had been instances of civil and human rights violations by the Soviet Union, establishment of a pro Soviet regime in Ethiopia (1974), dispatch of Cuban soldiers to Angola (1975) and harassment of Jews in the Soviet Union all of which soured the relation between the United States and the Soviet from time to time. They also continued to compete against each other to gain foothold in the resource-rich Third World especially in the Middle East and Africa.

Finally, the Soviet invasion of Afghanistan on the Christmas day in 1979 and replacement of its president with more strongly pro-Soviet leadership revived the American suspicion that the Soviet had not abandoned their expansionist ambitions.

Reagan Doctrine: Under Ronald Reagan, the Cold War heated up again as he believed that the spread of communism anywhere threatened freedom everywhere. Under the new policy, the Reagan Doctrine, the United States stood for financial and military aid to anti-communist groups and governments throughout the world to 'nourish and defend freedom and democracy' claiming that 'support for freedom fighters is self-defence'.

11. The Second Cold War (1979–85)

Invasion of Afghanistan by the Soviet Union ended the *détente* and resumed the Cold War which is known as the Second Cold War. During this period threat of a nuclear war reached new heights since the Cuban Missile Crisis. The 'intensity of this second Cold War was as great as its duration was short'.

In Afghanistan, political instability in the 1970s culminated in the **Saur Revolution** in April 1978, in which a Soviet backed Marxist-Leninist party – the **People's Democratic Party of Afghanistan** – captured power. The coup provoked a civil war between the Communist government and its non-Communist opponents which included among others radical Islamist group known as Mujahedeen, prompting direct Soviet intervention in Afghanistan in December 1979. Deployment of the Soviet army in Afghan was seen as invasion by the western media and constituted a dramatic proof of Soviet expansionism and also an attempt to implement the Brezhnev Doctrine.

A series of retaliatory steps were taken by the United States which effectively ended the *détente*.

1. The US government sent military aid to the anti-Soviet rebels and imposed a grain embargo against the USSR.
2. Under its new President Ronald Reagan (1981–89), the United States initiated the **'Reagan Doctrine'** and the **'rollback'**. Under this Doctrine, the United States took up responsibility of providing overt and covert support to anti-Communist fighters and movements in Asia, Africa and Latin America in order to 'rollback' the Soviet-backed regimes in these regions.
3. The resumption of the Cold War also revived arms race. In 1981, the United States started production of **neutron bombs** or enhanced radiation weapons which could kill people by massive radiation without destroying their cities. The United States deployed **Pershing II** missiles (nuclear capable ballistic missiles) in West Germany in 1983 and in the same year President Reagan initiated **Strategic Defense Initiative** (SDI) also known as '**Star Wars**' in which space-based weapons were to protect the United States from incoming weapons.

   In 1983, the US Navy conducted **FleetEx-83** largest fleet exercise since World War II in the Pacific. That was followed by the **Able Archer-83** in November the same year involving the NATO forces throughout Western Europe simulating a period of conflict escalation and coordinated nuclear attack.

   The Soviet Union responded by deploying **SS-20** nuclear capable missiles on its western border and in allied Warsaw Pact states. It also launched **Operation Ryan** in 1981 to collect intelligence on potential plans of the Reagan administration to launch a nuclear first strike against the Soviet Union. The Second Cold War further escalated in September 1983 when **Boeing 747** South Korean airline flight from New York to Seoul was shot down by a Soviet interceptor missile alleging that the flight was on a spy mission and flew deep into Soviet territory, killing all 269 passengers and crew aboard.
4. The revival of Cold War also found expressed in other fields too. The United States boycotted the **Moscow Summer Olympics** of 1980 to which the USSR responded by boycotting the **Summer Olympics** of 1984 held in **Los Angeles**, California.

12. | End of the Cold War (1985–91)

In March 1985, Mikhail Gorbachev, the new leader of the USSR, initiated political and economic liberalisation and gave impetus for cultivating warmer relations with the West. He put forth his doctrine known as the **'New Thinking'** in order to reform the international relations of the Soviet Union. It emphasised interdependence of the world, mutual security based on political rather than military instruments, de-ideologisation of international politics and priority of human interests over the interest of any class.

A. Initiatives Taken by Gorbachev

As part of this policy he established close relationships with many western leaders such as Ronald Reagan (the US President), Margaret Thatcher (British Prime Minister) and Helmut Kohl (German Chancellor). He also initiated number of steps to improve relation with the western world. In April 1985, Gorbachev suspended the deployment of SS-20 missiles in Europe. In November 1985, in **Geneva,** Switzerland, he started first of his four **Summit meetings** with the US President Ronald Reagan to discuss international relations and arms race. During the second Summit in **Reykjavik,** Iceland, in October 1986, both the leaders agreed in principle to remove INF (Intermediate range Nuclear Forces) systems from Europe. Culmination of these discussions took place in December 1987, in the **Washington Summit** when both Reagan and Gorbachev signed **INF Treaty** (Intermediate-Range Nuclear Forces Treaty). The Treaty provided for elimination of all nuclear and conventional missiles with the range of 500 to 5,500 km. and on-site verification inspections. The fourth Summit took place in **Moscow**, in May 1988, and both the leaders reaffirmed solemn conviction 'that a nuclear war cannot be won and must never be fought'.

B. Withdrawal from Afghanistan

In February 1988, Gorbachev announced the full withdrawal of the Soviet forces from Afghanistan.

C. Abandonment of the Brezhnev Doctrine

In 1988, Gorbachev announced abandoning of the Brezhnev Doctrine and allowed Eastern Bloc nations to determine their own internal affairs. Brezhnev Doctrine was replaced by **Sinatra Doctrine** by which Eastern Bloc nations were free to determine their own internal affairs. This policy of non-intervention in the affairs of the Warsaw Pact states proved to be the most momentous of foreign policy reforms of Gorbachev.

This caused a series of popular upheavals in Eastern Europe throughout the 1989 in which Communism was overthrown. The Revolutions of 1989 sometimes called as the **'Autumn of Nations'** started in Poland in June 1989 with free parliamentary elections and swept through Hungary, East Germany, Bulgaria, Czechoslovakia and Romania and witnessed ousting of the regimes established in Eastern Europe after the Second World War. In November 1989, the Berlin Wall was opened permitting East Germans to cross to West and its official demolition started in June 1990. The **collapse of the Berlin Wall** symbolised the **collapse of the Iron Curtain** and the end of European communist governments.

The above developments ended Soviet hegemony over Eastern Europe and effectively started the end the Cold War. The Warsaw Pact was declared 'non-existent' on 1 July 1991 in the final meeting of the Warsaw Pact leaders in Prague, Czechoslovakia. The breakup of the Warsaw Pact was soon followed by the dissolution of the USSR in December 1991. End of the Soviet Union marked the end of the Cold War and emergence of a New World Order.

13. Results of the Cold War

1. **Division of the world** – the notion of the 'Whole World as a Family' was shattered.
2. Arms race and efforts to gain a 'balance of terror' by the two blocs prompted other countries too to pursue arms race so that they are not reduced to sideline spectators in world politics.
3. **Military alliances** – NATO, SEATO, Warsaw Pact, CENTO, ANZUS and so forth, while instilling notion of security in members, to non-member states like India created suspicion and fear.
4. The **United Nations was rendered ineffective** – Korean crisis, Cuban crises and Vietnam War were some examples. As the United States and the USSR could not agree hardly on any international issue, the efforts of UN to settle disputes were frustrated by these powers by the use of 'veto' in the Security Council.
5. Emergence of third world – The nations of Asia, Africa and Latin America remained neutral, formation of **NAM** was a reflection of this thinking.
6. The ever-present possibility of a conflict erected an omnipresent **obstacle to world peace**.
7. **Barrier against progress** as huge resources were wasted in preparation for war and not for human welfare.

SUMMARY

The Cold War – It was a period of armed truce between the United States and the Soviet Union originated at the end of the World War II. It developed through different phases – the beginning (1946–1953), the Thaw (1953–1961), escalation (1961–1969), the détente (1969–1979), the Second Cold War (1979–1985) and the end of the Cold War (1985–1991).

Causes of the Cold War – Ideological differences, foreign policy of Stalin, suspicion of the United States and Britain towards the USSR and differing goals of the world powers in the post-World War II period.

Run-up to the Cold War – The Cold War had its root in the conferences such as the Yalta Conference and the Potsdam Conference held during the World War II and got consolidated with the emergence of the Eastern Bloc and the delivery of the Fulton Speech soon after the end of the War.

Origin and development of the Cold War – The Civil War in Greece, developments in Turkey, formation of the Truman Doctrine and launching of the Marshall Plan were the initial landmarks in the Cold War belligerence. The conflict further deepened with the developments in Czechoslovakia, formation of the NATO and the Warsaw Pact and division of Germany into West and East Germanys. As the Cold War deepened further, the conflict found expressed in the field of technology, in arms race and in space race.

Cold War in Asia – Formation of China, the Korean War (1950–1953), the First Indochina War (1946–1954), the Vietnam War (1954–1975) were major expressions of the Cold War in Asia.

Escalation – After a period of the Thaw, the Cold War escalated in the forms of the Berlin Crisis (1961) and the Cuban Missile Crisis (1962).

Détente – During this period there was general easing of tension between the two super powers found expressed in a series of summits between the leaders of the United States and the USSR, signing of the SALT I in 1972 and the Helsinki Accords in 1975.

The Second Cold War – It began with the invasion of Afghanistan by the Soviet Union in 1979.

End of the Cold War – The new Russian leader Mikhail Gorbachev initiated reforms in his own country and cultivated warmer relations with the West. He withdrew the Russian troops from Afghanistan and abandoned the Brezhnev Doctrine which in turn catalysed the Revolutions of1989 in the Eastern Bloc and also the disintegration of the USSR in 1991. The end of the Soviet Union marked the end of the Cold War.

Questions of Previous Years Civil Services Examination

1. Do you feel that the Vietnamese fought the 20th century's longest and bloodiest war for their liberation and integration of their country? Analyse. (2022)
2. Do you agree with the view that the formation of NATO marked a revolution in American attitude to the world problems? (2019)
3. Outline the circumstances leading to adoption of Marshall Plan. (2018)
4. Outline the circumstances leading to *Détente*. (2016)
5. Trace the significant role played by Ho Chi Minh in Vietnam's struggle for freedom. (2016)
6. 'The Truman Doctrine and the Marshal Plan were considered by the Russian Bloc as a weapon against Russia in order to restrict her influence'. Critically examine. (2015)
7. 'Europe faced peace in 1945 politically disorganised and economically crippled'. Elaborate. (2010)
8. Why did Vietnam go through thirty years of war after the Second World War? (2009)
9. Critically examine the various dimensions and phases of the Cold War between 1947 and 1962. (2005)
10. 'The Brussels Treaty of 17 March 1948 paved the way for the formation of NATO'. Examine. (2003)
11. One of the most important impacts of the Second World War was the 'division of Europe', eastern and western. Elucidate. (1998)

CHAPTER 16

Decolonisation

In this Chapter

1. Introduction

Decolonisation refers to the surrender of political sovereignty to the colonised people by their colonial masters. The second-half of the 19th century was a period of colonialism, while the second-half of the 20th century was marked by reversal of colonialism, that is, decolonisation.

Decolonisation began in 1946, when the Philippines became the first colony to attain independence after the World War II from the United States. Between 1945 and 1965, more than 50 nations emerged independent from European masters in Asia and Africa. Decolonisation was completed in the last decade of the 20th century after Britain returned Hong Kong in 1997 and Portugal returned Macao in 1999 to China. The wave of decolonisation changed the face of the world as it freed more than 740 million from colonial subjugation.

In most of the cases, the colonial powers relinquished their control at the threat of violence and militant mood of the nationalist fighters. In other cases, the colonial powers were driven out after fierce liberation wars fought by the colonial people.

Decolonisation may take any of the broad four forms as given below:

1. Self-government for colonies inhabited by large number of white settlers. Examples - Australia and Canada
2. Transfer of sovereignty by the empire to the colony leading to independence of nations. Example - India
3. End of control of formal empire is followed by informal controls in the form of neo-colonialism. Example - Latin America
4. Replacement of one imperial power by another. Example - Indochina where the United States replaced the French.

2. Factors of Decolonisation

- **Nationalist resistance** and anti-imperialist struggle of the colonial people were important factors. During the World War II, nationalist forces had become militant and there were anti-imperialist upsurge in many colonies. Armed resistance had even been resorted to by the people in the colonies when the imperialist powers tried to re-establish their rule in colonies.

- **Colonial soldiers** who fought in the World War II were appalled at the contrast between the primitive conditions in their countries and modern life conditions of their masters. They returned home with fired desire for independence and were no longer willing to accept foreign rule.
- **Japanese conquest** of the European colonies in Asia during the World War II had destroyed the notion of European invincibility, which in turn boosted confidence of people in colonies.
- **Solidarity of anti-imperialist movements** and the support they extended to each other was another factor. For example, Indian nationalists opposed the deployment of Indian soldiers to restore the French and the Dutch rule in Indochina and Indonesia in 1946. International forums such as the NAM and the Organisation of African Unity had eradication of colonialism as their main objectives and they extended support to national movements.
- In the **new world order** of the post-Second World War, 'colonial empires appeared as quaint survivors of a pre-war age'. For example, starting with the Atlantic Charter, which had called for independence of colonial peoples, the general perception of the world community was against colonialism.
- The **United Nations** condemned colonial system as violation of the UN Charter and in 1960 had issued 'Declaration on the Granting of Independence to Colonial Countries and Peoples'.
- **New Super powers** - the United States and the USSR - were against the existing style of imperialism or the 'old style imperialism'.
- **Domestic realities** in European countries such as severe economic crisis, high cost of maintaining the colonies, ruined military forces; political compulsions of welfare state and doubtfulness of continued loyalty of colonial forces were also significant in forcing imperial powers to free their colonies.
- Decolonisation was also often affected by **superpower competition**. The United States believed that delay in granting independence would lead to spread of communism in those countries.
- In the new political climate imperialism was **no longer perceived as a symbol of superior civilisation**. Ideas such as sovereignty and self-determination, right of the people and cooperation among the nations were dominant themes not only in colonies but also among the people of Europe.

3. A Survey on Decolonisation

The British colonial empire was the largest. India, Ceylon, Burma, Malaya, Cyprus, Hong Kong, the West Indies and territories in Africa and the mandates (Transjordan and Palestine) were the major British possessions. France with the Indochina and territories in Africa and in the West Indies and its mandate in Syria was the second largest colonial empire.

There were significant differences between decolonisation process of Britain and France. While Britain was ready to grant independence after the World War II (exceptions were colonies with large white settlers such as Kenya), the French were firmly determined to hold on its colonies - such as the Indochina, Morocco and Algeria and even their small enclaves in India. Moreover, the British were interested in continuing their political, cultural and strategic interests in their former colonies even after granting them freedom through the mechanism of the **British Commonwealth**. The British also encouraged colonies to adopt British parliamentary form of government with multi-party system, thus 'guiding' the colonies and not resisting them. France did not care for any of these.

Holland (Dutch East Indies), Spain (Spanish Morocco, Sahara and Spanish Guinea), Italy (Libya, Somalia and Eritrea), Portugal (Angola, Guinea and Mozambique) and Belgium (Congo, Ruanda-Urundi) were other European colonial powers.

A. Asia

a. India - 1947

With the passage of Indian Independence Act in the British parliament India was granted full independence but the Muslim majority areas in the northwest and northeast were grouped together to form a new country, Pakistan in the same year.

b. *Sri Lanka – 1948*

Known as Ceylon, it gained independence in February 1948 from Britain. Here three-quarters of the population were Sinhalese – followers of Buddhism – while a fifth were Tamils who follow Hinduism. There were two categories of Tamils in Sri Lanka. The first were descendants of Tamil-speaking people migrated to Sri Lanka centuries back and were known as **Sri Lankan Tamils or Jaffna Tamils**. The second group the **Indian Tamils or Up Country Tamils** were descendants of labourers brought to Sri Lanka to work on plantations during British colonial period.

After independence, the Sinhalese majority started discriminatory steps such as declaring Sinhalese as official language and driving Tamils out of civil service. **The Ceylon Citizenship Act of 1948** also barred citizenship to Indian Tamils, turning some 700,000 Indian Tamils stateless. Discriminatory steps were further extended in 1970s with 'state sponsored colonisation schemes' of settling Sinhalese into Tamil areas. After decades of ethnic tensions, the militants known as the LTTE (Liberation Tigers of Tamil Eelam) started armed struggle demanding a separate nation in northern Sri Lanka called 'Eelam' for the Tamils. Starting from 1983, Sri Lanka underwent a period of civil war turning the island country into a battleground. Finally, in 2009, the Tamil insurgents were defeated by the government forces. During 26 years of conflict more than one lakh deaths and large displacement of civilians took place and hideous atrocities committed on both sides.

c. *The Philippines – 1946*

It was a Spanish colony since 1521, the year **Ferdinand Magellan** landed in Philippines. The United States acquired it in 1898 following the **Spanish-American War**. Realising that the Spanish rule had been replaced by American rule, the Philippine revolutionaries clashed with American forces but was suppressed. In 1902, the US Congress passed the Philippines Act providing for limited self-government for the Philippines. During the World War II, it was invaded by the Japanese but was liberated by the US forces in 1945. In July 1946, the Philippines was granted independence by the Treaty of Manila and a government patterned on that of the United States was formed.

Even though independent, she was a dependency of the United States on military, economic and political matters. Under the **Bell Act** of 1946, the United States provided $800 million in war damages and for reconstruction. But the Philippines had to agree to certain conditions which included preferential tariffs on the goods imported from the United States, no restrictions on currency transfers from the Philippines to the United States and 'parity rights' (equal economic rights to the Americans) to the natural resources such as minerals and forest products equal to that of Philippine citizens. By the **Military Bases Agreement** in 1947, the United States also secured 99-year lease of its military bases such as Clark Air force Base and Subic Bay Naval Base in order to protect its strategic interest in Asia in the background of the Cold War. In 1951, both the countries also signed the **Mutual Defense Treaty**.

In the post-independence period Philippines witnessed a communist peasant rebellion known as the Huk Rebellion. Harry Truman, the US President alarmed at the worldwide expansion of communism, provided military supplies to the Manila government and by 1954 it was suppressed.

The next important development was the dictatorship of Ferdinand Marcos. Though elected as president in 1965, he established a dictatorship in 1966 which continued till 1986, the year in which he was forced to flee after a huge public outcry. Another crisis to the new country was from the separatists. In the southern Philippines, the Moro Muslims formed the **Moro National Liberation Front (MNLF)** and resorted to armed struggle for independence in 1973. An agreement between the government and the rebels was signed which granted autonomy to the Southern Philippines. Even after it, a splinter group of the MNLF, Abu Sayyaf Group, continued the struggle and acts of kidnapping and terrorism.

> Siam or Thailand was the only country in South-East Asia that was not a colony of the Western powers. Though located uncomfortably between the French Indochina and British Burma, Siam maintained its independence by playing off the British and the French one another and through

skilful diplomacy. During the Cold War, Thailand was a major ally of the United States and a member of the SEATO aimed at containing communism in Asia.

d. Burma – 1948

Now known as Myanmar, it was granted independence by Britain in January 1948. The post-independence period was of turmoil for Burma as military regimes, democratic forces, ethnic minorities and the communists were engaged in a protracted struggle. Though Myanmar chose the path of parliamentary government, in 1962, military leaders under General Ne Win staged a coup and captured power. The constitution was suspended, the press was controlled, opposition political parties were banned and the country was closed off to the outside world. The military controlled one-party ('Burma Socialist Programme Party') regime aimed to transform Burma into a true socialist state. In 1988, Ne Win was forced to resign after nationwide protests.

A new military junta known as the **State Law and Order Restoration Council** (SLORC) captured power and renamed the country Myanmar. Though the **National League for Democracy** under Aung San Suu Kyi succeeded in forcing the military regime to conduct multiparty elections in 1990, in which NLD won 80 per cent of the seats, Aung San was kept under house arrest and military rule continued. In 1997, the SLORC took a new name – the **State Peace and Development Council**. Though parliamentary elections were held again in 2020 and the NLD won a landslide victory, the military rejected the election results and declared a state of emergency in February 2021. During all these, civil wars on ethnic and religious lines continued in Myanmar. In the northern state of Kachin, minority ethnic groups continue their fight for self-determination and in the Rakhine state in the west the fight between Rohingya Muslims and other groups continue unabated even now.

e. Malaysia – 1957

The Malay Peninsula was a British colony. Though Japan had conquered it during World War II, Britain reoccupied it after the defeat of Japan. The **Political structure** of Malaya was fragmented – nine states each ruled by a sultan and two British settlements – Malacca and Penang. **Demography** was multi-racial – Malay and Chinese were major groups, while Indian and Europeans constituted minorities.

In 1948, the **Federation of Malaya** was created in Peninsular Malaysia, as a protectorate of the British. Nevertheless, the Federation came under emergency as **Chinese communist guerrillas** of the Malayan National Liberation Army resorted to guerrilla violence for an independent Communist state. The British suppressed the insurgency by establishing internment camps known as 'New Villages' to resettle all Chinese suspected of helping the guerrillas.

In 1957, the Federation of Malaya became independent of British. In 1963, with the amalgamation of Singapore and the British Borneo (Sarawak and Sabah) the Federation of Malaya emerged as **Malaysia**. After a series of racial riots between the Malays and the Chinese erupted on account of political and religious tensions in 1964, Singapore was expelled from Malaysia which became an independent republic in 1965.

f. Singapore – 1965

Singapore is located at the southern tip of the Malay Peninsula. The modern city of Singapore was founded in 1819 by Britain's Stamford Raffles as a British trading post in South East Asia and was designated as **Crown Colony of Britain**. During the Second World War though it was captured by Japan, the British recaptured it and started granting increasing measures of autonomy. Realising that Singapore was too small to function as an independent state, it was joined to the Malaysian Federation in 1963.

Ethnically, Singapore was diverse – more than 70 per cent Chinese, 13 per cent Malay, some 10 per cent Indian and the rest of mixed ethnicity. Ethnic riots in 1964 between Chinese and Malays forced Singapore to leave the Federation and emerge as fully independent little nation with a parliamentary form of government in 1965. The race riots convinced the leaders of Singapore to adopt a constitution emphasising multiculturalism and multi-racialism and to follow non-discriminatory policies based either on race or religion. Subsequently, under its Premier **Lee Kuan Yew** (1959–90), Singapore emerged as one of the richest nations of the world.

South-East Asia comprises of eleven countries – Singapore, Thailand, Vietnam, Malaysia, Myanmar, the Philippines, Indonesia, Cambodia, Laos, Brunei and East Timor.

g. Indonesia – 1949

Indonesia was a Dutch colony. It consisted of more than 13,000 islands. During World War II Japan conquered it and the Japanese were initially welcomed as liberators. But their brutality against the natives of Indonesia catalysed nationalist feelings among the Indonesians.

After the defeat of Japan in the War, the Dutch tried to regain control of Indonesia but was opposed by the nationalists under their leader Sukarno leading to grant of independence in December 1949 by the Dutch.

Indonesia faced many crises as a nation. Its diversity was notable – more than 13,000 islands inhabited by more than 300 ethnic groups speaking 250 languages. It also had all the major religions in the world. Hence, clashes on religious and ethnic lines were frequent. A fragile economy, corruption in government and security problems were other important issues.

Sukarno, who led the independence struggle, now declared himself as the life-time president. Sukarno described his autocratic system as 'Guided Democracy'. His leanings towards the left and acceptance of aid from the Soviet Union and China were irritants to the military and the Islamists. After an attempted coup by a faction of the army in 1965, Sukarno was forced to transfer important political and military powers to a General called Suharto. In 1968, Suharto was formally declared as the President and Sukarto was put under house arrest till his death in 1970.

Suharto turned Indonesia into a police state known for its brutality and bloodbath which caused the death of nearly 1 million people. Suharto described his regime as a 'New Order' and initiated 'de-Sukarnoization' of Indonesian society. In 1998, a severe economic crisis forced Suharto to step down and Indonesia's transition to democracy was inaugurated. In 2001, Megawati Sukarnoputri, daughter of Sukarno, was elected as the president.

h. East Timor – 2002

East Timor is the eastern part of the island of Timor and was a Portuguese colony. It declared independence in 1975 but was annexed to Indonesia as one of its provinces in 1976 by Suharto. Suharto's action caused strong resistance and a savage war. After a long struggle under their leader **Jose Ramos Horta**, a referendum was conducted in 1999 under the UN in which East Timorese voted for independence. The result provoked the pro-Indonesian groups who resorted to violent attacks on Timorese. Finally, in 2002, East Timor became independent and thus became the first new sovereign state of the 21st century. East Timor also known as Timor Leste, is the only Asian country to be located completely in the Southern Hemisphere.

i. Indochina – 1954

It had been a French colony but had been occupied by Japan during the Second World War. The return of the French to Indochina after the defeat of Japan led to the Indochina War. The French forces were defeated and in 1954 the Indochina (Vietnam, Laos and Cambodia) became free.

After independence, civil war broke out in **Laos** between royalists and the communists known as the **Pathet Lao**, which had the support of North Vietnam. In 1975, the monarchy was overthrown and the Laotian communists established the Lao People's Democratic Republic in December 1975. The new government signed agreements with Vietnam for stationing Vietnamese armed forces and advisors in Laos and adopted one-party socialist republican political system which continues till now.

Cambodia too witnessed a civil war between right and left groups after being independent. Following a five-year struggle **Khmer Rouge or Red Khmer**, a communist group, under their leader **Pol Pot** captured power in 1975. They proclaimed the new state of Kampuchea and instituted a reign of terror. China provided advisors and aid to the Khmer Rouge and the Maoist inspired regime in its effort to achieve total communism overnight implemented autocratic and xenophobic policies and resorted to genocide. They abolished private property and private households and to create an egalitarian agrarian society forced the urban population to villages. Though the

Communist regime in Laos was friendly to Vietnam, the Communist Khmer Rouge of Cambodia was not. In December 1978, Vietnam attacked Cambodia and Pol Pot was toppled from power in January 1979 and a pro-Vietnamese regime was established in Cambodia.

Vietnam's invasion and influence in Cambodia was of concern to China, which attacked Vietnam in February 1979. Though the proclaimed Chinese intention was to 'teach Vietnam a lesson', the very short invasion of 17 days did not cause any change in the situation but added one more chapter of misery, death and destruction for the people of the peninsula. The Vietnamese forces withdrew from Cambodia only in 1989 and in 1993 after the UN-sponsored elections, Cambodia became a constitutional monarchy.'

The North' and 'the South' divide shows socio-economic and political categorisation of world nations. The North comprises all First World and most of Second World countries, while the South denotes the Third World nations. This categorisation is not on geographical terms as some 'North' countries such as Australia and New Zealand are located in southern hemisphere.

B. Africa

Independence era was inaugurated in Africa in 1950s as African nationalism had intensified after the Second World War. The first to get independence was Libya in 1951, an Italian colony since 1912 taken from Turkey. It was followed by Egypt in 1954 from Britain and Tunisia in 1956 from France. The process continued in Ghana, the first sub-Saharan state to gain independence, which gained independence from Britain in 1957. In the next three decades, 47 countries emerged independent in Africa. Between 1960 and 1980, almost all British and French colonies in Africa attained freedom. In 1970s, the Portuguese colonies of Angola, Mozambique, Cape Verde Islands and Guinea Bissau too emerged free. In 1990, the South West Africa or Namibia which was a 'Mandate' of South Africa since the end of World War I gained freedom. In the Cold War scenario, the United States supported non-communist factions in Africa, while the communist groups were supported by Soviet Russia.

African-independent struggle took three forms - **peaceful transition, violent transition and three-sided conflict between native Africans, white settlers and European colonial masters**. Peaceful transition took place in countries such as Ghana, where tensions between African groups were minimal and European population was small. In the second category, in states such as Nigeria, independence movement and post-independence period were characterised by conflicts between different groups - ethnic and religious. Nigeria, for example, had roughly half Christian and Muslim population and large number of tribes such as Hausa, Yoruba and Igbo. In the last category, in countries like Algeria, Kenya and South Africa three-sided conflict took place before they could free themselves from colonial rule.

a. Ghana - 1957

Ghana was known as the Gold Coast and was a British colony. Here nationalists had been organised by Kwame Nkrumah on nonviolent lines for freedom. In 1957, the Gold Coast attained independence and took the name Ghana. Nkrumah as the first prime minister and later as its president for life introduced reforms in education, industrialisation and health. But, in 1966, in a coup, military captured power and Nkrumah was forced to take refuge in Guinea.

b. Congo - 1960

Known as Zaire was a colony of Belgium. It was given independence in 1960, but civil war erupted. There were more than 150 tribal groups making unity almost impossible, and the south eastern region of Katanga was rich in copper deposits and wanted to be independent. The United States and USSR supported the opposing groups. The UN also sent peacekeeping force.

c. Algeria - 1962

Algeria was a French colony which had more than one million French settlers known as 'colons'. As the French government refused to grant independence, the Algerian nationalists under their leader Ahmed Ben Bella organised the **National Liberation Front** or FLN to fight against the French forces. From 1954, the FLN employed guerrilla tactics,

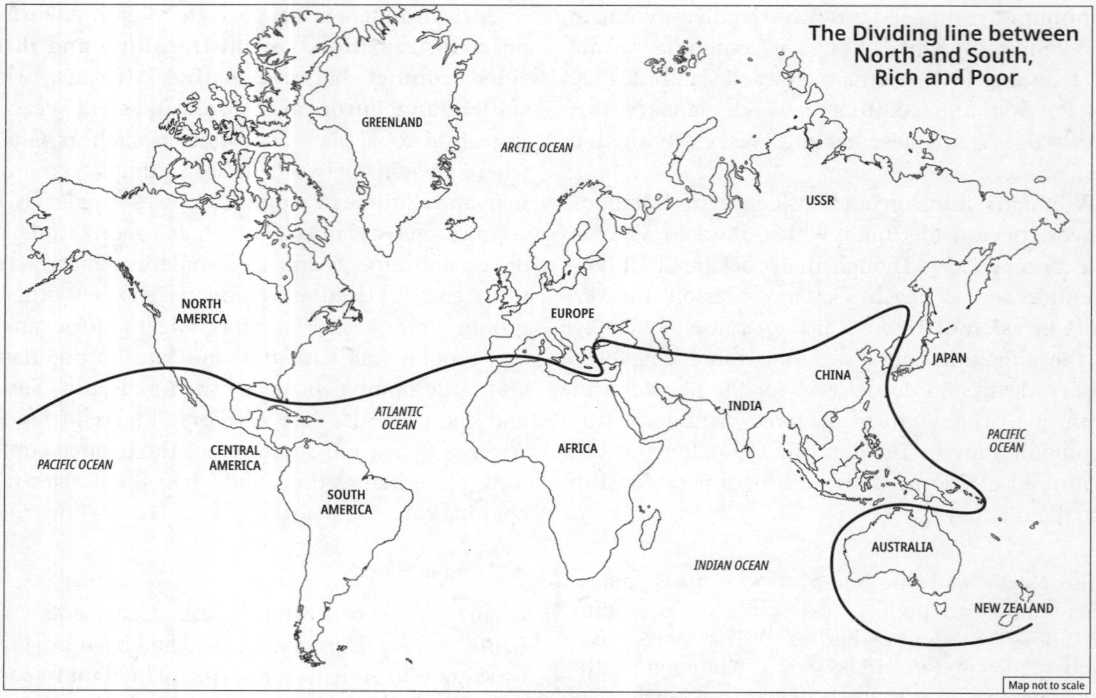

North and South

terrorism and torture against the French settlers and the Africans who supported the regime. The war lasted for eight years and had more than one million casualties. At the same time, the European Algerians launched massive demonstrations demanding integration of Algeria with France. Some French generals in Algeria even threatened to invade France. The new French President Charles de Gaulle was in favour of granting independence and in 1962 Algeria became independent and Ben Bella became the first president. Like in many other African countries, Algerian President Ben Bella turned to authoritarianism and was overthrown in a coup in 1965.

d. *Kenya – 1963*

This was another British colony in Africa but unlike in Ghana, British refused to grant independence as it had large number of British settlers. By the early 20th century, more than 30,000 British settlers had occupied best farmlands in Kenya to cultivate cash crops like coffee and tea using native labour. As a result, the Europeans constituting less than 1 per cent had come to hold most of the political and economic power in Kenya.

Nationalists in Kenya were organised by **Jomo Kenyatta**, while an underground group - mainly of Kikuyu tribe – **the Mau Mau** organised guerilla war against the white settlers. The British tried to suppress it by declaring emergency and transporting Kikuyu tribes to concentration camps and to enclosed villages. Finally, in 1963, the British were forced to grant independence and Kenyatta became the president. Kenyatta was a votary of **African socialism** which aimed at providing every person the right to participate fully and equally in political affairs. But independence did not end the troubles for the Kenyans as Kenyatta instituted one-party rule and turned despotic. Moreover, ethnic conflict with Somali rebels in the north too plagued the country for long.

e. *Angola – 1975*

Angola was a Portuguese colony and gained independence in 1975 after armed struggle. As the Portuguese had left Angola without conducting elections or handing over power to one-party, dominant liberation movements engaged in power struggle. As a result, Angola witnessed civil war between **MPLA** (Popular Movement for the Liberation of Angola), a Communist group, and **UNITA** (National Union for the Total Independence of Angola). In the Cold War background, Soviet Russia and Cuba supported the MPLA, while UNITA received support from the United States and from South Africa. In 2002, Jonas Savimbi, the leader of UNITA, was killed and UNITA abandoned the armed struggle.

f. Zimbabwe – 1980

In Southern Rhodesia (Zimbabwe), a colony of Britain, the white settlers were opposed to the idea of Black majority rule, hence opposed granting it independence. After a fierce guerrilla movement against the white minority rule, free elections were held in 1980 in which both Black and White participated. The nationalists became victorious and Robert Mugabe became the Prime Minister.

g. South Africa – 1934

In 1910, Britain had established the Union of South Africa by joining four colonies – **Cape, Natal** and the Boer Republics of **Transvaal and Orange Free State** together. It was a dominion under the British Empire. By the Status of the Union Act passed by the South African Parliament in 1934, South Africa became a sovereign nation state within the British Empire. Though more than 70 per cent of the population were black Africans, the whites dominated all aspects of life – blacks could not vote, had to do manual labour and their living and working conditions were horrible.

In 1948, the National Party, a white-only party, formed government under the Prime Ministership of Daniel Francois Malan and introduced a **policy of apartheid** (apart-ness in Afrikaans language). It was a policy of discrimination and segregation of races. Though discrimination had been implemented from 1910, until 1948, the word apartheid was not common. Emergence of newly independent nations such as India and the transfer of power to the natives were alarming to the whites who wanted to preserve their supremacy by segregating and suppressing the native Africans. Many laws were passed to implement apartheid. The **Prohibition of Mixed Marriages Act** of 1949 prohibited marriages between Europeans and non-Europeans and was aimed at maintaining 'purity' of the Whites. The **Population Registration Act** provided for categorisation of people on the basis of race. The **Group Areas Act** of 1950 segregated residential areas of different races. From 1960 to 1983, more than 3.5 million non-white South Africans were forcibly relocated to neighbourhoods reserved for them. Separate schools, buses, trains, toilets, park benches, beaches, hospitals and even churches were set up for blacks and whites to implement apartheid. By making use of the **Suppression of Communism Act,** of 1950 the government suppressed any protest against apartheid.

The **African National Congress**, which was formed in 1912, organised breach of apartheid laws by entering in whites-only areas. In 1960, police opened fire on anti-apartheid protesters in Sharpeville killing 69 people. The government banned African National Congress and the Pan Africanist Congress, two parties that opposed apartheid and jailed their leaders. The **Black Conscious Movement** too emerged in 1960s in South Africa to raise Black self-awareness and to unite Black students and intellectuals and urging rejection of apartheid. Its leader Steve Biko was beaten to death by police in 1976.

> Nelson Mandela was a crucial figure in the struggle against apartheid. He became the leader of African National Congress' armed wing and was arrested in 1961 for sabotage. Mandela spent more than 27 years in jail and after being released was elected as South Africa's first African president in 1994.

International pressure too emerged against apartheid. The UN called for economic sanctions and arms embargo against South Africa. The UN general assembly also suspended South Africa from participating in its work. In 1986, the US passed the **Comprehensive Anti-Apartheid Act** imposing sanctions against South Africa and forcing many US corporations to move out of South Africa. The act severely restricted lending to South Africa and also imposed ban on import of agricultural goods, iron, coal, steel, uranium and textiles from South Africa.

Increasing international pressure and end of white rule in Zimbabwe – last of the white-ruled states that supported apartheid – in 1980, forced the

South African government under P.W. Botha to ease apartheid. As part of it marriage and sexual relations between people of different races were permitted and pass laws (black Africans had to carry passes) were abolished. In 1989, the South African President F.W. de Clerk lifted the ban on ANC and released political prisoners. In February 1990, Nelson Mandela was released after 27 years in prison. In 1994, non-racial and democratic elections were held and the ANC emerged victorious with 62 per cent votes. Nelson Mandela became the first Black president of South Africa.

4. What Were the Challenges Before the African Nations?

A. Creating a National Identity

The colonial powers had imposed borders without any logic or concern for ethnic or social landscape on the ground. These artificial borders caused division of people of the same tribe into different countries or brought warring tribes to a single country. It was difficult to forge a sense of national identity out of conflicting groups. For example, **Somali** people were divided between French Somaliland, British Somalia, Italian Somalia and Northern Kenya. As a result tribal warfare within countries and across borders was a constant factor in Africa. Another example was Rwanda, where the Belgian colonial policies had exacerbated divisions between **Hutus and Tutsis** leading to genocide in 1994.

B. Cold War Pressures

In the context of the Cold War, America and Russia tried to expand their influence in the newly independent African countries. As a result African nations had to bear the push and pull of two super powers. Interference by these countries put obstacles in establishing strong economies and in maintaining political stability. For example, in Angola, the civil war lasted for nearly 30 years as the United States and the USSR supported one or other group.

C. Setting Up of Governments

People of Africa did not feel a sense of allegiance to their government as they were haunted by memories of the old European regimes which were brutal, distant and exploitative. Even after independence, people did not look at the government as a benevolent organ that exists for everyone's welfare.

Though almost all nations drew up democratic constitutions, many of these suffered through the periods of authoritarian rule and witnessed military dictatorship and political instability.

D. Lack of Leadership

As higher ranks in administration had been reserved for Europeans during the colonial period and higher education facilities were very few, immediately after their independence African countries were left with poor and inexperienced civil leadership.

E. Corruption

Corruption was rampant in African states. Even though African countries were rich in resources, they remain poorest in the world which shows the undeniable connection between poverty and corruption. It also points to the fact that honesty is not just morally good but it is what makes one's country rich.

F. Building Economic Self-Reliance

Though gained political independence, they continued to remain as economic dependencies of their former masters. European colonial masters had maintained these countries as sources of raw materials and market for their manufactured goods. For the purpose they cultivated cash crops such as rubber and coffee and developed mines while neglecting to build factories. Post-colonial economy lacked basic infrastructure and manufacturing infrastructure which was essential to add value to their raw materials. Even oil rich countries lacked refineries to process crude oil. As a result these countries had to depend on imported goods from Europe.

G. Civil War

Religious, cultural, ethnic and political factors caused bloody civil wars in many of the African states. If it was between the central government and the mineral-rich region of Shaba (also known as Katanga) in Zaire, in Sudan and Chad the fight was between Muslim north and Christian south. In Ethiopia, the Islamic groups and the Marxist central government known as Derg were engaged in a protracted war from 1974 to 1991.

H. Socio-Cultural Drawbacks

Lack of skilled labour force and low level of literacy hampered real growth in many African countries. It also reflected in bureaucratic inefficiency, corruption and nepotism. In spite of gaining independence, by the end of the 20th century, the African countries were at the bottom of all indexes of development and population living in poverty had doubled.

> **The Fourth World** – The nations within the Third World but are most impoverished and least developed are known as the Fourth World. They are characterised by extreme low per capita income and limited natural resources.

5. Latin America

Latin America can be defined as all of the Americas south of the United States. It consists of the entire continent of South America in addition to Central America including Mexico and the islands of the Caribbean Sea such as Jamaica, Cuba and Hispaniola (Haiti and the Dominican Republic). It is twice the size of the United States and has more varied terrain than the US and is one of the most multi-ethnic and multicultural regions of the world. The inhabitants of the region have had a shared experience of conquest and colonisation by the Spaniards and Portuguese since the late 15th century and hence most of the countries are Spanish-speaking (the exception being Brazil, the population of which speaks Brazilian Portuguese). The term 'Latin America' originated in the 19th century, referring to those whose national language – like Spanish – was derived from Latin, in order to differentiate from the 'Anglo-Saxon' English-speaking people of North America.

In the early 19th century Latin Americans initiated movements for independence from their European masters. These movements were closely related to contemporary developments in Europe and North America. **The Enlightenment** and ideas of French philosophers such as Voltaire and Rousseau had been inspirations to Latin Americans. The **French Revolution** also catalysed the spirit of freedom in Latin America in two ways. First, the French Revolution was a persuasive model of the overthrow of an absolute regime to be imitated. Second, the pre-occupation of Spain and Portugal with the **Napoleonic Wars** provided the people of the New World, an opportunity to challenge their European overlords. For example, the Spanish crown had allied with Revolutionary France in 1795, which set off a series of developments that widened economic and political distance between Spain and its American colonies. By being an ally of France, Spain pitted itself against England, the dominant sea power of the period, which in turn cut off communications between Spain and the Americas, forcing Spanish crown to loosen the restrictions on its colonies' commerce. The Spanish Americans now exploited this situation to their best interests who could now trade legally with other colonies, as well as with any neutral states such as the United States. Thus, the wartime liberalization of colonial trade sharpened Creoles' desire for greater economic self-determination leading to initiation of their fight for freedom. Similarly, another contemporary development that had an influence on Latin Americans was the **American War of Independence**. The victory of the American colonies over their subjugators was viewed as an example of how persistent struggle could attain overwhelming success against huge odds. The subsequent establishment of the United States as a new nation and the drafting of the Constitution was seen as an imitable model. Translations of speeches of the founding fathers of the United States, including that of Thomas Jefferson and John Adams, had been in circulation in Latin America. For all these reasons the manifestos and slogans of the Latin American revolutionaries closely resembled those of these countries. Apart from the idealistic inspiration they also enlisted material support from these two regions in course of their revolutionary wars and by 1826 all the South American countries were free of foreign rule.

A. Independence of Latin Americas

Latin America became free of European colonialism after a series of revolutions in the 19th century. Latin America was not a united region, as such the territories were freed in sections with the ultimate goal of liberating an entire viceroyalty into which the continent was divided. Consequently, the fight for independence was long, slow and uneven, and each area had its own leaders and history and the areas that declared independence looked different than they do today. Most of these revolutions were led by the Creoles or the 'colonial whites' (pure-blooded Spaniards who were born in the Americas) who resented their exclusion from high positions in the government and the church. Many of the Creoles were wealthy but were poorly respected by the European-born Spaniards. Since **the Creoles** remained connected to Europe through their ancestry and were often educated abroad, ideas of self-determination had great appeal for them. At the same time not all Creoles were believers in independence and democracy and there existed an opposition of Creole royalists who supported the Spanish Crown and colonial rule. Now we will have a brief look at the major contours of Latin American independence.

The Island of **Haiti**, a colony of France was the first to witness a revolution. In 1791, Negro slaves under a leader Toussaint L'Ouverture rose in revolt against their masters and captured the entire Island. Though Toussaint emerged as the ruler, Napoleon Bonaparte now sent a strong force under his brother-in-law General Le Clerc who by treachery captured and sent Toussaint as a prisoner to France. Now the slaves once again rose in rebellion forcing the French troop to withdraw leading to the independence of Haiti in 1804.

The first major Latin American colony to proclaim independence from Spain was **Venezuela**. In 1806 Francisco de Miranda, one of the Creoles, made an unsuccessful effort with the help of American and English supporters to land forces in Venezuela to liberate it from Spain. Miranda's army was defeated and he was sent to prison. The next stage in Venezuelan independence started with the efforts of **Simon Bolivar**, a rich Creole rancher and erstwhile friend of Miranda. Bolivar captured Caracas and in 1814 the Venezuelan Republic was proclaimed with Bolivar as its head with the title 'Liberator'. Bolivar then defeated the Spanish forces in Columbia and declared the establishment of the Republic of Columbia in 1819. A constitution for the United States of Columbia comprising both Columbia and Venezuela was drafted. In 1822, one of the lieutenants of Bolivar, Antonio Jose de Sucre liberated Ecuador from Spanish forces which was now united with Columbia and Venezuela with the name the **Republic of Gran Columbia**. Gran Columbia was the first union of independent nations in South America.

Gran Columbia, 'Great Columbia' or Greater Columbia was a state that encompassed much of northern South America and part of southern Central America from 1819 to 1831. These terms are used historically to distinguish it from the current Republic of Columbia. Gran Columbia was dissolved in 1831 due to the political differences that existed between supporters of federalism and centralism, as well as regional tensions among the peoples that made up the republic. The former republic was replaced by the republics of Venezuela, Ecuador and New Granada. In 1858, New Granada was replaced by the Granadine Confederation which in 1886, adopted its present-day name – the Republic of Columbia. Panama, which voluntarily had become part of Gran Columbia in 1821, remained a subdivision of the Republic of Columbia until 1903 when it became independent under intense American pressure as the United States wanted territorial rights in the future Panama Canal Zone, which Columbia had refused.

Meanwhile, liberation efforts started in southern Latin America. In 1810 in Buenos Aires, Argentina, the revolutionaries under rich Creoles overthrew the viceregal administration of Joseph Bonaparte. A representative assembly called the Congress of Tucuman issued the Argentine Declaration of Independence in July, 1816. **José de San Martín**, an Argentine native who had been trained as a military officer in Spain and had fought the French forces in the Peninsular War on the side of the Spanish forces in Europe returned to Argentina and in 1817, he crossed the Andes into Chile, where a rebel army under **Bernardo O'Higgins** had been fighting the Spanish since 1810. Joining forces, the Chileans and Argentines defeated the Spanish and freed Chile in 1818 and Peru in 1821. In 1824, Simon Bolivar completed the conquest of Peru. Soon the south-eastern region declared itself a republic with the name Bolivia in honour of Simon Bolivar, their Liberator. Bolivar's friend de Sucre became the first President of the new Bolivar state.

After Napoleon captured Portugal in 1807 the Portugal ruling family had taken shelter in Brazil. Prince John, as the regent of the Portuguese ruling family in Brazil, took steps to modernise Brazil and introduced reforms. In 1821 his son **Dom Pedro** became the regent in Brazil who in 1822 declared Brazil's independence from Portugal. Uruguay which was a province of Brazil broke away and became an independent country in 1828.

In **Mexico**, the revolt started in 1810 under a Creole priest **Father Hidalgo**. Though he could capture some cities he was defeated and shot dead in 1811. The leadership of the rebels was now assumed by an adventurer by name of **Augustin de Iturbide** who by preaching racial equality attracted a large number of followers. In 1821 he captured Mexico City and declared the establishment of an independent Mexican Empire with himself as the ruler with the title of Augustin I. Very soon his rule became suppressive and he was forced to exile and Mexico adopted a republican constitution modelled after the United States.

Commonalities of Latin American countries: They all were European colonies – Brazil by the Portuguese, Haiti by the French and others under Spain. All were underdeveloped both in agrarian and industrial terms. All these countries had high illiteracy, high poverty and unstable political systems to endure. Under such circumstances crimes, assassinations and coups were common occurrences. Most of these were also heavily dependent on foreign countries, especially on the United States, for economic aid. In the background of Cold War politics, they were also susceptible to foreign intervention if any regime was unacceptable to the Capitalist Bloc as happened in Guatemala (1954), Brazil (1964), the Dominican Republic (1965), Chile (1970) and Panama (1989).

B. Problems Faced by the Latin American Countries

1. **Political:** In most Latin American countries the political systems were in a nascent stage and inadequate to deal with the enormous challenges faced by these countries. The democratic tradition was absent, governments were dominated by wealthy landlords and run by military dictators known as **caudillos**. Though constitutions – usually modelled after that of the United States – were drafted they remained as mere documents meant to legitimise the dominance of upper sections, the entrenched oligarchy, rather than a tool to implement democracy or to provide for the masses a more equitable share of the wealth they produced. Similarly, though some experiments in elected governments were made from time to time, sooner their reform efforts threatened the interests of the landed interests they enlisted the support of the army to overthrow these reforming governments as happened in Guatemala (1950), Bolivia (1964), Brazil (1964), Argentina (1966) and Chile (1973).
2. **Interstate wars:** This was another characteristic of Latin American history after their independence. The newly independent Latin American countries did not possess internationally or even domestically recognised boundaries. This caused border wars, especially in Central America, mainly provoked by efforts to reunify now-independent territories. These conflicts were very costly as military expenditures averaged about 77 per cent of total budgets in Latin America between 1822 and 1860. Uruguay fought a long-drawn war against Argentina for 14 years (1838–1852). The large Latin American powers such as Brazil, Argentina and Chile were engaged in efforts to annex smaller states like Uruguay, Paraguay and Bolivia for many years. During the War of the Pacific (1879–1883) Chile fought against the combined forces of Peru and Bolivia and acquired Peru's south-eastern region and Bolivia's only outlet to the sea. Another war of significance was fought during 1864–1870 in which Paraguay fought against the combined forces of Brazil, Argentina and Uruguay in which more than half of Paraguay's population was killed.
3. **Economic:** Though the Latin American countries were rich in natural resources they were weak in economic terms. They were underdeveloped both in the agrarian and industrial spheres. As labour was abundant and cheap, the wealthy landowners did not care for modernisation in agriculture. Emphasis upon production for export made agriculture less diversified and the promotion of a one-crop economy tied

the economy of these countries to the vagaries of the external market forces. Whatever industries existed, they faced problems of inadequate capital, machinery and technical knowledge. Prospective of the home market was low as the majority of the population was poverty-stricken and hence with low purchasing power. The export market for Latin American industrial products was also bleak as they had to face competition from the industrialised nations. Many of the countries were dependent on the export of a limited range of goods – many a times raw materials – copper in the case of Chile, tin by Bolivia, sugar and tobacco by Cuba. High dependency on exports of limited items made the economies of these countries very fragile as a fall in the world price of such commodities meant disaster.

4. **Demographic:** High population growth was another challenge faced by Latin American countries. The population tripled between 1800 and 1900 touching 70 million at the beginning of the 20th century and by 1979 it crossed 350 million. Concomitantly, issues with a large population such as shanty towns; scarcity of water, electricity and jobs; unhygienic living conditions in the cities, and a wide gap between the rich and poor existed in these countries. As a result, Latin America presents a picture of contrast where the height of wealth coexists with the depths of poverty, and a splash of fashion and sophistication entwines with the remnants of a semi-feudal culture.
5. **Foreign interventions and control:** Apart from the political interferences from foreign countries such as the United States, Latin American countries also had to endure foreign interventions and control of their economies. It found expressed in the following major ways – investments in agriculture and industries by foreigners; and loans and credits by international donors. For example, the oil industries of Bolivia and Venezuela and Chilean copper mines were owned by American companies. Similarly, the US Fruit Company owned most of the lands in Guatemala. The governments of the region also had to depend on loans from Europe and North America and profits on loans too went into foreign hands. These countries, under the terms of their borrowings, were bound to follow economic policies known as '**neo-liberalism**' which involved privatisation, reduction in social spending and other austerity measures to the detriment of the common people.
6. **Issues of foreign debt and finance:** As seen above, general backwardness forced the Latin American countries to borrow heavily from foreign banks especially those in the United States. The borrowing was at its apex during the decade from 1973 to 1982 and by 1985 the Latin American debt was more than 368 billion US dollars. During crisis situations such as a decline in export earnings or as in 1979–1981 when the American interest rates were doubled these countries failed to pay even the interest on the loans which was added on to the existing debt. Such situations pushed these countries into a **debt trap** as they were forced to borrow new loans from institutions such as the International Monetary Fund (IMF), merely to make payment of interest on the original loans.
7. **Social discrimination:** The elite minority that controlled the political and economic affairs of the newly formed Latin American countries were intolerant of indigenous cultures and were promoters of individualism. Most of them had a high contempt for the more helpless sections of society. These elite dismissed native Indians and Africans as inferior and exalted the 'superior' nature of the whites.
8. **Social tensions, crime and violence:** The uneven distribution of the benefits of economic progress along with economic insecurities, unemployment, political instability and others cause large-scale violence and crimes in many Latin American countries. El Salvador, Honduras and Venezuela have the highest murder rates globally, with El Salvador having 61.7 homicides per 100,000 people. Additionally, those three countries, as well as Brazil and Guyana, have five of the ten highest overall crime rates in the world. Venezuela has the highest kidnapping rate in the world as five people on average were kidnapped for ransom every day and Venezuela's capital city of Caracas was described as 'the kidnap capital of the world' in 2013.
9. **Military rule:** This was characteristic of many Latin American countries for many decades. As a consequence of the violent struggles for

independence in most of Spanish America, the military grew in importance and military leaders often became the initial heads of state.

10. **Drug trafficking:** Latin America faces the challenge linked to organised crime, especially related to drug-related markets. According to the United Nations Office on Drugs and Crime (UNODC), Latin America has had the highest homicide rates for several years at the global level. In Columbia, armed conflict thrived on the trade of cocaine as well as on other illicit economies (such as oil and illegal gold mining).

Profiles of some major Latin American countries

Argentina: It is one of the Latin America's largest countries in terms of land area and is also among the most biodiverse countries on Earth. It is located very near the southernmost point of Latin America, and shares borders with Chile to the west (and south); Bolivia to the north; and Paraguay, Brazil and Uruguay to the east. It has a robust economy and one of the highest Human Development scores in Latin America

Brazil: It is the largest Latin American country and is the third-largest country in the Americas behind only Canada and the United States and is home to the majority of the Amazon rainforest. Brazil is the longest and most biodiverse country in the world, stretching from the equator to the Tropic of Capricorn. It is bordered by the Atlantic Ocean to the east, and shares border with (counterclockwise from top) French Guiana, Suriname, Guyana, Venezuela, Columbia, Peru, Bolivia, Paraguay, Argentina and Uruguay.

Costa Rica: The Central American country of Costa Rica is bordered by Nicaragua to the north, the Caribbean Sea to the northeast, Panama to the southeast and the Pacific Ocean to the southwest. San José is the capital and largest city. Costa Rica consistently ranks high in terms of human development and is known for its educated workforce and stable democracy. It also ranked as the happiest country in Latin America, as per the World Happiness Report 2023. Costa Rica is also known for its beaches, volcanoes and incredible biodiversity of the protected jungles that cover roughly 25 per cent of its land area.

The Dominican Republic: It is often referred to as the DR, and this Caribbean nation is one of the two countries (the other being Haiti) that jointly occupy the island officially known as Hispaniola. The DR is the most popular tourist destination in the Caribbean, on account of its beaches, biodiversity and abundance of year-round golf courses.

Mexico: It is located in the southern part of North America and is the third largest country in Latin America, after Brazil and Argentina. It is bordered to the north by the United States; to the south and west by the Pacific Ocean; to the southeast by Guatemala, Belize and the Caribbean Sea; and to the east by the Gulf of Mexico. Mexico is one of the chief economic and political powers in Latin America and home to the world's largest population of Spanish speakers – about two and a half times that of Spain or Columbia. Mexico City, the capital, is one of the most populous cities and metropolitan areas in the world.

C. How Far Did Latin Americans Succeed in Facing the Challenges?

1. **Throwing off the US dominance:** Venezuela was the first country to throw off the US influence in political affairs when in 1998 **Hugo Chavez** preaching a radical socio-economic programme was elected president. Other countries such as Brazil (2002), Argentina (2003), Chile (2005), Bolivia and Ecuador (2006) soon followed this path by electing presidents who stood for greater freedom in economic and political affairs away from US control.
2. **Economic independence:** Towards the end of the 20th century in many of the Latin American countries resistance against US domination began to emerge and support for socio-economic reform solidified. As a result, governments with left leanings came to power and introduced reforms, and abandoned neo-liberal capitalism though did not abandon capitalism altogether. For example, Hugo Chavez fully nationalised the oil industry of Venezuela in 2007 apart from ending his country's longstanding military ties with the United States. This was followed by the nationalisation of some more sectors such as

telecommunications, electricity supply and the gold industry. Chavez introduced the **Bolivar Plan** 2000 also called Bolivarian Missions, a social welfare programme aimed at improving the public health system, developing housing projects, providing subsidised food and other consumer goods, and provisions for easy loans to start small enterprises. All these resulted in a reduction in poverty in Venezuela which was 54 per cent in 1998 to 28 per cent in 2008.

The formation of the **Bank of the South** in 2009, to provide loans to any Latin American country to implement approved social and infrastructural projects and the emergence of other regional funds such as the **Andean Development Corporation** and the Venezuelan Development Bank called **BANDES** have all eclipsed the importance of the IMF in the region. The Bank of the South or Banco Sur was established as a monetary fund and lending organisation by Argentina, Brazil, Paraguay, Uruguay, Ecuador, Bolivia and Venezuela and is claimed as an attempt to achieve regional independence and endogenous development.

Another expression of economic independence was the diversification of markets and investment. Venezuela, the leading oil exporter in the Western hemisphere moved closer to China to reduce its dependence on the United States. This route was followed by many other countries especially raw material exporters such as Brazil, Peru and Chile to the extent that China has now become Brazil's largest trading partner.

3. **Economic progress:** Some of the Latin American countries especially the countries in the '**Southern Cone**' comprising Chile, Uruguay and Argentina made economic progress with the support of foreign investment. Similarly, European immigration too played a significant role in the development of these countries. Discovery and exploitation of minerals were added factors of economic progress. Chile acquired economic prosperity with the discovery of mineral deposits such as silver, copper and nitrate. In Brazil, a huge reserve of iron ore was discovered in 1967. In Venezuela, exploration of its huge oil reserves could transform that country from an agrarian to an increasingly industrialised one. With all these, by the beginning of the 21st century, some of the Latin American countries acquired greater economic prosperity as demonstrated by Brazil which by 2011 emerged sixth largest in the world and one of the world's great emerging economies along with India.

In conclusion, it may be stated that Latin America is a huge territory comprising countries that have different colonial heritages and histories, radically different geographies, demographics and ethnic compositions. These countries have different levels and types of economic and social development, political traditions and institutions, modes of insertion into the international economy, and attitudes toward international policies and relationships. For example, Latin American countries such as Brazil, Chile and Argentina enjoy healthy economies while many other Latin American countries are still developing and have the corresponding challenges to overcome. The political and economic powers in Latin American countries had been concentrated in a few hands. Moreover, as seen above, in many instances, the results of the material progress were mainly accrued by the European and North American capitalists by way of investments, ownership of lands, banks, mines and industries, and also by marketing Latin American products. Though Latin Americans have initiated a move away from neo-liberalism this has not been on a single trajectory. While Venezuela, Bolivia, Cuba, Ecuador and Argentina moved decisively away from it, countries such as Brazil, Nicaragua and Uruguay adopted a middle path with a mixture of policies. Others such as Mexico, Chile and Guatemala continued to remain close to the United States which bound them to the US with separate trade agreements.

A reorientation in the outlook of the United States, Canada and the European countries towards Latin American and Caribbean nations not simply as sources of commodities, arenas for investment, and export markets but as potential partners in confronting the broad global agenda, from climate change to public health, non-proliferation to fighting organised crime is highly desirable for a more inclusive global order.

6. Verdict on Decolonisation

1. Gradual process – Decolonisation was a gradual process that extended for many decades. Though the process started soon after the end of the World War II, it came to an end only in 1999 with the return of Macao to China.
2. European unwillingness – Attitude of the European powers vis-à-vis with decolonisation was different. While Britain took the stand that it cannot stop the nationalist resurgence, but only guide the process, the other European powers, except Italy, were determined not to let go of their colonies and were ready to suppress it with all forces at their command.
3. Unprepared for independence – It was a paradox that while the time for gaining independence finally came, many of the colonies were not ready for it. Many factors such as lack of education, lack of officers to man both the bureaucracy and military and lack of experience in governance were important factors for it. It is worthy to note that India was an exception in this regard, where Western education, political awareness, Indianisation of civil services and implementation of self-government, though gradually, had prepared people to shoulder responsibilities of administering the country.
4. Plethora of challenges – This was an obvious fall-out of long colonial rule. Exploitation of colonial resources and people by the colonial masters meant the colonies lacked basic infrastructural facilities and modern industries, shortage of skilled manpower, deepening of social divide on caste, communal and tribal lines and food shortages. Newly independent nations were left to resolve these issues and in fulfilling these tasks, they were thrown in the throes of neo-colonialism.
5. Emergence of neo-colonialism – To meet the huge developmental challenges, the new nations required capital and aid. Though agencies such as IMF and countries like the United States were supportive by granting loans and aid, these were tied to fulfilment of certain conditions. These conditions, such as opening up of their economies to foreign investment, austerity measures in governance and termination of social welfare programmes essentially meant imposition of a new type of colonialism, that is, new-colonialism over these countries.

7. Impact of Decolonisation

- The **Third World** emerged as a powerful force in world politics.
- Emergence of independent nations in 1950s and 1960s **tilted the balance of power** in the UN. Whereas, in 1946, the UN had just 51 members and with the joining of the 'third world' it rose to 127 by 1970.
- **Widened the agenda of the UN** as issues of concern of these new nations such as decolonisation, racial issues and developmental issues began to acquire more attention.
- The Eurocentric world came to an end, and **Europe lost its grandeur**.
- **Britain lost its predominance** in world affairs and became a second-rate power.
- In the **context of Cold War**, both the super powers poured economic and military aid in an effort to enlist more nations to their side.
- **Partition and civil war**. Of the newly independent states, only a few could establish stable governments, while in the rest of them dictators or military juntas captured power. Violence and struggle were part of transition in Asian and African colonies.

SUMMARY

Factors of Decolonisation – Strengthening of nationalism and nationalist resistance against the colonial powers, solidarity of anti-imperialist movements of different countries, exposure to the outside world during the World War II, Japanese conquest which destroyed the notion of European invincibility, opposition to colonialism by the UN, opposition to colonialism by the superpowers, domestic compulsions of the colonial powers, realities of the post-World War II period.

A survey of Decolonisation – The colonial empire of the Britain was the largest and of France the second. Other important colonial powers of Europe were Holland (Dutch East Indies), Spain (Spanish Morocco, Sahara and Spanish Guinea), Italy (Libya, Somalia and Eritrea), Portugal (Angola, Guinea and Mozambique) and Belgium (Congo, Ruanda-Urundi). In Asia the countries gained freedom were India (1947), Sri Lanka (1948), the Philippines (1946), Burma (1948), Indochina (1954), Malaysia (1957), Singapore (1965), Indonesia (1969) and East Timor (2002). In Africa the major countries that gained freedom were Ghana (1957), Congo (1960), Algeria (1962), Kenya (1963), Angola (1975) and Zimbabwe (1980). Latin America became independent after a series of struggles in the 19th century-Haiti (1804), Paraguay (1811), Venezuela (1814), Argentina (1816), Chile (1818), Columbia (1819), Mexico and Panama (1821), Brazil and Ecuador (1822), Peru (1824), Bolivia (1825) and Uruguay (1828).

Impact of Decolonisation – Europe lost its grandeur, Britain lost its predominance in world politics, caused emergence of the Third World, tilted the balance of power in the UN, widened the agenda of the UN, new pawns in the Cold War emerged and witnessed partition, violence and nations' struggle for survival.

QUESTIONS OF PREVIOUS YEARS CIVIL SERVICES EXAMINATION

1. The historical causes for the rise of anti-colonial movement in South-East Asia were cultural differences, spread of western education and the emergence of Communist ideas. Discuss. (2023)
2. How far did Latin American countries overcome centuries of subjugation and foreign intervention? (2022).
3. What happened to Malaya after it was liberated from Japanese occupation in 1945? Discuss. (2022)
4. Why was the apartheid policy introduced in South Africa? What were its main features? (2022)
5. The white-minority government of South Africa treated the natives very badly by denying them fundamental rights and made Apartheid as official policy. How were the people able to end Apartheid policy and establish a transitional rule? (2021)
6. The rise of nationalism across nations shattered the chains which held together the empires of modern Europe. Discuss. (2021)
7. Discuss the circumstances leading to the French exit from Algeria in 1962. (2020)
8. Critically examine whether it was true that after a century of dependency on Europeans, Africans were ill-prepared for the task of nation-building. (2020)
9. Explain why Latin America was beset with chronic political instability and endemic military conflicts throughout most of the 19th century. (2019)
10. Discuss the factors constraining development of Africa after decolonization. (2018)
11. Explain the features of Apartheid in South Africa. (2018)
12. What problems were germane to the decolonization process in the Malay Peninsula? (2017)
13. The anti-colonial struggles in West Africa were led by the new elite of Western-educated Africans. Examine. (2016)
14. 'Colonies are like fruits which cling to the tree only till they ripen'. Elucidate. (2006)
15. Give a brief account of the struggle against 'Apartheid' in South Africa. (2006)

CHAPTER 17

Asia in Focus

In this Chapter

A. The Chinese Revolution and the Communist China

1. Introduction

Chinese civilisation is more than 5,000 years old and has played a crucial role in world history. Since ancient times it was under the rule of various dynasties and the last dynasty to rule was the Qing or Manchu from 1644 to 1912. The Qing rulers had to confront problems on many fronts. The first of these was bullying of the Western imperial powers. Intrusion of Christian missionaries, internal unrest and upheavals, alarming degree of corruption of civil servants and weakening of the central power were some of the troubles faced by China in the 19th century. Though the incompetent monarchy was overthrown in 1912, it did not improve the conditions.

The post-monarchical period was one of increasing instability, caused at first by fight between different warlords and later by two political parties – the **Kuomintang and the Communists**. At the end of this fight, which is known as the Chinese Civil War, the Communists emerged victorious and founded the People's Republic of China in 1949.

2. | Western Intrusion

During the Age of Explorations the Chinese had followed a policy of isolation in international relations. They believed that their kingdom, what they called as the **Middle Kingdom**, was the cultural centre of the universe. On this assumption of cultural superiority they stood for limiting the influence of outsiders to a minimum. To avoid contamination from the Western people, the Chinese authorities imposed a number of restrictions on foreign trade. For example, foreign trade could be carried only through certain designated ports – **Canton and Macao** (a Portuguese settlement). The Western traders were required to have relations only with Chinese traders and not with government servants. The foreign traders were also prohibited from bringing their families with them or employing Chinese servants. Being self-sufficient in agriculture and with its extensive mining and manufacturing sectors, the Chinese had little interest in European goods, which was another reason for their isolationism.

For long, China could resist European advances towards their country by erecting hurdles as seen above. In spite of such hurdles, traders from various nations including the British and the Americans engaged in trade with China and the balance of trade was in favour of China as exports far exceeded imports. Initially the British trade with China consisted of selling British wool and Indian cotton and buying Chinese tea and silk. As the Chinese demand slackened and trade deficit mounted, Britain developed opium trade with China. By 1829, opium trade amounted more than 4 million pounds annually and by 1835 more than 12 million people in China were opium addicts.

i. The First Opium War

Alarmed at the development and concerned about economic and social impacts of opium addiction, the Chinese authorities prohibited the opium traffic. Authorities also destroyed British opium in the port city of Canton in 1839. This incident gave birth to the **First Opium War** or the **Anglo-Chinese War** (1839–42). China was defeated and was forced to sign the **Treaty of Nanking** (1842). This was the beginning of a series of defeats of China in their fight against the European colonial powers and also the beginning of a series of '**unequal treaties**' imposed on it.

By the Treaty of Nanking, China was compelled to grant extensive trading rights to the British which had far-reaching and devastating impact on China. By this Treaty the Chinese agreed to:

1. **Pay indemnity** to the British
2. Grant most favoured nation treatment to Britain and to cede the island of **Hong Kong** to the British
3. Open more ports for trade and to grant the **right of residence** to foreigners in these ports.

Soon, other nations secured similar concessions by signing separate treaties with China.

ii. The Second Opium War

The desire of Britain and France to gain more concessions and legalisation of opium trade in China led to another conflict – the **Second Opium War** (1856–60). China was defeated by the forces of Britain and France. By the **Treaty of Tientsin** (1858) and the by the **Convention of Beijing** (1860), China had to open 11 more ports to foreign ships, foreigners were to be permitted to travel in China, foreign diplomatic representatives were to be permitted in the capital Beijing and also had to legalise the use and import of opium. The Christian missionaries were also granted freedom of movement in China. Thus, defeats in the Opium Wars marked the beginning of the end of Imperial China and the beginning of a '**century of humiliation**'.

iii. The Sino-Japanese War

After the defeat in the Sino-Japanese War of 1894–95, China lost Taiwan and parts of Manchuria. China also lost its influences in Korea. Making use most of the situation, the Europeans tried to get more concessions. The colonial powers – Britain, France, Japan, Germany and Russia – carved China into their '**spheres of interest**', where these countries had exclusive rights on commerce and profits thereon. The United States, the new entrant in the colonial race, objected to this and pushed for an **Open Door Policy** in China for all colonial powers. The United States was apprehensive of European powers and Japan carving China among themselves, hence announced that trade with China should be opened to all.

3. Internal Troubles

Apart from foreign incursions, China faced many internal troubles in the 19th century. China was extremely undemocratic, economically backward and militarily weak. By 1850, it had a huge population of 430 million but food production was insufficient resulting in hunger and distress. Opium addiction was another issue. In spite of all these, the Qing rulers showed neither inclination to assess the situation in realistic manner nor have the political will, military strength or popular support to meet these challenges.

i. Taiping Rebellion

Discontent found expressed in many rebellions, the first of which was the Taiping Rebellion started in 1851 in Guangzhou (Canton) province in south-eastern China. Taiping means 'great peace'. It was led by Hong Xiuquan whose declared aim was to establish a '**Heavenly Kingdom of Great Peace**' after overthrowing the Manchu. Being a follower of Christianity Hong Xiuquan envisioned a theocratic Chinese nation, considered Buddhism and Taoism as idolatrous and his followers desecrated ancient Chinese temples. In 1853, he captured Nanking and made it his capital. Though the rebellion spread to 14 out of 18 provinces of China by 1864, it was suppressed with the help of the British and French forces. The Europeans supported its suppression as they preferred a weak government under the Manchus to a strong government of Taiping. The rebellion was defeated mainly by regional armies and not by the central government and in the process the provinces began to assert their independence. At least 20 million had died in the battles and in famine during the rebellion.

ii. Boxer Rebellion

In 1900, once again rebellion broke out. This rebellion known as the **Boxer Rebellion** was against the foreigners and was led by 'the Society of Righteous and Harmonious Fists'. Members of this group opposed privileges granted to foreigners and adoption of Christianity by many of the Chinese. They were also critical of the Chinese ruler for failing to contain foreign imperialism in China. They attacked the Europeans in Beijing and the Chinese Christians. Once again the Chinese were defeated by an army that consisted not only the Europeans but of Japanese and Americans. By the **Boxer Protocol**, the peace treaty signed by the Qing ruler in 1901, China had to agree to pay huge reparations for failing to protect foreigners from the attack. It also had to ban anti-foreign groups and to permit foreign military garrisons permanently stationed in Beijing.

4. Decadence of the Manchu

China was in effect ruled by Empress Dowager Cixi, as regent of minor kings for nearly five decades. She was called as the 'dragon lady' and the 'Old Master Buddha' who controlled the government for 47 years from 1861 till her death in 1908.

She supported the **Self-Strengthening Movement** – a period of institutional, economic and military reforms by way of Westernisation. The reformers emphasised promoting industries and communications and modernisation of the army. But they failed in recognising the significance of reforms of political institutions and social values. Being conservative and superficial, compared to the modernisation programme of Japan of the same period, the Chinese reform efforts did not yield the intended results. The Movement thus turned out to be an effort to protect the structure of the existing Qing government.

5. The Chinese Revolution

Hatred towards the foreigners and discontent with the dynasty continued to simmer. In 1905, Sun Yat-sen organised the **Revolutionary Alliance,** an alliance of revolutionary groups aimed at spreading nationalism, revolutionary ideas and the overthrow of the Manchu dynasty. Finally, revolution broke out among the soldiers in Wuchang in 1911. Governors in provinces too rose in rapid succession. As the provinces declared independence and repudiated the Manchus, the emperor sought support from a retired army general **Yuan Shih-kai** to suppress the rebellion. But Yuan

Shih-kai made a deal with the revolutionaries and garnered their support to capture power. In February 1912, **Emperor Pu Yi** was forced to abdicate and the Qing dynasty that ruled China since 1644 came to an end. The Revolution took place without any bloodshed. **China was declared a republic** with Yuan Shih-kai as its President (1912–16). He ruled as an autocrat and suppressed democratic aspirations. In 1915, Yuan declared himself the Emperor of China but he died in 1916. After his death Yuan Shi-kai's leading generals emerged as warlords and started fighting for control of China.

Sun Yat-sen (1866–1925) was born in a peasant family in Canton. He acquired Western education in Hawaii and acquired a medical diploma at Hong Kong. He travelled extensively in Europe and in the United States before returning to China to transform China into a republic. Though he was elected by the delegates from the provinces as the 'Provisional President' of the new Republic of China in December 1911, he handed power to Yuan Shi-kai in a deal to secure abdication of the Manchu emperor. He organised the Chinese people and enlisted the support of the communists in his fight first against Yuan Shi-kai and after Yuan Shi-kai's death against the warlords. He died in 1925. He is known as the 'Father of Chinese Republicanism' and was the most prominent revolutionary before Mao.

6. Warlord Era

The period from 1916 to 1928 was the Warlord Era. During this period, there was no central government in China. China was fragmented into hundreds of small states controlled by warlords and their army. During this period warlords fought and bargained for themselves and China went through a period of disorder and instability.

7. Emergence of Nationalism and Modern Politics

By the beginning of the 20th century, large number of Chinese youngsters who had attended foreign institutions were exposed to radical and modern ideas. They returned to China with dreams of establishing their country on national and modern lines.

i. The May Fourth Movement

Out of such groups that believed in liberal and national ideas emerged the **May Fourth Movement**. It began on 4 May 1919 with demonstrations in Beijing and it marked the birth of Chinese nationalism. The **May Fourth Movement** was the Chinese outburst against the provisions of the Treaty of Versailles to hand over the Chinese territories held by Germany to Japan. At the Paris Peace Conference Chinese demands had been rejected and Shantung Peninsula had been given to Japan. The May Fourth Movement thus was an expression of anger against the weakness of China's government and also against Japan's encroachment on China.

ii. The National People's Party

The **National People's Party** or **Kuomintang (KMT)** was formed in 1912. Founded by Dr Sun Yat-sen, the Kuomintang had 'Three Principles of the People' as its aim. These were-

Nationalism: Ending the foreign rule and instilling loyalty of the people to the nation instead of to the family or the province,

Democracy: Based on peoples' sovereignty and representative government, and

Livelihood: To ensure material progress and economic security for all Chinese.

Based on these ideals, Sun Yat-sen instilled hope among the Chinese people of a republican China which is free and strong. In 1917, Sun Yat-sen established his government in Canton, in southern China. Sun Yat-sen and his Kuomintang party were supported by the Soviet Russia by providing military and political advisors to Canton from 1923. During this period Chinese national movement emerged under a disciplined leadership enjoyed popular support and set forth clear objectives. By 1925, the Canton government emerged as an effective government with an army and tax collecting apparatus.

In 1926, the Kuomintang, now under Chiang Kai-shek, marched to the north – the **Northern Expedition** – and defeated the military lords and occupied Peking in 1928. The Nationalists also shifted their capital to Nanking. It also secured diplomatic recognition and financial assistance from the West including the United States. At the same time, the Kuomintang failed in implementing the promised reforms such as the Livelihood Principle. It also established a party dictatorship with secret police and indoctrination.

iii. The Chinese Communist Party

In 1921, the **Chinese Communist Party (CCP)** was founded in Shanghai. The communists were inspired by the Russian Revolution of 1917 and consisted mostly of intellectuals. It put forward a revolutionary programme against imperialism and feudalism. They emphasised the revolutionary method of relying on the masses and started organising workers movements.

Mao Zedong

Mao Zedong (1893–1976). Mao was born in a peasant family. He was one of the founding members of the CCP in 1921. Traditional Marxist idea of revolution was that it would be brought about by the urban workers. But Mao deviated from this path by basing his revolutionary programme on the peasantry. Mao developed Maoism by combining the basic tenets of Marxism with the actual practice of the Chinese Revolution. It entailed blazing a revolutionary path from rural areas to encircle the cities and seizing state power with military force. He was the Chairman of the Communist Party of China (1931–76) and Chairman of the People's Republic of China (1949–59). By the time of his death, China emerged as a nation with political stability, economic prosperity and also as an international power having nuclear weapons.

Chiang Kai-shek (1887–1975): He was a military leader who turned into a republican revolutionary after the end of the Manchu Dynasty. He was associated with Sun Yat-sen in their efforts to overthrow the dictatorship of Yuan Shi-kai. He became the leader of the KMT after the death of Sun Yat-sen in 1925. From 1928 to 1949, he was the president of the Republic of China (Nationalist government in China). His government was corrupt and inefficient. As the leader of the KMT, Chiang expelled the communists from his party and tried to prevent the spread of communism in China. After being defeated by the Communists in 1949, he fled to the Island of Taiwan establishing there the Republic of China on Taiwan. Here with ample American aid and support, he transformed Taiwan into a modern nation.

8. Civil War in China

Initially, both the Kuomintang and the Communists cooperated in the **Northern Expedition,** the struggle against the warlords. They formed the **First United Front** (1922–27) by which the communists were absorbed into KMT and became responsible for organising the urban workers. This collaboration ended in 1927, after they succeeded in defeating the warlords. As the Kuomintang gained strength and controlled more and more regions, Chiang Kai-shek grew overconfident and launched the '**White Terror**' to destroy the communists. Chiang Kai-shek and many of his supporters such as the landlords and capitalists were also alarmed by the growing influence of communists in the KMT. In this **anti-Communist purge,** thousands of Communists were killed. The First United Front thus ended and the civil war between the Nationalists and the Communists started. Chiang Kai-shek also severed the link with the Soviet Russia and expelled the Russian advisors.

The civil war between the Nationalists and Communists took place in two stages – the first from 1927 to 1937 and the second from 1945 to 1949. In the civil war, the KMT was supported by the United States and the CCP was supported by the Soviet Union.

After their breakup with the Kuomintang, the Communists spread their influence among the peasants in central and southern China and also acquired the technique of guerrilla warfare. They organised the peasants and formed their own army – **the Red Army**. The Communists also organised the Soviet style semi-autonomous bases called the **Chinese Soviet Republics** and one of such bases – Kiangsi became the communist headquarters. The Communists' promise of land reform was hugely popular among impoverished peasants.

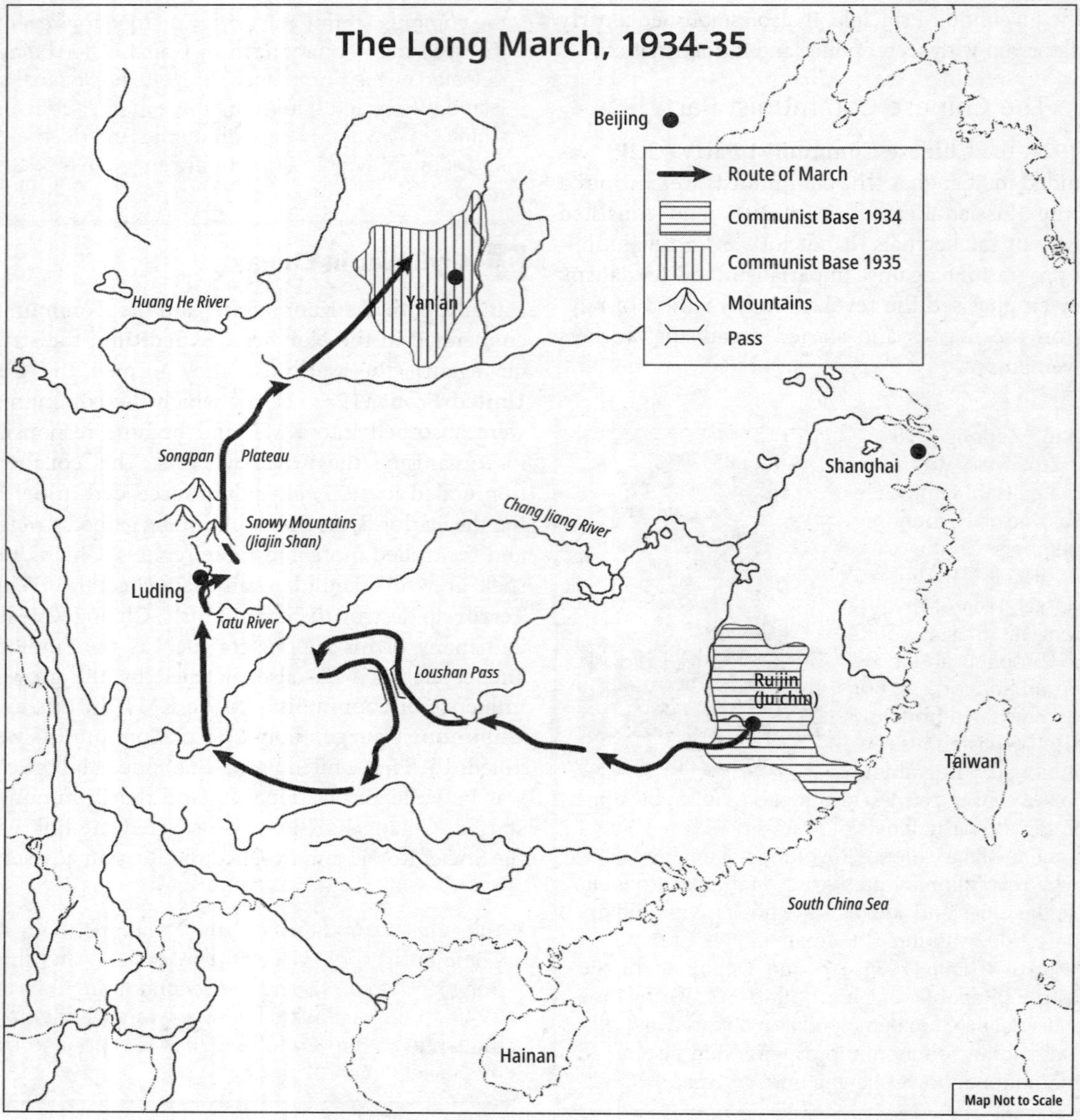

The Long March

Chiang now launched **'Extermination Campaigns'** – five campaigns were launched starting with the first in 1930 – against the communists who by this time had established themselves in China's southern and western provinces. Though the communists could survive initial attacks, they found it increasingly difficult to withstand the assault. The fifth Extermination Campaign launched in 1933 with more than five lakh troops was aimed to encircle and starve the communists out of their strongholds. Threatened with extinction, the Communists, nearly one lakh members, under the leadership of Mao undertook a mass migration to Yenan in northwest Shensi Province. The hazardous 6,000 miles of trekking known as the **Long March** took place during 1934–35. The survivors, merely 7,000 or more, settled in caves in northwestern China. Yenan was to remain the headquarters of the communists till their final victory over the Nationalists.

Here, the Communists reorganised themselves from an urban-based party of workers led by intellectuals into a rural-based Maoist revolutionary party consisting mainly of peasants. They gained popular support through their peasant friendly measures such as land redistribution, rent reduction, establishment of cooperative societies and with their strong resistance against the Japanese aggression.

The Long March was highly significant in the history of Communism in China. The Long March enabled the Communists to survive against KMT assault. They also acquired a strong base in Yenan from where they could consolidate their position and continue the civil war. It also established unquestioned leadership of Mao as his tactic of 'retreat to advance' proved successful. The March also offered an opportunity for hard physical training and political education and prepared the party cadres for their final assault against their enemies. Before the Long March the Communists were on the brink of extinction and if not for the Long March the Nationalists would have won the civil war. The survivors of the Long March which included Mao, Chu Teh, Chou en Lai et al constituted the hardcore of reliable and the disciplined force of Chinese communism who went on to build the People's Republic of China in 1949.

In 1937, Japan invaded China (the Second Sino-Japanese War). Faced with a common enemy, both the Nationalists and the Communists joined hands and formed the **Second United Front** (1937–45). During this period the Communists continued to expand their influence among the people (CCP membership rose to more than one million) while simultaneously engaging in a guerrilla war against the Japanese. By helping the peasants the Communists showed that they hold progressive and supportive policies and also demonstrated they practice what they preach. At the end of the World War II, the Communists controlled approximately one-quarter of the Chinese mainland, while the Nationalists controlled the remainder.

9. The Communist Revolution

After the defeat of Japan in World War II, which ended the Japanese threat, a full-blown civil war broke out between the KMT and CCP in 1945. Chiang launched a major offensive once again against the communists but the Red Army which had been now organised as the **People's Liberation Army** (PLA) could organise counter attacks and force the KMT troops to retreat even from their capital Nanking. In October 1949, the CCP declared the formation of the **People's Republic of China** or the PRC with capital at Peking. The Nationalists retreated to the island of Taiwan. Chiang considered himself the president of all of China, while Mao claimed Taiwan as part of the PRC. The status of Taiwan is a dispute that still lingers today.

The Communists could defeat the Nationalists with superior organisational structure and purpose, peasant support and with Mao's leadership. For their success, the Communists owed much to the weaknesses of Kuomintang forces as to their own strengths.

i. Weaknesses of KMT

Political: Chiang was dictatorial and his leadership could not unite people on nationalist lines. KMT officials were incompetent and corrupt. Officials, especially tax collectors, were hated by all.

Economic: Post-World War II period was a period of inflation and unemployment, which made life miserable especially in the cities. But Nationalist government imposed heavy taxes and lost peoples' support. Instead of allocating economic resources for reconstruction, Chiang spent it on fighting the Communists. Economic miseries forced people to resort to strikes. Chiang responded to protests and criticism by intellectuals and newspapers with censorship and suppression which drove more people to Communist camp.

Military: Chiang had more troops than Mao but it had many drawbacks. Most of the KMT soldiers were drafted against their will. Soldiers were poorly trained and did not have adequate food or clothing. The Nationalist army was not coordinated by a central command. Many of its Generals led independent units were corrupt. They competed with each other for ration and ammunition. All these caused defection in huge numbers from the Nationalist army to the Communist side during the civil war.

ii. Strengths of CCP

Propaganda: The Communists employed effective propaganda to enlist the support of the masses. Mao declared that 'the battle for China is a battle for the hearts and minds of the people' and in this battle, he added, land reform as 'the mother of all other work'. They took over lands from landlords and distributed them to poor peasants and labourers. This strategy had many benefits. Though most of the people who received the land were not dedicated Communists, it became imperative for them to support the Communists to continue to enjoy the land or they would lose everything if the Communists fail. Hence, they supported and enrolled in the Red Army. Moreover, by destroying the landlords, Mao could destroy the traditional power structure in the villages which was now replaced with peasant leadership under the Communists. Further, the unflagging fight against the Japanese convinced the Chinese people of the communists' dedication to the Chinese cause.

Military: The PLA of the Communists was organised under a central command and had a well-thought plan. They were dedicated to the Communist cause, and were led by leaders of better qualities and the guerrilla tactics enabled them to take advantage of the larger, conventional army of the KMT. Another significant factor was the huge quantity of weapons the Red Army captured from the Japanese in Manchuria.

Leadership: Mao's leadership role too was significant in the success of the Communists as demonstrated during the Long March.

10. Consolidation of the Communist State Under Mao

The new regime under Mao faced many challenges. It included total devastation of the national economy, galloping inflation, disruption of communication systems, decline in foreign trade and the threat of famine. Internationally, the Communist regime was isolated, except for Soviet Russia other nations adopted a hostile attitude.

i. Political Reforms

The Communist victory in the civil war put an end to the internal turmoil and foreign interventions. For the first time in many decades, China was united and was at peace. It brought **political stability** and created conditions for the implementation of policies that transformed China into a political, economic and military power. Establishment of **centralised state power** provided for territorial unification and the emergence of a modern **nation-state.**

After the Revolution Mao retained absolute power and 'enemies of the people' – those who did not follow Communist line were imprisoned or executed. In 1954, a constitution was enacted providing for parliamentary democracy in form but dominated by Communist party. It is a single-party ruled state and political power is distributed between the President, the State Council and the National People's Congress (NPC). The State Council is the administrative branch and is headed by the Premier, while the NPC is the single legislative body consisting of members selected by the Communist Party of China. Politically the CCP still retains its monopoly in power and does not tolerate any political dissent. The Politburo and the Standing Committee of the Politburo are the highest authorities in China.

> Current Communist countries are China, Vietnam, Laos, North Korea and Cuba. The political and economic systems in Communist courtesies are different from democratic nations. Elections are single-party affairs and Communist parties maintain total power in governance. Similarly their economic systems are controlled by the party.

ii. Economic Reforms

Since 1949, China has transformed from the status of 'the sick man of Asia' into one of the most rapidly growing industrial powers in the world. The political and institutional foundations for this transformation had been laid in the post-Revolutionary years. Two important institutions in this regard were the party apparatus which imposed strict discipline over its members and a socialist economy modelled after the Soviet Russia. Some of the important economic measures were as follows:

Land Reforms: Land reforms were initiated soon after the Communist capture of power. It was carried out in three stages. In the first stage, the properties of the landlords were confiscated and redistributed among the peasants. It ended in 1953, and the cooperative system was introduced. Cooperatives were a piece of lands owned and worked by a group of farmers. By 1958, the Communes-state owned farms operated by a large group of farmers were introduced.

Five-Year Plans: These were a series of socio-economic development initiatives launched since 1950s containing detailed strategies, targets and directions. The First Five-Year Plan (1953–57) was aimed at laying the foundation for China's industrialisation and socialist transformation. In economic terms, the First Five-Year Plan was successful – heavy industries greatly expanded and agricultural output witnessed substantial improvement.

> **A Hundred Flowers Bloom:** It was launched in the background of the success of the First Five-Year Plan. It invited ideas from intellectuals and public. Mao equated open expression of ideas with the blooming flowers. By **'One Hundred Flowers Movement'** Mao wanted to be seen as a leader who was open to new ideas.

The Great Leap Forward: The Great Leap Forward into Communism, as it was officially known, was a socio-economic campaign. Launched in 1958, it aimed at transforming China from an agrarian nation to a modern industrial society. Mao wanted China to out produce Britain, the mother of the industrial revolution. It was a five-year plan for forced agricultural collectivisation and rural industrialisation. Private plot farming was abolished and collective farms controlled by the Communist Party were introduced. New agricultural techniques and experimental methods were practiced. Backyard steel furnaces were constructed on farm lands and urban neighbourhoods to increase industrial production. Millions of agrarian labourers were transported from farms to industries leading to the breakup of families. The Great Leap failed. Food shortages, severe industrial depression and demoralisation of labour were the immediate results. Though launched as a five-year plan, it was called off after three years. During the period of its implementation more than 40 million died of starvation, torture or of forced labour. Politically it sidelined Mao and he relinquished the office of the Chairman of the People's Republic of China.

iii. Social Reforms

The establishment of Communist rule in China transformed social relations. The Land Reform campaigns of 1950s destroyed China's gentry – landlords as a social class and introduced social equality. The Marriage Law of 1950 provided for equal rights for women. It declared marriage as an institution based on equality and mutual consent. It replaced the centuries-old patriarchal family system with an independent nuclear family and thus transformed social relationships.

iv. Foreign Policy Under Mao

China with a history of long foreign intervention now stood for protecting its sovereignty and remaining independent of foreign powers. In 1950, Chinese troops took part in Korean War not just to protect communist North Korea but also to prevent the spread of American influence in the region. Tibet which had declared independence from China in 1912 was annexed to China.

Though Mao had retained good relations with Stalin and had received aid from the Soviets during the civil war, border disputes with Soviet Russia and de-Stalinisation measures in Russia strained Chinese relation with Soviet Russia leading to Sino-Soviet Split in the 1950s. Many border skirmishes with the Soviet Russia convinced China to consider Russia as a bigger threat than the United States. On its border with the Soviet Russia, China maintained a strong border force.

The United States had suspended its diplomatic relation with China after the Communist victory. It remained in force for many decades. Outbreak of the Korean War in which America and PRC were pitted against each other widened the wedge. The United States recognised the Republic of China (Taiwan) as China's true government and supported its seat in the UN.

As the Cold War entered a period of détente in the 1970s, China realised the benefit of improving relation with the United States. On their part, the United States was not directly involved in conflicts with communist forces in South East Asia after the Vietnam debacle. In 1970s, relation improved between the United States and China, in 1971, China was given the permanent seat in the UN and in 1972 American President **Richard Nixon** visited China.

v. The Cultural Revolution

It was a socio-political movement launched by Mao in 1966 to purge China of **Four Olds – Old Ideas, Old Habits, Old Culture and Old Customs**. Launched after 17 years of capturing power, by it Mao aimed to reinvigorate the communist revolution by strengthening ideology, purging the **'impure' elements** of Chinese society and weeding out opponents whether real or imagined.

Mao's position in government had been weakened after the failure of the 'Great Leap Forward'. Mao also came to believe that Communist party leadership was moving in a **revisionist direction,** embracing bourgeoisie values and preferring expertise to ideological purity. Mao wanted to destroy his enemies and reassert his control over the communist party by unleashing the masses. As one of the critics observed 'It was a power struggle waged ... behind the smokescreen of a fictitious mass movement'.

It started with 'May 16 Notification' issued by the party in 1966 warning of counter-revolutionary 'revisionists' infiltrating the party to create a 'dictatorship of the bourgeoisie'. It exhorted the masses to 'clear away the evil habits of the old society' claiming that some old elements were trying to subvert communism. Anything of feudal or bourgeoisie was to be destroyed. Students were encouraged to attack counter-revolutionaries and criticise party leaders accused of deviated from Maoism.

A Propaganda Poster of Cultural Revolution

School and university students carrying the **red book**, who saw themselves as the Chairman's sentinels, responded by setting up paramilitary groups called the **Red Guards** in classrooms and on campuses. They resorted to **red terror**. Teenagers in red armbands and in military clothes ransacked shrines, churches, shops and anything they perceived as 'feudal elements' and unleashed violence as brutal as that of Stalin's Russia. Intellectuals and people deemed class enemies were persecuted and officials were purged, others were killed and still others committed suicide on despair.

In their desire to wipe out the Four Olds, the Red Guards destroyed historical sites and cultural relics. Mao ordered the party and the army not to suppress the movement. In 1968, millions of urban students were sent to rural areas to learn from the peasants to create a new society devoid of any gap between urban and rural or labourers and intellectuals. Though the Revolution lasted a decade, most of its extreme brutalities occurred in the first few years. As the Red Guards grew more extreme and started battling one another, the PLA was sent to suppress them.

> ***Little Red Book*** was a pocket-sized book containing collection of quotations from Mao. During the Cultural Revolution, the Little Red Book became the sacred text of the Revolution and promoted the personality cult of Mao. Reading sessions of the Red Book were common in China even in the skies where airhostesses preached Mao's wisdom to passengers.

The Cultural Revolution officially ended in 1976 after the death of Mao. During these ten years of turmoil and bloodshed millions of lives were lost. The anarchy and terror resulted from the Revolution disrupted the economy and industrial production dropped by 12 per cent in 1968.

The CCP termed the Revolution as an error in 1981 and party leaders accused Mao's wife Jiang Qing and her accomplices known as the **'Gang of Four'** of masterminding the chaos. Jiang was sentenced to death in 1981 which was later reduced to life imprisonment.

> Hong Kong was returned to China by Britain in 1997. It was under the British for 156 years and had a capitalist economy. As per the transfer agreement, China promised to preserve capitalist economy of Hong Kong and to follow 'One country two systems' in its relation with Hong Kong.

vi. Evaluation of Mao's Reforms

The period of Mao was an epoch of startling accomplishments and also of disastrous failures.

1. **Collectivisation** – It refers to the creation of collective farms, where farmers jointly engage in farming activities. Under this system the peasants were ensured of an income and they were educated. But people lost their land and collectivisation was a forced affair in many instances.
2. **Five-Year Plans** were inspired by the Soviet model. Decades of fighting had ruined the Chinese economy and Mao wanted to rebuild it as quickly as possible. Priority areas were identified and individual factories were told what exactly their contribution should be. The Five-Year Plan raised output and in many areas such as coal, iron, steel and fertiliser production exceeded the target by 1957. Though it enabled China to get back on economic track, the Plan involved huge environmental and human costs.
3. **Hundred Flowers Movement** was aimed as an outlet for the people and intellectuals to discuss problems faced by China and suggest solutions. By this, Mao expected people would suggest socialist ideas as the best way forward. Instead, a lot of criticism was directed against the CCP and its leader Mao. The idea backfired and Mao withdrew the Movement as he considered that the people crossed the reasonable limit of criticism. Thus, a movement that was intended to enlist shared and agreed on solutions to problems faced by China and which had great potential to change Chinese society, if done in a constructive way, ended in suppressing free debate and minimised dissent.
4. **One China Policy** – With this policy, China asserted that there is only one sovereign state under the name China. It strengthened China as a nation and upheld its national identity. But it caused victimisation of minorities, suppression of regional aspirations and limitation on religious freedom.
5. **Cultural Revolution** – With this, the objectives of CCP were made clear but came at a huge human cost. It also incorporated a Cult Personality of Mao.
6. **Human Cost**: The Chinese Revolution entailed a huge human cost – not only those millions who died during the revolutionary struggle but also those millions that were persecuted after the Communists captured power. To get a fair picture of the human cost these figures need to be added with some more million human lives lost during the political misadventures of the Great Leap Forward and the Cultural Revolution.

Ping-Pong Diplomacy: It refers to improvement in bilateral relation between America and China by engaging in tab e tennis matches under the slogan 'Friendship First and Competition Second'. It started in 1971 when Mao extended an invitation to the US table tennis team to make an all-expense paid visit to China. The US table tennis team visited China in April 1971. During the tour, the US and Chinese players participated in a series of exhibition Ping-Pong matches. Crossing of the 'Bamboo Curtain' by the US players was followed by a visit by the Chinese table tennis team to the United States and President Richard Nixon's visit to China in 1972.

11. China Under Deng Xiaoping

After Mao's death in 1976, the new leadership under Deng Xiaoping initiated the '**Four Modernisations**' in agriculture, industry, defence and in science and technology to rejuvenate China's economy. Changes affected during the Cultural Revolution were reversed. It also opened up the country to the outside world. In 1980, China joined the IMF and the World Bank and western investment was encouraged. The government established a number of areas of foreign investment such as **Hi-tech Industry Development Zones** and **Special Economic Zones** facilitating inflows of foreign capital, technology and managerial practices. This economic liberalisation and a policy of government regulated capitalism is known as '**market socialism**'. Critics argue that what exists in China is 'bureaucratic capitalism' where the functioning of the capitalist market is closely controlled by the Communist Party of China. After the adoption of elements of capitalism and free-market reforms, China in due course of time emerged as the second largest economy in the world.

Tiananmen Square Massacre in 1989 was an assault on the democratic movement of students demanding freedom of speech and democracy. At Tiananmen Square, students of Beijing had assembled peacefully to protest against inflation and for political reforms – democratic institutions and an end to corruption. The Chinese government responded with overwhelming force and more than 3,000 students were gunned down.

12. China as a Global Power

China, a Communist Republic, now consists of 23 provinces, 5 autonomous regions (Xinjiang, Tibet, Inner Mongolia, Guangxi and Ningxia) and 4 principalities (Beijing, Shanghai, Tianjin and Chongqing), which are directly under the central government. China has a unicameral legislature known as the NPC. National suffrage is 18 years and above. The CCP is the major party, though some minor parties exist, but all are controlled by the CCP. Majority of the Chinese are non-denominational in matters of religion though roughly 10 per cent follows Buddhism.

China has emerged as a global **economic powerhouse** and is expected to surpass America as the biggest economy of the world in 2028. In military terms China is much behind the United States, even though China's increased spending on military technology and development of secretive weapons are likely to improve its position. But in its effort to become a global superpower, China faces many challenges – a tough neighbourhood, lack of trusted powerful allies and a firm American stand on international issues such as the issue of Corona Virus. Even if China happens to overtake the United States in economic and military terms, its claim to global power status shall be dwarfed by its closed-one party political system, incapability of Mandarin to replace English as the world's language and its location amidst several powerful and competing nations. With these countries especially, Russia, India and Japan, China has a border disputes. So long as China is entangled in thorny relation with these nations, the ability of China to freely interfere in political and military affairs in other parts of the world will be greatly curtailed and its dream of super power status will be hampered.

SUMMARY

The Chinese Revolution and the Communist China – Chinese for many centuries followed a policy of isolation and resisted European advances to open up their country. But, with the Opium Wars (1839–1842), China was forced to allow European access in China. Under a decaying Manchu Dynasty, China also witnessed many internal troubles such as the Taiping Rebellion and the Boxer Rebellion. By the beginning of the 20th century spirit of nationalism emerged in China and formation of the National People's Party also known as Kuomintang in 1912 and the May Fourth Movement of 1919 were expressions of it. The Chinese Communist Party was formed in 1921.

Civil War in China – It took place between the Nationalists and the Communists. The Nationalists conducted extermination campaigns against the Communists and the Communists undertook the Long March under their leader Mao Zedong and survived the annihilation attempts. The Civil War ended with the victory of the Communists and the formation of the People's Republic of China in 1949.

China under Mao – reforms in every sphere – in political field it meant enactment of a constitution which provided for parliamentary form of government but under the dominance of the Communist party, establishment of centralised state power and bringing stability in governance. In economic field reforms such as Five-Year Plans, land reforms, the Great Leap Forward aimed at transforming China from an agrarian to modern industrial society were implemented. In socio-cultural spheres introduction of social equality by destroying the landlord class, implementation of equal rights for women and the Cultural Revolution were notable.

China after Mao – Under Deng Xiaoping China underwent Four Modernisations – in agriculture, industry, defence and in science and technology.

China as a global power – China by the beginning of the 21st century emerged as an economic power house and plays a pivotal role in the global supply chain. At the same time China faces challenges in its ambition to become a great world power even from its neighbourhood and beyond.

Questions of Previous Years Civil Services Examination

1. 'The failure of Kuomintang against the Communist onslaught was unimaginable and it was Mao Tse-tung whose tenacity and innovative approach had accomplished the unthinkable'. Discuss. (2015)
2. The announcement of the creation of the People's Republic of China on 1 October 1949 by Mao Zedong ended the civil war between the Chinese Communist Party (CCP) and the Nationalist Party (KMT). Elaborate. (2012)
3. Critically analyze the causes and results of the Chinese Revolution of 1949. (2006)
4. Discuss the circumstances leading to the Chinese Revolution of 1949. (2006)
5. Divided into spheres of influence by foreign powers, China in the 19th century presented a sorry spectacle. How did China react to it? (1995)

B. Transformation of Japan Into a Modern State

1. Introduction

As in the case of China, Japan too resisted Western advances for long. But the response of the Japanese after the failure of their resistance was different from that of the Chinese. Japan opened up its country to Western ideas and institutions. They deliberately copied many aspects of Western civilisation while retaining Japan's spiritual tradition and in the process transformed into an industrialised modern nation. This story of transformation of Japan into a triumphant modern nation constitutes one of the most spectacular annals of modern world history.

In 1853, the US Commodore, **Matthew Perry**, sailed into Tokyo Bay and forced the Japanese to grant concessions to Westerners. His message was clear 'permit to trade in peace or face the consequences in war'. By the **Kanagawa Treaty** of 1854, the United States gained the right to dock at two Japanese ports, though not for trade. **Townsend Harris**, the first American consul-general to Japan, gained further concessions in Japan by signing a commercial treaty with the Shogun in 1858, providing for diplomatic intercourse and opening of eight Japanese ports to American traders. By this Treaty, the United States also secured extra territoriality, that is, Americans who were accused of crimes in Japan could only be tried in foreigners' courts and under foreign laws and not in Japanese courts. That was the beginning of a series of treaties with foreign powers the Shogunate was forced to sign.

> Shoguns were hereditary military dictators of Japan who ruled the country for many centuries under the nominal authority of the emperor. Tokugawa was the last Shogun family to rule Japan from 1603 to 1867. They imposed a conservative feudalistic rule, closed Japan to foreigners and prohibited Japanese from travelling abroad. Daimyos were powerful feudal lords during the Shogunate and Samurais were hereditary warriors and retainers of the Daimyos.

2. Meiji Restoration

The sudden influx of foreign people and money unsettled the Japanese lifestyle. Unhappy with the developments and by the threat of foreign encroachment, the pro-imperial Samurais (the warrior nobles) captured the government and forced Tokugawa Yoshinobu, the last Shogun, to resign in November 1867. They encapsulated their belief in the slogan **'Revere the Emperor, Expel the Barbarians'** and restored the rule of the emperor in January 1868. The young emperor Mutsuhito took the name Meiji or 'enlightened rule', hence the incident is known as the **Meiji Restoration** of 1868 and his reign of 45 years is known as the **Meiji Era**. As an expression of change in power, the capital was shifted from Kyoto to Edo which was renamed as Tokyo. The Restoration was significant as it ended the feudal aristocracy that ruled Japan in emperor's name for almost seven hundred years and re-established the emperor to power. Though the Samurais, especially of south-west Japan, who feared that Meiji restoration would affect their interest, rose in revolt as **'the last gasp of a fast dying feudal society'**, they were suppressed and the old regime thus came to an end.

It also marked the transformation of Japan from a feudal nation into a modern industrial state. By ending the Tokugawa Shogunate it initiated parliamentary system in Japanese politics. The Meiji Revolution unlike the revolutions in the West was of top-down or a **'revolution from above'** and not a middle-class mass movement. It was the aristocrats of the old regime that spearheaded the revolution.

3. Reforms Under Meiji

The period from 1868 to 1912 is known as the Meiji Era. The Meiji Emperor was well awake to the need for reform and modernisation. Extensive reforms introduced by the Meiji, under the motto **'a rich country, a strong military'** transformed Japan into a powerful modern state. This transformation was basically westernisation, as Japanese leaders studied and accepted western institutions and practices to suit the Japanese needs. Diplomatic missions were sent to Europe and the United States and the Japanese adopted good institutions and practices from these countries. They adopted the American system of universal public education, Germany's centralised form of government, Britain's naval tactics and the Western model of industrialisation.

i. Political

In 1871, the emperor abolished the feudal system transforming the peasants into free landowners and daimyo and samurais were pensioned off. All domains were abolished and replaced with prefectures whose governors were appointed by the central government. In 1889, the emperor promulgated a constitution based on the constitution of the Imperial Germany. It provided for a constitutional monarchy, a bi-cameral parliament known as the Diet and Rights and Duties of the subjects. It was an emperor-entered constitutional order. The Emperor was the supreme commander of the armed forces, ministers were responsible to him and he could veto bills passed by parliament. New judicial system and legal codes were also enacted on western lines.

ii. Military

Armed forces too were modelled after the European forces. Universal military service was introduced, the navy was modelled after the British and army on German. By the early 20th century, the modernised army with its more than five lakh trained soldiers emerged strongest military power in Asia. As a clear expression of this transformation, Japan defeated Russia – a powerful European nation, in the Russo-Japanese War in 1904–05.

iii. Economic

The lands surrendered by the feudal lords (daimyos) were redistributed to peasants. As a result the country was restructured into prefectures which allowed the central government to collect land revenue more extensively. A land survey was conducted, fixing an owner to every piece of land and land tax was fixed at 3 per cent of assessed value. It also facilitated land tax collection in currency rather than in forced labour or in the form of products of the land.

Modernisation of the economy was undertaken **under the government leadership** as private capital was insufficient and foreign loans would curtail the economic independence of the country. The government built roads, ports railways, telegraph lines and even manufacturing units and later on transferred to private owners. The government also supported **Zaibatsu** (large business families or monopolies) by measures such as subsidies. Japanese scholars were sent to the West to study modern science and language, while foreign experts were invited to teach in Japan.

Realising that private investors lacked initiative and the knowledge to run modern industries, the government took up the role of setting up them resulting in the emergence of **state-financed model enterprises**. Thus, instead of laissez faire of the British it was the German philosophy of state-led development that fuelled Japan's industrial growth. High portions of national revenue were set aside for importing Western technology and expertise to set up modern industrial units. All these resulted in rapid industrialisation and surplus production.

In 1873, the national **banking system** was established based on the American model and in 1883 a central bank known as the Bank of Japan was established. By the mid-1880s, a uniform national currency the 'yen' was also issued. In 1893, to finance the peasants and manufacturers agricultural and industrial banks were also established.

On the negative side, there took place exploitation of peasants and labour. To the Meiji elite the end justified all the means, hence they also exploited women and child labour and taxed heavily on peasants for Japanese modernisation.

iv. Socio-Cultural

In 1871, the Ministry of Education was formed to oversee the Westernisation of education. A large number of schools – elementary, middle and high – were built and compulsory elementary education was introduced for boys and girls resulting in universal literacy. For higher education, scientific and technical subjects and foreign languages were introduced while retaining Confucian philosophy. Education emphasised principles like individualism, egalitarianism, scientific outlook and other Western concepts.

4. | Japan as an Imperial Power

Side by side, Japan adopted a policy of imperialism. The initial focus of Japanese imperial activity was Korea. In 1876, Japan employed **'gun boat diplomacy'** (the same method pursued by Perry against Japan in 1853) and signed a treaty with Korea securing trade rights and extraterritoriality. The aim of Japanese government was to forge a close political connection with Korea, but it clashed with that of China. This conflict of interests with China over Korea led to the **Sino-Japanese War of 1894–95**. Japan won victory over China and secured Formosa, Liaotung Peninsula and Pescadores Islands apart from the right to construct railway in southern Manchuria. Japan later on had to return Liaotung Peninsula to China under pressure of European powers.

Next imperialist action of Japan was that of sending soldiers to China as part of the multinational force to suppress the Boxer Rebellion. In 1902, **Anglo-Japanese Alliance** was signed by which the British recognised Japan's special interest in Korea.

Though the treaty of 1895 had forced China to recognise Korea as an independent state, the Russians soon emerged as a competing rival of the Japanese positions in Korea who conquered the Liaotung Peninsula in 1898. In 1904, Japan declared war – the **Russo-Japanese War** – to secure its position in Korea and defeated her in 1905. With the victory Japan secured half of Sakhalin Island and economic concessions in Manchuria such as control over the Russian railway lines in southern Manchuria and recognition of Japan's exclusive rights in Korea. After defeating the Russians, Japan extended its control over the Korean government leading to the disbandment of the Korean Army and its **annexation to Japan**.

The World War I was a golden opportunity to Japan to expand its power in Asia. The Anglo-Japanese alliance of 1902 facilitated Japan's entry into the war on the British side. By joining the war, Japan aimed to secure German possessions in the Pacific and in the Shantung Peninsula. At the Paris Peace Conference 'the Powers' conceded to these demands.

In the latter part of the 1920s, discriminatory measures of the Western countries such as the **Oriental Exclusion Law** passed by the US Congress, which placed Asians in the inferior category and the imposition of high tariffs on Japanese goods created psychological and economic impact on the Japanese. A number of rightist organisations too emerged preaching **internal purity** – the revival of unique Japanese spirit – and **external expansion**.

The Great Depression of 1929 had devastating effect on Japan as her foreign trade fell off by one-half. The Japanese economy was in trouble and many people blamed the government for the situation. Making use of the crisis military harnessed support of the people and gained control of the government. Though the military leaders kept **Emperor Hirohito** as the head of the state, policy decisions were taken by the military. They stood for extreme nationalism and intended to solve Japan's economic miseries by establishing a Pacific empire and exploiting the region's resources, markets and people. The following steps were taken for this purpose:

1. Manchurian Invasion of 1931 – Japan invaded Manchuria, the north-eastern province of China with an eye on its rich iron and coal and established a puppet government there.
2. In 1936, to counter the Russian and Western powers in Asia Japan and Germany signed the Anti-Comintern Pact.
3. Japan invaded China in 1937. Important cities including the capital Nanjing as well as Beijing were captured and the invaders slaughtered thousands of Chinese people.
4. In 1940, Japan signed the Tripartite Pact with Germany and Italy to support each other, if the United States enters World War II.
5. Japan also attacked American and European colonies in the Pacific and Southeast Asia. These were French Indochina, Pearl Harbour, Guam, the Wake Island, the Philippines and the British colonies of Hong Kong, Malaya and Singapore. Next, they conquered the Dutch East Indies or Indonesia, British Burma and targeted India. The newly conquered territories brought more than 1 million sq ml land and more than 150 million people under Japanese control.

5. Japan After the World War II

Japan was defeated in World War II, and their country was occupied and their colonial empire was dissolved. Japan was under the US occupation for seven years from 1945 to 1952. Instead of punishing Japan for the War, the US supported Japan's economic recovery and in its socio-political transformation to forge a strong partnership with it. The **Supreme Commander for the Allied Powers** (SCAP) headed by **General Douglas MacArthur** and mainly staffed by Americans implemented far reaching reforms in Japan.

- **Demilitarisation** – Japan was deprived of its armed forces and was permitted to keep only a small police force. The American occupiers on their belief that non-militaristic Japan required larger reforms than just disbanding the army sought to smash authoritarian political structure, granted right to freedom of speech, press, assembly and religion.
- **Democratisation** – Real power was handed over to the people and abolition of traditional strongholds of power was the core of this reform.
- A **new constitution** was drawn up (May 1947) with a constitutional monarchy, universal adult franchise, two house parliament known as the Diet and a prime ministerial government. The Emperor was deprived of his divine status but was retained as 'symbol of the state and of the unity of the people' and Japan came to be called as '**imperial democracy**'.
- Article 9 of the new constitution renounced war 'as a sovereign right of the nation and the threat or use of force as means of settling international disputes'.
- Lands of big landlords were redistributed and trade unions were permitted to function. The Constitutional guarantee of the right to work and bargain collectively led to the emergence of

powerful labour movements whose membership touched five million by 1947.

- Educational system was divested of its militaristic, extreme nationalistic and indoctrinating features and was replaced by teachings of peace and democracy.
- Once the Cold War set in Europe, the Americans were strongly committed to promote economic recovery of Japan to develop it as 'Asia's bulwark against communism'. This also coincided with the Korean War which brought immense military orders to Japanese industries from the United States.

6. | Post-Occupation Japan

In September 1951, 49 nations signed a treaty, the **Treaty of San Francisco,** to end the state of war still existed with Japan. In April 1952, the United States ended its occupation and Japan regained its sovereignty.

Though the United States ended its occupation of Japan, it retained the right to station her troops in Japan by signing a pact with her. Okinawa Island was also retained under the US control. Though officially claimed that these forces were to protect Japan from attack, the American bases continued to be a bone of contention as the local people detested violence and rape committed by off-duty American soldiers. It was also argued that Japan would again be a target of nuclear war if the USSR decides to attack these bases.

The two decades from 1950 were a period of '**high speed growth**' and Japan recovered from the destruction and poverty to prosperity at a stunning pace. During this period Japan's GNP grew at an average rate of more than 10 per cent annually and its capital formations averaged 22 per cent per year during the same period which came to be called as '**economic miracle**'. Global economic recovery and the general growth in the post-war years, high quality of trained human capital, a more open international trade environment under General Agreement on Trade and Tariffs (GATT), tax concessions and low-interest loans by the government to firms in sectors designated for growth, cheap energy supply from the Middle East and the Korean War were important factors in Japan's economic miracle. Japan's transformation into a high-technology industrial house and urban society was also characterised by the diversification of its markets and sources of raw materials and integration of its economy into the global system transforming it to the position of a leading industrial country in the world.

SUMMARY

Transformation of Japan into a Modern State – The Meiji Restoration by which the emperor was restored to power in 1868 was a turning point in Japan's modern history. Under the Meiji large number of reforms in politics, military, economy and in socio-cultural fields were initiated transforming Japan into a modern state and also an imperial power. Military leaders of Japan stood for establishing a Japanese Empire in the pacific and took many measures such as invasion of Manchuria (1931), signing of the Anti-Comintern Pact with Germany (1936), invasion of China (1937), signing of the Tripartite Treaty with Germany and Italy (1940) and attacking and capturing of the American and European colonies in the Pacific and in South-East Asia. After being defeated in the World War II Japan was under the occupation of the United States for seven years. In 1952, the United States ended its occupation and within two decades Japan recovered from the destructions of the war and emerged a leading industrial nation of the world.

Questions of Previous Years Civil Services Examination

1. 'The Russo-Japanese War helped in the rise of Japan as a global power'. Explain. (2014)
2. 'The years 1853–94 witnessed the transformation of Japan'. Explain. (1998)

C. The Middle East

1. Introduction

The Middle East is the region around the southern and eastern shores of the Mediterranean Sea, corresponding to western Asia and north-eastern Africa. Countries in this region are Iran, Iraq, Kuwait, Saudi Arabia, Yemen, the United Arab Emirates, Oman, Bahrain, Qatar, Egypt, Sudan, Jordan, Syria, Lebanon, Turkey, Palestine territories and Israel. Of these, Iran and Turkey are non–Arab states while Israel is a Jew state. Turks, Persians and Kurds are other major ethnic groups in the region other than the Arabs. The countries in the Middle East except Israel are Muslim majority states (Iran, Iraq and Bahrain mainly Shia and others mainly Sunni) and in many of these states the legal system is based on Islamic law. Most of these regions were part of the Ottoman Empire and with its decline aspired to become independent and modern. To meet these goals, they had to overcome illiteracy, corruption, ignorance, vested interests and foreign interventions.

> The Middle East is an intersection of Asia, Africa and Europe, while the West Asia though significantly overlaps with the Middle East is the Western part of the Asian continent.

During the First World War, three important developments took place that became crucial to the Middle East history. First, in 1916, the British government instigated Arab leaders to rise against the Ottoman Empire, an ally of Germany, in return for **British support for independent Arab states** to be carved out of Ottoman's Arab provinces including the Palestine. The Arabs supported the Allies in the World War I and hoped for independence. Second, in 1917, Lord Arthur Balfour, the British Foreign Minister in his **'Balfour Declaration'** supported establishment of 'a Jewish national home in Palestine'. Lastly, Britain and France entered into a secret deal – the **Sykes-Picot Agreement** – to divide among themselves the Arab territories of the Ottoman Empire. After the War, the territories taken from Turkey were designated as Mandates of the League of Nations – Palestine and Transjordan under the British and Syria and Lebanon under France.

In the 20th century, the Middle-East witnessed prosperity due to the oil industry. In the 1920s and 1930s, enormous oil deposits were discovered by American and European companies in the region around the Persian Gulf. Subsequently, the European powers tried to dominate the region to protect their energy sources. Though the oil resources brought in material prosperity, it did not bring peace to the region as conflict soon emerged between traditional Islam and Western materialism.

> Arabs are an ethnic group found mainly in the Middle East. Arabic language and Islam religion are the common bond among the Arabs (though half of the Arab population of Lebanon are followers of Christianity). Beyond the Middle East, Arabs live in the African countries of Morocco, Algeria, Tunisia and Libya.

2. Why the Middle East is Important?

1. **Geopolitics – Strategic location**: It is the crossroads between continents and connects the Western nations and Russia with Asia and Africa

2. **Geo-economics – Oil wealth**: Many countries in the region such as Iran, Saudi Arabia, Iraq and Kuwait are rich in oil, approximating about two-thirds of the oil reserves of the world.
3. The **Suez Canal** connecting the Mediterranean Sea and the Red Sea is one of the busiest waterways in the world and the shortest maritime route from Europe to Asia.
4. It is the **birthplace of three religions** – Judaism, Christianity and Islam.
5. In the **context of the Cold War**, the Middle East was also one of the regions favoured by the superpowers for establishing their ideological hegemony.

3. Arab Nationalism and the Pan-Arab Movement

The Middle East witnessed the emergence of **Arab Nationalism** by the end of the 19th century. The Arab nationalists espoused the glories of Arab civilisation and considered the Arabs as a single nation bound together by common historical, cultural, linguistic and religious heritage. The Arab nationalists stood for politico-economic cooperation among the Arab nations. They also aimed at ending the Western influence in the region and removal of pro-Western rulers in Arab states on their perception that the Western states to be pro-Israel.

Pan-Arabism stands for bringing the Arab countries of North Africa and West Asia into a single unit known as the Arab world. It became dominant in the 1950s and 1960s and was an expression of strengthening of the Arab nationalism. The following were the major contours of this Arab resurgence:

1. The **Arab League** was founded in 1945, in Cairo. It was the first effort to coordinate the political, economic and socio-cultural programmes of the Arab member states and to safeguard their independence. But internal squabbles on issues such as the 1979 Egypt–Israel peace treaty after which Egypt was expelled from its membership and the US intervention in the Gulf War at the request of Saudi Arabia caused a deep rift in the League.
2. The **Baath Party** founded in Syria in 1947 with its motto 'Unity, Liberty and Socialism' and having its branches in other Arab countries were another expression of pan-Arabism. It gave emphasis on **Arab Socialism** with its twin objectives of political independence and economic development. It stood for establishing social justice in the Arab societies and to free the Arab world from Western control. It rejected Marxism and class struggle and gave emphasis on cooperation between classes to ensure equal distribution of wealth along with governmental measures for the underprivileged.
3. **Gamal Abdel Nasser** and his leadership role. Though primarily an Egyptian nationalist, Nasser desired greater inter-Arab cooperation to free the Arab world from western domination. The Suez Crisis of 1956 was the heyday of pan-Arabism. Though the outcome of the war was a military setback to Nasser, the failure of the western powers to overthrow Nasser boosted the Arab morale and Nasser became the natural focus of pan-Arabist hopes.
4. The **United Arab Republic** (UAR) was established in 1958 by Egypt and Syria. But domination by Nasser led to the secession of Syria from the UAR and its end in 1961.
5. Creation of the **Federation of Arab Republics**, a loose confederation of Libya, Egypt and Syria. Founded under the initiative of Libyan ruler Muammar Gaddafi in 1972, it envisaged formation of Arab states stretching across North Africa and the Middle East. But differences emerged and it came to an end in 1977.
6. Constant **struggle against Zionism** and opposition against imperialism were two important features of the Arab nationalist foreign policy.
7. At the same time the Arab unity had its drawbacks. The **lack of unity of aims and cooperation** were important factors in the Arabs' failure in the war against Israel in 1948. This was evident when the Arab governments pursued their agendas and captured territories in Palestine – Jordan captured the West Bank and Egypt annexed the Gaza Strip during this war.
8. The humiliating **defeat of the Arab powers by Israel in 1967** was another defining moment in Arab unity. It further exposed the Arab governments' inability to integrate or cooperate in their fight against Israel and pan-Arabism began to be overshadowed by political Islam.

9. Pan-Arabism as a movement for the renaissance of the Arab golden age came to be depicted as the **revival of the Islamic Empire** by the Islamist movements in the 1970s. This idea of **pan-Islamism** was based on religion and not by a secular form of ideology. This rival trans-national ideology of Islamism viewed Arab nationalism as Western inspired concept to undercut the Muslim unity. This resurrection of religious conservatism in Arab societies caused the decline of alternative streams such as pan-Arabism.
10. End of overt Western imperialist domination in the region and the growing acceptance of **the reality of Israel** had also removed much of the rationale for inter-Arab solidarity.
11. Since 1970s many Arab state leaders such as Anwar Sadat and Hosni Mubarak of Egypt, Hafiz al-Assad of Syria and **Saddam Hussein** of Iraq pursued policies promoting their states' interest rather than that of Arab unity.
12. Factors like **sectarian differences** such as Sunni–Shia divide and social differences between the two Levantine countries – Lebanon and Syria – which are comparatively secular and the religious Saudi Arabia too fuelled the decline of pan-Arabism.

Though the idea of Arab political unity was corroded by the mid-1970s, the unity sense of the Arab people who are bound by a common culture, facing similar problems and having shared aspirations, has penetrated deep into Arab consciousness in great measures. This was facilitated by the spread of the Internet and mass media as was evident during the **'Arab Spring'**.

4. Turkey and Modernisation

As seen already in another chapter, the end of the World War I had resulted in the breakup of the Ottoman Turkish Empire. Defeat in the war and the secret wartime agreements between the British and the French to parcel out the Ottoman territories amongst themselves had sealed the fate of the Ottoman Empire. It was now threatened by the Greeks who invaded it and the Allies occupied Istanbul and Izmir. Against the occupation and the partition plan in the **Treaty of Sevres**, the Turkish revolutionaries rose in rebellion giving birth to the **Turkish War of Independence** that lasted from 1919 to 1923.

The resistance was organised under Mustafa Kemal and was aimed at ending the foreign occupation of the Turkish speaking areas. Kemal's forces defeated the Greeks, and in 1922 they marched on **Istanbul**, the capital of the Ottoman Empire and deposed the Sultan. Now the Allies signed a new treaty with Turkey – the **Treaty of Lausanne** in July 1923, by which Turkey could retain all lands they conquered and the Allies left Anatolia and Eastern Thrace. But Turkey lost territories such as Syria, Palestine, Mesopotamia and Arabia. In October 1923, Kemal declared the establishment of '**Republic of Turkey**' with its capital at **Ankara**. He introduced reforms to transform Turkey into a modern secular nation. Kemal's reforms were based on his belief or **'Kemalism'**, that Turkey needs to be Westernised both politically and culturally to modernise. With this aim he:

1. Segregated Islamic laws from the laws of the nation.
2. Abolished religious courts and the Caliphate.
3. Established a new legal system of modern civil codes on the European model.
4. Established a national system of public education, and children between six and sixteen were made to attend.
5. Replaced Arabic script with Roman script as medium of expression of the Turkish language and knowledge of the new writing was made mandatory to hold public offices. This change was made as Kemal believed that Arabic was insufficient to express Western ideas.
6. Ban on alcohol was lifted, Sunday was declared as a weekly holiday instead of Friday, and the Islamic calendar was replaced with Gregorian calendar.
7. Women were empowered – schools were established for girls, they were given the right to vote and to hold public offices.
8. Fez was abolished and he encouraged Western dressing for all and exhorted women to discard veil.
9. As a part of economic reforms, he started model farms, agricultural colleges and banks for agricultural credit. He built a large railway network and established state enterprises to produce goods such as munitions, salt, sugar, alcohol and tobacco.

> Mustafa Kemal or Ataturk, the 'Father of the Turks', was an officer in the Ottoman Army. Though played a minor role in the Young Turk Revolution in 1909, Kemal emerged prominent in the post-World War I period. He became the founder of the Republic of Turkey and its first President from 1922 until his death in 1938. His reform programmes were known as Kemalism, six concepts enumerated as republicanism, nationalism, populism, reformism, statism and secularism. Though an elected president, Kemal was a dictator, nevertheless a benevolent one, who kept a strong hold on his country's affairs and permitted no opposition parties.

Turkey, though it remained neutral during most of World War II, joined the Allied side at the end of the war in February 1945. After the war, the Soviet expansionist designs prompted Turkey to seek military and economic assistance from the United States. It also joined both **NATO** and the **CENTO**. During all these periods Turkey continued on democratic path till 1960 when the military captured power after a coup. The period subsequent to it witnessed the emergence of political and religious extremism leading to instability and further military interventions in 1971 and 1980.

Since the year 2002, with the victory of conservative Islamic party, the **Justice and Development Party** (AKP) in parliamentary elections, the Turkish constitutional secular principles are under challenge. Measures such as higher taxes on alcohol and lifting of the ban on religious and conservative dresses in public institutions are some of the causes of confrontation between the secularist opposition and the AKP.

5. Egypt and Arab Resurgence

Egypt, a province of the Ottoman Empire, was a dependency of Britain since 1882. After the World War I, Egyptian nationalism emerged and was found expressed in 'Wafd' (meaning delegation) movement. It was led by **Saad Zaghloul** and stood for the country's independence. The British tried to suppress Egyptian nationalism by exiling Saad Zaghloul to Malta but people en masse rose in revolt forcing the British to grant independence to Egypt in February 1922.

Though the British abolished their protectorate, the new **Kingdom of Egypt** remained a puppet regime of the British as it had to meet certain conditions set by the British. It included the British protectorate of the Suez Canal (as more than half of the shares of the canal were owned by the British and French) and provisions for the protection of minorities and foreigners in Egypt. In 1936, by signing another treaty – the **Anglo-Egyptian Treaty of Friendship and Alliance**, the British withdrew all its troops from Egypt except in the Suez Canal but continued to supply and train Egypt's army and offered to defend it in case of war. In this way the British could maintain varying degrees of political control and military presence in Egypt till 1952.

In July 1952, military conspirators led by **General Muhammad Naguib** and **Colonel Gamal Abdel Nasser** instituted a coup and toppled the monarchy of King Farouk, which they considered pro-British and corrupt. The **Republic of Egypt** was now established and General Naguib (1953–54) and Colonel Nasser served its first and second presidents (1956–70). As per the 1954 Anglo-Egyptian Agreement the British withdrew its forces from all Egyptian territory by June 1956.

In the decades following the coup, industrialisation programmes were implemented and a period of infrastructural building and urbanisation was inaugurated. Nationalisation of the Suez Canal, construction of the Aswan High Dam and the Helwan Steel Works were some of the achievements of Nasser. As a follower of **Arab Socialism,** Nasser took the state as the vehicle for transformations and turned Egypt into a centrally planned economy. Agrarian reforms, such as limits on land ownership and desert reclamation, were introduced, many sectors of economy were nationalised and expanded social, health and educational services were provided. But Egypt under Nasser did not have civil liberties and political freedom. In all three elections (1956, 1958 and 1965) that he contested, Nasser was the sole contestant.

Nasser was succeeded by **Anwar Sadat**, one of his close associates, in 1970. He reversed many of the policies of Nasser and initiated a new era especially in foreign relations.

1. Agreements were signed in 1974 and 1975 providing for mutual disengagement by Israel and Egypt in the Suez Canal region and return of Sinai oilfields to Egypt by Israel.

2. In 1975, the Suez Canal which had been closed in 1967 was opened for merchant ships of all countries including Israel.
3. In 1977, he visited Israel, the first Arab leader to do so. He addressed the Israeli parliament Knesset, and emphasised Israel's right to exist but called for the creation of an independent Palestine and for Israeli withdrawal from all occupied territories.
4. In 1978, Sadat signed the Camp David Accord.
5. In 1979, Egyptian-Israel Peace Treaty was signed.
6. He broke away from the Soviet alliance and became an ally of the United States.
7. Sadat also introduced greater political freedom by reinstituting a multiparty system and a new economic policy known as 'Infitah' or 'open door' by which private investment was encouraged and government controls were relaxed.

At the same time, Anwar Sadat tried to transform Egypt from a secular nation to an Islamic state. Measures such as declaring Islam as the state religion and making Sharia (Islamic law) as the principal source of legislative rules created division in society as non-Muslims were now designated as 'protected people' and were subjected to persecution. He also loosened control on Islamist groups such as the Muslim Brotherhood, which had been kept under suppression by Nasser.

The Camp David Accords (1978). This was signed by Anwar Sadat and the then Israeli Prime Minister Menachem Begin in 1978 under the mediation of the US President Jimmy Carter in Camp David, a retreat for the US president near Washington D.C. The Accords ended the long hostility between Israel and Egypt. On its part, Egypt recognised Israel and opened the Suez Canal to Israeli ships, while Israel agreed to return Sinai to Egypt, agreed to begin the withdrawal of its forces from the West Bank and to begin the process of granting autonomy to Palestinians in the West Bank and the Gaza Strip within five years.

Though warm relations with Israel brought the US friendship to Egypt, it resulted in Egypt's isolation in the Arab and Islamic international fraternity. The PLO and the Arab League rejected the Accords and the latter expelled Egypt from the Arab League. The PLO, 16 Arab states and Iran ended their diplomatic relation with Egypt. It also led to Sadat's assassination in October 1981 by Islamic fundamentalists. Hosni Mubarak succeeded Anwar Sadat in 1981 and continued in power till 2011, the year in which he was forced out during the **Arab Spring**.

Arab Spring refers to a series of pro-democracy uprisings in the Middle East and North Africa in 2011. The Revolution challenged the entrenched authoritarian regimes in these regions started in Tunisia and Egypt in January 2011. In both these countries the old regimes were toppled peacefully and new governments came to power. But when it spread to Yemen, Bahrain, Libya and Syria in the subsequent months they turned into protracted fight between revolutionaries and ruling regimes. The Arab Spring also found reflected in the forms of constitutional changes and political reforms in other countries such as Algeria, Jordan, Morocco and Oman.

6. | Iran and the Islamic Revolution

Iran was known as Persia. In 1925, Reza Khan with the title Reza Pahlavi became the ruler of Persia and changed the Greek name Persia to a traditional name **Iran** or **the land of the Aryans**. During the World War II, the Anglo-Soviet forces invaded Iran to secure the Allied supply line and prevent its takeover by Germany. They also replaced Reza Khan, who was suspected to be a Nazi sympathiser, by his son **Mohammad Reza Pahlavi** as the new Shah (ruler) of Iran.

With the origin of the Cold War, Soviet Russia tried to set up a communist government in the northern part of Iran bordering the USSR upon which the Shah signed a defence treaty with the United States in 1950. In 1951, though the Iranian Premier **Muhammad Mussadiq** nationalised Iran's petroleum industry, he was overthrown in 1953, by the CIA in a covert operation. This was the first instance of America overthrowing a foreign government during the Cold War. Subsequently, American companies secured 40 percent of Iran's petroleum industries and Shah Mohammed Reza Pahlavi became a close Cold War ally of America in the Middle East.

During nearly four decades of his rule, Reza Pahlavi supported Western institutions and industries in Iran. With his country's oil wealth, Western investment and the support of US weapons he attempted to transform Iran into a modern nation and as the strongest military power in the Persian Gulf region. In 1963, the Shah launched his **'White Revolution'** aimed at transforming Iran into a global power by implementing a series of economic and socio-political reforms. Infrastructural development, agrarian reform, promotion of literacy and emancipation of women were the main aspects of the reform. He built railways, roads, public schools and extended the rights of women such as their right to vote. Tehran, the capital of Iran, became a modernised city.

But Pahlavi's rule was autocratic and brutal. He did not permit political opposition and employed terror and torture by his secret police known as **SAVAK** to suppress any opposition to his rule. Islamic leaders were critical of his reforms as they saw it as westernisation. Iranian nationalists too opposed it. Another anti-Western force in Iran was conservative Shiite Muslims and their leader **Ayatollah Ruholla Khomeini** who was living in Iraq and later in Paris after being exiled in 1964. In the 1970s, discontent grew and demonstrations broke out in the major cities of Iran. Ayatollah Khomeini, though in exile, spurred the people by his tape recorded speeches. In January 1979, the Shah fled the country and his regime collapsed. Ayatollah Khomeini returned to Tehran on February 1, and began an anti-Western authoritarian theocratic state under the Guardianship of the Islamic Jurists.

> Ayatollah Ruhollah Khomeini was a Shia Muslim leader and the leader of the Iranian Revolution of 1979. He became the Supreme Leader, the highest ranking political and religious authority, as per the new constitution of the Islamic Republic of Iran. He rejected both capitalism and communism and gave the slogan 'Neither East or West – but Islamic Republic'. He regarded the United States as 'Great Satan' and the Soviet Union as 'Lesser Satan'. A follower of puritanical Islam, Khomeini decried all Western influences and wanted to build his nation on the simple teachings of Islam and also his country's return from westernisation and modernisation.

Many reasons were attributed to the Islamic Revolution in Iran. Conservative reaction was an important factor. The Islamic religious leaders known as the mullahs were opposed to Pahlavi's rule as they had lost their influence and viewed his secularisation measures as anti-Islam. Corruption, extravagance and the oppressive nature of Shah's rule had alienated Intellectuals from the regime. Many also saw him as a dictator installed by non-Muslim Western powers. Rising unemployment and inflation which touched 50 per cent in the 1970s too were factors that caused discontent. Outlets for political participation were minimal and protests were often met with suppression, detention and torture. Discontent developed into street demonstrations, strikes in the oil fields and student demonstrations in universities and transformed into revolution.

i. Iranian Revolution 1979

The overthrow of the absolute monarchy of Reza Pahlavi was known as the **Iranian Revolution or Islamic Revolution**. Iran was declared an Islamic republic with a theocratic constitution. The new regime which was based on **populism, nationalism** and **Islam** nationalised much of industries, Islamized education and laws, prohibited Western practices and replaced a thriving capitalist economy with Islamic economic practices. Under the new system the Supreme Leader was the highest authority for supervising the policies, Commander-in-Chief of the armed forces, sole authority to declare war and peace and appointing authority of the highest officials. Next to the Supreme Leader, the President elected by universal franchise was the head of the executive, except on matters retained by the Supreme Leader.

The Iranian Revolution was followed by **Cultural Revolution** in 1980, found expressed in the purging of Western and non-Islamic influences from academics and university campuses. As a part of political vengeance, officials associated with the Shah regime were executed. Domestic opposition was suppressed, Western music and alcohol were banned and punishments prescribed by Islamic law were meted out. In foreign policy, Iran now started an unrelenting hostility towards both the superpowers and engaged in exporting Iran's brand of Islamic revivalism to other Muslim countries. Thus, the Iranian Revolution marked a fundamental transition in Iran's political structure, legal system, socio-cultural-economic life and in foreign policy.

Compared to any other revolution, the Iranian Revolution was different. It took place in a country that was undergoing changes and enjoying relative prosperity on account of its oil resources. The Revolution was also relatively non-violent though violence and chaos took place in post-revolutionary period.

Islamic Revolution in Iran had significant repercussions beyond Iran. It strengthened Islamic forces and their opposition to Western influences. Some of its expressions were the capture of the US Embassy in Tehran by radical Muslim students in 1979, assassination of Egyptian President Sadat in 1981, bombing of the American embassy in Lebanon in 1983 and issuance of fatwa by Khomeini in 1989 against the British citizen Salman Rushdie for writing the book *The Satanic Verses* alleging it as blasphemous.

ii. The Iran-Iraq War (1980–88)

In 1980, the Iraqi ruler Saddam Hussein invaded Iran. Ayatollah Khomeini's exhortation for Islamic revolutions across the Muslim world was seen as a threat by Saddam Hussein. **Pan-Islamism** preached by Iran was perceived as an existential threat to Bath Party of Iraq and Arab Nationalism it stood for. This was more so as Iraq was a neighbouring country of Iran with Shia majority population. Saddam also wanted to take advantage of post-Revolutionary chaos in Iran and its unpopularity and isolation from the Western world. He also intended to obtain Iran's oil resources. There was also a long history of border disputes between the two nations. The war lasted from 1980 to 1988. Though Iraqi forces had early successes and could advance into Iran, by 1982, they were pushed out of Iran and in the subsequent offensive the Iranian forces entered Iraq. The War ended in 1988, with Iranian forces being defeated and Khomeini accepting a UN brokered truce.

7. Iraq and the Gulf Wars

Iraq, the '**cradle of civilisation**' of antiquity emerged as an independent state in 1932, when the British which held the mandate over the region gave independence to it. Even after independence the King Faisal, ruler of Iraq maintained friendly relation with the British and became a member of the **Bagdad Pact**. Set up in 1955, the Bagdad Pact provided for joint defence and economic policies and aimed at preventing Soviet infiltration into the Middle East.

Iraq's experiment with constitutional monarchy came to a brutal end when King Faisal was killed by an army faction in 1958. The incident took place in the wake of British humiliation in the 1956 Suez Crisis and strong Arab opposition to Faisal's pro-British policies. Iraq was declared a republic and it withdrew from the Bagdad Pact which effectively ended the British influence in the Middle East.

Though a republic since 1958, Iraq was ruled by a series of dictators since then and the last was Saddam Hussein. Saddam Hussein, a member of the **Baathists, a pan-Arab socialist movement**, emerged president of Iraq in 1979. During his despotic rule spanning almost a quarter of a century he dragged his oil-rich nation to poverty, waged war against Iran and killed thousands of Iraqis including the Kurds who were killed by chemical weapons. His desire for regional hegemony and the pursuit of Weapons of Mass Destruction (WMD) caused a collision with the Western powers and to the Gulf Wars.

i. The First Gulf War of 1990

On 2 August 1990, Saddam Hussein attacked and annexed Kuwait, as his '19th province'. This invasion triggered an international crisis known as the First Gulf War or the Persian Gulf War that lasted from August 1990 to February 1991.

a. Reasons

- Saddam wanted to gain hegemony in the region.
- He faced a financial crisis on account of the recently concluded war with Iran.
- Saddam wanted to acquire Kuwait's oil reserves.
- Saddam Hussein considered Kuwait as an artificial state carved out by Western powers out of the Iraqi coast.
- He accused Kuwait, of syphoning crude oil from the oil fields located on their common border by horizontally drilling into Iraq's territory.

- Saddam was infuriated by the fact that many gulf countries including Kuwait was exceeding their oil-production quotas set by the OPEC leading to drop in oil prices costing Iraq a huge income.
- He also wanted to cancel a massive debt Iraq owed to Kuwait.
- He expected support from the Arab nations.

b. ***Response***

- Arab League condemned the aggression.
- Kuwait and Saudi Arabia sought support from the United States.
- As NATO sent its troops, Saddam declared the war as 'jihad' or holy war to garner the support of the Muslim world. With the same aim he offered to evacuate from Kuwait if Israel withdrew from the occupied territories.
- UN called for Iraq to withdraw from Kuwait, imposed a trade embargo and the UN Security Council sanctioned the use of force if Saddam failed to withdraw from Kuwait by 15 January 1991.
- The US considered the invasion a blatant aggression and threat to their interest. The United States was apprehensive of an oil crisis if Saddam succeeded in gaining control over Kuwait and Saudi Arabia which had 20 per cent of the world's oil reserves.
- Above all, if Saddam succeeded in annexing Kuwait, it would cause a great geopolitical threat as Iraq's army of one million and possessing American weapons (the United States had supplied weapons to Iraq during the Iran-Iraq War) would cause a threat to regions stability.

The international response against Saddam Hussein's invasion evolved into **Operation Desert Storm**. It started with the US-led massive air raids with **smart bombs** – bombs that could find their target with pinpoint accuracy – on Iraq's air defences, oil fields and communication lines. It was aimed at winning the war in the air and to reduce the combat on the ground to a minimum level. It was followed by a massive ground offensive in Kuwait. Though Iraq launched missiles against Saudi Arabia and Israel, it did not affect the course of the war and within three days Iraqi forces were defeated and Kuwait city was retaken. On 28 February 1991, the United States declared ceasefire.

By the peace treaty, Saddam agreed to recognise Kuwait as a sovereign state and to destroy his **Weapons of Mass Destruction** (WMD). Iraq was required to submit to inspections for weapons of mass destruction. Economic sanctions were to continue till compliance and **UNSCOM** (UN Special Commission) was appointed to inspect and verify Iraq's compliance.

Operation Desert Fox in 1998 was resumption of brief hostility with Iraq. The United States and Britain conducted raids on government and military targets in Iraq suspected of being associated with WMD.

ii. The Second Gulf War of 2003

The war again erupted in the Gulf region in 2003. Known as the Second Gulf War or the Iraq War, this conflict was precipitated by the following developments.

- After the **9/11** terror attacks on the United States on 11 September 2001, the US administration took a strong stance against international terrorism and complete disarming of Iraq was seen by the US administration as a renewed priority.
- The US President George Bush made his '**Axis of Evil**' speech in January 2002, in which he described Iraq, Iran and North Korea constituting 'an axis of evil, arming to threaten the peace of the world' and sought to rally American people in support of his War on Terror.
- The **US intelligence** claimed that Iraq was building WMD, though there was no concrete evidence to prove this claim or to link Hussein with terrorists.
- The American administration also formed the '**Bush Doctrine**' which emphasised 'unilateralism' and 'pre-emption'. It was claimed that America was 'threatened less by conquering states than are by falling ones'. Further, it was argued that the United States had the right to secure itself by resorting to unilateral pre-emptive strike to destroy 'the threat before it reaches the US borders'.
- The UN Security Council passed the **Resolution 1441** on November 2002 asking Iraq to

permit inspection and comply with all previous resolutions.

As Saddam refused permission to the UN inspectors, the United States and Britain issued an ultimatum to Saddam on 17 March 2003, to abdicate and leave the country within 48 hours. On his refusal, forces of these nations and supported by some other nations – 'the coalition of the willing' invaded Iraq – **'Operation Iraqi Freedom'** – on March 20. The Bush administration claimed that the operation was 'to disarm Iraq, to free its people and to defend the world from grave danger'. As one of the objectives of the invasion was **'regime change'**, Saddam Hussein was captured in December 2003 and was executed in December 2006, after being convicted by a court.

Following the collapse of Saddam regime, Iraq was occupied by the coalition forces, while Iraq itself was immersed in sectarian violence between Shias and Sunnis. It also inaugurated a long-lasting insurgency against the coalition forces by a diverse mix of militias which included not only Arab and Iraqi nationalist groups but also foreign Islamist volunteers linked to al-Qaeda, for whom Iraq was a 'new field of Jihad' in the battle against the US forces. In December 2011, the United States declared an end to the Iraq War.

Unlike the Persian Gulf War there was strong public opinion in the United States, in Europe and the Middle East against the invasion on Iraq and the subsequent occupation. Anti-war protests took place in America, the long standing US allies such as France and Canada were opposed to it, and for the majority of people in the Middle East the invasion and occupation of Iraq was a new brand of anti-Arab imperialism by the Western forces. The invasion also lacked the UN mandate.

8. The Israel–Palestine Conflict

On the eastern coast of the Mediterranean Sea, Palestine is close to the hearts of Jews, Christians and the Muslims. The connection of Jews with this land traces back to 3,000 years during which Jewish kings had ruled the area from Jerusalem. But the Jews were expelled from the region by the 1st century AD. The Christian claim to the land is based on the fact that they lived in the region after the ouster of Jews. The Arabs conquered the area in the 7th century A.D. Palestine now comprises three regions – Israel, the West Bank and the Gaza Strip – and Zionism and Arab nationalism have conflicting claims over this historical homeland.

> Jerusalem is one of the oldest cities in the world. It was a humble village on a hilltop and emerged as a Holy City in historical times. In 1000 BC, King David had conquered it, renamed it as The City of David and made it his capital. In 960 BC, David's son Solomon built the first Jewish temple here. In 335 A.D., the Roman Emperor Constantine built the Church of the Holy Sepulcher or the Church of Resurrection. In 691, a Muslim shrine known as Haram al Sharif or the Dome of the Rock was built here. The walled area of less than one square km within Jerusalem is known as the Old City and is home to important monuments of many religions – the Temple Mount and Western Wall or the Wailing Wall for Jews, the Church of the Holy Sepulcher for Christians and the Dome of the Rock and al-Aqsa Mosque (the third holiest site in Islam after Mecca and Medina) for Muslims. The Old City is one of the World Heritage Sites of UNESCO. Israel looks for complete and united Jerusalem as its capital, while Palestinians want East Jerusalem as the capital of a future Palestine state.

From the 16th century, this region was part of the Ottoman Turks. By the 19th century, the Jews scattered in different parts of the world desired to have their national homeland here. After the defeat of the Ottomans in World War I, Palestine had been placed under Britain as **Mandate of the League of Nations**. At that time its population consisted 70 per cent Arab and 30 per cent Jew and Christian. There was huge immigration of Jews from different parts of the world to Palestine and as a result Jewish population rose from 58,000 in 1919 to 9,60,000 by 1934. The immigration was intensified after the Nazis started persecution of the Jews which prompted Britain to relax conditions of immigration into Palestine. Soon conflicts emerged between the Jews and the Arabs. Apart from religious differences, what irritated the Palestine, Arab hostility against the Jews was economic. Jews were more prosperous, well-educated and their purchases of land caused the displacement of Arab cultivators and unemployment. This coupled with a mass exodus from Nazi Germany was perceived as a threat by the Arabs leading to violence, guerrilla attacks and terrorism in the 1930s.

Major factors behind the Arab-Israel conflict are deep religious divide, nationalism and issue of control over holy places. Arabs also consider Israel as an outpost of imperialism in their region.

In April 1947, Britain announced their intention to end the Mandate in Palestine and referred the matter to the UN. The UN General Assembly now voted for creating two states – one for the Jews and the other for the Arabs – by partitioning Palestine. On 14 May 1948 the British ended their mandate and the Jews declared the establishment of an independent state of Israel. Soon war broke out between the new state of Israel and its Arab neighbour states – the six Islamic countries of **Egypt, Iraq, Jordan, Lebanon, Syria and Saudi Arabia** invaded Israel. The war caused exodus of Palestinians from the area controlled by the Jews, while the state envisaged by the UN for the Palestine Arabs never came into being. Since then this land has seen relentless terror and counter terror transforming it into one of the most troubled parts of the world. Though many efforts were made to find a solution, 'absence of meaningful peace' still eludes the region.

Diaspora and Zionism. The globally dispersed community of the Jews after their expulsion from Palestine is known as the Diaspora. The movement to establish a Jewish national homeland in Palestine, where a Jew kingdom had existed in ancient times, is known as Zionism. It emerged in the late 19th century and proclaimed the Jews scattered over the world as a nation.

i. Arab-Israel Wars

Five major wars and numerous local conflicts took place between the Arabs and Israel. In these wars Israel was supported by the United States and the Arab states got the Soviet support.

a. The First Arab-Israeli War (1948–49)

Six neighbouring Arab states of Israel – Egypt, Iraq, Saudi Arabia (its forces fought under Egyptian command), Syria, Lebanon and Jordan – invaded Israel to destroy the new state. Israel defeated the enemy, captured more than half of Palestine territory forcing more than 6,00,000 Palestinians to flee to the neighbouring Arab countries such as Jordan, Lebanon and Egypt. The Arab states too captured Palestine territories – Gaza Strip by Egypt and West Bank by Jordan. It also caused exodus of Jews from Arab countries into Israel.

b. The Suez War of 1956

Colonel Gamal Abdel Nasser of Egypt was a staunch pan-Arab nationalist, hostile to Israel and stood for liberating Palestine from the Jews. Nasser signed an arms deal with Czechoslovakia, an ally of the Soviets which was viewed by the Capitalist bloc as Egypt's shift towards the Soviet bloc. In July 1956, Nasser nationalised the Suez Canal, which was largely owned by the British and French firms, triggering a crisis known as the **Suez Crisis**. As the United States and Britain had withdrawn their offers of loan, Nasser argued that revenue from the Canal was essential to build the proposed **Aswan Dam** on the River Nile. Egypt also closed the canal to Israeli shipping and blockaded the Gulf of Aqaba connecting to the Israeli port of Eilat.

The Suez Crisis soon became a part of the Cold War as the Soviet Union with an aim to increase their influence in the Middle East, offered loans and supplied arms and military experts to Egypt. In this fast-changing scenario Britain, France and Israel entered a secret deal to invade Egypt. Subsequently Israel invaded Egypt in October 1956 with the air support of Britain and France. Though Egypt was defeated, international pressure – the **United States, the USSR and the UN were opposed to it** – forced Israel to withdraw from both the Gaza Strip and the Sinai Peninsula it had conquered from Egypt. The Suez was also returned to Egypt. Though the Suez Crisis was a military disaster for Egypt, it was seen as a political victory as Egypt could claim uncontested control over the canal for the first time. Egypt reopened the canal on its terms for ships of all nations except Israel.

The Palestine Liberation Organization, Fatah and Hamas. The Palestine Liberation Organization (PLO) is an umbrella organisation of many Palestine groups. It was established in 1964 with the aim of creating an Arab Palestine state by reclaiming lands captured by Israel. Fatah is a Palestine social democratic political party and the largest of the multiparty confederation called PLO. Hamas founded in 1987 is an offshoot of Egypt's **Muslim Brotherhood** and is a militant organisation striving to establish an Islamic state in Palestine by destroying Israel. While it runs clinics and schools as part of its social welfare programmes, its military wing al-Qassam Brigade organises armed attack against Israel. Hamas rejects ceding of any land to Israel and denounces the 1993 peace deal between Israel and the PLO. Ideologically Fatah is secular and Hamas is Islamist. In their strategy too both are different. Fatah stands for negotiations with Israel, while Hamas resort to armed struggle to establish Palestine. Fatah recognises Israel, while Hamas does not recognise its existence. Now Gaza and West Bank are ruled by Hamas and Fatah, respectively.

c. The Six Days War of 1967

Israel launched a pre-emptive war against Syria, Jordan and Egypt as these states had massed troops and had been conducting military manoeuvres along their border with Israel. These Arab states had also been sending Fedayeen squads to conduct guerrilla raids into Israel. The crisis was precipitated after Egypt once again closed the Gulf of Aqaba to prevent Israeli access to the Red Sea. The Arab forces were defeated within six days and Israel captured **Golan Heights** from Syria, the **West Bank** and the **East Jerusalem** from Jordan and the **Gaza Strip and Sinai Peninsula** from Egypt. Israel more than doubled its size by these new acquisitions and importantly they also acquired sole control of Jerusalem.

d. The Yom Kippur War of 1973

It was launched on 6 October 1973, the day of Yom Kippur, the **Jewish Day of Atonement** and the holiest day for Jews. It was organised by Anwar Sadat who succeeded Nasser as the President of Egypt. Egypt and Syria launched a two front attack on Israel to regain territories they lost in the 1967 war. The Arab states also reduced their oil production and OPEC raised oil prices substantially to put pressure on the Western powers. The Arab states also put an embargo on the United States by suspending oil supply. Though the Soviet Union supplied weapons to Egypt and Syria and armed units from Iraq, Jordan and Saudi Arabia joined the fight on the Syrian front they were defeated by Israel. During the crisis, the United States supplied weapons to Israel and alarmed at the prospect of direct military intervention by the Soviet Union put its nuclear forces on worldwide alert. Finally, under the UN initiative ceasefire was established in October 1973.

Shuttle Diplomacy was a new lexicon in international politics emerged at this time. The term owes its origin to a number of trips made by Henry Kissinger, the US Secretary of State between Israel, Syria and Egypt in an effort to broker a peace deal.

e. The Lebanon War of 1982

In 1982, Israel invaded Lebanon to drive out the Palestinians and the PLO which had built a network of settlements in Lebanon from where they launched terror attack and shelling on northern Israel. Israeli forces created a buffer zone in south Lebanon. The expulsion of the PLO from Lebanon forced the PLO to change its tactic and it was forced to take negotiation route leading to the signing of the Oslo Accords.

ii. The Oslo Peace Accords of 1993

By this Israel recognised the PLO in return for peace. The Oslo Peace Accords or the Declaration of Principles was signed by the Israel Prime Minister **Yitzhak Rabin** and the PLO leader **Yasser Arafat** in White House, USA. The treaty is named after Oslo, Norway, where the negotiations took place. The Accords provided for self-rule to Palestinians in the West Bank and the Gaza Strip. The Jewish extremists were opposed to the Accord and Rabin was assassinated in 1995 by one of its members. In 1994, the PLO created the **Palestine Authority** with its capital at Ramallah to administer West Bank and Gaza Strip as agreed in Oslo Agreements.

Palestine Authority (PA) also called by the Palestinians as the Palestine National Authority (PNA) was created after the Oslo Accords of 1993. It was envisaged as an interim governing body till Israel and Palestinians find a final solution to the conflict. The PA is led by 'Head' or 'President'. Yasser Arafat headed this Authority till his death in 2004 and was followed by Mahmoud Abbas. The Palestine Legislative Council (PLC) is the legislative body of the PA.

After Israel withdrew its troops and settlers from Gaza in 2005 Hamas began engaging in Palestine political process and in 2006 it won a majority in Palestine legislative elections. After a bitter power struggle with Fatah, Hamas captured Gaza by ousting forces loyal to Fatah in 2007. Since then Hamas is the de facto governing authority in Gaza and the territory officially recognised as the PA is divided between Hamas in the Gaza Strip and Fatah in the West Bank. Attempts for reconciliation between Hamas and Fatah have been failures.

Though efforts continue to be made to resolve the Israeli-Palestine conflict, many issues continue to be bottlenecks in the process. The expansion of Israeli settlements in the West Bank, control of Jerusalem, status of Palestine refugees and their right of return and violence perpetrated by Palestinian militants against Israeli civilians and military forces are some of these.

iii. Timeline of the Arab-Israel Conflict

1. In the 1st century A.D., Jews were displaced from Palestine by the Romans.
2. In the 7th century, the Arabs settled in Palestine.
3. 1897 – the **World Zionist Organization** was founded in Basle in Switzerland, and aimed at establishing a Jewish national homeland in Palestine.
4. 1917 – Arthur Balfour, the British Foreign Minister in his **'Balfour Declaration'** supported the idea of a Jew state in Palestine but specifically stipulated that 'the civil and religious rights of existing non-Jewish communities in Palestine' shall not be affected.
5. 1919 – Palestine became a British mandate under the League of Nations.
6. 1930s – the Nazi persecution causes an exodus of the Jews to Palestine.
7. 1937 – the **British Peel Commission** proposed creation of two separate Arab and Jew states in Palestine but it was rejected by the Palestinians.
8. 1939–45 – during the World War II large number of Jew refugees from Europe took shelter in Palestine.
9. 1942 – American Zionists adopted **Biltmore Program** by which they resolved to create a Jewish state in Palestine.
10. 1947 April, the British announced their intention to end their mandate in Palestine and referred the issue to the UN.
11. 1947 May, the UN General Assembly appointed **UNSCOP** (United Nations Special Committee on Palestine) to devise a solution to Palestine issue.
12. In the November of 1947, the UN passed the **Resolution 181** providing for the division of Palestine, as proposed by the UNSCOP, in half to create independent Arab and Jewish states by October 1948, end of mandate and withdrawal of the British forces.
13. In 1947–48, the Civil War broke out between Jews and Arabs in Palestine following the **'UN Partition Plan for Palestine'**.
14. On 14 May 1948, leaving a power vacuum in Palestine, the British ended their mandate and Ben Gurion, leader of the Jews in Mandatory Palestine declared the creation of an independent state of Israel on the same day. The city of Jerusalem was divided between Israel and Jordan.
15. On 15 May 1948, the Arabs invaded Israel initiating the first of the Arab-Israeli Wars.
16. 1964 – the **Palestine Liberation Organisation** was set up to create an independent state of Palestine.
17. In the September of 1978, the **Camp David Accords** ended 30-year conflict between Israel and Egypt. It was signed by the US President Jimmy Carter, Israeli Prime Minister Menachem Begin and Egyptian President Anwar Sadat and prepared a framework for peace.
18. In the March of 1979, peace was signed between Israel and Egypt.
19. 1987 – the Palestinians started a boycott known as **'intifada'** or 'uprising' against Israel.
20. 1993 – the **Oslo Peace Accords** were signed by Israeli Prime Minister Yitzhak Rabin and the PLO leader Yasser Arafat. By this, Israel agreed for self-rule for Palestinians in the West Bank and the Gaza Strip (known as the occupied territories) beginning with the town of Jericho and PLO agreed to recognise the State of Israel.
21. 1994 – the PLO set up **Palestine Authority** with its capital at Ramallah to administer the West Bank and Gaza Strip

22. In the September of 2000, **Ariel Sharon**, the former Israeli Prime Minister and political leader, visited the **Temple Mount** in Jerusalem prompting the Palestinians to launch the 'Second Intifada'.
23. 2002 – Israel constructs a barrier wall around the West Bank to protect itself from Intifada.
24. 2013 – peace talks were revived by the United States but was suspended after **Fatah and Hamas** formed a unity government in Palestine Authority. Hamas is a designated terrorist organisation by the United States.
25. 2020 – signing of the **Abraham Accords** between Israel, the United Arab Emirates and the United States and later on by Bahrain. It normalised relations between Israel, the UAE and Bahrain making them the third and fourth Arab countries to do so after Egypt (1979) and Jordan (1994).
26. In the April of 2021, the Palestinians demonstrated against an Israeli court's order of eviction of several Palestine families from Sheikh Jarrah in East Jerusalem.
27. On 7 May 2021, Israeli forces clashed with Palestine demonstrators at the **Al-Aqsa Mosque compound** in Jerusalem. Hamas launched rockets into Israel to which Israel responded with air strikes and artillery fire into Gaza.
28. On 21 May 2021, Israel and Hamas agreed cease fire under mediation of Egypt. By that time thousands of Palestinians had been displaced, more than 250 Palestinians and around 15 Israelis had been killed apart from causing huge destruction to property.
29. Currently Israel has official diplomatic relations with five Arab countries: Egypt, Jordan, the UAE, Bahrain, and Morocco. As seen already, Egypt was the first Arab state to sign a peace treaty with Israel, in 1979 and Jordan followed in 1994, a year after Israel and the PLO recognized each other via the Oslo Accords. In 2020, by the Abraham Accords the UAE and Bahrain normalized ties with Israel. In the same year (2020), Morocco too established official ties with Israel. In 2022, Israel, the UAE, Bahrain, Morocco, Egypt, and the U.S. established the **Negev Forum** to advance multilateral cooperation.
30. The first meeting of the **Moroccan-Israeli Joint Défense Cooperation Steering Committee** took place in Rabat in January 2023. In March 2023, **Israel and the UAE signed a customs union agreement** to implement the free trade deal reached in 2022. The UAE also officially recognized Israeli drivers' licenses, to implement a memorandum of understanding signed in 2022.
31. Israel-Arab relation is also on the path of progress through 'Minilateral' mechanisms which involves mostly interaction between diplomats and officials, not politicians. The meet of **I2U2 group** — (Israel, India, the UAE, and the U.S.) held in February 2023 in Abu Dhabi on food security; the meet of Israel, Egypt, and the EU in February 2023 in Cairo to strengthen their 2022 tripartite memorandum of understanding on natural gas exports to Europe; **the first water dialogue** held between Israel, Morocco, and the EU in March 2023; and signing of a memorandum of understanding by Israel, Jordan, and the UAE to advance their trilateral electricity-water swap deal are the latest significant developments in this regard.

Minilateralism: This is a concept in international relations where small groups of nations collaborate either to tackle problems or to pursue mutual goals. The most notable aspect of Minilateralism is its emphasis on shared interests instead of shared values or ideological alignment which enables nations to collaborate on critical issues without agreeing on everything or without holding the same worldview. Thus, it offers a flexible and innovative approach to diplomacy, particularly in tackling global challenges like climate change, health care, and food security. For example, in 2021, India, Israel, the UAE, and the US announced "Partnership for the Future" which soon emerged as the I2U2 Group. In the context of the rise of middle powers (states with moderate influence on the international stage) Minilateralism offers a viable way forward for countries seeking to address issues that cannot be tackled in isolation. Though Minilateralism has been in existence for long from the Concert of Europe of the 19th century to the Quad (Australia, India, Japan, and the US) of today, its relevance has increased in the new global order where major global powers are grappling to tackle conflicts, such as the war in Ukraine and the growing divide between the US and China.

SUMMARY

The Middle East – This region is significant in world history for more than one reason. Its geopolitics, geo-economy and cultural importance as the birthplace of three religions had significant role in many of the developments in the world in modern times. The Arab nationalism and the Pan-Arab Movement, Arab resurgence in Egypt, modernisation of Turkey, Islamic Revolution in Iran, the Gulf Wars and the still unresolved Israel–Palestine conflict are major landmarks that left deep imprint in history in modern period.

Questions of Previous Years Civil Services Examination

1. Arab nationalism was not only a cultural movement, but also an anti-colonial struggle. Comment. (2023)
2. The Arab countries looked up to Nasser as a leader who could withstand the pressure exerted by the Western countries on Egypt to make peace with Israel. Critically examine. (2021)
3. 'The British were slated to withdraw from Palestine in May 1948, and both sides prepared for that day. Violence between Arabs and Jews, already endemic, escalated'. (2020)
4. Analyze the role of Egypt after the Second World War in bringing about Arab unity. (2019)
5. Trace the growth of Arab nationalism after the First World War. How far was it a reaction to Oil Imperialism? (2016)
6. Discuss the circumstances leading to the Suez Crisis of 1956 and examine its repercussions on global politics. (2014)
7. What were the events that led to the Suez Crisis in 1956? How did it deal a final blow to Britain's self-image as a world power? (2014)
8. 'The Arab nationalism had a peculiar character. It stood for national independence for separate Arab states as well as for the unity of all Arabs irrespective of their state boundaries'. Examine. (2012)
9. 'Arab nationalism and oil-these were the principal factors in complicating the relations of Middle Eastern countries with the outside world'. Elucidate. (2009)
10. Discuss the aims of the establishment of the Arab League and assess its role in safeguarding the interests of the Arab nations. (2001)
11. Turkish renaissance guided by Kemal Pasha revolutionized the Turkish life at many levels. Amplify. (1996)

CHAPTER 18

The New World Order

In this Chapter

1. Introduction

The decades at the end of the 20th century and the beginning of the 21st century has seen a lot of transformations in Global Order. The collapse of the Soviet Bloc, the emergence of a unipolar world, efforts to reinvent the NAM and transformation of the European Community in European Union were some of the significant ones.

2. The Non Aligned Movement (NAM)

The NAM is an international forum that officially does not align with or against any major power blocs. It stands for multilateral coordination between the countries of the South and to be 'non-aligned' from either of the two super powers and the military blocs – NATO and the Warsaw Pact – under them. It was born out of a desire to 'create an independent path in world politics that would not result in member states becoming pawns in the struggles between the major powers'.

Non-alignment was a foreign policy initiative of retaining autonomy of policy (not equidistance) between the two super powers and the **Non Aligned Movement** was the platform for the newly independent countries to come together to protect this autonomy. Preservation of newly gained independence and remaining independent in global affairs were the two aims of NAM. Its flagship campaigns were for decolonisation, against apartheid and for universal nuclear disarmament. Peaceful coexistence, third world nationalism and opposition to western hegemony were the consistent themes of the NAM.

As of now, it has 120 members and 17 Observer States and 10 Observer Organizations. After the UN, NAM is the largest grouping of the world nations. NAM member countries constitute two-thirds members of the UN and 55 per cent of the world population. NAM does not have a constitution or a permanent secretariat. All members have equal weight within the organisation and decisions are taken on consensus but not necessarily on unanimity. Its Summit Conferences are convened usually every 3 years.

A. Panchsheel or the Five Principles of Peaceful Coexistence

NAM traces its origin to the **Panchsheel**, the basic tenets of India's foreign policy, initiated by Jawahar

Lal Nehru in the 1950s. These principles were incorporated in an agreement signed between India and China in 1954. These were–

1. mutual respect for each other's territorial integrity and sovereignty
2. mutual non-aggression
3. mutual non-interference in internal affairs
4. equality and mutual benefit
5. peaceful co-existence.

B. The Bandung Conference

The idea of the NAM took shape in the **Bandung Asian-African Conference** held in April 1955, in Bandung, Indonesia. The 29 Heads of State that attended this Conference were the first post-colonial generation of leaders of Asia and Africa and they formulated the '**Ten Principles of Bandung**'. These were:

1. Respect for fundamental human rights and of the objectives and principles of the UN Charter.
2. Respect for the sovereignty and territorial integrity of all nations.
3. Recognition of equality among all races and of the equality among all nations, both large and small.
4. Non-intervention or non-interference in the internal affairs of another country.
5. Respect for the right of every nation to defend itself, either individually or collectively, in conformity with the UN Charter.
6. Non-use of collective defence pacts to benefit the specific interests of any of the great powers and non-use of pressure by any country against other countries.
7. Refraining from threatening or using force against the integrity and independence of any country.
8. Peaceful solution to all international conflicts in conformity with the UN Charter.
9. Promotion of mutual interests and of cooperation.
10. Respect for justice and international obligations.

C. Founding of the NAM

These ideas acquired a concrete shape when the Non-Aligned Movement was founded in September 1961 in Belgrade, Yugoslavia. The five leaders that gave shape to the concept of NAM were the Indian Prime Minister **Jawahar Lal Nehru**, Indonesian President **Sukarno**, Egyptian President **Gamal Abdel Nasser**, Ghanaian President **Kwame Nkrumah** and the Yugoslav President **Josip Broz Tito**. For them the NAM was not to be a movement for 'passivity' in international politics but was a forum to reflect the interest of its members in an independent manner. It stands for steering clear of two power blocs but did not mean neutralism or isolationism in international affairs. It was a positive and dynamic concept of judging each issue on merit and taking an independent stand.

NAM was formed in the **backdrop** of two international developments:

1. **Decolonisation** – By emphasising on multilateralism and mutual non-aggression, the NAM leaders wanted to use the newly acquired political freedom to attain a wider objective of socio-economic and cultural independence.
2. **Cold War** – Emergence of bi-polar world and the formation of the two military blocs – the NATO and the Warsaw Pact – in the post-World War II period necessitated multilateral cooperation between the Third World countries.

Some basic elements define the nature of NAM:

1. The right of independent judgement in international affairs
2. Opposition against imperialism and neo-colonialism
3. Use of moderation in relations with all big powers
4. And the recently added element of restructuring of the international economic order.

D. Membership Criteria of the NAM

1. The country should have an independent policy based on the co-existence of states and on non-alignment.
2. Country should support national independence movements in a consistent manner.
3. Country should not be a member of a multilateral military alliance concluded in the context of great power conflict.
4. Country should not have granted military bases to a foreign power in the context of great power conflicts.

E. What Did the NAM Do?

1. NAM was a key factor in the decolonisation process and in the founding of a number of new sovereign nations.
2. It played a fundamental role in preserving the world peace by its opposition to military blocs of the Cold War, supporting disarmament conferences and by discouraging arms competition.
3. It could accentuate the end of the apartheid regime in South Africa and the racial discrimination.
4. Its member countries supported the UN in peacekeeping efforts in different parts of the world.
5. NAM facilitated friendly and cooperative relations between the member nations.
6. It prevented a total division of the world into two antagonist blocs.
7. NAM reoriented its priorities and adapted itself to the changing world realities. At its beginning, the NAM was mainly concerned with peace and security while from mid 1960s it emphasised anti-colonialism. In the 1970s, it focussed on economic development of non-aligned countries, while in the 1980s it concentrated on disarmament. Since the 1990s, the NAM focussed its attention mainly on environmental and economic issues.

3. Relevance of NAM

As the NAM was formed to thaw out the Cold War and to support the decolonisation process, it is argued by many scholars that NAM has lost relevance in the post-Cold War period. They describe the NAM as a term 'of a particular era and a particular geopolitical landscape'.

A. Why is the NAM Irrelevant?

1. Cold War came to an end
2. Decolonisation has become a reality
3. Military blocs tumbled down
4. The bipolar world now became unipolar
5. Apartheid regime in Africa has come to an end
6. Universal nuclear disarmament lost its relevance as member states such as India are declared nuclear power states.
7. Economic cooperation between countries, for example the European Union, tends to emphasise the concept of peaceful coexistence.
8. NAM also lacks an effective and visionary leadership, as it had at the time of its formation.
9. NAM neglected autocracy and human rights violations in member countries, perhaps due to its policy of non-interference in internal affairs of countries. It also failed in preventing war between Iraq and Iran which lasted for 8 years. NAM failed in preventing two of its members – Iraq and Kuwait – starting a conflict that escalated into a war. It also failed to prevent the civil war in Yugoslavia, another member state.

Others argue that though the end of the Cold War has made it necessary to redefine and reinvent the NAM, it still has an important role to play. In the context of the growing gulf between the poor and rich countries and in the background of emerging global challenges the NAM still has relevance.

B. Why is the NAM Relevant?

1. **NAM principles** of independence, national sovereignty and peace. NAM opposes aggressive unilateral measures in international relations, foreign occupation and interference in internal affairs which are still in existence but in a unipolar world. NAM as a moral force can voice the concerns of developing nations and oppose the injustices and arm-twisting policies by powerful nations.
2. Shift from political to **economic relevance**. Inequalities manifested by globalisation and the implications of neo-liberal policies necessitate NAM. NAM holds the view that poverty, social injustices and economic underdevelopment as the major factors for the growing threat to the world peace and security.
3. **One of the largest international organisations.** NAM represents more than 55 per cent of the world population. Its membership has grown to 120 countries. All African states except the newest South Sudan and the majority of the states of South Asia, South America and the Caribbean are its members.
4. **Democratisation of the international system.** The NAM considers the UN Security Council as distorted and undemocratic, which needs reshaping. It looks for ways to strengthen the representation and power of the 'non-aligned' states by restructuring and democratising the UN.

5. Promoting **South–South cooperation**. The Group of 77 (G77), which is a coalition of 134 developing countries in the UN, aims to promote collective economic interests of the global south.
6. Promoting **North–South dialogue**. NAM is the forum where the member countries can discuss international issues rather than solving them. Such issues of common concern can then be discussed with the countries of the North in their efforts to promote an equitable global order.
7. It is the **strong front** of the Third World countries on international forums especially in the UN.
8. Though the Cold War has come to an end and the socialist bloc has withered away, **pressing problems** of the world remain. The NAM faces twofold challenges. The first is the attainment of the **long-standing goals** of the movement itself which includes economic cooperation, promotion of peace, development and the democratisation of international relations. The second is the **emerging challenges** such as terrorism, environmental degradation, energy security, food security, refugee crisis, migration, interventionism, regime change and also making the UN more effective.
9. NAM's stand on **cultural diversity** and human rights. While the NAM recognises the universality of human rights and social justice, it is fiercely opposed to cultural homogenisation. Thus, it stands for religious tolerance and the protection of cultural diversity.

The last Summit Meeting of the NAM was held in Baku, Azerbaijan, in 2019, and the leaders upheld the Bandung Principles to meet the challenges of the contemporary world. Multilateralism, equality and mutual non-aggression shall be the new emphasis of NAM for its revitalisation to the present times. Thus, what the NAM requires is **redefining its role** in the emerging international scenario. The shared objectives of NAM to work together to ensure socio-economic development and for a more just and equitable world order remains relevant even today as they were in the past. In short, the world is 'still far from being a peaceful, just and secure place', hence the relevance of NAM.

4. | The European Union

The European Union (EU) is a political and economic union of 27 European countries. It evolved out of a purely economic union. Now it has a wider scope that spans policy areas ranging from climate and environment and health to external relations, security, justice and migration. The EU citizens share a single market, enjoy guaranteed rights and possess a common history. Though the member states remain sovereign and independent, they pool some of their 'sovereignty' in areas where it makes sense to work together. **United in Diversity** is the slogan of the EU.

The idea of a European Common Market was conceived after the two big wars in Europe and from the realisation that it was better to work together than fight against each other. In 1946, Winston Churchill called for the creation of a '**United States of Europe**'. The idea was given further thrust by two French visionary administrators **Jean Monnet** and **Robert Schuman** who wanted to restructure the dynamic of Franco-German relations. Their vision was to bind Germany and France, the two countries that fought three fateful wars against each other in less than a century, into a web of economic inter-dependence that would ultimately spill over into politics.

Why the desire for unity?

1. Economic inter-dependence was expected to bring a speedy rapprochement between France and West Germany.
2. Economic inter-dependence was expected to render war unthinkable on both political and economic terms.
3. Economic cooperation by all Western European states was seen as the best way to recover from the ravages of World War II.
4. Joint action by the Western European states and their economic prosperity were perceived as the best bulwark against the spread of communism from Eastern Europe.

5. | Evolution of the European Union

A. The European Coal and Steel Community–ECSC

In 1950, Robert Schuman, the then French foreign minister, came out with the Schuman Plan, envisaging coordination in coal and steel production among the European countries. Out of this plan emerged the ECSC. It was established by the **Treaty of Paris** in 1951 with six countries – France, West Germany, Italy, Belgium, Netherlands and Luxemburg – as members. They removed tariffs on trade in coal, iron and steel between their countries. This move was significant as most of the coal and steel resource regions such as the Ruhr Valley and Alsace-Lorraine were located in these six states. To coordinate the process, an agency called the 'High Authority' with its headquarters at Luxemburg was also created. The High Authority apart from supervising the whole process of coal and steel industry provided support to weaker manufacturers for modernisation. The ECSC was a huge success and steel production increased by more than 50 per cent within a few years.

B. The European Economic Community–EEC

The success of ECSC prompted the creation of the European Economic Community (EEC) so that the principles of the ECSC could be extended to the whole economy. With the **Treaty of Rome** signed in 1957, the EEC came into being in 1958. By this, the above six countries agreed to gradually remove all tariffs and quotas and to create a common market of goods, capital and labour. Hence, the grouping was also known as the **European Common Market**. To implement the EEC's objectives, four institutions – the European Parliament (in Strasbourg), the Council of Ministers and the European Commission (in Brussels) and the European Court of Justice (in Luxemburg) – were created. This too was a great success, experienced 'economic miracles' and emerged as the world's biggest exporter and also the biggest importer of raw materials.

C. The European Community–EC

In 1967, the institutions of ECSC, EEC and EURATOM (an organisation to develop atomic energy by these six countries) were merged and renamed as the European Community (EC).

D. The European Union–EU

The **Maastricht Treaty** of 1991 was signed in Maastricht, Netherlands, transforming the EC into European Union. By this treaty, the member countries agreed to work for 'a new stage in the process of creating an even closer union among the people of Europe'. They also committed to introduce uniform tax rates, adopt a common currency, common citizenship and a common foreign and security policy. The Treaty also contained a section known as the Social Chapter aimed to protect the workers and to regulate the working conditions. The European Union was formally inaugurated in 1993.

The **Treaty of Lisbon**, which took effect in 2009, amended the two existing treaties – the Treaty of Rome and the Maastricht Treaty – and updated regulations for the EU, established a more centralised leadership and foreign policy apart from streamlining the process for enacting new policies.

E. Expansion of the Membership

In 1973, three more countries – Britain, Ireland and Denmark – joined the EC. In 1981, Greece was granted membership and Portugal and Spain in 1986. In 1995, with the induction of the wealthy states of Sweden, Finland and Austria membership was further expanded. After the disintegration of the Soviet Bloc all of the post-communist European states applied for the EU membership which was granted in 2004. In 2007, Bulgaria and Romania were admitted. The last state to enter the EU was Croatia in 2013. Today it has 27 members. These are Austria, Belgium, Bulgaria, Croatia, Cyprus, Czechia, Denmark, Estonia, Finland, France, Germany, Greece, Hungary, Ireland, Italy, Latvia, Lithuania, Luxemburg, Malta, Netherlands, Poland, Portugal, Romania, Slovakia, Slovenia, Spain and Sweden. As per its decision not to continue in the EU, the United Kingdom is no longer a member of the EU from January 2020.

F. The Goals and Values of the European Union

1. To ensure peace in Europe.
2. To ensure people have good lives.
3. To ensure that things are fair for all people and nobody is left out.
4. To ensure that the languages and cultures of all people are respected.
5. To ensure a strong European economy.

6. Organs of the European Union

1. The **European Commission**: This body suggests laws for the EU, monitors their implementation, manages the EU budget and helps to shape the EU's overall strategy.
2. The **European Parliament**: Its members are elected by all people of the EU member countries and this body discusses the laws for EU. It is the forum for political debate and decision-making at the EU level and is the only directly elected institution of the EU.
3. The **Council of the European Union**: It consists of government ministers from each EU country who have authority to commit their governments to the actions agreed on in the meetings. The Council of the European Union together with the European Parliament constitutes the main decision-making body of the EU. It expresses the voice of the member governments, adopts EU laws and coordinates EU policies. It is located in Brussels, Belgium.
4. The **European Council**: It is made up of the Heads of States or Governments of all the EU member nations and the President of the European Commission. It represents the highest level of political cooperation between the EU member states and set the political agenda of the EU. It is different from the above mentioned the Council of the European Union.
5. The **Court of Justice of the European Union**: It is the judicial branch of the EU.
6. The **European Central Bank**: It is the central bank of the Eurozone.
7. The **European Court of Auditors**: It is the investigatory audit agency to ensure the sound management of the EU funds.

7. Achievements of the European Union

1. **Peace in Europe**: Since its formation there were no wars in Europe. In 2012, the EU was awarded the Nobel Peace Prize for its role in keeping peace in Europe.
2. Freedom of movement: Now the people of the EU can **move freely** across the member countries and can live, work or study in any of these countries. In this context creation of the 'Schengen Area', an area without borders, in 1985, is a notable development. Through this area people can move freely for work or tourism without checks and controls. Of the 27 members of the EU, 22 are its members.
3. **The EU coin**: Its own coin 'Euro', introduced in 2002, facilitates business. Now people can buy and travel in most of the member countries which have adopted this currency. Out of the 27 members, 19 use the Euro, and this is known as the **Eurozone** and forms a common economic and monetary union consisting of a central banking system (the European Central Bank), a common currency and a common economic region. The Euro has emerged as the second largest and the second most traded currency after the US dollar.
4. Expansion of trade: The EU is the **largest trade bloc** in the world, the biggest exporter of manufactured goods and the biggest import market for over 100 countries. It accounts for a third of the world's Gross Domestic Product and is 'the biggest and richest capitalist market place in the world'.
5. Contribution to humanitarianism: The EU and its member countries are the world's leading **donor of humanitarian aid** to the victims of man-made and natural disasters worldwide.
6. **Single market**: It means over 500 million EU citizens are free to move and settle where they wish in the Union. It is based on 'four freedoms' – for people, goods, services and capital flows freely between the member nations.
7. The **Charter of Fundamental Rights of the European Union**: It provides for certain political, social and economic rights for its citizens and residents. The European system of social welfare which came to be known as the 'European social model' offers the best living standards, the strongest guarantees of gender equity and generous unemployment assistance.

8. Crisis in the European Union

Widening of the EU membership to relatively poor countries such as Portugal and Greece and Eastern European countries, many of them struggling to establish democratic institutions and with living standards much below the EU, was costly. It caused movement of labour from East European countries to the West leading to the flooding of wealthier nations with job seekers. This huge migration also ignited ethnic tensions and issues of integration. The inclusion of poor countries also meant supporting these countries with 'structural adjustment' funds to bring them up to the EU average. Rapidly increasing migration from Africa and Asia has also put the EU under pressure in recent times.

The EU also struggled to overcome a debt crisis known as **Europe's Sovereign Debt Crisis** in some of the Eurozone countries such as Greece in 2010. During the crisis many EU countries experienced the collapse of financial institutions and high government debt. Such crises have created centrifugal forces which pull European public opinion apart. There was social unrest in affected countries such as in Greece where the citizens voted against austerity measures. The financial crisis recurred in Italy in 2016. In 2016, in a referendum the United Kingdom voted to leave the EU in what is known as '**Brexit**'. Such developments have caused many to view the European Union as the **'New Sick Man of Europe'** and have put a question mark on the viability of an expanded EU and the common currency.

Nevertheless, the European Union with its geographical size, population strength, economic might and social standards has contributed to the re-emergence of Europe as a crucial force in international field. The EU has as many soldiers as the United States has and its population outstrips America's by 200 million. It maintains permanent diplomatic missions world over and has representation in important world bodies such as the UN and WTO. With all these, the EU is trying for a major role, along with Beijing and Moscow, in a world dominated by the United States.

9. The New World Order

Nations of the world interact on different planes and such patterns of interactions could be called as the World Order. It denotes the distribution of power among world powers. The World Order is not permanent and undergoes constant changes. The World Order that came into being after the Second World War was characterised by the Cold War and the emergence of the Third World. With the end of the Cold War, new forces such as globalisation, economic integration and the formation of regional groupings facilitated the emergence of a New World Order. The collapse of the Soviet Union and the disintegration of the Soviet Bloc also implied the emergence of a unipolar world. Many of the former Soviet satellite states also became members of the NATO. The Gulf War of 1991 is considered the first expression of the New World Order.

The New World Order is characterised by the dominance of the United States and its **unilateralism**. With worldwide interests and military presence as evident from military installations and military bases and lakhs of military men deployed overseas, the United States dominates world affairs. In all the world crises the United States directly or indirectly gets involved – either as an instigator, a participant or as a mediator. It is also the largest economy of the world and home to the largest number of MNCs. The United States is also the highest defence producer in the world and the country with the highest defence spending. The United States also holds approximately two-thirds of the total value of global arms exports. The US's share in world trade is the largest and it also dominates the world bodies such as the IMF and the WTO. Its attack on Afghanistan and Iraq after the 9/11 terror attacks on America were two glaring examples of the unilateralism of the United States. The United States also rejected the Kyoto Protocol 1997, which sought to reduce gas emissions to prevent global warming. Another expression of the US unilateralism was the imposition of 'safeguard tariffs' on steel and handing out huge subsidies to American farmers in violation of the spirit of the Uruguay Protocol.

Another feature of the New World Order is the **marginalisation of the United Nations**. In the unipolar world, the role of the UN seems to be shrinking while the United States actively promotes its interests in the UN and expects the world to support it. In the UN Security Council, other permanent members either collaborate with the United States or are looking the other way. Some examples in this regard are the pressure brought upon the UN Security Council to pass a resolution requiring Iraq to dismantle its Weapons of Mass Destruction and subsequent invasion of Iraq in 2003 by the forces under the United States.

The rise of China and the European Union may prove **counter-weight to the US dominance** and a tri-polar or multi-polar World Order may be the outcome. As nuclear technology played a significant role in the World Order of the Post World War II period, the developments in information technology and communication (an example is the **Global War for 5G**)